ADMINISTRATION OF PUBLIC EDUCATION

ADMINISTRATION OF PUBLIC EDUCATION

THIRD EDITION

STEPHEN J. KNEZEVICH

Dean, School of Education
University of Southern California

HARPER & ROW, PUBLISHERS
New York, Evanston, San Francisco, London

Sponsoring editor
Michael E. Brown

Project editor
Robert E. Ginsberg

Designer
Jared Pratt

Production supervisor
Will C. Jomarrón

**ADMINISTRATION OF PUBLIC
EDUCATION, Third Edition**

Library of Congress Cataloging in Publication Data

Knezevich, Stephen J
    Administration of public education.

    1. School management and organization. I. Title.
LB2805.K53 1975   379'.15   74-6669
ISBN 0-06-043738-3

Rededicated with even more reason than before to my wonderful wife—

Doris L. (Boggs) Knezevich

CONTENTS

PART IV
THE PRACTICAL DIMENSIONS AND OPERATIONAL CHALLENGES IN EDUCATIONAL ADMINISTRATION

PREFACE

The preparation of this new edition provided an opportunity to assess the magnitude of change in the profession during the relatively brief period of only five years. Once again a number of startling new developments have had a profound impact on school administration. The great social ferment that started earlier has continued and has spawned new pressure on schools. The teacher militancy of the early 1960s spread swiftly across the land. Early in the 1970s it split teachers and administrators into separate professional societies, but it also generated feelings of greater unity and impending merger between the previously warring teacher union and teacher association factions. Technology is no longer merely talked about, but is an integral part of daily school operations.

Once again updating statistics and sharpening writing style, the traditional concerns in textbook revision, were overshadowed by even greater needs to introduce basic concepts of the new management science, to describe the new administrative competencies required to maintain effectiveness, and to review the implications of accountability. Of no less significance is the dramatic shift from the robust expansionary mood of the 1950s and 1960s, when enrollments, personnel, and budgets grew at record rates, to the retrenchment mood of the 1970s, when growth rates leveled off in all dimensions. The teacher shortage has been replaced by a teacher surplus.

A cosmetic revision would be inconsistent with the spirit that launched this text in educational administration in 1962. The first edition was unique, for it presented in a general school administration book a comprehensive review of administrative process, leadership concepts, and theory development, in addition to highlighting major trends and issues, basic facts, and research findings in the substantive content that historically have been associated with the field. The second edition made this the first basic text in education written from the systems point of view. It bridged the gap between theory, models, and systems. It attempted to catch the flavor of the turbulent times and stressed the role of the administrator as a change agent and mediator among the diverse pressures and demands upon schools.

For this third edition, basic data have been updated and administrative concepts have been reordered in the chapters that have been retained, chapters on new and emerging developments have been introduced, and many chapters have been placed in a new sequence to make this edition more relevant and to give a more accurate portrayal of what school administration in the 1970s is all about. To illustrate, significant shifts in the posture of the federal government with reference to education, such as the creation of the National Institute of Education, the growing interest in the adaptation of management-by-objectives-and-results (MBO/R) to educational administration, and the increasing pressure for administrator appraisal systems, are a few of the new ideas or extensions reviewed for the first time in this edition. The prime substance of introductory courses in educational administration in the next 10 to 25 years may well be the administrative processes of decision making, communication, and planning; administrative theory; management of innovations; models and the systems approach; and management science systems. These materials are now all grouped in the first major section. The third edition projects the image of educational administration as a field dedicated to the search and eventual implementation of new ways of managing educational institutions to make them more effective and more productive.

Reactions from graduate students and professors of educational administration who have used the various editions of *Administration of Public Education,* which now span a period of more than ten years, influenced the production of the third edition. It has been used as a basic source book by many who prepared for end-of-course, master's, and written doctoral examinations in educational administration. The overwhelming majority reported that the recent and relevant hard data presented in previous editions were most valuable and a distinguishing feature of past volumes. It is easier to write sweeping and unsupported generalizations than to dig out the most recent and accurate facts, but quantitative data provide the documentation for generalizing and identifying trends, and no truly scholarly effort can ignore the facts in the field. Such basic information about various dimensions of educational administration are continued in this edition, but streamlined to minimize the probability of drowning the reader in voluminous data. Some argue that statistics on enrollments, expenditures, and number of school districts grow obsolete and tend to "date" a book. The truth is that every book is dated from the moment it is copyrighted by its writing style, its perspectives, and its omissions of new significant developments in the field, as well as by dates attached to facts and figures. Accurate figures do not grow obsolete; new information emerges to support existing trends or to suggest a change in trends. The student and professor are challenged to search for more recent data as time passes, and to facilitate such efforts the basic data sources are indicated throughout this volume.

This book is addressed to the student of educational administration, be he or she a practitioner of long standing, a graduate student preparing to enter school administration, or a teacher desiring to learn more about administration. It is a source book on the many dimensions of educational administration. It is dedicated to a panoramic view of a complex field rather than an in-depth analysis of each major dimension of administration. Special stress is placed on professional competencies in leadership, decision making, innovations management, planning, and management science techniques as well as in comprehending the structure of public education, the administrative hierarchy and team, and the operational problems in schools. The social and political dimensions of the art of administration are described as well. As suggested previously, the broad conceptualizations about administration are documented by facts and hard data from the real world. The 26 chapters include more material than can be studied carefully in a single semester or quarter course. Each instructor will doubtless choose the specific chapters to be pursued that contribute most to his own style of instruction or to his particular course syllabus. The broad scope of subject matter presented allows for flexibility and provides fresh material for new approaches to basic courses in school administration.

The 26 chapters are grouped into 4 major sections. Within each section, fundamental concepts are introduced and form recurring themes. The book is designed as a teaching-learning vehicle; for this reason basic concepts recur in varying situations and illustrations and some concepts are repeated in varying contexts to promote comprehension and to enhance retention.

No man is an island; many persons influence and stimulate the successful completion of a complex undertaking. My mentors over the past 30 years include the following men who greatly influenced my career: Dr. Forrest E. Conner, executive secretary emeritus of the American Association of School Administrators, and Dr. Glen G. Eye, Dr. John Guy Fowlkes, and the late Dr. Russell T. Gregg, all of the University of Wisconsin-Madison. A number of professional colleagues have used various editions of this text and offered suggestions on how it might be improved in the third edition. These include Dr. Robert P. Moser of the University of Wisconsin-Madison, Dr. Edward B. Sasse of Southern Illinois University, Dr. John Maguire of Barry College, Miami, Florida, and Dr. Thomas T. Tucker, Jr., of the University of Nevada-Reno. The writer acknowledges the many professional courtesies received and his debt to the aforementioned and to other professional colleagues.

The outstanding assistance from a diligent and dedicated secretary at Wisconsin, Cleo H. Coenen, deserves very special recognition. Cleo's contributions to the production of the manuscript greatly facilitated the completion of a complex assignment. My former graduate assistants at the University of Wisconsin-Madison, Dr. (Sister) Patricia Magee of Kalamazoo, Michigan, Dr. Stephen Owen of Wisconsin, and Dr. Bal K. Thaper of India provided much help in researching important data for the third edition. To my good friends Susan Stemnock of the Educational Research Service and Dr. Arch K. Steiner of the National Institute of Education go my appreciation for supplying the often difficult to find but always current statistical data used herein. The finishing touches were added in California. Mrs. Jean I. McCulloch and Julie D. Thompson of Los Angeles deserve recognition for their aid. Lastly, but by no means least, I acknowledge the assistance of Mrs. Stephen J. Knezevich for her help in the preparation of the index for all three editions of this book.

Stephen J. Knezevich
Glendale, California

I

THE PROCESS, SCIENCE, AND INNOVATIVE DIMENSIONS OF EDUCATIONAL ADMINISTRATION

Administration had its origins when society began to organize to achieve its goals. Although it was classed among the ancient arts, its systematic study is a more recent event. Such study and research have paralleled the growing complexity of social institutions.

In Part I the fundamental nature of public school administration, a relatively new field that is distinctly American in flavor, is analyzed. These chapters break from the traditional mold of viewing administration as a cluster of substantive problems unique to educational institutions. (The discussion of such concerns is delayed until Part IV.) The chapters of this part focus on an analysis of the general contributions, basic processes, and emerging developments of public school administration. Administrators of all types of organizations seek to comprehend what planning, decision making, and communication are all about. Likewise, administration is concerned with people and this emphasis places a premium on leadership concepts and competencies for all who would become administrators. Administration is a dynamic field. Recent developments in administrative theory, the use of models, and the implementation of management science techniques testify to the fact that administrators must dedicate themselves to a lifetime of learning. The advent of more powerful technologies, the increasing incidence of conflicts, and the growing demands for innovations in education generate pressures for the acquisition of new management competencies, which are also reviewed in this part.

In previous editions only a few chapters were dedicated to the process, science, and innovative dimension; there are eight chapters now grouped in this first part.

1

ADMINISTRATION: AN INDISPENSABLE FUNCTION

The needs and interests of an individual and a society of people are many and varied. For much of history the home, as a cultural institution, was the prime mechanism for satisfying the individual's educational demands as well as for providing him with food and shelter. As the complexity of life increased, specialized institutions were created to deal with basic and subsidiary needs. Man arrived at a point where he had to organize and manage his resources through specialized institutions to attain educational, political, economic, and social goals.

Administration is an integral part of an organized society. It is crucially needed for maintaining and expanding the relevance, effectiveness, and productivity of complex institutions. The survival of organizations is dependent on the quality of administrative services available. Too often taken for granted, and not infrequently castigated, the importance of administration to the welfare of complex social mechanisms created specifically to attain predetermined objectives is seldom fully appreciated.

What does administration contribute to the operation of an enterprise? The following is a partial list: Administration:

- Exists to implement the decisions of a legislative body.

- Influences the results to be achieved, the direction to be pursued, and the priorities to be recognized within the enterprise.
- Has a decisive impact on strategies selected and utilized to reach predetermined objectives.
- Determines, in large measure, the organizational climate and working relationships.
- Can help to make personnel employed more productive (or, when it falters, less effective).
- Helps to assemble and to insure prudent use of resources.
- Unifies and coordinates the human and material resources available to the enterprise.
- Appraises the quality and quantity of outcomes actually accomplished.
- Shapes, to a considerable degree, the image and prestige of the enterprise.

Drucker considered administrators (managers) to be a "basic resource," the "scarcest resource," and perhaps the most precious resource in an enterprise.[1] These ideas will be expanded when the dimensions and processes of administration are explored in subsequent chapters.

Administration, or the need for it, has been in evidence whenever there

[1]Peter F. Drucker, *The Practice of Management,* New York: Harper & Row, 1954, p. 111.

3

were complex tasks to be performed and two or more people were involved; it has a long history. Administrative activities are described in the most ancient records of significant events in a culture. Constructing pyramids in Egypt, outfitting Phoenician ships, developing Babylonian commerce, constructing the temples of ancient Israel, operating governments in the city-states of ancient Greece, equipping and sustaining Hannibal's legions, carving roads to the distant reaches of the Roman Empire, propagating and preserving the Christian faith, supervising medieval feudal domains, governing colonies in a distant hemisphere all demanded some degree of skill and understanding of the administration of institutions, organizations, or activities. Management of today's corporations requires similar, although more sophisticated, procedures and talent.

Who the first administrator was is lost in the mists of antiquity. The ancient philosophers Socrates, Plato, and Aristotle referred to the art of administering social institutions, as did Thucydides and, later, Julius Caesar. In the Middle Ages St. Thomas Aquinas and William of Occam dared to write on the problems of managing the church and the state. About 300 years later Thomas Hobbes argued for a theory of government based on a "social contract" with individual citizens.

THE NATURE OF ADMINISTRATION

Classical and medieval writers pictured administration as action oriented. To "perform," "take charge of," or "accomplish" something described the activities of administrators. This is the executive dimension. A strong hint of the same view remains in present-day writings, with special emphasis on

what is to be accomplished. Although administration is among the ancient arts and many great thinkers of history deliberated upon it, its formal study (particularly research and scholarly publications devoted to it) is more recent. The productive activities of cameralists in the 1700s gave governmental management the beginnings of a scientific orientation that resulted in a general improvement of governmental practices in the Austrian and German cultures.[2]

The need for the formal study of the administration of public education grew out of the increasing complexity of educational institutions. School administration as a unique area of formal study and research is a twentieth-century phenomenon. It was first in evidence in rapidly developing urban school districts. It now encompasses rural areas as well where the organization of school districts produced more complex administrative units. Although Henry Barnard wrote *School Architecture* prior to the Civil War and other specialized tracts or reports on administration were published in the last half of the nineteenth century, it was not until the 1920s that a collection of writings was in evidence that could be called a literature for the field.

Public school administration, or for that matter the administration of private schools, is relatively new and distinctly American. The illusion that anyone with a good general education can become an effective administrator was common in Europe and other

[2]The work of the Cameralists flourished in the 1700s, although its roots can be traced to efforts by Osse in 1550. See Albert Lepawsky, *Administration: The Art and Science of Organization and Management*, New York: Knopf, 1949; or Albion W. Small, *The Cameralists*, Chicago: University of Chicago Press, 1909.

countries until recently. The dominance of American business corporations over their European counterparts can be traced in large measure to the greater effectiveness of American managerial talent. The business leaders in this nation devote much study to learning to execute managerial leadership roles. Their European counterparts, who at one time depended solely upon experience, are now beginning to recognize the importance of specialized managerial development programs.

There are many types of educational administrators. Local school administrators—superintendents, assistant superintendents, directors, and principals —represent the largest group. Then there are intermediate school district administrators. Officials of the state department of education constitute another level. University and junior college presidents, chancellors, and deans are all educational administrators. The rapidly developing federal agencies concerned with education, of which the United States Office of Education is only one, have generated the need for ever-increasing numbers of special types of educational administrators. Within the past few years there have come into being new educational agencies such as educational research and development centers as well as regional educational laboratories that require administrative staffs. Private industry now employs educational leaders to direct in-house training programs as well as to spearhead the development of educational hardware and software to be sold to school systems. School administrators are simply a subset of the total field of educational administrators. The numbers and types of educational administrators increase with each new decade.

Administration is a means to an end, a facilitating mechanism. The ends or objectives of education serve as the starting point in the study of educational administration. The form that educational administration should assume is determined in large degree by the functions of education in society.

Administration as a means to an end

The Supreme Court of the United States declared in 1954: "Today, education is probably the most important function of state and local governments. . . . In these days, it is doubtful that any child may reasonably be expected to succeed in life, if he is denied the opportunity of an education."[3]

This declaration on the importance of education rendered by the highest tribunal in the land corroborates similar statements issued by individuals and groups from all walks of life. The American system of education has served the nation well, for never before in history have so many been educated so well.

Specific statements on purposes of education in the United States have been recorded over the years in such writings as *Cardinal Principles of Secondary Education, The Purposes of Education in the American Democracy,* and *Imperatives in Education.* That a high degree of similarity exists among the various declaration is evident from Table 1–1.

To help students attain "worthy home membership" was an objective in 1918. A similar need was expressed in 1952 as an understanding of "family life." The objective "vocation" in 1918 became "economic efficiency" in 1938, "occupational skill" and "ability to consume wisely" in 1952, three elements of a "productive dimension" in

[3]*Brown* v. *Board of Education,* 347 U.S. 483 (1954).

TABLE 1–1

EDUCATIONAL AIMS AND IMPERATIVES

1918 "Seven cardinal principles"[a]	1938 "Four groups of objectives"[b]	1952 "Ten imperative needs"[c]	1960 "Four dimensions of the task of the school"[d]	1966 "Imperatives in education"[e]
1. Worthy home membership	1. Self-realization	1. Family life	D. Productive dimensions 15. Home and family	1. To discover and nurture creative talent
2. Health		2. Health	C. Personal dimensions 9. Physical: bodily health and development 10. Emotional; mental health 11. Ethical: moral integrity 12. Esthetics: cultural and leisure pursuits	2. To make urban life satisfying
3. Command of fundamental processes		3. Ability to think and communicate clearly 4. Arts (esthetics) 5. Science	A. Intellectual dimensions 1. Possession of knowledge: concepts 2. Communication of knowledge: skills 3. Creation of knowledge: habits 4. Desire for knowledge: values	3. To strengthen the moral fabric of society 4. To deal constructively with psychological tensions
4. Worthy use of leisure time		6. Use of leisure		6. To make the best use of leisure time

5. Vocation	2. Economic efficiency	7. Occupational skill 8. Ability to consume wisely	D. Productive dimensions 13. Vocation: selective 14. Vocation: preparative 16. Consumer: personal buying, selling, investment	7. To prepare people for the world of work 5. To make intelligent use of resources working
6. Citizenship	3. Civic responsibility	9. Civic understanding	B. Social dimensions 6. Man to state: civic rights and duties 7. Man to country	8. To keep democracy
7. Ethical character	4. Human relations	10. Human relations	B. Social dimensions 5. Man to man: cooperation in day-to-day relations 8. Man to world: relationships of peoples	9. To work with other peoples of the world for human betterment

[a] National Educational Association, *Cardinal Principles of Secondary Education*, U.S. Bureau of Education, Bulletin no. 35, Washington, D.C.: GPO, Commission on Reorganization of Secondary Education, 1918.

[b] Educational Policies Commission, National Education Association, *The Purposes of Education in an American Democracy*, Washington, D.C.: The Association, 1938.

[c] Educational Policies Commission, National Education Association, *Education for All American Youth: A Further Look*, Washington, D.C.: The Association, 1954

[d] L. M. Downey, *The Task of Public Education*, Chicago: Midwest Administration Center, The University of Chicago, 1960.

[e] American Association of School Administrators, *Imperatives in Education*, Report of the AASA Commission on Imperatives in Education, Arlington, Va.: The Association, 1966.

1960, and "to prepare people for the world of work" in 1966. In the early 1970s "career education" became popular for a similar concept. Words change to fit the mood of the times, but the basic beliefs as to what the needs of education should be have not varied greatly over the years.

This special study of the "Four Dimensions of the Task of the School" revealed further that each of the 16 elements within the four dimensions was interpreted differently in different geographic areas.[4]

Recent reappraisals of education have led to a rediscovery of its potential power. More and more, education is being perceived as a significant force for amelioration of social injustices and as a creative agency for improvement of man and his society as well as a conserver and transmitter of our most noble traditions. Through the philosophical debates described by Plato to the Great-Society goals enunciated by Lyndon B. Johnson runs the theme that education can be a powerful force in the building of an ideal society or a better world. Related ideas on the impact of the school on society were expressed by John Dewey, who around the turn of the century viewed the school as a strategic outpost on the social frontier; by George Counts, who just prior to the Great Depression concluded that the just society might evolve from educational planning; and before them by Kant, by the eighteenth-century French liberals, by Froebel, by Pestalozzi, and by Plato.[5]

Practical considerations in years gone by eclipsed the schools' dynamic role in the solution of social ills. This

is difficult to translate into action, and a preference was noted through most of history for a conservative educational program that rejected the notion that schools could be used for social regeneration. As a consequence, throughout history schools were usually assigned roles of meeting rather than anticipating current social demands; the school was often behind, sometimes abreast, but hardly ever in advance of society's needs. As civilizations and empires rose and fell, the schools followed the Aristotelian view that education should seek to maintain the status quo. While schools cannot be charged with preparing the way for any nation's cultural collapse, they have been at least powerless to prevent it. Even in the United States, the schools have been closely associated with the status quo, and until recently there has been relatively little inclination to give serious consideration to social progress through education.

An educational system that strives to do more than merely transmit cultural heritage becomes explosive and controversial. Schools conceived as vehicles for contributing to cultural change become controversially involved in political and social issues as well as in the technological developments of an era. Agreement on educational inadequacies seldom yields a consensus about what new educational directions should be pursued.

During the 1960s schools were criticized with increasing frequency for failing to contribute more substantially to the solution of persistent social problems. To date they have been called upon to consider and act on broad social issues that are not strictly educational problems and thus have become the focal point for action in resolving civil rights issues, combating poverty, reducing unemployment, and

[4]Lawrence M. Downey, The Task of Public Education, Chicago: Midwest Administration Center, University of Chicago, 1960.

[5]John S. Brubacher, A History of the Problems of Education, New York: McGraw-Hill, 1947, p. 623.

easing social tensions.[6] If the United States has reached a point in history where public elementary and secondary schools are ready to shed their traditional conservatism and assume an active role in the improvement of society, we must develop an immensely more complex educational system than one aimed at preparing an intellectual elite for higher education or transmitting the cultural heritage. Education must have a larger share of the nation's wealth if it is assigned roles beyond that of transmitting the cultural heritage to those intellectually capable of comprehending it. Education in the United States today is being conceived as a vehicle for satisfying national and state social and economic policies as well as local and individual concerns.

Educational institutions represent only one social agency concerned with the development of people. Mass media, churches, other governmental (but nonschool) agencies as well as the home are concerned with intellectual, social, personal, and productive development of the citizenry. The public school system, however, remains the formal, and perhaps the foremost, social institution for promotion of educational objectives in the United States. Other agencies within the culture build on the foundations laid in the schools.

Those who advocate the systems approach to school administration, particularly those who call for MBO (management-by-objectives), criticize existing statements of educational objectives for being much too general. Objectives have been talked about for a long time, but they have rarely influenced an administrator's actions.

[6]American Association of School Administrators, *Imperatives in Education,* Arlington, Va.: The Association, 1966, p. 6.

If objectives are to influence what an administrator does, they must be written in precise terms and the anticipated outcome must be capable of measurement. More will be said in later chapters about "management-by-objectives" as a management system that gained considerable popularity in educational administration in the early 1970s. The preparation of administrative objectives has become an important art in school administration.

Dimensions of school administration

Every educational institution requires a pattern of administration to propel it efficiently and effectively toward realization of its goals, to maintain and sustain it on an even keel, to steer it through often uncharted problem areas, and to keep it energized and prepared to weather challenges of fast-changing times. That administrative or managerial leadership is important to organized institutions is a relatively new concept. Peter Drucker called administration an essential service that, once begotten, proves indispensable.[7] He declared that management is "the organ of society specifically charged with making resources productive."

An administrator can be likened to a catalytic agent. In chemistry, as in organizations, the presence of a unique ingredient can stimulate a desirable interaction between two or more factors that previously showed little propensity to react even though placed in proximity to each other. There is no assurance that the mere presence of enough money, quality personnel, or sufficient equipment will yield excellence. Another force is needed to translate potential into reality—administrative leadership. The more dynamic the

[7]Drucker, op. cit.

institution, the more voracious its appetite for resources. One of the most significant challenges confronting an administrator is the allocation of scarce resources among the various competing goals of the educational institution.

Administration is not just anything that an administrator does. Describing the behavior of some persons in administrative positions would reveal a degree of preoccupation with non-administrative tasks, such as teaching a class or two, typing letters, filing reports, and perhaps even taking tickets at a basketball game.

Effectiveness in administration is judged by how well objectives of education are realized and not by some real or imagined standards for the proper administration of schools. As goals change or new priorities evolve, it becomes necessary to reexamine the existing system of administration. Thus, a simple one-room school was adequate to realize a limited curriculum for a pioneer and fundamentally rural society. A more comprehensive educational program had to be fashioned to meet the challenges of a fast-moving, primarily urban and industrial society. This required a fundamental change in the organization and administration of public education. Relevance and accountability demanded new administrative styles and strategies in the late 1960s and the 1970s.

The various tools and techniques classified as parts of the systems approach to school administration require precise statements of objectives. The school, from the systems point of view, is a network of interrelated subsystems, each charged with the responsibility to accomplish part of the overall task of converting educational inputs into desired outputs. The educational enterprise is perceived as a unified systematic vehicle for translating resources made available to it (in the form of money, people, facilities, and processes) into outcomes or benefits related to educational goals. The systems approach to administration emphasizes the importance of phrasing both short- and long-range objectives in such a way that they can be translated into operationally meaningful activities capable of implementation and subsequent evaluation. Under the systems approach the administrator must continually keep his eye on objectives, sensing subtle changes almost as rapidly as they occur. In this sense the administrator becomes a strategist with primary responsibility for orienting the resources of the institution toward its dynamic goals.

Educational administration can be approached from several viewpoints. Traditionally, the study of school administration has been limited to a review of a cluster of substantive or operational problems unique to schools. Early texts were devoted almost entirely to developing special knowledge, describing so-called "best practices," or recommending solutions to problems encountered in administering professional personnel, financing schools, or constructing school plants. Operational problems in educational administration are proper subjects for inquiry and are reviewed in Part IV. Although they represent the "technical" subject matter in this special field, they constitute only one dimension of educational administration.

Administration of public education can also be considered a process, similar to management of other types of public and private institutions. Emphasis on process, or the cycle and sequence of activities employed to attack specific problems, may reveal what all types of institutional managers are concerned about. More will be said about this in the next chapter.

Katz argued that "successful administration appears to rest on three basic skills" that he called "technical, human, and conceptual."[8] He questioned the "quest for the executive stereotype" and suggested emphasis on "what a man can accomplish." Performance demands technical skill that stresses method, process, procedures, or techniques. In addition, human skill is necessary for the administrator "to work effectively as a group member and to build cooperative effort within the team he leads." The technical dimension emphasizes things and physical resources; the human side focuses on working with people, that is, human resources. Conceptual skill enables the administrator to put it all together and "involves the ability to see the enterprise as a whole."

There are political, economic, and social considerations as well as the traditional educational concerns for the school administrator. This book combines the various existing and emerging views on the process of administration as well as the operational problems unique to schools. This edition places more emphasis on the administrative process and management science than ever before. The exploration of all facets and approaches to educational administration separates this text from those published in previous years as well as many current ones.

Fields outside education prefer the term "management." For the purposes of this volume management and administration are synonymous. In recent years educators have come to accept management as a complimentary rather than a demeaning term.

It is not unusual in private industry and commerce for a capable executive in one corporation to move to another company concerned with an entirely different product (or set of substantive problems) and to continue to perform as effectively as he did in the first post. For example, an executive of one of the largest oil companies was selected president of one of the largest fruit companies. This "transfer of training" in management is based, supposedly, on a comprehension of fundamental management processes. There is considerable merit in the idea that administration is administration no matter what the institution or organization, and some educators believe the selection of future school administrators should not be limited to professional teachers. They argue that teaching experience is not crucial and that administrative experience in education or even in another field is a more than adequate substitute for teaching. The executive of the oil company referred to above had special knowledge of antitrust laws, and the fruit company was experiencing difficulties with many antitrust suits against it. The new president of the fruit company brought needed technical knowledge as well as skill in the administrative process to his new concern.

In all fairness, it must be reported that not every great ex-general or ex-admiral is successful as a business executive, and not every business executive who moves to an entirely different industry can boast of success. However, the executive with the knowledge of technical problems and an understanding of basic administrative processes will have a considerable advantage over the person who does have a firm grasp of the process of

[8]Robert L. Katz, "Skills Of An Effective Administrator" in *Skills That Build Executive Success*, Cambridge, Mass.: *Harvard Business Review*, 1964, pp. 21–30.

administration but who lacks intimate knowledge of operational aspects of an institution.

The fact that people are a part of, and are influenced by, operations within social institutions may be considered a special emphasis or extension of one of the administrative processes or an aspect of the problems concerned with personnel in educational organizations or public relations; however, most writers insist much more is involved. Ever since the famous "Hawthorne experiments" during the 1930s and 1940s, there has been an awakened interest in human relations. Administration is viewed as a complex of interpersonal relations based on the science of individual and group psychology. As Argyris indicated, "Increasing emphasis is being placed by behavioral scientists on developing a valid systematic theory of the human behavior in organizations to go beyond the scope of traditional organizational theory based on such principles as task specialization, chain of command, unity of direction, and span of control."[9] Other writers, such as Getzels, postulated that administration was a social process and developed a model to depict the relations within the social system.[10] Leadership, which is concerned with stimulating or influencing people within organizations, is discussed in Chapter 4.

Emphasis on the process of administration as well as on human behavior in organizations stimulated concern for an adequate theory of administration.

[9]Chris Argyris, "The Individual and Organization: An Empirical Test," *Administrative Science Quarterly*, vol. 4, no. 2, September 1959, p. 145.

[10]Jacob W. Getzels, "Administration as a Social Process," Andrew W. Halpin, ed., in *Administrative Theory in Education*, Chicago: Midwest Administration Center, University of Chicago, 1958, pp. 150–165.

Griffiths considered this "a movement toward a more scientific approach to administration."[11] It must be pointed out that all attempts to improve administration from the time of the empirical studies of the cameralists were "movements toward a more scientific approach to administration." Science can be based upon purely empirical observations or upon a theoretical framework used to synthesize empirical observations. Attempts at creating a theoretical basis to guide administrative activity in education are still in the infancy stage.

Administration defined

School administration is defined as a social process concerned with identifying, maintaining, stimulating, controlling, and unifying formally and informally organized human and material energies within an integrated system designed to accomplish predetermined objectives. A school administrator fulfills such demands by developing strategic plans and executing policies within a unified system related to organizing, allocating, and coordinating formally and informally organized human and material resources (the basic sources of energy) within the organization, being ever mindful of the missions of the educational institution. It is through administration that the often contradictory social energies within an organization are adroitly synchronized to produce a unity of operations. Administration is concerned with directed and controlled human energy, whether or not it is supplemented by the energy of mechanical or electronic devices. As will be developed later, the importance of leadership stems from its potential

[11]Daniel E. Griffiths, *Administrative Theory*, New York: Appleton-Century-Crofts, 1959, p. 21.

for activating and converting human energy within an organization (the inputs) to produce desired outputs. In this sense, the school is a special kind of a conversion or delivery system, that is, is capable of converting the talents and other resources into learning gains for the student and other objectives desired by society.

This definition suggests that the starting point for administration is the goals of the educational institution and implies that policies and plans are related to goals. The question of what to do in school precedes the problem of how to do it. The bases used for organizing, allocating, and coordinating available resources are institutional objectives.

The definition above views administration as an executive activity. It borrows from Alexander Hamilton the idea that policy making and executive activity are separate and distinct areas, and considers administration to be concerned with the latter. Although a precise separation between policy formulation and policy execution is seldom possible, the degree of overlap should not confuse the fundamental issue. Executives are concerned primarily with the implementation of policy. Hamilton stated: "The administration of government, in its largest sense, comprehends all the operations of the body politic, whether legislative, executive or judicial; but in its most usual, and perhaps its most precise significance, it is limited to executive details, and falls peculiarly within the province of the executive department."[12]

It is not suggested that administrators do all the work within the organization. Administrators make things happen by working with and through

[12]Alexander Hamilton, *The Federalist,* no. 72, New York Packet, March 18, 1788.

other people. How the various people involved are related to each other (organized); what tasks are assigned them (allocation); how many efforts are stimulated, coordinated, and unified; what material resources must be procured and utilized constitute the functions of the administrator. The term "administrator" as used herein refers to persons concerned primarily with strategic planning and the execution of policies and is therefore synonymous with executive.

Administration—an art or a science?

The debate over whether administration is an art or a science continues to stir interest. Those who consider it a science suggest that as specific conditions (variables) are controlled, certain activities will lead to predictable outcomes. They advocate the use of scientific methods in problem solving, the development of models based on identification of significant factors and relations among them, and the use of sophisticated mathematical tools, where appropriate, in the solution of administrative problems. Development of a conceptual framework or model is aimed at broadening the scientific base of administration and at explaining and unifying separate empirically derived laws. The systems approach is another way of making administration more scientific. The ultimate goal of providing a more scientific base to administration is the prediction of outcomes in institutional operations. As a result, administrative behavior, it is claimed, will be less intuitive and less subject to serious error. Purely scientific administration, however, is sharply criticized when it attaches excessive importance to readily securable and quantifiable data rather than to data relevant to broad educational and social direction.

Artistry in administration depends to some degree on the intuition and experience of the practitioner. People in an organization are individual personalities. The behaviors influencing the behavior of human beings are numerous; it is not possible to control enough variables to predict outcomes of human behavior with a high degree of accuracy. The importance of the artistic component in administration is recognized in the systems approach, which is characterized by a high degree of reliance on the scientific method and an interdisciplinary team or task force with specializations in scientific tools, methods, and techniques. Science has its limitations, for as some writers point out, the significant problems confronting administrators in top echelons are too complex and are interspersed with too many political, psychological, and sociological intangibles to be resolved via pure science, that is, without any artistic component.[13] In essence, the scientific approach assists a decision maker in improving his intuition and judgment. Systems analysis serves to sharpen the artistic component of administration but is not a substitute for it.

The artistic view stresses possession of know-how derived from experience and intuition. Intuition or experience alone is no guarantee of success in the practice of educational or other types of administration, but then neither is science. To illustrate, oil and water colors are available to all, as are fine brushes, good canvasses, and stirring scenes. The possession of these materials along with scientific facts about color mixing, color harmony, and composition of spaces will not automatically produce a great artist. How well one applies knowledge and materials to the canvas is the measure of artistic genius. The administrative genius is one who not only has the scientific facts in grasp but senses when to utilize them and to what degree in each situation. Stated simply, good judgment is essential for success in administration, and this goes beyond mere possession of data. It is the application of elements known to all that distinguishes the administrative artist.

It is the opinion of the writer that the scientific insights provided by the systems approach will remove much of the guess work. Administration is fundamentally a practice, an application of knowledge to meet varying situations. Because of this, administrators rely on a considerable amount of artistry as well as objective study of the facts or technical knowledge and know-how. Not everybody who scores high on objective tests of technical administration proficiency is destined for greatness. One of the challenges facing the profession is the selection of people who have the potential to be outstanding practitioners instead of merely majors in educational administration with a very high grade-point average. Administration, then, is an art that is improved through the understanding of science. This is in agreement with Drucker's contention that while there are professional and scientific dimensions to management, it is a "practice" (that is, an art) and "can never be an exact science."[14] Some of the scientific bases of administration, particularly the systems approach, are presented in this book; the artistry must be developed with another type of experience.

Administration must be guided by a social ethic as well as by scientific knowledge and artistry. The work of

---

[13]Gene H. Fisher, "The Role of Cost, Utility, Analysis, and Program Budgeting," in David Novick, ed., *Program Budgeting*, Washington, D.C.: GPO, 1965, p. 39.

[14]Drucker, op. cit., p. 9.

Mary Parker Follett and others in the 1920s was characterized by a tendency to treat administration as an art, a science, and an ethical practice, with an implied criticism of those approaches to administration that tend to overstress any one aspect to the neglect of the other two. A similar trinity of values was evident in Greek thought, in which knowledge, artistry, and goodness of purpose were conceived to be indispensable and related aspects of responsible human action.

THE CULTURAL SETTING FOR ADMINISTRATION

Administration does not operate in a vacuum, nor can any institution be divorced from the mores of the culture in which it is located. Public education is part of the American way of life. Schools influence events within a nation and are in turn influenced by forces that operate throughout the nation. The two are inextricably entwined. Patterns and styles of administration must be adapted to the clientele and community served.

Educational attainment

One measure of the impact of the schools on the society served is the level of learning among the people. Educational attainment of this nation's population is relatively high and keeps improving. Illiteracy among the population 14 years old or older has been reduced from 11.3 percent in 1900 to 1.0 percent in 1969.[15] This trend suggests that presently less than 1.0 percent of those 14 years old or older can be classed as illiterate. This is an im-

pressive accomplishment when compared with other cultures. It is estimated that around 1970 over one-third (34.2 percent) of the adult population of the globe—780 million—could not read or write."[16] As the world population grows the number of adult illiterates will exceed 800 million in 1980, even though the percentage will drop to an estimated 30 percent. Illiteracy in certain areas of some developing countries runs as high as 90 percent, and almost 84 percent of the total population for the continent of Africa. In many countries the female population is almost entirely illiterate. There are signs that a world-wide attack on illiteracy may reduce it substantially in the years ahead, but it will be a long time before the accomplishments of the United States are equaled.

The median number of years of schooling completed by the adults is a more positive indicator of learning achievement. The United States has moved from a nation of eight grade elementary school graduates to a nation of high school graduates within less than one generation. To illustrate, the median number of years of schooling completed climbed from 8.4 in 1940 to over 12 at present.

The birthrate

A great increase in births in the late 1940s reversed the declining trends established in the 1930s. The number of live births hit a peak in 1961 with a total of 4,268,000 and then began to decline.[17] In 1965 the number of live births in the nation fell below the 4 million mark for the first time in a

[15]U.S. Bureau of Census, *Illiteracy in The United States*, Current Population Reports Series P-20, no. 217, Washington, D.C.: GPO, November, 1969.

[16]National Educational Association, "The World Problem on Illiteracy," *Research Bulletin*, vol. 50, no. 2, 1972, pp. 53–58.

[17]*The U.S. Book of Facts, Statistics, and Information for 1967*, New York: Washington Square Press, 1966, p. 47.

decade. It continued to drop in the late 1960s. By the early 1970s live births appeared to level off at about 3.5 million annual rate and the nation was approaching what some call "zero population growth."

The birthrate (births per 1000 population) was 24.1 in 1950, declined slightly to 23.7 in 1960, and then fell to 19.4 in 1965; this last figure is similar to the 1940 rate. The birthrate dropped even further in the early 1970s to 18.2 in 1971. The rate of population growth during 1971 (1.00 percent) was lower than that for 1945 (1.05 percent). The peak postwar population growth rate was 1.83 percent in 1956; this had dropped to 1.64 percent in 1960. Declining birthrate in the 1960s and 1970s will call for yet another adjustment. The cycle facing school administrators was a robust expansionary mood that presented school systems with unprecedented enrollment growths in the 1950s, to a more conservative small growth mood in the late 1960s and early 1970s, to a possible declining elementary and secondary school population anticipated in the late 1970s. What happens in the nation's live birth pattern has a profound impact on the schools. Migration, rather than birthrate, may cause pupil enrollment growth in some suburban areas of the nation during the 1970s, but this will not be the typical experience in school systems as a whole.

The rural farm sector

The nation's farm industry has been adjusting first to a depression, then a war, and finally a postwar economy that first saw surpluses and then experienced the specter of food shortages in the 1970s. These dramatic developments obscured the farm industry's basic problems. New techniques have enabled fewer farmers to produce the food needs for a much larger nation. The average agricultural worker in 1820 supplied food and fiber for less than four persons. Currently, each farm worker equipped with present-day machines, hybrid seeds, and commercial fertilizers can produce food for more than 23 persons, and progress in agricultural output is far from complete. Farm output per hour is now more than four times that in 1939. In 1930 the farm population exceeded 30.5 million and represented one-fourth of the total population of the nation. The percent of working population engaged in agricultural pursuits was less than 4 percent in the early 1970s. The trend away from the farm continued in the 1970s, because the forces of mechanization have not reached their full potential. The exodus has been primarily away from the small farms.

The changes in the rural farm portion of the nation have stimulated the reorganization of rural school districts as well as the expansion of the curriculum and the extension of the educational program beyond the traditional elementary grades.

The urban scene

What is happening in urban and suburban America is perhaps even more dramatic. In 1790 only 5 percent of the people in the United States lived in cities, and there were only 24 urban areas in the nation. A century later those residing in urban communities accounted for 35 percent of the total population in the country. The proportion in urban areas climbed to 40 percent by the twentieth century, and 20 years later passed the halfway mark. The trend toward urbanization continued so that in 1950 64 percent, by 1960 almost 70 percent, and by 1970,

73.5 percent of the population lived in urban areas. By the mid-1970s at least three out of every four persons will be residing in an urban population center.

The shift of population from the country to the city was the first great change in living patterns. Of no less importance during the twentieth century was the second change—the formation and rapid expansion of metropolitan areas. Most of the national population increase since 1950 was recorded in the standard metropolitan areas (SMA's). The SMA is defined as a core city and its surrounding urban and suburban territory having a population of 50,000 or more. In 1950 there were 168 SMA's, by 1960 this number had jumped to 224, and by 1970 the figure reached 243. In other words, the current growth is predominantly metropolitan. By 1970 about two out of every three persons (68.6 percent) resided in an SMA. It is estimated that by 1975, 73 percent of our national population will live in metropolitan areas—about 164 million people.[18] At that time 60 percent of the population may be concentrated in the 25 largest metropolitan centers. It can be said of metropolitan areas that most of the students, teachers, and school plants are there because most of the people, labor force, production, and markets are located there.

The metropolitan area comprises three rather broad and crudely defined subareas: (1) the central city or central core (the Greek word metropolis means "mother city"); (2) the suburb or urban fringe which is somewhat densely built up and located outside the central city; (3) the rural-urban fringe which is outside both the central city and the suburb. Further analysis of population distribution shows that by far the largest national population increase was in metropolitan areas outside the central cities, with a substantial percent being outside both central cities and suburbs. This is a fairly recent phenomenon. In the 1920s less than 10 percent of the nation's population increase was in the rural-urban fringe; most of the population increase was then found in the central cities.

The 1960 census was the first to record population losses in 11 of the 12 largest cities. In 1960 there were almost as many who lived outside rather than within the central city of a SMA. The 1970 census showed, however, that the majority (54.2 percent) lived outside of the central city of the SMA. This is a fact of great significance to school administration.

Schools serving the rural-urban fringe have experienced growth greater than that experienced elsewhere in the United States. Out-migration from the central city and the changing social composition of the central city, brought about by the new minorities, have created new problems for administration in these communities as well. An absolute decline of 0.3 percent in the white population of central cities was noted in 1960–1966 for the first time in American history. The non-white population in central cities increased by 23.9 percent during the same period. For the identical period the white population of the suburbs grew 21.3 percent and the nonwhite population grew 10.1 percent.[19] This pattern was not reversed in the 1970s.

Metropolitanism is a twentieth-century phenomenon born of technological advances in transportation systems that made possible a diffusion of homes and industry. A restless people

---

[18]S. W. Lee, "The Dimensions of U.S. Metropolitan Change," *Looking Ahead*, Monthly Report by the National Planning Association, vol. 15, no. 5, June 1967.

[19]*City, Bimonthly Review of Urban America*, vol. 1, no. 2, July 1967, p. 2.

moving from older neighborhoods in the central city to outer regions of metropolitan areas creates problems for schools as well. The concept of a single school district embracing all of the territory of an SMA is being talked about more frequently in the 1970s than ever before and is encouraged by lower court decisions suggesting it as an approach to achieving racial balance in central city schools.

The possible development of so-called "strip cities" will pose new problems for school administration in urban areas. It is forecast that one continuous strip of population may eventually extend from Boston to Washington, D.C., and on to Atlanta. Another may stretch from Milwaukee to Chicago to Toledo to Cleveland, and a third may extend from San Francisco to Los Angeles, and on to San Diego. The location of population in the United States will continue to pose problems for all social institutions.

Productivity and wealth

In 1950 one man could produce as much in 40 hours, using the machines of the day, as three men could in 70 hours in 1870. It is estimated that 100 years from now it will only take one man 7 hours to accomplish what is now done in 40. At the turn of the century a 10-hour day was the goal for the labor force. The present standard is a 40-hour week, but the 30-hour week does not seem far away.

Output per man-hour in the private economy rose at the rate of 2 percent a year in the 35 years before the end of World War II. Between 1947 and 1965 the increase in productivity was about 3.2 percent.[20] During much of

[20]*Technology and the American Economy,* Report of the National Commission on Technology Automation, and Economic Progress, Washington, D.C.: GPO, vol. 1, February 1966, p. 2.

the 1960s productivity increases were about 3.6 percent annually. A productivity growth rate of 2 percent a year doubles every 36 years, while a growth rate of 3 percent a year doubles in about 24 years. In other words, the product of an hour's work is now likely to double in less than 20 years if the present increase in productivity —about 3.6 percent a year—continues.

The growth of the American economy is one of the marvels of economic history and has been the source of unmatched living standards for the American people and security for the nation. Paradoxically, despite great wealth based on rapidly improving technology about 25 million Americans in the 1970s were living at poverty levels. Public schools are struggling for tax dollars in a land of plenty. Delicate balances in our environment have been upset by technological change, and pollution of air and water has resulted. The labor force increased at the annual rate of 1 percent from 1947 to 1953; this reflects the low birthrates of the 1930s. Between 1953 and 1960 it jumped to 1.5 percent. Reaching full employment remains a challenge. In 1971 there were about 84.1 million people in the civilian work force with about 5.9 million workers (about 5.9 percent) unemployed. The occupational structure of the American labor force continues to change. Education is now a more potent force than ever before in determining the employment capabilities of the individual. It is considered to be an integral part of the nation's manpower development strategies.

The school scene

Enrollments in public elementary and secondary schools grew rapidly in the 1950s, grew at a slower rate in the 1960s, and hit a peak of 46.081 million students in the fall of 1971. In the fall of 1972, for the first time since 1943–1944, public school enrollments *decreased* from the previous year to the total of 45.75 million students. Enrollments fell below 45.5 million in 1973–1974. Historical records show school enrollments climbed from 1869–1870 until 1933–1934; decreased, 1935–1936 through 1943–1944; and increased again, 1945–1946 through 1971–1972. By the fall of 1977 public school elementary and secondary enrollments are expected to be 1.5 million below the fall of 1972 figures due largely to rapidly falling elementary enrollment.

Combined public and nonpublic school enrollment may level off near 52 million in this decade. Enrollment gains in the 1950s were most significant in the elementary schools; relatively smaller gains were recorded at the secondary school level. Significantly larger increases are noted at the secondary level in the last half of the 1960s and relatively more modest gains are registered for the elementary grades. Thus, elementary school enrollment in the fall of 1967 was up only 1.4 percent over the previous year, while secondary school enrollment gained 3.0 percent. In 1972–1973 elementary school enrollments began to decline while secondary school enrollments set new records. About 85 percent of the school-age population (aged 5 to 17) attends the public schools, a higher proportion than in previous years. The private schools in the United States accommodate about one out of every eight pupils. There is a tendency to take for granted the educational opportunities in the United States. Estimates from UNESCO indicate that schooling is available for only about 45 percent of the world's 550 million children between the ages of 5 and 14.

The total number of classroom teachers in public elementary and secondary schools is now in excess of 2.1 million. This figure will likewise level off during the 1970s. Other instructional staff members total about 142,000. There are about 105,000 principals and assistant principals. There are almost 70,000 central office administrators and supervisors. This is a total of about 2.43 million full-time professional personnel. Typically during the past decade there was a 4 percent annual increase in instructional staff members. The present decade (1970s) is more likely to end with a net decrease rather than increase in professional personnel.

Annual current expenditures for public elementary and secondary education amounted to less than $2 billion in 1939–1940. Ten years later it more than doubled. By 1959–1960 current expenditures reached about $12.9 billion, and in 1969–1970 about $33.6 billion. In 1973–1974 current expenses were almost $49.25 billion and the total for all purposes $55.9 billion. If the trend of almost tripling expenditures in a decade continues, annual expenditures for public education alone could reach the staggering sum of $100 billion by 1979–1980. It will be a tremendous challenge to design an educational finance system capable of delivering dollars that can support expenditures of this magnitude. Obviously a leveling off in increases will occur at some time. Inflation has taken a tremendous toll in school operations as well as elsewhere.

The administrator is a creature of his environment. The simple pioneer culture of the previous century generated a set of demands that in part defined standards for measuring his performance. The relatively stable society of the 1930s produced superintendents who fashioned tools and developed skills necessary to cope with the challenges of the period. Today the role of the superintendent is dramatically different, for the problems that confront him did not even exist 15 years ago. It should be equally apparent that the problems that he has the good fortune to solve today may not be the ones to confront him 15 or 25 years hence. Some thinkers have conceived of superintendency and principalship as impossible positions. This they may be if school administration remains static during an era of technological revolutions and social upheavals. The perceptions of tools and resources available to administration are destined to be reshaped to meet emerging challenges. A world in ferment is a world unsafe for schools guided by administrative techniques developed to meet the demands of a previous, more stable era.

If all the school plants, equipment, books, teaching films, and other supplies were destroyed, we would still manage to provide education. It might not be of excellent quality, but it would be available. On the other hand, if the facilities and equipment remained intact, but professionally prepared teachers and administrators disappeared, education would nearly halt. People with special skills and professional talents remain the most important resource in education. It is imperative, however, that such people have the professional preparation and abilities necessary to cope with emerging conditions if their full effectiveness is to be realized.

At one time an administrator was judged effective if he was able to operate schools efficiently at fairly static levels. As late as the 1930s any attempt to bring about significant changes within the school system was highly suspect, and the person who tried new approaches was labeled pro-gressive. The reverse is true today. There is an active search for innovation, and administrators are criticized for not changing fast enough. Sensitivity to new demands brought about by changing times is most important if administration is to remain abreast of its challenges.

Factors influencing the structure of public education

The general framework for the operation of public education in the United States affects its administrative structure as well. This framework includes: (1) the local school districts as the basic operating units; (2) the intermediate administrative district as an important service and supervisory unit; (3) the state department of education as the leadership, regulatory, and coordinating agency; (4) the United States Office of Education and other agencies through which the federal government extends its interest and cooperation; and (5) professional societies and other informal educational organizations. Each of these will be studied further in Part II of this book.

The pattern observed in the United States differs considerably from that found in most countries of the world. The existing structure took time to evolve. It was influenced by struggles that molded a nation out of a wilderness. It felt the impact of such ideals as freedom, democracy, and equality of man. Political patterns, legal decisions, and democratic ideals created a system of public education unique in history.

The political system. One of the significant factors influencing the structure of public education and its administration is the nature of the

American political system. The plenary source of governmental authority resides in the individual states. The federal government, on the other hand, possesses delegated rather than inherent power.[21] Creation of a federal government was dependent upon agreement among the states to delegate certain powers to Congress and the President. Federal regulation and control of national affairs are limited by the Constitution of the United States. Congress has authority over citizens of states to the extent specified or clearly implied in the Constitution. If the federal government desires powers not expressly or implicitly granted it, it must seek an amendment to extend its sphere of influence. Such an amendment requires approval of Congress and of three-quarters of the states. On the other hand, elastic interpretations of the implied powers of the Constitution, particularly those in the general welfare clause, have led to a gradual expansion of the influence and involvement of the federal government far beyond what could be justified by a strictly legalistic interpretation of the Constitution.

Still, the Constitution does restrict federal power. The Tenth Amendment, which is part of the Bill of Rights, declares that "the powers not delegated to the United States by the constitution nor prohibited by it to the states, are reserved to the states respectively or to the people." This amendment reinforces the belief that the plenary authority resides in the states.

Of what significance is this for structuring public education? The Constitution makes no mention of education. It follows, therefore, that the federal government has no authority to determine the pattern for public education or to control its operations directly. Stated positively, public education is reserved to the "individual states." It is a state function—a fact that has been upheld repeatedly by the courts. The federal government demonstrates interest in public education and participates in financing public schools as part of its concern for the "general welfare" of the nation. It lacks authority to operate schools directly. Such power could be granted the federal branch, but only by constitutional amendment ratified by three-fourths of the states. The likelihood of this occurring is remote. There is no national system of public education simply because Congress and the President lack the specific or clearly implied authority to design and structure a national system directly. Recent events suggest that although the national government has no direct control of public education, it can significantly influence the direction and operation of education through grants, guidelines, and funding of competitive educational operations as well as through federal court decisions.

Democratic ideals. Not all factors that influence the organizational pattern for education are based on political concepts. Many are related to the democratic way of life. Expression of these ideals was fuzzy at first, but was clarified in struggles of a young but maturing nation which celebrates its two-hundredth anniversary in 1976. Colonies that were destined to become a world power in less than two centuries were populated by immigrants from many countries who carried to these shores customs and attitudes of their native lands. These customs and attitudes had to be modified somewhat to fit New World con-

[21]Newton Edwards, *The Courts and the Public Schools,* Chicago: University of Chicago Press, 1955, p. 1.

ditions. Primitive conditions in the New World generated fresh responses, for without creativity survival was in question. The climate was favorable for the creation of institutions. Out of the struggle to build a new nation came the fundamental concepts of our way of life which have influenced public education.

The history of education in the United States was not the same in all states or colonies. Education developed differently in New England than in the middle and southern colonies. The public school system, as known today, evolved from ideas and practices born in New England. In contrast, the southern colonies were more influenced by Old World patterns and tended to stress education as a private rather than a state concern. As a result, what Cubberley called the "awakening of an educational consciousness" was much delayed in the southern states.

The first schools were organized to satisfy primarily religious purposes: to overcome temptations of that "old deluder Satan [who works hard] to keep men from knowledge of the scriptures, as he did in former times in keeping them in an unknown tongue." The Massachusetts law of April 1642 (from which the above quotation is taken) was perhaps the earliest colonial law regarding education. Its purpose was to compel parents and schoolmasters to provide children with a general education, for this was in the best interest of the civil and religious authorities. The "old deluder" law, enacted in 1647, was an extension of the 1642 law and decreed that:

Every township in this jurisdiction, after the Lord hath increased them to the number of 50 householders, shall then forthwith appoint one within their town to teach all such children as shall resort to him to write and read, whose wages shall be paid either by the parents or the masters of such children, or by the inhabitants in general, by way of supply, as the major part of those that order the prudentials of the town shall appoint.[22]

The New England colonies, with the exception of Rhode Island, developed similar statutes during the latter part of the seventeenth century. The law ensured that all children would acquire a minimum of education necessary for governmental and religious purposes. This was an abrogation of the common-law concept, created by the Romans, that education as well as other aspects of child development were to be controlled completely by the parents.

The rugged environment where survival demanded the best in a man; the distrust born of experience of centralized power, whether embodied in a king or a colonial governor; and a faith in the right and wisdom of people to determine their own fate all contributed to what has been called grass-roots democracy. These beliefs produced their imprint on schools as well. If school operation was to be consistent with grass-roots democracy, a maximum amount of authority for operation must be awarded to those served by it. Thus a high degree of local control over education reflected developing traditions as well as the desire to keep schools close to the homes of the pupils.

The end result of the belief that education is a function of the state and that a high degree of local responsibility for the operation of schools is desirable has been the creation of 50 state school systems. That there is no national system of public education in the United States does not mean

[22]Quoted in L. M. Thurston and William H. Roe, *State School Administration*, New York: Harper & Row, 1957, pp. 51–54.

that public education serves no national purpose. It has and can continue to do so. Allocation of federal funds for school programs furthers national goals. The decisions of the Supreme Court have made certain that no one's rights shall be abrogated by the manner in which public education is organized.

The differing degrees of autonomy over educational operations delegated to local districts in various states have made each state system unique. Decentralization has the advantages of keeping educational facilities close to the child's home, of encouraging parental interest in the child's educational welfare, and of permitting a greater degree of flexibility and adaptation to changing conditions. The chief disadvantage of decentralization, particularly in its extreme form, is the uneven quality of public education that can result within a state and throughout the nation. Occasionally parents, because of religious beliefs or economic motives, have resisted sending their children to school. The authority of the state in enforcing compulsory education has been clearly expressed by the courts.

The public schools may well be the most democratic of American institutions. The first obligation of the administrator is to use a style of operation that is consistent with democratic values, then to provide an organization in which it can flourish, and then to provide opportunities for young people to learn and practice democracy. The commitment to democracy as a way of life and a condition for operating educational institutions is part of the social ethic for school administration as well.

These, then, are the salient features of the cultural matrix in which school administration must perform, and there are a host of local variations from the national picture.

SUMMARY

Administration is a crucial function in a highly organized society. Neither schools nor other institutions could remain effective or survive for long without some type of administrative structure and personnel. The practice of administration is as old as man's first attempts to organize to achieve his goals. Although the practice is old, the formal study, research, and literature about administration have appeared on the scene fairly recently. Public school administration as a field of formal investigation is an even more recent development than administration per se and is a distinctly American contribution. School administration can be examined as a cluster of substantive problems, a process, a pattern of relations among people in a social organization, or a system of interrelated components. All perspectives will be in evidence in this book.

School administration is defined as a process concerned with the execution of policies within a unified system related to organizing and allocating human and material resources to accomplish predetermined objectives. It is a means to an end. The ends of education can serve as an appropriate starting point for the study of the administration of public education. Administration is an art that can be improved through scientific understanding, and it should be practiced with certain ethical considerations in mind.

School administration is part and parcel of the American scene and influences and is influenced by this culture. Commitments to democratic practices, local control, and "education for all" form some of the traditions which must be comprehended in the practice of administration. World change promises to continue and creates another dimension in which administration must perform.

QUESTIONS

1. Whom do you feel might deserve the title of first administrator?
2. In what way do the classical or other definitions of school administration differ from the one presented here?
3. Do you think school administration will ever reach the stage where it will be a "pure science"? Justify your stand.
4. Is it possible for the public school to rise above its cultural matrix and, therefore, be able to ignore or change the trends therein?
5. What is the significance of the fact that the state is the plenary source of authority in our political system?
6. Would the public schools have been patterned any differently, in view of our democratic traditions, if education were a function of the national rather than the state government? Justify your stand.
7. What influence does the Supreme Court have on the structuring and operation of public education? Should its influence be expanded or curtailed? Why?

SELECTED REFERENCES

American Association of School Administrators, *Imperatives in Education*, Washington, D.C.: The Association, 1966.

Brubacher, John S., *A History of the Problems of Education*, New York: McGraw-Hill, 1947.

Cubberley, Ellwood P., *The History of Education*, Boston: Houghton Mifflin, 1920.

Educational Policies Commission, National Education Association, *An Essay on Quality in Public Education*, Washington, D.C.: The Association, 1959.

Edwards, Newton, *The Courts and the Public Schools*, Chicago: University of Chicago Press, 1955.

Lee, S. W., "The Dimensions of U.S. Metropolitan Change," *Looking Ahead*, Monthly Report by the National Planning Association, vol. 15, no. 5, June 1967

Technology and the American Economy, Report of the National Commission on Technology, Automation, and Economic Progress, *Washington, D.C.:* GPO, vol. 1, February, 1966.

2

THE ADMINISTRATIVE
PROCESS: THE GENERAL
FUNCTIONS OF AN
ADMINISTRATOR

What activities characterize the work of the administrator? How can one justify an administrative position? Is there a universal process of administration? Probing for satisfactory answers to these questions has been going on for a long time. Emphasis on process in the administration of public education is a relatively recent development. Process was ignored, by and large, prior to 1950, for the essence of educational administration, as described in the popular texts, was considered to be operational problems such as personnel administration and business management. Since 1950 there has been a growing interest in process in school administration.

Socrates hinted strongly at a universal administrative process, that there existed administrative functions that were common to varied endeavors:

"Do you say, then Socrates," said he, "that it is in the power of the same man to manage a chorus well, and to manage an army well?" "I say," said Socrates, "that over whatever a man may preside, he will, if he knows what he needs, and is able to provide it, be a good president, whether he have the direction of a chorus, a family, a city, or an army."
. . . "Do not, therefore, Nichomachides," he added, "despise men skillful in managing a household; for the conduct of private affairs differs from that of public

concerns only in magnitude; in other respects they are similar; but what is most to be observed, is that neither of them are managed without men; and that private matters are not managed by one species of men, and public matters by another; for those who conduct public business make use of men not at all differing in nature from those whom the managers of private affairs employ; and those who know how to employ them, conduct either private or public affairs judiciously, while those who do not know, will err in the management of both."[1]

It is significant that Socrates recognized "management" as a social process, concerned principally with relations between people.

Aristotle disagreed with Socrates and in the first chapter of *Politics* refuted the claim of universal traits for the good manager.[2]

Throughout history there have been vague references by a number of writers to administration as a process. Modern thinking about the subject, however, is about 100 years old and evolved out of the movement to apply scientific methods and reasoning to

[1]Plato and Xenophon, *Socratic Discourses*, J. S. Watson, trans., Ernest Rhys, ed., New York: Dutton, book 3, chap. 4, 1956.
[2]Albert Lepawsky, *Administration*, New York: Knopf, 1955, p. 87.

25

management. Men such as Frederick W. Taylor, writing at the turn of the century, stressed the need for employing scientific methods as opposed to strictly intuitive or rule-of-thumb approaches to the production problems of burgeoning industrial complexes. Taylor, however, placed major emphasis on a logical, systematic, and thorough analysis of shop-level problems of production. As important as this may be, it should not be confused with high-level policy decisions aimed at determining what should be produced. The scientific management movement associated with Taylor represented a turning point in approaching managerial problems. By present-day standards, knowledge, and emphasis it appears somewhat pedestrian, but for his period it represented a significant breakthrough, at least for shop-level management. There are caustic critics of Taylor's brand of scientific management today, as there were at the turn of this century.

The study of management as a separate field is an even newer development. Classic management concepts that focus on process and stress basic elements or principles abstracted from a variety of substantive problems encountered in organizations began with the writings of Henri Fayol. Like Taylor, Fayol was involved in industry. Printed originally in French in 1916, his work was not widely read in the United States until many decades later.[3] Fayol believed there were administrative functions common to all types of organizations. He viewed the five basic elements of administration as "planning, organization, command,

coordination, and control."[4] These famous five have been repeated, adapted, and extended by other writers concerned with identifying the elements of the process of administration. Sears, in 1950, was one of the early writers on "the school administrative process" and declared "no reason was found for departing significantly from Fayol's classification."[5] Early in 1951, Fowlkes recognized educational administration as a complex process that included formulation, execution, and appraisal of policies.[6] In his excellent summary of the administrative process, Gregg concluded that "only during the present decade (the 1950s) have writers in the field of educational administration dealt specifically with an analysis of the administrative process."[7]

PROCESS ANALYSIS BY QUESTIONS

One way of abstracting what an administrator does is to seek answers to the kinds of questions that confront administrators in all types of organizations. These broad queries—whose answers reveal the essence of administration—are:

1. What is to be done? (The answer will reveal the broad objectives and specific goals to be attained.)
2. How will the work be divided? (The answer will determine manpower use,

[3]Joseph L. Massie, "Management Theory," in James G. March, ed., *Handbook of Organizations*, Chicago: Rand McNally, 1965, p. 388.

[4]Henri Fayol, "Administration industrielle et générale," in Constance Starrs, *General and Industrial Management*, London: Sir Isaac Pitman & Sons, Ltd., 1949.

[5]Jesse B. Sears, *The Nature of the Administrative Process*, New York: McGraw-Hill, 1950, p. ix.

[6]John Guy Fowlkes, "The Process of Educational Administration," *School Executive*, vol. 71, September 1951, pp. 44–46.

[7]Russell T. Gregg, "The Administrative Process," in R. F. Campbell and R. T. Gregg, eds., *Administrative Behavior in Education*, New York: Harper & Row, 1957, p. 271.

assignment of responsibility and authority, and utilization of material. This is basic to organizing an institution.)

3. How will the work be done? (The answer will reveal policies and procedures that govern operations. It involves specification of methods and techniques already in existence and those to be developed.)

4. Who will do the work? (The answer will suggest assignments and discern requirements, availability, training classification, and utilization of personnel.)

5. What will the work be done with? (Facilities, money, and material required to carry out the work should become more evident as the solution to this question is pursued.)

6. When will the work be done? (This involves preparing a time schedule and sequence of activities based on factors determined previously in the assignment of tasks.)

7. How well should the work be done?

8. How well is the work being done? (These last two questions are concerned with the appraisal function. The first seeks to establish standards for evaluation; the last is concerned with determining how well the standards of quality have been satisfied.)[8]

The universal tasks of the administrator become evident in the search for solutions to the above eight questions. These activities distinguish the administrator's contributions to the welfare of an organization. For example, in an educational institution the teaching function is distinct from the administrative function. Teachers utilize instructional materials, prepare lessons, instruct pupils, correct tests, and do other work related to the teaching and learning processes. The teaching process produces something of greater value (outputs) than the raw materials (inputs) utilized in the process. The contribution of the administrator goes

[8]Department of Air Force, *The Management Process,* Air Force Manual, 25–1, Washington, D.C.: GPO, 1954, pp. 3–5.

beyond performing incidental teaching duties. He should be concerned with pursuing the goals to be attained, providing teachers with resources required to attain objectives, stimulating quality performance, sensing modifications necessary to cope with external forces that may distract the institution from teaching goals, and appraising how well goals are being realized. The administrator works with and through people to achieve the purposes of the institution.

DESCRIPTIVE TERMS

A more popular method of identifying the elements of administrative process is listing terms to which special meanings have been attached. The purpose of the descriptive words is to identify matters that should be of fundamental concern to an administrator. Some of the descriptive word lists produced at various times by writers are summarized in Table 2–1.

Planning

Planning is included as an administrative process in all but one of the lists in the table, and in that list it was incorporated in programming. What most writers call planning is in reality a definition of goals or objectives. In other words, it is the output of objectives rather than a generalized process or set of techniques that is stressed by most who produced such word lists. The implication is that every institution should know where it is going and administrators should engage in planning to give direction to the activities of an institution. Asking an executive the question: "Just what are your goals or purposes in recommending this course of action?" is likely to

TABLE 2–1

DESCRIPTIVE TERMS USED BY VARIOUS WRITERS TO SUGGEST THE FUNCTIONS OF THE ADMINISTRATOR

Fayol[a] (1916)	Gulick and Urwick[b] (1937)	Newman[c] (1950)	Sears[d] (1950)	AASA[e] (1955)	Gregg[f] (1957)	Campbell et al.[g] (1958)	Newman and Sumner[h] (1961)	Johnson et al.[i] (1967)
1. Planning	1. Planning	1. Planning	1. Planning	1. Planning	1. Decision making 2. Planning	1. Decision making	1. Planning	1. Planning
2. Organizing	2. Organizing 3. Staffing	2. Organizing 3. Assembling resources	2. Organizing	2. Allocating resources	3. Organizing 4. Communicating	2. Programming	2. Organizing	2. Organizing
3. Commanding	4. Directing	4. Directing	3. Directing	3. Stimulating	5. Influencing	3. Stimulating	3. Leading	3. Communicating
4. Coordinating	5. Coordinating 6. Reporting		4. Coordinating	4. Coordinating	6. Coordinating	4. Coordinating	4. Measuring and controlling	4. Controlling
5. Controlling	7. Budgeting	5. Controlling	5. Controlling	5. Evaluating	7. Evaluating	5. Appraising		

[a] Henri Fayol, "Administration industrielle et générale," in Constance Starrs, *General and Industrial Management*, London: Sir Isaac Pitman & Sons, Ltd., 1949.

[b] Luther Gulick and L. Urwick, eds., *Papers on the Science of Management*, New York: Institute of Public Administration, 1937.

[c] William H. Newman, *Administrative Action*, Englewood Cliffs, N.J.: Prentice-Hall, 1950, pp. 4–5.

[d] Jesse B. Sears, *The Nature of the Administrative Process*, New York: McGraw-Hill, 1950.

[e] American Association of School Administrators, *Staff Relations in School Administration*, Thirty-third Yearbook, Arlington, Va.: The Association, 1955, pp. 17–22.

[f] Russell T. Gregg, "The Administrative Process," in R. F. Campbell and R. T. Gregg, eds., *Administrative Behavior in Education*, New York: Harper & Row, 1957, p. 274.

[g] R. F. Campbell, J. E. Corbally, Jr., and John A. Ramseyer, *Introduction to Educational Administration*, Boston: Allyn and Bacon, 1958, pp. 179–186.

[h] W. H. Newman and C. E. Sumner, Jr., *The Process of Management*, Englewood Cliffs, N.J.: Prentice-Hall, 1961, pp. 10–11.

[i] R. A. Johnson, F. E. Kast, and J. E. Rosenzweig, *The Theory and Management of Systems*, 2nd ed, New York: McGraw-Hill, 1967, pp. 121–127.

produce embarrassment or fumbling to articulate a cogent response.

The systems approach to administration places stress on planning as a process as well as a means of orienting the institution towards goals.[9] In this point of view it becomes a mechanism by which a system can adapt to change. As someone put it, planning is the intelligent cooperation with the inevitable. As such it is future oriented. The dynamic environment confronting organizations, the need to identify and define emerging roles for the organization, and the need to relate the organization to various environmental systems make the planning function critical and a matter of high priority.

Under the systems approach the administrator is a strategist with primary responsibility for orientation toward goals, planning, and coordination, rather than a tactician engaged in day-by-day operating decisions. A hierarchy of plans is developed including broad plans in the form of goals and objectives, plans for repetitive actions, plans for nonrepetitive problems, and strategic or long-range plans.[10] The systems approach includes the design of tools and techniques to facilitate the planning function. These include the planning, programming, budgeting system (PPBS), management by objectives and results (MBO/R), the program evaluation and review technique (PERT) and simulation techniques.[11] Skill in the employment of sophisticated planning techniques and tools becomes vital in the use of the planning process as a means for facilitating system change.

Dror's definition of planning as "a process of preparing a set of decisions for action in the future, directed at achieving goals by optimal means" is an excellent one for administrators.[12] It helps to bring operational clarity to a term that is popular but too often described in vague terms.

Organizing

Organizing as a primary function of the administrator is listed by almost as many writers as is planning. It is through organizing that the tasks of an institution are subdivided and then related and arranged to create an operating unity. Purposes give direction and, therefore, precede and justify the organization ultimately adopted. Problems of organization will be examined in greater detail later in this chapter.

The AASA suggested that the term "allocating resources" would include organizing, staffing, budgeting, and supply management.[13] Campbell et al. included arranging for the selection and organization of staff, for housing, for equipment, and for budget, and suggested "programming" as a more appropriate word than "organizing."[14]

In some of the descriptive word lists executive activities related to staffing or gathering other resources were considered separate and distinct from organizing. This approach suggests a narrower concept of organizing, which would confine it to creating a skeleton, form,

[9]R. A. Johnson, F. E. Kast, and J. E. Rosenzweig, The Theory and Management of Systems, 2nd ed., New York: McGraw-Hill, 1967, pp. 21–42.

[10]Ibid., pp. 31–34.

[11]See Chaps. 7 and 8 for a more detailed analysis of each.

[12]Yehezkel Dror, "Planning Process: A Facet Design," International Review of Administrative Sciences 29, no. 1 (1963), pp. 44–68.

[13]American Association of School Administrators, Staff Relations in School Administration, Thirty-third Yearbook, Washington, D.C.: The Association, 1955, p. 19.

[14]R. F. Campbell, J. E. Corbally, Jr., and John A. Ramseyer, Introduction to Educational Administration, Boston: Allyn and Bacon, 1958, p. 181.

or pattern of relations to be used as a basis for grouping and executing institutional functions. Newman typifies this line of thought when he suggests "assembling resources" as a process of "obtaining for the use of the enterprise the executive personnel, capital, facilities, and other things needed to execute plans."[15] This was apart from the organizing or grouping of organizational activities. Gulick and Urwick's "staffing" is a narrower concept suggesting a single type of resource. At the other end of the spectrum is the use of programming to describe "arrangements for the selection and organization of staff, for housing, for equipment and for budget."[16]

To Fayol and the later classical writers, to organize was to determine the general structure or form with every detail in its place. Formal organization, therefore, emphasized structure, and these writers practically ignored the effects of the human factor and informal groupings in organization.[17]

Under the systems concept, "the organizing function helps to coordinate people and resources into a system."[18] To organize implies the development of interconnections between the various subsystems and the total organizational pattern. In another sense, organizing implies, in the systems concept, design of methods and determination of activities required to achieve objectives of the institution.

Directing or stimulating

What Fayol referred to as "commanding" others have called "directing";

[15]William H. Newman, *Administrative Action*, Englewood Cliffs, N.J.: Prentice-Hall, 1950, p. 4.
[16]Campbell et al., op. cit., p. 181.
[17]Massie, op. cit., p. 388.
[18]Johnson et al., op. cit., p. 15.

still others use terms that appear more consistent with the present-day connotation of making things happen through other people. Recent writers in the field of educational administration show a decided preference for such words as "stimulating," "influencing," or "leadership."

"Planning," "organizing," and "assembling resources" set the stage. The next essential step in administration is to start action and keep the system moving toward its goals. This step, be it called "commanding" or "'stimulating," is concerned with the authority —issuing directives, consulting, decision making—necessary to keep the institution going.

Fayol's term "commanding" must be examined in the light of the times during which it was used. He considered knowing the personnel, eliminating the incompetents, and setting a good example as part of "commanding." The term is thus similar in meaning to "directing," "stimulating," and "influencing." More recent descriptive word lists compiled by writers in school administration reject the authoritarian connotation of "commanding" and "'directing" to describe the manner in which authority is used as a means of motivating change within schools.

Coordinating

Most writers considered coordinating a prime function, and no one suggested a different term. Newman did not include the term in his list but devoted an entire chapter to coordination. He viewed it as "the synchronizing and unifying of actions of groups of people."[19] It was his opinion that coordination "should not be regarded as a separate and distinct activity, however,

[19]Newman, op. cit., chap. 22.

because it is a part of all phases of administration."[20] Coordination ensures teamwork toward realization of objectives. As soon as more than one person works in a given school district, some means must be developed to unify individual efforts and to prevent one group from working at cross purposes to another. Coordination strategy used will be influenced by the manner in which the institution is organized; the patterns of communication within and among the various buildings and departments of the system; the selection, orientation, and in-service development of the staff; the nature of the supervisory program; and the type of sensing and control methods built into the system.

Controlling or appraising

What many called "controlling" was suggested in the terms "reporting and budgeting" used by Gulick and Urwick, "evaluating" employed by the AASA and Gregg, and "appraising" adopted by Campbell et al. As a part of the total cycle of administrative activities this phase can be both a culminating and an initiating activity. It takes place during or after planning and organizing have occurred. One result of appraisal may be the development of new or modified plans and changes in organization or allocation of resources.

The concept of control in administration received renewed emphasis from the later classical writers on management theory as well as from advocates of the systems approach. In the systems concept, control is defined as "that function of the system which provides direction and conformance to the plan or, in other words, the maintenance of variations from systems objectives within allowable limits."[21]

Control is a way to keep the organization locked onto targets and should be more concerned with the prevention of disabling, substandard performance than with punishment for wrongdoing or rigid expectation for behavior. Some means are necessary for measuring the outputs of the organization, comparing the end products with previously determined standards, and developing mechanisms to adjust inputs or other factors to keep the system moving according to previous plans. The control function demands information on various operations which would allow the administrator to detect deviations that might create difficulties. Once deviations from expected norms are detected, corrective action must be instituted to complete the feedback loop.

Control in this sense becomes the embodiment of cybernetics. In cybernetics the elements of control include a controlled characteristic or condition; a sensor to gather information on inputs, processing, outputs, and environmental conditions; a control unit to appraise data on all factors within the system, that is, to detect significant deviations and pass corrective information to a fourth factor (a corrections-activating unit); and a corrections-activating unit that responds to interpretations of data from the control unit and stimulates corrective action.[22] The whole cycle can be summarized as an information-measurement-feedback-correction process. The feedback loop is most critical.

Decision making

Of late, writers on school administration have introduced "decision making" as part of the administrative

---

[20]Ibid., p. 390.
[21]Ibid., p. 72.

[22]Ibid., pp. 78–80.

process. Many years prior to this, Barnard and then Simon proposed that decision making could be used as a means of understanding human behavior in organization. Simon suggested:

Organization behavior is a complex network of decisional processes, all pointed toward their influence upon the behaviors of the operatives—those who did the actual physical work of the organization. The anatomy of the organization is to be found in the distribution and allocation of decision-making functions. The physiology of the organization is to be found in the processes whereby the organization influences the decisions of each of its members—supplying these decisions with their premises.[23]

Barnard wrote: "Acts of decision are characteristic of organization behavior, and that descriptions of the process of decision are relatively more important to the understanding of organization behavior than in the case of individuals."[24]

A decision can be defined as a conscious choice made from among a well-defined set of often competing alternatives. The sequence of activities called decision making results in the selection of a course of action from alternative courses intended to bring about the future state of affairs envisaged. At least two alternatives must be available in the process, and at times the possible choices are far more numerous. The output of the decisional process is rules or policies to guide subsequent behavior. The importance attached to decision making lies in its influence over subsequent behavior in the organization.

John F. Kennedy made the following statement in his 1961 State of the Union Message to Congress: "Capacity to act decisively at the exact time action is needed has been too often muffled in the morass of committees, timidities, and fictitious theories which have created a growing gap between decision and execution." This decision gap has been a matter of concern to administrators of lesser institutions. It may result from slowness in passing information that is vital to decision making up the channels to where the decision is to be made, or from slowness in passing the decision (action selected) downward to the points where it becomes operative. (More will be said about this later in connection with layering.) It has even been suggested that strict adherence to channels of authority be ignored in favor of the more flexible policy of permitting the man at the top to be in contact with lower-level executives to obtain more quickly the responses and information necessary to decision making in a fast moving world. (A more detailed analysis of decision making is presented in Chapter 3.)

PROCESS ANALYSIS BY STATEMENT OF PURPOSE

Tead identified the "elements which together defined the responsibilities of administration as a total process" as follows:

1. To define and set forth the purposes, aims, objectives, or ends of the organization.
2. To lay down the broad plan for the structuring of the organization.
3. To recruit and organize the executive staff as defined in the plan.
4. To provide a clear delegation and allocation of authority and responsibility.
5. To direct and oversee the general carrying forward of the activities as delegated.
6. To assure that a sufficient definition and standardization of all positions have taken place so that quantity and quality of performance are specific-

[23]Herbert A. Simon, *Administrative Behavior*, 2nd ed., New York: Macmillan, 1957, p. 220.
[24]Chester I. Barnard, *The Functions of the Executive*, Cambridge, Mass.: Harvard, 1938, pp. 186–187.

ally established and are assuredly being maintained.

7. To make provisions for the necessary committees and conferences and for their conduct in order to achieve good coordination among major and lesser functional workers.
8. To assure stimulation and the necessary energizing of the entire personnel.
9. To provide an accurate evaluation of the total outcome in relation to established purposes.
10. To look ahead and forecast the organization's aims as well as the ways and means toward realizing them, in order to keep both ends and means adjusted to all kinds of inside and outside influences and requirements.[25]

A DUAL CLASSIFICATION OF DESCRIPTIVE TERMS

Attempts to identify universal administrative activities are efforts to distill the essence of administration from the myriad daily duties that confront an administrator. The universal activities are abstractions of operational activities unique to an institution. Less commonly recognized is the fact that descriptive word lists, questions, or statements are abstractions of different orders. Thus, determining what shall be the relation between teachers,

[25]Ordway Tead, *The Art of Administration*, New York: McGraw-Hill, 1951, p. 105.

building principals, special subject matter supervisors, and assistant superintendents in charge of elementary or secondary education can be abstracted as part of the organizing process. It can also be viewed as planning—that is, deciding in advance what the relation will be among various position incumbents. Through the planning process several alternative courses of action are developed. Further distillation of the process of organizing shows it to comprise such elements as planning, decision making, executing or operating, and appraising. These then are abstractions of a higher order than organizing or assembling resources. What is the essence of planning or decision making? Thinking, particularly the rational process of deliberation, represents the ultimate abstraction of the administrative process. Taylor argued that the "processes important in problem solving are also often important in decision making or creative thinking."[26]

To indicate the dual nature of these abstractions, the writer offers a dual classification of terms that describe the essence of administration. These are shown in Table 2–2.

[26]Donald W. Taylor, "Decision Making and Problem Solving," J. G. March, ed., *Handbook of Organizations*, Chicago: Rand McNally, 1965, p. 48.

TABLE 2–2

DUAL CLASSIFICATION OF TERMS DESCRIBING THE ADMINISTRATIVE PROCESS

First-order abstractions	Second-order abstractions
Planning	Goal orienting
Decision making	Organizing
Executing or operating	Assembling and allocating resources
Appraising	Leadership
	Coordinating
	Controlling
	Performing ceremonial functions

Second-order abstractions

Goal orienting. The term "goal orienting" was selected because it more accurately describes the output of what other descriptive word lists had indicated as "planning." An administrator must know where he wants to go before designing ways of organizing or allocating resources for various programs. Meaningful evaluation is all but impossible without specification of prior objectives. Without purpose an institution simply drifts.

Schools are complex social institutions pursuing multiple objectives. They have goals related to individual and to societal development. They must meet local, and therefore unique, responsibilities as well as satisfy national purposes. They must help develop educated clientele and at the same time satisfy the personnel who provide educational and instructional services. The emerging management system entitled MBO, as its title implies, places special emphasis on objectives in the management of institutions.

Organizing. Knowing where you want to go begs the question of how to get there. Organizing the institution provides the structure to facilitate the task of achieving objectives. It is concerned with determining (1) how work shall be divided, (2) the nature and number of positions to be created, (3) what relations shall exist between various positions, and (4) establishment of communications between positions. An organization can be defined formally as a system of structured interpersonal relations with the roles and expectations prescribed for incumbents of various positions. Within the organization is a hierarchy of positions differentiated on the basis of authority, status, and roles. The relations and interactions among members, or position incumbents, of an organization are prescribed or structured in a formal manner. This does not preclude the existence of an informal organization. Organizing is a vital responsibility of an administrator and for that reason will be explored in greater detail later in this chapter.

Assembling and allocating resources. The term "assembling and allocating resources" implies the twofold task of assembling or acquiring resources as well as determining how much shall be allocated to each objective. Human resources ranging from janitors to top executives must be assembled. Financial resources to pay for goods and services and physical resources to house the institution must be acquired.

"Assembling resources" should not suggest that the administrator simply asks for and then receives what is needed to reach goals. Resources are scarce, and various social institutions compete for limited funds, personnel, and facilities. Those that are made available must be allocated among competing purposes within the institution. It suggests the need to develop an understanding of and skills relating to what might be called the "economics of school administration." Economics focuses on the problem of allocating scarce means to the various ends of society. It is concerned with how we employ scarce resources to achieve the many, and often competing, goals subscribed to by people and groups in society.

Leadership. The term "leadership" is offered in place of "commanding," "directing," "stimulating," or "influencing." Resources represent a potential. There is no built-in guarantee that more staff, more money, or more facilities will produce a more effective educational program. How to stimulate personnel to best performance, how to inspire continuous professional development, and how to maximize the output of educational services are challenges to leadership. The administrator must work through others to achieve institutional goals. Leadership is a people phenomenon.

The close relationship between leadership and the first-order activity, "executing and operating," should be evident. There is some justification for placing leadership among the first-order activities. In the opinion of the writer, however, there is even better argument for placing it among the second-order abstractions. (A more detailed analysis of leadership is presented in Chapter 4.)

Coordinating. There is good argument for considering coordinating as part of the leadership function. Coordination, particularly in institutions of large size, involves activities other than leadership. How the institution is organized, the informal organizational patterns, and the quantity and quality of supervision of employees affect teamwork and the degree to which dysfunctional behavior within an institution is prevented.

Controlling. In spite of some undesirable connotations, "controlling" more nearly describes this aspect of the administrative process than do the broad terms "evaluating" or "appraising." The challenge is one of maintaining quality standards; being ever ready to institute what the astronauts refer to as "midcourse corrections." The administrator is responsible for controlling in the sense of detecting problems before they threaten the welfare of the entire system, and having the ability and the courage to institute corrective action to ensure

that the institution fulfills its educational missions. Evaluation is a part of control, as are supervision and other built-in devices.

Under the systems approach, control is a means of gaining quality performance, and errors are inevitable. This makes imperative a control system that can detect changes in operating characteristics by measuring at critical points, by continuously interpreting conditions, and by planning for corrective actions. No administrator can afford to remain ignorant of changes that might throw the system out of control.[27]

Performing ceremonial functions. There are times when an administrator must take part in certain community functions as a representative of the institution. These activities are referred to as the "ceremonial" responsibilities and may improve external and internal relations. Ceremonial functions often amount to no more than attending a meeting or greeting a distinguished visitor. The administrator makes no contribution to such gatherings other than just being there. Ceremonial activities are time consuming but may have a significant impact on the institution and the image of the administrator.

First-order abstractions

First-order abstractions are a part of each of the second-order functions. Thus, goal-orienting behavior involves appraising past actions as well as planning and then establishing a new set of goals and standards.

Because the first-order abstractions constitute a higher level of analysis, there is some overlap among such terms as "planning" and "decision

[27]Johnson et al., op. cit., p. 125.

making." Table 2–3 presents the steps suggested by four writers to achieve a similar, but differently phrased, function of administration: (1) Newman's "analytical planning," (2) Griffiths' "decision making," (3) Umstattd's "inductive procedure in problem solving," and (4) Dewey's analysis of a complete act of thinking. The obvious similarities support the contention that further abstracting the planning and decision-making processes to reveal their essence will show a common base in thinking. The differentiation between planning and decision making can be made on the basis that one is the preparatory and the other the culminating phase of reflective thinking. The second-order abstractions "as-sembling and allocating resources" and "leadership" suggest action. Action starts the execution of the plan or the decision to do something, and this is followed by appraisal (the culminating activity). In this sense administration can be conceived of as "thinking" and "action" along the lines suggested in the second-order activities.

Detailed list of 16 major administrative functions

The traditional lists of administrative functions ignore such emerging concerns as change and conflict management. Fayol's original list of five can be multiplied by three to present a more comprehensive picture of the

---

TABLE 2–3

STEPS IN PLANNING, DECISION MAKING, PROBLEM SOLVING, AND THINKING

1. Analytical planning[a]

Clarify the problem
Determine the alternatives
Get the facts
Analyze the facts
Decide on action

2. Decision making[b]

Recognize, define, and limit the
    problem
Analyze and evaluate the problem
Establish criteria or standards
Collect data
Formulate and select preferred
    solutions (test them in advance)
Put into effect preferred solutions

3. Problem solving[c]

Become aware of the problem
Collect and analyze information
Assemble and organize information
Set forth possible solutions or hypotheses
Eliminate weak hypotheses
Apply solution to the situation

4. Thinking[d]

Stimulate through felt need
Locate and clarify problems
Suggest possible solutions
Hypothesize, to initiate and guide
    observation, and gather facts and ideas
Mentally elaborate; reason to determine
    consequences of the suggested hypoth-
    eses of solutions
Experimentally corroborate hypotheses
    selected by overt or imaginative action

---

[a] William H. Newman, *Administrative Action*, Englewood Cliffs, N.J.: Prentice-Hall, 1950, pp. 88–89.
[b] Daniel E. Griffiths, *Administrative Theory*, New York: Appleton-Century-Crofts, 1959, p. 94.
[c] J. G. Umstattd, *Secondary School Teaching*, Boston: Ginn, 1953, p. 155–156.
[d] John Dewey, *How We Think*, Boston: Heath, 1933, rev. ed., pp. 106–116.

major process concerns of the administrator. This writer offers yet another list which seeks to describe the essence of administration. It is a more comprehensive and detailed identification of 16 major administrative functions to reflect present-day as well as traditional responsibilities.

Anticipating. The administrator is responsible for anticipating what future conditions may confront the educational institution. Administrators are expected to look ahead and beyond day-by-day problems. Planning as a process of sensing future conditions and needs is synonymous with the anticipating function.

Orienting. It was indicated in Chapter 1 that administration had an impact on the direction the organization was to pursue. The administrator fulfills this function by ensuring that objectives are generated and then used in the operation of the institution.

Programming. Objectives are a declaration of intent or hope. They are not self-executing. Programming begins with the generation of alternatives or strategies that can be used to reach an objective. It ends with the selection of the alternative or strategy to be followed.

Organizing. This function focuses on creating the structural framework for interrelated positions required to satisfy the demands of objectives and programs.

Staffing. People are needed to implement a strategy. Identifying, employing, assigning human resources needed to pursue an objective and fulfill program demands are all parts of the staffing function.

"Resourcing." This unusual word is used to describe the process of acquiring and allocating the fiscal and material (nonhuman) resources needed to pursue an objective and/or program. The administrator is held responsible for procuring needed resources.

Leading. Stimulating or motivating personnel to action and toward objectives is one of the major responsibilities of an administrator.

Executing (Operating). There are day-by-day or operating functions that command the attention of all administrators. These are related to the actual performance of assigned responsibilities.

Changing. The identification of something to change to, introduction of an innovation, and management of change to produce maximum benefits and a minimum of dysfunction have emerged as very important administrative functions in recent years.

Diagnosing—Analyzing Conflict. Conflict or problem diagnosis and subsequent analysis are relatively new competencies demanded of administrators.

Deciding–Resolving. This function focuses on resolution of choices, that is, determining which of the many possible courses of action will be pursued. It may be a conflict-laden or conflict-free decision situation.

Coordinating. Where there are many in an organization, there is always the possibility that some may be working at cross purposes. The administrator has the responsibility to unify the activities of various components and to focus the functions of discrete units onto objectives.

Communicating. This function is concerned with the design of information channels and networks as well as the supply of relevant information in the form most useful to various points in the system. It provides for the information-flow (up or down, in or out of the system) essential to other functions such as unification, motivation, and decision making.

"Politicking." Once again a slang term is used for want of a better one. It suggests that administrators must function with various internal and external power configurations related to the institutions.

Controlling. This is controlling in the best sense of the term, namely, monitoring progress toward objectives, keeping organizational activities locked onto objectives and ready to implement corrective-action strategies when the organization strays too far from objectives.

Appraising. The administrator requires the courage to assess or evaluate final results and to report the same to his constituency.

THE ORGANIZATION OF INSTITUTIONS

Through the organizing process, a group of people is patterned into a unified body with the ability to act toward the environment in an effective manner. As differentiation of responsibility emerges[28] in an organization, a system of structured interpersonal relations is created with roles and ex-

[28]Ralph M. Stogdill, "Leadership, Membership and Organization," in C. J. Browne and T. S. Cohn, eds., *The Study of Leadership,* Danville, Ill.: Interstate Printers and Publishers, 1958, pp. 31–45.

pectations prescribed for incumbents of various positions. Organization is primarily a matter of form, or structure, and bears the same rudimentary relation to administration as does the science of anatomy to the field of medicine.[29] Organizing provides a systematic means of differentiating and coordinating resources (both human and material) to attain the purposes of the institution.

Individual members of a group or institution do not have identical amounts of intelligence, special abilities, professional experiences, or emotional drives. Organization of the institution makes it possible to capitalize on human differences.

THE INFORMAL ORGANIZATION

The act of organization should produce a system of cooperation among incumbents. But positions are occupied by people. The fact that human beings, with all their strengths and weaknesses, are an integral part of organization gives rise to the possibility, if not the reality, of interactions not intended or anticipated in formal structuring of the institution. The informal organization within an institution grows out of the personalities of position incumbents and is the consequence of their frequent contacts.

According to Simon, "the term informal organization refers to interpersonal relationships in the organization that affect decisions within it but either are omitted from the formal scheme or are not consistent with that scheme."[30] Not every gathering of employees outside the prescribed pattern can be called an informal organization. The potential to become an informal

[29]Lepawsky, op. cit., p. 219.
[30]Simon, op. cit., p. 148.

influence group is present in such incidental contacts as:

1. Teachers having the same "planning" or (nonteaching) period and meeting fairly regularly in the teachers' lounge.
2. Administrators with offices close by going out daily for coffee.
3. Principals from various schools playing golf together.

In addition to social relations, outside recognized roles, there must be activity or discussion that will influence decisions in a manner not consistent with, or anticipated by, the recognized chart of operations. Thus, a group of ten or more elementary principals may gather once a week to bowl in the same league, play bridge together, or in general be involved in the same social circle. If as a result of these interpersonal relations, which strictly speaking are not a recognized part of the formal school system, there develops a rather consistent pattern of shop talk out of which grows a consensus that influences decisions at the formally called meeting of principals, then an informal organization is a fact. This usually is not hidden for long from other people who have been in the organization for some time.

Not all informal organization has its roots in social interactions. Any frequently recurring meetings not formally sanctioned or a part of the formal way of transacting business are potentially informal organizations. Thus, a group of administrators with common interests may gather in one office to deliberate on educational problems that have not been regularly assigned to them. The meeting may not be a procedure suggested in the rules of organization, but it may affect decisions of consequence to the formal operation. Likewise, an individual may enjoy prestige as an authority on an aspect of school operation that had never been stipulated in the formal organization chart as his domain, and other administrators may consult him about that aspect of school operation.

The informal organization seldom consists of only one group. Usually there are many informal clusters or influence groups. The more heterogeneous the professional preparation, experiences, or philosophies of members, and the more complex and rapidly growing the organization, the greater the possibility that a sizeable number of such informal groups will form. People of like mind and interests seek each other.

The informal organization may introduce valuable innovations which may be adopted later as part of the formal pattern of operation. It serves to facilitate communication within the organization. The so-called grapevine has a useful function and is usually accurate in transmitting information from one person to another by word of mouth. It may function as a means of informally informing an executive about a sensitive issue that would be difficult or embarrassing to present through formal communication channels. On the other hand, informal organization can create problems of morale if influence groups degenerate into warring cliques, and the so-called "invisible government" or "kitchen cabinet" bypasses formally recognized channels of decision making. An additional problem arises when a new administrator is not aware of the informal, undefined roles his predecessor played in the organization. Knowing the power structure in the school system means knowing the informal organization. Not all activities and interactions of employees follow precisely the official organization chart of the institution; unofficial procedures and norms may regulate performance.[31] Informal organizations, therefore, exist in most systems though their presence is not always recognized.

PRINCIPLES OF MANAGEMENT

In addition to identifying the five elements of administration, Fayol stipulated the following fourteen principles of management, none of which he considered immutable:[32]

1. Division of work. (He recognized the value of specialization of effort so that each individual may work on a limited number of objects.)
2. Authority. (He declared it to be important but recognized responsibility as its corollary.)
3. Discipline. (He believed that superiors have a right to obedience, application of due energy, and outward marks of respect from employees.)
4. Unity of command. (He stressed that an employee should receive orders from one superior only, and disagreed with Taylor's "functional foremanship" concept.)
5. Unity of direction. (He advocated one leader and one plan for a given group of objectives.)
6. Subordination of individual interest to general interest.
7. Remuneration of personnel. (He believed the rate of remuneration was independent of employer's will and employee's worth and should be based on such factors as cost of living, availability of personnel, and economic conditions.)
8. Centralization. (He believed that the comparative merits of centralization vs. decentralization depended on conditions of each institution.)
9. Scalar chain. (He defined this as the line of command or the flow of authority from the highest to the lowest rank.)
10. Order. (He believed in "a place for

everything and everything in its place.")
11. Equity.
12. Stability of tenure of personnel.
13. Initiative. (He recognized its importance.)
14. *Esprit de corps*. (He believed harmony and unity among personnel to be most important.)

It must be reemphasized that Fayol did not wish to inject inflexibility in administration by insisting that all the principles be adhered to strictly. He considered the principles of management to be changeable with the circumstances.

DEPARTMENTATION

"Departmentation" is the term applied to subdividing the work of an institution into units of various sizes for the purpose of administration.[33] Several bases may be used for departmentation. The grouping of activities can be by:

Products or services. Departmentation by services such as teaching, guidance, health, attendance, and business is fairly common in educational institutions.

Location. In schools of large size and complexity, there may be area or deputy superintendents. In another sense educational services are organized according to the attendance area of which a particular building is the center.

Time. A large manufacturing firm or restaurant may group operations on the basis of shifts for particular workers. In some schools special groupings may be necessary if there is a night as well as a day school, or a summer school as well as a regular term.

---

[31]P. M. Blau and W. R. Scott, *Formal Organizations,* San Francisco: Chandler Publishing Co., 1962, p. 6.

[32]Massie, op. cit., pp. 391–392.

[33]Newman, op. cit., p. 125.

Customers. The federal government has departments and bureaus serving farmers, Indians, children, small business, and the like. Schools are commonly organized according to age level of the learner. Thus, educational activities are grouped according to whether they are intended for elementary school children, secondary school youths, or adults.

Processes. In manufacturing, a sequence of operations such as cutting, machining, processing, packing, and shipping may serve as the basis for departmentation. In education institutions teaching is the dominant process and therefore is seldom used as a basis for departmentation. However, the counseling process may be separated from the teaching process.

Functions. How to differentiate functions from other categories is a difficult task. Schools can group activities on the basis of such functions as administration, supervision, public relations, counseling, teaching, and research. Functional departmentation appears to be increasing in popularity, although a precise delimitation of the term is lacking. Thus, guidance or business services can be classified as functions as well as services.

Subject matter. This basis is useful in public school systems. Secondary school departmentation is usually based on subject matter.

The hierarchy

After departmentation there remains the problem of arranging relations and establishing levels of authority necessary to discharge responsibilities. The hierarchy of authority gives a vertical dimension to an institution. The concept that every organization consists of gradations of authority, starting with the top administrative post and ending with operatives or workers, is referred to as the "scalar principle."[34] The number of levels of authority is related to the size and/or complexity of the organization. Chain of command is another phrase used to describe how authority is distributed from its ultimate source to positions at successively lower levels. In education, people acting through their representatives in the legislature and on the school board are the ultimate source of authority. The chief executive officer of the board of education derives his authority from actions of the board or the legislature. All other school administrators and employees derive their authority from the same source. In other words, the administrative hierarchy for schools is created in the formal sense by the board of education or the legislature.

The scalar organization characteristic of business and industry (see Figure 2–1) can, with some modifications, be applied to public schools only (see Figure 2–2). Instead of top management, middle management, and supervisory management, four levels of administration, differentiated on the basis of scope of authority, are identified: (1) general administration, (2) central-office administration, (3) building administration, and (4) classroom administration.

Decisions or other activities at the general administration level influence all segments of the educational institution. In other words, authority exercised at this level is not limited in scope. The board of education, the general superintendent, and the deputy superintendent make up general administration.

[34]Dalton E. McFarland, *Management Principles and Practices,* New York: Macmillan, 1958, p. 165.

FIGURE 2–1

Organizational pyramid for business or industry.

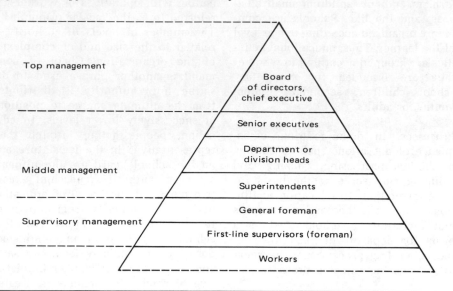

Source: Based on Dalton E. McFarland, *Management Principles and Practices,* New York: Macmillan, 1958, p. 163.

FIGURE 2–2

Organizational pyramid for public school administration.

Central-office administration is somewhat narrower in scope and subordinate to general administration. The authority of executives at this level is exercised over a rather broad segment of the school system, nonetheless. Assistant superintendents in charge of broad areas, such as elementary education, secondary education, curriculum, personnel, or business, as well as directors of major divisions, supervisors, or special consultants, occupy positions at this level of administration.

Closer to the teacher and pupil is building administration. The primary focus here is the individual school, which may be housed in one or more buildings. At this level are administrators such as the elementary, junior high school, and senior high school principals, assistant principals, and other specialists attached to one or a limited number of schools.

Farthest removed from general administration and with the most limited field of operations is classroom administration. It is the closest to the teaching function, as the title suggests. It may be considered the gray area where the activities of certain personnel move from nonadministrative to administrative functions. For example, teachers may perform nonteaching activities, such as checking and reporting attendance or collecting and distributing school supplies and textbooks. These constitute classroom administration. At a more sophisticated level, but still within this realm, are the activities of the subject matter department heads.

Unity of command

For unity of authority or command, one chief executive must have ultimate responsibility. In the field of education this one person is directly responsible to the board of education. Each individual within the system, in turn, reports primarily to one executive or superior.

A modification of unity of authority, however, can develop at lower echelons in education, as well as in business and military establishments. It is perhaps too much to expect one executive to maintain a high degree of expertness in all teaching and educational areas. The teacher in a given building looks to the principal as the person primarily responsible for general development of the overall educational program in the school building. On the other hand, the same teacher may look to the special subject supervisor for specific direction in development of better teaching in his special field. A supervisor is responsible for supervision and improvement of methodology and program in a given field. Here, then, is a situation where there is a dual supervision (the principal and special subject supervisor) over a teacher. This need not be confusing for the teacher, since he expects a different kind of supervision from each. The supervisor is limited strictly to technical guidance in a specific teaching field or, in the case of elementary schools, to a limited range of subjects. The principal has a more general responsibility for all teachers. An analogous situation is found in the army post hospital, which is, strictly speaking, under the direction of the post commander but is also under the technical supervision of the Surgeon General. In business it is not unusual to find workers reporting to the foreman and to the company specialist in a given process.

In present-day practice, dual supervision or joint command does work, despite the organizational tradition that no man can serve two masters.[35] As pointed out by Lepawsky, "the fact that this nonhierarchical conception of organization can be enforced in the military sphere, where hierarchy and authority are so rigidly enforced, is a tribute to its validity."[36]

This points to limitations that exist in all administrative principles. There are few, if any, absolute rules for administrative behavior in organizations. Statements regarding functions of the administrator and desirable approaches to organization are true only within limits. The trend toward greater specialization in educational institutions will bring problems of unity of command versus dual supervision into sharper focus.

Delegation of authority

When work must be divided, authority must be delegated to accomplish the task. Delegation of task responsibilities originates at the level of general administration. In most states, the board of education is empowered by the state legislature or its constitution to operate and control the public school system. Most school boards recognize the superintendent as the chief executive officer and delegate authority as well as responsibility to him for the operation of the system. The superintendent, in turn, by grouping tasks of the school system in various ways, creates an administrative organization that calls for the distribution of some degree of authority along with responsibility. The process of delegation involves:

1. Assignment of duties by an executive to subordinates.
2. Granting of permission or authority to make commitments, to utilize resources, and to determine other action necessary to perform delegated duties or responsibilities.
3. Creation of an obligation on the part of each subordinate to the executive for satisfactory performance of duties.[37]

The larger the school system, the greater the series of redelegations to the point where the duty or responsibility can be performed by personnel without further assistance. In the process of delegation, responsibility for execution of a phase of the educational program is assigned, and permission is granted to make commitments and to utilize resources necessary to ensure performance of the responsibility. The executive does not rid himself of responsibility through delegation. Responsibility for a task rests with the executive who delegated the duty as well as with the person who accepted it.

Authority granted to execute a delegation should be equal to responsibility. It is unfair to hold a person accountable for results without allowing him the opportunity and resources required to achieve such results. Authority should not be confused with overall power; it is merely permission to make certain commitments, to utilize resources and to take whatever actions may be necessary to perform delegated duties. Note that the subordinate is accountable for the manner in which he utilizes authority delegated. When an administrator delegates duties and authority to others, he should clearly specify the standards of performance expected as well as the limits and the extent of authority granted. Subordinates' reports on achievements to date and the exercise of authority granted provide the executive with the data needed to maintain the pulse of the institution without

---

[35]Lepawsky, op. cit., p. 333.
[36]Ibid.

[37]Newman, op. cit., p. 166.

actually performing all the work thrust upon him.

Authority and power

Power is often equated with authority. Authority is an important dimension of an office and is necessary for achieving tasks assigned. Simon defined authority as "the power to make decisions which guide the actions of another."[38] In effect, it determines relations that exist between two individuals occupying different positions within the organization. As Barnard pointed out, "authority is another name for the willingness and capacity of individuals to submit to the necessities of cooperative systems."[39] Virtually no organization is able to get along without some hierarchy of authority.

There are various kinds of authority. "There exists a kind of authority known as technical authority which adheres to the individual because of his recognized expertness in a given field."[40] Because technical authority adheres to the person, it goes with him as he moves from one position to another. It cannot be delegated or given in any other way to an individual not recognized by others in the organization as possessing the degree of expertness required. Technical authority is a reputation earned. It is a demonstrated capability, not an assigned responsibility.

The perceptive organizational theorist Max Weber greatly influenced subsequent thinking and research on authority and power. He recognized both as a means of obtaining social control, but noted subtle differences between them. Power is a form of raw energy that enables a person to carry

out his own will despite the protestations of others. It is based on involuntary compliance, with resistance overcome through threats or use of physical, economic, or social force. *Power accrues from holding access to or the actual possession of resources—* physical, personal, economic, social, or psychological—*that someone else desires.* If the control over what someone else wants is removed or curtailed, the person's power over others will be reduced accordingly. In a negative sense, power may be control over punishment (or negative rewards) that a person seeks to avoid. In a power-play situation, the subordinate complies not because he wants to but because he must or face deprivation of some kind.

Authority, on the other hand, is voluntarily obeyed. The person influenced sees the commands as emanating from a person or system that has legitimacy beyond raw control over something desired or something to be prevented. Group norms within the organization are a primary force for achieving social control through a special kind of authority.[41] The key difference is that the individual goes along because he feels he should rather than because he must.

Persuasion is yet another form of voluntary compliance. It is similar in many respects to technical authority except the persuasive person has no formal or legitimate position in the hierarchy. You go along, that is, are persuaded to do something, because of the cogency of the arguments or faith in the persuader. It is compliance without consideration of personal wants (power) or the position of the other person (authority). The similarities, differences, and relationships among power, authority, and persuasion are diagramed in Figure 2–3.

---

[38]Simon, op. cit., p. 125.
[39]Barnard, op. cit., p. 184.
[40]Newman, op. cit., p. 161.

[41]See Blau and Scott, op. cit., pp. 27–32.

FIGURE 2-3

Relations and differences among power, authority, and persuasion.

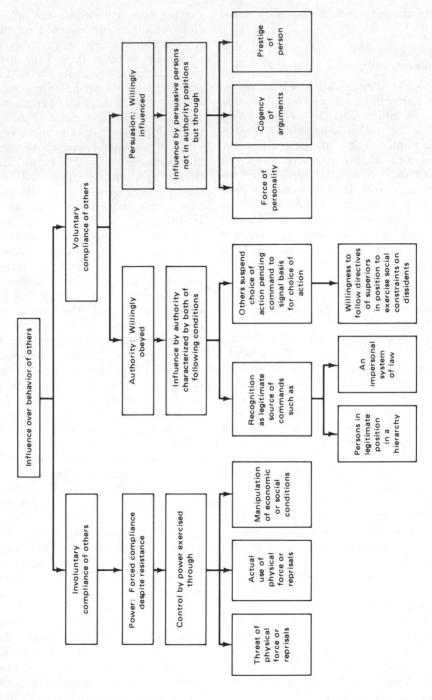

Source: Based on Max Weber's theoretical analysis as presented in P. M. Blau and W. R. Scott, *Formal Organizations*, San Francisco, Chandler Publishing Co., 1962, pp. 27–32.

Span of supervision or control

Creation of a variety of subordinate positions in an administrative organization gives rise to the issue of how many persons an administrator can control or supervise. "Span of supervision" or "span of control" is concerned with optimum numbers reporting directly to a recognized higher level in the hierarchy. The rule has been: The larger the number of people reporting directly to an executive, the more difficult it is for him to supervise and coordinate them effectively. The controversy revolves around how many persons of administrative rank can be supervised effectively by an executive.

The following factors influence optimum numbers for effective supervision or for a most desirable span of control.

1. Time available by the executive for supervision. The more time the executive is willing and able to devote to this task, the larger his span of supervision.
2. Mental capacity and personal adaptability of the executive doing the supervising. Individual differences explain in part why the effective span of supervision varies among executives.
3. Complexity of the situation supervised. The effective span of supervision is smaller where the executive must refocus his thinking to control each of the diverse tasks than when he can concentrate his efforts on limited and similar tasks of a work force.
4. Other duties of the executive. If the executive is responsible for general planning and control as well as for supervision of a number of other administrators, his effective span will be far smaller than that of an individual of similar ability and experience not confronted with broad responsibilities.
5. Stability of operations. The greater the turnover among the teaching or administrative staff, the more difficult it becomes to supervise effectively a large span of operations.
6. Capability and experience of subordinates. The more capable, the better

prepared professionally, and the greater the experience of principal and teacher, the easier it becomes to supervise larger numbers. This implies that as administrators and teachers become more capable through greater professional preparation and experience, the effective span of supervision will increase.[42]

There is no optimum span of supervision for all executives. Nonetheless, the complexity of relations in an institution multiplies rapidly as the number of persons in the institution increases (see Table 2–4).

Flat and tall structures

The type of supervision span adopted influences the shape of the organizational structure. A large span of control means that a given executive supervises a large number of people, and a relatively flat organizational structure results. The term "flat" should be interpreted to mean "relatively flatter than other types of organizational patterns." In a flat organization there are only a few administrative levels between the lowest and highest executive echelons in the hierarchy. Although the hierarchical distance between operatives and executives, or between the lower echelon and the top executives, is short in the flat pattern, this does not imply that contact between persons at various levels in the hierarchy is better. A flat structure is more likely to be a successful organization when those supervised have a high degree of competence and when turnover is low. The flat structure may overburden top-rank executives, making it impossible for them to devote sufficient time and attention to all their subordinates.

When complexity, magnitude of responsibilities confronting each execu-

[42]Newman, op. cit., p. 161.

tive, and staff turnover require a short span of supervision, a tall organizational structure results. Such a structure is characterized by many administrative levels between the lowest and the highest positions in the hierarchy. This does not necessarily imply an inferior organizational pattern. The many hierarchical levels in the tall or pyramidal organization may be no more detrimental than the difficulty of gaining access to superiors in the flat organization. In an organization it is important that those with assigned operational responsibilities have easy access to persons with supervisory responsibility over operational activities.

Layering

The existence of many administrative echelons in a tall organizational structure may result in layering (see Figure 2–4). Difficulties in contacting another administrator while following the chain of command may be compounded by the existence of several layers in the command. If all communication is required to flow up and down through proper channels, a request initiated at a relatively low level may take an excessively long time to reach a coordinate level in a different division. In such circumstances, an informal arrangement to facilitate communication is likely to develop between same-level administrators in different divisions—the transhierarchical bridge.

STAFF AND LINE

The staff-and-line concept views the organization in terms of vertical and horizontal components based on differentiation of functions. The vertical dimension establishes the hierarchy of authority—the "line" component that is assigned responsibility for discharging the operational functions of the institution. Line positions grow out of departmentation, as the superintendent assigns duties and grants permission to

---

TABLE 2–4

EFFECT OF GROUP SIZE ON RELATIONS WITHIN THE GROUP

Number in group	Number of relations	Increase in relations with each addition to group
2	1	—
3	3	2
4	6	3
5	10	4
6	15	5
7	21	6
8	28	7
9	36	8
10	45	9
15	105	—
20	190	—
50	1225	—

Source: Chester I. Barnard, *The Functions of the Executive,* Cambridge, Mass.: Harvard, 1938, p. 108.

position incumbents. Authority down the line is never absolute but is based on delegation. In general, line officers are responsible for activities related directly to providing educational services to children, youth, and adults.

The staff concept gives a horizontal dimension to the organization. A staff officer provides special services or fulfills certain responsibilities that a line officer at any given level of the administrative hierarchy would perform if the latter had (1) the time and (2) the specialized knowledge to do it. In other words, the staff component represents an extension of the line executive's responsibility and, as such, can be attached to an executive at any echelon. In general, however, the staff concept has been limited primarily to those at the general administrative level. The function of the staff, it is said, is primarily advisory and consultative. Authority over operatives in a given department is assigned to line officers, not to staff officials.

The staff-and-line concept was developed to a high degree of proficiency by the Prussian Army just prior to the turn of the century. Although the concept probably dates back to before the Prussian Army, this military organization was among the first of modern organizations to make extensive and highly developed use of it. The staff-and-line concept can be applied in business and education without adoption of the disciplinarian framework or the other aspects of the military.

Staff officers and line officials complement, rather than compete with, each other. The growing need for technical experts in new fields tends to stimulate a larger staff complement. Creating a staff organization is one way to make use of specialized executive skills.

The staff person has functional authority but no direct authority over operating personnel. He has permission to prepare and issue directions with respect to a given group of educational activities only in the name of the line executive to whose office he is attached. It is his relation to the

FIGURE 2–4

Effect of layering and the transhierarchical bridge on interorganizational communication.

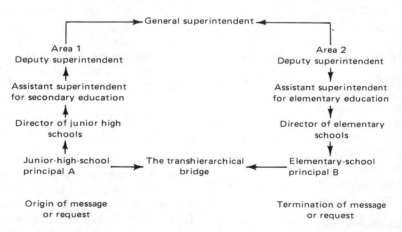

line executive rather than authority inherent in his own position that brings others to be influenced by his recommendations. A supervisor as a staff person has no formal authority over teachers but must depend on persuasion or prestige related to his special knowledge in a field. The staff officer has technical authority—the authority of a specialist, which adheres to the individual, moves with the individual, and cannot be assigned to him. If the supervisor seeks to implement without relying on persuasiveness of his arguments, he must do so in the name of the general superintendent (a line officer). Such recommendations will then fall on the chain of operating command to principals and teachers. This assumes that the superintendent goes along with recommendations by virtue of his confidence in the supervisor as an expert in curriculum and would have issued the recommended change had he had time and knowledge to prepare it.

Concepts such as staff and line are useful terms in assigning duties and locating specific responsibilities, but there is a danger in rigid interpretation.[43] The main missions of staff officers are to conduct auxiliary activities and to serve as advisors to line executives. Duties assigned to a staff person helping an executive plan or supervise the activities of others may include any or all of the following:

1. Assembling, summarizing, and interpreting facts
2. Recommending courses of action
3. Discussing plans with other executives to obtain their reactions
4. Preparing written orders necessary to activate a plan
5. Explaining or interpreting orders issued

[43]Lepawsky, op. cit., pp. 320–321, and Newman, op. cit., p. 181.

6. Evaluating the manner in which orders are working
7. Being ready to initiate new plans
8. Promoting an exchange of information among operating officials
9. Informing and advising operatives

A critique of the staff-and-line concept

An organization with staff officials can experience complex problems of relations between the narrow specialists who observe a given phenomenon from one perspective, and the general executives, who have breadth of vision but not special knowledge in the area. The staff agencies also increase expenses. It is not unusual in times of financial cutbacks to find reductions in force occurring first among staff positions.

Charts that depict staff-and-line relations are idealized pictures of operations within an organization. Seldom is the chain of command limited to the paths indicated on an organizational chart. Direct contact between a teacher and a superintendent is more common in a large school system than it is between a worker and the chief executive of an industry of any size. One reason for this is the nature of the education profession; teachers and administrators are members of the same profession. Furthermore, top industrial executives seldom hire operatives, whereas most school superintendents are actively involved in the employment of individual teachers.

There is ample evidence that such concepts of organization as unity of command, hierarchy of authority, and line and staff are undergoing considerable modification as the functions of an organization and the qualifications of people available to fill positions change. This is noted in the armed forces as well. Implicit in line organization is the fact that one person at any level can be replaced by another of the same rank. However, in an age of specialization this is not true. A captain in the Air Force may be able to pilot jet fighters or multiengine planes, whereas another is knowledgeable only about engineering, electronics, missile work, or navigation. Specialization has made people of equal rank unlike. Much the same has occurred in teaching. Certification laws and accreditation requirements often do not permit one teacher to be replaced by another.

Specialization in education has confused the relative hierarchical status of the staff-and-line positions. The creation of new posts at the central-office administration level precipitates the question of who is superordinate and who is subordinate to whom.

Some definitions are in order. The term "superordinate" is preferred to the term "superior." It designates a position in the hierarchy of the organization that is considered higher in rank, endowed with greater authority, or more prestigious than that of one or more other positions in the system. Coordinate positions are those of relatively equal rank, authority, or prestige. Subordinate posts enjoy less rank, authority, or prestige than one or more other positions in the hierarchy. It can be seen that these three designations are relative and are viewed from an organizational standpoint rather than from any social system outside the organization. Differences in salary among position incumbents serve only to obfuscate the issue.

Identification of comparative rank, authority, or prestige is fairly simple within a single branch of the organization. For instance, few will argue that the senior high school principal is subordinate to the assistant superintendent in charge of secondary education. Ranking becomes more difficult

when several branches are involved. For example, is the elementary school principal coordinate with the junior or senior high school principal? Is the special subject supervisor superordinate, coordinate, or subordinate to the elementary school principal? In a system where there is an assistant superintendent for curriculum and none for secondary education, is the high school principal subordinate, coordinate, or superordinate to the assistant superintendent for curriculum?

One way out of the dilemma is to ignore the relative designations of rank or authority among the main branches of the hierarchy. This does not preclude conflict, however. Another solution is to have the superintendent or the board clearly define the status of each position. This will not bring uniformity among separate systems if research in the area involves more than one system. A third approach is to establish a standard that recognizes the hierarchical distance from a focal point such as the superintendent or board of education. Positions once removed from the superintendent's office are judged superordinate to all positions twice or more times distant from the focal point, regardless of the branch of the hierarchy. Thus, all assistant superintendents reporting directly to the superintendent are superordinate (in a hierarchical sense) to principals or directors who report to him through the office of an assistant superintendent. The high school principal is subordinate to the assistant superintendent for curriculum or the assistant superintendent for business (logistical support) services. The supervisors (staff personnel) are coordinate with the principals if the former report to an assistant superintendent. Not all problems are solved by this approach, however, for look what happens to principals when there is an assistant superintendent for elementary education but none for secondary education. More consideration must be given to these problems in future years.

An organization chart for public education

The organization chart (org chart) with its familiar pattern of lines and boxes is found almost everywhere. The most important position is at the apex. In schools, the school board is placed there, and immediately underneath is the superintendent. As stated previously, charts seldom depict reality, because they do not take account of informal relations. Also they quickly become obsolete in a dynamic school system. Frequently, the obvious fact that people rather than charts are being reorganized is overlooked. The personalities of the people holding the positions, rather than the best thought on administration, may dictate who reports to whom. Although it has been said that the architect of an organization chart that satisfies everybody should be acclaimed the best fiction writer of the year, few can resist the urge to pattern boxes and solid and dotted lines between the spaces in the top box and those in lesser boxes. The typical org chart of a school district focuses on operational aspects of the system. From the systems point of view operations represent only one facet of the total. In a time of relative stability, maintaining smooth and efficient operations may well be the sole preoccupation of the chief administrator. But the present period is one of considerable ferment. Change is demanded by the people of the community, the state legislature, and federal officials. A more realistic org chart should depict a structure that facilitates introduction of promising social

innovations. An org chart showing various major functions in school administration is presented as Figure 2–5.

Division I: operations division. School operations is the first major division. It is clear enough and sufficiently common so that no further explanation of it is necessary. Administration of elementary, secondary, and special educational centers constitutes the prime function of this division. The other five divisions are discussed below.

Division II: innovation and development. Within this division are branches concerned with identifying new and promising practices through research or other means, developing the program and staff necessary to take advantage of an innovation, and planning for fiscal and facility adjustments necessary for implementation of change. Program development is a major branch in the overall educational planning system. After a promising social innovation has been found effective in pilot situations, it moves into the program development branch, becomes a part of curriculum planning, and, if successful, is included in the school's operations. Its introduction rests on the efforts of special staff consultants working through special in-service development meetings with the instructional staff in Division I (operations division). Instructional media are developed. Program evaluation through testing and surveys is included as part of the total development task. What was previously recognized purely as supervision of existing operations is now conceived as well as consultant services to direct and facilitate program development and implementation. In other words, supervision is viewed not as a way to maintain the status quo but as a way to

FIGURE 2-5

Functional administrative organization.

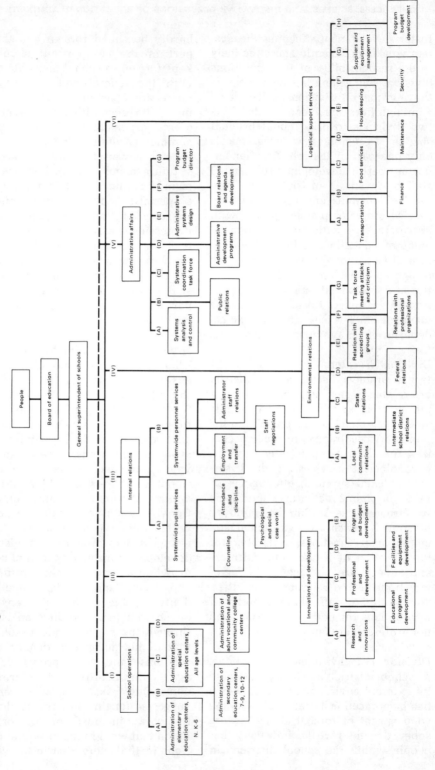

foster development. Keeping the system working efficiently and effectively is the responsibility of the operations division, but generating new ideas is the mission of Division II. Top-level administrators must coordinate these two divisions to bring about prudent change. Designing new programs is only one part of the job. Another important part is developing professional staff by means of district-inspired in-service programs and cooperative in-service programs planned jointly with universities or with the state department of education. A final important part of educational development is the design and development of new facilities and equipment—an activity traditionally assigned to school business management services. This is a radical departure from previous organizations.

Division III: internal relations. The internal problems of a school district are related to serving pupils and maintaining job satisfaction and morale among personnel employed. Within the pupil services branch are such specialized functions as counseling services, psychological services, medical services, dental services, attendance affairs, discipline activities, and home welfare agencies. Within the employed personnel branch are recruitment and employment functions, programs for identification of future administrators and supervisors, the agency to facilitate transfer and retirement activities, administrative staff relations, and staff negotiations for both professional and nonprofessional staff.

Division IV: environmental relations. A school district must also relate to its external environment. This branch has been facetiously referred to as the "department of foreign affairs." More sober thought reveals, however, that people within the school district can hardly be called foreign and that no part of the environment should be kept foreign to school tasks. Relations with the federal and state governments are a part of this division. Dealings with accrediting bodies are another responsibility. Involvement in community affairs, PTA relations, and special power-structure studies constitute a major branch. Because criticism of public schools is never absent, a special task force to deal with it is suggested as another major branch. Professional associations have an impact on school district relations, and on occasion may invoke sanctions or, in the case of unions, precipitate strikes; these functions are related in part to internal relations through staff negotiations.

Division V: administrative affairs. There is need for a special division to ensure the continued effectiveness of the administration of the institution. Systems control and analysis constitutes a major branch and includes such agencies as those for information systems, operations research and surveys, and special reports on operational conditions. Public relations is another branch. Planning organizational changes is a significant activity within this division. A special branch is included to promote administrative development through special in-service growth programs for school principals, supervisors, and assistant superintendents. All the various divisions must be coordinated. Coordination is done through the superintendent's office or that of his designated deputy. Board relations and the preparation of agenda for board meetings are time-consuming tasks. A special branch is suggested for this purpose. Within this branch are included concern for legislation that would influence total operations in the school district.

Division VI: logistical support services. What has been previously identified as school business services is called in Figure 2–5 logistical support services. These include security of school district property, food services, transportation, housekeeping, maintenance, purchasing, storage and inventory of supplies and equipment, and finance. The finance function is subdivided into treasury, accounting, payroll, budgeting, and audit functions. The special functions of this division are discussed at length in Chapters 26 and 27.

The organization depicted in Figure 2–5 is an unusual pattern based on functions of significance to the operations, maintenance, and development of educational organizations. There is nothing sacred about any organization chart. It should change as new demands and responsibilities are placed upon the educational institution.

THE SCHOOL SYSTEM AS AN ORGANIZATION

All organizations are characterized by the following key factors: goals, structure, a social system of people within it, communication networks, distribution of authority, resources, cultural and environmental constraints, service functions, and a dynamic life cycle. The goals give direction to efforts and justify the organization's existence. They are dynamic in nature; new goals emerge and priorities within existing goals are constantly reordered.

Every organization has a structure that must be kept in balance and adapted to goals. The structural pattern defines relations among persons and groups within the organization. Tasks are allocated on the basis of some pattern that hopefully facilitates achievement of tasks. Rules and poli-

cies are a part of the framework. Specific decision points may be identified as well. The structure is demonstrated as a bureaucracy or hierarchy of positions.

Social systems develop in organizations simply because people are involved. People have different desires and skills. They group themselves in informal associations for various purposes and exhibit a characteristic pattern of interaction. Ways are defined for accepting or rejecting nonorganizational individuals or groups. The organization gives its members opportunities to express values such as encouraging or resisting innovations and changes.

Communication networks for receiving, processing, and transmitting information or intelligence are part of the organization. Preferred methods for communication become specified. Informal networks are of no less significance than formally conceived channels of communication.

Distribution of authority to strategic leverage points is another significant characteristic of an organization.

An organization cannot fulfill its challenges without resources and logistical support plans. Various types of resources—fiscal, human, and material—are required. Resources sustain activities but create logistical problems.

There are cultural and environmental constraints placed on all organizations. Operational constraints may make goal attainment difficult. Every organization has external relations to maintain.

The services an organization provides to its clientele and/or society justify its continued support. This is a more concrete way to express its goal orientations.

All organizations have a dynamic life cycle. They are created, struggle to exist, are modified by forces within and outside, mature, grow old, and sometimes die.

SUMMARY

There exists a universal process of administration. Fayol, early in the twentieth century, gave impetus to the idea that there are administrative functions common to all organizations. The administrative process represents an abstract picture of administration. It is the result of distilling the essence of administration from the many activities of the administrator.

The administrative process has been described in different ways. Descriptive word lists are the most common way, and there is a striking similarity among such lists. Because some terms represent different levels of abstraction, the dual system of classification was developed to describe the nature of the administrative process in a relatively small number of terms. Among the first-order abstract terms that convey what an administrator does are planning, decision making, operating or executing, and appraising. The second-order abstract terms are goal orienting, organizing, assembling and allocating resources, leadership, coordinating, controlling, and performing ceremonial functions; these represent a lesser degree of abstraction than do first-order terms. Meanings of these terms do not differ radically from those presented in other descriptive word lists. Carrying the process of abstraction further shows that planning, decision making, and problem solving are closely related to what Dewey called reflective thinking. In effect, it can be said that administration is concerned with thinking and action.

Goals and standards precede organizing. An organization is a system of structured interpersonal relations, with roles and expectations prescribed for incumbents of various positions. Organization is primarily a matter of determining form and structure and relations. Individual differences are better utilized when there is a systematic differentiation of roles in formal organization. There are informal organizations in all formal ones. The informal grows out of the personalities of fellow workers as a consequence of frequent social and other contacts. The informal organization may introduce positive changes, but may create problems as well.

Departmentation is the process of subdividing or grouping the work of an institution. Seldom, if ever, is only one of the many bases of departmentation used in an institution.

The hierarchy of authority gives a vertical dimension to an institution. The scalar principle declares that every organization consists of various gradations of authority, starting with the top administrative post and ending with the operatives. "Chain of command" implies much the same idea. It is suggested that an organizational pyramid for schools could be identified on the basis of the breadth or scope of authority in the systems. These broad gradations of authority are (1) general administration (including board members and general superintendent), (2) central-office administration (assistant superintendents, directors, and supervisors), (3) building administration (principals and assistant principals), and (4) classroom administration (department heads and teachers).

Unity of authority or command calls for one chief executive to assume ultimate responsibility. Each individual, in turn, is responsible to one executive or supervisor. A modification of this is developing in our age of specialization. Joint command or dual supervision need not pose insurmountable problems if a teacher looks to the supervisor for technical assistance in a specialized field and to the principal for all other or general administrative directions.

The process of delegation involves (1) assigning duties, (2) granting authority to make commitments and utilize resources, and (3) creating an obligation on the part of the subordinate for reporting and for satisfactory performance. The responsibility for performance of the task remains with the executive who delegated the duty, as well as with the person who accepted it. Technical authority resides in the individual who has developed the expertness and goes with him as he moves from position to position. The executive cannot automatically create a technical authority through the process of delegation.

Span of supervision or control is concerned with the number of persons of administrative rank who can be supervised effectively by an executive. It is dependent upon a variety of factors, such as time, complexity of the situation, and stability of operations. A large span of supervision will result in a flat organization, that is, relatively few administrative levels between the lowest and highest executives. A limited span of control in a large and complex institution will create a pyramidal or tall organizational structure. The danger of layering is most pronounced in tall organizations, and devices such as the transhierarchical bridge have been developed to facilitate communication. The decision gap is layering viewed from another vantage point.

The staff-and-line concept permits an analysis of organization into its vertical and horizontal components. The line officers are concerned with discharging subject matter functions. Staff officers serve as advisory or consultative persons for line officers and are involved in the discharge of auxiliary activities to facilitate the proper functioning of line responsibilities. Staff-and-line officers complement rather than compete with each other. Staff officers have functional authority only, and no real authority, over line personnel. The idealized version of staff-and-line positional relations can be depicted in a formal chart of organization. Such a chart fails to show the informal organization, and seldom are actual operations limited to the formal paths of interrelations indicated.

The age of specialization has created new problems for school organization not anticipated by present concepts. Even ideas such as staff and line are beginning to crumble and remain only because better ways of depicting the personnel structure have not been developed or accepted. Identifying who is an administrator has become more complex.

The formal chart of organization (org chart) for most school systems focuses primarily on operations at the expense of system development. A new organization chart is presented based on school operations, innovations and development, internal relations, external relations, administrative systems, and logistical support services.

QUESTIONS

1. What is the administrative process?
2. Which of the functions of the administrator is most important?
3. In what ways are planning and decision making similar? Dissimilar?

4. What can an understanding of a universal process of administration contribute to a better understanding or better practice of school administration?
5. What is meant by informal organization? Have you ever been in a school system that had an informal organization? Describe it.
6. What is the best basis for the departmentation of a school system?
7. What is "layering"? What effect does the development of a "transhierarchical bridge" have on layering?
8. What are the factors that influence an effective span of supervision?
9. Who is more important in a school organization, a staff officer or a line officer?
10. Can there be an organization without communication? Justify your stand.

SELECTED REFERENCES

Barnard, Chester I., The Functions of the Executive, Cambridge, Mass: Harvard, 1938.

Gregg, Russell T., "The Administrative Process," in R. F. Campbell and R. T. Gregg, eds., Administrative Behavior in Education, New New York: Harper & Row, 1957.

Lepawsky, Albert, Administration, New York: Knopf, 1955, chaps. 1, 4, 8, 10, and 11.

Newman, W. H., and C. E. Sumner, Jr., The Process of Management, Englewood Cliffs, N.J.: Prentice-Hall, 1961.

3

DECISION MAKING, COMMUNICATION, AND PLANNING

Although the scope of the administrator's functions was described in the previous chapter, three important processes—decision making, communication, and planning—deserve further analysis. Their interrelationship has been argued by noting that one outcome of planning is a decision action, and that decisions would be difficult if not impossible to implement without a communication system.

DECISION MAKING

The importance of decision making in the administration of organizations has been recognized since the writing of Barnard in 1938,[1] Simon in 1947,[2] and Bross in 1953.[3] The influence of these writers has been felt in the field of educational administration as well as elsewhere. There are different conceptualizations of decision making. Thus, Newman and Sumner "use the expression 'decision making' as a synonym of planning."[4] Dorsey viewed the decision process as an extension of or a series of interrelated communication events.[5] Simon conceived of decision making "as though it were synonymous with managing."[6] A decision was defined in Chapter 2 of this book as a conscious choice from among a well-defined set of often competing alternatives. A decision by a school administrator commits the district or other division of the school to a course of action. If it is a questionable action the school system may suffer and the decision rendered is called a poor one. Decision making is a sequential process that culminates in a single decision or a series of choices that stimulate moves or actions. At least two alternatives must be generated, and more often than not the number of possible actions is far greater. The results of the decisional process are policies or rules that guide subsequent behavior. The importance attached to decision making lies in large part in its influence over the organization's subsequent behavior.

Decision making may be considered a culminating activity, or the final

[1]Chester I. Barnard, Functions of the Executive, Cambridge, Mass.: Harvard, 1938.

[2]Herbert A. Simon, Administrative Behavior, New York: Macmillan, 1947.

[3]I. D. J. Bross, Design for Decision, New York: Macmillan, 1953.

[4]W. H. Newman and C. E. Sumner, Jr., The Process of Management, Englewood Cliffs, N.J.: Prentice-Hall, 1961, p. 253.

[5]J. T. Dorsey, Jr., "A Communication Model for Administration," Administrative Science Quarterly, December 1957, p. 309.

[6]Herbert A. Simon, The New Science of Management Decision, New York: Harper & Row, 1960, p. 1.

phase in rendering a choice among alternatives, plus all activities that occur prior to it. When Simon declared that decision making was synonymous with managing, he referred to the whole process, which includes finding occasions for making a decision, identifying possible courses of action, and choosing among many different courses of action.[7] Decision making can be considered synonymous with politics as well as management; some political scientists define politics as making and executing authoritative decisions for society. On the other hand, Dorsey[8] emphasized that because the decision rests upon the receipt of some kind of communication and can be effectuated only through communication to others, communication is the more important of the two. Pfiffner and Sherwood declared that decision making and communication were interdependent and in practice inseparable though not identical.[9]

Economists, political scientists, statisticians, psychologists and behavioral scientists, management scientists, specialists in operations research, and systems analysts all express a lively interest in writing and research in the area. The economist's long-standing interest stems from how consumers make choices and how economic organizations determine the most promising course of action. The behavioral scientist is a relative newcomer to the area. Even more recent are the activities of the operations researcher and the systems analyst in sharpening decision-making skills. In the systems approach, the organization is viewed as an integrated decision system.[10] The

systems approach tends to blend communication and decision making and refers to the new unity as an "information-decision system."

Interest in decision making in educational organizations had to await the development of an appropriate perspective for examining the functions of the administrator. When the focus switched from primary concerns for operational problems, such as personnel or school-plant construction, to the examination of the process or the theory of administration, decision making emerged along with communications as an area of particular significance.

The process of decision making

Taylor[11] reported evidence that suggested that when viewed in terms of process, problem solving, decision making, and creativity are essentially the same. Each is a variety of thinking and involves similar activities and sequences. He suggested the need for a general theory of thinking. Taylor differentiated these intellectual activities in terms of the result, not the process. Thus, creativity is a type of thinking that results in the production of ideas; decision making is a choice among alternative courses of action; and problem solving is a solution of problems.

The antecedent of all these efforts is John Dewey's classic work, whose title comes right to the point—*How We Think*.[12] Dewey's steps called for:

1. Stimulation to thinking through the existence of a felt need.

[7]Ibid.

[8]Dorsey, op. cit.

[9]J. M. Pfiffner and F. P. Sherwood, *Administrative Organization*, Englewood Cliffs, N.J.: Prentice-Hall, 1960, p. 309.

[10]R. A. Johnson, F. E. Kast, and J. S. Rosenzweig, *The Theory and Management of Systems*, 2nd ed., New York: McGraw-Hill, 1967, p. 281.

[11]D. W. Taylor, "Decision Making and Problem Solving," in J. G. March, ed., *Handbook of Organizations*, Chicago: Rand McNally, 1965, pp. 48–82.

[12]John Dewey, *How We Think*, Boston: Heath, 1910.

2. Location and clarification of the nature of the problem.
3. Suggestion of possible solutions.
4. Hypothesis or development of a vehicle which can initiate and guide observation and gathering facts and ideas.
5. Mental elaboration, or reasoning to determine the consequences of the suggested hypotheses of solution.
6. Experimental corroboration of the hypotheses selected by overt or imaginative action.

All writers since Dewey have stressed that:

1. There must be a situation that calls for a decision before there can be decision making (felt need).
2. It is imperative to define or diagnose the nature of the problem (location and clarification).
3. The problem can be analyzed by gathering data pertinent to it (further clarification).
4. Alternative courses of action must be generated or preferred solutions formulated (suggestion of possible solutions).
5. Each alternative course of action should be appraised, preferably through the use of a model that portrays the essential properties of the phenomena under study (hypothesizing).
6. Consequences of each possible choice must be examined through sophisticated processes such as cost-benefit analysis or informal consideration of what might happen after the decision were made (mental elaboration).
7. After the choice is rendered and the decision put into effect, the decision should be evaluated (experimental corroboration).

Simon spoke of the initial phase of the decision-making process as "intelligence activity,"[13] by which he meant surveying the environment to identify conditions that call for new action. This, in effect, is similar to sensing the need for a decision. The second phase

he called "design activity" and the third "choice activity." He believed that decision-making skills could be developed and that good decision makers, therefore, are made and not born.[14]

Newman and Sumner identified the four phases in rational decision making as (1) diagnosis, (2) discovering alternatives solutions, (3) analyzing and comparing alternatives, and (4) selecting the plan to follow.[15] Diagnosis starts the rational process by identifying and clarifying the problem. What obstacles might impede achievement are located and isolated for analysis. Differentiation between symtoms and sources of trouble is another aspect of diagnosis. Sometimes critical limits or constraints are placed on the pursuit of acceptable solutions. Diagnosis, therefore, calls for specifying the trouble, identifying probable causes, outlining requirements for an appropriate solution, and stating the constraints or limits upon the search for a solution. Alfred P. Sloane, Jr., of the General Motors Corporation, emphasized the importance of getting all the facts possible and examining the problem from all angles prior to making a decision.

Diagnosis leads to discernment and clarification of issues. It sets the stage for the search for alternatives. Imagination and originality are prime requisites for finding ways to overcome obstacles. Creativity is essential in the generation of new and useful alternatives.[16] The various stages in the creative act are:

1. *Saturation.* Immersing oneself in the situation so as to know the problem and its setting from all angles.

---

[13]Herbert A. Simon, *The New Science of Management Decision,* New York: Harper & Row, 1960, pp. 2–4.

[14]Ibid.
[15]Newman and Sumner, op. cit., pp. 261–262.
[16]Ibid., pp. 78–87.

2. *Deliberation.* Serious study of all sides of the problem by analyzing, reviewing, rearranging, and rethinking all points of view and noting previously obscure relations.
3. *Incubation.* Allowing ample time for ideas to gel.
4. *Illumination.* The coming of the sudden great idea or solution, the closing of the "insight gap," the emergence of the most promising notion.
5. *Accommodation.* Further development of the idea by reframing and modifying it on the basis of other people's reaction to it.

Individual creativity can be facilitated by guarding against attitudes and habits that constitute psychological barriers to creativity, by seeking the fresh viewpoint or approach to the problem under study, and by serendipity (the gift of discovering the unexpected).

Group approaches to creativity, such as brainstorming, work best if the problem is simple and specific. Brainstorming is most likely to be productive when (1) the group refrains from criticizing or evaluating ideas presented, (2) even wild or freewheeling ideas are encouraged, (3) large numbers of different ideas are produced, and (4) "hitchhiking" on another's ideas occurs, such as when various notions are combined and expanded. A permissive atmosphere, along with willingness to adapt and borrow ideas of others enhances the process of defining or generating alternatives.

Analyzing and comparing alternatives is necessary to ascertain the advantages of each. This reduction process, often regarded as the essence of decision making, can be accomplished through the traditional decision-making methods described by Simon.[17] Habits

of individuals and the standard operating procedures characteristic of organizations influence choices in a decision situation. Operations research, a cluster of procedures and tools within the systems approach to administration, provides other ways of comparing alternatives. Operations research stresses construction of a model of the problem under consideration, the use of interdisciplinary teams in attacking a problem, and the use of quantitatively oriented tools to cope with alternatives. Cost-effectiveness analysis is a similar technique for appraising one alternative against another.

The final act in the process as visualized by Newman and Sumner is arriving at the choice of action. What most people think of as decision making is simply the culminating activity or the final act that determines the course of action.

Decision making is not a fragmented or isolated activity unrelated to total operations; rather, it is a sequential and continuous process. As a process, it introduces a rational way of determining which courses of action to follow. However, it is not suggested that values have no role in decision making. The decision is evaluated in terms of the ultimate values of the individual or organization as well as by objectively determined outcomes. Logic processes facilitate objective decision making but do not determine which one of several alternatives should be selected.

Types of decisions

Simon offered a taxonomy based on programmed and nonprogrammed decisions.[18] The two classifications were not intended to be mutually exclusive,

---

[17]Simon, op. cit., pp. 9–14.

[18]Ibid., pp. 5–26.

but rather represented two points on a continuum ranging from highly programmed decisions at one end to highly unprogrammed decisions at the other. Programmed decisions are used in basically repetitive and routine activities, that is, when definite procedures can be worked out. Such decisions cover the regular operational or routine problems of an organization that do not need a unique response for each recurrence. In contrast, nonprogrammed decisions encompass the novel and unstructured issues where standard operating procedures may not apply because the situation is new or because too many variables are involved. Nonprogrammed decision-making situations are those for which the decision maker must rely on intelligent, adaptive, or problem-oriented behavior.

Simon contended that programmed and nonprogrammed decision making within an organization are based on different techniques. Thus, improvement of programmed decision making can come from the development of internalized standard operating procedures of written policies and careful allocation of programmed decision-making responsibilities within the hierarchy. In contrast, improvement in nonprogrammed decision making stems primarily from training in orderly thinking. Use of the scientific approach to decision making or problem solving is imperative. It begins with a simple question such as "What is the problem?" or with what in the military is called an estimate of the situation. New techniques related to operations research and systems analysis can be employed in programmed as well as nonprogrammed decisions.

Decision making takes place in situations where a variety of constraints are forced upon the organization and its administrators. These constraints, such as completing the task within a specified time or within existing budgetary resources of personnel and money, set conditions surrounding a decision and to some extent influence the use of traditional or modern methods of decision making.

Economists speak of decision making under certainty, under risk, and under uncertainty. In the first instance, the decision maker knows all the alternatives and the specific consequences of each. This is the classic concept of the economic man who has all the pertinent data and always acts rationally. Decision making under risk is similar to choosing under certainty, in that all alternatives and all strategies leading to particular consequences are known. The difference is that one alternative does not invariably lead to a given set of outcomes; the end result of pursuing a given course of action occurs with a probability that can be computed but not with certainty. Decision making under uncertainty has some characteristics of the previous conditions. It differs from the risk situation in that the probabilities of outcomes are not known and cannot be computed.

The difficulties of decision making are compounded when incomplete or invalid information prevents the administrator from knowing all alternatives and when incomplete or inaccurate study of analysis makes it impossible for him to foresee the consequences.

Another type is group decision making where decisions are made with the participation of the people who carry out the decision in the daily work of the school. This can be done by a majority decision or by demanding group consensus. In the latter approach "all participants contribute their thoughts and feelings and all share in the final decision."[19] It is very difficult to operate in this mode because consensus is often impossible to achieve.

Methods and tools of decision making

Traditional methods emphasize the value of experience to habituate individuals to standard operating procedures. Recently developed approaches, derived from systems concepts and operations research, stress other dimensions for improvement of the decision process. The use of mathematical models and tools, such as linear programming, statistical decision theory, and Monte Carlo techniques is developed in greater detail in Chapter 7 of this book. The program evaluation and review technique (PERT) is a way to sharpen decision-making abilities. Game theory, which is basically decision making in conflict situations, reveals the dynamic qualities of decision-making situations so that for every action there may be a possible reaction calling for determination of new choices of action.

Evaluation of the decision-making process in the school situation leads to cost-effectiveness studies. Every alternative has its own set of resources (costs) necessary to attain a goal. These costs must be weighed against the degree of effectiveness likely to be attained in pursuing a given alternative. Cost-effectiveness analysis is held by many to be synonymous with systems analysis. Sophisticated mathematical analysis is part of the process. Suffice it to say at this point that cost-effectiveness studies represent one way of improving decision making in education.

[19]R. A. Schmuck et al., *Handbook of Organization Development in Schools*, Palo Alto, Cal.: National Press Books, 1972, p. 258.

Decision levels in educational administration

A school system can be conceptualized in terms of decision points, that is, places in the hierarchy where specific kinds of decisions are reached and from which the determined course of actions emanate. This implies a delegation of authority and consequent responsibility. The various decision points are interrelated to focus on goals of the organization. At the top or superintendency level decisions are rendered on exceptional problems or on choices within an unusual situation. The many detailed operating decisions should not be determined here; rather, the emphasis on the superintendency level is on overall planning and strategy decisions. At the middle level (building, attendance-center, and supervisory administrators), decision-making responsibilities related to implementation of strategy or general policy developed are translated into operational activities. Basic operation decisions, therefore, are allocated to the middle echelon. Exceptions to standards operating procedures, controls, or appraisals are referred to the top echelon. At the lowest level (classroom, department, or general service activity), basic decisions on teaching procedures or service methods are determined. The authority to make such decisions is delegated from middle-echelon officers. The greater involvement of teachers in the decision-making process is one characteristic of education today. Professional negotiation is one way teachers gain access to the points where decisions are reached. Collective bargaining is an agreement-making process. Decision making can also be viewed as a bargaining or agreement-determining process.

The foregoing model assumes that

responsibility for various types of decisions is clearly specified within the organization. Decision making is a characteristic of all mankind. Choices are forced upon the housewife determining what shall constitute the menu for the evening meal, the college girl wondering what to wear, as well as the top-echelon executive concerned with the destiny of a complex enterprise. What differentiates decision making by the top-level or middle-level administrator from that by others is the nature of the decision to be made. Administration by exception implies that administrators at the general superintendency level are consulted only when an unusual operating decision must be made. Operational decisions evolve from the implementation of strategy; plans are formulated at the top echelon, and responsibility for execution rests with the middle-echelon administrators and service-echelon personnel in the school system.

Barnard observed that one choice is that there shall be no decision: "The fine art of executive decision making consists in not deciding questions that are not pertinent, in not deciding prematurely, in not making decisions that cannot be made effective, and in not making decisions that others should make."[20] The statement suggests the need for judgment and implies that decision making is an art. It is an art, however, that can be enhanced through science, particularly the utilization of some of the more sophisticated models and mathematical techniques. Although the systems approach is based on objective analysis in decision making, it does not preclude the decision maker's use of intuition and judgment. Science becomes a way to sharpen intuition and judgment, recog-

nizing their contributions as well as their limitations. Dr. A. C. Enthoven, Deputy Assistant Secretary for Systems Analysis of the Department of Defense in the 1960s, declared:

The analyst at this level is not computing optimum solutions or making decisions. In fact, computation is not his most important contribution and he is helping someone else to make decisions. His job is to ask and find answers to the questions: "What are we trying to do?" "What are the alternative ways of achieving it?" "What would they cost and how effective would they be?" "What does a decision maker need to know in order to make a choice?" (and) to collect and organize this information.[21]

Most concur that the really difficult problems involve too many variables to be decided in a strictly quantitative fashion and that the unrecognized constraints under which the decision maker must operate are far too complex to enable complete routinization of decision making. It is repeated: The contribution of the systems approach to decision making is to sharpen the intuition and judgment of the decision maker.[22] To a large degree decision making will be, like the iceberg, deeply rooted in the judgment capabilities of the decision maker.

COMMUNICATION

As stated earlier there is a close relation between communication and decision making. Prudent decision making is based on data that suggest alternative courses of action and facilitate comparison and evaluation of alter-

[20]Barnard, op. cit., p. 194.

[21]A. C. Enthoven, "Decision, Theory, and Systems Analysis," *The Armed Forces Comptroller,* vol. 9, no. 1, March 1964, p. 39.

[22]Gene H. Fisher, "The Role of Cost, Utility, Analysis, and Program Budgeting," in David Novick, ed., *Program Budgeting,* Washington, D.C.: GPO, 1965, p. 40.

native choices. Some system must be developed, therefore, for communicating such data to decision makers. An information-decision system is vital in systems analysis.

Organizations and communication

The many working parts of an organization necessitate establishment of a means of interchanging thoughts and coordinating efforts. Some writers contend that an organization cannot survive unless a means of communication is developed among various operating levels. An organization can be conceptualized as an elaborate system of communication. Thus, an organization may be seen as composed of sets of individuals with differentiated responsibilities, each set having a high degree of internal communication and some degree of external communication. Without communication, coordination would be all but impossible. It would be difficult to reach agreement on such important matters as how goals are to be achieved or what appraisal procedures shall be used. It is possible to comprehend the network of relations in a functioning organization by examining patterns of interpersonal contacts. These networks of positional and personal relations are a function of the formal and informal communication systems.

There are various conceptions of the term "communication." It can suggest the media of mass communication such as radio, television, newspapers, and magazines. Communication may be considered equivalent to public relations. Thus, it is said when school administrators fail to communicate effectively with school patrons problems arise. This, in turn, implies that better public relations is the answer to better communications. In another sense, communication may identify a specific field of study. Thus, English courses may be called courses in communication skills. Communication sometimes refers to semantics or special problems in the use of the language arts.

Considerable improvement is evident in the means available for communication, but relatively little has been accomplished to enhance better understanding between individuals and groups, particularly within organizations. Only a limited amount of research is available that focuses on interlocking networks of communication within school systems. There has been research in other fields, however, from which can be gained a better understanding of communication in school administration.

Concepts of communication

The many definitions of communication consider it (1) imparting or exchanging attitudes, ideas, and information by use of human abilities or technological media; (2) transmission and reception of ideas; (3) the broad field of human interchange of thought and opinions; and (4) a process of giving and receiving facts, ideas, and feelings.

More simply, communication may be defined as a process in which a communicator attempts to convey an image to a communicatee. This viewpoint considers the communicator as one who desires to impart an idea or a message to another person or group. He is the initiator of the process. Further review of terms such as communicator, communicatee, and image are in order. A *communicator* attempts to convey an image; he is the prime motivator of the communicatory activity. A *communicatee* experiences some degree of awareness that another is attempting to convey an image.

Whether the communicator succeeds in conveying the image, in its genuine or a distorted form, is measured on the communicatee's side of the picture. Note the implication of varying degrees of awareness on the part of the receiver of the image. An *image* is a representation of a communicator's purpose or intent. It may be an idea, a signal, a message, a picture, a diagram, a bit of information, an attitude, a feeling, or an emotion. Communication need not be confined to its language form. The image arises in and from the communicator. On the other hand, the interpretation or influence of the image is judged by the communicatee. The image is more popularly referred to as the message.

This process is usually charted as:

communicator (originator of information)→
image (information or message)→
instrument (transmitter)→
channel (medium)→
communicatee (receiver)→
impact.

Noise, or static, may occur in the channel and interfere with the communication process.

Communicatory activity can be examined in terms of (1) structural factors (parts or positions connected), (2) organizational functions, (3) content, (4) psychological concomitants of communication, and (5) other properties.

Perceived and unperceived communication

Communication is not necessarily a two-way activity. A communicator may attempt to convey an image to a communicatee, but there is no assurance that the image transmitted will be received in part or in toto by the latter. By definition, any attempt to convey an image, whether consummated or not, is communication. This distinction necessitates the designation of two types of communication—one unperceived and the other perceived. A communication is unperceived when the attempt to convey a message results in no measurable degree of awareness on the part of the communicatee. The latter has no consciousness of the message, that is, it falls below the threshold of consciousness. If a superintendent sends a message to a principal, this is an act of communication. It is unperceived communication if the principal finds himself too busy to read the letter or loses it, or if it never reached him in the first place. A communication is perceived, on the other hand, when the attempt to convey an image results in some measurable degree of awareness on the part of the recipient. This does not imply any degree of congruence between the message sent by the communicator and its interpretation by the communicatee. It merely implies that the communicatee was aware that someone was trying to tell him something. The impact, or degree of congruence, between the original message and its interpretation is related in part to the credibility attached to the sender (communicator) by the receiver (communicatee or audience).

Factors in communication

In essence, communication is concerned with who says what through which channel or medium to whom and with what impact. The establishment of channels, or pathways, through which images or messages may travel is an essential part of organizing. Thus, in a school system it may be stipulated that all communication shall follow the chain of command. The superintendent desiring to contact elementary school teachers must do so through the office of the assistant superintendent in charge of elementary education and the elementary school principals. The medium may be a teachers' meeting or a letter.

In organizing, consideration must be given to how individuals in coordinate positions, such as elementary school principals, junior high school principals, and senior high school principals, can facilitate close and continuing communication to expedite learning or unify efforts. The principals' meetings, as well as informal social gatherings, may be means recognized for this purpose.

The invention of the telephone facilitated communication, but because it provides no corroborating evidence of message transmittal and receipt, it does not solve the general problem inherent in all types of oral communication—the difficulty in determining the accuracy of the interpretation of the oral message. Some insist that anything worth saying is worth writing down and that therefore all important communication should be reduced to writing to permit subsequent verification. To do so is time-consuming. Further, there is no guarantee that a written word will convey the same meaning to all individuals. Communication is one of the least understood areas in administration; yet few writers question the importance of creating a communication structure within any institution.

Communication is, in effect, a means to accomplish the objectives of an organization. It is central in all previously determined administrative functions such as planning, organizing, decision making, assembling and allocating resources, coordinating, leadership, and appraising. The organizational structure can be conceptualized in terms of communication events that connect pairs of individuals and establish patterns of context among individuals and other groups. Communication events, when repeated, tend to take on a characteristic form in terms of structure, function, content, psychological concomitants, and other properties. This implies that relations between individuals as reflected in characteristic communication events are appropriate and useful ways of understanding operational characteristics of an organization.

"Communication" is derived from the Latin word *communis* meaning "common." Through it a commonality of purpose and attitude between sender and receiver is established. Without communication, commonality of thoughts and opinions and of purposes or executions according to plan would be impossible to achieve. It is through the communication system that a decision reaches various levels in the enterprise. As the organization becomes more complex, through increased specialization, barriers to communication in many spheres of activities develop. Achieving coherence and control in organization becomes more difficult, and obstacles to the flow of communication are more readily apparent.

Research on communication

Berelson and Steiner summarized some of the significant research and points of view with reference to communication. These were:

1. People are likely to seek out congenial communications (those favorable to their predispositions) in controversial matters just after coming to a decision on the matter.
2. Rumors spread in direct proportion to the receptivity of the audience.
3. If the substance of the rumor is congenial to persons hearing it, it will be passed on to others and/or changed into more personally satisfactory forms.

4. Objective information on the subject that is not tied into the rumor itself is the best counterattack.
5. Misperception and misinterpretation of a communication follow one's psychological propensities to evade or distort a message.
6. The effect and use of the printed word in communication are related to the level of education—the higher the education, the greater the reliance on what is in print, and the lower the education, the greater the preference for oral and visual presentations.
7. People seek out and will respond to persuasive communications consistent with their predispositions to believe on an issue.
8. Facts are not effective in changing the opinion of an audience whose emotional predispositions run in a contrary direction—the stronger the psychological factors, the less the impact of an adverse communication; facts alone are not likely to win many converts where controversial issues are involved.
9. The higher one's intelligence, the more likely that the person will gain information from mass media.[23]

An organization becomes "too big" when information essential to effective operations fails to reach those mainly responsible for policy development as well as operations. Developing formal and understanding the informal communication networks (information system) within an educational system are matters of high priority in school administration. The significance of communication in an organization's planning, decision making, and leadership increases in direct proportion to its complexity. Organizational ineffectiveness, if not destruction, stems from difficulty in the exchange of messages among various points in the hierarchy. In the relatively small organization it is possible for the administrator to know personally most of the clients

[23]B. Berelson and G. A. Steiner, *Human Behavior*, New York: Harcourt Brace Jovanovich, 1964, pp. 527–554.

served and personnel employed—parents of students as well as the total teaching and supportive staff. This is not possible in complex urban operations. To obtain a feel for operations and to sense difficulties before they erupt into serious situations, the administrator must depend upon the flow of messages from key positions and the interpretation of information received from various important decision points.

One writer likened the administrator in a complex organization to a man driving a car with another person sitting next to him. When the driver is at the wheel, he has a feel for the total system by personally viewing the road, the pedestrians, the automobile traffic about him, the weather conditions, and the vehicle he is driving. Considerable confidence in arriving at his destination, no matter how many turns in the road, is not unusual under such conditions. But let it be assumed that the driver (the administrator) is blindfolded and must depend upon information communicated to him by the person sitting next to him. Clarity and promptness of communication are absolutely essential to the driver. Any breakdown in communication could be disastrous. The situation could be complicated further if the person sitting next to the blindfolded driver were forced to look out through the back window to give information to the man at the wheel, who thus receives the information after the event has occurred.

Communication thus far has been examined in terms of a process rather than in terms of the message or information being transmitted. The latter constitutes a separate discipline known as "information theory" or the "mathematical theory of communications" which is beyond the scope of this book.

The content of the message is no less important than the process of getting the message from one point in the organization to another. Determining the nature of information necessary to maintain awareness of operations, to detect potential trouble spots, or to evaluate performance is one of the most crucial unsolved problems in school administration. Calling for voluminous reports in the hope that somewhere within the mass of data is a clue merely intensifies the problem. An administrator can be suffocated under a pile of useless reports or what has been called "systematically organized ignorance."

The most serious deficiency concerns the pertinence, timing, and organization of information (in the form of reports) moving from operating levels upward to levels responsible for effective planning and decision making. The nature of the essential information for control and evaluation is not known with the precision necessary for effective administration. The simple question, "What do I need to know about each part of the school system to sense what is going on?" remains very difficult to answer.

Lane et al.[24] stressed that the internal and external communication system that permeates an organization has a profound impact on effectiveness in attaining organizational goals. They outlined the psychological and sociological factors that complicate the communication process and pointed out that the practicing administrator should recognize that communication problems in education "are not solved merely by increasing the flow of information," that "exposure does not guarantee effective communication,"

that "people may hear but do not always listen," that "a message may reach a person's desk but not his mind," and that "people may become almost immune to much of the enormous volume of messages that reaches them daily."[25] Sociopsychological forces point to the complexity of the process and simply a few words in a message or switching to a new channel or medium may not overcome barriers to communication. Predispositions, or the individual's personality factors, influence what is read or heard, individual perceptions, and what is or is not believed in a message.

PLANNING

The brief reference to planning in the previous chapter requires further expansion in light of growing references to the fact that administrators should be "educational planners" and the establishment of planning departments in local and state school systems. With a world in ferment administrators must develop special competencies that will allow them to anticipate future demands and to get the system ready to cope with change. Planning is an important mechanism for such purposes. To repeat the basic definition, planning is a process of preparing a set of decisions for future actions directed at achieving goals by optimal means. The concern here is for the planning methodology as rational thought and action rather than simply an exhortation to invest in something important called planning. Planning does not exist in a vacuum. Goals and objectives for it must be set. It has a specific context such as facilities, urban, fiscal or resource allocation, or program planning. It has

[24]W. R. Lane, R. G. Corwin, and W. G. Monahan, *Foundations of Educational Administration: A Behavioral Analysis,* New York: Macmillan, 1967, chaps. 3 and 4.

[25]Ibid., p. 90.

a time frame such as short-range or long-range planning, tactical or strategic planning.

Planning is sometimes equated with data processing simply because of the large volume of information required to meet its objectives. Information inputs are needed to define what conditions presently prevail, what is the nature of the problem under study, and what are the expectations. Forecasting is not the same as planning, although the estimates of likely future conditions are important to the decisions influenced by planning activities. Information is so vital that many argue that the quality of planning to reach a given objective is only as good as the accuracy, recency, and organization of the data available and the rationality of procedures employed.

Logically the educational planner should pursue a series of steps such as:

1. Appraising the political, economic, and social environments that will face the schools at some future point in time.
2. Determine what changes in learner and school patron needs will be evident in the projected new environment for education.
3. Project (develop a scenario of) the desired goals to be pursued and administrative roles to be played in the type of future school environment envisaged.
4. Establish vehicles within a system for the communication and information flow to facilitate the involvement of institutional and other personnel in the planning process.
5. Translate the broadly defined planning objectives into a series of functional programmatic efforts.
6. Develop more detailed planning activities within each of the programmatic efforts.
7. Report the findings and conclusions of the planning efforts.
8. Design a set of decisions leading to actions consistent with the findings and conclusions that will enable the organization to more effectively fulfill future missions.

It is apparent that the magnitude of change confronting educational institutions will require competencies in a broad range of new techniques useful in planning, such as PERT, forecasting techniques, planning models, simulation, MBO/R, PPBS, and quantitative analysis. Most of these are described in greater detail in Chapters 7 and 8. Specific books on these techniques are available for those who seek to develop skills as well as general understandings about them.

The higher one moves in the hierarchy, the more of one's time and effort must be dedicated to anticipating future demands on the institution through planning. If a special department within the school is created for planning, its missions must be clarified, qualified personnel must be identified or trained, other resources should be commensurate with the tasks assigned, and lead time must be available to complete tasks assigned. Most planning departments in local and state school systems are in the infancy stage searching for more definitive status and functions.

There is no guarantee that planning will produce results. The quality factor is as important here as elsewhere. If the dimensions of planning are not understood, if too much is attempted at once, if the data available is inadequate, or if unrealistic expectations prevail that plans must be 100 percent true or accurate, then planning activities will be initially suspect and eventually lose much credibility among administrators. The existence of a planning department should not be misconstrued as a substitute for planning elsewhere. Such a division should employ the resource persons to facilitate planning at all administrative levels. Planning must be integrated within the total management system and administrators must be committed to follow its findings, by and large, or the investments in such efforts are not likely to have much of a payoff for schools. The proof of its value lies in what happens to the organization at some future time. As stated previously, the future will arrive whether the institution is ready or not.

SUMMARY

Decision making, communication, and planning are interrelated. One outcome of planning is a decision action and decisions are difficult to implement without a communication system.

Recognition of the importance of decision making in administration goes back at least as far as the writings of Barnard in 1938. Definitions or simple analyscs tell only part of the story. Decision making has been variously defined as planning, a series of interrelated communication events, managing, or a conscious change. The output of the process is policy to guide subsequent behavior. Some consider decision making and communication as interdependent and in practice inseparable.

Scientists from many disciplines are concerned with decision making. The behavioral scientist is a relative newcomer to the field. There is a striking similarity between problem solving, decision making, and creativity. The antecedent of all is thinking.

There are many phases in the decision-making process, including diagnosing the situation, discovering alternatives, analyzing, and selecting a plan to follow. Creativity is essential in the generation of alternatives. Decision making is a sequential and continuous process.

Simon suggested the classification of programmed (or fairly routine) decisions and nonprogrammed (or novel) decisions. Different techniques are required for making each type of decision. Often decision making must take place in the face of a variety of constraints. It may take place under certainty, risk, or uncertainty. Many methods and tools are available for the process. Traditional methods rely on experience, and more recent methods employ systems techniques and procedures.

A school system may be conceptualized in terms of decision points. Planning and strategy decisions take place at the highest echelons. One choice is that no decision be registered.

Communication is a process whereby a communicator (the initiator) attempts to convey an image to a communicatee (the recipient). The image is a representation of a communicator's purpose or intent. The total process can be charted as:

communicator→image→instrument
of transmission→channel
communicatee→impact.

It is not necessarily a two-way activity, for a communication may be perceived or unperceived. The impact, or degree of congruence, between the original message and its interpretation is related to the credibility attached to the sender by the receiver.

Communication is central to many administrative activities. It is essential to the survival of an organization. One indication that an organization is becoming too big is difficulty in reaching or relating to its various parts. The nature of the essential information for control and evaluation is not known with the precision necessary for effective administration. The internal and external communication system that permeates an organization has a profound impact on its effectiveness in attaining goals. Predispositions, or the individual's personality factors, influence what is read or heard, individual perceptions, and what is or is not believed in a message.

Administrators are being challenged to anticipate future demands and to get the system ready to cope with change. Planning, as rational thought and action, is a means for attaining such purposes. It does not exist in a vacuum, but rather operates in a special context such as urban planning or program planning to mention but a few.

Planning requires massive data inputs to define what conditions prevail, the nature of the problem, and what expectations exist. Forecasting is used in planning but is not all that planning is about.

The higher one moves in the administrative hierarchy, the greater the priority placed on the planning functions. Planning does not guarantee results. The quality factor prevails here as elsewhere. There are a number of reasons why planning is not always successful, such as attempting too much at once, inadequacy of data, and lack of adequate resources.

QUESTIONS

1. What are the essential elements of the decision-making process?
2. In what ways are creativity and decision making related?
3. How does a programmed decision differ from a nonprogrammed one?
4. Why is it said that decision making and communication are interrelated?
5. What tools are available to enhance decision making?
6. What is communication?
7. Describe the essential elements of the communication process.
8. What are some of the significant points about communication discovered through research?
9. Why is communication essential to the survival of an organization?
10. What factors influence the quality of planning in an organization?

SELECTED REFERENCES

Berelson, B., and G. A. Steiner, *Human Behavior,* New York: Harcourt Brace Jovanovich, 1964.

Dewey, John, *How We Think,* Boston: Heath, 1910.

Dorsey, J. T. Jr., "A Communication Model for Administration," *Administrative Science Quarterly,* December 1957.

Kaufman, R. A., *Educational System Planning,* Englewood Cliffs, N.J.: Prentice-Hall, 1972.

Lane, W. R., R. G. Corwin, and W. G. Monahan, *Foundations of Educational Administration: A Behavioral Analysis,* New York: Macmillan, 1967.

McGrath, J. H., *Planning Systems for School Executives,* Scranton, Pa.: Intext Educational Publishers, 1972.

Newman, W., and C. E. Sumner, Jr., *The Process of Management,* Englewood Cliffs, N.J.: Prentice-Hall, 1961.

Simon, Herbert A., *The New Science of Management Decision,* New York: Harper & Row, 1960.

Taylor, D. W., "Decision Making and Problem Solving," in J. G. March, ed., *Handbook of Organizations,* Chicago: Rand McNally, 1965, pp. 48–82.

4

ADMINISTRATORS WORK WITH PEOPLE: HUMAN RELATIONS, MOTIVATION, AND LEADERSHIP

The previous chapters, if read apart from what follows, could leave an erroneous impression of the nature of the administrative challenge. It might be concluded prematurely that administration is concerned with things and functions and not with people. People make the organization productive or unproductive; they constitute the most important resources. How well an administrator can work with and for people will, in large measure, determine his success. As will be evident from the following discussion, it took a while for this obvious fact to emerge in the writing and research on the management of organizations.

EMERGENCE OF THE HUMAN ELEMENT IN ORGANIZATIONS

Max Weber,[1] the European social scientist, developed the classical model for the bureaucratic organization around the end of the last century. He designed patterns of relations to guide activities within a complex formal organization, with the hope that the patterns would enhance productivity or stimulate more effective services for the organization's clientele. Since then the term bureaucracy has gained an undesirable connotation. In popular usage bureaucratic structure implies a morass of red tape and the rigid application of policies that guide an organized institution's activities that is almost devoid of human consideration. The popular concept bears little resemblance to the purposes of operation of Weber's model of management.

Admittedly mechanistic, Weber's concept was characterized by a division of labor within the organization based on functional specialization, a well-defined hierarchy of authority, a system of rules covering rights and duties of position incumbents, a system of procedures covering work to be performed, a situation where impersonality prevailed in interpersonal relations, and a pattern for selection and assignment of individuals to various positions based on technical competency.[2] It was a monolithic concept concerned primarily with internal operations of what was for all practical purposes a mechanical system, not

[1] Max Weber, *The Theory of Social and Economic Organization*, A. M. Henderson and Talcott Parsons, trans., Talcott Parsons, ed., New York: Free Press, 1947.

[2] R. H. Hall, "Concept of Bureaucracy: An Empirical Assessment," *American Journal of Sociology*, July 1963, p. 33.

with the relations of the organization to its environment. The Weberian model was distinguished further by its universality: it could be implemented in a wide variety of organizations such as business enterprises, governmental agencies, military operations, and educational institutions. The bureaucratic model has had a profound influence on research and thinking about formal organizations, and some consider it the most important single statement on the subject. The formal charts of organization are diagrammatic translations of Weber's bureaucratic model.

This depersonalized form of organization had as its purpose the minimization of the impact of human capriciousness. This was accomplished by institutionalizing authority and carefully presenting procedures to be followed in all cases. Underlying it all was the belief that man was basically unpredictable, lazy, more often emotional than rational, disorganized in his approach to problems, and that such predispositions could interfere with achieving maximum efficiency. Weber recommended an organizational form to overcome the limitations of human resources working within it.

Weber was not the only one to stress form and structure and to minimize human relations, the psychological factors behind human productivity, and the impact of the informal group relations on operations within a large organization. Frederick W. Taylor, working at about the same time as Weber and who is credited as founder of the scientific management movement (not to be confused with the more recent management science approaches), is also criticized for stressing primarily the mechanical as opposed to the human aspects of production. Henry Fayol, working and writing during the same period, likewise paid little heed to the human element within a productive enterprise. Many writers find it difficult to avoid criticizing these pioneers, creatures of their time who attempted to make more orderly that which in practice tended toward chaos and limited productivity. Our present knowledge, however, is derived from the experiences and thinking of these early workers. The limitations of the early thinkers should not blind one to their many significant contributions to the improvement of management of organizations. It is evident even now that if one were to focus on the administrative processes and consider decision making, communication, and planning as the fundamental competencies in educational administration, that the human element might be lost in the shuffle.

An early reaction to the mechanistic and impersonal perceptions of organizations by Weber, Taylor, and Fayol came from Mary Parker Follett, who was among the first to recognize the importance of human factors in administration.[3] Her influence and contributions, which some place on a par with those of Florence Nightingale and Marie Curie, became known through a series of speeches pointing out the growing professionalization of business management and the significance of the human element.

The Hawthorne experiments

An experiment at the Western Electric Company's Hawthorne plant in Chicago almost unintentionally provided significant information on the impact of human relations on the productivity

[3]H. C. Metcalf and L. Urwick, eds. *Dynamic Administration: The Collected Papers of Mary Parker Follet,* New York: Harper & Row, 1942.

in an organization. Few experiments, particularly those that focus on small groups, have been quoted or referred to more often in the literature on administration than the Hawthorne or Western Electric studies, which took place in the late 1920s and early 1930s.

During World War I research in ways to increase productivity focused on how to measure the impact of physiological fatigue or other physical factors in the environment. Thus it was believed that the amount of light available in the work area would influence a worker's output. This environmental factor received special attention in experiments prior to those conducted by Mayo and Roethlisberger. It was anticipated that productivity would rise as light levels improved and this did in fact occur in the Hawthorne experiments. The unusual and unexpected result was that production was maintained at a high level even though illumination was reduced later to a point where it approximated bright moonlight. The last effect violated the common-sense prediction that production would decline if illumination was decreased since it rose when lighting was increased. In short, it had to be concluded that alternating the levels of illumination per se had little effect on productivity. The search for working conditions most conducive to high productivity was in the tradition of Taylor and the scientific management proponents. The explanation for the anomalous behavior in the illumination experiment had to be found in psychological rather than physiological factors related to work.

The Western Electric studies were concerned also with how the use of incentives to work could be combined with improved work conditions. The search for the most efficient and productive work arrangements began with the now famous six girls in the relay assembly room. The girls assembled electrical relays in a special room where they could be observed, but were told to perform at a comfortable pace and not to make a race out of the test. In spite of presence, absence, or great variations in a number of variables thought to affect productivity, such as work space or illumination, the output of the six girls continued to rise over the two years of the study. This raised the same kind of questions that emerged in the earlier illumination studies. The experimenters expected one set of results but experienced some unexpected or different ones as well. It was at this point that researchers began to be concerned with psychological factors. The six girls, it was reasoned, received special recognition by the fact that they were selected for an experiment. This improved their morale and had a positive influence on their productivity. An informal group was identified by the researchers, that is, a team that became a minisociety of its own within a big company. Interaction among members of the social group that had its own rules and sanctioned procedures was noted.

Eager to learn more about the effect of forces other than physical conditions of work, in 1927 Western Electric turned to Harvard professors Elton Mayo, an industrial psychologist, and F. J. Roethlisberger, a sociologist, for explanations of the phenomena. In this second research project they measured the influence of rest pauses, lunch breaks, and length of the work day and work week. The locale was the bank wiring observation room, whose name derived from the fact that wires were attached and soldered in rows or banks to a telephone switchboard component in this work area. What started as a limited project lasted more than five years, and its summation was not published until 1939.[4]

Physical conditions of work—noise, light, and amount of space—were varied, but the major experimental variable in the bank wiring observation room was a series of wage incentives. The number of workers involved was increased to fourteen, and thus the relations were more complicated than in the previous relay assembly room experiment. It was assumed by management that an employee would work hard for extra pay, but management failed to realize that the worker's first concern during these early years of the great depression was to keep a job. This meant playing it safe by keeping production levels steady in the face of all the incentives management was willing to offer.

The puzzled investigators concluded that neither wage incentives alone nor change in physical conditions could explain restriction of output. The emergence of the social group with its own code of behavior was demonstrated once again, as it had been in the earlier relay assembly room. It became evident that people in continuous contact tend to form informal social organizations; a group code is developed and differentiation of roles occurs within the informal group.[5]

The Hawthorne experiments stimulated the development of behavioristic models of organization. Administration was viewed more as a social process than as the mechanical manipulation of production factors. The human factor gained new prominence. The existence and importance of in-

formal group relations within the formal organizational structure gained the recognition due to it. Oddly enough the researchers were looking for something different from what they found; this is a classic illustration of serendipity.

The informal organization grows out of the social needs of people. The human relations movement pictured the organization as a system of individuals interacting, informal intergroup relations, as well as formal relations defined by the organizational chart. Psychologists and sociologists became more interested in the study of organizational behavior. The human relations movement is credited with changing the organizational style of administrators to place less emphasis on the rigid interpretation of efficiency suggested by F. W. Taylor and greater attention on obtaining the cooperation of employees and helping them identify more closely with the organization and its goals. Administrators are expected to be sensitive to people and to develop social skills for working with people, as well as to be competent in the technical aspects of their responsibilities.

The term "Hawthorne effect" grew out of the experiments as well. Those who believe it to exist interpret the Hawthorne effect as producing a positive change in behavior, learning, or output simply through knowledge of participation in an experiment. The gain stems from demonstrated concern for the needs of the worker and the special attention accorded him during the period of study.

---

[4]F. J. Roethlisberger and W. J. Dixon, *Management and the Worker*, Cambridge, Mass.: Harvard, 1939.

[5]M. S. Olmsted, *The Small Group*, New York: Random House, 1959, pp. 30–31.

BARNARD AND THE COOPERATIVE SYSTEM

In the late 1930s, Chester I. Barnard lectured and wrote about the organization, not as a mechanistic vehicle but as a system composed of human beings working cooperatively.[6] By a cooperative system, Barnard meant a group of persons some or all of whose activities are coordinated. The system was held together by a common purpose as well as by the willingness of certain people to contribute to the operation of the organization. People are in a position to cooperate more effectively if they can communicate with one another. Within every complex organization there are small operating groups and units that must interact if objectives are to be achieved. Barnard was among the first to differentiate between the formal and informal aspects of organization. Formal organization is consciously coordinated according to predetermined plan; informal organization grows out of the formal plan and is basically unconscious, indefinite, and structureless.

Barnard placed great emphasis on leadership, but paid greater heed to cooperation as the creative process in organization. He recognized leadership as being influenced by such variables as the individual, a group of followers, and the existing conditions.

Motivation

Administrators work with and through people to accomplish the purposes of the organization. Sensitivity to the human factor is an important first step. How to motivate teachers and others in the school system is a very significant next step. The administrator must be concerned with what makes people behave as they do. In more common parlance, what "turns on" a given staff? The search for understanding whether it is external motivators

or internal motivators that drive people to do what they do is a neverending one. What motivation strategies will be employed depends in part on how the administrator pictures the people with whom he works. In other words, what the superintendent or principal believes to be fundamental human nature influences his choice of rewards and punishments as well as his administrative style.

Whether man is good or evil, an end or a means, a pilot choosing or a robot imprisoned by circumstances, or a self-regulated being or externally regulated individual are contradictions that frame the fundamental issues in the continuing debate on human nature and how to work with members of an organization. Not everyone agrees on how to work with people; some are optimistic about human nature, and others are pessimistic.[7]

Tradition holds that people are essentially opposed to work and lack the capacity for self-direction and personal responsibility. Machiavelli in *The Prince* (1515) pictured man as rebellious, aggressive, selfish, greedy, and uncooperative, and therefore to be controlled by whatever means available to those who want to gain and maintain power or who have the responsibility to maintain order in government. Spencer, who adapted Darwin's law of natural selection to human beings, declared that even among the human race the fittest survive. Because the fittest are the aggressive, and the urge to dominate and to acquire material possessions is so great, many contend that conflict within an organization is unavoidable and something more than reason and self-control is required to develop

---

[6] Chester I. Barnard, *Functions of the Executive,* Cambridge, Mass.: Harvard, 1938.

[7] See H. P. Knowles and B. O. Sanberg, "Human Relations and the Nature of Man," *Harvard Business Review,* vol. 45, no. 2, March–April 1967, pp. 22–40, 172–178.

effective working relations within organizations. People's tendency to prey on others to satisfy personal desires must be restrained by society: This is perhaps the original sin. Modern theories of organization take exception to this pessimistic perception of humankind and believe that the individual has the capacity to be virtually self-motivated and self-controlled. Cooperative social relations are natural to man, according to this point of view, and he has the propensity to become psychologically involved in corporate activity. Equally important is the concept that a person's reaction to life is influenced most by the way he is treated by others.

McGregor[8] identified two opposing points of view about human beings in organization, one called Theory X and the other Theory Y. Theory X postulated the assumptions about human nature and behavior such as people dislike work, shirk responsibilities if they can, are not creative by nature, are innately lazy and unreliable, treasure security above all else, are inclined to be ruthless, are ungrateful, possess little ambition, and yearn for external direction. The administrator who subscribes to the Theory X view of people with whom he works will design rigid organizational patterns and controls based on imposed authority (institutionalized authority along the lines of the Weberian bureaucratic model). He will employ careful supervision, give detailed directions, insist on complete compliance, and will use threats of firings or economic harm to motivate the recalcitrants.

In contrast Theory Y's basic assumptions about human nature are people consider work natural as play, strive to establish cooperative social relations, do not enjoy being loners, are basically self-directive, want to help and contribute, exhibit self-control, are naturally creative, seek opportunities for creative expression and strive for excellence in everything they do.

Under proper condition most individuals will seek greater responsibilities and use much of their imagination, ingenuity, and creativity in solving organizational problems. The administrator who holds these views of his fellow workers will design an organizational structure and use an administrative style that will place more reliance on self-control than on external supervision, will give individuals greater freedom to act, and will emphasize recognition for achievement to motivate rather than fear of punishment. McGregor declared that traditional bureaucratic assumptions and methods of organization and control rather than basic human nature were responsible for lazy, indifferent, unwilling, intransigent, uncreative, and uncooperative dispositions of employees.

Management-by-objectives-and-results (MBO/R) is an approach to administration that is concerned with motivation of employees among other things. It is a participative management style. Teachers and administrators are motivated by an opportunity to work toward meaningful goals which they helped to define. MBO/R rests in part, on the Theory Y conceptualization of human nature.

Maslow[9] attempted to explain human behavior on the basis of a hierarchy of needs. The basic physiological needs of hunger and thirst usually are placed at the bottom of the hierarchy. Assuming physiological cravings are

[8]Douglas McGregor, *The Human Side of Enterprise,* New York: McGraw-Hill, 1960.

[9]A. H. Maslow, *Motivation and Personality,* New York: Harper & Row, 1954.

satisfied, motivation of human behavior moves up the scale toward safety needs, need for social affection, need for esteem, need to understand, esthetic needs, and need for self-actualization. Self-actualization is highest in the hierarchy. It is perhaps the most difficult to attain and refers to one's craving for self-fulfillment, that is, becoming what one might be. A satisfied need no longer motivates. In contrast, it is difficult to stimulate a person to pursue a higher need such as self-actualization if a more basic need such as hunger is not satisfied.

Administrative organization and leadership in education are influenced by the administrator's perceptions of those with whom he works—teachers, students, board members, noncertificated employees, and people in the community. Human resources are assets without which an organization could not achieve its potential. The development of competence and skill among professional staff members represents an investment in valuable human resources rather than an expenditure for in-service education. Recognition of human beings as assets that require further development to enhance growth is a logical outcome of the human-relations approach. Leadership emerges as a most significant factor when the human element and psychological factors gain appropriate recognition in organizations.

LEADERSHIP

Separating research findings from the romance that surrounds leadership is a sizeable task. Leadership has been conceived of as (1) an attribute of personality (symbolic leadership); (2) a status, title, or position recognized in a formal organizational chart (formal leadership); and (3) a function or role performed in an organized group (functional leadership). Leadership is, in essence, concerned with human energy in organized groups. It is a people phenomenon. It is a force that can initiate action among people, guide activities in a given direction, maintain such activities, and unify efforts toward common goals. Leadership is of prime importance to administrators because people are a part of all organizations. It demands understanding of fellow workers and their interrelationships to accomplish the objectives of the organization.

Symbolic leadership

In an ancient, but common and highly romanticized concept, the leader is seen as a person with well-developed and important personality traits. According to this view, "leaders are born, not made," that is, some have it, some don't. The leader stimulates and unifies the activities of others along certain paths because of the way he looks and his personality. This is the charismatic approach to leadership and bears a strong kinship to trait psychology. The gifts possessed by those endowed with leadership characteristics are many in number. Usually they include vaguely defined traits such as dependability, friendliness, enthusiasm, forcefulness, or perseverance.

Physical size is too often thought to be related to leadership. It has been pointed out that in 14 of the 15 presidential elections from 1904 to 1960 the taller candidate was elected; more often than not the difference was little more than a fraction of an inch. It is not unusual for a superintendent to specify that his principal be a "tall man" (6 feet in height or better) in the belief that shorter men fail to fulfill the leadership role in the community. One wonders how a man of shorter stature like Napoleon accomplished as much as he did. There is no evidence that height or girth has anything to do with leadership, but the myth that they do persists in spite of the evidence to the contrary.

The search for leadership, according to this point of view, is oriented toward seeking those with desired personality traits that are well developed. Over the last 50 years a large volume of research has consistently refuted the notion that leadership is an attribute of personality. A variety of people with significantly different personality, environmental, and hereditary backgrounds have become successful leaders. Only about 5 percent of the traits reported in over 100 studies appeared in four or more studies. Why, then, does the notion persist?

The romantic concept of the leader as an individual endowed with almost magical attributes can be traced to a longing for security.[10] The leader becomes idealized as a prestige figure with almost unlimited powers and with none of the faults and shortcomings found in ordinary humans. He becomes the "father image" or the "security symbol." The leader is perceived as a "knight on a white horse" and is described as larger in physical size, stronger, more intelligent, more mature, more cultured, and more impressive than you or I or any other of his followers. The longing of followers for security and dependence is satisfied through such a symbol, and in this sense, the leader is more a symbol than an individual personality.

The highly romanticized version of leadership is likely to develop when the functional relation between "fol-

lowers" and the symbolic leader is remote. The distance, in a physical and functional sense, between the people and the leader is so great that opportunities for interaction or joint participation in the discussion of issues rarely, if ever, occur. For example, the president of a large nation seldom if ever has close personal contact with most of the citizens, nor does a king with his many subjects. It has some value during times of stress when the symbol becomes the focal point for rallying the people. It would not be difficult to cite instances where the myth of the leader as one endowed with superhuman characteristics and even infallibility has been skillfully developed and perpetuated by presenting to the people only those aspects of the symbolic leader's activities or personality which would support such a myth.

In general it is possible to create such a leadership image or symbol in the minds of people having a remote relation to a leader. The myth can be exploded if there is frequent and intimate contact between the leader and the led, and if such experience exposes the leader as different from what he was supposed to be. The myth can be perpetuated, however, if the leader reveals himself or permits contact only when he is ready and under conditions he specifies. This gives rise to speculation that through the use of the mass media and publicity almost anyone can be made into a leader and project the image of one endowed with godlike qualities and surrounded by a magical aura. The procedure is often identified with the so-called "Madison Avenue" technique for developing a desired leader image for a certain group of people or for the whole nation.

This concept of charismatic leadership may have application in the field

---

[10]Irving Knickerbocker, "The Analysis of Leadership," in C. G. Browne and T. S. Cohn, eds., *The Study of Leadership,* Danville, Ill.: Interstate Printers and Publishers, 1958, pp. 3–4.

of school administration. The superintendent in a large school district often finds it difficult, if not impossible, to have close and continuing contacts with large numbers of teachers, principals, and school patrons. Under such conditions the superintendent may be forced to create an image of leadership which is highly prized by the majority of professional personnel and laymen. The desired image can be developed through a well-planned and coordinated program of publicity (sometimes called public relations), including television appearances, well-prepared speeches before teachers' or principals' meetings, selected interviews, pictures, and statements released for the press. The educational leader is "created" by the power of the "image makers," who specialize in press, radio, and TV relations.

Formal leadership

The leader has been visualized as a person ensconced in a position recognized in the formal organizational chart as a leadership post. The person and the position become confused. The terms "status leader," "titular leader," "hierarchical leader," and "formal leader" are interchangeable. The individual occupying a given status in the organization or holding a specific title of office or placed in a certain position in the hierarchy or granted special authority in the formal chart of organization is automatically considered a leader. This recognition may disappear when he vacates status, title, position, or office.

The school superintendency is recognized in a formal way as a leadership position; thus the title of leader is accorded the person ascending to this office. Mere occupancy of a position is no guarantee that its incumbent will actually be what subsequently will be defined as a "functional" leader. Nonetheless, the leadership potential of a person occupying the position of superintendent of schools is far greater than that of an individual with the status of a regular classroom teacher. The manner in which most schools are organized makes it difficult for a classroom post to be as effective a platform from which to perform the leadership role as is the superintendent's or principal's post. Teachers attempt to rectify this by joining teachers' associations and seek election to office to gain a platform to project plans and programs.

The organizational pattern inevitably makes some positions better platforms for demonstrating leadership qualities than others. Administrative positions in school systems are leadership platforms. There is good reason for structuring schools with such potentially great influence points. Formal leadership is an important attribute of organization, for without it the execution of policies would be more difficult and the identification of primary responsibilities more confused. It would be almost impossible to operate without leadership positions. There is a danger of going to extremes with highly directive behavior styles replacing concerns for motivation and human relations when too much emphasis is placed on formal leadership.

Functional leadership

Leadership is not solely an attribute of personality, nor can there be any assurance that it will emanate only from specified positions in the hierarchy. It cannot exist in isolation, but is related to interpersonal relations and group operations. Leadership emerges as a group phenomenon, a function essential in organized groups. This demands learning more about the behavior of individuals within groups. The focus changes from unique personality traits to the organized group situation, where the leadership role is differentiated from others. The emphasis shifts to the situation and the characteristics of the group, and away from individual traits as separate and distinct from the group. Functional leadership is viewed as a role performed within an organized group. A leader is that person who has something to contribute to the more effective functioning of the group. Group needs or demands, rather than individual personality traits, become the determinants of leadership. Criteria for leadership are based on what the leader does to help the group define its goals, achieve its objectives, or maintain its strength as a body. Unless a person can fulfill one or more of these group functions, he is not a functional leader no matter how charming his personality or how impressive the title of his position.

Others have attempted to define leadership in terms of behavior that initiates new structures. This is the change-agent role that is reviewed more fully in another context in the chapter that follows.

Stogdill[11] defined leadership "as a process of influencing the activities of an organized group in the task of goal setting and goal achieving." Others add group maintenance as a third dimension in this complex and difficult role. Research in the behavioral sciences views leadership as a product of interpersonal relations and as a function or role within a specified social system. To comprehend functional or operational leadership better, one must examine the organized group within which there is a dynamic rela-

tion among members and a differentiation of roles. In other words, leadership can be conceived in terms of the dynamics of human social behavior.

The functional conceptualization assumes that leader activities or roles can be learned. The principal and superintendent must develop sensitivities to the workings of the group (its dynamics), and the needs of groups to fulfill a leadership role. In addition he would develop special competencies necessary to better articulate what the group desires and how group objectives can be realized in a most expeditious manner. The next logical step is to examine the nature and dynamics of groups.

The nature of groups

What is a group? To begin with, it consists of at least two people who maintain social interaction and share a common purpose. Through interaction members arrive at commonly defined goals and act in a unified manner toward the environment. Leaders do not emerge until there is differentiation of member roles.[12] A group is more than a collection of individuals in physical proximity to each other or held together mechanically. A mass of people in a crowded railroad station does not become a group until its members perceive common goals and start to interact. A group has a personality and dimensions to measure its characteristics or "personality." Hemphill identified ten characteristics of a group:

1. Size: the number of members in the group
2. Viscidity: the degree to which the group functions as a unit
3. Homogeneity: the degree to which the group members are similar in age, sex, background, etc.

[11]Ralph M. Stogdill, "Leadership, Membership, and Organization," in Browne and Cohn, ibid., p. 38.

[12]Ibid.

4. Flexibility: the degree to which the group has established rules, regulations, and procedures
5. Stability: the frequency with which the group undergoes major changes in organization
6. Permeability: the degree to which the group resists admission of new members
7. Polarization: the degree to which the group works toward a single goal
8. Autonomy: the degree to which the group operates independently of direction by other larger groups
9. Intimacy: the degree to which the group members are acquainted with one another
10. Control: the degree to which the group restricts the freedom of members' behavior[13]

Cartwright and Lippitt[14] declared that groups are the inevitable result of human propensities and are ubiquitous; they "mobilize powerful forces which produce effects of utmost importance to individuals"; they "produce both good and bad consequences"; they can be better understood through knowledge of group dynamics and their desired consequences enhanced thereby; and they may generate subgroups.

The leader and the group

Leadership can serve as a focal point around which people may cluster and eventually form an organized group. It is not unusual to find religious groups that are unified through belief in a prophet or lesser religious leader. Through the group and its leaders, members anticipate finding a means of satisfying needs or of protecting themselves against threatened loss of need satisfaction. Individuals tend to leave

a group when it no longer satisfies real or imagined needs.[15]

The leader is involved in a network of relations with others who make up the group. Leadership, therefore, is not an abstract phenomenon. Individuals will accept direction of their activities if the leader's behavior appears to provide a means of need satisfaction.

Leaders arise within a group for various reasons. One may be to satisfy a desire for concerted action toward objectives. Any collection of people is forced to turn to a single person to execute actions. Such a simple activity as the ordering of discussions necessitates some degree of organization and the selection of someone to fulfill the role of leadership. The part an individual plays in the total dynamic pattern of the behavior of the group defines him as a leader.

The first National Training Laboratory in Group Development defined and compiled a number of functional roles of group members. The leader and other group members should be sensitive to persons, knowingly or otherwise, who opt to play any one or more of the following roles that may facilitate or impede the productivity of the group:

1. Group task roles
   a. Initiator-contributor: member who contributes new ideas or different ways of examining group problems.
   b. Information seeker: member who seeks clarification of ideas presented to the group, asks for authoritative information, or probes for more pertinent data.
   c. Opinion seeker: member who seeks clarification of pertinent values rather than facts.
   d. Information giver: member who offers the pertinent fact, generalization, or experience to the group.
   e. Opinion giver: member who is ready to offer his belief or suggestions which are not based on facts.

[13]John K. Hemphill, "The Leader in His Group," in Browne and Cohn, ibid., p. 369.
[14]D. P. Cartwright and R. Lippitt, "Group Dynamics and the Individual," *Group Development*, Washington, D.C.: National Training Laboratories, 1961, pp. 11–24.

[15]Knickerbocker, op. cit., pp. 5–11.

f. Elaborator: member who develops a more extended rationale built on previously submitted ideas.

g. Coordinator: member who pulls together activities or ideas and clarifies relations.

h. Orientor: member who defines or raises questions about group directions or goals.

i. Energizer: member who stimulates or arouses others to action.

j. Evaluator-critic: member who reviews the accomplishments (good and bad) of the group.

k. Procedural technician: member who expedites group activity.

l. Recorder: member who records group events.

2. Group building and maintenance roles

a. Encourager: member who praises and agrees with others and promotes warmth and solidarity within the group.

b. Harmonizer: member who relieves tensions, mediates and reconciles differences, etc.

c. Compromiser: member who works within difficulties in an effort to resolve apparent disagreements.

d. Gatekeeper and expediter: member who keeps communications channels open, "keeps them talking."

e. Standard setter or ego ideal: member who expresses proposed standards for group accomplishments.

f. Group observer and commentator: member who expresses on and evaluates how the group functions

g. Follower: member who goes along with others more or less passively.

3. Individual roles

a. Aggressor.

b. Blocker.

c. Recognition seeker: member who uses group to call attention to himself.

d. Self-confessor: member who uses group to express personal nongroup-created feelings.

e. Playboy: member who uses group to show off his lack of involvement.

f. Dominator.

g. Help seeker: member who seeks sympathy response from group.

h. Special-interest pleader.[16]

Recent experiments in group behavior and human relations revealed the following characteristics of effective group relations:

1. Training in effective human relations makes leaders and others more sensitive to needs of individuals.

2. The group becomes more sensitive to needs of individuals.

3. The individual shares in the setting of group goals, which affects his own situation, and in determining methods used in attaining goals.

4. Expressions of individual differences are more likely in permissive siuations than in autocratic, manipulated ones.

5. Utilization of decision making by consensus makes the individual important.

6. The individual is encouraged to feel independent, delegated responsibility and authority, and encouraged to grow and improve.

7. A wide range of individual contributions are needed.

8. Individual action and responsibility are more likely to be stimulated by shared decision making.

9. Leadership skills are acquired not inherited.[17]

Groups vary in maturity and productivity. Skills are required to maintain effectiveness, and techniques can be acquired to resolve group problems. A group cannot function unless it has something to do and has the energy to keep operating. The three most common group problems are conflict (brought on by frustrations from impossible jobs, conflicting interests, the use of the group by some to acquire status, etc.); apathy (brought on by preoccupation with unimportant problems, inadequate procedures, and a feeling of powerlessness, etc.); and inadequate decision making.[18] Group

---

[16]K. D. Benne and P. Sheats, "Functional Roles of Group Members," in *Group Development*, Washington, D.C.: National Training Laboratories, 1961, pp. 51–59.

[17]See L. P. Bradford and G. L. Lippitt, "The Individual Counts . . . In Effective Group Relations," in *Group Development*, Washington, D.C.: National Training Laboratories, 1961, pp. 25–32.

[18]L. P. Bradford et al., "How to Diagnose Group Problems," *Group Development*, Washington, D.C.: National Training Laboratories 1961, pp. 37–50.

problems can be overcome by diagnosis and feedback.

The leader and the situation

Leadership can arise out of any given situation. This view is almost, but not quite, a contradiction of the trait theory. A person is not chosen to lead simply on the basis of intelligence or originality, but rather may become a leader if personal characteristics such as intelligence or originality are seen as a means of satisfying group purposes. He is followed because he promises to get—or actually gets— what his followers want. A leader is a product, not of specific or universal characteristics possessed by all such persons, but of his functional relations to specific individuals in a specific situation. If he is removed from this specific situation and placed in a different one, it is highly unlikely that he will be a leader. Thus, a leader of a white supremacy movement is not likely to be a leader of an international society of anthropologists. A boy accepted as a leader on the football field will not automatically become a leader in a college club devoted to the pursuit of higher mathematics. An educational leader in one type of community may receive no such recognition in a completely different type of community. Changing the situation or the group's purposes results in a variability of leaders' characteristics that upsets all but the broadest statistical efforts at analysis.

This suggests that the best leader (and, similarly, the best teacher) is one who knows the group best or fits into the group best; thus, the question arises whether the leader is someone who has characteristics similar to those of other members of the group and who, seeing the group moving in a given direction, hastens to get out in front.

Personal factors associated with leadership

After surveying the literature on personal characteristics associated with leadership, Stogdill concluded that the following were associated with leadership and classified them as follows:

1. Capacity: intelligence, alertness, verbal facility, originality, judgment.
2. Achievement: scholarship, knowledge, athletic accomplishments.
3. Responsibility: dependability, initiative, persistence, aggressiveness, self-confidence, desire to excel.
4. Participation: activities, sociability, co-operation, adaptability, humor.
5. Status: socioeconomic position, popularity.[19]

To achieve leadership, an individual must possess traits that are relevant to the characteristics, activities, and goals of the organized group. This is a compromise between the pure trait approach and the strictly situational approach. In other words, traits related to leadership must be as varied as the situations likely to develop for a group. As group purposes or objectives change, so will the characteristics of the person likely to be selected, or likely to succeed, as a leader.

For example, a certain community during the depression years was fundamentally conservative in outlook, was satisfied with a limited educational quality, and was extremely tax-conscious. The young superintendent employed agreed with these views and was accepted as the educational leader of the system. But World War II brought changes in the composition of the community and improved its economic situation. People began to clamor for improvement in quality of the schools and for experimentation in new approaches in education and

[19]Ralph M. Stogdill, "Personal Factors Associated with Leadership: A Survey of the Literature," in Browne and Cohn, op. cit., p. 58.

were willing to pay the necessary additional taxes. The same superintendent either failed to recognize the change in the community or was unable to adapt his pattern of administration to meet it. The people of the community began to ask for a new leader for their schools. Similarly, the 1970s brought into being conditions that were closer to the depression years than to the expansionary 1960s. Once again the changing situation called for new kinds of leadership roles for the school executive.

Leadership styles

"Getting things done" is a frequently stated purpose for administration. Determining the direction of the institution through selecting goals and establishing standards, organizing the institution, and assembling and allocating resources is only a start in the right direction. There must be a force to direct the resources in the organizational structure toward institutional goals and standards. Leadership provides that force.

Early research characterized three styles of leadership: autocratic, democratic, and laissez faire. For the sake of semantic consistency it appears more appropriate to refer to these three styles as autocratic, democratic, and anarchic.[20] A variant of these styles is manipulative leadership.

In the *autocratic* style of leadership the leader determines policy and assigns tasks to members without consulting with them. The leader is personal in his praise and criticism of individuals but remains aloof from the group. There are no group-inspired decisions. The leader decrees what shall be done, and the others have no choice but to accept it. The rationale behind this style was stated by Adolf Hitler:

Nothing is possible unless one will commands, a will which has to be obeyed by others, beginning at the top and ending only at the very bottom. . . . We must train our people so that whenever someone has been appointed to command, the others will recognize it as their duty to obey him, for it can happen that an hour later they will be called upon to command, and they can do it then only if others in turn obey. This is the expression of an authoritarian state—not of a weak, babbling democracy—of an authoritarian state where everyone is proud to obey, because he knows: "I will likewise be obeyed when I must take command."[21]

In the *democratic* style of leadership although the leader participates in policy formation, policies also involve group action or decision. Members decide with whom they would like to work. The group, in effect, determines the division of the tasks to be accomplished. The leader is supposedly objective in his praise and criticism and participates in group activities as deemed appropriate. In the fields of business and industry this is often referred to as the participative management style. (More will be said about this style in the following discussion.)

The *anarchic* style of leadership grants complete freedom to group or individual decision without leader participation or direction. The primary role of the leader is merely to supply materials, remaining apart from the group and participating only when asked. His comments on member activity are infrequent, and he makes no attempt to interfere with or participate in the course of events determined by others. Anarchy is a "leaderless" social situation.

[20]C. G. Browne, " 'Laissez faire' or 'Anarchy' in Leadership?" in Browne and Cohn, op. cit., pp. 305–309.

[21]See Clyde M. Campbell, ed., *Practical Application of Democratic Administration*, New York: Harper & Row, 1952, p. 29.

The following four methods[22] may be used by a leader to direct the group's activities: (1) force, resulting from the control or access to resources desired by others; (2) paternalism, where emphasis is placed on loyalty and gratitude to the leader; (3) bargaining; and (4) mutual means. The policy of the organization may determine which of these methods shall be used by the appointed leader.

In *manipulative* or *pseudodemocratic* leadership, the leader makes his desires known and then appoints a committee, ostensibly to deliberate, but primarily to approve his proposals. The committee, without much thought or discussion, automatically endorses what the leader hopes to achieve. Group members go through the motions of cooperative action, but to no avail, since the decision has been reached beforehand. It has been suggested that this type of leadership is tolerated or successful when the leader rewards those who support him and refrains from rewarding, or actually punishes, those who do not. Under the manipulative leadership style "the group members not only follow orders but take full responsibility for creating the orders as well."[23]

Because the words democratic, pseudodemocratic, autocratic or authoritarian, and anarchic have developed desirable or undesirable connotations, Getzels and Guba have developed another group of terms to describe leadership styles.[24] The terms suggested are nomothetic, idiographic, and transactional.

The *nomothetic* leader stresses requirements of the institution and conformity of role behavior to expectations, even at the expense of individual personality and individual needs. He emphasizes the authority vested in the status or position he holds and the rules and procedures, and he imposes sanctions as necessary. Effectiveness is what the nomothetic leader expects from his followers.

The *idiographic* leader is most concerned with his perceptions and his predispositions. Organizational demands upon the individual are minimized. The leader's authority is delegated, and his relations to others are tailored to individual personality needs. The idiographic leader is more concerned with his own ego or personality and those of the other members of the institution than he is with institutional demands.

Transactional leadership represents a compromise between the nomothetic (stressing institutional demands) and the idiographic (emphasizing individual needs). The transactional leader appreciates the need to achieve institutional goals, but at the same time hopes that individual personalities will not be violated as they strive toward these goals. He recognizes the importance of institutional roles and expectations, but he also hopes that pursuing institutional goals can result in fulfillment of individual personality drives. At one time he may stress the nomothetic dimension and at another the idiographic dimension of the leadership situation.

The comparative newness of the terms nomothetic, idiographic, and transactional has made it possible to utilize such terminology without introducing political overtones or immediate qualitative connotations. It may

[22]Irving Knickerbocker, "Leadership: A Conception and Some Implications," in *Leadership in Action*, Washington, D.C.: National Training Laboratories, 1961, p. 81.

[23]Ibid., pp. 36–37.

[24]J. W. Getzels and E. G. Guba, "Social Behavior and the Administrative Process," *School Review*, vol. 65, December 1957, pp. 423–441.

well be only a question of time (depending upon whether or not such terminology comes into popular usage), however, before they too gather connotations of good and evil. Some years hence the transactional leader may be identified as the "good guy," in contrast to the nomothetic "tyrant" or the idiographic "slob."

Democratic school administration

Democratic leadership emphasizes group and leader participation in the formulation of policies that serve as guidelines for institutional operations.[25] It is an approach that places much stress on the participation of the entire group in the formulation of courses of action. Ideally the formulation of policy under democratic leadership involves those who are to be influenced by it. In the school situation this means that teachers and others deliberate with administrators, and from such action educational policies develop. It does not mean that teachers only, or lay people only, or school members only decide questions of policy. Note its similarity to professional negotiation and collective bargaining concepts. In the case of negotiation teachers may express the opinion that their involvement in certain kinds of educational decision making is a right rather than a privilege that grows out of a particular administrative behavior or style of superintendent.

There is an all-too-prevalent misconception that democratic administration excludes those in leadership positions from participation in policy making and limits the task of superintendents or principals to organizing faculty committees, which in turn determine policy. This is more characteristic of the anarchic style of leadership

than of the democratic. The confusion of anarchic with democratic administration can devitalize the school executive's role in policy formulation and execution. Under this misinterpretation the role of the leader is limited to counting the hands raised for or against the policy being voted on. A democratic leader is not indecisive until all the votes are counted; his special insights and information can be of value in the formulation of policies. The group interacts with but does not replace the expert.

For some time teachers have expressed a desire to participate in the determination of policies, particularly in such areas as curriculum, salary schedules, and working conditions.[26] Studies before the advent of collective negotiations have shown that teachers who have an opportunity to participate regularly and actively in making policies are much more likely to be enthusiastic about their school system than those who have limited opportunity to participate. To this extent democratic leadership can promote a higher degree of faculty morale. It is a means by which the creative talents of many teachers can be tapped and for that reason is called creative, as well as democratic, leadership. Today, teachers are demanding such participation through professional negotiation, which will be explained in detail in a later chapter.

Advantages of democratic school administration. Benne[27] pointed out some of the benefits of democratic leader-

[25]Browne, op. cit., p. 304.

[26]"The Teacher and Policy Making," *Administrators Notebook,* vol. 1, no. 1, May 1952, Chicago: Midwest Administration Center, University of Chicago.

[27]K. D. Benne, "Leaders Are Made Not Born," in *Leadership in Action,* Washington, D.C.: National Training Laboratories, 1961, p. 19.

ship: It promotes greater group productivity; democratic planning is a way to forestall crises in group life; and personalities shaped by democratic participation are more mature, more capable of objectivity, and less aggressive.

Problems of democratic school administration. The superintendent who has long practiced the autocratic style of leadership is not likely to change overnight. Value patterns are not easily modified—changing human behavior is a complex and arduous task. Evidence seems to indicate that the authoritarian personality may be a fundamentally insecure one. In other words, the authoritarian person is driven to autocratic behavior to achieve security. There is a need for authority and for the title of office as a shield behind which to hide real or imagined personal shortcomings. Some administrators of this type are arrogant and domineering toward staff members but meek and submissive toward board members or others considered as superiors. The autocratic leader views the world as essentially friendless and therefore strives for power and toughness and becomes rigid in dealing with people (a Theory-X man). He is reluctant to delegate authority or to permit subordinates to participate in policy matters which he feels are his concern. A person who envisions the world as being populated with scheming incompetents who look after their own hides and are after his at all times would find it most uncomfortable to enact the role of a democratic leader.

It would likewise be extremely difficult for an individual to adopt the democratic leadership style if he had a low opinion of the professional competence and personal sincerity of teachers. Democratic school adminis-tration rests on the belief that the professional personnel in the classrooms are individuals who know enough to do the right thing at the right time and who desire to build better schools rather than merely to feather their own nests. The better professional preparation of teachers has made the democratic style of leadership more of a practical possibility than ever before. Today's teachers are better educated than ever before and are more alert and better informed about school problems. This attitude tends to promote rather than inhibit the practice of professional negotiation.

The other side of the coin is that some teachers find it difficult to accept the democratic style of leadership if most of their professional career has been spent under an autocratic or manipulative style of leadership. Once the suspicion of fellow workers is overcome, it takes time to develop maturity and skills to participate effectively in group activities. Individuals with limited experience in group situations may find such participation a waste of time. Furthermore, some people enjoy being told what to do. In addition, relatively inexperienced committees concerned with policy formulation tend to legislate rather than deliberate educational policy. The easy way to solve dilemmas is "to make a rule." Intelligence does not result from the compounding of ignorance. Individuals with limited information in a particular area and only rudimentary skills in group operations do not become endowed with an expert's knowledge as soon as they gather into a group. Decisions reached without adequate understanding of the problem are questionable, whether they are made by an uninformed group or delivered by an uninformed individual in a leadership position.

Another problem connected with

the use of the democratic leadership style arises from failure to differentiate between policy formulation and policy execution. Democratic leadership rests on the idea that members of the group or their representatives shall be involved in the formulation of policies. The execution of formulated policies is another matter. It can become confused unless a single person is assigned responsibility for execution. The status or titular leaders (those who are placed in formal positions with leadership potential) are necessary to execute policies arrived at through democratic deliberations. Democratic school leadership does not imply, nor should it encourage, execution of adopted policies by all members of the group.

To point out the dangers involved in employing this style of leadership is not to imply that it is a questionable practice. No matter what style is adopted, dangers must be recognized and appropriate action taken to correct them. Great strides have been made in understanding the dynamics of group work and the application of group effort to facilitate democratic school administration. More remains to be done.

Jenkins[28] viewed this complex function and observed that leadership is better evaluated in terms of goals and purposes of groups; that it is not the same in groups working at different tasks or in the same group that has added or shifted to new responsibilities, that it is only as effective as the group will let it be; that it is one thing the total group is responsible for and hence that its success or failure can be credited or blamed in part on the group; and that it is a useful function in helping a group progress toward

[28]D. H. Jenkins, "New Questions for Old," *Leadership in Action,* Washington, D.C.: National Training Laboratories, 1961, pp. 23–25.

its goals and in keeping the group in a healthy working condition.

HUMAN BEHAVIOR IN ORGANIZATIONS

The behavior and motivations of individuals in organized groups are receiving attention from behavioral scientists. The sociologist views the organization as a society of people interacting at various levels, rather than as an impersonal system of positions. Viewing an organization as a social institution consisting structurally of a system of roles can improve understanding of the mechanisms by which the individual actualizes himself through the organization and, simultaneously, the organization actualizes itself through the individual.

An understanding of terms basic to a sociologist's or a social psychologist's discussion of organizational behavior is necessary. The most frequently used terms are:

1. Position: the location of a person or persons (often called an actor or class of actors) in a system of social relations.
2. Expectation: an evaluative standard applied to an incumbent of a particular position; a responsibility of obligation placed upon a person who occupies a given position in the organization. It is anticipatory in nature.
3. Role: a series of somewhat unified expectations applied to an incumbent of a particular position. An actor's role in a social system is defined by the obligations and responsibilities attached to his position. The role places the actor in organizational perspective and relates him to other individuals playing roles in the social system.
4. Incumbent: a person or actor who is holding an office or position at a particular time.
5. Alter group: a group which, because of a certain status or relations, may contribute legitimately to the definition of a role another is to play in the institution. It is sometimes referred

to as a "counterposition" or "referent group."[29]

These terms can be illustrated as follows. A supervisor has an idea of what his role should be. The teachers, who compose an alter group, are in frequent contact with the supervisor and develop their own concept of what the role of the supervisor should be. The superintendent and the assistant superintendent participate in the definition of the role of subject matter supervisors and, therefore, compose another alter group for the supervisor. There can be many referent groups that have an impact on a role incumbent.

Role occupancy has at least two aspects: behavior which is necessary to reach the institutional or group goals and behavior which satisfies the individual's own needs.[30] The institutional obligations may be called the nomothetic dimension. The satisfaction of personal needs, or need disposition, may be identified as the idiographic dimension in a given organization. These dimensions of human behavior in organizations, according to Getzels,[31] permit a differentiation between effectiveness and efficiency. Behavior is effective if it contributes to attainment of institutional goals. Effectiveness is measured along the nomothetic dimension. An effective person may be productive, as measured by institutional demands, but such accomplishments may be possible only through expenditure of a large amount of psychic energy. This is likely to

occur when the type of behavior demanded to realize institutional goals is against the better judgment or ethics of a person and thus upsets him. Such behavior is termed inefficient, even though effective, because the individual must expend an undue amount of psychic energy or self-discipline to perform the role or to live up to expectations. In a positive sense the behavior is efficient if it is consistent with the need dispositions of the role incumbent.

Application of these concepts of human behavior in organizations can contribute to a better understanding of morale and personnel satisfaction. A principal may perceive his role in terms of certain expectations, but other referent groups, such as teachers, superintendents, boards of education, and lay people may have their own perceptions of how the principal should fulfill his institutional obligations.

Let us concentrate on teachers as serving in counterpositions to the principal. Teachers are not a homogeneous group. Their backgrounds, interests, and experiences vary widely. Relations between a heterogeneous group of teachers and the principal can be important. Inability of either teachers or principal to cope with conflicting or ambiguous expectations with reference to the principal's role may arouse feelings of tensions and dissatisfaction. Bidwell's[32] study provides evidence to support this. Dissatisfied teachers claimed they could not predict how their principal would act. They opined that administrators shifted procedures from day to day and held conflicting expectations regarding what or how to

[29]Adapted from Neal Gross, W. S. Mason, and A. W. McEachern, Explorations in Role Analysis, New York: Wiley, 1958, p. 67.

[30]J. W. Getzels, "Administration as Social Process," in A. W. Halpin, ed., Administrative Theory in Education, Chicago: Midwest Administration Center, University of Chicago, 1958, p. 165.

[31]Ibid.

[32]Charles E. Bidwell, "Some Causes of Conflicts and Tensions Among Teachers," Administrators Notebook, vol. 4, no. 7, March 1956, Chicago: Midwest Administration Center, University of Chicago.

teach. These teachers were extremely tense about relations with administrators and were unable to predict what their superintendent or principal would expect them to do. They could not determine how to act toward administrators. Feelings of tension and insecurity were generalized into a widespread dissatisfaction with the school system in general, including relations with fellow teachers, pupils, and patrons.

On the other hand, satisfied teachers felt quite secure in relations with their superiors. They had no difficulty predicting how administrators would act and what was expected of them. They saw the superintendent and/or principal as behaving in a consistent fashion, holding clear and consistent expectations of teacher behavior, and giving ample warning of any changes in procedures that would affect them. They displayed no tension; instead, feelings of security were generalized into satisfaction with the operation of the entire school system and their role in it.

The startling conclusion was that one administrator worked with both satisfied and dissatisfied teachers. In other words, the same administrative behavior resulted in feelings of security and of tension, respectively, in two groups of teachers. A single set of actions by the administrator may not always produce confidence and security in teachers who hold different expectations. The role of the administrator was perceived differently by the two groups having contact with him.

Bidwell concluded "there is no doubt that a teacher's feeling of security or tension regarding his own behavior is very closely related to his view of proper behavior on the part of the administrator."[33] If the administrator acts as a teacher feels he should, the teacher will tend to be comfortable. On the other hand, if a teacher is of the opinion that the administrator is not fulfilling his role as the former sees it, he will often feel that the administrator's expectations are conflicting and ambiguous, and feelings of tension will result.

Human behavior in an organization cannot be understood by analysis of personality apart from the organization. Human behavior in an organization is affected by need satisfactions of the person and the institutional expectations for his performance. Levinson[34] observed that "if the two sets of needs do not mesh, then a man has to fight himself and his organization, in addition to the work that must be done."

SUMMARY

Leadership is a commonly used term and has many definitions. The various concepts can be classified, for purposes of analysis, as (1) symbolic or charismatic leadership, (2) formal or titular leadership, and (3) functional or operational leadership. The symbolic leader is considered to possess almost magical individual powers or traits and is most likely to flourish when the distance from, and opportunities for interaction with, followers are remote. The myth of the leader as a person in possession of some universal trait of leadership has been exploded by research, but still persists. Formal leadership is based on the idea that position in the hierarchy determines who leads. Functional leadership is related to the activities of groups. The leader arises because he

[33]Ibid.

[34]H. P. Levinson, "Management By Whose Objectives?" *Harvard Business Review*, vol. 48, July–August 1970, pp. 125–134.

possesses the talents the group finds of value in defining or attaining its goals. Leadership competencies can be acquired and the study of group dynamics may contribute to that end. Most complex institutions contain more than one group. The dimensions of a group define its personality.

Leadership is a force that activates the human resources within an organization. Various styles have been utilized (and labeled) to achieve this purpose, such as autocratic, democratic, anarchic, manipulative, nomothetic, idiographic, and transactional. Styles are differentiated on the basis of who is involved in the formulation of policies, or whether emphasis is placed on the institutional or the personal dimensions of the social situation.

The keystone of democratic leadership is that the formulation of policy should involve those who are influenced by it. The creative talents of many teachers can be tapped through democratic leadership. This style of leadership precipitates problems but nevertheless holds much promise. It does not resist the application of professional negotiation to schools.

An organization can be described as a social system with structured and informal relations among people. This is a view of the organization "from the bottom up." It is based on the research of sociologists and social psychologists and introduces concepts such as expectation, role, and referent group into the field of administration. An analysis of behavior must recognize the limits of human rationality; emotions, mores, and the human ego influence human behavior to a considerable extent.

The perception of the role of an actor by various referent groups may affect the satisfactions and dissatisfactions of such referent groups. Leadership and the study of human behavior in organizations are concerned with people and are two sides of the same coin.

A recurring theme in this book is that administrators make things happen through the efforts of other people. Most institutions are too large or too complex for one person—administrator or anyone else—to accomplish all tasks. The involvement of human energy from many sources creates a host of problems, among which are activation and unification of efforts toward organizational goals. This places a premium on the leadership qualities of the administrator. Leadership is an important force in the operation of educational systems.

QUESTIONS

1. Why are leaders necessary in organizations?
2. Would leadership in a small school system be different in action or style from that in a very large school system? Justify your stand.
3. How does functional leadership differ from symbolic leadership? From formal leadership?
4. Would it be possible to have an organized institution without a leader? Justify your stand.
5. Describe the essential characteristics of the following leadership styles: (a) nomothetic leadership, (b) democratic leadership, (c) manipulative leadership, (d) idiographic leadership.

6. It is said that people are a part of organization. What does this mean to you?
7. What is the significance of the statement that "an organization can be viewed as a social system?"
8. How does the scientific management movement differ from the "human relations" movement in organizational development?
9. Define the following: (a) referent groups, (b) role occupancy, (c) efficient behavior, (d) congruent expectations.
10. How does human behavior within organizations differ from human behavior outside organizations?

SELECTED REFERENCES

Bidwell, Charles E., "Some Causes of Conflicts and Tensions Among Teachers," *Administrators Notebook,* vol. 4, no. 7, March 1956, Chicago: Midwest Administration Center, University of Chicago.

Browne, C. G., " 'Laissez faire' or 'Anarchy' in Leadership?" in C. G. Browne and T. S. Cohn, eds., *The Study of Leadership,* Danville, Ill.: Interstate Printers and Publishers, 1958.

Campbell, Clyde M., ed., *Practical Application of Democratic Administration,* New York: Harper & Row, 1952.

Getzels, J. W., and E. G. Guba, "Social Behavior and the Administrative Process," *School Review,* vol. 65, December 1957, pp. 423–441.

Group Development, Selected Reading Series One, Washington, D.C.: National Training Laboratories, 1961.

Knickerbocker, Irving, "The Analysis of Leadership," in C. G. Browne and T. S. Cohn, eds., *The Study of Leadership,* Danville, Ill.: Interstate Printers and Publishers, 1958.

Leadership in Action, Selected Reading Series Two, Washington, D.C.: National Training Laboratories, 1961.

"The Teacher and Policy Making," in *Administrators Notebook,* vol. 1, no. 1, May 1952. Chicago: Midwest Administration Center, University of Chicago.

Stogdill, Ralph M., "Leadership, Membership, and Organization," in C. G. Browne and T. S. Cohn, eds., *The Study of Leadership,* Danville, Ill.: Interstate Printers and Publishers, 1958.

5

MANAGING CHANGE AND THE LEGACY OF TECHNOLOGY

Traditionally, the administrator was pictured as the one responsible for maintaining the status quo efficiently. Weber's bureaucratic model was an organizational pattern to preserve and perpetuate existing concerns and was not designed to encourage the pursuit of the new or the management of change. Various forces acting singly and in concert have committed the late twentieth-century world to continuing, if not radical, change. Technological advances in transportation, communication, and the production of goods and services have generated pressure for significant modifications in social institutions. This has necessitated a reevaluation of the priorities awarded to goals and services and the structuring of new ones. As a result since World War II the primary role of the administrator has come to be viewed as that of a change agent or an introducer and manager of innovations into the educational system, rather than simply as a maintainer of existing operations at efficient levels. Bureaucratic organizations long recognized for high productive capability are now under attack for their relatively low innovative capacity. Drucker called for a shift in administrative posture toward building and managing innovative systems rather than stable

or fixed organizations.[1] How to build and manage a human group capable of anticipating and accepting the new emerges as an important administrative competency. Leadership, some argue, is demonstrated by the ability to make needed changes.

In ancient Greece the philosopher Xenophon attacked Sophists of his day as innovators who were leading youths away from ancient virtues. Socrates was judged guilty of corrupting the youth of Athens by discussing purposes, values, and methods not in harmony with those of his contemporaries who were then stressing the immediate-success approach to education. Innovators today need not fear that they, like Socrates, will be forced to drink hemlock. On the contrary, those who resist what may appear to be radical departures in education are more likely to be banished from their positions of leadership.

Innovation is today's popular term, whereas progressivism was "yesterday's," that is, 40 or 50 years ago. Progressivism of the 1920s and 1930s died fighting for educational reforms in an era when people were unrecep-

[1]Peter F. Drucker, *The Age of Discontinuity,* London: Wm. Heinemann, Ltd., 1968, p. 51.

tive to and even suspicious of change. Today, innovation is not just something to be tolerated; it is a way of life.

Schools have changed in past years, even though the alterations are not always striking or as fast in coming as some would like. It is erroneous to assume that schools of today are replicas of educational institutions of 100 or 200 years ago. Today's schools neither look nor feel like their historical counterparts. The professional behavior of teachers, the comprehensiveness of educational opportunities, the methods of instruction, the design of facilities, and the amount learned in school are all quite different today from what they were a generation or two, much less a century or two, ago.

By 1870 the graded school pattern—then an innovation—was installed in practically all school districts in the major cities of the nation. In moving from the inefficient, unsystematic nongraded instructional approach that produced little learning and many elementary school dropouts, many systems went to the opposite extreme of rigidity and over-systematization. This gave rise almost immediately to a passing parade of plans for improving instruction that stretches back into the previous century. Many plans were named after cities, such as Pueblo, Cambridge, Gary, Dalton, and Winnetka, where the experimentation or innovation took place. In short, efforts were instituted to ameliorate the many undesirable features of the graded approach to instruction that were apparent at least three-quarters of a century prior to the existing writings on the elusive nongraded school.

The present alphabetical curriculum in science and math, which has spawned BSCS (biology), PSSC (physics), CHEM (chemistry), and SMSG (math), is far more conservative than the curriculum reforms advocated by the proponents of progressive education early in this century. The present-day "revolution" concentrates on altering the substantive content of school experiences and strives to restructure, rather than to replace, the traditional disciplines. It uses more sophisticated terms to describe the subject matter format. Altering course content has long been a respectable pastime for scholars. Hardly a decade has passed, during the last century as well as the present one, when some elementary subject has not been added, deleted, or significantly modified. More drastic curriculum reform based on formats radically different from the traditional subject matter approach (such as the core curriculum, broad fields, and the vaguely defined experience curriculum) had been rejected with some degree of finality by 1940.

The desire for reform in education never dies. It becomes dormant for a while, only to return with greater vigor and in a new guise. The drive toward more school innovation merely represents a recent reform movement. Those who champion innovation reveal an eclectic point of view at best. The lack of a common philosophy and/or psychology to serve as a foundation for the construction of many new programs is readily apparent. For better or worse, there are no great minds to match John Dewey or E. L. Thorndike, who gave philosophical or psychological foundation to previous reform efforts.

The point being made is that school administrators have been confronted with change before: It is the pace of change that is different. More new developments in shorter periods of time will be in evidence in the years ahead.

INNOVATION DEFINED

Conflicting concepts of innovation are common in the literature. Miles defined innovation as change that is thought to be more efficacious in accomplishing the goals of the system.[2] Change is considered an undefined, primitive term, with innovation classified as a species of the genus change. Thompson viewer innovation as "the generation, acceptance, and implementation of new ideas, processes, products, or services."[3] It implies a capability to change or adapt. Paul Mort and his students, since at least the late 1930s, executed approximately 200 studies dealing with the adaptability of public school systems.[4] They preferred the term "adaptation" to "innovation," and defined "adaptability" as the capacity of an institution to respond to its role in society and to new insights related to new techniques of operation. Mort and his group were more concerned with identifying factors associated with school systems of high adaptability than with innovation per se.

Dictionary definitions reflect popular usage of terms during a given period and do not always incorporate new and emerging concepts. At present, the dictionary recognizes innovation as dealing with change in something established; hence, a novelty. The verb "to innovate" means "to introduce new ideas or things." Synonyms for the verb form include "alter," "con-

vert," "exchange," "modify," "qualify," "shift," and "substitute." Some synonyms for innovation have uncomplimentary as well as complimentary connotations. The most frequently used synonym for innovation is change. Change means creation of something different, for whatever reason.

In a strict sense change is neutral; it does not necessarily beget progress. It is possible to regress, to change for the worse rather than the better. One hopes that doing something differently will produce improvement, but there is no inherent guarantee that this will be the case. Innovation may create an illusion of progress. When this occurs, the phenomenon known as discontinuance results. Discontinuance is the abandonment of a new approach or activity and the reversion to a previous pattern of behavior. This suggests one of the more perplexing problems in the cataloguing of what constitutes a new approach: When can an administrator be sure that what is introduced has become a permanent part of the system? This will be probed in greater depth later in this chapter.

"Invent," "originate," "create," and "discover" are not synonyms for "innovate." Innovating, strictly speaking, is not the same as discovering or creating new things, methods, or instruments. There must be invention—the devising of new things or methods through study and experimentation—before there can be innovation. Change cannot occur unless there is first something to change from.

Innovation is conceptualized here as a process concerned primarily with strategies that may effect the move from one type of instructional system to another or the substitution of one system of administration for another.

[2]Matthew B. Miles, ed., *Innovation in Education*, New York: Teachers College, 1964, pp. 13–18.

[3]Victor A. Thompson, "Bureaucracy and Innovation," *Administrative Science Quarterly*, vol. 10, no. 1, June 1965, pp. 1–20.

[4]Paul R. Mort, "Studies in Educational Innovation from the Institute of Administrative Research: An Overview," *IRA Research Bulletin*, vol. 3, no. 1, October 1962, pp. 1–8.

INVENTION, INNOVATION, AND IMPROVEMENT

Three concepts are offered to describe what has been referred to simply as innovation. Invention is concerned with the generation of previously unknown things, events, or activities, while innovation is concerned with diffusion; improvement is the purpose behind it all. The ultimate goal of improvement may be lost when unusual emphasis is placed on change for the sake of change. An invention is the product of a creative mind. This display of originality need not be confined to physical gadgets. Thus, social inventions such as novel teaching methods, unique instructional patterns, or new ways of organizing educational systems are possible. Grading (and recently nongrading) of schools, ability grouping, team teaching, and laboratory methods of instruction are illustrations of social inventions in the field of education. MBO/R and PPBS are others that apply specifically to administration. In popular usage, innovation implies inventing new forms, approaches, or behaviors as well as the process of diffusing them.

Qualities of mind, personality, or position essential for inventing are not necessarily the same as those for disseminating or implementing the invention. Intellectual, scholarly, and creative ability are needed to generate new models of instruction or new administrative systems. The creation of social inventions demands comprehension of conceptual frameworks and theory, a disciplined research approach, time to think, and resources to develop.

The inventor of novel things, events, or activities for education need not play all roles in the change process. Inventions are born in laboratories and are products of creative minds wherever they may be. Involvement in the operational activities of an administrative post, which is necessary to facilitate diffusion of the invention, might well frustrate the inventor. The innovator—the person responsible for disseminating a new idea—would find it difficult to realize success without a position in the administrative or supervisory hierarchy. Innovation as a process is a field activity rather than a laboratory operation. State departments of education and public school systems are intimately involved in innovation; yet they may or may not produce an invention. The first step in the process of innovation for the administrator as a change agent is the identification of social and physical inventions that warrant consideration.

External criteria must be developed for judging change as good, bad, or indifferent. People viewing a new practice from different perspectives or in terms of different value systems will end up with different evaluations. Improvement is a value judgment. Thus, innovation should proceed on the evidence that an invention deserves implementation, that is, according to one's subjective opinion, it has a probability of improving existing practices. This is the normative aspect of the problem. Educational administrators are becoming more sophisticated and are demanding hard data that a new approach has been adequately tested and found to be effective in such field test. It is what an "innovation" can do rather than the fact that it is new that is important.

Recognizing that invention precedes innovation and that the purpose of each is improvement tends to minimize worship of new gadgets as essential parts of innovation. Eye, Netzer, and Krey warned:

Recognition, however, must be granted to the fact that the gadgetry of any profession seems to be the rallying point for the quacks of the profession. In this sense all need to be aware of the danger of gadgetry. There have been, there are, and probably there will continue to be "operators" in the educational profession who are willing to single out any vehicle of change and deal with it as though it satisfied all of the professional program needs.[5]

INNOVATION AND SOCIAL CHANGE

Determining what strategies are most effective in getting them to modify previously crystallized behavior becomes a matter of high priority for administrators intent on serving as change agents. Educational change can be viewed as a special case of general social change, therefore, the extensive research concerned with social change may be a starting point for identifying viable strategies for introducing change.

Berelson and Steiner[6] summarized the conclusions from significant research on social change. Much of what follows is adapted from this source. It is possible for large and complex social changes (for example, using team teaching in all grades) to be assimilated with a minimum of social disruption if the modifications are desired by the people involved. The reverse is also true. Even a rather small change, if not desired, will acquire considerable social and personal cost for implementation. The strategies of the educational innovator are more likely to succeed when the people affected are involved in and committed to changes. If teachers are ignored, even small modifications from existing

[5]G. G. Eye, L. A. Netzer, and R. D. Krey, *Supervision of Instruction*, 2nd ed., New York: Harper & Row, 1971, p. 73.

[6]Bernard Berelson and G. A. Steiner, *Human Behavior*, New York: Harcourt Brace Jovanovich, 1964, pp. 613–623.

practices will be resisted. More will be said about the fact that in innovations you must change people as well as things. Changes imposed on a school system by outside groups (for example, an undesirable approach to teacher evaluation imposed by a legislature) are not likely to be accepted without considerable struggle. The exertion of pressure upon teachers to effect alterations in behavior may result in a false compliance and considerable likelihood of discontinuance. It tends to create the illusion of progress by stressing overt compliance, but ignores the likelihood of covert resistance.

The more the proposed change appears to threaten or actually threatens traditional values of the group affected, the greater will be the resistance to it. If modification of behavior is demanded despite resistance, a considerable cost in social and personal disorganization can be anticipated. The slower the rate of social change, the greater the commitment to discussions by those to be affected by the modifications; the more the new proposals are introduced through existing and familiar institutions, the less likely the change will be considered a serious disruption of a prevailing way of life. Allowing more time and exerting less pressure for adjustment will permit greater opportunity for rationalizing the change with existing practices.

Social change is more likely to be precipitated in heterogeneous rather than homogeneous societies. When most teachers of a system received professional preparation at the same or similar schools, belong to the same age group, and so on, innovation will prove more difficult than when a pattern of heterogeneity prevails.

Social change is more likely and more readily accepted in material aspects of the culture, such as in technology, than in the nonmaterial aspects, such as value patterns. Thus, a teaching machine will be readily accepted by teachers who consider subject matter of great importance and employ a psychology of learning consistent with that upon which the machine is based. Furthermore, innovations are more readily accepted in less emotionally charged, less sacred, and more technical sectors of practice, such as tools and tactics; in the simple rather than the complex dimensions of a profession; in the nonsymbolic as opposed to the symbolic facets; in form rather than in substance of a practice; in elements congenial rather than strange to the profession; and in periods of pressure, crisis, and stress rather than in normal times. Note the last clause. Alterations in teacher behavior are more likely to occur when the school is subject to criticism or when a respected leader expresses dissatisfaction with results than when everyone is well satisfied with the school.

There is a tendency toward stability following drastic social change. In other words, reorganizations follow disruption and are aimed at reestablishing a new security base. (This is one reason that continual change leaves much to be desired.) Within a profession major changes are not likely to be stimulated by those in the lowest social stratum. In other words, major changes in professional practice are not likely to be led by those held in lowest esteem or by those traditionally in control. Change agents are more apt to be the deviant, marginal, and disaffected groups, but they must have some status base. Studies show innovators to be younger than resisters and more oriented to the outside world. Such persons are able to adopt new ideas or practices in less

time and discontinue them less often.

Changes can precipitate social conflict. The more substantial or encompassing the professional conflict over a proposed change, that is, the more central the change is to basic value patterns of the profession, the greater the pressures will be to bring a resolution of differences. A social conflict is likely to intensify when the goals sought by disputants are more fixed; contact or openness between parties is limited; the groups are bound together by close ties; ideology is involved; the participants on each side are committed to a cause; and the rules for resolving conflict are uncertain or unstable. Furthermore, a sharpening of the conflict will tend to bring participants who differ to associate with those who believe as they do. This has a tendency to deepen the strife, polarize participants, and harden antagonistic positions. Thus, cliques are born and become more noticeable in school systems experiencing conflict.

Of no less significance is that human conflicts are seldom resolved simply by eliminating the original source of the dispute. As more people besides the originally warring parties become part of the argument, rational settlement becomes more difficult. A threat from forces outside a group will result in a subordination of internal conflicts to achieve the common goal. Removal of the external threat, however, usually causes resumption of internal differences.

Throughout the course of disagreement, individuals with differing points of view will become polarized around the controversial issues; leaders will emerge to represent one side of an issue or another, with new leaders usually taking a more extreme position than the original ones; word-of-mouth communication will be used more, because this medium is more adaptable to partisan purposes than the media of mass communication; arguments will tend to move from specific to broader issues, from the original to ones not previously contemplated, from divergence of opinions on issues to personal antagonism.

The effect of crisis on social relations depends upon preexisting conditions in the community. If the community is not homogeneous, crisis will tend to deepen the chasm.

The diffusion of social inventions in educational institutions can precipitate social conflict if the process of innovation is mishandled. Knowing appropriate strategies and sensing the nature of the teachers are most important qualities for an innovator. Only the naive will assume that many and numerous changes are good; this would imply that social conflicts never occur in school situations and that people are equally willing to accept any position presented them.

Other studies focus on specific changes in educational institutions and occurred after Berelson and Steiner's compilations. Resistance to innovations is not always traceable to the stubbornness of professional groups. Overloading may be a factor. Overloaded workers find that they must devote so much energy to staying on top of known situations that they have little time, thought, or energy to develop or accept new approaches. Unrealistic goals, lack of skill in promoting innovation, and alienation from surrounding environment militate against change as well. Studies indicate that rejection of change is related to ignorance, default (lack of interest), preference for maintaining status quo, societal mores, interpersonal relations, erroneous logic, substitution, fulfill-

ment, and experience.[7] Carlson[8] identified the three barriers to change that are partially responsible for the slow rate of change in schools as: absence of a change agent, a weak knowledge base, and "domestication" of the public schools. In short, one who seeks to promote change must understand incentive and motivation and must ascertain whether financial, political, professional, or personal incentives are most likely to stimulate realization of objectives.

Social change occurs when pressure from various sources demands a response. Figure 5–1 presents an idealized illustration of the flow of forces from pressure to response. The time element is not portrayed. It should be noted that not all ideas define issues or give birth to social movements.

Like all social change, innovation in education can result from such conditions as (1) plain drift (aimless and uncertain activity over a period of time), (2) accident (primarily unplanned and uncertain events), (3) revolution (violent activities and upheavals), and (4) plans and purposes. Revolutions in education are bloodless. They may take the form of giant upheavals such as mass resignations of school boards, administrators, and/or teachers to bring about or resist modifications in practice. Most writers imply that change should be planned and purposeful.

The horizontal dimension of innova-

---

[7]G. Eichholz and E. M. Rogers, "Resistance to the Adoption of Audio-visual Aids by Elementary School Teachers: Contrasts and Similarities to Agricultural Innovation," in Miles, op. cit., chap. 12.

[8]R. O. Carlson, "Barriers to Change in the Public Schools," R. O. Carlson et al., *Change Process in the Public Schools,* Eugene, Ore.: Center for the Advanced Study of Educational Administration, University of Oregon, 1965, pp. 3–8.

tion measures whether change is system-wide or confined to only a few classrooms of a few buildings. The substantive dimension specifies what is changed, that is, the practice abandoned or the new procedure adopted. When substantive changes in curriculum occur, the question arises whether all or simply part of the offerings are modified. The rate of innovation is another dimension that has intrigued researchers and writers.

Duration of implementation is yet another dimension of innovation. When novelty wears off, there may be reversion to previous conditions. It is not clear how long a new social invention must be practiced (by whatever number of persons) before it can be credited as an innovation. Some current writings imply that an invention becomes an innovation the moment it is adopted. As long as there is suffi-

cient fanfare accompanying adoption, the fact that the invention was adopted in the morning and abandoned by late afternoon appears to make little difference. This pedestrian approach is beginning to disappear.

If one recognizes as an innovation *any* new practice implemented for *any* period of time by *whatever size* group, the inevitable conclusion is that schools do change continually. If it must be system-wide dramatic change (however defined) in some facet of education such as curriculum (for example, a completely new content for the teaching of science in all grades), personnel (for example, an entirely new approach for deploying all teachers), or administration (for example, implementation of MBO/R), then the inevitable conclusion is that schools have not changed much. Stated another way, the rate and magnitude of

---

FIGURE 5–1

Flow of forces from pressure to response in the accomplishment of social change.

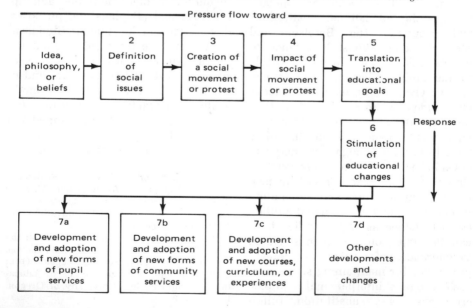

change necessary for a school to be considered forward-looking and dynamic have been ill-defined.

Those who say schools fail to adopt "promising practices" are referring evidently to major and dramatic shifts. Some look only at curriculum and ignore the changes in school financing, managing fiscal resources, constructing new facilities, utilizing electronic data processing, and so on. Though few writers can speak with authority on innovations in education from a total-system point of view, the fact that they are generalizing from an inadequate sampling does not deter their stinging rebukes of public education.

PRIORITIES IN INNOVATION

The fact of invention precedes the act of innovation. The decision to adopt a social invention is one of the crucial points in the process of innovation. It is questionable whether the confusion and extra effort that accompany attempts to alter peoples' behavioral patterns are justified if there is a low probability that the shift will yield significant additional benefits.

Prudent innovation is based on scientifically validated social inventions. When a change is not supported by research or is inadequately field tested, its advocates are tempted to select evidence to support preconceived notions and rudely dismiss facts to the contrary as being spurious or planted by "antiinnovation-minded" persons.

Education would do well to impose the discipline other fields demand on the search for better solutions to plaguing problems. The medical profession, for example, refuses to tolerate extravagant and premature claims for cures; it demands more than statements from renowned physiologists and distinguished practioners or testimonials from cured patients. Those who report cures that cannot be verified are subject to disciplinary action by the profession. Similarly, a new way of teaching reading or a new approach to mathematics should not be adopted on the basis of only a supporting opinion of a well-known personality in education. In addition, it must be demonstrated not only that a social invention (a new type of grading or nongrading, or a new grouping technique) truly results in improvement, but also that it produces no harmful side effects. What is gained if a pupil learns more math and science only to develop a lifelong hatred and subsequent avoidance of both? The lot of a change agent would be a happier one if more disciplined appraisals of the so-called promising practices were in evidence.

Resistance to a highly proclaimed "promising practice" can come from many sources, not the least of which is the emptiness of inadequately conceptualized or developed proposals. The dashed hopes of previous generations who supported poorly conceptualized, inadequately tested, and shabbily developed—but widely heralded—instructional panaceas are significant testimony to the experienced educator. Substituting a new untested dogma for an old one does not necessarily constitute progress.

MODELS OF THE INNOVATION PROCESS

Figure 5–2 presents a model to describe the innovation process. It bears a kinship to Dewey's model of the thinking process. The model looks upon the condition of "felt need" or disequilibrium as the trigger of subsequent activity. Felt need arises from dissatisfaction with the current state of affairs. It is usually the byproduct of external and/or internal forces acting upon the institution. Criticism in a local newspaper editorial is an illustration of an external force; dissatisfaction among teachers or students is an example of internal force. The point is that there must be an environment conducive to innovation before invention receives serious consideration.

A leader may be viewed from this perspective as one who purposely sows dissatisfaction with existing approaches. He may highlight the institution's shortcomings in an effort to set the stage for change. In doing so he runs the risk of being unpopular, but unless there is created within a group a longing for something different, change is difficult to achieve.

The model views the second stage as conceptualization of the problem. This in turn leads to a search for an invention which holds promise of contributing to the solution of the problem. If none exists, it leads to the design of a model for invention. Once an invention is identified or designed, experimentation to ascertain the effectiveness of the new procedure is a most necessary part of the total development.

Evaluation, unfortunately, is ignored more often than not. Miles[9] declared that evidence indicated that "Educational innovations are almost never evaluated on a systematic basis." It appears that creators of experimental programs have little question about the efficacy of recommended changes. In light of this assumption, evaluation becomes superfluous. Miles pointed out that less than 0.5 percent of experimental programs in one large state was systematically evaluated.

In the proposed model it is implied that should the results prove negative, other approaches or different inventions must be sought. This starts the process of experimentation and evaluation all over again.

Assuming that an approach has been proved desirable, the next step is development for classroom use. In the laboratory stage of experimentation many variables are controlled to ascertain the impact of one—namely, the social invention. There is a great deal of difference between the laboratory and the classroom. Often an invention must be modified, redesigned to some extent, or better engineered to enable its use by the typical classroom teacher rather than only by the master teacher.

Pilot programs, or small-scale field tests, perfect and develop the social invention. The significance of this step can be illustrated by analogy to a rocket. If the design of a rocket and its propellant are scientifically and mathematically accurate, the combination of the two should send the pay-

---

FIGURE 5–2

Model of the innovation process.

1. Disequilibrium
   ↓
2. Conceptualization
   ↓
3. Identification or design for invention
   ↓
4. Experimentation
   ↓
5. Evaluation (return to step 2 if necessary)
   ↓
6. Pilot programs
   ↓
7. Diffusion
   ↓
8. Successful installations
   ↓
9. New balance or equilibrium

---

[9]Miles, op. cit., p. 657.

load into orbit. Faulty switches or careless workmen can negate sound design, however, and if they do the rocket may explode on the launching pad. Many new practices fail to work, not because they are unsound conceptually or unproved by experimentation, but because of human failures. Pilot programs, that is, actual field tests, are a means of working out the "bugs."

Diffusion of the "debugged" and experimentally proved new social invention follows. Various strategies must then be developed to facilitate the spread of new practices. The ultimate outcomes of diffusion are successful installation of the social invention and a new equilibrium for a given period of time.

There are others such as the Guba-Clark model for educational change. It has four stages—research, development, diffusion, and adoption—with a total of eight subcomponents.[10] The subcomponents fit into the model as follows:

1. Research
2. Development
   a. Invention-Formulating new solutions.
   b. Design-Engineering and packaging of the invention.
3. Diffusion
   c. Dissemination-Informing or creating widespread awareness of the invention.
   d. Demonstration-Presenting the invention in an operational mode to enhance its image.
4. Adoption
   e. Trial-Tryout or test of the invention in a particular context.
   f. Installation-Operationalizing the invention within an institution.
   g. Institutionalization-Complete assimilation into the system as an ongoing

program to reduce it to the status of a "non-innovation."

The literature on change has multiplied during the past decade to the point where annotated bibliographies on change or some aspect of it are no longer uncommon.[11]

DIFFUSION STRATEGIES

Dissemination of social inventions calls for a comprehension of appropriate strategies. There can be no real innovation until the change reaches the classroom level. Motivation of teachers is a basic element. To inaugurate change, the innovator must sense whether one or a combination of motives, such as those based on political, personal, professional, financial, or negative factors, are likely to succeed with particular types of teachers. The impact of teachers on innovation was reported by one researcher concerned with the implementation of BSCS biology:

The data would suggest that there really is no such thing as BSCS curriculum presentation in the schools. . . . Each teacher filters the materials through his own perceptions and to say that a student has been through the BSCS curriculum probably does not give us as much specific information as the curriculum innovators might have hoped.[12]

Knowingly or otherwise, teachers may negate the effect of a new approach by nominally accepting the innovation

[10]Egon G. Guba, "Methodological Strategies for Educational Change," a position paper for the conference on Strategies for Educational Change, Washington, D.C.: November 8–10, 1965.

[11]A recent annotated bibliography is Louis M. Migetre, Sanford Temking, and C. Peter Cummings, *An Annotated Bibliography on Administering Change,* Philadelphia: Research for Better Schools, Inc., October 1971, p. 333.

[12]J. J. Gallagher, *Teacher Variation and Concept Presentation in BSCS Curriculum Program,* Urbana, Ill.: Institutions for Research on Exceptional Children, University of Illinois, 1966, p. 33.

but continuing to behave as always. Past experience suggests that a wide variation in teacher classroom performance is to be expected even though the same instructional materials may be used.

What some have referred to as "quality assurance" for the implementation of innovative practices in education has importance. Models and strategies are necessary to enhance the "quality assurance" factor, for as Gallagher indicated on another occasion:

Those interested in curriculum development have not finished their job when they have packaged a cognitively valid and consistent set of materials. They must establish, in addition, how these materials are operationally introduced in the classroom environment. Otherwise, they will be left with certain unqualified assumptions as to how their package is unwrapped in the classroom.[13]

The administrator as a change agent needs educational change models and related strategies to facilitate the careful and competent "unwrapping" of an R-and-D-Center–designed and developed curricular and instructional package. The "unwrapping" is accomplished by one or more teachers, principals, and perhaps other administrative and support personnel.

The discrepancy between promise and practice is the bane of administrators as well as the original researchers and developers. Many trace the failure of a new approach to work well in the pilot stage but not in uncontrolled situations to the human factors involved. Teachers, the human components of any curriculum and instructional system, may or may not adjust to and incorporate the novel approaches in an acceptable manner. Many writers are now concluding that distortion of the social invention during the spread of its precepts and concepts to the uncontrolled real world is not only common but should be anticipated by developers of novel systems. Teachers and administrators are the ultimate users or, better, translators of new systems. They need special competencies to make the innovation operational.

The Wisconsin R and D Center for Cognitive Learning generated a staff development model to facilitate acquisition of requisite competencies.[14] It was designed to help teachers better understand and acquire competencies in working in a new instructional organization known as Individually Guided Education in the Multiunit Elementary School (IGE/MUS-E).

The general staff development model can be outlined as:

Ground zero: No IGE/MUS-E awareness
Stage one: IGE/MUS-E awareness
Stage two: IGE/MUS-E interest
Stage three: IGE/MUS-E entry level skills and concepts gained
Stage four: IGE/MUS-E operational skills and concepts demonstrated
Stage five: IGE/MUS-E concepts and skill refinement
Stage six: IGE/MUS-E professional competence achieved

A series of in-service meetings at various points in time plus actual teaching experiences can be designed to achieve the objective in the model. Completion

---

[13]J. J. Gallagher, *Analyses of Teacher Classroom Strategies Associated with Student Cognitive and Affective Performance,* Cooperative Research Project No. 3325, Urbana, Ill.: University of Illinois, 1968, p. 43.

[14]Stephen J. Knezevich, *Strategies For Educational Change: The Wisconsin R & D Center General Implementation and Staff Development Models for IGE/MUS-E,* Working Paper No. 93, Madison, Wis.: University of Wisconsin, Wisconsin R and D Center, February 1972.

of Stage Three is necessary before actual start of IGE/MUS-E teaching.

Adequate resources are necessary. All systems must ascertain how much money, staff, space, new equipment, etc., is required to stimulate as well as to install new social inventions. This calls for uncommitted money, time, skills, and goodwill. When the entire professional staff is committed to production work—that is, to teaching—innovation will be limited. Change has political ramifications as well as ideological ones. Time is another dimension in the overall strategy. What is a reasonable time schedule for the conversion? Lastly, strategies for precipitating a modification of teaching behavior must examine what means are most appropriate for what group of teachers (demonstrations, visits, clinics, conferences, etc.).

ROLE OF THE ADMINISTRATOR IN INNOVATION

Planned change requires a mechanism, a means, or an organization to facilitate dissemination among classroom teachers, building administrators, and others, as well as a carefully designed and developed social invention. Brickell[15] outlined the dynamics of instructional change for the New York State public schools. A basic assumption in this and other works is that adoption of new modes of behavior or techniques by classroom personnel and modifications in what is taught are dependent upon fundamental changes in people.

The essence of the problem is how to change teachers and administrators who are accustomed to acting in a given way—how to generate an atti-

[15]Henry M. Brickell, *Organizing New York State for Educational Change,* Albany, N.Y.: State Education Department, 1961.

tude of creative interest and willingness to alter fixed patterns or to adopt significantly different ones. The educational system as a whole must be geared to the process of innovation if the products of research are to reach the operational level of school systems —namely, the classroom. This includes the state department of education, institutions of higher learning that prepare the teachers, laboratory schools, local school systems, and individual attendance units. Dissemination of school inventions requires state laws and state education department regulations conducive to the spirit of innovation.

Of no less significance is the development of a new posture for local school administrators and supervisors if innovations are to prevail. Public school administrators and supervisors are conceived as change agents as well as technicians able to keep the system operating efficiently. This is not intended to devalue effective and efficient use of resources, for there is no virtue in waste or inefficiency. The administrator or supervisor who cannot even keep the school system operating efficiently at existing levels of performance is not likely to manage change to improved achievements. The administrator or supervisor who is to be a change agent as well as a technical expert must acquire sufficient understanding of research and of practical school situations to evaluate whether an invention has merit and if it can be used effectively by teachers or administrators to improve educational practice. Administrators and supervisors are released from daily classroom activities to enable them to learn what is happening in research laboratories and among developers of ideas significant for the classroom level. They can be likened to the research and development department of an industry that keeps the firm in tune with times and producing products to meet the changing demands of consumers. Workers immersed in the challenges of quantity and quality and industrial production seldom have time to generate the products of the future.

Identification of promising practices is only the beginning of the change agent's role. The administrators and supervisors must develop strategies for the dissemination of new ideas to classroom levels. The change agents must command the respect of professional personnel as well.

School systems require change agents to remain viable social institutions. The change agents who occupy administrative and supervisory positions must be sensitive to new technology that can be applied to education, be skilled in strategies for promoting change, command the respect of professional colleagues, and be dedicated to challenges. To fulfill the role of change agent, administrators and supervisors need competence in systems techniques and approaches.

entire organization will be stimulated to search).

3. Emphasizing recognition (such as professional esteem or satisfaction rewards) for search and innovation in addition to the usual extrinsic organizational rewards of income, power, and status (esteem striving replaces status striving).
4. Building a creative atmosphere free from external pressure that demands successful inventions in short periods of time (indulgence in time and resources is needed in the organization's evaluation of the innovator).
5. Producing an environment of freedom to innovate.
6. Designing greater structural looseness, less stratification, and less emphasis on narrow nonduplicating, nonoverlapping definitions of duties and responsibilities.
7. Using group processes more and more with freer communication systems, broader work assignments, less emphasis upon authority, greater interpersonal communication and multiple group membership.
8. Thinking in terms of innovative areas rather than in form of research and development departments alone.[16]

The complexity of creating and maintaining a structure conducive to innovation should be apparent.

INNOVATION AND ORGANIZATIONAL STRUCTURE

People represent one facet in innovation, social inventions another, and the work situation—the structure that facilitates or confines their actions—yet another.

Thompson examined the structural characteristics of the innovative organization. He viewed the general requirements as:

1. Allocation of special resources to innovation in an organization (uncommitted money, time, skills, and goodwill).
2. Creating diverse inputs needed to facilitate generation of new ideas (such as wide diffusion of uncertainty so the

SPREAD OF INNOVATION

The start of a movement toward new ways of doing things is usually modest. In the beginning there is a small group of innovators,[17] approximately 2 or 3 percent, who make the earliest decision to try out a new process. They are characterized by a high degree of awareness, usually consult with experts away from the local area, are well educated, are considered leaders, and are not likely to be concerned

---

[16]Thompson, op. cit.
[17]E. M. Rogers, "What Are Innovators Like?" in R. O. Carlson et al., op. cit., pp. 55–61.

with what others think of a decision they feel is worth a trial.

The "early adopters" wait a little longer than the first small group. They are typically about one-eighth of the total population and tend to be younger, readers of special bulletins, well educated, and leaders. They in turn are followed by the "early majority, the majority, and then the laggards."

THE NORTH CENTRAL ASSOCIATION STUDY ON INNOVATIONS

A national inventory of innovations in 7237 regionally accredited high schools,[18] about 72 percent of the total sample, was reported as of December 1966. Accredited high schools tend to be larger and better financed than their nonaccredited counterparts. This study aimed at documenting what kinds of innovations found their way into practice. The status of 27 innovations, in the three broadly defined areas of curriculum, technology, and organization, were determined on the basis of whether they were fully implemented and operating, whether they were being tried on a limited basis, when the practice started, whether plans were definitely made to adopt it next year, whether the practice had been tried and abandoned, and whether the practice was not used at all.

PSSC (physics), CHEM (chemistry), CBA (chemistry), SMSG (mathematics), UICSM (mathematics), ESCP (physical science), SSSP (physical science and humanities), were classified as specific curriculum innovations. Television instruction, programmed in-

struction, teaching machines, language laboratories, data-processing equipment, telephone amplification, and simulation or gaming were classified as technological developments. Flexible scheduling, team teaching, allowing college course credit in high school, nongrading, use of teachers' aides or paraprofessional personnel, honor-system study halls, work-study programs, school-within-a-school concept, cultural enrichment programs, student-exchange programs, optional class attendance, and extended school year were considered organizational innovations. Implementation of any or all innovations was determined on the basis of at least one class using the practice.

The 12 most commonly implemented innovations were: SMSG (in over 36 percent of the schools), PSSC (in 43 percent), CHEM or CBA (in almost 50 percent), programmed instruction (in use in 29 percent but abandoned in 5 percent), language laboratory (in 75 percent), electronic data-processing equipment (in 28.3 percent), team teaching (in about 41 percent of the schools, a greater proportion than the 22 percent estimated in 1964), college-credit courses in high school (in some 28 percent), teachers' aides (in 20 percent), work-study programs (in almost 50 percent), student-exchange programs (in 36.5 percent), cultural enrichment programs (in 31 percent). For the nation as a whole, an average of 6.1 of the 27 innovations were implemented; the average number per state varied from 3.3 to 8.6. The larger the school enrollment and the greater the pupil expenditure, the larger the number of innovations implemented.

Relatively few schools reported using SSSP, telephone amplification, nongraded school organization (4.7 percent), school-within-a-school organization, optional class attendance, and ex-

[18]Gordon Cawelti, "Innovative Practices in High Schools: Who Does What and Why and How," *Nation's Schools*, April 1967.

tended school year programs. Schools appear to be changing at a faster rate than in previous years.

Relatively high abandonment rates were reported for PSSC (3.2 percent), CBA and CHEM (combined 4.3 percent), SMSG (6.1 percent), ETV (3.8 percent), programmed instruction (4.9 percent), team teaching (4.3 percent), and honor-system study halls (6.0 percent). Various reasons, such as teacher resistance, teacher turnover, and inadequate facilities, were listed for abandoning a previously inaugurated new practice.

The study clearly indicates that schools across the nation are adopting new approaches, that some inventions are more readily accepted than others, but that discontinuance can follow diffusion.

LEGACY OF TECHNOLOGY

Technology is on everybody's list of forces necessitating change in educational administration. "Technology" is derived from a Greek word meaning "systematic treatment." Technology is defined as:

1. The terminology of a particular subject, that is, technical language.
2. The science of the application of knowledge to practical purposes, that is, applied science.
3. The application of scientific knowledge to practical purposes in a particular field.

Technology focuses on application and emphasizes the practical use of knowledge. Most often the term is used to refer to the product or procedure resulting from the application of scientific knowledge. Typically, literature dealing with technology in instruction describes a fairly recent physical or social invention that could be adapted to instructional purposes. Thus, television and the computer are physical inventions with implications for instruction; programmed instruction and the systems approach are social inventions. In a broad sense, the adaptation of a new invention to educational purposes can be construed as "the application of scientific knowledge to the practical purpose of education." More specifically, there are many new and old inventions (which trace their origins to scientific insights) that can improve various aspects of education.

Connotations of the term "technology" are as significant as its conceptual base. The ideas of "improvement," "a better way of doing things," "flexibility," "individualization of instruction," and in general all that is "good" are the positive connotations of technology. Technological change has eliminated most of the menial work, and it has increased the productive capacity, and thereby the earning power, of people. But there are negative dimensions as well. For example, technology has upset the delicate balance between man and his environment by contributing to air and water pollution. In the field of education, it has upset social relations among professionals by necessitating alteration of established patterns of teaching behavior. Social costs and dislocations often accompany change to accommodate technology. Tension and mental illness among humans are compounded by the quickening pace of change. The challenge that confronts the administrator is to maximize the benefits of technology and to minimize its debilitating spin-offs.

TECHNOLOGY IN INSTRUCTION

Education has felt the impact of technology throughout history. The development of the alphabet and of writing 5000 years ago greatly influenced ancient systems of education and instruction. The invention of paper and writing instruments furthered the utility of the alphabet and writing, and demanded skill in penmanship for those who would take advantage of these technological breakthroughs. Written records became important documents worthy of preservation, and the need for accessible storage of information led to a concern for some system of binding. In short, the creation of a manual system of written communication many centuries before the birth of Christ, consisting of many interrelated elements such as the alphabet, writing instruments, paper, penmanship, and binding, had a profound effect on the transmission and extension of knowledge through the ages.

Limitations as well as advantages in a manual system of written communication soon became apparent. The process was so expensive that few could afford handwritten volumes. Few could read, for few written records were available to the masses. Gutenberg's invention of printing from movable type represented another technological breakthrough that profoundly affected the instructional process in particular and educational institutions in general. Printing included elements of a manual written system (the alphabet and paper) and added a new element (movable type). The printing process made it possible to reproduce written thoughts in large quantities for rapid and relatively inexpensive dissemination. Education today remains indebted to technology related to printing.

After printing ceased to be a novelty, it became obvious that the quality of printed thoughts was at least as important as the circumstance that they were presented in print. Validity, organization, comprehensiveness, and manner of presentation of ideas became the basis for selecting one printed book for use in schools as opposed to another. The content of educational ideas and experiences maintains its importance no matter how advanced the technology for presenting it. There is always a danger that in the short run the glamor of a new gadget in education may obscure the shabbiness of the ideas or experiences being disseminated. The quality of materials presented by an invention must be assessed along with the device.

The recency of the invention is important in a discussion of technology. The demand for greater use of technology in education does not refer to the alphabet, paper, writing, instruments, movable type, chalkboards, or globes. These were yesterday's wonders. The modern technological developments that seem destined to have an impact on instruction are discussed below.

Modern technological developments

Technological developments related to photography. The invention of photography gave rise to the still photograph, glass slide, filmstrip, silent motion-picture film, sound motion-picture film, microfilm, and microfiche. "Audiovisual instruction" utilizes much of the technology of photography. The term "audiovisual education" is being discarded in favor of today's more popular term "educational technology." A combination of optical and mechanical devices focuses light on a light-sensitive chemical plate or film to fix an image which can be brought out after appropriate developing and printing of the plate or film. The projection of a visual image from a film onto a screen depends upon another optical-mechanical system known as the projector. This system is based on lenses, transparent film, powerful light sources, motors, and electricity. The projected image can appear in color or in black and white and can be accompanied by sound. Color-film technology represents an extension or refinement of black-and-white film technology. The 16-mm. sound film made its initial great impact in schools immediately following World War II. The 8-mm. sound film is sometimes considered part of the new technology in education, although the basic chemical, optical, and mechanical components are the same as for the 16-mm. sound film. The breakthrough is that the sound track is placed on the film. The smaller size of the film simplifies storage, and the greater economy thus achieved may encourage greater use of the sound film in the classroom. Microfilm and the microfilm reader represent an extension of this technology as well.

A visual image, in black and white or in color, still or in motion, with or without sound, can be helpful in promoting the learning of concepts and even of skills. It is not visual images in general, however, that result in learning gains; specific images related to promoting particular kinds of learning must be identified and made available for use with the technology of producing and projecting images with or without the accompaniment of sound. Again and as always, the technological device is only a means; its greatest misuse can arise from a confusion of the means-end dichotomy.

Technological developments related to the recording and reproduction of sound. Pioneering efforts by Edison to record and reproduce sound on cylindrical and on flat recording surfaces were limited to mechanical approaches. Subsequent technological developments in electronics produced other ways of recording sound on discs as well as on magnetic wire or tape. Electronic recording procedures improved fidelity and made possible stereophonic audio reproduction as well.

Music, speech, and English teachers have long adapted recording and reproduction of sound to improve instruction and learning. Foreign-language laboratories are essentially a collection of devices for listening to and recording sound on magnetic tape. Commercial-education laboratories teach stenography by devices that vary the speed of dictation individually and pipe it to various stations. The technological breakthrough here is the packaging of recording and listening devices for individuals or groups of students in libraries or classrooms.

It must be emphasized that what is recorded on magnetic tape to influence the student's learning is of no less importance than the fact that it is placed on magnetic tape. The psychology of learning behind the so-called "magnetic-tape learning laboratories" must be examined to assess accurately the impact of the technology.

Technological developments related to long-distance electronic transmission of sound. Radio was among the first of the electronic communication marvels. Audio transmission of school lessons via AM radio can no longer be considered part of the new technology. FM radio, which improved fidelity even in the face of atmospheric interference and distortion, is used presently for instructional purposes and in some states is considered an innovation.

Technological developments related to long-distance electronic transmission of visual and audio images. The transmission of visual as well as audio images over distance via electronic means is television. Statewide or regional educational television (ETV) stations are in use across the nation. Varying degrees of success have been reported in the use of TV in instruction. Television is similar to sound film, except that events can be televised as they occur and images can be transmitted over long distances and are reproduced primarily by means of electronic devices with limited use of optical and mechanical components. The method permits greater centralization of image projection.

ETV can no longer be considered new, since it has been around for more than a decade, but videotape, which stores visual and audio images without much loss of fidelity, is counted a new technology. Videotape is similar to sound film. It allows greater flexibility in adapting instructional materials to individual school class schedules, but it does not fundamentally alter the basic technology. Videotapes are being packaged in a cassette or cartridge similar to magnetic audiotape and can be played back when plugged into a TV set.

Again, instruction via television—whether videotaped or not—is only as effective as the preparation and quality of the instructor being televised or taped. Television may distort, but it can never improve, the quality of the lesson being disseminated.

Technological developments related to electronic processing, storage, and retrieval of information. The computer is an electronic device (with some mechanical components) for the manipulation, storage, and retrieval of data. It multiplies man's intellectual powers and enables him to complete tasks that could be done in no other

way. Third-generation and even newer equipment coupled with appropriate programming can be adapted to instruction. The use of computer technology in instruction and in administration requires new ways of presenting learning sequences, new roles for teachers, and new ways of organizing for instruction. Computer-assisted instruction (CAI), and computer-managed instruction (CMI), a blend of technological development in computers and in programmed instruction, are available in ever increasing numbers.

The tutorial mode of the computer is on everybody's list of modern technology; in fact CAI is sometimes equated with instructional technology. More will be said about the uses of the computer in instruction and administration in subsequent sections of this chapter.

Technological developments related to programmed instruction. Systematic arrangement of materials to be learned can be traced back to Socrates' style of questioning, the catechetical instruction of the early Christian church, and the early nineteenth-century interests in the psychology of learning. Programmed instruction is based on a sequence of actions or experiences that follow a preset order and facilitate evaluation of learned knowledge, insights, or performance at an established standard. CAI is basically programmed learning employing the computer, which either writes out questions and responses via typewriter or presents them visually, with or without audio complement, through a cathode-ray tube. Programmed instruction can be presented in written or printed form (for example a programmed text) as well. It is itself a systematic approach and does not depend upon a mechanical or electronic device to realize its purposes, although the computer gives the approach great flexibility.

Technological developments related to the systems approach. The systems approach is more a social than a physical invention. It is a generalized process for applying scientific knowledge to practical purposes. It is a way of coping with the change process in the instructional system. It calls for the specification of missions in terms of behavioral outcomes, an interdisciplinary attack on problems, emphasis on the whole and the interrelatedness of elements, the generation of models, and sophisticated quantitative reasoning tools. The concept of instructional systems is related to the systems approach, and will be discussed in Chapters 8 and 9.

Technological developments related to biochemical or pharmacological means. A 1967 summer seminar on the chemistry of learning and memory, sponsored by a foundation, suggested that in all probability within 10 years it will be possible to alter the intellectual capacity of children through the use of drugs. This report was made by some of the world's leading biochemists and other scientists. Although in hindsight it seems overly optimistic, there may someday be a whole arsenal of drugs available that can affect various parts of the learning process. Such a technology might well trigger a major social controversy.

Status of instructional technology

Before proceeding further, it is necessary to clarify what is meant by instruction. A useful statement by Corey[19] defined instruction operation-

ally as "the process whereby the environment of an individual is deliberately manipulated to enable him to learn to emit or engage in specified behaviors, under specified conditions, or as responses to specified conditions." Instruction can be considered intentional environmental manipulation, that is, a purposeful alteration of conditions within the realm of consciousness of learners.

Educational television. ETV has been praised and damned during its brief history. Television, according to Mitchell, "stands today (1966) as perhaps the most expensive and disastrous single failure in the history of educational technology."[20] He recognized the unlimited potential of ETV as a teaching tool but concluded that up to 1966 the millions poured into ETV by government, foundations, business, and industry had failed to release its real contribution to the educational process. At this writing (the mid-1970s) ETV has yet to reach its full potential or anywhere near the impact on instruction predicted by its proponents in the 1950s.

To repeat and expand on a previous observation, instruction via television is no better than the quality of the teacher in front of the TV camera. It is the teacher before the TV camera, not the electronic connections that ultimately terminate at a TV tube or screen, that stimulates learning. ETV makes possible wider dissemination

[19]S. M. Corey, "The Nature of Instruction," in B. C. Lange, ed., *Programmed Instruction,* Sixty-fifth Yearbook of the National Society for the Study of Education, part 2, Chicago: University of Chicago Press, 1967, p. 6.

[20]Statement of Maurice B. Mitchell, *Technology in Education,* Hearings before the Subcommittee on Economic Progress of the Joint Economic Committe Congress of the United States, 89th Congress, Second Session, Washington, D.C.: GPO, 1966, p. 12.

of the performances of outstanding teachers, albeit at the cost of doing without a live personality to observe in front of the classroom. ETV, however, for all practical purposes limits the teacher's mode of presentation to the lecture format, with or without visuals. The learners are primarily passive recipients. ETV can be used as a supplement to, or a replacement for, the live classroom teacher. Its effectiveness will be influenced by how skillfully the classroom teacher employs it. It can also be valuable for independent study, particularly among adults, but here again some coordinating person must be available to determine how well the learner is reaching his objectives through television as an instructional medium.

Programmed instruction. Programmed instruction is a system that has the potential to individualize the pace at which a person learns, but a considerable amount of development is needed before its potential can be realized. Lindvall and Bolin[21] identified steps in applying programmed instruction.

Programmed instruction is a disciplined approach based on careful, detailed study of the instruction process. Exaggerated expectations and subsequent deflation were experienced during its first decade of existence. According to Lange,[22] there were three major phases in its development. The beginning phase was characterized by a false sense of development engendered by enthusiasm for and over-selling of initial program designs. The

[21]C. M. Lindvall and J. O. Bolin, "Programed Instruction in the Schools: An Application of Programing Principle in Individually Prescribed Instruction," in B. C. Lange, ed., *Programed Instruction*, Chicago: University of Chicago Press, 1967, pp. 178–216.

[22]B. L. Lange, "Future Developments," in B. C. Lange, ed., ibid., pp. 286–287.

secondary phase was disillusionment with primitive initial applications of the technology. Disillusionment grew as users discovered that the approach to learning failed to match claims of early proponents; many schools in the 1960s adopted programmed instruction in selected areas and dropped it because it failed to produce learning gains and cost savings. The third phase was improvement of the new technology by the remaining core of imaginative and dedicated developers, which resulted in increasing use once again.

Programmed instruction can be implemented with or without the help of machines of various degrees of sophistication. It is a way of presenting what is to be learned in an orderly, psychologically defensible, sequential pattern. The machine is less important than the developed programmed instructional materials. Sometimes the "machine" is only a device that covers the answer to a question presented through a slot to the learner. Sometimes a sophisticated machine is coupled with a computer that, through special circuits and commands, activates a typewriter to raise questions, submit answers, or indicate reactions to responses by the learner. With computer connections the programmed material can be presented visally on a cathode-ray tube. By using a light pen, the student can place his response to a question directly on the screen.

Computer-assisted instruction. CAI, or CAL (computer-assisted learning), is programmed instruction based on computer technology. It is a blend of two technologies—programmed learning and computer-based electronic data processing. It captured the imagination of many educators in the 1960s. The status of CAI, particularly its readiness for use in the typical classroom, was subject to debate and conflicting interpretation in the 1960s. The author's investigations as chairman of three special commissions probing various aspects of technology in education led him to the following conclusion: even in the late 1960s CAI was an underdeveloped technology. Several large computer manufacturing firms invested over $150 million to develop an operationally feasible CAI system. They terminated these huge development costs in the early 1970s, which amounted to an admission that the costs and speed with which the computer could be adapted to instruction and become an economic alternative to the live teacher were grossly underestimated.

Nonetheless, progress in generating new computer-managed instructional programs continued among individuals and school systems in the 1970s. Hoye and Wang[23] produce an annual index of available computer-based instructional systems in the United States. In 1969 this index listed 410 computer-based learning programs, which by 1973 more than quadrupled to a total of 1766. Problems remain of adapting instructional materials to machine-usable form as well as problems of economics. CAI has focused on the more trivial aspects of education such as drill and practice. The teletype system of presenting questions to students via typewritten statements and demanding pupil responses through the teletype is a slow and unnatural way for a pupil to address a problem. Communicating directly with a computer via voice contact rather than teletype is under study, but this is at least a decade away.

The high cost of CAI cannot be ig-

nored. As Arnstein[24] said in testimony before the Congressional panel on technology in June 1966: "There is not now in existence anywhere in the United States, a tested, validated, usable computer-assisted teaching program which is economically competitive with 'live' teachers." This remained true in the mid-1970s even though computer operating costs showed signs of declining from very high levels.

A realistic appraisal suggests that CAI needs 10 more years of development before it moves out of the laboratory stage. Industry has grossly underestimated the time, difficulty, and cost of developing CAI. As of November 1967, the U.S. Office of Education had spent approximately $34,000,000 on research and other projects concerning application of new computer technology to education. Over 60 projects and over $10,250,000 of this total was for CAI. It is the writer's opinion that expenditures on the order of $1 billion dollars will be necessary to perfect CAI. Clearly, the availability of the computer does not imply its immediate use in schools. A long and costly period of programming the computer to perform educational tasks is required.

Future of instructional technology

Technology will continue to shape instruction in public education. An increased expenditure of resources will be necessary to enable schools to accommodate change more rapidly and to take advantage of existing technology.

[23]Robert E. Hoye and Anastasia C. Wang, *Index To Computer-Based Learning*, Englewood Cliffs, N.J.: Educational Technology Publications, 1973.

[24]Testimony of George G. Arnstein, *Technology in Education*, Hearings Before the Subcommittee on Economic Progress of the Joint Economic Committee, Congress of the United States, 89th Congress, Second Session, Washington, D.C.: GPO, 1966, p. 110.

Many issues are raised in reference to the impact of technology on instruction. Can learning be a completely automated process? Can it be controlled from start to finish on the basis of preestablished criteria or by means of an information system that can be implemented without human intervention? A completely automated instructional system would be predominantly an electronic process, supplemented by mechanical devices, which could be carried out without human intervention. It would include a self-adjusting control maintained by continually measuring desired or planned results and triggering corrective procedures. This is an exaggerated view of the impact of technology on instruction. A system need not exclude people. A total systems approach includes people, purposes, procedures, machines, supplies, and other resources. An automated instructional system, however, minimizes human intervention.

In another publication this writer predicted that "present and preliminary insights into the pharmacological stimulants of learning will only begin to be defined more sharply by the mid-1980s."[25] "Chemically-assisted instruction" or enzyme-assisted instruction may not be feasible until the twenty-first century, but "get smart" pills may be talked about with increasing frequency during the rest of this century. Educational strategies will by 1985 be dramatically different from what they are now due primarily to the technological thrusts of computers, lasers, and holography. The impact of electrophysiology and pharmacology will not be felt that soon. All these portend a continuing emphasis on the change agent role of educational administrators.

TECHNOLOGY IN ADMINISTRATION

Of no less interest are those technologies specifically concerned with administration as a function. The systems approach and the use of models will be reviewed in subsequent chapters. The present discussion concerns computer-based electronic data processing (EDP).

The computer is no ordinary invention. It may well be one of the most significant tools in the history of humankind. It may have an effect as profound as that of the wheel, the movable-type printing press, and the machines that powered the industrial revolution.

The computer was invented and then perfected by physical scientists primarily to satisfy the need for rapid computation. It has been adapted to other functions. Manufacturers of computer hardware have become concerned with refining and adapting computer systems to meet the needs of educational institutions. Computers were introduced in schools much more slowly than in industry or the federal government.[26] By 1961 less than 5 percent of the nation's public school districts employed EDP gear in some way. Based on 1965 data, one group of writers declared: "EDP is not an advanced art in the field of education. Primitive paper-and-pencil techniques still prevail for most educational information processing."[27] Frustration

[25]Stephen J. Knezevich, "The Educational Program in 1985," in *Educational Futurism 1985*, W. G. Hack et al., Berkeley, Cal.: McCutchan Publishing Co., 1971, p. 55.

[26]American Association of School Administrators, *EDP and the School Administrator*, Washington, D.C.: The Association, 1967, p. 4.

[27]J. I. Goodlad, J. F. O'Toole, Jr., and L. L. Tyler, *Computers and Information Systems in Education*, New York: Harcourt Brace Jovanovich, 1966, p. 55.

was common in the early years because equipment designed for other purposes was inadequately adapted to the challenge of educational tasks while operating costs skyrocketed beyond preliminary estimates. It is not unusual, however, for a field to experience difficulties early in its use of a new technology. By the late 1960s schools were moving rapidly toward utilization of computer-based technology to attack educational problems. In the early 1970s computers were so common in educational administration that they had lost some of their early glamor. By the end of the 1970s it will be the exceptional school district that fails to use or have access to a computer system.

Nature of a computer

A computer combines electronic devices with some mechanical attachments. It is a man-machine system. The machine dimension cannot fulfill its potential unless the human element designs programs to direct computer operations. The computer multiplies intellectual efforts. How well it does this is influenced to a considerable extent by the user.

A computer is basically an electronic device for processing information. There are two main types. The digital computer manipulates data that can be expressed in separate units; it counts precisely and sequentially; its distinguishing quality is a memory; and it is the most common type sold and used today. The analog computer, in contrast, has no memory and reflects data in relative forms; it is less likely to be used in the administration of education.

Digital computers differ in memory capacity, flexibility in inserting data and delivering output information, speed in executing operations, and

versatility. Computers developed rapidly after the first one was created in 1944. The first-generation electronic devices employed vacuum tubes that generated tremendous heat and were not reliable during extended operations. The use of vacuum tubes and traditional circuitry produced a bulky, room-size machine that required sizable amounts of floor space. The second-generation computers used the much smaller transistors instead of vacuum tubes, thus greatly reducing bulk while at the same time increasing reliability. The third-generation computers retained the smaller and more reliable transistors and replaced traditional circuits with minaturized, or integrated, circuits. The new circuitry enhanced the computer's internal memory, improved its speed, and reduced its cost, and at the same time decreased its bulk. These improvements in the third-generation machines made them suitable for attacking educational problems. Further reduction in size of circuitry have appeared along with increased speed of operations. Computer hardware changed rapidly during the 1960s.

Operation of a computer

Computer operation can be explained on several levels.[28] The kind of technical information that would be of interest to electronic engineers or specialists in data processing will not be presented here. Rather, the discussion will focus first on some misconceptions about the computer and then on a general, nontechnical explanation of its operation.

Few experience direct contact with EDP. This does not inhibit the public's interest nor lessen the public's awe of

[28]American Association of School Administrators, op. cit., p. 12.

this "amazing" and "fantastic" device. The computer is often interpreted as an all-powerful, incomprehensible, infallible, and independent "superbrain." Uneasiness about the computer is related to its "science-fiction-machine" attributes. One sociologist viewed the electronic computer as an assault on man's ego. The infernal machine is credited with accomplishments beyond human capabilities. A hard look at its limitations as well as its splendors should produce a more realistic image.

Second-, third-, and subsequent generation computers consist of a variety of cabinets of different sizes and colors and a work bench with a typewriter, control buttons, and flashing lights. Inside the cabinets and the work bench are multicolored wires, electrical circuits, and panels of electronic devices. Off to one side, magnetic tapes whirl on colorful spindles. Mechanical gadgets attached to the main frame of the computer receive data via punched cards and deliver data in printed form. More important than physical appearance are basic operations. There are four basic operations in computer-based data processing.

1. Input: introducing information to be analyzed by the computer.
2. Storage: holding items in abeyance.
3. Processing: manipulating data according to plan.
4. Output: getting processed data out of the computer in such forms as punched cards, magnetic tape, or typewritten report.[29]

Input. Two kinds of inputs are necessary to get the computer into operation: Data to be analyzed or manipulated must be introduced, and because the computer does only what it is told to do, a series of instructions to the machine must be introduced that command it to manipulate data in a par-

[29]Ibid., p. 13.

ticular way and to issue a report of a given type. Each type of input data must be translated and organized into machine-usable form and inserted via cards or tape at a particular point and with a given speed.

The punched card, which was developed prior to the computer, is one of the most popular methods of feeding data. Developed by Hollerith, the punched card is some times referred to as the Hollerith or the IBM card. It is a thin, rectangular cardboard with standard dimension ($7\frac{3}{8}$ x $3\frac{1}{4}$ inches). Data to be inserted into the computer are coded into a series of punched holes arranged in a particular sequence. The operator works at a special machine, the key punch, which places the round or rectangular holes in a given series of positions. The arrangement of holes on the card is important. Twelve punches can be made in a column and there are 80 columns on the IBM card. Numbers require only one punched hole; letters of the alphabet require two. The ordinary computer cannot read ordinary writing or typing. Special devices, known as optical scanners, may be attached to a computer to give it the capability of reading type by interpreting characters, noting position of marks, or sensing the presence or absence of a notation.

Paper tape with holes punched in a coded pattern will accomplish the same purpose as the IBM card. Convenience determines which is best.

Magnetic tape is similar to punched tape, but has electronic signals stored in given positions rather than visually obvious holes on paper tape. Introducing data into the computer by means of cards takes far more time than introducing data by running off a reel of magnetic tape. Input data, such as the program, which is to be used over and over again, may be magnetic tape.

Magnetic tape, when interpreted by a special magnetic "reading head," generates electronic impulses the computer understands. Electronic impulses are the language of the machine. The holes in the punched cards or paper tape close a circuit that produces the impulse the machine is capable of interpreting.

Storage and retrieval. Not everything inserted in the computer—data to be processed or instructions about operations—can be handled at one time. All or part of a given input must be held in abeyance for various periods of time. Information may be stored in devices within the computer (internal storage) or in equipment outside the main frame (external storage). The capability to preserve inserted data is one of the remarkable qualities of the digital computer. Storage is sometimes called the computer's memory because the process suggests the human brain's quality of retaining experiences. The computer will remember only what it is programmed at a given point in time to remember. It is more accurate to say that data are stored as directed by a program rather than to suggest that a computer can recall items processed in a previous and unrelated program run.

One computer differs from another in the type of storage device as well as the quantity of information that can be stored within the main frame. The amount of external storage is limited only by the availability of storage devices and the manner in which they are connected to the main computer. To illustrate, magnetic tape and discs can store thousands of bits of data, but if it is external, the storage device must be placed on line, that is, connected with the main frame of the computer. Retrieval is the preferred

term for obtaining data from internal or external storage. Rapidity of retrieval, that is, speed of access to stored items, varies from one type and generation of computer to another.

Comprehension of computer storage depends on recognizing that a computer is an electronic device. It is sensitive to electrical impulses. What is being stored is not akin to the bits of paper placed in the typical file. Electrical charges are stored. As stated in the discussion of inputs, the computer reacts to electrical signals and "reads" the presence or absence of an electrical charge at some point. A device that can retain and release an electrical charge is a storage device for the computer.

The key to computer storage is a pattern created by the presence or absence of an electrical charge. A binary number system (consisting of only two digits), in which the decimal values of the places (from right to left) are 1, 2, 4, 8, 16, etc., is used. The absence of electrical charge is 0 and the presence of electrical charge is the number 1. For example, the decimal number 4 becomes 0100, five becomes 0101, seven becomes 0111, and 9 becomes 1001 in the binary system. Binary numbers can be translated back into the everyday number system. The computer must recall where a particular fact is placed as well as retrieve it accurately. Instructions—that is, the computer program—determine whether the item recalled from storage is destroyed upon retrieval or retained for other occasions of retrieval.

External storage may be on magnetic tape, magnetic drums, special discs, or data cells. The devices may be placed on line, or filed and connected manually as needed. Reels of magnetic tape and discs are light and of comparatively small size; this facilitates movement and storage of these components.

Processing. Processing, or manipulation of data according to some plan, is the primary function of a computer. Storage is a convenience. So important is the processing function that the main frame of the computer is referred to as the central processing unit (CPU). Processing is based on a program of instructions (called "software" in contrast to "hardware," which is the machine itself) to direct the computer to act on each item of information in a particular way. For example, the program may command that something be added to an item stored in a given register or that two numbers be multiplied or that one number be compared with another and the larger reported out. The act of processing is a significant characteristic of the computer, but of no less importance is the program of instructions that coordinates the processing.

The computer lacks imagination, initiative, and creativity. It does only what it is told—no more, no less. It is finicky and sensitive to the manner in which it is addressed. Programming a computer is less laborious now than ever before, but considerable expenditures are necessary to get the computer in operation. Delivery of the machine is only the beginning move toward computer operations. The difficult and time-consuming task of preparing a series of programs to direct computer functions is necessary. There are libraries of programs for common activities, such as extracting square roots or making statistical computations. Unusual processing or report preparation via computer necessitates the investment of time, money, and talent for special programming. A small error in programming can distort results or make the machine inoperable.

Programs designed for computers of one brand or one generation will not work in another. There are different programming languages as well. Greater programming compatibility is being developed in new, more complex models. Perhaps someday the laborious task of programming will be automated.

Programming is an important part of the cost of installing, maintaining, and operating an EDP system. It is a cost in addition to machine purchase or rental. It is done by people with specialized talent and skill. A task that may take only a few seconds of computer time may require many hours, weeks, months, or years of program-writing time. Programming costs in the hundreds of thousands of dollars are required to render one subject of one grade level into CAI format.

All activities performed by a computer must be regulated in some fashion to ensure that everything moves in a proper sequence and without confusion. A central control panel or switchboard is imperative. As implied previously, control is usually done automatically through a program of instructions inserted in the computer. It can be done manually by the operator, but this is slow and cumbersome.

Output. Upon completion of the processing, the data must be released from the computer. This is the reverse of input and calls for translating the electrical impulses into a form meaningful to human beings. The program includes directions about how its output will be recorded, that is, whether it will be printed on sheets of paper, on punched cards, or on a reel of magnetic tape. Auxiliary machines, called peripheral gear, are activated by the computer to produce the output in the desired form. High-speed printers may be purchased to release data faster. The slowest parts of computer operation are input and output. Processing is accomplished with almost lightning speed, but output printing is comparatively slow.

Impact of EDP on school administration

Computer-based EDP will affect the organizational hierarchy of a school and the types of specialized personnel employed, as well as the execution of tasks ranging from preparation of payroll checks or grade reports to CAI and administrative decision making. The computer is a powerful device that will affect all aspects of education.

Often EDP enters the educational institution at a low level—for example, to speed up and accurately maintain the ever-growing volume of school fiscal operations. These tasks can readily be adapted to EDP because similar tasks in other fields have already been programmed. Often the school business officer is the first to urge installation of EDP and to suggest its potential in other aspects of education. Clearly, EDP should not be confined to one aspect of education, for it has the capacity to contribute to many different areas.

The question of where EDP fits into the school organizational hierarchy is subject to debate. The fact that it often enters the system to speed up fiscal services and reporting should not be interpreted to mean that primary control should emanate from the business office. EDP cuts across all school operations, and the position of the person in charge should reflect this. To keep the superintendent informed of the state of EDP in the school district, there should be an individual qualified to serve the EDP needs of the school district as a whole. He can be a director or an associate superintendent for information systems, depending upon the size of the school system.[30]

Many specialists (a director of data processing, programmers, computer operators, key-punch operators, and information-systems analysts) will have to be employed to make the EDP system operational. Small school systems may well depend upon a regional agency, such as the intermediate unit, to supply EDP needs. EDP services may also be made available through a university, the state department of education, or some specialized groupings of school districts.

The Committee on EDP of the American Association of School Administrators recommended that the superintendent and key school administrators be involved in determination of needs and in the design and operation of a school's EDP system.[31]

Computer-based EDP can be justified in schools (and elsewhere) when the following conditions prevail:

1. Greater speed in processing information is a necessity and apparent to all.
2. Complexities of data processing can be simplified only with electronic assistance.
3. Investment in computer equipment is offset substantially by the monetary and qualitative values placed on the beneficial results of its use.

Establishing an EDP system requires more than renting or buying hardware. The information-processing requirements of the school must be analyzed to determine who is responsible for what reports, where information originates, how gathered information is

[30]Ibid., p. 30.
[31]Ibid.

treated, what resources are available to accomplish tasks, what is done with the information collected and processed, and what are the unmet information needs.[32] Designing an EDP system begins with a description of people, data, procedures, financial resources, and machines to be employed to attain specific and general information needs of the educational institution. The computer is an element in a total system composed of people, organizational procedures for data collection or dissemination, computer programming, and fiscal and material resources to make the program operative. EDP hardware requirements are based on information demands, not vice versa.[33]

EDP is a means and not an end. Facts and figures are manipulated according to some prearranged plan to yield more useful information. The school administrators of today must grant high priority to the design of a comprehensive EDP system. The computer specialist has technical knowledge to contribute, but professionals in education with broad understanding of the missions and administration of schools must share responsibility for EDP design and operations.

Establishment of an information system is mandatory in all districts seeking to take advantage of the computer. Data on professional staff, students, financial transactions, facilities, supplies, and equipment can all be inserted in a computerized information system. The ability to bank data, that is, to insert information and subsequently retrieve it from the computer with great speed in its original or in a manipulated form is the significant advantage of EDP.[34]

A specialized information system

can be developed to help the administrator instantaneously retrieve data in the form required to arrive at a prudent decision and to make possible the simulation of decisions so that the administrator can determine consequences of alternative approaches to a given problem.

By the mid-1960s computers were harnessed to perform such educational tasks as maintaining school census files and reports, recording attendance, accounting, issuing grades and student report cards, scheduling classes (particularly at the secondary school level) managing the payroll, budgeting and accounting, controlling inventory, maintaining personnel records, and accounting for property. One writer by 1966 outlined 100 uses for EDP in schools.[35] Kaimann and Marker cited a wide variety of current literature on the tactical and strategic application of EDP to school administration.[36] There are few administrative record-keeping tasks that cannot be done faster and more accurately with computer-based EDP.

Despite a slow start, computer-based EDP is becoming increasingly more important in school administration. It is a technological development that will enable administrators to cope better with both mundane and sophisticated problems. The computer enhances the capability of the administrator and gives him the means to do many things that would otherwise be impossible. Future school administrators will have to be prepared in understanding the nature and potential of computer-based EDP; practicing school administrators should gain a working

[32]Ibid.
[33]Ibid.
[34]Ibid. p. 6

[35]G. E. Anderson, Jr., "100 Uses for School Data Processing," *Nation's Schools,* October 1966.
[36]R. A. Kaimann and R. W. Marker, *Educational Data Processing,* Boston: Houghton Mifflin, 1967, parts 2 and 3.

understanding of EDP as rapidly as possible.

As an AASA report on EDP declared: "It takes more than a machine to produce a technological revolution."[37] People and plans are involved. Sophistication in theory as well as skills and insights into generation of models are required of those who seek to maximize the computer potential. Fields that traditionally use theory have moved most rapidly toward sophisticated utilization of computer systems.

The future of technology in education

Education cannot by any stretch of the imagination be classed as a "high technology industry." Nonetheless, technology will continue to trigger significant changes and challenge educational administrators.

Kahn and Wiener[38] prepared a list of what they called "One Hundred Technical Innovations Very Likely by the Last Third of the Twentieth Century." Some of these that are likely to have important implications for educational institutions include the following (the numbers attached are those used by Kahn and Wiener):

1. Multiple application of lasers and masers for sensing, measuring, communication, cutting, heating, welding, power transmission, illumination, destructive, defensive and other purposes.
13. Major reduction in hereditary and congenital defects.
17. New techniques and institutions for adult education.
22. More sophisticated architectural engineering (e.g. geodesic domes, "fancy"

stressed shells, pressurized skins, and esoteric materials).
24. Three-dimensional photography, illustration, movies, and television.
29. Extensive and intensive centralization (or automatic interconnection) of current and past personal and business information in high speed data processors.
30. Other new and possibly pervasive techniques for surveillance, monitoring, and control of individuals and organizations.
33. New and more reliable "educational" and propaganda techniques for affecting human behavior—public and private.
34. Practical use of direct electronic communication with and stimulation of the brain.
38. New techniques for very cheap, convenient, and reliable birth control.
43. New techniques and institutions for the education of children.
58. Chemical methods for improving memory and learning.
63. Mechanical and chemical methods for improving human analytical ability more or less directly.
70. Simple inexpensive home video recording and playing.
71. Inexpensive high-capacity, worldwide, regional, and local (home and business) communication (perhaps using satellites, lasers, and light pipes).
72. Practical home and business use of "wired" video communications for both telephone and TV (possibly including retrieval of taped material from libraries or other sources) and rapid transmission and reception of facsimilies (possibly including news, library material, commercial announcements, instantaneous mail delivery, other printouts, and so on).
75. Shared time (public and interconnected) computers generally available to home and business on a metered basis.
81. Personal "pagers" (perhaps even two-way pocket phones) and other personal electronic equipment for communication, computing, and data processing programs.
83. Inexpensive (less than $20) long lasting, very small battery operated TV receivers.

[37]American Association of School Administrators, op. cit.

[38]Herman Kahn and A. J. Wiener, *The Year 2000*, New York: Macmillan, 1967, pp. 51–55.

84. Home computers to "run" household and communicate with outside world.
85. Maintenance-free, long-life electronic and other equipment.
86. Home education via video and computerized and programmed learning.
88. Inexpensive (less than one cent a page), rapid high-quality black and white reproductions; followed by color and high detailed photography reproduction—perhaps for home as well as office use.
94. Inexpensive road-free (and facility-free) transportation.
97. New biological and chemical methods to identify, trace, incapacitate or annoy people for police and military uses.

A sizeable number of the innovations on the list by Kahn and Wiener may well appear by 1985, whereas others might be delayed until the end of the century.

Kahn and Wiener[39] generated another list called "Ten Far-out Possibilities," with the following selected as having implications for education after the year 2000.

1. Life expectancy extended to substantially more than 150 years (immortality?).
5. Interstellar travel.
7. Practical and routine use of extrasensory phenomena.
9. Lifetime immunization against practically all diseases.

INNOVATION, RISK, AND SURVIVAL

It is much easier to operate an institution along well-established patterns than to seek out new courses of action. Charting a new course requires knowing the way toward the goal of continuing improvement. The administrator's ability to discriminate and select the most promising from among the variety of unproved inventions and his talent for identifying and implement-

[39]Ibid., pp. 56–57.

ing the strategies most likely to stimulate the professional staff to modify existing behavioral patterns and to gain community acceptance will be put to the test.

There is a considerable risk in innovation. Not everything that is tried will prove effective, and when a change fails, the innovator may be criticized for squandering limited resources. The management of prudent change may well emerge as one of the most important competencies for educational administrators in the last quarter of the twentieth century. Compulsive innovation, the propensity to change just for the sake of change, is a questionable practice. Nevertheless, the worship of traditional practices is as futile as compulsive innovation.

Change does not guarantee improvement, but there is no possibility of improvement without it. The issue is not whether schools should or should not change. Education continues to evolve. The process cannot be stopped for long, but its pace can be influenced. The problems are deciding what to change to and sensing the organization's readiness to accept varying rates of change. The late Dag Hammarskjöld's advice on mountain climbing is appropriate for school administrators committed to accepting change as an adventure and a fact of life rather than simply something to be tolerated: "Don't move without knowing where to put your foot next, and don't move without having sufficient stability to enable you to achieve exactly what should be the next step. One who is really serious in his determination to reach the top does not gamble by impatiently accepting bad footholds and poor grips."

Defensible and prudent innovations based on carefully drawn conceptual design, experimentation, and validation to substantiate conclusions, hold the greatest promise for improvements in education. Fads produce the cycles of extremism in education that testify that haste in implementing unsubstantiated innovations can make waste.

SUMMARY

The role of a change agent is complex and difficult. This responsibility is an addition to, rather than a replacement for other functions assigned to administrators. Change is an essential fact of life if an organization is to respond to disruptive forces, to adapt to emerging environmental demands, to sense new goals and directions, and to survive as a viable organization. Determining what, when, and how much change an organization can and should assimilate taxes the judgmental powers of the most effective administrators.

Change made without regard to improvement, that is, for its own sake, may engender conflict, destroy previously established sensitive balances and relations, reduce productive capabilities and thus waste resources, and even create the kind of turbulence that can split and destroy. Society in ferment cannot survive without innovation, but by the same token it faces the risk of severe wounds and probable extinction through imprudent change.

At issue is not whether education has changed but whether the schools are changing fast enough. The alphabetical curriculum revolution in science and math is conservative compared with the curriculum reform efforts of the progressives of 40 to 50 years ago. The desire for reform in education never dies, but merely fades for awhile, waiting for the proper stimulus to return.

There are many definitions of inno-

vation. Most assume that change is always a movement for something better. Change is a means to an end, namely, improvement. Invention precedes the act of innovation. Innovation may be the result of plain drift, accident, revolution, or specially developed plans. Whether a school can be judged innovative depends on how innovation is measured. Staff development models help to facilitate change in people as well as in things.

A model for the process of innovation includes the elements of disequilibrium, conceptualization, identification or design of new practices, experimentation, evaluation, pilot programs, diffusion, wide implementation, and a new equilibrium. Diffusion is based on appropriate strategies and recognition of the human factors involved. Innovation in education can be considered a special type of social change, and research on social change can be used to guide educational efforts. The national inventory of innovations in some secondary schools showed schools are adopting new approaches but discontinuance of some is not unusual.

Technology is the application of scientific knowledge to practical purposes. The term is often used to mean a particular invention or approach. It has been judged to be beneficial, by and large, for its contributions rather than its negative dimensions receive the most attention. Technology has influenced education down through the ages, starting with the invention of the alphabet and continuing with printing and the modern marvels. Types of technological developments in instruction include those related to photography, recording and reproduction of sound, long-distance electronic transmission of sound, electronic transmission of audio and visual images, programmed instruction, electronic data processing, the systems approach, and biochemical or pharmacological devices. These are means; the quality of ideas being projected via the new technology is even more important than the means.

Many new technologies related to instruction have been acclaimed as ways to improve learning. ETV and programmed instruction have been put to the test, and thus far the full potential of each has failed to be realized. CAI remains a fascinating experiment. CAI is not as yet economically competitive with live teaching. It is a promising development that needs further expenditures of some $1 billion and at least 10 more years before it is ready for general classroom use.

Computer-based EDP has been adopted only slowly by schools because of its initial design for other fields and its high cost. The computer is an electronic device that depends partly on mechanical gear but mostly on electrical impulses for action. Its major elements in operation are input, storage, processing, control, and output. There have been three computer generations thus far and more are in the offing. The computer is not creative, imaginative, or endowed with a human memory. It must be programmed, that is, given precise directions, to become operative. The costs related to pro-gramming are a major element in EDP operations. A problem that takes seconds to run through a computer may take months to program.

EDP is transforming school administration. There are hundreds of uses for EDP in education, some more sophisticated than others. Establishing an EDP system calls for more than hardware. The information-processing requirements of the system must be analyzed in detail prior to purchase or rental of equipment. Top-level administrators should be involved, along with information specialists, in the design of an EDP system.

Future and present school administrators must comprehend the nature and contributions of EDP. EDP enables administrators to do many things that could be done in no other way. But it takes more than a machine to alter school operations significantly. A knowledge of theory, models, and the systems approach (the subjects of subsequent chapters) are necessary to maximize the potential in EDP.

Education is not a high technology industry. Nonetheless, a number of new technical innovations may appear during the remainder of this century and will call for further modifications in education. The management of change may be a most important competency for the next 25 years.

QUESTIONS

1. Trace the history and development of some major educational reform movements in American public education since 1800.
2. Why are present efforts at curriculum-content innovation judged to be conservative?
3. Is it better to use the three concepts of invention, innovation, and improvement to research the nature of change in education or simply one concept of innovation? Justify your stand.
4. What factors are conducive to stimulating change? What factors inhibit innovation?

5. What organizational conditions are most likely to bring about change?
6. What is technology?
7. Why has ETV failed to reach its potential thus far?
8. What is the status of CAI at present?
9. Why was EDP slower to be adopted by educational institutions than by government or industry?
10. Where should the director of EDP be placed in the school's chart of organization?
11. What are the uses of EDP in school administration?
12. What are the conditions which justify implementation of EDP in schools?

SELECTED REFERENCES

American Association of School Administrators, *EDP and the School Administrator,* Washington, D.C.: The Association, 1967.

Berelson, Bernard, and G. A. Steiner, *Human Behavior,* New York: Harcourt Brace Jovanovich, 1964, chaps. 15 and 16.

Brickell, Henry M., *Organizing New York State for Educational Change,* Albany, N.Y.: State Education Department, 1961.

Cawelti, Gordon, "Innovative Practices in High Schools: Who Does What and Why and How," *Nation's Schools,* April 1967.

Corey, S. H., "The Nature of Instruction," in B. C. Lange, ed., *Programmed Instruction,* Sixty-fifth Yearbook of the National Society for the Study of Education, part 2, Chicago: University of Chicago Press, 1967.

Eye, G. G., L. A. Netzer, and R. D. Krey, *Supervision of Instruction,* 2nd ed., New York: Harper & Row, 1971.

Goodlad, J. I., J. F. O'Toole, Jr., and L. L. Tyler, *Computers and Information Systems in Education,* New York: Harcourt Brace Jovanovich, 1966.

Hack, Walter G. et al, *Educational Futurism 1985,* Berkeley, Cal.: McCutchan Publishing Corp., 1971.

Hoye, Robert E., and Anastasia C. Wang, *Index To Computer Based Learning,* Englewood Cliffs, N.J.: Educational Technology Publications, 1973.

Kahn, Herman, and H. J. Wiener, *The Year 2000,* New York: Macmillan, 1967.

Kaimann, R. A., and R. W. Marker, *Educational Data Processing,* Boston: Houghton Mifflin, 1967.

Thompson, Victor A., "Bureaucracy and Innovation," *Administrative Science Quarterly,* vol. 10, no. 1, June 1965, pp. 1–20.

Toffler, Alan, *Future Shock,* New York: Bantam Books, 1970.

6

THEORY AND MODELS TO FACILITATE A BETTER UNDERSTANDING OF ADMINISTRATION

Educational administration, an ancient art, emerged as a discipline for special study during the twentieth century. The early preparation programs for school administrators stressed acquisition of such important skills and techniques as budget making, scheduling, public relations, planning school facilities, and personnel relations. Prior to 1950, little consideration was given to other important aspects of school administration that could not be reduced immediately to a skill or technique. The prime requisite for success was to acquire a "big bag of tricks," or something that "worked" without knowing why it worked.

Members of the early faculties of universities who were engaged in the preparation of educational administrators were selected on the basis of successful experience as superintendents or principals; "success" was equated with maintaining efficient operations in their school systems rather than with introducing innovations. This changed during the 1960s when inexperienced specialists in selected university disciplines were added to departments of educational administration. Among these were those whose primary interests were in theory rather than practice, although there were some with practical experience in the field who developed an interest and spe-

cialization in theory. A similar history is found in the evolution of professional schools for medicine, law, and engineering. At one time medical education, for example, was more of an apprenticeship than a program of professional preparation in a university. The future medical practitioners observed the established practitioner in action and thereby gained the insights of many years of experience.

The important issue is why should we be concerned with theory in a practice-oriented field such as administration? In other words, what can a theory of administration, or selected dimensions of it, contribute to greater success as a superintendent or principal? This and the two chapters that follow attempt to respond to such queries.

"Empiricism" is the term used to describe an approach to learning characterized by dependence on observation or experience alone, without regard to science and theory. It is interesting to note that in the field of medicine, it is not a complimentary term. Empiricism in medicine may be conceived as "a practice of medicine founded on mere experience without aid of science." This is followed by such words as ignorant and unscientific practice, charlatanry, and quackery. Present-day emphasis on developing theories of educational administration is an attempt to move away from the empiricism characteristic of so much research study and practice in this area.

It was declared in the first edition (1962) of this book that construction of a theory of educational administration was in the infancy stage. Interest has increased among practitioners and professors of educational administration, but few fresh ideas have emerged. Even more alarming is the appearance of a semantic barrier between practitioners and alleged theorists and a consequent breakdown in communication. In the years since 1962, the chasm between the two components of the field has widened, and efforts to allow theory to influence in any significant way the practice of school administration have been limited. The preponderance of research in the field has showed little regard for theoretical underpinnings.

Closely related in spirit to the relatively unproductive original theory movement in educational administration is the systems approach. It is more practice-oriented, and leadership in the development of systems administration came from persons other than those who lead the theory movement. The so-called "management science" movement likewise placed more emphasis on the application of concepts to the improvement of the practice of administration than did the original theory developers. Nonetheless, the contributions of the early theory developers deserve study for they represented a significant departure in the field.

DEFINITIONS OF SCIENCE

The theory movement is an effort to provide a scientific base for the practice of administration. Science can be defined as systematic knowledge considered as a distinct field of investigation; a branch of study concerned with observation and classification of facts, especially with the establishment of verifiable general laws; and accumulated and accepted knowledge. T. H. Huxley viewed science as organized common sense. Knowledge, the systematizing and classifying of knowledge, and the ability to verify the existence and objectivity of knowledge (to the extent that it can be verified by confirmation of other workers) are significant components of science. Kerlinger[1] considered as static those views that emphasize science as a body of facts or a way of explaining observed phenomena. The dynamic view regards it as an activity of scientists and emphasizes imaginative problem solving.

The manner in which knowledge is obtained and verified is important. Knowledge may result from:

1. Accepting authoritative statements of others: the method of established belief.
2. Intuition: the a priori or self-evident method.
3. Revelation: the method of sudden, often divine, inspiration or message.
4. Experience: the method of science.

Science is rooted initially and finally in experience as a way of knowing. It does not rest on pure reason alone, although logical analysis by induction or deduction is involved. For example, science refuses to accept the argument that planets move in circles because they are heavenly bodies and intuitively, or through revelation, one knows that heavenly bodies, being

[1]F. N. Kerlinger, *Foundations of Behavioral Research*, New York: Holt, Rinehart & Winston, 1964, p. 1.

perfect, must move in perfect orbits such as circles. Through observation and subsequent computation planets are found to move in elliptical rather than circular orbits.

The scientific method of coming to know is based on observation (experimentation is controlled observation) and subsequent description, which may or may not employ classification or other methods of ordering and systematizing data. Observation and description are not ends in themselves, but rather are means to first explain and then predict the outcome of events. It can be said that science is concerned with observation, description, explanation, and prediction. A heuristic or problem-solving emphasis underlies this approach: The purpose of all this activity is to discover general laws or relations. Kerlinger said that "the basic aim of science is theory," and he defined a theory as a general explanation of natural events.[2]

The philosophies of realism and pragmatism look to science as a way of investigating and reasoning that supplements formal (Aristotelian) logic expressed in syllogism. Science generates major premises (the starting point of deductive inference) based on facts by investigating reality through the techniques of objective observation and description. Inductive inference, that is, generalizing only after accumulating a series of discrete, verifiable observations, yields generalizations important to the potential productivity of the method of formal logic. Butler declared:

As the syllogism has been the form in which thinking has been cast by way of examining its validity, scientific method has virtually become the form in which investigation is cast in order to guarantee its validity and also in order to yield actual results in knowledge and the con-

trol of experience which probably would not be achieved without this method.[3]

The syllogism is a form of logic used to relate one specific proposition (minor premise) to a general proposition (major premise) and to draw a conclusion (which is possible only if the specific statement is included within the class of subjects within the major premise). A comparison between the steps in the syllogism (essentially a deductive form of reasoning) and the steps in the scientific method (essentially an inductive approach to thinking) is presented in Table 6–1.

It should be noted that the first two steps of the scientific method are primarily sensory and concerned with observation. The third is rooted in experience but is somewhat more advanced ("preconceptual"). It is worth repeating that the scientific method is a disciplined type of experience characterized by being systematic, controlled, and objective.

Theory, on the other hand, is founded on experiential data but does not stop at observation. Only narrowly can science be considered a fact-gathering activity. There is a need for a conceptual framework to guide fact gathering. Theories enable the development of such a conceptual framework to direct the search for objective evidence and to explain and eventually to predict observed and described phenomena. The present-day concern for theory building in educational administration is an extension of the scientific method to more sophisticated levels. It portends greater use of the syllogistic form to deduce valid knowledge. It attempts to explain why things should be accomplished in a given

---

[2]Ibid., p. 10.

[3]J. Donald Butler, *Four Philosophies and Their Practice in Religion,* New York: Harper & Row, 1951, pp. 318–319.

way. A conclusion derived by the use of formal logic must be tested in the world of reality. Science is initially and finally rooted in experience, but unless research has the development or testing of theory as its aim, its quality will be limited.

EARLY SCIENTIFIC APPROACH TO ADMINISTRATION

The development of a theory of administration is part of the continuing movement toward a more scientific approach to administration that can be traced to the Cameralists in the seventeenth and eighteenth centuries. During the early part of the twentieth century the school survey, the advent of budgeting in public education, and the "scientific" planning of school facilities were scientifically oriented movements. During the 1940s and 1950s the creation of classification schemes (taxonomies) to describe administrative activities was a further step toward a science of administration. These early scientific efforts were, however, primarily investigative and emphasized sensory perception and description (with or without the aid of classificatory devices). They stopped short of creating general hypotheses, theories, and models. In other words, they were empirical and focused on the first three steps in the scientific method described above.

Cameralism

The Cameralists, a group of German writers active from the middle of the sixteenth to the end of the eighteenth century, approached civic problems in the small German states from a common viewpoint and developed a coherent civic theory and a system of administration. They were concerned with enhancement of the physical wealth of the state by stressing the importance of good management and the application of scientific know-how in the maintenance of state functions. The outstanding Cameralist scholar was Georg Zincke.[4] Zincke contributed

[4]Albert Lepawsky, *Administration*, New York: Knopf, 1960, p. 97.

TABLE 6–1

SYLLOGISM VERSUS THE SCIENTIFIC METHOD

Syllogism	Scientific method
Major premise or proposition	Define the problem to be solved or the event to be explained
Minor premise or proposition	Observe all factors relating to the problem or event
Conclusion (if possible)	Describe or classify the observable phenomena
	Formulate a hypothesis or hypotheses which may meet all conditions and, thus, explain the observation
	Test hypotheses by putting them to work in controlled situations in which the event or problem is the only variable factor
	Predict events explained by tested and verified hypotheses

more to the preparation of administrators than any other Cameralist. As professor at Leipzig, he taught courses in the science of law and of Cameralism. His bibliographies contained over 2000 titles, many of which dealt with such distinctly administrative topics as financial administration, political economy, fiscal science, and public administration. Zincke declared:

If the means of livelihood for a land and people are to be flourishing, good management must prevail among and over them. It follows that the ruler, or those who assist him in these important matters, must have the knowledge necessary to insure good management, and must exert the utmost endeavor to secure the application of this knowledge throughout the land. This is necessary not only for the sake of promoting good management in the land, and to put the people in the way of ready means, but it is necessary in order to secure the sources of the prince's own ready means. It follows that a prince needs genuine and skillful Cameralists. By this name we mean those who possess fundamental and special knowledge about all or some particular part of those things which are necessary in order that they may assist the prince in maintaining good management in the state.[5]

The Cameralist approach was not followed to any great extent outside Germany and Austria; other cultures and states were, some time later, to rediscover many of the Cameralists' concepts. Cameralism is "an administrative technology."[6] Max Weber, working in Germany around the turn of the century, continued in the tradition of the Cameralists with his development of the bureaucratic model described in Chapter 4. F. W. Taylor, early in this century, complained that his proposed scientific management

was misinterpreted as simply a group of efficiency devices, rather than a "complete mental revolution" toward work and responsibilities.

The school-survey movement

The school-survey movement during the second and third decades of the present century can be traced as far back as the Lutheran Reformation, when a school study attempted to determine the condition of Latin schools and universities which declined because of the violence of religious and vocational changes.[7] The twentieth-century surveyors observed, described, and evaluated school practices to detect weaknesses. Recommendations based on analysis of data stimulated the introduction of scientific practices in financial management, school-plant planning and construction, and organization of attendance centers. Although relatively unconcerned with a conceptual framework for administration, these observations and descriptions of administrative practices started the scientific study and investigation of school administration. The scientific approach, however, remained at the experiential level and fell short of creating fertile hypotheses capable of revealing the essential nature of administration. It failed to generate general explanations and predictions which might grow into theories and models.

Taxonomies

Observations produced data related to a variety of administrative functions, and classification became necessary to handle the volume of information generated. One group of writers suggested

---

[5]Quoted in ibid., pp. 98–99.
[6]Albion W. Small, *The Cameralists*, Chicago: University of Chicago Press, 1909.

[7]Frederick W. Eby, *The Development of Modern Education*, 2nd ed., Englewood Cliffs, N.J.: Prentice-Hall, 1952, p. 647.

a classification based on three elements: job, know-how, and theory.[8] The "competency pattern" was defined as a behavior pattern designed to "reflect the best in intelligent action" obtained by "searching out and separating the good patterns" from the ineffective. The qualitative aspect of the competency pattern was a "selected and carefully designed blueprint reflecting the kind of behavior deemed best for present day living."[9] The job was divided into critical tasks, which in turn were grouped into seven operational areas: "organization and structure, finance and business management, student personnel, curriculum and instruction, staff personnel, school plant, and transportation."[10] This classification scheme for administrative behavior followed the traditional substantive problems of administration rather than the more recent emphasis on process, theory, and models. *Know-how* was viewed as attitudes, skills, knowledges, and understandings of major importance to success in administration. To illustrate, know-how included the skill required in "getting people to work together," an attitude that upholds the "efficacy of the group process," knowledge "of group dynamics," and understanding that "plans are more effectively made as a group endeavor."[11] A know-how was created for each of the tasks confronting the administrator. *Theory* referred to "the basic beliefs that a person accepts as the guide for his way of living." It included "what we mean when we talk about the democratic theory of social living, the worth

and dignity of all individuals, our concepts of the nature of truth, etc."[12] This is more akin to a philosophy of life than to a theory as defined in this book.

Another tridimensional classification postulated that the basic components of educational administration are the job, the office holder, and the situation, and assigned each administrative activity to one of the three categories. This classification does not constitute an explanatory model or a theory useful in predicting outcomes.

Other less comprehensive classification schemes were devised for grouping the tasks and abilities of the school administrator. All reflect the practical nature of administration and emphasize the desired qualities in administration.

Taxonomies are not theories, although they may be useful as precursors to theories. They are sterile by nature and contribute little to the production of new knowledge. Nonetheless classification schemes are valuable in handling efficiently large volumes of accumulated facts. Halpin pointed out some of the snares in devoting large quantities of time and effort to taxonomies:

1. The number of classification schemes that can be generated is limited only by the size of one's vocabulary.
2. There is the risk of mixing different types in the same classification, such as mixing oranges and battleships indiscriminately.
3. It may be assumed, somewhat naively, that placing two taxonomic schemes side by side will somehow produce a theory.[13]

---

[8]Orin W. Graff and Calvin M. Street, *Improving Competence in Educational Administration*, New York: Harper & Row, 1956, chap. 3.

[9]Ibid., p. 19.

[10]Ibid., p. 204.

[11]Ibid., chap. 12.

[12]Ibid., pp. 216–217.

[13]Andrew W. Halpin, "The Development of Theory in Educational Administration," in Andrew W. Halpin, ed., *Administrative Theory in Education*, Chicago: Midwest Administration Center, University of Chicago, 1958, pp. 7–9.

ORIGINS OF CONCERN FOR A THEORY OF EDUCATIONAL ADMINISTRATION

The concern about the lack of theory to guide the study of educational administration can be traced to 1954. Some place the origins of theory in educational administration about 40 years earlier, but this is questionable, for although the word was not strange to the field, the definition was far different and less precise. Furthermore, the alleged concern for theory prior to 1954 had little impact on the mainstream of thinking and writing in school administration. Much of the impetus since 1954 has come from early annual meetings of the National Conference of Professors of Educational Administration and from a publication by Coladarci and Getzels.[14] The writers were primarily interested in educational and social psychology. They claimed that research in educational administration relied too heavily on empiricism. (This remains true many years after their publication.) Overemphasis on practical attitudes was judged to be an obstacle to development of theory in educational administration. Formulation of a theory of administration in fields other than education has a much longer history, as evidenced in the writings of Max Weber around the turn of the century, of Barnard in the 1930s,[15] and of Simon in the 1940s.[16]

Dissatisfaction with the piecemeal approach, the lack of consistency, and the overemphasis on techniques and skills in educational administration eventually stimulated long-overdue concern for a theory of administration in education. There was a growing recognition of the shortcomings of scientific approaches that failed to achieve the development of conceptual framework to explain observations and descriptions. At this writing, the great majority of practicing school administrators appear to view theory as a purely intellectual exercise that has little to offer to the solution of persistent problems. They evince no great desire to learn more about theory. During the late 1950s and much of the 1960s interest in theory was confined to some, but by no means all, professors of educational administration. Leadership in theory building was confined to the university level. The systems administration and emerging management science movement may generate greater interest in theory among practitioners.

DEFINITIONS OF THEORY

Feigl defined theory as "a set of assumptions from which can be derived, by purely logico-mathematical procedures, a larger set of empirical laws."[17] This widely accepted definition of theory is very popular in the literature of educational administration. Theory becomes a means of furnishing an explanation for empirical laws and unifies previously heterogeneous areas of subject matter characterized by those empirical laws. Feigl further suggested that the term "scientific explanation" be employed "wherever more specific or more descriptive statements are derived from more general or more hypo-

[14]Arthur P. Coladarci and Jacob W. Getzels, *The Use of Theory in Educational Administration*, Stanford, Cal.: Stanford, 1955.

[15]Chester I. Barnard, *The Functions of the Executive*, Cambridge, Mass.: Harvard, 1938.

[16]Herbert A. Simon, *Administrative Behavior*, New York: Macmillan, 1947.

[17]Herbert Feigl, "Principles and Problems of Theory Construction in Psychology," in *Current Trends in Psychological Theory*, Pittsburgh: University of Pittsburgh Press, 1951, p. 182.

thetical assumptions."[18] This definition removes much of the ambiguity that surrounds the term. To illustrate, other definitions of the theory include one or more of the following: a style or jargon for recording descriptions; classification, inventory, or typology schemes; a bold guess or a suggested working hypothesis; a program of research; or an elaborate model in the form of an analogy or a mathematical equation.[19]

The various elements of Feigl's view of theory deserve further exploration. Theory arises in empirical phenomena —that is, in observations and descriptions of events—but does not stop there. It involves further contemplation or speculation to produce a pattern or system from which hypotheses can be drawn. At this point, definition of the term "hypothesis," which is the first part of the phrase "hypothetico-deductive system" becomes necessary. One view is that a hypothesis is a proposition or condition that is assumed (a set of assumptions), perhaps without proof of the validity of the assumptions, in order to draw logical consequences. It is generated as a means of explaining some condition or occurrence. Evidence is lacking to substantiate it, but this is not crucial because the hypothesis is conceded just to start action or argument and, therefore, can subsequently be accepted, rejected, or modified. In this sense, a hypothesis is a provisional or unverified conjecture regarding causes or relations of certain phenomena.

Kerlinger defined a hypothesis as "a conjectural statement of the relation between two or more variables."[20] Implied is the fact that the variables can be measured in some way. A legitimate hypothesis, in a scientific sense, must involve two or more measurable variables, and a relation among the variables must be specified. The theory is tested by deducing hypotheses from it, measuring the variables involved, and then testing the relation stated to determine its validity in the world of reality. This is what Kerlinger meant when he declared that "hypotheses are important bridges between theory and empirical inquiry."[21] In this sense, the hypothesis is truly "a powerful tool for the advancement of knowledge." The creation of hypotheses is not easy; it requires great imagination and considerable familiarity with the subject.

Theory has potential not only for explaining and predicting events but also for gaining new knowledge through application of formal deductive logic to verified major premises. In some cases the pattern of logic is purely symbolic and hence mathematical in essence (as in the term "logico-mathematical procedures"). A theory is, thus, a complete system for gaining new knowledge or giving direction to research by describing and classifying experience, creating and testing hypotheses about what was experienced, applying logico-mathematical procedures, and subsequently testing empirically the conclusions reached from deductive inferences. Preparation in logic is a decided asset in the process.

Considering a theory as a hypothetico-deductive system capable of producing new knowledge does not imply reversion to prescientific thinking in which a thesis or major premise was proposed and its validity tested primarily by the syllogistic form of deductive reasoning. Rather, it is the application of deductive logic to premises inductively arrived at to gain leads about how further scientific

---

[18]Ibid.

[19]Ibid., p. 181.

[20]Kerlinger, op. cit., pp. 20–22.

[21]Ibid., p. 24.

efforts can be most efficiently utilized in the pursuit of new knowledge. A theory is evaluated not only in terms of its usefulness in explaining and predicting but also in terms of its generation of new ideas that can be tested for validity in the world of reality.

Kerlinger, in 1964, submitted a definition of theory that may be a little easier to understand: "A theory is a set of interrelated constructs, definitions, and propositions that presents a systematic view of phenomena by specifying relations among variables, with the purposes of explaining and predicting the phenomena."[22] Note the three main components of Kerlinger's definition of theory:

1. A set of propositions is drawn from well-defined and interrelated constructs
2. Interrelations are noted among the variables to highlight a systematic view of the phenomena described by the variables.
3. The purpose is to explain the phenomena and to help predict from certain variables to other variables.[23]

The writer, acting independently in preparing a paper presented to the Southern Regional Council on Educational Administration in 1963, submitted a definition of a theory (or model) that is remarkably similar to that published by Kerlinger in 1964: "A theory (model) is a cluster of interlocking and interactive concepts systematized into an abstracted intellectual pattern capable of interpreting generalizable trends and interrelationships that prevail within a set of varied facts within reality (or a part of it)." In this definition, the three major points are that a theory is:

1. A constellation of interlocking and interactive concepts.

2. Concepts subsequently systematized into a pattern.
3. Functional, that is, helps to explain or understand all or part of reality.

DEFINITION OF CONCEPT

Concept and theory are closely related. A concept has been defined as any term with an accepted meaning; such a definition suggests that all words in the dictionary are concepts. For the purpose of this book, a concept is an intellectual interpretation or image of a process, event, or thing. In other words, a concept is a mental image derived from imagination, memory, and/or sensory experiences and subsequently intellectually processed, organized, or abstracted to reveal all that is associated with a process, event, or thing. It is the product of intellectual distillation. Concepts are the starting points, essential elements, or building blocks in the creation and comprehension of theories. Theory building begins when a collection of concepts are interrelated to produce a system of connected ideas or unified thought patterns that help to explain, understand, or predict reality.

AN ILLUSTRATION OF THEORY BUILDING

Greenwood[24] used an abbreviated outline of Durkheim's work on suicide as an illustration of theory building. Durkheim started his search for societal cause of suicide by garnering all available facts (the empirical approach). From these facts the following were apparent:

[22]Ibid., p. 11.
[23]Ibid.

[24]Ernest Greenwood, "The Practice of Science and the Science of Practice," in W. G. Bennis, R. D. Benne, and R. Chin, eds., The Planning of Change, New York: Holt, Rinehart & Winston, 1961, p. 82.

1. Countries predominantly Protestant have higher suicide rates than countries predominantly Catholic.
2. Christians have higher suicide rates than Jews.
3. Countries with higher literacy rates have higher suicide rates than countries with low literacy.
4. Those in white-collar liberal professions as a group have higher suicide rates than those in manual occupations.
5. The unmarried have a higher suicide rate than the married.
6. The divorced have a higher suicide rate than the married.
7. The childless married have a higher suicide rate than the married with children.
8. The average size of family is inversely related to the suicide rate.

The above observations are "interesting" to know. Durkheim sought the common thread that would help to explain empirical generalizations. He wondered what it was that Protestant countries, white-collar professions, the unmarried, divorced, and childless had in common to account for higher suicide rates among them. Attempting to find a pattern among known variables eventually led to Durkheim's theory of the social cause of suicide. He reasoned that a closely knit group that controlled its members with strong bonds prevented them from evading social obligations by self-elimination. In addition, these ties gave them the support necessary to perform obligations in the face of otherwise disabling personal stress. Suicide was then stipulated to be a function of the degree of group integration that provides the psychic support to group members for handling acute stress.

This illustrates the evolution from empirical observations to empirical generalizations to the creation of a model or a theory. In transcending empiricism, the researcher explained apparently unconnected phenomena. He had a basis for predicting under what conditions certain individuals were prone to suicide and why there was a high probability that others facing a similar seemingly disabling personal stress would not commit suicide.

SOME MISCONCEPTIONS ABOUT THEORY

Griffiths proposed the following series of statements to indicate what a theory is *not*:[25]

1. A personal affair. Personal procedures developed as an individual style of administrative behavior lack the breadth, depth, and necessary consistency to be called a theory.
2. An idle dream. Idle daydreaming or aimless speculation is undeserving of the term "theory."
3. A philosophy. Philosophy is concerned with directions based on a set of values to indicate what the administrator ought to do. Theories of administration are concerned with what is, rather than what ought to be. This is-ought dichotomy separates a theory from a philosophy. Controls on behavior of the administrator may be related to values, but this part will not be controlled by a theory of administration.
4. A taxonomy. A taxonomy does not permit the development of testable hypotheses as does a theory.
5. Impracticality or complete divorcement from reality.

THE VALUE OF THEORY

The usefulness of a model or theory in producing explanations or predictions is evident from the following quotation by Einstein:

[25]Daniel E. Griffiths, *Administrative Theory*, New York: Appleton-Century-Crofts, 1959, pp. 13–19.

In our endeavor to understand reality we are somewhat like a man trying to understand the mechanism of a closed watch. He sees the face and the moving hands, even hears it ticking, but he has no way of opening the case. If he is ingenious, he may form some picture of a mechanism which could be responsible for all the things he observes, but he may never be quite sure his picture is the only one which could explain his observations. He will never be able to compare his picture with the real mechanism and he cannot even imagine the possibility of the meaning of such a comparison. But he certainly believes that, as his knowledge increases, his picture of reality will become simpler and will explain a wider and wider range of his sensuous impressions.[26]

This quotation suggests that there may be many explanations of observable phenomena that are right or good as judged by their capability to accurately describe conditions or to predict events. At no time, however, can the creator of theories in administration (or any other field) be quite certain that his picture is the only one that can explain observations, and there is no way directly to compare the world of reality with this concept.

A theory of school administration can be used as a means of profiting from experience, for it permits the systematizing and ordering of experiences in accordance with a conceptual framework. Thompson suggested:

1. That the administrator can use theory as a basis for deriving answers or approaches to specific situations.
2. That theory can condition the administrator to think of the administrative process as a complex of simultaneously variable factors rather than a set of specific techniques.
3. That theory allows the administrator to incorporate knowledge produced by

several disciplines and influences the procedures he uses in gathering significant facts relevant to administration.[27]

Theory switches the focus from isolated things or specific events to processes and patterns and relations. It is an intellectual tool that allows one to rise above the morass of detail so as to see the basic substance of educational administration.

Intuition can be viewed as an understanding reached without conscious reasoning. A practitioner cannot afford the luxury of doing nothing simply because there is an insufficiency of scientifically validated knowledge at the time a decision must be reached. He carries with him a store of ideas acquired through long experience, and he acts on the basis of such insights. This experience and knowledge, seldom systematized and verbalized, and therefore often uncommunicable, is his personal property and he uses it when he operates intuitively. Intuition is a pretheoretical type of thinking.

One group of writers claims that use is made of concepts, conceptual schemes, or theory even while a most vociferous attack is leveled at unfamiliar concepts in the name of naive realism or common sense. "Common sense itself is a loose collection of conceptual schemas, and is the end product of cultural accretions, of folk wisdom, habitual modes of thought and hidden assumptions about human nature, and the social arrangements of man."[28]

John Dewey contended that theory is perhaps "the most practical of all things because the widening of the range of attention beyond merely pur-

[26]Albert Einstein and Leopold Infeld, *The Evolution of Physics*, New York: Simon and Schuster, 1938, p. 33. (Quoted in Andrew W. Halpin, ed., *Administrative Theory in Education*, Chicago: Midwest Administration Center, University of Chicago, 1958, p. 17.)

[27]James D. Thompson, "Modern Approaches to Theory in Administration," in Andrew W. Halpin, ed., pp. 20–24.

[28]W. G. Bennis, R. D. Benne, and R. Chin, eds., óp. cit., p. 194.

pose and desire eventually results in the creation of wider and farther-reaching purposes and enables us to make use of a much wider and deeper range of conditions and means than were expressed in the observation of primitive practical purposes."[29]

The well-conceived theory, through its capability of portraying an accurate mental picture of how an organization works, can be an immensely valuable means of deriving better practices and improving school administration in general. The theory can be a means of suggesting how administrative phenomena may be observed, how they may be explained, and how they may predict future events through an analysis of past observations and relations.

Operationism is the attempt to link concepts with existing networks of accepted concepts and through them to experience. New concepts will be necessary to continue theorizing about educational administration.

Hempel formulated the basic tenets of operationism as follows:

1. Meanings are operational. To understand the meaning of a term, it is necessary to know the operational criteria.
2. Every scientific term should be defined by means of one unique operational criterion. If two different operational procedures yield the same results, they are defined as different concepts.
3. Hypotheses incapable of operational test are rejected as meaningless.[30]

SOME THEORIES OF EDUCATIONAL ADMINISTRATION

The literature on theorizing in school administration was relatively sparse

[29]John Dewey, Sources of a Science of Education, New York: Liveright, 1929, p. 17.
[30]Carl G. Hempel, "A Logical Appraisal of Operationism," in P. G. Frank, ed., The Validation of Scientific Theory, Boston: Beacon Press, 1956, pp. 53, 54.

during the 1950s and early 1960s and consisted mostly of a recapitulation of earlier writers' thinking on the importance, definition, and development of theory. Although the volume of literature on theory in educational administration increased during the remainder of the 1960s, the content did not change much. There was little effort to generate new theories to explain or predict phenomena in school administration. Today there are signs to indicate a breaking away from such simple and uncritical acceptance of the few primitive theories. It is the writer's opinion that theory development has been stifled in part by overemphasis on a universal theory that would describe, explain, control, and predict the totality of administration. It is suggested that a meaningful and functional global model is more likely to follow than to precede theories concerning specific aspects of administration. The sterility that characterizes existing theory development will not be overcome until models are generated of specific aspects of administration and are related to meaningful problems confronting administrators. This is discussed further in Chapters 7 and 8.

The question of whether there should be but one theory of school administration is related to the belief that wrong theories should be rejected. It is questionable whether any explanation of observable phenomena, much less any prediction of events, will be the outgrowth of a single concept that grew to perfection at one time and will remain unmodified through the ages. The history of the physical or natural sciences is full of seemingly logical explanations of events that were altered radically as a result of new knowledge derived from unusual experiences or the development of new instruments. There are today conflicting theories in the natural science field that attempt to explain the same phenomenon in different ways. It should not be surprising, therefore, that there are and will continue to be conflicting theories in a behavioral science such as administration.

The presentations that follow are not intended to plead a case for any theory, but merely recount the theories developed to date.

The work of Barnard and Simon

It is fitting to begin the discussion of administrative theory with the work of Barnard and Simon. Barnard's *Functions of the Executive* has been a source of inspiration to many writers.[31] His views on administration and organization come closest to formulating a comprehensive theory (in a hypothetico-deductive sense). Many of the existing concepts of formal and informal organization, institutions and cooperation among people, communication, decision making, and leadership can be traced to his work. Barnard was among the first to formally and carefully describe administration in terms of basic processes. He considered formal organization as the "concrete social process by which social action is largely accomplished." He attempted to formulate a conceptual framework for the study of formal organizations. He regarded organization as "an impersonal system of coordinated human efforts."

Simon was among the first to recognize Barnard's influence in his own work. His *Administrative Behavior* attacked some of the questionable and contradictory "principles" of administration.[32] Simon was much concerned with administrative behavior and cre-

ated the concept of the "administrative man." His primary contribution was elaboration of the nature and importance of decision making in the administrative process. Others have carried forward and modified his thinking about the decision-making process. Simon's work contributed more to theory building than to the design of a comprehensive theory of administration.

The work of Mort and Ross

Mort and Ross suggested a series of principles from the "common sense of the culture" as a guide to "wiser administration."[33] They compiled a synthesis of value concepts derived from the literature of political science, history, education, and allied fields.

Their analysis was loaded with value terms and to that extent is concerned with what ought to be rather than what is. Particular stress was laid on the knowledge of mechanics, the servicing and handling of the tools and agents essential to perform the responsibilities of administering educational units. Understanding forces, purposes, ethics, and criteria related to the selection and use of knowledge were emphasized as well.

Mort and Ross divided the "common-sense" principles into three major groups with subclassifications. Principles were conceived of as a relatively stable and universal body of cultural values. The first set of principles was the "humanitarian group" and included values related to:

1. Structural democracy, the idea that control should be placed as close to the people affected as possible.
2. Operational democracy.
3. Justice, whose essential quality is bal-

[31]Barnard, op. cit.
[32]Simon, op. cit.

[33]Paul R. Mort and Donald H. Ross, *Principles of School Administration*, New York: McGraw-Hill, 1957, p. ix.

ance so that there is protection of the individual against a system and of the system against the individual.

4. Equality of opportunity, each person shall have his chance to reach whatever flowering his inner potential promises.

The second set of principles was the "prudential group" and consisted of:

1. Prudence of caution.
   a. Consideration to economy.
   b. Checks and balances.
   c. Liberty and license.
   d. Responsibility and authority.
2. Prudence of understanding.
   a. Simplicity.
   b. Loyalties.
   c. Inertia.

The third set of principles was the "tempo group," consisting of:

1. Adaptability, or the capacity of an organism to change to meet new developments.
2. Flexibility, which recognizes the desirability of carrying on a given function in ways particularly adapted to the needs of an individual or to differences in individuals in the school system.
3. Stability, which is used in the light of considering education as a means of passing on cultural heritage and connotes freedom from upsetting change within the system, without opposing change as such.[34]

The principles are not in complete agreement with each other.

SOME DESCRIPTIONS OF THE ADMINISTRATIVE PROCESS

Various attempts to describe the administrative process by abstracting administrative activities were reported in Chapter 2. These are taxonomies, or a means of classifying what an administrator does, rather than theories. They are useful in explaining what is involved in administration, but

have little predictive value. Although these descriptions fall far short of being comprehensive hypothetico-deductive systems, some are concerned with the development of organizational theory, and will be discussed here.

The work of Getzels and Guba

Perhaps the most often-quoted model of educational administration is the one developed by Getzels and Guba, which views administration as a social process.[35] Administration is conceived of "structurally as the hierarchy of subordinate-superordinate relationships within a social system. Functionally this hierarchy of relationships is the locus for allocating and integrating roles and facilities in order to achieve the goals of the social system."[36] It is assumed that administration always functions in an interpersonal way and as part of a larger social system.

The social system is conceived of in terms of two major dimensions that are conceptually independent but phenomenally interactive. The first, the institutional dimension, defines roles and expectations that will fulfill the goals of the system; it is the nomothetic, or normative, dimension of activity in a social system. The second, the personal dimension, is influenced by personalities and need-dispositions of individuals. Individual personality and need-dispositions constitute what Getzels referred to as the idiographic dimension in the social system.

The observed behavior of individuals in the organization is based on interaction between the institutional and the personal dimensions. In other

[34]Ibid.

[35]Jacob W. Getzels, "Administration as a Social Process," in Andrew W. Halpin, ed., op. cit., chap. 7.

[36]Ibid.

words, the observed behavior is influenced simultaneously by both the nomothetic and the idiographic dimensions. Thus, the individual with certain need-dispositions might cope with patterns of expectations for his behavior consistent with institutional demands.

The equation $B = f(RP)$ means that the observed behavior (B) is a function of a given institutional role (R) as defined by the expectations attached to it and the personality of the particular role incumbent (P) as defined by his own need-dispositions. Figure 6–1 presents Getzels and Guba's model of

administration as a social process; Figure 6–2 presents a modification of the model adapted to educational administration.

The significance of this model is that it spotlights administrative relations as a function of interaction between the nomothetic and idiographic dimensions. It suggests the possibility of role conflicts when a role incumbent is required to conform simultaneously to a number of expectations which are contradictory or inconsistent, and of personality conflicts when there is a discrepancy between the pattern of expectations attached to a

FIGURE 6–1

Getzels and Guba's model of administration as a social process.

Source: J. W. Getzels, "Administration as a Social Process," in Andrew Halpin, ed., *Administrative Theory in Education,* Chicago, Midwest Administration Center, The University of Chicago, 1958, chap. 7.

FIGURE 6–2

Getzels and Guba's model of administration as a social process modified to apply to school administration.

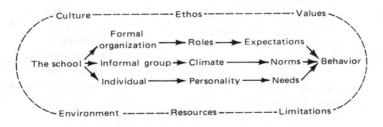

Source: L. W. Downey, "Who Shall Train Our Administrators," in D. E. Tope, ed., *A Forward Look: The Preparation of School Administrators, 1970,* Eugene: Bureau of Education Research, University of Oregon, 1960, p. 97.

role and the pattern of needs of the individual.

The work of Litchfield

Litchfield's work bears a close relation to that of Barnard and Simon. Among his major propositions were the following:

1. The administrative process is a cycle of action which includes the following specific activities: decision making, programing, communicating, controlling, and reappraising.
2. The administrative process functions in the areas of: policy, resources, and execution.
3. The administrative process is carried on in the context of a larger action system, the dimensions of which are: process, the individual, the total enterprise, and ecology (interaction).
4. Administration is the performance of the administrative process by an individual or a group in the context of an enterprise functioning in its environment.
5. Administration and the administrative process occur in substantially the same generalized form in industrial, commercial, civil, educational, military, and hospital organizations.[37]

The work of Agryris

Closely allied to the Getzels-Guba model is the theory developed by Argyris. It is aimed at revealing an understanding of the mechanism by which the individual actualizes himself through the organization and simultaneously the organization actualizes itself through the individual.[38] This approach places special emphasis on understanding organization not by the study of it or individuals alone, but rather by the study of the individual-organization. To the organization as viewed in the formal chart of organization must be added all activities that individuals manifest to express their personality, all informal activities designed by individuals to help them adapt to the formal structure, all activities designed by individuals to fulfill their idiosyncratic needs, and all activities that are the result of the interaction.

The framework of ideas developed by Argyris was as follows:

1. The development of the human personality can be hypothesized to follow the direction and dimensions outlined in the following model. It is assumed that human beings in the culture tend to develop from infants to adults—from:
   a. A state of passivity to a state of increasing activity.
   b. A state of dependence upon others to a state of relative independence.
   c. Having erratic, shallow, quickly dropped interests to having deeper interests.
   d. Being capable of behaving only in a few ways to behaving in many different ways.
   e. Having a short time perspective (that is, the present largely determines behavior) to a much longer term perspective where behavior is much more affected by the past and future.
   f. Being in a subordinate position in the family and society to aspiring to an equal or superordinate position relative to their peers.
   g. A lack of awareness of self to an awareness of and control over self.
2. Most human problems in organiza-

[37]Edward H. Litchfield, "Notes on a General Theory of Administration," *Administrative Science Quarterly*, vol. 1, no. 1, June 1956, pp. 3–29.

[38]Chris Argyris, "The Individual and Organization: An Empirical Test," *Administrative Science Quarterly*, vol. 4, September 1959, pp. 145–167.

tion arise because relatively healthy people in our culture are asked to participate in work situations which coerce them to be dependent, subordinate, and submissive, and to use few of their more than superficial abilities.

3. There are three major sets of variables which cause dependence: formal organization structure, directive leadership, and managerial controls such as budgets and incentives, quality control, etc.

4. The degree of subordination that these variables cause tends to increase as one goes down the chain of command and as the organization takes on characteristics of mass production.

5. Healthy human beings in our culture tend to find subordination frustrating.

6. Individuals will adapt to frustration and conflict by creating any one of the combinations of the following informal activities:
   a. Leave the situation.
   b. Climb the organizational ladder.
   c. Become defensive.
   d. Become apathetic, disinterested, and non-ego-involved in the organization as its formal goals.
   e. Create informal groups to sanction the defense reactions in (c) and (d).
   f. Formalize groups in the form of trade unions.
   g. Deemphasize the importance of self-growth, creativity, etc., and emphasize the importance of money and other material rewards.
   h. Accept the ways of behaving outlined above as being proper for their life outside the organization.

7. Management will tend to view most informal activities as detrimental to the formal organization.

8. Such reactions will tend to increase employees' subordination, which in turn will increase frustration, failure, and similar reaction, which in turn will increase the informal activities.

Testing of assumptions developed by Argyris led to the general conclusion that employees modified the organization by creating an informal employee culture that coerces and sanctions behavior that helps to guarantee employee actualization. In accordance with this theory, employees provided greater opportunities to express more mature predispositions differ significantly from employees required to express behavior closer to the infant end of the personality model.

Critique of the role concept

Both the Getzels-Guba and the Argyris models make extensive use of the role concept in a scheme to explain social behavior. According to one group of writers, the role concept "has yielded few significant hypotheses of theoretical importance."[39] It has served to emphasize cultural and social structural dimensions in analyzing social behavior. Human behavior is influenced to some degree by expectations that individuals hold for themselves or which others hold for them. The role concept has spotlighted the dualistic conflict between the individual's needs and the organization's demands.

Perhaps of even greater significance is the consideration of these early efforts as the theories of educational administration. In the more than 20 years since the inception of the theory

[39]Neal Gross, Ward S. Mason, and Alexander W. McEachern, *Explorations in Role Analysis*, New York: Wiley, 1958, pp. 319–320.

emphasis relatively few efforts have been expended in generating new conceptualizations or theories of administration and too much stress has been placed on what is implied to be the theory of administration. Administrative techniques have outrun theory and efforts to bridge the two have not paid off as yet.

TRENDS AND CRITIQUES OF ORGANIZATIONAL THEORY

The theory movement in educational administration is relatively new (less than a quarter of a century old), has failed to generate an adequate number of new theories, and, by and large, has had to borrow and adapt theories from other disciplines. As indicated earlier, it has had limited impact on both practice and research in the field. For the present at least identification of trends and critiques of organizational theory will have to be based on what is being experienced in other fields where considerably more action is evident.

March edited a sizeable volume of over 1200 pages that "sought to summarize and report the present state of knowledge about human organizations."[40] He identified the "33 frequently cited books in studies of organizations."[41] These reflected thinking in such disciplines as sociology, anthropology, management, economics, political science, and psychology. Organizational analysis took its rise among practitioners in the early years of such efforts although some organization theorists were part of the history. In the *Handbook of Organizations* are 28 scholarly chapters authored by distinguished writers who described the state of organization theory and research.

In the field of business management criticism of theory as being divorced from reality and as failing to provide sufficient practical guidance to managers began to appear in the early 1970s. To illustrate, Lee[42] critiqued what he called the "Modern Human Resource Management" theories that grew out of the writing of such behavioral theorists as Douglas McGregor, Frederick Herzberg, Chris Argyris, Rensis Likert, Robert Blake with Jane S. Mouton, and Abraham Maslow. Lee cited resistances to applying Modern Human Resource Management theories to practice. Most such theorists were professors who learned and generated theories by observing rather than by being involved in management of people. The limitations of the detached observers' insights were evident in the following statement from Douglas McGregor who was first a theorist and then President at Antioch.[43]

Before coming to Antioch I had observed and worked with top executives as an adviser in a number of organizations. I thought I knew how they felt about their responsibilities and what led them to behave as they did. . . . I was wrong! It took the direct experience of becoming a line executive and meeting personally the problems involved to teach me what no amount of observation of other people could have taught me.

Some studies indicated that human relations training (role playing, group dynamics, etc.) "had no measurable effect on plant behavior after return to work."[44] The gap between human relations theory and practice in indus-

---

[40]J. G. March, ed., *Handbook of Organizations*, Chicago: Rand McNally, 1965.

[41]Ibid., p. xii.

[42]J. A. Lee, "Behavioral Theory vs. Reality," *Harvard Business Review,* vol. 49, no. 2, March–April 1973, pp. 20–28, 157–159.

[43]Quote in ibid., p. 28.

[44]Cited in ibid., p. 22.

trial management does not seem to be closing.

Mockler started his review of the impact of theories of management by stating: "Business executives have often criticized management theory as an 'ivory tower', 'impractical', and 'out of touch with the real world.' "[45] He considered it justifiable criticism. He argued that theories are influenced by the conditions of practice and cited a number of writers who supported the situational theory of management. The situational framework provided a pragmatic turn to management theory which "offers the hope that a more unified and practical body of management theory will be developed in the 1970s and 1980s."[46]

What theory in educational administration sorely needs is a much broader conceptual base that addresses itself to more dimensions of the practical art of management. The systems theorists, reviewed in the next chapter, offer much more hope in bridging the gap between a conceptual understanding of what is being done and the art of doing it.

FROM THEORY TO MODELS

Models are a bridge between the purely abstract and the practical. They are a connection between theory and the systems approach (the substance of the following chapter), though the kinship is stronger with theory. The construction of a model of the system under investigation is an essential step in operations research, a type of systems study. Model building represents one way of spanning the differences that presently exist between the theo-

retical orientation of professors of educational administration and the everyday concerns of practicing administrators. The synthesis of theory and practice is more likely to occur when the focus is on generation of models of specific aspects of administration rather than global models of the total administrative process.

Models to be described and examined herein are creatures of the mind and not of the flesh. It is postulated that the functional beauty of models as intriguing "mind-holds" promises much for the improvement of educational administration. They are significant intellectual tools for probing, describing, and comprehending complex phenomena.

For practical purposes, model is synonymous with theory. It is a conceptual framework, a theoretical scheme. Model building starts by gathering related concepts that are significant in the situation under scrutiny and concludes when a system or pattern of connected ideas is produced that improves comprehension of the situation. A model, therefore, can be defined as an abstracted intellectual pattern, generated from a cluster of interlocking and interactive concepts, which has the capability of interpreting generalizable trends and interrelations that prevail within the real world.

Some authorities argue against this close identification of model and theory. Maccia[47] draws a distinction between a "model of" and a "model for." In the former phrase, the model represents something, and in the latter it is represented in something. Maccia

[45]R. J. Mockler, "Situational Theory of Management," *Harvard Business Review,* vol. 49, no. 3, May–June 1971, pp. 146–155.
[46]Ibid., p. 154.

[47]E. S. Maccia, "Models and the Meaning of 'Retroduction,'" Educational Theory Center, Occasional Paper 62–110, Columbus, Ohio: Bureau of Educational Research and Service, Ohio State University, mimeographed.

contends theory and model are "logically equivalent terms" only when "representational models" are implied.

The term "model" has the advantage of not possessing the impractical connotations associated, albeit unjustifiably, with the word "theory." This subtle semantic difference may facilitate' the use of conceptual framework by administrators to attack the everyday long-range problems of school operations and development.

According to *Webster's Unabridged Dictionary,* a model is (1) that which exactly resembles something, a copy; (2) a miniature representation of a thing; (3) something intended to serve as a pattern; or (4) an example for imitation. These definitions are not wholly consistent with the viewpoint presented herein.

A model is a representation of reality, that is, a simplified version of the real world containing only those aspects that are important to better understanding or control; it is a symbolic approximation of the real situation. It is thus more akin to an image, a symbol, or an analogy than to an aerial photograph or a precise miniature of the real situation, as suggested by the dictionary definition.

A model is incomplete in the sense that it is not a perfect facsimile of the actual world. As an abstraction, it includes (in the opinion of the creative person who devises it) only those elements necessary to the comprehension of the total system or an aspect of it. In the model, some factors in the real situation (hopefully not too significant) are neglected, at least temporarily, to reduce the variables under consideration. A model, therefore, becomes a means of rising above the minutiae not germane to grasping the substance of some aspect of administration. The beauty of abstraction is that it enables one to focus on those phenomena within the total complex whose variables and functions are pertinent. In developing the model, the theorist specifies what factors are significant and what relations are assumed among them. This is not to imply that variables left "outside" the model are ignored; they may be introduced at a later time to ascertain subsequent effects. This incompleteness is one of the many virtues of a model. As Baumol put it: "The model should be a sufficiently simple version of the facts to permit systematic manipulation and analysis."[48] He emphasized further that the more "realistic" model may often be the poorer model, for adding more "realism" may seriously complicate the investigation of complex phenomena. More than one investigator has been overwhelmed by the magnitude of administration and the difficulty of controlling all variables. Administration becomes more amenable to research, and school operations are comprehended more clearly, when models are developed that focus on those factors pertinent to understanding or control. It is not surprising, therefore, that a model "appropriate for the examination of one problem arising out of a given set of circumstances may be totally useless and even misleading for the investigation of another problem arising out of these same circumstances."[49]

There is a danger inherent in any attempt at abstraction. Gross oversimplification and along with it a distorted picture of operations can result. To be functional, a model must be a sufficiently close approximation of relevant facts in the real world. One model is better than another in terms of whether

[48]William J. Baumol, *Economic Theory and Operations Analysis,* Englewood Cliffs, N.J.: Prentice-Hall, 1961, p. 393.
[49]Ibid.

it oversimplifies or distorts less than another as well as whether it describes more accurately the key factors and is useful in making accurate predictions. The quality of a model is affected by factors included and omitted as well as by its ease of manipulation or internal consistency. Deciding which factors can be safely ignored (or at least held in abeyance) in the creation of a model is always a matter of judgment.

Sooner or later the model must be tested in the world of reality. If the model, as a system of internally consistent propositions, fails to describe or predict accurately conditions under which events in the actual world are likely to occur, it is the model and not the world that must be abandoned. Scientific inquiry has a built-in self-correcting character. No scientist or theoretician should permit himself to be trapped into devotion to his model (the offspring of his intellectual life) to the point where experimentation, experimental findings, and validation are avoided or ignored. Models are never more than approximately valid, and those with inaccurate premises can magnify errors and produce thoroughly undependable conclusions.

Working without models is like working without one of the necessary prerequisites to clear and scientific thinking. One reason for this, as suggested previously, is that a model is a constructed simplification of some part of reality that retains only those features regarded as essential for comprehension or control. It is the result of stripping away the rituals, behaviors, activities, details, or façades which obfuscate and confuse rather than clarify and unify.

Models enable the scientist to perceive relations that underlie pertinent facts, and hence, their use in the physical and most behavioral sciences is extensive. One of the indications of scientific maturity in any field is the degree of its reliance on the creation, testing, and use of models. Educational administration may never attain the rigorous and tightly structured theories characteristic of physics, since the movement of planets and of electrons seems to be determined by fewer antecedents and stimuli than human behavior. Nonetheless we can establish, on at least a probabilistic basis, functional relations between antecedents and consequences in human behavior. This may enable us to reduce, even if we cannot eliminate, the margin of error in administrative decisions.

Bross[50] suggested that models can be classified as physical, verbal, symbolic, and mathematical.

Physical models, whether of the solar system, of atoms, of buildings, or of airplanes, are rather commonplace. The small physical model is easier to manipulate than its full-sized counterpart. It is not necessary to reproduce each and every single detail on a smaller scale. Hence, creation of a model should not be confused with miniaturization. As stated previously, only those characteristics of the real thing necessary to understand the facets under question are copied in detail in a physical model. Thus, a physical model of an airplane need not include the seating arrangements, when its purpose is to understand the plane's flight characteristics. The proportional size of wings to aircraft body and tail stabilizing units would be important. The common physical models used to demonstrate the moon moving around the earth sooner or later develop snags as imperfect gears, bent wires, and friction produce a less-than-per-

---

[50]Irwin Bross, *Design for Decision,* New York: Macmillan, 1953, pp. 161–182.

fect representation of the solar system in motion. For this reason physical models are used rather infrequently by physical scientists and then primarily for instructional purposes.

Because words, however voluminous, are employed to describe and explain relations, causes, and predictions, the *verbal model* emerges. It consists of interrelated and interactive concepts expressed in words and sentences, that is, the language of a culture. Because verbal concepts represent a concrete thing or a specific activity, the verbal model is more abstract than its physical counterpart. Unfortunately, the same word often means different things to people with different experiences. There are many "vessel words" into which people pour their own meanings and which, hence, have no commonly agreed upon interpretation. Confusion rather than elucidation results from the imprecise use of words to describe and predict complex events.

The *symbolic model* evolves from the verbal model as specially constructed symbols are substituted for words and phrases. It involves a greater degree of abstraction but has the advantage of easier manipulation.

As various symbols are related to each other in a quantitative manner, the *mathematical model* emerges. A mathematical model is in this sense a special type of symbolic model. With a mathematical model more precise computations can be made. The internal consistency of concepts can be more readily judged. Many writers believe the most powerful models are sets of mathematical equations. A mathematical model expresses the effectiveness of the system as a function of a set of variables at least one of which is subject to control. Thus, the economist is able to relate complex business phenomena in terms of mathematical equations as well as graphical presentations. The economist speaks of the "production function" of a given industry. The productivity of an educational system can be viewed as a function of such variables as amount of financial support, clarity of educational goals, availability of specialized labor resources, and so on.

Another classification specifies *iconic, analog, function, quantitative,* and *qualitative* models.

The *iconic* model, a scaled-down or pictorial representation of a thing or system, corresponds in part to Bross' physical model. The globe representing the earth, the "model" plane representing its operational counterpart, the blueprint representing the building, the photograph representing the person, the map representing the terrain and space of a given area, and the timetable representing the pattern of operations are all iconic models. An iconic model is typically two- or three-dimensional and represents a static event.

The *analog* model employs something similar, that is, with close correspondence of fundamental characteristics. Animals used in medical experiments aimed at understanding more about humans and the wind tunnel used to test flow of fluids around a submarine or airplane are analog models.

The *function* model is simply a grouping of models by functions or purpose performed.

The *quantitative* model facilitates measurement or aids in observations. The test models are designed to measure certain events or characteristics.

The *qualitative* model classifies by subject described. Examples are economic models, education models, social models, and business models.

Deutsch[51] classified models according to four functions: organizing, heuristic, predictive, and measuring (or mensurative) functions.

The *organizing* function is the ability of the model to order and relate disjointed data and to show similarities or connections which previously had remained unperceived. Other writers have labeled this the "ah-ha experience." Isolated pieces of information become more useful when placed into a meaningful pattern. It is naive to assume that "facts speak for themselves." Reeling off facts (data) in rapid succession will inevitably beget the question "Now what does all this mean?" To be useful, facts must be interpreted within the framework of some stated or implied model. This can be called explanation or interpretation, that is, a special case of the organizing function. As Baumol stated:

Basically, the need for theory arises because facts unfortunately do not speak for themselves. . . . Facts supply us with correlations, not with structural relationships. At times all of us are prepared to reject conclusions which appear to be implied by the facts because these conclusions conflict with the rudimentary theoretical structures which we implicitly accept.[52]

As a *heuristic* device, the model leads to discovery of new facts and new methods. Anything which is heuristic must have, by definition, a "discovery emphasis."

The *predictive* function of a model goes beyond explanation and prophesies that certain events will occur when other phenomena are observed.

A model may suggest a means of accurately *measuring* operations. Scales

[51]Karl W. Deutsch, "On Communication Models in the Social Sciences," *Public Opinion Quarterly,* vol. 16, no. 3, Fall 1952, pp. 356–357.

[52]Baumol, op. cit., p. 391.

are then proposed along with dimensions for the evaluation of certain systems.

NEED FOR MODELS IN EDUCATIONAL ADMINISTRATION

Educational administration is one of the last and slowest of the behavioral sciences to evince concern for theories and models. Progress has thus far been painfully slow. There has been a tendency to become infatuated with a few existing models and a failure to develop new ones. Professors seem to be overly preoccupied with reading about a few models and worshipfully presenting them to students. More emphasis must be given to stimulating the generation of a variety of models concerned with the many aspects of educational administration, and less emphasis must be given to converting the uninformed and noble savages to disciples chanting the praises of the limited and far from perfect models.

Models that strip away the minutiae and "administrivia" are needed for a better understanding of the activities and behavior of professional personnel, the allocation of resources for the support of schools, the coordination of administrative echelons, information processing, and decision making. If different purposes must be satisfied, different models of the same situation will probably be needed. When many models that accurately describe or predict events within the many aspects of administration have been created, there may emerge from a set of interlocking and interacting models a global model to portray the essence of school administration.

Concern for model development is an attitude, a frame of mind, a predisposition to find a rational answer to multifaceted problems. Realization of the full potential of the scientific method has been prevented, however, by preoccupation with empiricism. Facts have been gathered, but the field has lacked an adequate theoretical framework. In addition, there has been a tendency to refer to "criteria" in school-plant planning, to principles of accounting, to "fundamentals" of transportation, or to "basic concepts" of instruction, when all too often these are high-sounding terms for recommended routine practices rather than carefully developed conceptual schemes. It is easy to become mired in unrelated facts or empirical generalizations when sophisticated models are lacking.

Useful and accurate models of any aspect of educational administration will take many years to evolve as an imperfect model is modified or merged with others trying to describe and explain or predict the same thing. To quote Bross: "Few scientists are so fortunate or clever as to devise a useful model on the first attempt."[53] Even a model used successfully for years may encounter a situation whose outcome it will not be able to predict accurately, and hence a new model must be developed. It is contended that poor and inaccurate models are better than none, for a field that lacks models is still depending on disconnected and purely empirical observations.

EXAMPLES OF MODELS IN EDUCATIONAL ADMINISTRATION

An accounting model

Depicting the school system in terms of an accounting model calls for verbalization and systemization quite dif-

[53]Bross, op. cit.

ferent from the mechanical routine of posting financial transactions into accounts. The model includes categories of inputs and outputs that can be measured. The dollar is a rational and stable unit for measuring certain things. In the accounting model, an image of the system is created in terms of what happens to the money that flows in and the products that flow out, with particular emphasis on translating fiscal resources into desired outputs. This approximates the systems approach and cost-effectiveness analysis.

A building model

The school-plant can be visualized as a physical translation of the instructional process in terms of structural techniques, materials, and architectural design. Few would consider constructing a building without first generating the iconic model for the structure, namely, the blueprints. To move beyond the iconic model to the symbolic model, it is necessary to identify the key spatial and other environmental factors that affect the teaching-learning process.

A decision-making model

Models based on decision making as the essence of administration are illustrations of universal or global types. It is the nature of the decision, rather than the process itself, that differentiates the administrator from others in an organization. A theory of decision making emphasizes the process of arriving at decisions, particularly scientific, rational, or "best" decisions, by anyone (not only the administrator). Procedures based on scientific problem solving and quantitative tools to enhance decision making will be reviewed in the next chapter.

A specific decision demands knowledge of the situation or the problem. For example, a number of models may be necessary in deciding which person should be employed as a teacher. Thus, models of the instructional process in the building, of the meritorious teacher, of the clientele served, or of the social system called the school where the person is to teach may be reviewed during the decision making.

Skill in developing and using models, therefore, can enhance the decision-making capabilities of an administrator. Note that the emphasis is not on a model or theory of decision making, but on the use of models in decision making.

MODELS AS A MEANS OF IMPROVING RESEARCH IN EDUCATIONAL ADMINISTRATION

Professors of educational administration (as well as others) have long wrestled with the problem of what constitutes doctoral-level research. Determining whether a model or theory is involved in the study may contribute to the resolution of some aspects of this dilemma. If a proposed study suggests no conceptual framework to unify, explain, or predict observable generalizations, it cannot meet the first criterion for doctoral-level study. The first (but not necessarily the only) step in analyzing a proposed doctoral research project in school administration should be to determine whether the study is undergirded by a relevant model or theory or whether it rests on empirical and highly pragmatic approaches.

A model has a focusing effect and minimizes the chances of aimless research. If a model is capable of interpreting generalizable trends and interrelations within a set of varied facts,

then the research hypothesis is a deduction from the model and its verification is a validation of the model. Deductive explanations are the logical consequence of well-established premises or intellectual patterns. This is the hypothetico-deductive approach used to start investigations. Any study without this basis is merely exploratory.

Educational research has not influenced practice to any great extent because, generally speaking, it has been of poor quality, and has provided few suggestions for the improvement of practice. Much of the research in educational administration has been concerned with gathering isolated facts rather than evolving theories or testing the validity of a given model. The objection is not to empirical observations or generalizations, which are indeed important in research, but rather to the studies that remain at this level. If research in educational administration is to influence practice, it must move beyond the mere gathering of facts to the scientific and creative level of explaining and interpreting facts. Models emerge, or are modified or justified, as the researcher moves from collecting to interpreting facts. As one writer put it:

There is . . . no genuine progress in scientific insight through the Baconian method of accumulating empirical facts without hypotheses or anticipation of nature. Without some guiding idea, we do not know what facts to gather. Without something to prove, we cannot determine what is relevant and what is irrelevant.[54]

A TAXONOMY FOR MODELS IN EDUCATIONAL ADMINISTRATION

A taxonomy of function models presented herein is based in two broad

[54]M. Cohen, *A Preface to Logic,* New York: Meridian, 1956, p. 148.

categories, namely: organization-oriented (OO) function models, which focus primarily on the organizational dimensions of administration; and administrator-oriented (AO) function models, which emphasize an administrator's characteristics or administrative behavior within the system. The general system model, an all-encompassing type that seeks to unify the OO and AO models, is global in approach, and will be examined in the next chapter.

Organization-oriented models

The major types of OO function models are (1) social-system models; (2) economic models; (3) decision-rendering, or power, models; (4) communication models; (5) service models; (6) structural models; and (7) dynamic models. As will be noted in the following paragraphs, some overlap exists among these types. In addition, a miscellaneous category is needed for those models that fit in none of the other classes.

Social-system models. Such models picture the school as an organization of human efforts and behavior to promote the attainment of social goals. They concentrate on factors related to describing, analyzing, or predicting human behavior in a given system. They may identify individual needs as aided or inhibited by the demands of the organized institution. The underlying assumption is that it is difficult if not impossible to comprehend what goes on in an organized society without looking at how human beings are related to each other and how they behave in the face of given constraints. Many models begin by describing the institutional dimension, as expressed by roles and expectations and the individual dimension, as evinced by personal need predispositions. Interaction between these two fundamental dimensions of the organizational and cultural matrix produces social behavior. In a sense, the individual actualizes himself through the organization, and simultaneously the organization realizes goals through the individual's behavior. The models constructed by Parsons, Getzels and Guba, and Argyris are of this type, although in only one case is the model specifically directed at school administration as a social process.

Other models analyze the organization as a social system not in terms of individuals resolving personal needs within institutional demands, but rather as coalitions of individuals pursuing conflicting goals. (For example, a faculty senate meeting of a large university, or "multiversity," could dramatically demonstrate the existence of coalitions attempting to influence the outcome of controversial issues.) How the organization copes with internal and external coalitions is significant to its productivity.

Still other models emphasize conflict between those who have access to the power and control the reward system of the organization and those who do not have formal and legal access to power but strive to control the reward-distribution system. Collective bargaining is the classic illustration of the conflict model, that is, how a social system manages human conflict.

The work of Max Weber and its recent extensions represent a mechanistic variation of the social-system models. Here bureaucracy is suggested as a form of social organization effective in organizing the behavior of many to attain desired social goals.

Human relations models, coalition models, and conflict-resolution models are other examples of social-system models.

In short, models of this type view the organization as a social system in which human behavior is the result of the many forces within the system and determines to a large degree the productivity of the system. Individual needs, institutional demands, role behavior, coalitions, and resolution of conflicts are key factors within the system.

Economic models. These models focus on those aspects of an organization concerned with procuring, allocating, and utilizing resources. In other words, the emphasis is on what is done with resources to fulfill the productive goals of an organization. Economics can be defined as the study of how society allocates scarce resources or means among competing ends. Few organizations have all the resources required to satisfy competing purposes. How human and material resources of a school system are obtained, made available to meet the various objectives of education, and effectively managed constitutes the economics of school administration. Specific examples are the finance models (which seek to identify and relate into a defensible pattern the key national, state, and local fiscal resource factors, their magnitude, their method of distribution among schools, and their impact on the quality and quantity of education in society) and the logistical models (which seek to identify and organize into a unified system factors related to supplying, maintaining, transporting, storing, and accounting for human, fiscal, and material resources for schools in a manner which optimizes utilization of the resources

to productive purposes). Logistical models can be subdivided further into budgeting and accounting models (focusing on the allocating, recording, and safeguarding of the flow of fiscal resources for specified purposes within the system); personnel-allocation models (stressing staff assignments to various roles such as instruction, counseling and administration); transportation models; and school facilities models. Efficiency and the production function of education are rather vaguely defined at present, but future models may suggest a defensible measuring stick. Operations research is readily applicable to economic models. Certain mathematical techniques such as linear programming can be used to attack allocation problems such as scheduling of transportation facilities.

Decision-rendering, power, or political models. These models examine the organization in terms of the locus and flow of decisions (or the power and authority to make them) on policy and administrative matters. They may be called political models to distinguish them from the previously discussed social and economic models. People and positions are categorized in terms of formal and informal decision points or power levels. The formal chart of organization is an iconic model of key decision points. Within such models a flow diagram of the decisional processes within large, multifunctional, and hence, complicated organization can be developed. Identifying key factors that determine how formal or informal power and authority are distributed within the establishment becomes germane. While it can be argued that decision-rendering models should be separate from power and authority models, their combination is also valid because power can be measured in terms of its effect on the decisional process.

Communication models. These represent the organization as a giant processor of information or a vast network wherein data are generated, transmitted, and received by various positions. Without communication, coordination would be all but impossible and prudent decision would be the result of pure chance. Each position in the hierarchy becomes a kind of switchboard with varying degrees of influence. Models of this type stress how an organization secures information, how the communication (formal and informal) reaches various parts, or what is done with the data. Structural and functional relations are developed in terms of the communication function.

Service models. These models focus on the instructional and allied functions of a school organization. Teaching models, learning models, counseling models, welfare (health, lunch, and the like) models, student-body-activity models, and curriculum models are types of service models, for all are connected with the service function of an educational organizational. The opportunity for overlapping with other types is most evident. The emphasis determines the basis for typing models.

Structural models. These models analyze the structure of an organization, with less emphasis on decisions, communications, and social relations and more emphasis on line-and-staff relations, tall and flat patterns, departmentation, and span of control. Overlap with other types of OO models is a distinct possibility.

Dynamic models. These models view the organization as evolving—coming to be, battling to maintain equilibrium, living and thriving, and possibly dying. More recently these types have been referred to as general systems models. The word "dynamic" is used in the sense of a moving force or energy that affects equilibrium. The dynamic model is an adaptation of the biological models. Closely related is innovation and how it is met, resisted, or encouraged in an organization. To illustrate, some key factors in an organizational-change model might be the organization's sensitivity to its clientele and/or environment, ability to design in operational terms new services, ability to identify alternative solutions to change, feasibility and speed of developing new organizational arrangements, and ability to slough off old practices.

What disturbances (within or outside) do to the system is of prime concern in the dynamic model. It suggests ecological problems as the organization copes with its environment. This is sometimes called the boundary maintenance concerns of a system. The organization may live through a cold war with certain elements in its community, a guerrilla war with specified factions within the system, or a hot or open war with self-appointed critics of the system. How it meets those factors that create disequilibrium is a subject of concern for dynamic models. The organization is seen as a viable entity, interacting with its environment and carrying built-in mechanisms of varying degrees of effectiveness to meet challenges. Change, planned or unplanned, is a significant theme in such models. How crises are faced as the organization develops is of concern in related models. For example, Lippitt and Schmidt developed the thesis that "certain recognizable non-financial crises occur in the life cycle of an organization."[55]

Administrator-oriented models

The major AO function models are (1) leader models, (2) innovator models, (3) policy-scientist models, (4) mediator or resolver of conflict models, (5) technician-expert models, (6) organization-man models, and (7) decision-maker, or influence, models. Again, the need for a miscellaneous category is evident.

Leader models. Models of the administrator as leader abound in the literature. The impact of the leader on organizational activities is the focus of some models. Other models identify key factors in the leadership role or focus on measurement of leadership behavior.

Innovator models. These models stress the role of the administrator as a change agent. Some incorporate this as part of a general configuration for the leadership-behavior model, but there is sufficient difference to warrant separation. Such models are closely related to the dynamic models of the OO class, but focus on the person rather than the organization.

Policy-scientist models. These models focus on the role of the administrator as an architect or influencer of policy formulation. The key personal and experience factors are identified to conceptualize the policy scientists.

[55]G. L. Lippitt and W. T. Schmidt, "Crises in Developing Organization," *Harvard Business Review,* vol. 45, no. 6, November–December 1967, pp. 102–112.

Mediator or resolver of conflict models. With the possibilities of conflict and confrontation increasing the roles of the administrator as a mediator or resolver of conflicts have been receiving greater emphasis. How to analyze and develop strategies for overcoming conflicts or coping with and containing confrontations may be the focal points for such models.

Technician-expert models. Such models see the administrator in his traditional practice-oriented role as an expert in human relations, finance, school plant, personnel employment, etc. The administrator is viewed as one who needs to possess (if he already does not) certain technical competencies in order to cope with operational problems.

Organization-man models. These models commit the administrator to organizational objectives with special stress on such qualities as loyalty, harmonious relations, and getting the job done.

Decision-maker, or influence, models. These models emphasize the role of the administrator as a determiner of the course of action or the one responsible for making the choice among alternatives.

SYNTHESIZING MODELS AND PRACTICE

Emphasis on the development and use of models in administration will be an important first step in the synthesis of theory and practice. Administrators are beginning to recognize the value of theorizing, or creating models, if for no other reason than the failure of the traditional empirical approaches to cope with today's challenges. As long as empirical data are used to test the usefulness and truthfulness of a model, the danger of creating models for the sake of sterile theorizing will be minimized. It was suggested earlier that models increase the probability of prudent judgments by identifying significant factors and revealing alternative courses of actions and consequences. Theory and practice are not polarized entities. Model building will enhance the practice of educational administration.

The professor of school administration can be conceived in terms of the administrator-scientist who develops and tests models for the discipline. Although research-oriented, he is intimately involved in the real world of administration where the products of his creative mind are continually evaluated. His instructional responsibilities include refreshing students with challenging concepts and models. Practitioners in the field bear the same relation to the professor of school administration as does the medical practitioner to the professor of medicine. The practitioner brings to the professor the difficult problems that thus far have defied solution and the two blend talents and contributions to create new breakthroughs in administration.

SUMMARY

The development of theory in educational administration is an extension of scientific principles beyond the levels of pure sensory perceptions. Administration is a practical science whose improvement by application of scientific approaches can be traced as far back as the Cameralists of the seventeenth and eighteenth centuries. Cameralism was an administrative technology developed and employed in Germany and Austria. The school-survey and similar movements in the second and third decades of the twentieth century stimulated a scientific study of educational administration concerned primarily with a fragmentary empirical aspect of administration. Such study resulted in improved techniques and procedures, rather than in an overall understanding of the nature of administration.

Science is concerned with knowledge gained as the result of verifiable observations and descriptions. Observations and descriptions are not ends in themselves but means to first explain and then predict events. Science is rooted initially and finally in experience as a way of knowing. It is inductive in character, although deductive inferences can follow verified major premises.

Taxonomies are schemes of classification that are useful in handling large volumes of related data. The number and extent of these schemes are limited only by one's vocabulary. They are not theories and are sterile in terms of generating new knowledge.

Theory, according to Feigl, is a set of assumptions from which can be derived, by purely logico-mathematical procedures, a larger set of empirical laws. It also can be defined as a cluster of interlocking and interactive concepts systematized into an abstracted intellectual pattern which helps interpret generalizable trends and interrelations that prevail within a set of facts. Other disciplines in the natural and social sciences developed theories and found them useful in producing new knowledge before the concern for theory in educational administration around 1954. Theories are hypothetico-deductive systems that make use of inductive and deductive patterns of logic. They give rise to a conceptual framework for the study of administration. "Model" is a term synonymous with theory. Theory building is based on concepts operationally defined.

Theories have sometimes been erroneously referred to as personal systems of operation, idle dreams, philosophies, or taxonomies. Values are primarily variables in a theory. A theory is concerned with what is rather than what ought to be.

Theories have been misconstrued as being impractical; in reality they can be as productive in the social sciences as they have been in the physical and natural sciences.

There have been various attempts at developing theories of educational administration and administration in general. Most of the existing theories are concerned either with understanding and describing human behavior in organizations or with decision making.

A theory represents a way of thinking about and unifying apparently unconnected empirical observations into a meaningful pattern. It is a significant intellectual tool for gaining greater insights into a discipline such as administration. There are few things so practical as a theory or model. The more complex the phenomenon, the greater the urgency for the creation and use of a model.

A model is for practical purposes synonymous with a theory and can serve as the bridge between the abstract and the practical. Models are significant intellectual tools for probing, describing, and comprehending complex phenomena.

A model is a representation of reality, a symbolic approximation of a real situation. It is incomplete and includes only those factors that are pertinent to comprehension of the operation of a system. The incompleteness facilitates manipulation and analysis. The danger in abstraction is that oversimplification can lead to distortion. Science has a built-in self-correcting mechanism that insists that a model be tested with data from the real world. One of the clues to the scientific maturity of a field is its degree of reliance on the creation, testing, and use of models.

Models may be classed as physical, verbal, symbolic, and mathematical. The symbolic model evolves from the verbal as symbols are substituted for words and phrases. As various symbols are related to each other quantitatively, the mathematical equation emerges. Mathematical models are the most powerful and are the easiest to manipulate. Models may also be classified as iconic, analog, function, quantitative, or qualitative.

Models can serve organizing, heuristic, predictive, and measuring functions. It is naive to assume that facts speak for themselves. Facts must be interpreted within some conceptual framework.

If different purposes are to be satisfied, different models of the same situation may be needed. Generation of functional global models will follow rather than precede the construction of models of specific aspects of the system. Concern for model development is an attitude or a frame of mind. It implies a desire to rise above the morass of details to glean the essence of a situation.

Models can be useful in decision making. It is highly unlikely that a burst of creativity in model development will immediately produce a useful model. Inaccurate models are better than none, for the effort demonstrates a concern for creating a conceptual framework and progressing beyond empiricism. Models are essential in doctoral-level research.

A taxonomy of function models in school administration postulates two broad classifications: organization-oriented (OO) and administrator-oriented (AO) models. Major OO types are social-system, economic, decision-rendering (political), communication, service, structural, and dynamic models. Major AO types are leader, innovator, policy-scientist, mediator, technician-expert, organization-man, and decision-maker models.

Improvements in and new approaches to school administration depend on the development and use of models. The professor of educational administration can be conceptualized in terms of the administrator-scientist who develops and tests models.

QUESTIONS

1. What factors led to the development of a concern for theory in educational administration?
2. What are the distinguishing characteristics of a theory?
3. Of what value are taxonomies?
4. Why is it said that theories are concerned with what is rather than what ought to be?
5. How does the scientific method of coming to know differ from the more formal methods of logic based on the syllogism?
6. What is a model?
7. Why are inaccurate models better than no models?
8. What types of iconic models are used in school administration now?
9. Why are models essential in well-developed research?
10. How can models be used to bridge the gap between the abstract and the practical?

SELECTED REFERENCES

Barnard, Chester I., *The Functions of the Executive*, Cambridge, Mass.: Harvard, 1938.

Bross, Irwin, *Design for Decision*, New York: Macmillan, 1953.

Deutsch, Karl W., "On Communication Models in the Social Sciences," *Public Opinion Quarterly*, vol. 16, no. 3, Fall 1952.

Feigl, Herbert, "Principles and Problems of Theory Construction in Psychology," in *Current Trends in Psychological Theory*, Pittsburgh: University of Pittsburgh Press, 1951.

Getzels, Jacob W., "Administration as a Social Process," in Andrew W. Halpin, ed., *Administrative Theory in Education*, Chicago: Midwestern Administration Center, University of Chicago, 1958.

Greenwood, Ernest, "The Practice of Science and the Science of Practice," in W. G. Bennis, R. D. Benne, and R. Chin, eds., *The Planning of Change*, New York: Holt, Rinehart & Winston, 1961.

Griffiths, Daniel E., *Administrative Theory,* New York: Appleton-Century-Crofts, 1959.

Halpin, Andrew W., "The Development of Theory in Educational Administration," in Andrew W. Halpin, ed., *Administrative Theory in Education,* Chicago: Midwest Administration Center, University of Chicago, 1958.

Lippitt, G. L. and W. T. Schmidt, "Crises in Developing Organization," *Harvard Business Review,* vol. 45, no. 6, November-December 1967, pp. 102–112.

Maccia, E. S., "Models and the Meaning of 'Retroduction,'" Educational Theory Center, Occasional Paper 62–110, Columbus, Ohio: Bureau of Educational Research and Service, Ohio State University (mimeographed).

7

THE SYSTEMS APPROACH TO EDUCATIONAL ADMINISTRATION: DEVELOPMENT OF NEW CONCEPTS, TOOLS, AND TECHNIQUES

The 1960s may be remembered as the time in history when the systems approach began to be talked about with increasing frequency in educational administration. Admittedly, some pioneers may have demonstrated something less than perfect, or simply a fascination for new terminology; nevertheless, the spirit of change was in the air. In the early 1970s there were definite signs that specific applications of the systems approach were being designed and implemented in schools. The use of systems, like the use of models, is a way of harnessing theory to the actual problems of administrators. The systems approach produces a set of procedures and an attitude toward viewing the functions of administration in terms of a sophisticated conceptual framework and scientific analysis. It also makes available a new battery of tools and techniques to attack persistent problems. Systems thinking represents a further extension of science in administration that started with the orderly analysis of shop-room level production problems by F. W. Taylor, was extended by the interpretation of experiences of general administrative concerns by Fayol, grew to a greater degree of maturity with the human-relations focus of the Hawthorne experiments, and reached a higher level of sophistication with the search for a theory of organizations to describe, explain, and predict administrative functions.[1]

HISTORICAL DEVELOPMENT

The systems approach testifies to the continuing evolution of administration from a conceptual and technical point of view. Its beginnings as an identifiable movement can be traced to the early 1940s. What is referred to as the "systems approach" herein is elsewhere call "systems analysis," "systems engineering," "systems management," "operations research," or "cost-effectiveness analysis." It is related to the disciplines of mathematics, physics, engineering, and economics. The orientation in this book favors

[1] Harold Koontz, "The Management Theory Jungle," *Journal of the Academy of Management*, December 1961, pp. 174–175.

approaches and models closely related to economics. Much of what is suggested stems from economic theory and analysis and existed many years prior to its application to problems of managing.

The systems approach is part of the stream of ideas associated with scientific management in its broadest sense and is closely related to operations research (OR). Churchman et al. tentatively defined operations research as "the application of scientific methods, techniques, and tools to problems involving the operations of a system so as to provide control of the system with optimum solutions to the problems."[2]

It is a multidisciplinary team, or task-force attack on problems. It has a strong quantitative orientation. Operations research and the systems approach are not the same, though the difference between the two has often defied specification. For the purposes of this book operations research is a part of the overall systems approach, specifically that part concerned with a range of mathematically oriented techniques.

During World War II, operations research racked up a number of spectacular successes, of which radar was one. Radar, developed by British scientists, was unfamiliar to the military in the early stages of the Battle of Britain. The military enlisted the scientists to design the equipment and to develop procedures for employing this novel detection device to solve some difficult defense problems. Through operations research and the application of new radar technology, the effectiveness of air defense during the Battle of Britain was increased an estimated tenfold.

Another illustration[3] in the military is the use of depth charges by naval forces in antisubmarine attacks. This study, like the one on radar, used a team combining skills and insights of scientists and military personnel. It called for careful compilation of operating data, generation of a model, and testing predictions against data from the real world. Analysis revealed that depth charges were traditionally set to detonate 100 feet below the surface. At that point, naval experts declared, detonation and the pressure of water had the greatest destructive power. The submarine had to be at a depth of 100 feet to experience the maximum destructive impact, and the attack often had to be delayed after the ship had been sighted to allow it to dive to 100 feet below the surface. During the delay, the submarine could turn in any direction, unknown to the attacker, and thus escape. The operations research team, using probability theory, determined that detonation at a point less deep than the point of maximum destructive force, such as 35 feet below the surface, would greatly increase the chances of the kill, for the likely position of the evasive ship could be determined with greater accuracy. The critical variable, according to scientists, was the position of the submarine at the time of detonation of the depth charge, not the point of maximum destructive force of the detonation. After much resistance and discussion by naval commanders, the results of probability analysis were put to a test and wonderfully validated in practice. The number of sinkings of enemy submarines increased almost exactly in proportion to the predictions of the operations researchers.

[2]C. W. Churchman, R. L. Ackoff, and E. L. Arnoff, Introduction to Operations Research, New York: Wiley, 1957, p. 18.

[3]A. Shuchman, Scientific Decision Making in Business, New York: Holt, Rinehart & Winston, 1963, pp. 2–5.

THE CONCEPT OF SYSTEMS

The concepts upon which the systems approach rests are not totally unfamiliar to the administrator. Traditional organization theory generally emphasized segments and is concerned with the separation of activities into tasks or operational units, but it insufficiently emphasized problems of interrelations—a factor of major significance in systems theory.

This is hardly a startling point of view. A favorite expression of the Gestalt psychologist during the 1920s and 1930s was that the whole is greater than the sum of its parts—a statement repeated frequently by those with a systems orientation. Few would disagree with another systems belief that change in one variable will affect others.

Johnson et al. defined the systems concept and a system as follows:

A system is defined as an array of components designed to accomplish a particular objective according to plan. There are three significant points in this definition: (1) there is a design or an established arrangement of materials, energy, and information; (2) there is a purpose or objective which the system is designed to accomplish; and (3) inputs of materials, energy, and information are allocated according to plan. (Italics in the original.)[4]

Others view a system as a collection of interactive and interdependent components that focus on a cluster of objectives for all organized entities.

Every system has boundaries that encompass the common purposes, varied functions, and interdependent parts. The boundaries are like the skin of an animal or the geographical borders of a political unit or subdivision.

The system has subsystems within, and the point of common contact, that is, the link between two subsystems is referred to as an interface. Everything outside the system is part of its surrounding environment, that is, is exogenous to the system. A system whose boundaries are impermeable to factors in the environment is called a closed system, for nothing outside can enter to influence inner operations. Closed systems are unstable in the long run, for they lack the mechanism to sense changes in the surrounding environment that have implications for the effectiveness of internal operations. If interplay is possible between the system and its environment, the system is referred to as open. Things that go into the system are called inputs; those that emanate from it are called outputs.[5] Systems is a way of thinking, a mental frame of reference, that can be used by the administrator in performing his traditional functions of planning, organizing, and controlling operations.

The word "systems" has long been in the dictionary, but purely as a plural of "system." The dictionary does not carry the concept presently associated with systems approach, systems analysis, or systems engineering. A system is defined as a complex unity formed of many, often diverse, parts subject to a common plan or serving a common purpose. Thus, a network is an organized or coherent pattern with interconnections or intercrossings of various parts at stated points. A group of related devices can form a network and be used to achieve common purposes. Scheme, network, and organism are synonyms for system. System suggests a plan or

[4]R. A. Johnson, F. E. Kast, and J. E. Rosenzweig, *The Theory and Management of Systems*, 2nd ed., New York: McGraw-Hill, 1967, pp. 403–404.

[5]C. J. Haberstroh, "Organization Design and Systems Analysis," in J. G. March, ed., *Handbook of Organizations*, Chicago: Rand McNally, 1965, pp. 1171–1211.

order. Chaos is the opposite of system. The term is not strange in the literature of education, for schoolmen have long talked about school systems and political systems. Emphasis on a systematic approach to administrative endeavors is hardly new or unusual.

The systems approach suggests a view of the school as a network of interrelated subsystems, each charged with accomplishing part of the overall task of converting inputs into desired outputs. The organization is seen as a network of subsystems and interrelated parts which make up the complex whole. School administration based on the systems approach perceives the educational enterprise as a unified, systematic way of translating resources made available to it in the form of money, people with varying abilities, facilities, and processes, into outcomes, outputs, or benefits related to the educational goals of society. The school system is not viewed as a conglomeration of separate elements, but as a man-made system which experiences a dynamic interplay among its parts and with its environment. A system or subsystem is a total array of resources, human and physical, concerned with the achievement of objectives.

The educational system of a culture may also be conceived as a kind of delivery or conversion system whose major components would be (1) a goal and priorities setting subsystem, (2) a resources subsystem, (3) a control subsystem, (4) a client service subsystem, (5) an educational manpower subsystem, (6) an environment relations subsystem, and (7) a student manpower reentry and retraining subsystem. This is a special illustration or one way of looking at a total system in terms of the functions or outputs of special and interrelated parts.

The *goals and priorities-setting sub-system* is concerned with specification of educational missions and/or reordering of priorities for goals to be emphasized within it. By and large, this particular subsystem is poorly defined in most cultures. Participants in the process are diffused, and relatively great difficulty is experienced in identifying truly potent influence leaders, either as groups or individuals. There is usually some degree of uncertainty as to who is clothed with authority to articulate goals. This may help to explain why goals change slowly and priorities are reordered less frequently than the turbulent times would suggest. On occasion the federal government, in the process of allocating funds for specific educational purposes, may behave as the goals and priority-setting subsystem for local school districts. Concerns for "federal control of education" stem, in part, from efforts of the national government, rather than the state legislature or local school board, to assume the role of the agency that determines what goals and priorities shall be attached to educational efforts.

Outputs of the *resources subsystem* are determination and allocation of human, physical, and fiscal resources required in pursuit of various educational missions. It includes a decision-making apparatus designating positions in the hierarchy authorized to make resource decisions. Every system pursuing goals consumes resources. The more complex its objectives and the more dynamic its growth, the more voracious its appetite for resources. The resources subsystem is usually both structurally and legally well-defined. Thus, state laws determine what kinds of taxing authority shall be available for school purposes and within what limits, what qualifications shall be demanded of human resources employed for instructional purposes in schools, the limits of procedures for borrowing, and so forth. Manpower and nonhuman resources are part of the subsystem. Its elements are recruitment, employment, assignment, and transfer of manpower resources as well as procurement, allocation, utilization, and management of physical and financial resources.

The *control subsystem* focuses on sensing the rhythm of operation and on plans for triggering adjustments necessary to keep the system locked onto attainment of stated targets within limits of predetermined permissible variations. Control may be institutionalized in one or more agencies at the local, state, or national levels. Thus, the control may be vested in a school board, the state department of education, or state legislature. Less well-defined are the limits of deviation before actualizing correcting mechanisms. This does not, of course, preclude the operation of informal control mechanisms as well.

The *client service subsystem* is the reason for creating the institution. It is the payload. Its output is a better educated student, as measured or implied in goals and priorities set. It is the dimension that identifies, receives, and involves learners in experiences judged to be educational. Typical conceptualization of the educational institution is in terms of this particular subsystem. It is usually well-defined and institutionalized by law in the form of school districts and attendance centers.

The *educational manpower subsystem* prepares instructional personnel for entry into the resources subsystem and for service in the client service subsystem. No country can hope to extend the range of its client service subsystem without the manpower to do so. The teacher manpower subsystem in the United States was designed in rudimentary form in the nineteenth century and has been in operation ever since. Control over the teacher manpower subsystem is usually outside the purview of both local and state school boards. At one time the very large cities, such as Chicago and St. Louis, had their own teachers colleges under the control of local boards of education, which prepared teachers needed for system operation. Interplay among the resources, the client service, and the educational manpower subsystems should be evident, even though the first two are parts of one institution in society and the latter is assigned to another.

The measure of the *environment relations subsystem* is the degree of meaningful and efficient interchange between various subsystems and the surrounding environment. If the educational system is to react to forces, it must design a mechanism to sense the magnitude and urgency of exogenous forces and to translate each into adaptive implications for the general education system. This subsystem is usually poorly defined. In these turbulent times, a more sophisticated mechanism probably will have to be fashioned to ensure responsive changes to stay in tune with the environment.

The function of the *reentry subsystem* is to enable the participant of the general educational system to move from his relatively protected environment to the world of productive labor. Effectiveness can be measured by success in placement of students who attended for various periods in productive and satisfying enterprises in society. This subsystem has been loosely defined and usually is outside the formal educational system. It may well be the most neglected subsystem. Most public schools demonstrate little more than passing interest in job placement and even less in retraining responsibilities for those whose skills were made obsolete by technological developments. The rapid growth of post-secondary vocational, technical, and adult educational institutions may fill this void.

GENERAL SYSTEMS THEORY

Specialists in one discipline sometimes have difficulty in communicating with specialists in other disciplines even though both employ the scientific method. While interdisciplinary studies and multidisciplinary approaches alleviate the problem to some extent, because they emphasize interrelations, the cross-discipline sometimes produces a new jargon that compounds the communication problems. An overall framework is needed to better relate specializations to each other so "that the *interdisciplinary movement* may not degenerate into *undisciplined* approaches."[6]

General systems theory is one effort to produce an overarching framework that embraces concepts and phenomena common to many disciplines. It provides scientists with the perspective necessary to carry out specialized research and still maintain a common base to compare concepts in a variety of disciplines. It is rooted in models "which are applicable to many systems, whether physical, biological, behavioral, or social" and aims at tying "all disciplines together in a meaningful relationship."[7] General systems theory is a reaction to the fragmentation that results from focusing on subparts and overlooking the pattern of relations in a network of subsystems. Its prime objective is to facilitate bet-

ter comprehension of complex situations by relating elements into a comprehensible pattern, structure, or framework.

The dynamic interplay between a system and its environment is characteristic of an open system. In other words, the system influences, and is in turn affected by, factors outside its boundaries. Change occurs in both, and the give and take produced is often referred to as a dynamic equilibrium. In a closed system, the influence of the environment is sealed off from the system, and the only interplay is among elements within the system.

Recognition of the two major types of systems—open and closed—is important in general systems theory. Systems concepts embrace a point of view in dealing with complex phenomena that is perhaps more important than the methods of analysis suggested. This view focuses on primary goals, fundamental processes, and interrelations among essential elements rather than on expertise in substantive areas.

MAJOR ASPECTS OF THE SYSTEMS APPROACH

The systems approach encompasses such nonexclusive major elements as (1) systems analysis, (2) systems design, (3) systems engineering, (4) systems management, and (5) systems evaluation.

Systems analysis

According to Black, "systems analysis is undertaken with a view to supporting decisions as to the design, selection, or operation of a system."[8] Hitch

---

[6]Johnson et al., op. cit., p. 7.
[7]Ibid., p. 6.

[8]Guy Black, *The Application of Systems Analysis to Government Operations*, Washington, D.C.: National Institute of Public Affairs, 1966, p. 3.

defined systems analysis for the military as "defining military objectives, designing alternative systems to achieve these objectives, evaluating these alternatives in terms of their effectiveness and cost, questioning the objectives and other assumptions underlying the analysis, opening new alternatives, and establishing new military objectives."[9] Thus, it becomes a continuous cycle of events.

The definitions by Black and Hitch are accepted as standard in the field. They suggest systems analysis as a method of analyzing a situation or a problem by identifying objectives and available resources and determining alternatives, including the optimal one, in using resources to attain objectives. It is a way to structure a problem. Their broadly defined systems analysis is similar to what in this book is called the systems approach. A more limited definition is given to systems analysis in this book. Systems analysis is only one dimension of a total view of administration. It is an analysis or a review of systems and operation. It starts with a description of systems as they presently exist, analyzes interrelations among variables, relates the benefit that accrues to the cost incurred, and prepares organizational and systems data pertinent to decision making. Systems analysis emphasizes models as frameworks for observation and analysis of the interrelations among variables—particularly between input and output variables—and seeks to quantify or translate into mathematical models relations within a system.

Systems analysts are only one of a number of different kinds of analysts; there are psychoanalysts, social analysts, political analysts, educational analysts, military analysts, and economic analysts. Analysis implies a detailed examination of a complex whole to ascertain the fundamental elements and relations among component parts. The process of resolution or dissection may provide significant insight into a situation and thereby enhance the judgment of decision makers. It is not possible to gather all the data or to break down a complex issue into all possible facets. Most major and long-range planning-decision problems will continue to be resolved primarily on the basis of intuition and judgment of the top-level decision maker.

It should not be assumed that the results of analysis will automatically lead to the most prudent decision. Fisher[10] stressed the two extreme perceptions of the contributions of analysis to decision making. At one extreme, it is argued that long-range planning-decision problems are far more complex than the bright, young, inexperienced analysts realize and are beyond the current capabilities of the analytical art; the conclusion is that decisions should be made purely on the basis of intuition, judgment, and experience. This is the zero analysis position. At the other extreme, it is argued that all problems can be attacked in purely quantitative terms that will dictate the correct decision to be made in any situation. This is the one hundred percent analysis position. The optimum position lies somewhere between the two extreme perceptions of the power of analysis. Thus, even a relatively incomplete set of quantitative models and calculations of cost and utility can sharpen the intuition and judgment of the decision maker.

The most plausible perception of the

[9]C. J. Hitch, "Plans, Programs and Budgets of the Department of Defense," *Operations Research,* January–February 1963, p. 8.

[10]G. H. Fisher, "The Role of Cost-Utility Analysis in Program Budgeting," in David Novick, ed., *Program Budgeting,* Cambridge, Mass.: Harvard, 1965, pp. 67, 68.

analyst is as one who enhances the decision-making capabilities of top-level administrators by framing problems so that appropriate objectives and relevant important environments are presented in bold relief, by collecting and arranging data significant to the decision, by stipulating the alternatives and how each might be tested, and by outlining possible costs and benefits of alternative actions. He may even have the ingenuity to invent new systems. In view of the many unprogrammed decisions, and time and cost pressures that preclude complete objectivity, the intuition and judgment of the experienced executive remain important elements in decision making.

Systems management

Congressman Morse[11] of Massachusetts stated that systems management is a refreshing and most promising new approach to the solution of public problems. He pointed out that although the United States is a wealthy nation, its resources are not unlimited, and our decision makers must assess carefully where to expend them in the face of rising population and complex problems. He argued that the systems approach, which combines logic and the techniques of acquiring, organizing, and analyzing key information, is critically needed. He introduced legislation to create a National Commission on Public Management whose mandates are (1) to collect or analyze information about the application of systems technique to nondefense, nonspace, and public problems, and (2) to develop programs that would use these techniques to solve specific problems. Being alert and interested in such ap-

[11] F. B. Morse, "Private Responsibility for Public Management," *Harvard Business Review*, vol. 45, no. 2, March–April 1967, pp. 6–21, 178, 180.

proaches, the American Association of School Administrators in 1966 activated its Commission on Administrative Technology to direct attention to developments and technology in the management of industry, government, or the military which could be adapted and applied readily to the improvement of educational administration. This Commission reported its findings early in 1969.

Systems design and engineering

After key elements, or variables, within a model of a system have been identified and related to system objectives, the system must be designed to achieve objectives in the most expeditious manner. This is the challenge of systems engineering. Its main purpose is to structure work assignments of groups to facilitate activity, with a minimal amount of overlap, to attain goals. The idea is not simply to accept what exists and incorporate plans in obvious patterns, but to design the optimum system for achievement of objectives. Following design comes the challenge of implementation, which necessitates allocation of resources, human and material, to facilitate the attainment of objectives.

THE SYSTEMS APPROACH IN SCHOOL ADMINISTRATION TODAY

The operational behaviors, or administrative activities, consistent with the systems approach are:

1. Viewing the organization as a delivery system.
2. Defining performance-based long- and short-range objectives—that is, identifying the mission of the organization.
3. Recycling of objectives—that is,

refining and generating new ones to meet the demand of the times and reordering priorities.

4. Introducing and managing innovations. Recognition of change as normal in viable organizations operating within an environment in ferment and creation of methods to facilitate prudent change.

5. Searching for alternative strategies to utilizing resources to attain objectives.

6. Creating models to study part or all of the system and to resolve problems.

7. Utilizing quantitatively oriented tools and procedures in analysis of systems.

8. Dedicating a high priority in the time schedule of top-echelon administrators to planning and programming activities.

9. Employing interdisciplinary teams of specialists in problem analysis, new systems design, operations evaluation, and the like.

10. Considering coordination of the ever-growing number of educational specialists within the system as a matter of high-echelon concern.

11. Implementing sophisticated, objective, and scientifically oriented procedures in decision making.

The measure of whether the systems approach has permeated school administration is the degree to which any or all of the above characteristics of systems are now in practice. Hard data are lacking. The best that can be submitted are tentative conclusions and opinions based on review of the literature, involvement in conferences and less formal meetings, and individual study of systems. These experiences are not adequate substitutes for hard data and perhaps someday this shortcoming will be repaired.

If school administrators were asked whether they viewed the school as a network of interrelated subsystems, each responsible for accomplishing part of the overall task of converting educational inputs into outputs, most would say that they did so view the school, even if the full meaning of the question was not clear. The point is that such systems concepts as "the whole is greater than the sum of the parts," "an enterprise should be perceived as a cluster of interrelated activities," and "the school is a unified systematic vehicle" have a familiar and favorable ring to educators. The crucial test is whether the implications of the concepts are evident and whether skills have been developed in the utilization of approaches consistent with systems theory, particularly those based on the use of models, the generation of alternatives, and the use of sophisticated quantitative-analysis techniques.

In general, school administration in the 1970s stands on the threshold of awareness of the concepts and procedures related to systems. A growing comprehension of concepts is beginning to develop the capability in the utilization of systems techniques and procedures (such as MBO/R and PPBS) that presently characterize the field. There are exceptions to all generalizations, and some parts of the country are better versed in the systems approach than others. There is more talk about systems, and references to it in professional literature are on the rise. To suggest a growing awareness is not to imply that systems has cornered a major share of publication space or that there exists more than superficial knowledge about it.

At what level systems shall enter the practice of educational administration stimulates lively discussions. Conceptualization of systems as primarily quantitative analysis of operations means that only those aspects of administration that can be quantified, that is, amenable to mathematical analysis, will receive the attention of systems analysis. Carried to an extreme position, statistics becomes the queen of subjects to be studied in gaining systems capability.

One of the issues remaining to be resolved at this point in time is what kinds of experiences are necessary to prepare the systems analyst in school administration? Is he to be a mathematician first without study or experience in actual administration? Or is it better to select the quantitatively oriented and experienced administrator who is given further opportunity to sharpen or develop even greater quantitative analysis skills?

Problems related to transportation routing, determination of optimum school lunch menus, computation of the number of cafeteria serving lines needed in a secondary school, and inventory control lend themselves fairly easily to quantitative analysis. Mathematical techniques such as queuing theory and linear programming may allow computation of optimal solutions under given constraints for some types of administrative problems. These are not, however, the crucial problems plaguing administrators today. Effective administrators who are the products of traditional preparation programs with field experience have found adequate solutions to transportation, inventory management, and school food service challenges. Sophisticated mathematical analysis may increase effectiveness by about 10 or 15 percent, but this is a relatively low payoff for additional analytical costs. The really perplexing administrative problems are those related to accountability, militancy of the professional staff, race relations, and implied or actual dissent and disruption in educational institutions. Unless the level of entry of systems enables the school administrator to manage problems of this magnitude better, it is not likely to be considered by practitioners to have much relevance in educational administration. In other words, systems analysis will be relevant to the degree that it enables an administrator to deal with the really difficult challenges full of intangible factors, which resist quantification or mathematical analysis by existing knowledge. It is contended that systems can help to sharpen the judgment of the decision makers even though they are confronted with situations that are not amenable to sophisticated quantitative analysis. The framing of the decision situation or generation of alternatives is useful in sharpening intuition and judgment. Mathematical analysis may further refine but not replace human judgment.

More will be said in the next chapter about the management science tools such as MBO/R and PPBS which are related to systems analysis but which contribute more to a broader range of significant problems confronting administrators.

There is always the danger of generalizing from simple cases—governed by a single objective, clear-cut control over resources, simple output measurement, and easily quantifiable data—in which analysts with the aid of mathematical tools were able to identify the best course of action. The mature perceptions of Sisson[12] suggest that "as we study more and more complex systems, we find that the selection of the optimum or best course of action be-

[12]R. L. Sisson, "Applying Operational Analysis to Urban Educational Systems: A Working Paper," Philadelphia: Management Science Center, University of Pennsylvania, 1967, mimeographed.

comes nearly impossible, even with the aid of mathematical tools." He added: "Unfortunately, however, it is very unlikely that we can find a mathematical structure which will permit us to manipulate a symbolic model of a situation as complex as a school district. Mathematics, as advanced as it is, has not developed techniques which permit manipulation of thousands of highly interacting variables required to model a school district."

Fisher[13] commented, "In practically no case should it be assumed that the results of analysis will *make* the decision. The really interesting problems are just too difficult, and there are too many intangible (e.g., political, psychological, and sociological) considerations that cannot be taken into account in the analytical process, especially in a quantitative sense." Again, it is repeated that quantitative analysis is not synonymous with the systems approach; it is a subset within the total approach.

TOWARD RESOLUTION OF SEMANTIC DIFFICULTIES

Systems analysis may be confused with utilization of computers in schools. Computer-based electronic data processing has preempted the term to describe a position classification or a survey procedure to ascertain status of information needs and processing requirements. A person described more accurately as an "information-systems analyst" may carry instead the unqualified title of "systems analyst." In some cases the systems analyst in data-processing operations is no more than a highly skilled programmer or computer operator capable of identifying best procedures for inserting, ma-

nipulating, or retrieving information in a computer-based information system. Individuals outside EDP as well as within have been prone to equate systems analysis with what some previously called special studies of school operation. What some call a "systems analysis of the school" is very much the same as what was previously referred to as a school survey.

THE SYSTEMS APPROACH AS A CLUSTER OF TOOLS

The systems approach can be viewed as a cluster of tools, methods, procedures, and techniques employed in systems analysis, design, development, or management. The scientific method and the interdisciplinary team or task force provide the framework within which the tools, methods, and techniques are applied. Emphasis is placed on quantitative analysis through the use of such sophisticated mathematical techniques as linear programming (for determining optimal courses of action where many known variables and conditions are involved); queuing theory (for determining number of service facilities required); Monte Carlo technique (for simulating an experiment to determine some probabilistic property); game theory (for decision making in conflict and competitive situations); and network programs (the use of the program evaluation and review technique [PERT] or the critical-path method [CPM] to plan the progress of complex projects). The reliance on and the need for skills in mathematics should be apparent. There are other systems related techniques such as MBO/R and PPBS that include more than mathematics.

Linear programming can be used in school administration to optimize transportation systems, plan best use

[13]Fisher, op. cit.

of food resources for school lunches, and solve some types of personnel-allocation programs. Queuing theory can be used to determine how many serving lines are needed in the school cafeteria given the student arrival rate, the food service rate, and the length of the lunch period or how long a wait in line would be tolerated.

A conceptual framework must be prepared to specify, relate, and quantify the important variables. Not everyone has the ability to produce a valid and usable model of an educational system or subsystem. Administration becomes more amenable to research and study when models are developed which reduce a situation to those factors pertinent to understanding or control.

PERT (NETWORK ANALYSIS) AS A SYSTEMS TOOL

PERT (an acronym of program evaluation and review technique) is one of the developments in administrative technology based on systems that can improve the planning, controlling, and decision-making skills of school administrators. It has been employed in other managerial endeavors for at least a decade, and during the 1960s was referred to with increasing frequency among school administrators. Experience in other fields suggests that PERT as a process has much to offer a school administrator.[14] For example, PERT helped administrators predict likely snarls in a complex project and facilitated prudent use of resources that contributed much to making the Po-

laris missile operational at least two years ahead of schedule. It is presently employed by many governmental agencies, both military and nonmilitary, to cope with complex projects and is accepted by forward-looking administrators in the business world as well.

Definitions

PERT is a technique for evaluating and reviewing progress toward a stated goal. It is more than a postmortem analysis and more than a gauge of what remains to be done. It is an administrative device for initially facilitating planning and subsequently controlling complex projects. It enables an administrator to arrive at decisions in an objective fashion that will enable more prudent utilization of resources available for completion of a project in a given period of time. It is not a historical approach or a way of attacking on-going activities. It is a means of dealing with processes not previously attempted, an activity for which there is no experience to serve as a guide.

How and why it can contribute to these ends will be evident on examination of its basic procedures and operations. A word of caution is in order: PERT is no more a cure-all than any other administrative technique. It is a tool and nothing more. It takes a craftsman to know when, where, and how to employ a given tool. Doubtless, it was the demand for new administrative skills to make operational as rapidly as possible the ever-increasing number of inventions that gave rise to PERT. The method is particularly useful when new things or new programs are to be implemented. Its primary contribution is in dealing with so-called "once-through" projects rather than repetitive activities. We live in a time when a new curriculum project, a new federal grant, a new school-

[14]See D. L. Cook, *Program Evaluation and Review Technique: Applications in Education*, OE-12024, Cooperative Research Monograph No. 17, Washington, D.C.: GPO, 1966, for illustrations of PERT in school testing programs.

plant, a new educational program must be implemented in a relatively short time and with constraints on resources. PERT can facilitate greatly the smooth implementation of novel programs.

PERT is an administrative planning-control and decision-making tool based on a work breakdown of complex programs, assignments of sequence for performance of tasks, scheduling of interrelations, and computation of time required to accomplish activities so that the objective is completed within the resource and time constraints. It (1) begins with a work breakdown of a complex goal into individual components, (2) develops a flow-plan (network development) to show sequence used in performing various work units, (3) establishes schedules for interrelated work events, and (4) provides a means of analyzing the time dimension for completing individual work.

This should have a familiar ring, since successful school administrators have followed similar patterns in an informal manner. As long as the project is not too complex, it can be planned in the "well-organized head" of the successful school administrator. In this sense, PERT represents a formalized, verbalized, and sophisticated statement of an orderly approach for accomplishing a task. In moving beyond the informal, nonverbal stage, the technique becomes available to a much wider range of activities.

An organized attack on a complex project by breaking it down into interrelated and meaningful units is a familiar advantage of PERT. There is a mathematical dimension as well which will be explored in greater detail in subsequent paragraphs.

PERT is basically a process. All processes must be tied to some substantive content. The person knowledgeable in a general technique but ignorant of the fundamental context in which it is to be used can hope for only limited success. PERT is not a substitute for knowledge gained through the study and experience of the substantive problems confronting administrators. By the same token this process cannot be made operative simply by concentrating on the substantive knowledge in a given field. Effectiveness is based on comprehension of the nature of the PERT approach and of the knowledge of the fundamentals of the work to be "PERTed." It is easier for a school administrator to understand PERT than for a PERT expert to understand all the substantive problems confronting various types of administrations.

Essential elements of PERT

"Think backward," "think small," "think togetherness," and "think time" are slogans that can aid comprehension of PERT. You "think backward" in the sense that you start with the end product and move backward to enumerate the steps taken (or events realized) to reach the end product. The ultimate goal, be it a constructed and furnished schoolhouse, a published curriculum guide, or an on-going staff development conference, is kept in view at all times. Each individual step or "work package" related to it is identified. All complex projects are tackled a piece at a time. You "think backward" in the sense of retracing steps, to reach a goal.

You must be able to "think small enough" to define each of the individual work units or work activities necessary to achieve the ultimate goal. In a certain sense you "think small" while you keep the big end product in mind. The translation of a defensible goal into specific events and activities that will lead to it is a challenging, time-consuming, and most necessary step in PERT as well as other administrative responsibilities.

Particular events that signal the completion of a definable work unit are among the most essential elements of PERT. An event is a milestone or a definable and significant completed achievement. It is either the start or the completion of a task. In itself it is instantaneous, a finite point in time that requires no time or resources. Thus, final architectural drawings completed, interior walls painted, teachers hired, housing plans started, guide to the teaching of modern math completed represent significant, definable, and measurable events.

The accomplishment of an event requires involvement in some kind of activity. Activities, in contrast to events, take time and consume resources. Thus, the event previously called "final architectural plans completed" necessitated the activity of many architects and draftsmen using such resources as time to think, paper and pencil, consultant services, and perhaps a copying machine. Events and activities, therefore, are very important building blocks in the utilization of PERT. Here again one notices the importance of understanding the subject matter of the program to be PERTed.

"Think togetherness" suggests that no event stands by itself and no activity is an end in itself. Events are related in a sequential fashion. A given activity cannot take place until the event(s) leading to it have been accomplished. Thus, it is difficult to produce "completed final architectural drawings" before the following events have occurred: "architect employed," "educational specifications completed," "preliminary architectural drawings completed," and "preliminary architectural drawings approved." In PERT the sequence of events and activities is important.

Other approaches, such as the Gantt Milestone Charts, have been used for many years to ascertain progress toward the completion of a complex task. PERT is similar to the Gantt charts in that both record the occurrence of the significant event and measure the time to complete the activity leading to the event. PERT differs from the Gantt approach by indicating the sequential relation of events and activities. In the case of school-plant construction, the significant and definable event of "roof installed" cannot occur until other events such as supporting structural systems or walls have been completed. These in turn must wait until footings have been completed, and footings cannot be poured before the site has been purchased and before architectural and engineering plans have been completed.

"Think time" points to a significant constraint in PERT. The measurement of elapsed time for an activity leading from one event to another or of the slack time is a significant aspect of PERT. The time dimension helps to identify the critical path of work that leads to the goal, and this in turn is useful in allocating resources to various activities in the total program as well as in estimating whether work will be completed on schedule. Much of the usefulness of PERT would be destroyed if one failed to think of the time it takes to complete activities. Not all activities can be timed precisely. PERT is distinguished from other network modeling by its use of three estimates for the expected duration of an activity: (1) most likely time, (2) optimistic time, and (3) pessimistic time. An average or *expected elapsed time* can be calculated from the three time estimates by the formula $t_e = (a + 4m + b)/6$, where a is the optimistic time, m is the most likely time, and b is the pessimistic time.

The PERT network

A sequential pattern showing interrelated events and activities and culminating in the achievement of the end product is called the PERT network (or model, diagram, or schematic).[15] Network modeling is a more general classification of which PERT is one system. The PERT network is simply a diagram, sketch, or pattern that shows the events and activities, and the time between them, required to attain the ultimate goal. Standard symbols are employed; events are designated by circles, and activities by straight lines and arrows leading from one circular symbol for an event to another. Events represent the significant units of work

[15]See PERT Orientation and Training Center, *PERT Fundamentals*, vols. I and II, Washington, D.C.: GPO, 1963, for an excellent and comprehensive presentation of PERT concepts and techniques in programmed instruction format.

that must be accomplished if the end product is to be realized. Each specific milestone is numbered, and the number is inserted in the circle to facilitate reading of the PERT network. Thus, there is usually need for a legend describing the numbered events. The time it takes to complete an activity is noted above the activity line in the network. Figure 7–1 illustrates a PERT network.

The following information can be gained from Figure 7–1. Event 2 is dependent upon the realization of Event 1 and the activity between them. Event 2 is independent of the accomplishment of Events 3 and 4. Activities 1-3 and 1-4 are said to be parallel to activity 1-2. (An activity is identified by the event numbers connected by the activity.) This is not true in all cases; for example, activities 1-3 and 3-6 are series-connected and not parallel. Event 6 is dependent upon the completion of prior Events 2 and 3 as well as activities 2-6 and 3-6. The network terminal event is 8. As said before, a special list would be needed to describe the events.

FIGURE 7–1

A simple PERT network.

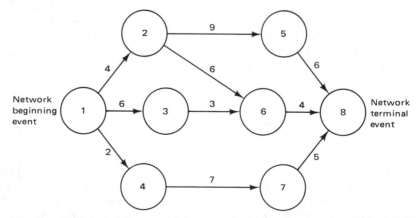

The time needed to accomplish activities is expressed in weeks or decimal fractions of weeks. In this particular case, no decimal fractions are used. Thus, 4 weeks are required to accomplish activity 1-2, 6 weeks to accomplish activity 2-6, and 7 weeks to accomplish activity 4-7. The time required to accomplish an activity is the "expected elapsed time" (t_e). This is an important PERT concept and useful in extracting more information from the network diagram.

An obvious ground rule of PERT is that an event cannot be completed until all activities leading to it have been completed. Event 6 is based upon the completion of Events 2 and 3 and two activities leading from them. Activity 1-2 requires 4 weeks and activity 2-6, 6 weeks. Therefore, if path 1-2-6 is followed, the activity time to accomplish Event 6 totals 10 weeks. On the other hand, activity 1-3 requires 6 weeks and activity 3-6, 3 weeks, so that if path 1-3-6 is followed, 9 weeks are needed to move from Event 1 to Event 6. It takes 1 week longer to reach Event 6 via path 1-2-6 than via path 1-3-6.

Computing earliest time. This brings us to another important PERT concept, namely, the "earliest time" for the completion of an event. This is symbolically designated as T_E. The earliest time is the longest time required for the execution of activities leading to an event. Accordingly, T_E for completion of Event 6 is 10 weeks, not 9 weeks. Stated in general terms, the earliest time an event can be completed is the longest time needed to reach that event through any path leading to it. Stated yet another way, the earliest time an event can be completed is equal to the summation of the expected elapsed time for each activity via the longest time path to the event. The earliest time implies no-sooner-than rather than the shortest time. Some writers refer to T_E as the earliest expected date. Computation of T_E is simplified greatly if there is only one path leading to an event.

The mathematical dimension of PERT allows certain computations that yield data useful in decision making about commitment of resources to certain activities. The mathematics involved are based on the arithmetic processes of addition, subtraction, and division. With simple mathematical manipulations, it is possible to determine such things as how long it takes to reach a network-ending event, where slack time is available in the project, and how to identify the critical path. Small networks, with 200 or less events, can be calculated manually. A computer can be used to save time and ensure accuracy when dealing with larger networks. A number of PERT computer programs are presently available.

Identifying the critical path. In Figure 7–1, Event 8 is the network-ending event. There are four paths to it. All start with Event 1 and can be identified as: path 1-2-5-8, path 1-2-6-8, path 1-3-6-8, and path 1-4-7-8. The T_E for completion of Event 8 is the sum of the t_e for each activity in any path leading to Event 8. T_E must be computed for each path. The following computations apply to path 1-2-5-8: 4 weeks to complete activity 1-2, 9 weeks for activity 2-5, and 6 weeks for activity 5-8. This is a total of 19 weeks for execution of all activities on path 1-2-5-8. The total activity time for path 1-2-6-8 totals 14 weeks; for path 1-3-6-8, 13 weeks; and for path 1-4-7-8, 14 weeks. It is apparent that the longest time path is 1-2-5-8 and, therefore, the T_E for Event 8 is 19 weeks.

These computations are related to the fundamental concept of critical path. The critical path is defined as the path which requires the longest time to progress from the network-beginning event to the network-ending event. Using Figure 7–1 and applying simple mathematics, it is apparent that 19 weeks are required to complete all activities along path 11-2-5-8 to reach Event 8. This is the longest time and, therefore, path 1-2-5-8 is the critical path in this particular network.

Computing slack time. The idea of slack time is valuable to administrators using PERT.[16] Slack time is more difficult to compute and explain than previous concepts because *two* other computations must be made before slack time can be obtained. The first is earliest time (T_E) and the second is latest allowable date (T_L). The computation of T_L begins with the T_E for the network-ending event. The mathematical manipulation works backward from the terminal to the beginning event because the T_E for the network-ending event is also its T_L. In other words, for Event 8, $T_E = T_L$. Computation of T_L cannot proceed unless the T_E is known for the network-ending event.

Reference to Figure 7–1 may make this clearer. Look at Event 5, and keep in mind that for Event 8 (the event that follows Event 5) $T_E = T_L$ and in this illustration is 19 weeks. The activity time (or expected elapsed time, t_e) between Events 5 and 8 is 6 weeks. The T_L for Event 5 is computed as follows: 19 weeks (the T_L for Event 8) minus 6 weeks (the t_e between Events 5 and 8) equals 13 weeks. The general rule is that the T_L for the event equals the T_L for the following

[16]For a more detailed analysis of PERT and an excellent programmed instruction approach to gaining PERT concepts and skills, *see Ibid.*

event minus the t_e between the two events. Note that in this particular case the T_L for Event 5 is equal to the T_E for Event 5: $T_L = T_E$.

Slack is equal to the difference between the T_L for a given event and the T_E for that same event: Slack time = $T_L - T_E$. For Event 5, 13 from 13 is 0, so the slack time available for the completion of Event 5 is 0 $(T_L = T_E)$.

This is not true for Event 6. That slack time is available is evident from the computation that starts backwards from the terminal event: 19 (the T_L for Event 8) minus 4 (the t_e between Events 6 and 8) is 15 (the T_L for Event 6). Since slack time = $T_L - T_E$ and the T_E for Event 6 is 10 weeks, 15 − 10 = 5. This means that the completion of Event 6 could occur 5 weeks later than the estimated earliest expected date for Event 6 and still not delay completion of Event 8 beyond the 19 weeks.

Event 3 is once removed from the network-ending event. It takes 3 weeks of activity after completion of Event 3 to realize Event 6. T_L for Event 6 was previously computed as 15. Subtracting the t_e of 3 weeks for activity 3–6 from 15 weeks (T_L for Event 6) yields 12 weeks as the T_L for Event 3. The T_E for Event 3 is 6 weeks. The slack time for Event 3 $(T_L - T_E)$ is 12 −6 = 6 weeks.

Use of PERT in decision making

The t_e for each activity, the T_E for each event, the T_L for each event, and the slack time for each event ($T_L - T_E$) in Figure 7–1 are computed and arranged in Table 7–1. Note that no slack (zero slack) is found for all points on the critical path. The critical path can also be defined as the path with the least amount of slack. This is the reason it is critical. Resources must be maintained for activities along the critical path. Some resources may be moved from events where slack time is available to events where there is none. In this manner, PERT can facilitate prudent decision making concerned with resource allocation and utilization.

It was stated that PERT is a powerful planning, control, and decision-making aid for administrators. Mathematical computations helped demonstrate why this is so. The network scheduling that shows the relation between events, what events are dependent upon other events, and the amount of time for the activity between the events enables administrators to make more prudent use of resources. It is apparent in this illustration that resources to complete Events 3 and 6 can be diverted to Events 2 and 5, which are along the critical path. Thus, manpower that might go to the completion of activity 1-3 can be switched to activity 1-2 for a time to ensure that Event 2 is completed on time since it is on the critical path, whereas Event 3 has a slack time of 6 weeks.

With PERT networks the administrator can produce a model of total operations and allocate resources necessary for the accomplishment of specific tasks on a mathematical basis.

PERT can also be viewed as a control device or a way to evaluate progress. Thus, if activity 1-2 takes longer than the expected elapsed time, then, unless additional resources are made available to reduce the time of activity leading to Event 5, the whole project will not meet the deadline. The value of PERT to contractors working on school buildings should be apparent. Whether the building will be completed on the scheduled date can be determined months in advance if the project has been PERTed. The number of weeks or days the project will be delayed can be computed with comparative certainty as well. A work-breakdown schedule in school-plant planning is shown in Table 7–2. Activity times are not shown.

The illustration of PERT use herein is the simplest, based on a one-time statement between events. This is more characteristic of the critical-path method (CPM). PERT networks may also involve situations where no definite time for an activity is known and

TABLE 7–1

COMPUTED t_e, T_E, T_L, AND SLACK TIME FOR THE PERT NETWORK DEPICTED IN FIGURE 7–1

Activities	t_e	T_E	T_L	$T_L - T_E$ (Slack time)
1-2	4	4	4	0
1-3	6	6	12	6
1-4	2	2	7	5
2-5	9	13	13	0
2-6	6	10	15	5
3-6	3	9	15	6
4-7	7	9	14	5
5-8	6	19	19	0
6-8	4	14	19	5
7-8	5	14	19	5

Italic indicates critical path (Events 1–2–5–8).

hence pessimistic time, optimistic time, and most likely time are estimated. Likewise, the brief review here was confined to PERT/time; PERT/cost is less well developed and too complex to be presented here.

INPUT-OUTPUT CONCEPTS

The terms "inputs" and "outputs" are associated with the systems approach. Simply stated, inputs are the array of resources of various types made available to achieve certain ends. Outputs are the products actually created by the system, and not simply those hoped for. The system is conceptualized as a converter, that is, a way of acting upon inputs to yield given outputs in an efficient or inefficient, effective or ineffective manner.

If an input is to be compared with an output, the unit of measurement must be the same or comparable. Thus, money is one common denominator for comparison—how much money goes into the system and how much is produced. A problem arises when inputs (teachers' salaries, cost of supplies, expenditures for operation) can be measured in terms of money but outputs (how much a pupil has learned, how much society has been improved) cannot.

Typically, it is hoped that some inputs, such as pupils, will be modified in some way when related to other

TABLE 7–2

WORK BREAKDOWN SCHEDULE FOR SCHOOL-PLANT PLANNING

	Event no.	Event described
Network terminal event	25	Start school-plant construction
	24	Contracts awarded
	23	Bids accepted
	22	Bids opened and evaluated
	21	Bids advertised
	20	Specifications and final drawings approved
	19	Start specifications and final drawings
	18	Preliminary drawings approved
	17	Start preliminary drawings
	16	Educational specifications completed
	15	State educational specifications
	14	School site purchased
	13	Start search for school site
	12	Architect hired
	11	Start search for architect
	10	Bond vote approved
	9	Start bond election campaign
	8	Bond vote authorized
	7	School survey completed
	6	Start financial survey
	5	Start plant survey
	4	Start education program survey
	3	Survey team hired
	2	Board approval of facilities study
Network beginning event	1	Start school-plant planning

system inputs, such as teachers and equipment. The conversion of some inputs into a desired output is significant. Being able to produce certain outputs is the fundamental reason for institutions such as schools.

A mechanical illustration of a heating system may help to clarify the input and output concepts. Fuel oil is an input. The objective is not to have fuel oil coming out of registers, but heat. The input of fuel oil is related to the desired output of heat by using some common energy measures such as BTU or calorie. How the conversion takes place, particularly its efficiency and safety, is significant. The total heating system requires fuel, a fuel-introduction subsystem, a fuel-burning subsystem, a heat-transfer subsystem (a way to heat air or water), a heat-distribution subsystem, a temperature-measurement and control subsystem; and perhaps even a human-control subsystem to assure proper ordering of fuel and setting of the temperature-control subsystem.

SYSTEMS CAPABILITY IN EDUCATION

The systems approach places unusual emphasis on the determination of both short-range and long-range objectives which are phrased in such manner that they can be operationalized—that is, translated into operationally meaningful activities capable of implementation and subsequent evaluation. Closely related to this is the planning function, likewise accorded high priority among administrative activities. Under the systems approach, the administrator continually keeps his eye on objectives, sensing subtle changes, and is the high-level planning officer in the organization.

The greater the complexity of an organization, the more likely it will have to depend upon the services of a variety of specialists. This growing complexity suggests that under the systems approach the top-level administrator becomes a coordinator of activities executed by the technical specialists in teaching, pupil services, or technical administrative activities.

Under the systems approach the administrator is a strategist with primary responsibility for goals, planning, and coordination; he is not simply a tactician engaged in day-by-day operating decisions. This is not to say that every administrator must master the tools, methods, and techniques of systems analysis, design, development, or management. Rather it is argued that the administrative staff must acquire a greater number and variety of talents. The systems approach is characterized by reliance on the scientific method employed by an interdisciplinary team capable of working within the scientific framework and with the tools, methods, and techniques associated with systems. An important further condition is the ability to construct models of systems or subsystems under study. Model building is an art, a way of thinking, rather than a science.

Striving toward excellence in the administration of modern school systems requires the addition of analysts to the professional staff to enhance the decision-making capabilities of top-level administrators. The primary contribution of analysts is to frame problems in such a manner as to reveal essential objectives and relevant important environments for decision making. This may entail collection and arrangement of data significant to decision making, definition of alternatives, determination of how each alternative can be tested, and outline of possible cost and benefits of alternative actions. The analyst does not substitute his decision-framing capabilities for the decision-making functions of top-level administrators. The intuition and judgment of the experienced executive remains important.

Systems capability is a blending of new talents and old. It calls for creative abilities in the development of models and sophistication in the use of appropriate mathematical techniques. Not everyone can be a systems analyst.

The systems approach is likely to flourish where certain conditions prevail. A condition of readiness precedes learning and utilization of the strange set of practices. Some of the more pressing improvements in education needed to create readiness for, and stimulate the use of, systems are:

1. The preparation of a more definitive set of educational objectives. Existing statements of educational goals are much too broadly conceived. Educational goals that can be defined in performance terms will be necessary to further systems capability in school administration. This tremendous and time-consuming task will take at least two and more likely five years of diligent effort.

2. Recognition of the need for the generation and use of models of at least parts of school operations. Few models of education as a whole or of its subsystems exist, and few administrators think in such terms. Those with a base in general and educational administration are in the best position to generate useful models. To do this, professionals in the field must acquire a better comprehension of the model-development process.

3. Development of quantitative reasoning and analysis capabilities. Powerful mathematical tools and models can be used only by those with special skills and ability. Mathematics and economic-analysis concepts have not heretofore been considered important

in the preparation of special types of administrators or administrative assistants. The issue arises of where school administrators go to recruit talent who have analysis competence. The short-term response may be to search for such personnel in other fields, such as economics or mathematics. The long-term answer is to redesign preparation programs to meet the need for new specializations in administration.

4. Greater emphasis on generating alternative means to utilizing resources to attain objectives. Generating many ways to approach a solution to a problem and analysis of consequences of each can enhance the decision-making capabilities of administrators.

5. A significant increase in administrative staff strength in local school districts for planning and systems analysis. Present numbers in the superintendency are hardly adequate to cope with existing operational problems. This is not a call for more of the same, but for the addition of administrative specialists who can generate alternatives, who can frame problems to facilitate prudent decision making, and who have the concepts and skills in utilization of systems techniques and procedures. Such specialized personnel represent extensions or new creations of administrative planning and analysis staffs in school districts.

6. Better means for dissemination of systems concepts and techniques. It is highly desirable that systems concepts, tools, and procedures be disseminated in education as rapidly as possible. It is the author's opinion that systems capability will help school administrators cope with complexity and will facilitate prudent change within the system. A massive in-service effort must reinforce some significant changes in professional-preparation programs for school administrators.

There must be an effort to move

beyond the confusion about and limited awareness of the systems approach that presently characterizes school administration. It must be a task-force effort of local school administrators acting in concert with specialized representatives of institutions of higher learning, federal agencies, and professional societies.

An overall view of systems approach concepts, procedures, and implications is sketched in Figure 7–2.

SUMMARY

The systems approach to educational administration was discussed with increasing frequency in the late 1960s. The systems approach is a way of harnessing theory to action problems facing administrators. It is a way of thinking about problems, a set of concepts, a collection of quantitatively oriented tools of analysis, and a group of procedures or techniques. It may or may not include utilization of computers. It is an extension of science in administration.

Its origins lie in fields other than education. Its beginnings, for all practical purposes, can be traced to the teaming of the scientist with the military experts in attacking the problems of warfare during the early years of World War II. Operations research, one of the main components of the systems research, scored spectacular successes during World War II. Operations research is basically a multidisciplinary task-force approach to problem solving based on scientific procedures.

A system is a unit with defined boundaries and endowed with an array of interrelated resources dedicated to achievement of stated objectives. Emphasis is placed on interrelations and recognition that a change in one part or element has an impact on others. The phrase employed by the Gestalt psychologists in the 1920s and 1930s, that the whole is greater than the sum of its parts, is used frequently in systems discussions. The school is viewed as a network of interrelated subsystems, each responsible for accomplishing part of the overall task of converting inputs into desired outputs. This is in contrast to the view of the school system as a conglomeration of separate elements—a view implied by those who would reform it by changing only one element within it.

General systems theory is an effort to produce an overarching framework that embraces concepts and phenomena common to many disciplines. It is a reaction to the fragmentation resulting from specialization and the focusing on subparts of the total knowledge at the expense of the patterns or relations in a network of subsystems.

Systems with boundaries that are impermeable to factors in the environment, that is, outside the boundaries, are said to be closed systems. If interplay or interchange is possible between the system and its environment, the system is open.

The systems approach includes systems analysis, systems design, systems engineering, systems management, and systems evaluation. Systems analysis is subject to many interpretations. To some it is the same as the systems approach, but for the purposes of this book it is restricted to the type of inquiry answerable to quantitative analysis. The systems approach is a way of analyzing a problem by identifying objectives and resources and determining alternatives in using resources to attain objectives. Analysis will not automatically lead to prudent decisions, for the really significant situations confronting administrators have too many intangibles that resist

FIGURE 7–2

Concepts, procedures, and implications of the systems approach.

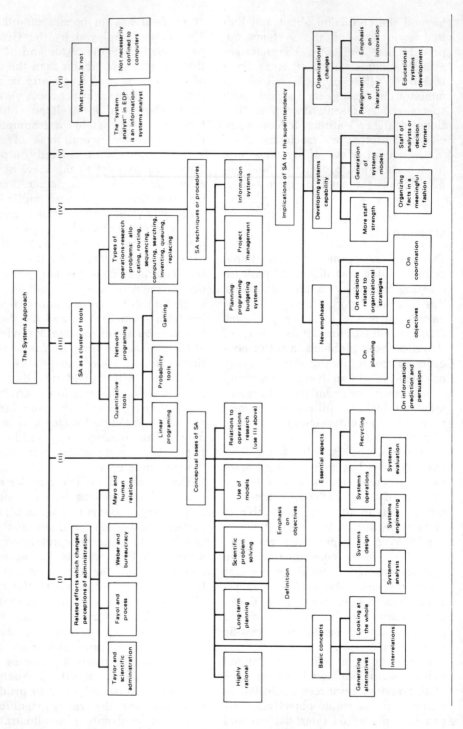

quantitative analysis. It can, however, be used to sharpen the intuition and judgment of the decision maker.

The salient features of the systems approach are:

1. Viewing schools as delivery systems
2. Using performance-based objectives
3. Refining and recycling objectives to determine new priorities
4. Emphasizing the importance of introducing and managing innovations
5. Searching for alternative strategies
6. Creating models for the study of problems
7. Utilizing quantitatively-oriented tools to analyze problems
8. Dedicating much time to planning
9. Employing interdisciplinary teams to resolve problems
10. Placing high priority on coordinating roles
11. Implementing rational decision-making procedures

The systems approach may enter education via the problems least vital to its survival, for many such problems are amenable to operations analysis. To make a significant impact, the systems approach must be used in the major policy decisions to improve the decision making capabilities of administrators.

Systems may be confused with computer-based electronic data processing. The systems analyst in data processing may be little more than a skilled programmer or data-flow analyst. Cost-effectiveness analysis, another systems technique, may be misinterpreted as cost analysis or confused with the practice of selecting educational program content on the basis of what costs less.

Models are important in systems studies. Many systems concepts are not new, but the clustering of such concepts and the use of sophisticated mathematical models are new. Mathematical techniques such as linear programming, queuing theory, Monte Carlo techniques, and game theory are part of the operations research repertoire of analytical tools. Network programming is a less mathematical approach to planning and assessing progress in complex projects.

PERT (program evaluation and review technique), a development in administrative technology related to network programming, may be related to the critical-path method (CPM). The term PERT was popularized by the military, particularly the Navy, in the development of the ballistic fleet missile system known as Polaris. CPM has been used in industry. It differs from PERT only in that seldom if ever does it consider expected elapsed time in terms of pessimistic time, most likely time, or optimistic time.

The systems approach in education must await preparation of a more definitive set of educational objectives, acquisition of skills in the generation of models of the situation under study, employment of specially prepared personnel with skills in quantitative reasoning and analysis, addition of personnel to administrative staffs, and development of better methods for the dissemination of systems concepts and techniques.

QUESTIONS

1. What is a system?
2. How does an open system differ from a closed one?

3. What is operations research?
4. Where is PERT most appropriate in educational administration?
5. Why are models important in the systems approach?
6. What are the essential contributions of the systems approach to educational administration?
7. What techniques or procedures are related to the systems approach?
8. What is operations analysis?
9. What are the essential elements of cost-utility analysis?
10. What changes must take place in educational administration before the systems approach can be implemented?

SELECTED REFERENCES

Black, Guy, *The Application of Systems Analysis to Government Operations,* Washington, D.C.: National Institute of Public Affairs, 1966.

Churchman, C. W., R. L. Ackoff, and E. L. Arnoff, *Introduction to Operations Research,* New York: Wiley, 1967.

Cook, D. L., *Program Evaluation and Review Technique: Applications in Education,* OE-12024, Cooperative Research Monograph No. 17, Washington, D.C.: GPO, 1966.

Fisher, G. H., "The Role of Cost-Utility Analysis in Program Budgeting," in David Novick, ed., *Program Budgeting,* Cambridge, Mass.: Harvard, 1965.

Haberstroh, C. J., "Organization Design and Systems Analysis," in J. G. March, ed., *Handbook of Organizations,* Chicago: Rand McNally, 1965.

Johnson, R. A., F. E. Kast, and J. E. Rosenzweig, *The Theory and Management of Systems,* 2nd ed., New York: McGraw-Hill, 1967.

Morse, F. B., "Private Responsibility for Public Management," *Harvard Business Review,* vol. 45, no. 2, March–April 1967, pp. 6–21, 178, 180.

Novick, David, ed., *Program Budgeting,* Cambridge, Mass.: Harvard, 1965.

O'Toole, J. F., Jr., *Systems Analysis and Decision Making in Education,* Santa Monica, Calif.: System Development Corporation, 1965.

PERT Orientation and Training Center, *PERT Fundamentals,* vols. I and II, Washington, D.C.: GPO, 1963.

Shuchman, A., *Scientific Decision Making in Business,* New York: Holt, Rinehart & Winston, 1963.

8

EMERGING DEVELOPMENTS: MANAGEMENT SCIENCE, ORGANIZATION DEVELOPMENT, AND CONFLICT MANAGEMENT

Schools are an integral part of a dynamic society, and their administration reflects the pressures and changes of the institution served. Educational administration has never remained static for very long. Emerging developments of the past decade testify to the fact that new management systems and new perceptions of administration are moving into educational administration at a faster rate than ever before. The theory movement in and the systems approach to administration were the comparatively new concepts introduced in earlier editions and continued in this one. Like management science concepts and techniques to be presented in this chapter these sets of ideas were generated outside of and eventually adapted to educational administration. It is apparent that the practicing administrator is committed to a professional lifetime of learning to acquire the new competencies demanded during future points in time.

Organization development (OD) is just beginning to create interest. Unfortunately, not everyone using the term interprets it the same way. Not so with conflict. The problem here is how to diagnose it, how to manage it,

and how to resolve it. After the disruptions of the 1960s, administrators have come to recognize conflict as a signature of the times and accept the importance of conflict management competencies.

MANAGEMENT SCIENCE

It is easy to confuse management science that came into being in the past decade and scientific management that has been around since the turn of the century. Scientific management focused on shop-level problems of production, dealing more with organizing individual work tasks to enable them to proceed toward completion in a most efficient fashion. Management science, in turn, is concerned with the organization as a whole and management in the broadest rather than narrowest perspective. It has more to offer to the executive level whereas scientific management is confined to the first line supervisory levels. Management science seeks to aid managers at various levels to make "decision making more explicit, more systematic, and *better* by using scientific methodology, principally mathematics and statistics."[1] It is closely related to operations research and the systems approach and can be considered an extension of these efforts to provide a more rational base to decision making and other administrative actions. The management scientist is typically the university-based expert on administration, and the manager is the practitioner grappling with real-world problems rather than in the comfort of an ivy-covered tower. The management scientist generates the new techniques that hopefully can be put into practice.

Grayson noted the gulf between the professor types who use sophisticated approaches to tackle relatively minor "nonexistent management problems" with "over-kill tools" and the practitioner types who "make and implement decisions, largely by rough rules of thumb and intuition."[2] As a result the contributions of management science to the improvement of management practices has been relatively small as yet.

Grayson cited some of the reasons why the tools of management science are underutilized even by those with good training and understanding in it.[3]

1. "Management scientists simply do not sufficiently understand the constraint of time on decision making, and particularly on decisions that count."
2. Management scientists continue "to construct models that call for substantial investments in design and data construction and most data are not in the forms that most models call for."
3. Management scientists lack the direct experience in power, politics, and

change resistance among people in the organization which militate against use of sophisticated decision tools.
4. Management scientists operate in a long response time environment, a luxury practitioners don't enjoy in situations which demand immediate responses.
5. The simplifying assumptions in the management science problems divorce their approaches from reality.

He called for the closing of the cultural gap between the world of management thought and management practice.

Some management science tools more closely related to quantitative analysis were identified in the previous chapter. Others such as PPBS and MBO/R will be reviewed in greater detail in the paragraphs that follow.

Program budgeting or PPBS

What is called PPBS by some and program budgeting by others traces its origins to the mid-1950s but its popularity in actual practice to the early 1960s. By the late 1960s these management science concepts were being adapted to the administration of educational institutions. The acronym PPBS is used more often in the literature than program budgeting. It translates into planning-programming-budgeting system. The first three letters represent processes and the last designates that those processes are integrated into a system. What is called PPBS will be discussed in Chapter 23 as well because the word budgeting stands out and the assumption is made that this is primarily a fiscal management tool, or merely a new way to prepare budget documents.

This writer has criticized the popular acronym as being incomplete because it placed the emphases on

[1]C. Jackson Grayson, Jr., "Management Science and Business Practice," *Harvard Business Review,* vol. 51, no. 4, July-August 1973, pp. 41–48.
[2]Ibid.
[3]Ibid.

processes rather than outputs.[4] The system is more precisely identified as PPBADERS, that is, planning, programming, budgeting, analyzing, deciding, evaluating, recycling system. Each of these needs further explanation:

1. *Planning:* The initial phase is more appropriately identified as a determination of goals and objectives. It is the output of planning, that is, the preparation of a set of objectives for the long and short range, that is of importance and not the process of planning per se.
2. *Programming:* This is the translation of objectives into a series of interrelated activities. In other words, the alternative strategies and related functions that contribute to the achievement of an objective are clustered and identified as a program. There can be no programs without objectives. A familiar dodge or misinterpretation of this process is the classification of activities into the traditional science program, English program, etc., without stipulating the objectives to be pursued. Programming is a frequently misunderstood dimension of this system.
3. *Budgeting:* In this step the fiscal and nonfiscal resources required to fulfill the demands of a program and its objectives are identified. It is *not* the budget document preparation stage which comes later. It would be better identified as the resource utilization plan for a program.
4. *Analyzing:* The planning, programming, and budgeting are accomplished to set up the crucial process

of analysis. Each of the alternatives are analyzed in terms of the costs (resources to be consumed) and benefits or effectiveness level in achieving an objective. There can be no analysis without specification of alternatives, and, of course, no alternatives unless objectives are known. Here is where the quantitative analysis tools are useful in PPBS.

5. *Deciding:* In the writer's opinion this is what PPBS is all about, namely, to help administrators make more prudent resource allocation decisions. One of the alternatives, with resource use specified and analyzed, is selected as the future course of action. The program budget document is prepared after decisions rendered as to alternatives to be pursued.
6. *Evaluating:* At a subsequent point in time the decisions made are appraised in terms of whether actual outcomes lived up to prior expectations.
7. *Recycling:* This is the built-in self-correcting phase that leads to further refinement. It is the feedback of evaluative data into the system and repeating all phases to refine objectives, programs, etc., and thus improve practices in subsequent years.

The writer has a preference for the acronym RADS, that is, identifying this management approach as the Resource Allocation Decision System. The idea behind it is that this is a decision system that is utilized by all levels and types of managers. It is not confined to school business managers alone. The focus is on particular kinds of decisions, namely, those related to how the limited resources of the school shall be allocated among the

[4]Stephen J. Knezevich, *Program Budgeting (PPBS)*, Berkeley, Cal.: McCutchan, 1973, chap. 1.

many and oft-times competing purposes of education. In other words, PPBS applied to schools is a decision technology concerned with the identification, analysis, and appraisal of public school expenditure alternatives in and through the application of the logic of economics.

Whether PPBS is new depends on whether one looks at some elements or the way the total system is put together. Thus, cost benefit analysis was in use long before PPBS appeared. Organizing expenditures in terms of program objectives has long been recommended. In education there has been a tendency to relate expenditures to broad educational functions, such as instruction, rather than simply to objects. With the PPBS, however, the functional-character classification "instruction" is much too broad and is not related closely enough to output categories. Nor is it appropriate to state simply how much is allocated to, say, mathematics instruction. The level of mathematical skills gained per unit of initial or additional resource allocation becomes important. The PPBS differs from the usual unit-cost analysis and from the allegedly scientific efficiency approach that attempts to determine what to teach on the basis of what costs the least. The fundamental idea behind the PPBS is what additional degree of effectiveness is gained from a unit increase in resource allocation. It is similar to the marginal-analysis concepts of economics. In short, PPBS was developed by economists at the RAND Corporation for the U.S. government. A number of existing techniques were melded into a new system. It is the system and not the individual components that are new.

It was the federal government, particularly through the Department of Defense, that popularized PPBS in the early 1960s. It has since spread to state and local governments as well as schools. A significant federally supported project of the Research Corporation of the Association of School Business Officials and Dade County, Florida schools in the late 1960s helped disseminate interest in PPBS in the schools.[5]

How many school districts are presently implementing PPBS depends upon how this management science technique is viewed. Some suggest that 387 school districts were implementing PPBS in the early 1970s, and others suggest 800 to 1000 were. The writer has identified about 500 school districts claiming to operate in the PPBS Mode in 1974. If it were demanded that all dimensions of the comprehensive PPBADERS model had to be in operation before laying claim to operating in the PPBS Mode, then few if any school districts could be said to be employing PPBS. An undetermined number have demonstrated an interest in it and are experimenting with some phase of it.

The introduction of PPBS into a school district requires a management strategy. A more realistic strategy would be an evolutionary one that would call for the implementation of PPBS in one part of the school district during a single fiscal year and then add other parts of the district as personnel competencies are made available. PPBS is not without its critics. Some extremist groups have attacked it as a mysterious and nefarious activity. There have been other and more rational criticisms of its shortcomings. Nonetheless its proponents are numerous and all indications support the notion that the decision system will

[5]W. H. Curtis, ed., *Educational Resources Management System*, Chicago: Research Corporation, Association of School Business Officials, 1971, p. 362.

spread to more school districts during the 1970s as special competencies in it are acquired.

MANAGEMENT-BY-OBJECTIVES-AND-RESULTS (MBO/R)

MBO/R took its rise in the private sector of business and industrial management at about the same time PPBS began in the public sector of government administration. Its basic concepts are traced to the writings of Peter Drucker and Douglas McGregor. It is a systems-oriented technique and is compatible with and complementary to PPBS. Both stress the importance of objectives for the management of educational institutions.

The large volume of writing about MBO/R in business and industry reveals that the term may be used in different ways and that its full meaning continues to evolve. Interest in this management science technique did not spread to educational institutions until the 1970s, or about four or five years later than the interest education showed in PPBS.

Most of the references to this system prior to about 1970 used the acronym MBO rather than MBO/R. It can be argued that the "R" (for results) is redundant if a strict interpretation of the "O" (for objectives) is adhered to. It has been noted, however, that in practice some interpret MBO to imply the generation of statements of objectives and little more. An objective may be defined as a statement of intent to achieve something at some future point in time. In other words, the question "what are your objectives?" can be interpreted to query "what is it that you hope to accomplish at some future point in time?" In the sense the "R" becomes redundant, because a result and an accomplishment are similar. The writer's preference for MBO/R is based on the contention that the system has at least two major components: management with objectives and management for results. After the generation of statements of objectives it is imperative to design and operate a results management subsystem to insure that the organization remains locked onto objectives.

There are two major points of emphasis or interpretation of MBO/R in the literature. One is the human relations orientation of MBO/R and the other the systems orientation. Within the broad human relations classification there are at least four subsets, namely, MBO/R as a results oriented administrator appraisal strategy; MBO/R as a motivation strategy; MBO/R as an administrator development strategy; and MBO/R as a special type of sensitivity training effort.

The most popular conceptualization of MBO/R in educational systems today is that it is a unique approach to administrator appraisal. Most schools that claim to implement MBO/R view it as a system to appraise its principals and other administrators, a fact that may generate resistance to MBO/R among such personnel. The unique dimension is that emphasis in evaluation is placed on objectives satisfied or results achieved and hence, the name results-oriented appraisal. This emphasis may also lead to defining administrative positions by objectives to be achieved rather than functions to be performed. The traditional approach to evaluation placed stress on traits or other inputs rather than outputs. A more extensive review of administrator appraisal is presented in the final chapter.

The use of MBO/R as a leadership strategy to motivate administrative personnel toward greater productivity represents an exacting dimension. The key to this motivation strategy is jointly determined objectives for each administrator. Each objective should be achievable, leading to a better understanding of what is expected of the administrator and what he contributes to the organization. It places emphasis on internal motivators of personnel such as a feeling of achievement or pride in accomplishment and self-actualization rather than pecuniary rewards alone. Most business and industrial concerns and practically all school systems have either avoided or found it very difficult to operationalize this dimension of MBO/R.

Closely related to the above is the concept of MBO/R as managerial development by objectives. The four subsets of the human relations conceptualizations of MBO/R are interrelated and overlap to some degree; they are not exclusive categories. The major emphasis here is to identify what competencies are required by administrative personnel to increase their productivity. Professional development programs are then designed with very specific objectives to help the administrator gain the new competencies or extend the proficiency level of those possessed.

Perhaps somewhat far out is the sensitivity training conceptualization of MBO/R. It may be considered an extension of the motivation or professional development dimensions. To discover what turns a person on it is useful to know or to become sensitive to the values he holds dear. This focus for the sensitivity training gives it a narrow interpretation and gains a utilitarian function.

The systems-oriented conceptualization of MBO/R does not neglect the human-relations concerns. Rather it broadens the ideas to encompass all aspects of the organization and not its people alone. This is a more recent interpretation in the evolutionary development. The entire organization is viewed as a goal-seeking mechanism. MBO/R is a device for overall planning and control of all dimensions of the organization.

The general systems model of MBO/R is shown in Figure 8–1. The process starts with identification of organizational goals which leads to setting first division then individual objectives consistent with these goals. At Step 7 in Figure 8–1 there is an assessment of the feasibility of the performance objective calling for a recycling back to Step 3 if no performance objective is found feasible in terms of time, money, or other constraints. Managing *with* the objectives starts thereafter at Step 8 with the identification of alternative strategies leading to development of work plans and tasks at Step 11. The results management phase covers Steps 12 to 14 and includes plans for monitoring operations to make sure the organization stays on target as well as evaluating and auditing the actual results. The refining and self-correcting mechanism is built in with the recycling phase noted as Step 15, which begins the process all over again.

MBO/R has relatively little in common with PPBS when MBO/R is conceptualized as a personnel appraisal or personnel management system. The general systems model of MBO/R brings it much closer to PPBS. PPBS places more emphasis on the analysis of resource use patterns, which is relatively informal in MBO/R. On the other hand the manner in which objectives are generated as well as the results management phases are more sophisticated in MBO/R than in PPBS.

MBO/R is not management by any type of objectives. The quality of objectives and the manner in which they are generated are crucial to the man-

FIGURE 8–1

General Systems MBO/R model.

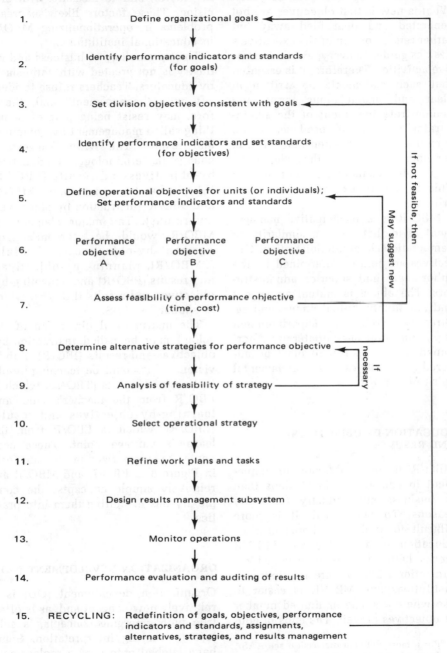

1.   Define organizational goals

2.   Identify performance indicators and standards
                      (for goals)

3.   Set division objectives consistent with goals

4.   Identify performance indicators and set standards
                     (for objectives)

5.   Define operational objectives for units (or individuals);
        Set performance indicators and standards

6.   Performance   Performance   Performance
      objective   objective   objective
         A   B   C

7.   Assess feasibility of performance objective
                 (time, cost)

8.   Determine alternative strategies for performance objective

9.   Analysis of feasibility of strategy

10.   Select operational strategy

11.   Refine work plans and tasks

12.   Design results management subsystem

13.   Monitor operations

14.   Performance evaluation and auditing of results

15.   RECYCLING: Redefinition of goals, objectives, performance
                  indicators and standards, assignments,
                  alternatives, strategies, and results management

If not feasible, then

May suggest new

If necessary

agement system. Likewise "know your objectives" is a statement that predates MBO/R by hundreds of years. What is new is that objectives are not generated and then filed away but rather remain on top of the executive's desk as guides to everyday administrative activities. Therefore, it is essential that such statements be written in clear and unambiguous terms and demonstrate the intent of the administrator to achieve, produce, or do something. Other important criteria for objectives is that they should be measurable, challenging, and realistic.[6] This is not an exhaustive listing of criteria.

MBO/R is a participative management style that bears a similarity to democratic school administration. Objectives are jointly determined by the subordinate and superior administrators. The object is mutual agreement and not simply mutual understanding. Directives from the superintendent stipulating that her unilaterally determined objectives for all must be adhered to violates the fundamental spirit of MBO/R.

EDUCATION-BY-OBJECTIVES-AND-RESULTS

MBO/R is more difficult to implement in educational institutions than in business and industry for many reasons. To begin with it is more difficult to apply to schools because education is a service and MBO/R works better in product-oriented organizations. Schools are multipurpose institutions and MBO/R is easier to use where a single or limited number of objectives prevail. The ends of edu-

[6]For a more detailed discussion see AASA National Academy for School Executives, *Management by Objectives and Results*, Arlington, Va.: The Academy, 1973, pp. 42–44.

cation are more difficult to define, to obtain agreement upon from the public in general, and to measure with precision. These factors likewise create problems in operationalizing MBO/R in educational institutions.

The terminology of business and industry is not greeted with enthusiasm by educators. Teachers refuse to identify with "management" and, therefore, may resist being part of something called management by objectives and results. The writer suggests a change in terminology to education-by-objectives-and-results (EBO/R). EBO/R[7] has two components: MBO/R and IBO/R (instruction-by-objectives-and-results). The major elements of MBO/R would be: personnel-management-by-objectives-and-results (PMBO/R), planning-by-objectives-and-results (PBO/R) and budgeting-by-objectives-and-results (BBO/R), which is similar to PPBS.

The instructional dimension of the school may be called instruction-by-objectives-and-results (IBO/R). Subdivisions of it could be teaching-by-objectives-and-results (TBO/R), which is EBO/R from the teacher's side, and learning-by-objectives-and-results (LBO/R), which is EBO/R from the learner's vantage point. These concepts are summarized in diagram form in Figure 8–2. EBO/R and MBO/R are relatively simple concepts; the complexity lies in putting them into practice.

ORGANIZATION DEVELOPMENT (OD)

Organization development (OD) is a relatively new concept and, as is often true with emerging concepts, is subject to varying interpretation. Some have latched onto it as a replacement

[7]Ibid.

FIGURE 8–2

Education-by-Objectives-and-Results (EBO/R): Managerial and Instructional Components

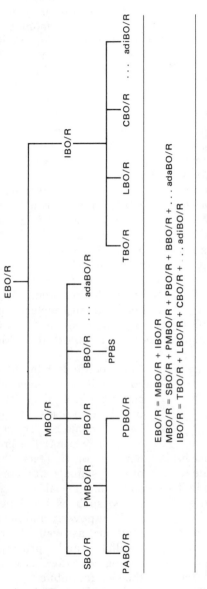

EBO/R = MBO/R + IBO/R
MBO/R = SBO/R + PMBO/R + PBO/R + BBO/R + . . . adaBO/R
IBO/R = TBO/R + LBO/R + CBO/R + . . adiBO/R

Where:
EBO/R = Education-by-Objectives-and-Results
MBO/R = Management-by-Objectives-and-Results
SBO/R = Supervision-by-Objectives-and-Results
PMBO/R = Personnel Management-by-Objectives-and-Results
PABO/R = Personnel Appraisal-by-Objectives-and-Results
PDBO/R = Position Description-by-Objectives-and-Results
PBO/R = Planning-by-Objectives-and-Results
BBO/R = Budgeting-by-Objectives-and-Results

PPBS = Planning-Programming-Budgeting System
adaBO/R = "Any dimension of administration"-by-
　　　　　Objectives-and-Results
IBO/R = Instruction-by-Objectives-and-Results
TBO/R = Teaching-by-Objectives-and-Results
LBO/R = Learning-by-Objectives-and-Results
CBO/R = Curriculum-by-Objectives-and-Results
adiBO/R = "Any dimension of instruction"-by-
　　　　　Objectives-and-Results

Source: These concepts developed by the writer were first published in AASA National Academy for School Executives, *Management by Objectives and Results*, Arlington, Va.: The Academy, 1973, p. 71.

for what was previously called sensitivity training. This is not the way the term will be used herein.

Organizations, like individuals, are dynamic. They are born, experience frustrations, mature, and may even pass from the scene. Concern for an organization's life history, sensitivity to the conflicts within that could influence achievement of goals, and restructuring it if need be to enhance its productivity is what OD is all about. A major responsibility of an administrator from the OD point of view is to be aware of the new demands facing the school as an organization and to marshal the staff competencies and other resources needed at crucial turning points in its history to sustain or increase its effectiveness.

Some writers view MBO/R as a key mechanism in OD. Through generation of objectives and then management for results there may be revealed a need to restructure the organization. The organization's growth patterns may be directed by operating in the MBO/R mode. The next edition of this volume may well have more substantial review of OD, but right now its concepts are only beginning to emerge.

CONFLICT MANAGEMENT

The traditional approach to conflict in the operation of schools was to hide it, ignore it, and above all never to admit that it exists in a school that you administer. Very little was written about conflict in school administration texts and other volumes until recently, presumably because there was no conflict and it made administrators uncomfortable even to talk about it. In contrast, much has been said about control. In a school system under control it was believed that conflict could be avoided.

The ferment and disruptions of the 1960s rather dramatically dispelled the myth that conflicts didn't exist, or if you ignored them, then conflicts would unobtrusively vanish. The emphasis has switched presently to where administrators are admonished to search out and identify incipient conflicts, rather than to hide them. Once identified, conflict can be managed, according to the prevailing point of view, assuming the administrator and the organization have acquired conflict-management competencies.

Conflict is inevitable in all complex organizations that are located in a society characterized by ferment and strife. It is a signature of the period, and it is folly to believe that schools exist in a conflict-free environment. The sources of tensions and disruptions in schools as elsewhere are many and varied. The following classification is offered as a way to get a handle on this phenomenon. The categories are not mutually exclusive and overlap among them should be evident, nor are these intended to be exhaustive.

1. *Goal conflicts:* In heterogeneous communities in times of great social upheaval, majority consensus on the purposes of education is hard to come by. To some, schools exist to transmit the great cultural heritage or to teach the 3R's. To others, schools are created to resolve the social problems of our times, such as breaking the harsh cycle of poverty and improving race relations as well. There are goal conflicts and priority disputes among educators as well as among the general public.
2. *Role conflicts:* There are many people who have specialized functions to perform in the school organization. Conflicts may take their rise in role differentiations with one group

of specialists battling for the authority or recognition of another. There are conflicting expectations for a given position from the various referent groups that interact with the person in that position. Thus, the principal sees his role set one way and teachers, students, and parent expect him to perform in different if not contradictory ways. Role conflicts are perhaps the most common cause of general organization tensions and dysfunctions.

3. *Interpersonal conflicts:* Wherever there are people, personality conflicts will arise.

4. *Intraorganizational conflicts:* Within an organization there may be power struggles among groups as well as among individuals. Attempts at a structural reorganization or a new set of working relationships between teachers and administrators brought on by negotiations will generate conflicts. Communication breakdowns add their bit to increased tensions leading to possible disruptions. Students are clamoring that their rights be respected along with those of other power groups.

5. *Interorganizational conflicts:* There are several sources of stress generated from outside the organization as well as those from within. A formal organization such as the city (through the mayor's office or some division such as the building inspector, the tax collector, or treasurer) may dispute what the school as a formal organization does. Battles with a state department of education, federal agency, or a local chamber of commerce are not rare.

6. *Societal conflicts:* This is perhaps a catch-all for the many informal group or individual citizen complaints against the school seen as part of "the establishment." Delegations at board meetings may be ad hoc groups, most are not formal organizations. Loosely-organized civil rights groups may picket a school building. Many of the great social conflicts spill over into the schools, simply because it is a visible and easy to get to platform.

With all the possibilities of conflict one wonders why more rather than less conflict doesn't come to schools.

Conflict analysis can proceed only if preceded by conflict identification, and that calls for a willingness to admit that conflict exists. The analysis leads to the generation of plausible alternatives for conflict management. It may begin by an analysis of the organizational climate. Crises may be anticipated and contingency plans created for courses of actions to be pursued if there is a student walkout, teacher strike, or a community demonstration on school property. In other words, a "game plan," with appropriate options, is prepared to identify responsibilities, or who is to do what in the event of a potentially disruptive activity.

Some internal tension may not only be tolerated but recognized as a constructive stimulant to improvement. Obviously, the extremes of tension and anxiety that reduce performance effectiveness of personnel and contribute to dysfunctional behavior are avoided and call for counter action to minimize their effects. One group of writers was of the opinion that "a conflict is sometimes best managed not by doing away with it, but by providing for occasions through which adversaries can introduce their conflicting claims into the business of the school whenever the claims are relevant."[8] By the same token, communities, school boards, and administrators dif-

[8]R. A. Schmuck et al., *Handbook of Organizational Development in Schools*, Palo Alto, Cal.: National Press Books, 1972, p. 136.

fer in the degree of conflict they can tolerate. It can be argued that conflicts kept undercover and not managed in the formal structure trigger the rise of informal networks that seek to cope with the conflict. All too often informal mechanisms lack the resources to analyze and deal with severe tensions and may further "exaggerate and distort the truth so that much harm is done."[9] The direct and constructive dealing with conflict through formal mechanisms recognized in the organizational hierarchy is the more effective management strategy.

Berelson and Steiner noted that "within an organization, conflict between leaders and subordinates tends to increase the number and concreteness of the organization's regulations, and vice-versa—i.e., regulations go along with conflict."[10] This introduces greater rigidity in operations and interactions among personnel. Informal understandings as to rules and responsibilities work well as long as conflicts are nonexistent or minimal.

Educational organizations are dynamic and are part of a society in ferment. Maintenance of equilibrium or stability is necessary to ensure the continued productivity and achievement of institutional goals. By the same token, however, disturbances without, conflict within, pressures that are external, and demands that are internal can be resolved to achieve equilibrium. In today's society many writers refer to the need of the organization to maintain a dynamic equilibrium, that is, the capability to identify the kinds of changes that are most likely to produce growth; the flexibility to assimilate promising methods,

structures, procedures, resources, and even revised goals; and the ability to accomplish all this without serious disruption of services to its clients in particular and society in general.

Homeostasis refers to the ability of a living organism to maintain a dynamic equilibrium between catabolic forces (destructive processes that release energy through utilization of the organism's food resources) and anabolic forces (constructive processes that contribute to the maintenance or growth of bodily conditions). It is a sensitive and fluctuating balance maintained through a variety of bodily mechanisms that keep the organism alive. The physiological concept of homeostasis has been applied to explain the growth processes of social systems. A delicate balance must be maintained in all dynamic social institutions if survival is to be assured. The equilibrium between constructive and destructive forces or processes, between stability and change, must be comprehended by those assigned responsibility for administration.

Homeostasis is similar to the systems approach. Within the body of the living organism there are self-regulatory mechanisms, based on the operation of interrelated systems rather than upon a single control mechanism working independently of other systems, that maintain the sensitive dynamic balance between life and death. The systems approach calls for the design of self-regulatory mechanisms within a social organization to keep it viable and responsive to the demands of a changing environment.

[9]Ibid., p. 137.

[10]B. Berelson and G. A. Steiner, *Human Behavior*, New York: Harcourt Brace Jovanovich, 1964, p. 377.

SUMMARY

Schools are part of a dynamic society that triggers a continuing effort toward development of more effective administrative systems. The theory movement in and the systems approach to educational administration were new concepts of the 1950s and 1960s introduced in previous editions. The management science techniques, organization development, and conflict management are among the more recent concerns in educational administration.

Management science is different from the scientific management movement that came into popularity around the turn of the century. Management science rises above the production room problems and seeks to aid managers at all levels to improve decision making by more systematic use of scientific methodology, particularly mathematics and science. As such it is an extension of the operations research and system management techniques. The management scientists who designed the new techniques were professors divorced from the practical problems. Very often the scientists understanding of time constraints, data limitations, and variable complexity faced by managers in the field produced models and strategies that failed to work as well as they might.

PPBS is one of the more recent management science techniques that took its rise in the management of federal departments. A more complete acronym would be PPBADERS for it is a planning, programming, budgeting, analyzing, deciding, evaluating, and recycling system. The processes are not as important as the end product. For that reason what is popularly referred to as PPBS is better identified as a resource allocation decision system (RADS).

In the late 1960s and early 1970s PPBS spread to schools with the help of a federally supported research project. Many school districts lay claim to operating in the PPBS mode. The actual number of schools using it depends on how PPBS is defined or how many dimensions of the system should be in actual practice before recognition for such operations.

MBO/R came out of the private business and industrial sector to be very recently adapted to the purposes of education. It is systems-oriented and stresses the importance of generating objectives of a specific quality followed by careful management to achieve desired results. MBO/R has been interpreted as a results oriented appraisal system, a motivation-by-objectives approach, a management development scheme, and a process akin to sensitivity training. These are the human-relations conceptualizations of it. It may also be viewed in the broader context of a general systems planning and control mechanism. It is this latter conceptualization that makes MBO/R compatible and complementary with PPBS. MBO/R also stresses the participative management style of involving those affected in decisions as to which decisions should be pursued.

Education-by-objectives-and-results (EBO/R) may be better accepted than MBO/R alone. Teachers and some others do not identify with management per se. MBO/R may be seen as EBO/R from the management side. Instruction-by-objectives-and-results (IBO/R) may be viewed as EBO/R from the instructional side of the system.

Organization development (OD) is a relatively new concept with varying interpretations. It recognizes the life cycle of the organization and focuses on ways of changing to keep the organization relevant to new challenges. MBO/R may be considered to be an OD strategy.

Conflict was ignored or not discussed for most of the history of educational administration. The object was control, and a person in control was often too embarrassed to admit the existence of conflict in the organization. Today conflict is recognized as inevitable; it is a sign of the times. There are goal conflicts, role conflicts, interpersonal conflicts, intraorganizational conflicts, and societal conflicts.

Conflict analysis leads to generation of plausible conflict management strategies. Some internal tensions may be tolerated if they serve to stimulate greater effectiveness. If too severe such tensions may be dysfunctional. Conflicts are inevitable and administrators must develop the competencies to cope with them.

QUESTIONS

1. What are the similarities and differences between management science and scientific management?
2. What are the relationships between operations research and management science?
3. Why have some of the management science techniques failed to gain greater acceptance and utilization among practitioners in the field?
4. Why is RADS a more accurate description of the management science technique more popularly known as PPBS?
5. In what ways are MBO/R and PPBS compatible and complementary management systems?
6. What is organization development?
7. Why is MBO/R more difficult to adapt and implement in educational systems than in profit making business and industrial organization?
8. Why have conflict management competencies assumed major significance in school administration?
9. What are the major sources of conflict in educational organizations?
10. What are the dangers and advantages of searching for conflicts in school administration?

SELECTED REFERENCES

AASA National Academy For School Executives, *Management By Objectives and Results,* Arlington, Va.: The Academy, 1973.

Beck, A. C. Jr., and E. D. Hillmar, *A Practical Approach To Organization Development Through MBO—Selected Readings,* Reading, Mass.: Addison-Wesley, 1972.

Grayson, C. Jackson, Jr., "Management Science and Business Practics," *Harvard Business Review,* vol. 5, no. 4, July–August 1973, pp. 41–48.

Knezevich, Stephen J., *Program Budgeting (PPBS),* Berkeley, Cal.: McCutchan, 1973.

Schmuck, Richard A., et al., *Handbook of Organization Development for Schools,* Palo Alto, Cal.: National Press Books, 1972.

II

THE STRUCTURAL FRAMEWORK FOR ADMINISTRATION OF PUBLIC EDUCATION

"Form follows function" is a truism. The structural framework for public education was influenced by the strugggles that molded a nation out of a wilderness, and it continued to feel the impact of informal agencies and of other governmental units. The pattern for the administration and operation of public education in the United States differs considerably from that found in most countries of the world.

The local school district is the basic structural unit. The numbers of these units continue to decline as local districts become larger and more efficient. The local unit does not and cannot exist alone. The intermediate unit, or regional educational service agency (RESA), is an essential component in a three-echelon state education system. The state education agency also has a leadership role in public education. Federal impact on education started with the need for the collection and dissemination of facts about education on a nationwide basis, but has expanded far beyond that today. It keeps changing but growing in importance with the addition of new agencies such as the National Institute of Education.

Although not an integral part of the formal public school system, the private schools, professional societies, and other informal agencies are part of the overall educational framework. They provide alternatives to and stimulation of public education.

9

THE BASIC UNIT: THE
LOCAL SCHOOL DISTRICT

The development of a system of public education with opportunities for learning available to more people than ever before in history can be regarded as one of the significant contributions of the United States to the progress of civilization. The American pattern called for transfer of control of schools from religious authorities or private corporations to public or civil authorities.[1] It resulted in formulation of the concept of education as a function of the state. Public education grew and prospered primarily because it was the will of the American people that it do so. Growth of the common school was a grass-roots movement. It was the product of local effort. County and state controls over public education came much later. The large degree of federal influence over public education was not evident until after World War II. It is not surprising, therefore, that in the United States the local district remains, although significantly modified in size and functions from its historic counterpart, the basic structural unit for the administration of public education.

EVOLUTION OF THE DISTRICT SYSTEM

The district system is an American invention. It was well suited to a pioneer culture where localism was cherished and democracy a passion. It was a system of school organization that evolved from the New England town. The New England town was a geographical entity of irregular shape whose boundaries were determined by difficult-to-traverse terrain such as hills or swamps. Its size varied from 20 to 40 square miles.[2] It included a center of population known as the village and a sizable rural area. Outlying settlements sprang up in rural areas and became known as quarters, squadrons, ends, skirts, or districts.[3] In the beginning, New England towns were village-centered. As the population increased and hunger for land grew among the early settlers, families moved to outlying settlements. Dispersion of population within the New England town, along with the growth of the spirit of democracy and localism, eventually gave rise to the district system.

[1] R. Freeman Butts and L. A. Cremin, *A History of Education in American Culture,* New York: Holt, Rinehart & Winston, 1953, p. 253.

[2] Ellwood P. Cubberley, *Public School Administration,* Boston: Houghton Mifflin, 1929, p. 56.

[3] Newton Edwards and Herman G. Richey, *The School in the American Social Order,* Boston: Houghton Mifflin, 1947, p. 111.

Colonial legislatures used the town as a civil subdivision of the state to govern and operate local political and school affairs. It was in town meetings that decisions on defense against the Indians and construction of roads, as well as on school affairs, were determined. The township provided the earliest framework for administration of public education in the United States. The New England town should not be confused with the surveyor's town or township created when the Middle West and Far West lands were laid out. The surveyor's township is a fairly regular geographical area with dimensions of 6 miles by 6 miles, having a total area of 36 square miles.

Not very long after people migrated to outlying settlements of the town they demanded their own church and school. Colonial laws required towns to maintain schools, but often difficult terrain and great distances made it difficult for children residing in outlying portions to reach the town school. The first attempt at a solution was the creation of the "moving school." It should be kept in mind that a school during the early years of our history was a very simple institution. It usually consisted of no more than a schoolmaster, who had little equipment to transport and few books; he carried most of the knowledge in his head. Most towns did not even have a school building; a rented room in a private home was the "schoolhouse." A school that consisted of little more than the schoolmaster was not difficult to move about the town. The difficulty was one of time rather than place. The schoolmaster moved from one part of the town to another, but the time periods allotted each part were not of equal length. In the town of Harwich, in 1725, there were six places where the master taught for varying lengths of time. The schedule called for the schoolmaster to make a complete circuit within the town every 3½ years; thus children enjoyed very long vacations from school, varying from 2 to 3 years in length.[4] Rise of the district system was significant because it marked the separation of school administration from general municipal administration, a separation which in most states continues up to the present time.[5]

The local district during early years embraced a limited geographical area so that all pupils could walk to the one-teacher school. It was a social invention of great consequence. It was carried away from New England by the people who headed westward. Many have said that the district system was as important to the earlier settlers of the Middle and Far West as was the ax that cleared forests, the gun that protected them and provided food, and the covered wagon that transported them westward. The local school district of limited geographical area made possible education of children in a pioneer culture.

There were evils as well as blessings in structuring educational operations into a pattern of small districts. The Massachusetts law of 1789 (which permitted creation of districts) and later laws of 1800 and 1827 (which gave districts the power to tax, raise money for schoolhouses, and select their own board members) placed a large measure of school control in the hands of the populace of the local district. This resulted in highly unequal resources to support education, as well as unequal interest and desire for public education. The consequence was unevenness in the quality of education that was provided in district schools. Legal action in state and federal courts

[4]Ibid., pp. 111–112.
[5]Ibid., p. 110.

to redress the historic inequalities had to wait for almost two centuries. In the early 1970s the famous *Serrano vs. Priest* court case was followed by others that attempted to force states to ameliorate the educational inequities. Many shortcomings necessitated the establishment of other educational administrative devices, such as township or county supervision over schools and eventually state departments of education, to counteract the ill effects of excessive decentralization. These were stopgap measures, and eventually it was recognized that reorganization of districts into larger units that could effectively discharge responsibilities of education was necessary. School-district reorganization has been motivated by the desire to form more effective local units and has been a perennial problem for well over 100 years.

The seemingly simple local school district is a complex unit. To explain it better, the school district will be examined as (1) a political entity, or civil subdivision of the state; (2) a legal entity, or quasi-municipal corporation; (3) a geographical entity; (4) a social institution; and (5) an educational entity.

The district as a political entity

As a civil subdivision of the state, the school district was developed to fulfill the state's function of education. Power of the legislature to create, alter, or abolish local school districts is limited only, if at all, by constitutional prohibitions.

As explained previously, in the United States political system the state is the plenary source of governmental power. Whatever subdivisions it creates are inferior to it. The school district has only those rights and responsibilities that the state delegates to it.

The legislature has plenary authority with respect to all matters of educational policy in public schools. In the absence of constitutional prohibitions, the state may pattern and control education in any manner it desires. The political result of all this is 50 state school systems plus separate ones in the outlying territories rather than a unified national pattern. Within each system, the educational traditions and desires of the people are manifested. For example, in some systems final authority over certain educational matters has been awarded to city councils or mayors rather than to local school boards. It is the legislature, speaking through its properly enacted statutes, that determines whether school-board members shall be elected or appointed. The state legislature by a single act may abolish all existing school districts and create a new set, as it did at one point in time in Iowa, Indiana, and West Virginia. The school district is a political or civil subdivision of the state, an instrument created to facilitate the realization of a definite governmental purpose. In absence of statements to the contrary in either the federal or the state constitution, whatever the legislature commands, the school district must obey.

Description of a school district as one of the many political units created by the state legislature must be tempered by the tradition of local concern for public education. Legislative members are representatives of people in the state. As political officials, they are responsive to the wishes of the electorate. Sensing desires of people at the grass-roots level to maintain a high degree of control over education without unwanted interference from the state, legislators have been hesitant, by and large, to adopt drastic changes unless emergency conditions prevail. These are the political facts of life. It was this hesitancy among legislators to modify local school-district structure without prior approval of district residents that served to slow effective reorganization until conditions in the last two decades demanded more forceful action. The question is not whether the legislature has complete authority over school districts, short of what may be prohibited in its own or the federal constitution, it is what legislators consider to be politically expedient use of legal authority to modify established educational patterns.

The federal government has no direct legal control over the operations of local school districts, even though recent events may suggest the contrary. Federal influence is felt at the local level though Supreme Court interpretations of what must be done to protect the civil rights of all citizens and through allocation of massive federal funds to stimulate specific types of educational programs. Although not a political entity within federal jurisdiction, the school district has been caught in the political and legal crossfire of federal demands and local community desires.

Often strife among the power groups within the community will be effected in the local school-district organizational pattern. Large concentrations of what were at one time minorities in sections of major cities have generated new political forces that have reopened debate on and instigated action concerning the organization and control of education in city and surrounding districts. Considerable confusion and contradiction became apparent in the late 1960s and continued in the 1970s. In one thrust, political voices seeking to ameliorate racial tensions and a better racial balance in an area recommended merger of the mother city and its suburbs to form a large and unified metropolitan school district. A contrary political movement, based on similar motives, called for fragmentation of educational control in very large city districts by distributing authority for decisions among neighborhood groups of similar racial characteristics. To illustrate, a federal judge called for the merger of the Henrico County, Virginia, school division, which has a predominately white school population, with neighboring Richmond city schools. Another ruled that several school districts surrounding Detroit, Michigan, be unified into one system with the city schools. This issue has not been at this writing resolved definitively by a U.S. Supreme Court decision. An illustration of the contrary is what happened in the New York City school system which was closed down by a teachers' strike in September of 1968 when, during a general trend toward decentralization, a local governing board of one ethnic background fired ten teachers, all of another ethnic group, without the permission of the central Board of Education. The crossfire between proponents of centralization and those of decentralization, ethnic considerations, and, at the same time, teachers' demands for job security made the dispute both complex and emotional.

The district as a legal entity

The affairs of the school district precipitate interactions among a variety of people including pupils, teachers, and contractors. A corporate structure is necessary to facilitate operations. In the eyes of the law, a school district is a quasi-municipal corporation, a special kind of corporation.

A corporation can be defined as a collection of many individuals united in one legal body that has perpetual succession under an artificial form, that is vested with the capacity to act in several respects as an individual might, and whose powers are specified and conferred upon it by some governmental agency. In a legal sense, a corporation entails the creation of an artificial person created so that many can act with the ease of one. Another significant feature of a corporation is that it gives the artificial body perpetuity and continuity. The death of any one or many members of the corporation has no effect on its legal existence. In contrast to the ordinary partnership, which ceases to exist after one partner dies, a corporation survives the death of any or all of its members and officers. Of no less importance is the limited liability enjoyed by officers of a corporation. This is related to the fact that the corporation is an artificial person and can sue and be sued in its corporate name. Human beings acting for it are not held personally responsible for corporate acts and are immune from personal assessability, except in the instances where fraud or collusion occur. This is important in school district operations. It means that board members, acting in good faith and in the absence of fraud and collusion, cannot be sued as individuals for their acts as corporate officers.

Most charters of incorporation are granted by state governments; some are granted by the federal government. There are many types of corporations. Some serve private purposes, and others serve public purposes. Private corporations are created to engage in activities that will result in economic gains to the owners. Quasi-public corporations are technically private in ownership and would be classified as wholly private if their activities did not have grave influence on the public welfare. Thus public utilities, such as gas and electric companies, rail-roads, and airlines, have a profound impact upon the public, and so are classified as quasi-public corporations even though they are actually privately owned.

Public corporations are created for political purposes only. They are not only creatures of the state but are instruments of it as well. They exist to facilitate governmental activities. Municipal and quasi-municipal corporations are only a few of the several types of public corporations. A municipal corporation is a public corporation that is local in character and exercises some function of government. The incorporated cities, towns, or villages are municipal corporations. They are granted a charter by the state that specifies the extent of their governmental powers. The municipal corporation has a twofold purpose: (1) to facilitate government by people in a local area and (2) to act as an arm of the state. A more technical definition of the municipal corporation is that "it is a body politic and corporate, established by public law or sovereign power, evidenced by seal, and perpetual succession, primarily to regulate the local or internal affairs of the territory or district incorporated, and secondarily to share in the civil government of the state in a particular locality."[6] In the absence of specific constitutional inhibitions, a state through its legislative powers may create municipal or public corporations of any description.

What then is a quasi-municipal corporation or a quasi-municipality? A school district is a special kind of municipal corporation. Hence, the word quasi, implying that the school district operates "as if" it were actually a municipal corporation, such

[6]Eugene McQuillan, *The Law of Municipal Corporations*, 3rd ed., 1949, vol. 1, Chicago: Callaghan and Co., p. 451.

as a city, but its authority is far more limited. The authority of a school district is limited to the performance of the education function. A school district is often referred to as a limited municipal corporation. As a quasi-municipal corporation it continues without structural change and exists in perpetuity unless altered subsequently by legal action. A school district, within the limits of its charter, can hold and convey property, sue and be sued, and act as a person. Its officers are not personally assessable for corporate acts.

A school district has only the authority granted to it by the legislature. It executes its function by virtue of delegated authority. The school district as a legal entity may exercise the following powers and no others: "(1) those expressly granted by statute, (2) those fairly and necessarily implied in the powers expressly granted, and (3) those essential to the accomplishment of the objects of the corporation."[7] If there is a question about a school board's legal authority in a specific matter, the doubt is resolved against the district and the power denied.[8] A school district (as a quasi-municipal corporation) and a city (as a municipal corporation) are separate entities even though their boundaries may be the same. The exception to this general rule exists where the specific intent of a law is such as to grant authority over the school district to the city, but city officials have no authority over school districts unless the legislature clearly intends that such a relation shall exist.

Since 1950 schools have been embroiled in an ever increasing number

[7]Newton Edwards, *The Court and the Public Schools,* rev. ed., Chicago: University of Chicago Press, 1955, p. 146.
[8]Ibid.

of state and federal court cases. The powers of the local district and its board are being redefined as a result of constitutional issues being debated.

The district as a geographical entity

A school district can be identified as a geographical area. It has boundaries that are known and specified. One way of describing a school district is to define the area it encompasses.

Methods of describing territory enclosed within a school district vary. There are two separate land-survey systems in the United States: the metes-and-bounds system and the rectangular-survey system. The most common is the rectangular survey; its major unit is the geographical, or surveyor's, township. This was the system used when the Northwest Territory was first surveyed.

All land descriptions must have a starting point. These are the base lines from which the survey proceeds to the north or south and to the east and west. Base lines are not the same for all areas of the nation. For example, the border between the states of Wisconsin and Illinois served as one base line in the survey of the Northwest Territory, and one of the principal meridians was selected as another base line or range line from which to proceed east and west.

The fundamental unit in land description is the township. The geographical township is an area 6 miles long and 6 miles wide, containing 36 square miles. The 36 square miles are subdivided into 1-square-mile areas known as sections (see Figure 9–1). A section of 1 square mile contains 640 acres. A system was developed to subdivide the section into four and then sixteen parts. The first step was to divide a section into four parts. These quarter-sections contained 160 acres each. Each quarter-section is identified by the general direction in which it is situated. The upper right-hand corner is the northeast quarter (NE ¼); the upper left-hand corner, the northwest quarter (NW ¼); and so on. The system for identifying the four parts of the quarter-section is the same as that for identifying the primary subdivision of the section. Thus, the 40-acre parcel could be described as the NW ¼ of the SW ¼ of Section 16. In this manner a precise definition of the land included within any school district (important in determining what land it can tax for school support) can be developed.

In 19 states, including the original colonies in the East and South, the more difficult system of metes and bounds is used. In this system, each parcel of land is individually described and bounded.

The district as a social institution

People live in school districts and pupils of varying socioeconomic backgrounds learn there. The school district represents one of the many social institutions developed by people to satisfy their needs. It is admonished frequently that "community school districts" should be formed. If this is to be achieved, the question of what constitutes a community must be answered.

A community school is a social agency serving people who associate naturally in a given local culture area. In the beginning, community schools functioned as community centers by providing educational opportunities to ensure a higher degree of development of the human resources living within the area. In turn, the community reciprocated by allocating a

FIGURE 9-1

The geographical township.

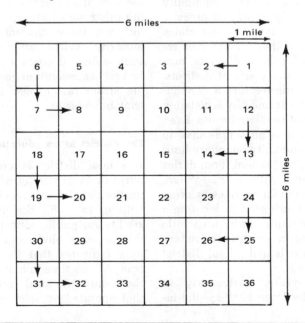

portion of its resources to the support of education and thus nurtured its development. The power of education works to the benefit of the people of the community.

The mere utilization of a school building as a meeting place for a variety of social or athletic activities after school hours or on nonschool days does not make for a community school. Such practices are commendable and can lead to better support of education, but there must be a more integral and intimate relation between the school and the community before the title of community school is merited. Not until the curriculum is related to the resources and needs of a cluster of people does the school begin to deserve the community appellation. Perhaps even more perplexing is the fact that the more popular definitions of community have a predominantly rural flavor. These conceptions do not fit well with the facts of life in an urban and highly mobile society. There is a need for a new conceptualization of the "community school" in densely populated areas.

At one point in time in some states the law declared that a merger or reorganization of school districts produced all community school districts. There is no guarantee that a community unit can be formed by legislation or the merger of unrelated units. Even in rural areas, it is no simple task to identify the community boundary lines and to formulate school boundaries that correspond with them. Where people go for school services is often considered one criterion in locating a community, but this contributes little to ascertaining community boundary lines when an enlarged school district is to be formed.

In recent years, particularly in the core of the large city, special-in-terest groups have emerged and appointed themselves representatives and spokesmen for a vaguely defined area or neighborhood within the city. Fragmentation of large urban school districts into autonomous subdivisions not unlike the ward schools around the turn of the century is becoming evident and is receiving publicity as an alleged solution to problems of educating disadvantaged groups. Rearranging the structure of urban districts under the guise of serving "community" educational interests may create the excessive decentralization typical of the New England states and large cities early in our history. It is said that those ignorant of the mistakes of history are doomed to repeat them. Dispersion of control of attendance centers to small groups in the city may create more problems than it solves. On the other hand some spokesmen for minority groups (whose numbers in some cases may make the minority the majority in the school population) have come to view the school as a social institution serving other social classes or even races but not those characteristic of the minority. Whatever the validity of such claims, it poses a complex problem whose resolution goes beyond simple structural changes in school district boundaries.

The district as an educational entity

A school district is created for the purpose of providing educational opportunities for its residents and for helping to fulfill the state's responsibility for public education. Although this appears obvious, an analysis of data indicates that it is not always true. At one time in history there were thousands of local school districts that operated no schools for learners.

Pupils who resided in such districts were transported to others that did operate schools. The function of the board of education in such a unit was merely to pay tuition for transported pupils. Nonoperating school districts exist because of tax advantages that accrue to residents, and this perverts the fundamental purpose behind the organization of school districts. These school districts have degenerated into tax colonies. Most states have all but eliminated nonoperating school districts through the enactment of (1) compulsory closing laws, which declare a district disorganized if no school is operated within it for a specified period of time, or (2) laws that require that by a specified date every school district in the state must be a part of one providing secondary school opportunities. In 1974–1975 fewer than 300 nonoperating schools existed, a substantial reduction from the more than 17,000 that existed in 1948. By the end of the 1970s the nonoperating school district may well disappear completely to the benefit of education in general.

The many facets of the school district

The school district has many dimensions. It may be perceived as an administrative unit and as an attendance unit. An administrative unit, also known as the basic unit of local school administration, "is an area in which a single board or officer has the immediate responsibility for the direct administration of all the schools located therein."[9] It is more often than

not the fiscal unit that is granted powers to tax within its boundaries or to raise other revenues for school operations.

An attendance unit[10] (school building) is a geographical area whose population is served by a single school-plant located within. In larger systems there are several attendance units within the administrative unit. The attendance unit or pupil learning center does not constitute a local taxing or fiscal unit and is not an independent system of administration. Strictly speaking, changes in boundary lines of attendance units (buildings where students attend) that would merge two or more previously independent operating units into one should be called consolidation. Consolidation, then, is the merger of two or more attendance units into one. Reorganization involves an alteration of boundary lines of the basic administrative unit. It is possible to have reorganization without consolidation. The confusion between consolidation and reorganization appeared early in the twentieth century when the fundamental purpose in forming larger administrative units was to replace many rural one-teacher schools with a single or central school. It was a time when the consolidation of attendance units overshadowed the alteration of district boundaries. One potential benefit of reorganization is consolidation of inefficiently organized attendance units into fewer but more efficient ones.

TYPES OF SCHOOL DISTRICTS

School districts are known by many names. There are common, city, town or township, county, union free high

[9]Howard A. Dawson and Floyd W. Reeves, *Your School District*, Report of the National Commission on School District Reorganization, Washington, D.C.: Department of Rural Education, National Educational Association, 1948, p. 47.

[10]Ibid., p. 46.

school districts, united and many others. The multiplicity of labels introduces confusion. Many terms simply reflect preferences within states for classifying school corporations. Often the legal designations exist for relatively short periods of time and then may be discontinued in favor of another label.

A city school district is usually a separate corporation from the general municipality or city proper. Prior to reorganization in some states it was not unusual to find boundaries of the city school district similar to those of the general municipality. Recent organizations created districts in which a city or large urban settlement was the nucleus of the district, which included a sizable adjoining rural area.

The county school district can be a basic, as well as an intermediate, unit of administration. It will be discussed more fully as an intermediate unit in Chapter 10. There are 13 states, located primarily in the South and referred to as the "county-unit" states, wherein all counties are basic school administrative units. Of these 13, Alabama, Georgia, Kentucky, New Mexico, North Carolina, Tennessee, Utah, and Virginia have independent school districts as well as county school districts serving as basic administrative units. In Florida, Louisiana, Maryland, Nevada, and West Virginia almost all basic units of school administration follow county boundary lines. These 13 states have relatively small numbers of basic units of school administration. The numbers of local districts in the county-unit states in the early 1970s ranged from lows of 17 districts in Nevada and 24 in Maryland to highs of 188 in Georgia and 190 in Kentucky.

Districts may be identified by the level of educational opportunity provided. There remain elementary school districts that provide elementary educational opportunity only. These educationally obsolete units are rapidly disappearing as they merge with districts that provide educational opportunities for Grades K through 12. A district can be organized to administer high school education only. California, Illinois, Kansas, and Wisconsin continue to have high school administrative districts: The board of education has control over education in a specified land area but is limited in providing educational opportunity for Grades 9 through 12 only. These districts are educationally obsolete, and their continued existence can be justified only on grounds of the special advantage that may occur in the financing of the construction of new school facilities. These should disappear by 1980.

The term unified district is applied to a merger of elementary and high school districts. Joint township or joint school district signifies a merger of adjoining districts.

EFFECTIVE SCHOOL-DISTRICT ORGANIZATION

A school district is a means to an end. It is created to provide educational opportunities for people facing the challenge of a given period of time. Standards that determine effectiveness of a local school unit are related to what constitutes a desirable educational program at some point in time. It is the program or educational function that determines the form or size of a district. This implies that as the educational program changes and becomes more complex, there is created a need to reevaluate the effectiveness of the basic unit of administration. It should be kept in mind that the local unit is only one part of the total educational structure, which includes the county (intermediate unit), state, and federal governments. The focus of almost all research described in the paragraphs that follow was efficient district size in rural, as opposed to urban, America.

District size

Dawson, in one of the most comprehensive of the early studies on district organization, developed minimum standards for elementary and secondary school districts in 1933. He concluded that each elementary school within the district should offer at least 6 years of instruction, have a desirable minimum of 7 teachers or an absolute minimum of 6, and have an average pupil-teacher ratio of approximately 40 to 1. To meet these conditions there would have to be a minimum enrollment of 240 to 280 pupils in the attendance unit. This pupil-teacher ratio is far above the 25 to 1 now recommended. Dawson's standards for the secondary-school attendance unit within the district called for 3 years of senior and 3 years of junior high-school instruction. A desirable minimum of 10 teachers was specified, with an absolute minimum of 7. If the average pupil-teacher ratio were 30 to 1 in a 6-year high school and 25 to 1 in a senior high school, the minimum number of pupils would be 210 to 300 in the 6-year high school and 175 to 250 in the senior high school.[11]

The National Commission on School Reorganization in 1948 reported its recommendations after a review and evaluation of standards proposed by various writers and researchers.[12] The Commission called for districts in which enrollments in attendance units for Grades K through 6 would be no less than 175 pupils and would have at least 7 full-time teachers. A more desirable minimum was specified as 300 pupils with 12 teachers. For attendance units for junior and senior high schools enrollment of no fewer than 300 pupils, or 75 for each age group, was recommended, plus a minimum of 12 full-time teachers. For schools organized to provide educational opportunities for Grades 9 through 12, a minimum of 200 pupils and 10 full-time teachers was recommended.

The 1948 recommendations of the Commission were consistent with those filed about 10 years earlier (1935 to 1937) by a United States Office of Education study group. The Office of Education study in 10 states suggested that all districts should be large enough to warrant one grade per elementary-school teacher plus 300 pupils and 10 teachers in junior and senior high schools.[13] These numbers should be residents within an area of the size that would ensure elementary pupils not walking more than 2 miles or riding in a school bus more than an hour each way. In addition, high-school pupils should not have to walk more than 2½ miles or ride more than 1½ hours each way to an attendance unit. The Commission recommended reducing maximum travel time to 45 minutes one way for elementary school pupils and an hour one way for secondary-school pupils.[14] One of the

[11]Howard A. Dawson, *Satisfactory Local School Units,* Field Study 7, Nashville, Tenn.: Division of Surveys and Field Studies, George Peabody College for Teachers, 1934, p. 39.

[12]Dawson and Reeves, op. cit., pp. 81–82.
[13]Henry F. Alves, Archibald W. Anderson, and John Guy Fowlkes, *Local School Units Project: Local School Unit Organization in Ten States,* U. S. Office of Education, Bulletin 1938, no. 10, Washington, D.C.: GPO, 1939, p. 12.
[14]Dawson and Reeves, op. cit., p. 82.

constraints on the geographical size of the effective school district was maximum bus-riding time to an elementary or secondary school building.

Standards for numbers of pupils in effective administrative units are related to those stipulated for attendance units. If the recommendations of the National Commission on School District Reorganization (a minimum of 75 pupils for each age group) were applied, the administrative unit of minimum size would contain 450 pupils in Grades 7 through 12 and at least an equal number in the elementary grades, for a total of 900. In view of the dropouts that usually occur at the secondary school level, there would be a need for more than 450 pupils in Grades 1 through 6. Considering only the number of pupils required to provide a comprehensive program of education at a reasonable cost per pupil, the absolute minimum enrollment in a basic administrative unit would be 1000. The Commission concluded that a satisfactory district should have at least 1200 pupils between the ages of 6 and 18.[15] Others have recommended a minimum of 1800 pupils in an administrative unit. These are minimum standards derived from a consideration of efficient size of attendance units only. Reorganization since the end of World War II demonstrated that those minimums were more likely to be too small for efficient operation than too large. An absolute minimum of 2400 pupils residing within the administrative unit was a more realistic goal in the 1950s. If the trend toward adding more social and broader educational responsibilities to schools continues and if technological developments such as computer-assisted and computer-managed instruction be-

come a part of educational institutions, then the minimum size school district should be 10,000 pupils. A study by the Educational Research Service in 1971 revealed widely disparate recommendations on minimum, maximum, and optimum size.[16]

The number of pupils residing within an effectively organized school district that can be educationally self-sufficient and can offer a comprehensive educational program would have to be at least 10,000. This, of course, assumes that there is no intermediate unit to provide special educational or business services to the local unit. Such a unit could reduce the necessity of forming administrative units with 10,000 or more pupils. There is evidence that districts enrolling 10,000 or more pupils would need a total population of 40,000 or more. Districts of this size would violate community boundary lines in rural and sparsely settled areas. It is more than likely that in the years ahead the minimum size of an administrative unit, particularly in sparsely settled areas, will approach 2,400 pupils rather than 10,000. This, of course, points to the need for the creation of an intermediate unit to provide certain educational services to the basic unit.

In the last analysis, all recommendations on the size of administrative units are relative to the educational program envisioned, technological developments, and other conditions within the society. Further expansion or enrichment of the educational program and/or the development of means of transportation other than those presently employed could make feasible units with enrollments different from those stipulated in studies ex-

[15]Ibid., p. 87.

[16]"Size of Schools and School Districts," *ERS Information Aid*, no. 8, June 1971, Arlington, Va.: *Educational Research Service*, p. 39.

ecuted in previous years. The continuing need for further reorganization was well defined by the Educational Research Services who noted that as late as 1971 "about 80 percent of our districts enroll less than 2500 pupils; about 40 percent, less than 300 pupils."[17] Stated another way "four-fifths of all districts in the country enroll only about one-fifth of all pupils."[18]

Relation of district size to learning

The Office of Education conducted a study of educational change in some 522 reorganized school districts.[19] In general, new districts with larger enrollment tended to make significant additions to the elementary- and secondary-school programs.

Another study concluded that the pupil who received his elementary education in a rural school and his secondary education in a small high school of 100 or fewer students suffered a form of educational double jeopardy. His achievement at the time he entered high school from a rural school was lower than the average for the state. During high school the extent of his disadvantage very likely increased. In short, the hypothesized merits of attendance at small schools appears to have no basis in fact, as demonstrated by tests of student achievements.[20] The Iowa study cited was based on the results of the Iowa Test of Educational Development, a series of achievement tests widely accepted and used throughout the country. Pupil achievement (in social studies, science, English, mathematics, literary appreciation, and vocabulary) in high schools of 100 or less (in Grades 9 through 12) was below that in the typical large school with 200, as well as in the typical moderate-sized school with 101 to 200. At the twelfth-grade level average pupil achievement in the typical large school was greater than in high schools with 100 or less. Feldt concluded that "by the time the pupils are tested in the fall of the senior year the difference in mean achievement of the largest and smallest schools approaches a full year's growth. Were pupils tested toward the end of the school year, the difference would undoubtedly exceed a full year's growth."[21]

Another significant finding of this study was that the rural pupil who entered a larger high school partially, but never totally, offset the limitations of his elementary training. The pupil who attended an urban elementary school and subsequently graduated from a large high school seemed, according to the Iowa Test of Educational Development, to have the most advantageous combination of educational experiences. Another revealing fact was that in this state the average student achievement on the test from 1948 to 1955 was relatively stable. Beginning in 1956 and continuing every year since that time the average pupil test performance in Iowa rose consistently. It is significant that school-district reorganization in Iowa began to move rapidly after 1955.

Stephens and Spiess[22] reviewed research on local school districts and concluded that most studies "pointed

[17]Ibid., p. 21.

[18]Ibid., p. 21.

[19]C. O. Fitzwater, *Educational Change and Reorganized School Districts,* U.S. Office of Education, Bulletin 1953, no. 4, Washington, D.C.: GPO, 1953.

[20]Leonard S. Feldt, "The Relationship Between Pupil Achievement and High School Size," Unpublished Paper, Iowa City: State University of Iowa, 1960.

[21]Ibid.

[22]E. R. Stephens and J. Spiess, "What Does Research Say About a Local School District?," *Journal on State School Systems,* vol. 1, no. 3, Fall 1967, pp. 182–199.

to a direct and positive relationship between size of school and pertinent factors: achievement, educational cost, breadth of educational program, extracurricular activities, professional staff qualifications, special services, and school plant." A more recent and more comprehensive review of research on the impact of size on pupil learning by the Educational Research Service revealed some contradictory conclusions and the continuation of the very small districts on such grounds was at least highly suspect.[23]

Rural district reorganization

One of the most dramatic developments in public education in the post World War II period has been the modification of school-district structure in the United States. These changes were made necessary by a variety of forces. The development of the telephone, radio, and television had an effect on communication. Better roads, automobiles, and trucks, along with airplanes and trains, knit the people of the nation closer together. On the farm the steel plow replaced the wooden one just as the tractor did the horse. Better seed, better fertilizer, and better agricultural techniques resulted in a revolution in the rural areas with fewer but larger farms. All these technological advances affected social institutions. Technological developments have also affected the manner in which people are distributed. The United States is now predominantly an urban rather than a rural nation. Such changes have stimulated reorganization of the structure of public education. Though reorganization was not accomplished

without battle, the animosity sparked by the mere mention of reorganization of inefficient district structures in rural areas has lessened.

The status of school districts in the United States from 1948–1949 to 1972–1973 is indicated in Table 9–1. In 1931–1932 there were 127,531 school districts. By the end of World War II (1941–1946) there was a relatively modest decline to 101,493. The history of the local school district reductions from 1931–1932 to 1973–1974 is summarized in Table 9–1. The rate of reduction intensified after World War II so that by 1965 the number of school districts had dropped to 26,983. The annual rate of decline in numbers of school districts slowed appreciably during the first half of the 1970s. Estimates for 1974–1975 indicate about 16,500 administrative units. In short, more than 110,000 school districts in the United States have been eliminated since 1931–1932, but most of the decline, almost 75 percent, were eliminated in the years between 1945 and 1965. The status of local school districts, number of nonoperating districts, and one-teacher schools in each of the states in 1948 and in 1972–1973 is summarized in. Table 9–2.

There remains considerable variability among basic administrative units in the United States. Thus, the Elko County, Nevada, School District is a single unit of administration and embraces a territory larger than the combined areas of the states of Connecticut, Massachusetts, and Rhode Island.[24] On the other hand, less than 4,000 pupils are enrolled in the 17,127 square miles of the single school dis-

[23]Educational Research Service, op. cit., pp. 7–20.

[24]American Association of School Administrators, School District Organization, *Report of the AASA Commission on School District Reorganization*, Washington, D.C.: The Association, 1958, pp. 80–83.

trict in Elko County, whereas the 638 school districts in Connecticut, Massachusetts, and Rhode Island have more than 2 million pupils. Some school districts encompass limited geographical areas but have sizeable enrollments. Enrollment in the New York City School District of about 1.2 million pupils is greater than that in 40 states. Enrollment in Chicago with approximately 558,000 pupils exceeds that in 21 states, and enrollment of over 277,-000 in Detroit exceeds that in 15 states.[25]

The Middle West is making progress but remains the less efficient school-district organization. In 1958 Kansas,

[25]Ibid.

Nebraska, North Dakota, Minnesota, South Dakota, Wisconsin, and Iowa, which make up one-seventh of the states and which had less than 7 percent of the public school children, accounted for 44 percent of the public school districts in the country. Over 80 percent of the nonoperating school districts, more than 50 percent of the one-room rural schools, and 55 percent of the districts with nine or fewer teachers were found in these states in 1958. Progress made since 1958 in these states has been most impressive. By 1972–1973 these states had reduced the number of school districts from over 22,100 to 3,659. These seven states had only 21.6 percent of all districts in the nation in 1972–1973, compared

TABLE 9–1

NUMBER OF LOCAL PUBLIC SCHOOL DISTRICTS AND PUBLIC SCHOOL ATTENDANCE CENTERS IN THE UNITED STATES, 1931–1932 TO 1973–1974[a]

School year	Local school districts	Public school attendance centers		Secondary schools
		Elementary schools		
		Total	One-teacher	
(1)	(2)	(3)	(4)	(5)
1931–1932	127,531	232,750	143,391	26,409
1941–1942	115,493	183,112	107,692	25,123
1945–1946	101,382	160,227	86,563	24,134
1951–1952	71,094	123,763	50,742	23,746
1955–1956	54,859	104,427	34,964	26,046
1961–1962	35,676	81,910	13,333	25,350
1965–1966	26,983	73,216	6,491	26,597
1970–1971	17,995	65,800	1,815	25,352
1971–1972	17,289	DNA	DNA	DNA
1972–1973	16,956	DNA	DNA	DNA
1973–1974[b]	16,814	DNA	DNA	DNA

Source: K. A. Simon and W. W. Grant, *Digest of Educational Statistics, 1972 Edition,* U.S. Department of Health, Education, and Welfare, Office of Education, No. (OE) Division 10024-69, Washington, D.C.: GPO, 1973.
DNA = Data not available.
[a] Does not include the single school district for education for each of the five outlying areas: American Samoa, Canal Zone, Guam, Puerto Rico, and Virgin Islands.
[b] NEA Research Estimates.

with 44 percent in 1958. Nebraska for years had the dubious distinction of being the state with the most school districts and still held that position with 1404 in 1972–1973. In 1960 about 26 percent of the states had more than 2000 districts. In contrast, in 1972–1973 no state had 2000 districts; only four had more than 1000 districts!

Nationally, the one-teacher school is being abandoned rapidly. In 1917–1918 there were 196,037 one-teacher schools in the United States, and they represented 70.8 percent of all public schools that year.[26] By 1958–1959 the number fell to 23,695 one-teacher schools. They comprised only 19.5 percent of the schools and only 1.1 percent of all enrolled in public schools. Of the classroom teachers in the United States, 2 percent were employed in one-teacher schools during that year. By 1970 the number of one-teacher schools had dropped to less

[26]National Education Association, "The Little Red School House," *Research Bulletin*, vol. 38, no. 1, February 1960, pp. 3–10.

TABLE 9–2

STATUS OF SCHOOL DISTRICTS IN VARIOUS STATES OF THE UNITED STATES, 1948–1949 AND 1972–1973

(1) State	No. of school districts		No. of nonoperating school districts		No. of one-teacher schools	
	(2) 1948	(3) 1972	(4) 1948	(5) 1972	(6) 1948	(7) 1967
Alabama	108	126	0	0	1088	30
Alaska	—	29	—	0	—	54
Arizona	322	298	0	3	84	32
Arkansas	1589	387	20	2	1517	25
California	2429	1059	39	1	820	24
Colorado	1884	181	392	0	872	20
Connecticut	172	166	2	0	115	0
Delaware	126	26	0	0	48	2
Florida	67	67	0	0	420	15
Georgia	189	188	0	0	1758	0
Hawaii[a]	—	1	—	0	—	0
Idaho	1011	115	320	0	214	24
Illinois	11,061	1090	315	0	7126	1
Indiana	1196	312	94	7	403	0
Iowa	4856	452	1335	2	5575	2
Kansas	5643	311	1270	1	3090	71
Kentucky	256	190	0	0	3127	320
Louisiana	67	66	0	0	778	3
Maine	493	289	21	56	728	42
Maryland	24	24	0	0	161	3
Massachusetts	351	410	0	47	128	12
Michigan	5434	602	1041	3	2952	50
Minnesota	7606	444	2418	3	4421	627
Mississippi	4194	150	0	0	1850	5
Missouri	8422	600	2067	2	5125	135
Montana	1800	732	327	57	915	275
Nebraska	6991	1404	1812	100	4516	1100

than 2150. About 45 percent of all one-teacher schools were in only two states—Nebraska and South Dakota. Twelve states have all but eliminated this institutional characteristic of the pioneer culture of the nineteenth century.

Fitzwater summarized the positive trends in school redistricting since 1945 as:

1. Continued progress in eliminating nonoperating districts.
2. Requirement in an increasing number of states that all reorganized dis-

tricts be unified or organized to operate both elementary and high schools.
3. Requirement by a growing number of states that all territory be within a district maintaining a high school.
4. Inclusion of more than one high-school district in a reorganized district.
5. Merger of previously established but small reorganized units into enlarged newly created districts; in other words, reorganization of previously too-small reorganizations.
6. Merger of small or medium-sized city districts with country districts surrounding them.
7. Union of all or nearly all districts

TABLE 9–2 (Continued)

(1) State	No. of school districts		No. of nonoperating school districts		No. of one-teacher schools	
	(2) 1948	(3) 1972	(4) 1948	(5) 1972	(6) 1948	(7) 1967
Nevada	211	17	22	0	88	18
New Hampshire	239	167	7	11	133	15
New Jersey	561	599	25	23	89	10
New Mexico	104	87	0	0	137	11
New York	4609	754	1765	20	1494	10
North Carolina	172	152	0	0	595	1
North Dakota	2267	375	279	34	2677	102
Ohio	1583	621	24	0	496	4
Oklahoma	2664	650	192	0	1324	63
Oregon	1363	339	336	0	399	24
Pennsylvania	2540	506	101	1	2744	27
Rhode Island	39	40	0	0	25	1
South Carolina	1737	93	45	0	1019	0
South Dakota	3409	231	801	4	3203	950
Tennessee	150	147	0	0	2095	50
Texas	5145	1135	900	5	1200	17
Utah	40	40	0	0	28	0
Vermont	268	271	5	1	552	80
Virginia	125	139	0	0	1178	17
Washington	628	316	39	0	137	12
West Virginia	55	55	0	0	2528	175
Wisconsin	6385	442	1074	0	4475	6
Wyoming	359	60	43	0	385	94
Totals	100,946	16,955	17,131	383	74,832	4,559

Source: Columns 2, 4, 6, and 7: data from unpublished surveys conducted by the Division of Rural Services, National Education Association. Column 3 National Center for Educational Statistics. Column 5 Research Division National Education Association, "Estimates of School Statistics," 1972–1973.
ᵃ One district.

within a county into a single administrative unit.
8. Formation of large suburban districts adjoining major cities.
9. Merger of independent city school districts with adjoining county school districts.
10. Consolidation of small high schools in the county-unit districts.
11. Formation of separately organized regional high-school districts embracing territory of several town or township school districts.[27]

On the negative side Fitzwater reported that in spite of all that has been accomplished since the report of the National Commission on School District Reorganization in 1948 there still are too many too-small districts.

The conclusion as we move into the last few decades of the twentieth century is that despite significant progress, more is necessary before an effi-

[27]C. O. Fitzwater, "Patterns and Trends in State School System Development," *Journal* *on State School Systems,* vol. 1, no. 1, Spring 1967, pp. 5–32.

FIGURE 9–2

Number of Local Basic Administrative Units (school districts) United States, 1945–1946 to 1972–1973.

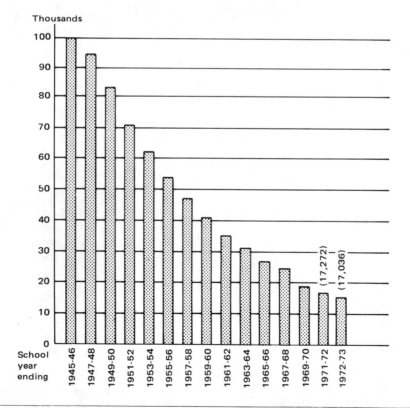

Source: U.S. Department of Health, Education, and Welfare, Office of Education, Digest of Educational Statistics and Fall 1969 Statistics of Public Schools. 1971–1972 and 1972–1973 data based on NEA estimates.

cient school-district organization is attained in the United States. The writer concurs with other opinions that few states, if any, can justify operating with more than 100 basic school administrative units. An average of 100 local school districts per state would mean no more than 5000 in the nation. This is a maximum, and the next generation may well see a total closer to 2000.

There is ample evidence that well-designed state legislation and school-financing programs have contributed mightily to the improvement of structural patterns for educational operation in each state. The success has been primarily in the rural areas, and trends to date demonstrate that districts too small to operate effective educational programs with a reasonable expenditure of financial resources are being eliminated. The rural dimension of effective school-district organization in the nation shows clear signs of approaching a desirable solution.

Urban district organization

While smallness is a problem in rural and some urban school operations, bigness, in terms of numbers of pupils and schools, plagues the great cities. At one point in history it appeared as if large urban centers had resolved the problem of efficient district organization and only the rural areas were likely to experience serious difficulties. The first efforts toward reorganization of attendance and administrative units took place in the cities. Many city school systems moved from a pattern of electing or appointing a board of education to control schools in each city ward toward a structural unity which placed concern for operation of all schools within the city in a single board of education.[28]

[28]Ibid., p. 20.

Since the end of World War II, mushrooming metropolitan areas, particularly in the suburban and rural fringe surrounding the core city, have produced a veritable jungle of school districts. Special attention is now being given to district organizational patterns in the suburban and nearby urban areas. There are few data at present that shed light on the optimum size of a district, beyond which no further advantage accrues from increasing enrollments. Even less is known about the point beyond which further growth brings special problems and disadvantages, such as increased cost for coordinating complex units, difficulties in staff communication, or loss of close contact with community feelings and attitudes toward schools.

Problems of race relations in the big cities, particularly the significant percentage increase in nonwhite students enrolled in the large urban school systems and the difficulties in breaking down segregated residential patterns in favor of open housing, have received considerable publicity in recent years. Some have pointed out that the difficulties have been intensified because the whites have left the large cities to live in the surrounding suburbs, and it has been suggested that metropolitan school districts be organized to merge the mother city with its suburban fringe. This has occurred in some places, particularly in the southern states. Examples of metropolitan school districts that encompass all land within a county including the big city center are Savannah and Chatham County in Georgia, the City of Greenville and Greenville County in South Carolina, the City of Albuquerque and all of Bernalillo County in New Mexico, the City of Nashville and Davidson County in Tennessee, the City of Miami and Dade County in Florida, and the City of Charlotte and

Mecklenburg County in North Carolina. The creation of metropolitan school districts represents less of a problem where the county is the basic school unit, as in Florida, West Virginia, and Nevada. In addition, where a metropolitan form of government for police and fire departments exists (as in Dade County, Florida), there is a greater likelihood of a metropolitan school district. The likelihood is less where suburban areas seek to preserve their political identity from the city and where the school district in the city is fiscally independent of the municipality.

As indicated previously, in an effort to achieve what is defined as racial balance some federal justices have called for merger of cities with one or more school districts in one or more counties to create a metropolitan district. The issue of whether a court can set aside legally constituted school corporations (districts) to achieve racial balance is as far reaching as it is socially sensitive. At this writing the U.S. Supreme Court has not arrived at a definitive decision.

**Internal organization of
large city systems**

The creation of the very large urban district brings forth unique problems in administration. It is not unusual to find the large city or metropolitan school district reorganized within its boundaries into subdistricts with special quasi-autonomous functions decided at the subunit level and others maintained at central headquarters for the system as a whole. This movement has been accelerating in the years following World War II; the decentralization of administration in large city school systems is not new. Bertolaet reported that as early as 1883 the Philadelphia school system created ten

geographical divisions within it and placed ten district (actually subdistrict) superintendents with considerable operating authority within each of the ten geographical areas.[29] There is a preference in the literature to refer to the administrator in a part of a large city school district as "district superintendent" when in reality he is operating in a subdistrict of the total city school district. This popular usage will be continued herein, even though it is inaccurate from a technical standpoint.

St. Louis created a number of district superintendencies in 1926. Detroit established the office of district principal in 1920. The Board of Education in New York City in 1906 provided for 46 decentralized units and appointed 26 district superintendents. Chicago began to use the title of district superintendent in 1898, and the number of such positions varied from 6 in 1902 to 12 in 1913. The administrative reorganization of the Chicago public-school system in 1955 by superintendent B. C. Willis created 16 district superintendencies, and this number had grown to 21 by 1962[30] and 27 by 1969.

The number of subdistricts in 23 large urban systems in 1929 varied from a low of 3 to 32 in New York City, as shown in Table 9-3. Decentralization into administrative subdistricts makes it possible to bring certain instructional services closer to the classroom teachers, the persons who have greatest need and use for such services. Other functions such as employing personnel, planning school buildings, and finance remained centralized

[29]F. W. Bertolaet, "The Administrative Functions of the District Superintendent in Chicago as Related to Decentralization," Doctoral Dissertation, Madison, Wis.: University of Wisconsin, 1964, pp. 3–6.
[30]Ibid.

in the general superintendent's office. Most large urban school districts in metropolitan areas have implemented or are contemplating some form of administrative decentralization and greater community participation in school administration.

There is an inherent danger in the creation of subdistricts within a large urban district. This danger point is reached when a subdistrict approaches autonomy, with its own separate school board for policy making and authority to levy additional taxes to be expended only in the subdistrict rather than in the educational system as a whole.

The search for solutions to educational problems in very large urban centers, particularly those problems related to racial balance or educational experiences and services for disadvantaged students, has led to proposals for the creation of autonomous subdistricts within the very large urban communities. There is no objec-

TABLE 9–3

NUMBER OF SUBDISTRICTS IN LARGE DECENTRALIZED SCHOOL DISTRICTS, 1969

School system	Number of subdistricts	Average enrollment of subdistricts
Montgomery County, Md.	12[a]	11,000[a]
Portland, Oreg.	7	12,000
San Diego, Calif.	10	13,000
Clark County, Nev.	5	14,000
Boston, Mass.	6	16,000
Garden Grove, Calif.	3	18,000
St. Louis, Mo.	6	20,000
Chicago, Ill.	27	21,000
Brevard County, Fla.	3	21,000
Atlanta, Ga.	5	22,000
Broward County, Fla.	5	23,000
Fremont, Calif.	4	24,000
San Antonio, Texas	3	25,000
Hillsborough County, Fla.	4	26,000
Baltimore County, Md.	5	27,000
New Orleans, La.	4	27,000
Fairfax County, Va.	4	33,000
Metropolitan School System, Nashville, Tenn.	3	34,000
New York, N.Y.	32	35,000
Philadelphia, Pa.	8	36,000
Detroit, Mich.	8	36,000
Dade County, Fla.	6	40,000
Los Angeles, Calif.	12	55,000

Source: Educational Research Service, "Size of Schools and School Districts," *ERS Information Aid,* no. 8, June 1971, Arlington, Va.: ERS, p. 29.
[a] Six districts effective July 1, 1971.

tive evidence in favor of this extreme form of decentralization; there is little rationality behind such a proposal; and there is nothing in experience to suggest its value. It resembles the ward school operations which plagued city school systems at the turn of the century. This experience demonstrated that the ward school was inefficient in meeting the needs of pupils and promoted interference in educational operations by ward politicians. There is real concern that fragmentation of the large city school district, even though stimulated by the hope of improvement, would repeat this bitter experience. The politics of decentralization may bring a return to the old and previously abandoned ward politics in education.

School-district organization is a means to an end, and no pattern can solve problems whose roots go deeper than simply structural realignment. Decentralization of the very large urban centers into subdistricts with specified authority for the improvement of instruction has many advantages. It can, however, be carried to the extreme of creating autonomous units that in effect fragment large city districts and intensify operational and educational problems.

The neighborhood school concept

Although education is legally a state function, the concern of the family unit for the intellectual, social, and personal development of children and youths should be stimulated and encouraged rather than subdued. The neighborhood school concept grew out of the desire to keep schools close to the people. There are economic advantages as well in keeping attendance centers within walking distance of the pupils' homes. The added cost of transportation in rural areas is justified by

the benefits of centralization of operations. Busing of pupils who live within walking distance of one school to another more distant one is being promoted for sociological rather than educational reasons. The neighborhood school is under attack, not because it is economically unsound or based on the wrong premises, but because of the difficulty in modifying segregated residential patterns in large metropolitan areas. Much the same can be said for the community school concept. The development of communities of people of similar socioeconomic level or nationality background may be advantageous, but when people of one skin color are placed in a given area, the term "ghetto," with all its undesirable connotations, is used in place of "community" or "neighborhood." At the present time the neighborhood and community school concepts are under serious attack and careful evaluation.

Reexamination of local control of education

As stated earlier, public education in the United States was a grass-roots movement. For most of the history of our nation, local control of education was recognized as one of the great virtues of the American way of life. This is now being challenged. Some people have gone so far as to brand local control of education a myth, an archaic practice, and an encrusted tradition. It is said to inhibit innovation, impede achievement of excellence, make difficult the amelioration of social injustices. It is accused of perpetuating de facto segregation and alleged to be a high price to pay for inferior education. This is a serious indictment of a democratic tradition and a distinctly American approach to the administration of public education.

What is attacked as local control is

not always the same. Some people criticize the neighborhood school, the existence of the local school district operationally independent from other governmental units, the policy-making powers of school boards, the legislative control of education by the state rather than the federal government, or even the authority of the school board to accept or reject a curriculum idea.

It should not be assumed, however, that there no longer exists any support for the concept of local control. On the contrary, there exists a full spectrum of reaction ranging from unequivocal approval to complete condemnation. Some people judge the system ridiculous, others sublime. Some appraise it a vice, others proclaim it a virtue.

Local control as defined herein means placement of policy-making authority, within legislatively defined limits, for the direct operation of education with the people or their designated representatives within a legally defined civil subdivision of the state known as the school district. It represents an effort to compensate for the removal of absolute control for the educational development of the child from the parent. Under the local-control concept, parental concern over the education of their offspring can be effectively expressed even though a preponderance of operational controls rests with the more distant units such as the state or the federal government. The qualifying clause "within legislatively defined limits" is significant in the interpretation of the concept of local control as developed herein.

No serious student of education ever championed the extreme position of unqualified local determination or implied that education is a local rather than a state function. There never was a time in this century when a local school system could do as it pleased.

No district is permitted to operate a school system as bad as some people within it want it to be. No parent can arbitrarily jeopardize and curtail the educational development of his child. The local-control concept does not mean a return to the inadequately organized school district or the one-room school, but it does suggest keeping people at home actively involved and concerned about education.

School terms, teacher certification, safety standards, graduation requirements, and instructional programs are determined often by the state and serve as constraints within which local policies must operate. For more than 100 years the expressions of people acting through selected lay school-board members have been tempered by state demands. No one has ever exempted school operations from specific state legislative enactments that are not in conflict with the state constitution or the United States Constitution. Restrictions upon the exercise of local initiative are more severe now than ever before, and there is no substance to the view that people within a local school district can do as they please.

Over the years local practices at odds with the prevailing consensus in the states of the nation have been corrected. Excessive decentralization, which produced almost 200,000 local school districts at one time, most of which are weak and ineffective, has been in large measure corrected. In 1974 there were approximately 16,500 school districts and this number grows smaller each year. As pointed out previously, it is questionable whether there is a need for any more than 5,000 basic administrative units. The process of strengthening local districts through reorganization continues. With the existence of thousands of local school jurisdictions there is bound to be a variation in quality in spite of efforts to equalize educational opportunity. Those impatient with local control generalize from the sorriest among them; those who champion the idea point with pride to the excellence demonstrated in the best.

The existence of variation among local school districts raises the question of what alternative structural patterns, or, better, what different allocations of decision-making authority over school operations, could conceivably right all wrongs. An attack on local control is an attack on the people or their designated representatives within a local jurisdiction. It assumes, further, that another group of people is more capable of generating and implementing innovations or ameliorating injustices.

What are the alternatives? One would be to shift the dominant decision-making authority over educational operations to a more distant unit such as the federal government. Some equate highly centralized control with innovation and with educational programs more responsive to present and future needs of society. Is there solid evidence that people who influence the decisions of the federal government are better suited than the people in local jurisdictions to assume direct operating responsibilities for education? An examination of the variety of federal experiences in education, as will be developed in subsequent chapters, indicates that confusion and contradictions abound in present federal involvements in education and does little to support such beliefs. The so-called "national commitment to education" is neither unified in one agency nor well coordinated among the many involved. It is extremely difficult to ascertain who speaks for the federal government on education. If there is frustra-

tion in local school operations, there is even more in federal educational efforts. Whatever the shortcomings of qualified local control of education, there is considerable evidence that the transfer of operational decision-making authority for education to Washington, D.C., would not be in the best interests of the national welfare.

With perhaps a single exception there is little to suggest that direct state operation of education will produce the fresh and imaginative approach to learning that some feel is lacking under the local-control concept. In short, there is little evidence to recommend greater centralization as an alternative to qualified local control on the grounds that the state or federal agencies are more likely to engender new and exciting advances in educational processes. As will be developed in subsequent chapters, there is a need for state and federal involvement in a decentralized system of education, even though neither level is an adequate substitute for limited control. The best educational framework is one in which people with vision are free to experiment, to be creative, and to speak out without fear of oppressive reactions. Local initiative can have virtue if properly nourished. It can degenerate into inertia when local leadership is bankrupt and when state and federal agencies fail to stimulate leadership at the local level. Local control can be visualized as a means for tapping the creative ability of thousands of lay citizens teamed with more than a million professionals. This will be expanded in subsequent chapters.

The propensity to castigate local control should be sublimated in favor of searching for an environment that would multiply its advantages and minimize its inadequacies. A creative decentralized school pattern for our times calls for local operational responsibility for education supported by adequate resources, blessed with leadership talents, and stimulated by enlightened partners at the state and federal levels. Shortcomings in present school organizations may call for reexamination, but not abandonment, of an approach that rests on the democratic premise that the people, not a self-appointed and distant aristocratic intellectual elite, are the safest repository of governmental controls.

There exists the ever-present danger that schools, as a social institution, may be subverted to the narrow purposes of a dominant power elite and, therefore, fail to demonstrate adequate concern for a sizable segment of their clients. The church, in previous centuries, failed in some of its missions when it became the tool of a favored minority.

It is far more difficult for a single power bloc to gain control of education in a decentralized pattern than when centralization prevails. Nonetheless, local boards must remain alert to the responsibility of the school system to serve all the people and not a favorite few. This is not to suggest that complacency should prevail and there should be satisfaction at present levels of accomplishment. Adjustment and modification are necessary if school districts are to go beyond present aspirations and quality levels. It is reemphasized that the democratic tradition of local control is still far more likely to achieve excellence in education than centralization and concentration of authority in a state, regional, or federal educational unit.

Fiscal relations with other municipal corporations

The problem of whether schools shall be fiscally dependent on or independent of general municipal corporations has been the subject of considerable debate.. At present the research and debate are far less intensive than that noted in the 1930s and 1940s. There are various degrees and types of fiscal relations between schools and municipalities. If the legally elected or appointed school board has complete and final authority to levy local property taxes and expend funds for education, the school district is said to be fiscally independent of other local governmental units. Approval of other municipal officials to determine the local tax, the size of the levy, or the size of the budget for a given year is not required by law. When the district lacks complete authority to levy property taxes for schools or spend money budgeted without prior approval from some other local governmental agency, the district is termed fiscally dependent.

There are other types and forms of fiscal control over school districts, such as who has custody of, and authority to disburse, school funds or who keeps school financial records. The critical issue, however, is control over the budget and the decision on the final school-tax rate.

There are relatively few new studies of fiscal authorities and relationships. A 1958 study of fiscal relations between schools and municipalities concluded that in 54 percent of the city school systems studied, the budget was not reviewed by any outside agency. In 18 percent of the cases where the school budget had to be reviewed by an agency, the review was merely for purposes of information. Of the city school systems studied, 72 percent were relatively independent in deciding the size of the budget.[31] In addition,

[31]National Education Association, "Fiscal Authorities: City School Boards," *Research Bulletin,* vol. 28, no. 2, April 1958, pp. 46–79.

62 percent were, for all practical purposes, fiscally independent in determining the amount and rate of the school tax. The city school systems at the time of this study composed less than 5 percent of the total number of local educational units. School districts outside of cities are more likely to be fiscally independent. Clearly, the large majority of school districts in the United States are so organized as to be fiscally independent from other municipal agencies.

Whether school districts should or should not be independent has been a subject of debate for more than 50 years. Political scientists generally favor fiscal dependence of school systems, but educators argue in favor of fiscal independence. The research in existence is not conclusive for either side.

The following arguments support fiscal independence for school systems:

1. Efficiency and simplicity are best measured in terms of realization of the education function.
2. The ends of education are important to the welfare of our democracy and can best be realized by those who devote considerable effort and time to their realization.
3. School boards become useless appendages unless they are able to control the fiscal implications of educational planning.
4. Public education in many cities is already a large complex organization operating under efficient and professional administrative management.
5. The boundaries of many cities are not coterminous with school district boundaries.
6. Education is a state function and the local board of education represents the people of the state as well as the people living in the school district.[32]

As Firman put it, the fundamental

issue is "whether or not educational policy formulation can be separated from financial policy formulation."[33] Educators declare unequivocally that the agency generating policy must have the power to finance the implications of policy action.

Firman developed eight practical tests to assess the relative degree of fiscal independence.

1. Budget. The school board has the power to establish the budget.
2. Taxing power. The school board has the power to levy taxes to finance, in part, the proposed budget.
3. Adequacy of tax base. There is an adequate tax base within the school district to realize funds when local taxing authority is exercised.
4. Tax and indebtedness limits. Maximum legal limits on tax rate and indebtedness are sufficiently flexible to raise the amount required for school support.
5. Tax and indebtedness leeway. Enough taxing and indebtedness authority remains after satisfying mandatory educational programs to permit the school board to go beyond and toward enriched experiences.
6. Accounting. The board can keep its own system of financial records, including control of auditing and reporting procedures.
7. Responsibility. The citizen can turn to one local governmental authority—the school board—for appeal and for responsibility determination.
8. Response to educational needs. Fiscal resources and powers are acceptable and flexible enough to permit the school board to adjust to emerging demands.[34]

His informal survey of 11 large cities led him to conclude that it is possible

---

[32]S. J. Knezevich and John Guy Fowlkes, *Business Management of Local School Systems,* New York: Harper & Row, 1960, p. 12.

[33]W. D. Firman, "Fiscal Independence of School Systems," *Trends in Financing Public Education,* Proceedings of the Eighth National Conference on School Finance, Washington, D.C.: National Education Association, 1965, pp. 117–124.
[34]Ibid.

for these cities to operate on the principles of fiscal independence.

McLoone argued that "viewing fiscal dependence-independence as a continuum permits better analyses."[35] He pointed out that direct selection of school-board members by voters as well as direct access to taxes and final determination of spending by local boards were the main factors in fiscal independence. Local boards have authority only over local tax resources, which are contributing less and less to the total school revenues as state aids and federal grants continue to increase. A new factor in the fiscal dependence-independence debate is the freedom of local educational agencies to utilize aids and grants from state and federal governments. Earmarked or categorical aids can make a mockery of the fiscal dependence-independence of school boards. The issue becomes particularly acute when change becomes a passion and tax resources under the control of local boards are either not large enough or local people are not disposed psychologically to support new programs. This suggests psychological as well as political and economic dimensions of the issue.

SUMMARY

The school district is the basic structural unit in public education. Born of the division of the New England town, the school-district system was carried to the rest of the nation outside the South.

The school district as a political

[35]E. P. McLoone, "Advantages of Fiscal Independence for School Districts," *The Challenge of Change in School Finance*, Proceedings of the Tenth National Conference on School Finance, Washington, D.C.: National Education Association, 1967, pp. 137–150.

entity is a civil subdivision of the state. It is a legal entity called a quasi-municipal corporation. The corporate status facilitates the execution of school affairs. A school district can be viewed as a geographical entity with definite boundary lines. The community school is a product of program, rather than mere utilization of physical facilities. More popular definitions of community have a rural flavor and fail to reflect urban conditions.

The most important function of the district is to provide educational opportunities to resident pupils. Non-operating districts have no reason for being. Criteria for determining the effectiveness of school districts are based on numbers of resident pupils necessary to provide a comprehensive educational program at a reasonable cost per pupil. Changes in technology have motivated reorganization of local school districts. The number of districts in the United States has been reduced significantly since the end of World War II. In 1974–1975 there were only about 16,500 basic units of school administration in the 50 states. Only in extreme cases can newly reorganized districts with fewer than 2400 enrolled pupils be justified.

There is evidence to show that effective district structure is an important step toward the improvement of quality in education; there is a definite relation between pupil achievement and school size; and there is considerable variability in the size of enrollments and geographical area of school districts in the United States.

What relations shall exist between the local school district and other local governmental units is determined by the state legislature. The problem of whether schools should be fiscally dependent or independent has been debated for some time. Most educators support fiscal independence.

QUESTIONS

1. What is a school district?
2. In what ways do quasi-municipal corporations differ from general municipal corporations?
3. What are the characteristics of effective school districts?
4. Distinguish among the following: (a) attendance units, (b) administrative units, (c) community school districts, and (d) city school districts.
5. What distinguishes a fiscally independent school district from one that is fiscally dependent?

SELECTED REFERENCES

American Association of School Administrators, *School District Organization*, Report of the AASA Commission on School District Reorganization, Washington, D.C.: The Association, 1958.

Firman, W. D., "Fiscal Independence of School Systems," *Trends in Financing Public Education*, Proceedings of the Eighth National Conference on School Finance, Washington, D.C.: National Education Association, 1965, pp. 117–124.

Fitzwater, C. O., *Educational Change and Reorganized School Districts*, U.S. Office of Education, Bulletin 1953, no. 4, Washington, D.C.: GPO, 1953.

McLoone, E. P., "Advantages of Fiscal Independence for School Districts," *The Challenge of Change in School Finance*, Proceedings of the Tenth National Conference on School Finance, Washington, D.C.: National Education Association, 1967, pp. 137–150.

National Education Association, "Fiscal Authorities: City School Boards," *Research Bulletin*, vol. 28, no. 2, April 1958.

National Society for the Study of Education, *Metropolitanism, Its Challenge to Education*, R. J. Havighurst, ed., 67th Yearbook of the Society, Chicago: University of Chicago Press, 1968, part I, especially chaps. 1, 4, 5, 8, and 16.

Stephens, E. R., and J. Spiess, "What Does Research Say About a Local School District?", *Journal on State School Systems*, vol. 1, no. 3, Fall 1967, pp. 182–199.

10

THE INTERMEDIATE UNIT: THE REGIONAL EDUCATIONAL SERVICE AGENCY

Although the intermediate unit of school administration has been a structural part of public education in the United States for about 150 years, it remains the least understood administrative unit. The problem is partly the result of terminology and partly the result of the unit's more distant relation with pupils, patrons, and professional personnel. The term "intermediate unit of school administration" is of fairly recent origin and certainly its popular usage can be traced to the years following the end of World War II. Emerging even more recently is the functional description of this unit as the regional educational service agency (RESA).

NATURE OF THE INTERMEDIATE UNIT

The intermediate unit of school administration, or the RESA, is a "betweener." Structurally and functionally, it lies between the state on the one hand and the local district on the other. It is an arm of the state but occupies territory that encompasses many local school districts. It may be charged by the state educational agency with certain educational responsibilities, but exists to provide selected educational services to the local district.

The geographical area of a Regional Education Service Agency (RESA) is smaller than the state but much larger than most individual local school districts. Its territory usually encompasses a fairly large region; it is an expression of regionalism in the administration of education. Thus, the Oakland schools, an intermediate school district headquartered in Pontiac, Michigan, serves 28 local school districts in its region located in an area of approximately 900 square miles. Sometimes the area of a RESA is coterminous with another political unit in the state, such as the county. Because the intermediate unit often had the same boundaries as the county, it became known as the county superintendency. This term continues even though in many states it is an inappropriate and confusing description in relation to the 13 county-unit states. In these states the county is the basic unit of school administration and the county superintendent is the equivalent to the local district superintendent and not the executive officer of an intermediate unit or RESA. In the New England states, as well as in Alaska, Delaware,

233

Hawaii, Idaho, Kansas, and Nevada, there is no county superintendent. In Alaska there are no counties or boroughs, and all schools outside organized districts are administered directly by the state board of education through the commissioner of education. In the New England states, the intermediate unit takes the form of the supervisory union. Idaho and Kansas recently dissolved all county superintendencies, and in Delaware, Hawaii, and Nevada the intermediate unit was never established.

Structurally, the intermediate unit is a confederation of local school districts within a county or associated without regard for counties or other political units. The identification of this unit as a "betweener" is evident in the following more formal definition: "An intermediate unit of school administration is an area comprising two or more basic administrative units and having a board, or officer, or both responsible for performing stipulated services for the basic administrative units or for supervising their fiscal, administrative, or educational functions."[1] Cooper and Fitzwater conceived of the intermediate unit as "a unit of school administration that performs administrative and supervisory functions and provides supplementary educational services in a designated area composed of two or more local administrative units."[2]

As the term "confederation of basic administrative units" implies, the intermediate unit of school administration has no direct authority over local school districts in the sense of determining the nature of the educational program, which teachers shall be employed, or how pupils shall be assigned to various attendance units in the local district. On the contrary, the extent of the services provided by this administrative level is determined to a large degree by the local districts of which it is composed. In other words, what the intermediate unit does is largely controlled by the local districts.

Emerson[3] referred to the intermediate school districts as "the middle echelon of a state school system made up of a state education office, numerous local school districts (public corporations), and less numerous intermediate school districts (also public corporations)." Thirty-two states have a three-echelon structure of school government with some type of intermediate school district administrative agency. The intermediate school district has many names: intermediate school district (in Michigan); county school district (in California, Illinois, and Pennsylvania); cooperative educational services agency (in Wisconsin); multicounty educational service unit (in Nebraska); board of cooperative educational services (in New York); and regional education service center (in Texas).

Stephens preferred the use of the more general term "regional educational service agency" (RESA) to describe districts that could be characterized by three qualities, namely: being regional in geographic area, extending beyond the political boundaries of a county; having a commitment to provide essential educational services to constituent local school districts; and being a legal component

[1]Howard A. Dawson and Floyd W. Reeves, *Your School District,* Report of the National Commission on School District Reorganization, Washington, D.C.: Department of Rural Education, National Education Association, 1958, p. 52.

[2]Shirley Cooper and C. O. Fitzwater, *County School Administration,* New York: Harper & Row, 1954, p. 103.

[3]W. J. Emerson, "Intermediate School District," *Journal on State School Systems,* vol. 1, no. 1, Spring 1967, pp. 33–45.

of the state school system.[4] He argued that one of the most dramatic of the "movements in school government in the United States during the past decade (1960s) has been the establishment of a service unit setting between the state education agency and the local school district, or the restructing of an already existing middle echelon unit."[5]

Historical development

The intermediate unit began as an adjunct to the state level of school government. It represented a downward extension of administrative control from the state level to one closer to local school districts.[6] There was a need for information relative to programs of study, teachers, school census, enrollments, expenditures, and buildings in many local school districts. Gathering such data, compiling reports, and relaying the information to the state department of education were early responsibilities of the intermediate unit.[7] It also managed for the state such details as apportioning state school funds, establishing local boundary lines, and supervising and employing teachers in one-teacher school systems.

The local school district (basic unit) was created long before the need for an intermediate unit became apparent. The state educational unit appeared on the scene before the intermediate or regional service unit as well. Cooper and Fitzwater cited a 1795

New York law that gave legislative encouragement to functions commonly ascribed to an intermediate unit. It provided the town commissioners with power to apportion state school money among several districts, to confer with school district trustees concerning qualifications of teachers, and to supervise, to some extent, the program of studies. The law remained on the books for only about five years and was not extended. The first state board of education was established in New York in 1784, but this board did not have control over public elementary and secondary schools. The state superintendency was created first in New York in 1812 and in Maryland in 1826.

Delaware in 1829 was the first state to enact legislation establishing the traditional county superintendency.[8] New York followed in 1843, Illinois in 1844, Virginia in 1845, Louisiana and Ohio in 1847, North Carolina in 1848, New Hampshire and Oregon in 1850, and California in 1852. By 1879, 34 of the 38 states then composing the nation, and 4 of the territories, had created the office of county superintendent. It was in an intermediate unit of administration.[9]

In the last half of the nineteenth and the early part of the twentieth centuries, most new states that developed structured plans for public education created local districts, intermediate units, and the state educational agency all at about the same time.

The supervisory union

In New England, the town served as the basic administrative unit for school purposes. A collection or federation of these towns was called the supervisory union.[10] The superintendent of this

---

[4]E. Robert Stephens, "A Profile of Exemplary Regional Educational Service Agencies," *Planning and Changing, A Journal for School Administrators,* vol. 3, no. 3, Fall 1972, pp. 33–40.

[5]Ibid.

[6]Shirley Cooper and C. O. Fitzwater, op. cit., p. 104.

[7]Ibid.

[8]Ibid., p. 136.

[9]Ibid.

[10]Ibid., p. 120.

intermediate unit was commonly referred to as the union district superintendent. About half of the superintendents in New England in 1950 were such superintendents.

Legislation authorizing formation of the supervisory union was permissive. Laws were enacted in Massachusetts in 1881, in New Hampshire in 1895, in Maine in 1897, in Connecticut in 1903, in Rhode Island in 1903, and in Vermont in 1906.[11] Membership in such unions was voluntary and frequently of short duration. Any member district could withdraw by majority vote at the annual school meeting. The transitory character of local district membership in the supervisory union created an unstable organization and prevented formation of long-range educational plans. This led subsequently to a revision that made membership mandatory for districts that did not employ superintendents. Cooper and Fitzwater described supervisory unions in various New England states as a pooling of local resources in one instance, a decentralization of the state department of education leadership in another, and a relevatively unimportant intermediate district in still another state composed largely of urban communities.[12] The union district superintendency in Rhode Island is relatively unimportant in the total pattern of school administration owing to the high concentration of population.

Most union district superintendents are appointed to office, but the method varies. Appointment is made by the state department of education in Connecticut, by the state board from nominations submitted by local boards in New Hampshire, and directly by joint action of school committees in Maine, Massachusetts, and Vermont.

[11] Ibid.
[12] Ibid., p. 121.

The formation of supervisory unions in New England is doubtless related to the relatively weak position of the county as a political unit in these states. In several of the New England states, the county exists for little more than judicial purposes. There is some evidence to suggest that the supervisory union superintendent in some New England states is assuming the role of a local district superintendent but continues to report to two or more different school boards.

The township

The township, for a short period of time, served as an intermediate district in New York and to some extent in Wisconsin and Illinois. The township exerted some intermediate functions in Michigan. In most instances the township (which in most midwestern states is a geographical unit of about 36 square miles) or collection of townships is much too small to serve effectively as an intermediate unit. It rarely provides such functions today.

The county superintendency

By far the largest number of intermediate units in the United States have land areas coterminous with the political unit known as a county. However, in about 1 out of every 8 states the county is not an intermediate unit. In 13 states (Alabama, Florida, Georgia, Kentucky, Louisiana, Maryland, Nevada, New Mexico, North Carolina, Tennessee, Utah, Virginia, and West Virginia), the county is the basic administrative unit, that is, it is the local not intermediate or regional service district; Alaska, Delaware, and Hawaii do not have superintendents of county-unit school districts or county superintendents of intermediate administrative units. In contrast in 1950, the county in 27 states was the intermediate administrative unit. Only 15 percent of these 27 states had a county board of education as well as a superintendent. Approximately 3050 school administrators in the nation some 25 years ago were superintendents of county units, county intermediate units, or comparable intermediate units of school administration.[13]

The county superintendency is established either by an act of the state legislature or by the state constitution. In 14 states the county superintendency is a constitutional office, and in these states it is very difficult to redefine the functions and responsibilities of the superintendency.

Selection of the superintendent

Historically, selection of the county superintendent has been by vote of the people. This method is losing popularity but continues to be used more widely than any other. Some 20 years ago in Arizona, Colorado, Illinois, Kansas, Minnesota, Mississippi, Montana, North Dakota, Oklahoma, South Dakota, Washington, and Wyoming most county superintendents were elected by popular vote.[14]

In contrast, in New England and New York all intermediate district superintendents are appointed. All county or intermediate unit superintendents in Arkansas, Indiana, Iowa, Michigan, Nebraska, Ohio, Pennsylvania, and Wisconsin are appointed by an intermediate board of education. In New Jersey county superintendents are appointed by the state commissioner of education, subject to the approval of the state board.

About 39 percent of the 913 county superintendents in the 13 county-unit

states were popularly elected in the early 1950s. In Kentucky, Louisiana, Maryland, North Carolina, Utah, Virginia, and West Virginia, all of which are county-unit states, the superintendent of the basic administrative unit was appointed to office by the county board of education. All the states selecting the county-unit superintendent by popular election are located south of the Mason-Dixon line and west of Indiana. The pattern is changing slowly in southern states such as Florida, where more county superintendents are being appointed to office each year, even though presently the majority continue to gain office by election.

Election of the county superintendent of schools, whether he serves the intermediate or the basic administrative unit, is difficult to justify. Politics, rather than the welfare of the educational program, supports this pattern. It is strongly recommended by most who have given careful study to the problem that the county superintendent be appointed to office by a county board of education. There appears to be a clear trend in this direction.

The term of office for the county superintendent varies and is usually prescribed by law. In 9 states he has a 2-year term; in 20 states, a 4-year term; in 2 states, a 3-year term; and in 6 states, an indefinite length of term. The short terms of appointment are carryovers from the political election or appointment system. Appointment by the county board of education for no less than 3 years, and preferably for an indefinite period, has greater justification.

Educational requirements for office are increasing. In most of the states where the county superintendent is an officer of the intermediate or basic unit, 4 years or more of professional preparation are now required. Many states require an administrator's cer-

[13]Ibid., p. 140.
[14]Ibid.

tificate based on 5 or more years of professional preparation in order to practice as a county superintendent.

REORGANIZATION OF THE INTERMEDIATE UNIT

The traditional intermediate unit, particularly the county superintendency, has long been subject to criticism. In addition, reorganization since 1941 has eliminated a large number of weak and ineffective school districts and reduced the number of one-teacher schools from over 100,000 to less than 1,000. Because each remaining district is stronger and staffed with a local district superintendent, assistant superintendents, and principals professionally prepared to execute their work, they no longer require the type of supervision and administration traditionally provided by the county superintendent for weak local districts. As a result some states during the 1950s and 1960s established what is today a most desirable trend—removing the county superintendent from partisan politics and creating the intermediate unit. County boards of education have been established where none existed; professional qualifications for superintendents of this unit have been upgraded; and salary and tenure of office have markedly increased. The questions arise whether this progress has been sufficient and significant, and indeed whether there is justification for the position in the first instance. A minority in the field of public education has called for abolishing all intermediate units on grounds that they no longer have any contribution to make toward better education.

It is submitted that unless all school districts in the United States are structured to include no fewer than 10,000

pupils, an intermediate unit of administration is essential for the maintenance of quality. The sparseness of population in most states, as well as the concern for maintaining community district boundaries, indicate that many districts will have less than 10,000 resident pupils. Formation of local school districts that follow county boundary lines does not by that fact make intermediate units expendable. It is the number of resident pupils within a basic administrative unit, rather than its geographic area, that determines such needs.

If school districts are structured along community lines, they will contain fewer than the minimum number of pupils needed to allow them to provide all the educational services at a reasonable cost per pupil. Another agency must be created to provide special services that the local district cannot provide either because there are too few pupils or because the cost would be prohibitive.

As stated previously, the work of the early intermediate units, particularly the county superintendencies, was to provide services to weak and ineffective school districts in a county. Fitzwater pointed out that the impact of local redistricting on county intermediate administrative units has varied widely.[15] An Idaho law called for dissolution of intermediate units when local redistricting was completed within a county. This state now has eliminated all intermediate units. Colorado, Minnesota, and Missouri have legislation that allows elimination of the office of county superintendent. By 1966, the county superintendency was voted out of existence in most counties in Colorado, and plans were de-

[15]C. O. Fitzwater, "Patterns and Trends in State School System Development," *Journal on State School Systems*, vol. 1, no. 1, Spring 1967, pp. 26–32.

veloped in that state to create a re-vitalized form of the intermediate unit known as the board of cooperative services.[16]

The 1960s may well be remembered as a decade of great significance in the development of more effective inter-mediate or regional service districts. The following significant reorganiza-tions in intermediate school adminis-trative agencies or units took place.[17]

1. In 1962 Michigan enacted legisla-tion requiring consolidation of county intermediate districts with school mem-bership of fewer than 5000 pupils. By 1973 the 83 original county units were reduced to 59. Thirty-eight were reor-ganized to produce 14 multicounty consolidations, most of which were 2-county mergers but one was a 5-county consolidation. The total num-ber of intermediate units in Michigan may be reduced to 20 in the near future.

2. In 1965 Nebraska enacted legis-lation creating 19 new multicounty ed-ucational service units covering the entire state. Unfortunately, counties had the option to move out of such units if so desired.

3. In 1965 Wisconsin abolished 72 county intermediate districts and re-placed them with 19 new cooperative educational service agencies.

4. In 1965 the state of Washington enacted legislation requiring the state board of education to develop a state-wide plan for reorganizing intermedi-ate units. The plan called for the cre-ation of 15 new intermediate units.

5. In 1965 Colorado enacted legisla-tion that permitted the abolition of the county superintendency and allowed for the creation of a board of cooper-ative services to replace such a unit where voters deemed it desirable.

6. In 1965 Pennsylvania enacted a statute calling for the reorganization of intermediate school districts. A study by the Pennsylvania State Board of Education released in 1967 proposed 25 intermediate units. A unique fea-ture was that the two largest cities, Philadelphia and Pittsburgh, were con-sidered as 2 of the 25 units.

7. New York has been consolidating intermediate school districts over the years and by 1968 had a statewide network of 55 boards of cooperative educational services. In some very large and populous counties, such as Suffolk County, Long Island, there were more than one such regional ser-vice units. This is one of the few ex-ceptions where the new intermediate unit served a geographic area that was smaller than the county.

8. In 1947 Iowa permitted county boards to merge 2 or more adjacent county intermediate units subject to the approval of the state board. In July, 1966, the first 2 counties merged to form the first multicounty interme-diate district in the state.

9. Acting under a 1965 law, Texas, through its state board of education, saw 20 regional education service cen-ters become operative and encompass all districts in the state by July 1967.

10. In Ohio a study has called for the replacement of the existing 88 county intermediate units with a new pattern of area education districts with a minimum pupil population of 35,000 to administer programs and services that could not be provided effectively by the local districts.

11. Oregon introduced legislation that would facilitate consolidation of county intermediate units.

12. The Elementary and Secondary Education Act of 1965 encouraged the creation of multicounty cooperative service programs. Title III under this act provided a basis for funding of

[16]Ibid.
[17]Ibid.; Emerson, op. cit.

special projects based on a regional approach to educational planning and services. This has helped make the revitalized intermediate unit an innovative educational agency.

Another approach to the intermediate unit was suggested in a special study of Nevada. That state had 17 school districts, of which 15 are sparsely settled. Regional services directly out of the state education agency were suggested as a better solution than the establishment of multicounty intermediate units.

Some of the dominant trends as evident by the actions of some 20 states intent on reforming the intermediate unit include:

1. Promotion of multicounty educational service districts for a region.
2. State education agency review authority over the role and functions of the RESAs.
3. Control of RESAs by popularly elected governing boards from representatives of constituent local districts.
4. Extensive use of advisory bodies to the RESA.
5. Provision of highly diverse specialized educational programs.
6. Limitations on the direct tax levying capabilities of the RESA.
7. Cooperative arrangements with neighboring institutions of higher learning to provide selected educational services.[18]

Role of the unit

The general or fundamental purpose of the intermediate or regional service unit should be to provide to two or more local school districts educational services that could not be provided by such districts in an efficient manner or at a reasonable cost per pupil. The intermediate unit has been redesigned to meet the educational needs of the local school district.[19]

The kinds of services provided will be those most needed and most significant in each area of the nation. The range of intermediate unit services available to enrich educational opportunities in local school districts is virtually unlimited. The following outline indicates some of the possibilities:

1. Adult education
2. Audiovisual library
   (Equipment, films, etc.)
3. Communication
   (Reports, bulletins, handbooks, etc.)
4. Cooperative or centralized purchasing
5. Curriculum laboratory
6. Curriculum leadership
   (Conservation, safety, radio and TV programs, etc.)
7. Services for exceptional children
   a. Gifted
   b. Mentally retarded
   c. Physically handicapped (crippled)
   d. Partially sighted (sight-saving class)
   e. Speech defective
   f. Hard of hearing (lip-reading class)
   g. Homebound
8. Financial services
   a. Accounting
   b. Auditing
   c. Financial counseling
   d. Reporting
9. Health services
   a. School nurse
   b. School doctor
   c. Dental health and hygiene personnel
10. In-service education
    a. Teachers
    b. Administrators
    c. School-board members
    d. Bus drivers
    e. Clerical personnel
    f. Custodians
    g. School-lunch personnel
11. Instructional materials center

[18]E. R. Stephens and W. S. Ellena, "Regionalism in Education: Terms, Trends, and Benefits," *School Administrator*, pp. 19–20.

[19]Robert M. Isenberg, ed., *The Community School on the Intermediate Unit*, Yearbook, Washington, D.C.: Department of Rural Education, National Education Association, 1954, chap. 7.

12. Instructional supervision
13. Legal services
14. Library services
    a. Books, films, recordings
    b. Exhibits, collections, models
    c. Professional librarian and materials
15. Professional personnel services
    a. Teacher placement
    b. Substitute teachers
    c. Salary-schedule development and coordination, sick-leave policy determinations, etc.
16. Pupil personnel services
    a. Attendance supervision
    b. Guidance and counseling
    c. Testing
    d. Psychological and psychiatric services
    e. Mental health clinic
17. Pupil-transportation services
    a. Administration of transportation
    b. School-bus maintenance
    c. Bus-driver training
18. Recreation programs
19. Research
20. School-building services
    a. Planning and maintenance
    b. Building clinics
    c. Architectural services
21. School-lunch services
    a. Coordination
    b. Supervision
22. Special teachers
    Art, music, agriculture, homemaking, physical education
23. Special consultants and coordinators (Reading consultant, science consultant, etc.)
24. Trade and industrial education[20]

The advent of computer-based electronic data processing in education points to yet another valuable service that can be provided effectively and efficiently by an intermediate unit.

The different educational services would require different numbers of pupils for efficient and economical operation. To illustrate, an attendance supervisor with clerical assistance can serve 6000 pupils; a health nurse 2000 pupils; a dental hygienist 2000 pupils; a school psychologist about 3000 pupils; a guidance counselor about 600 pupils.[21]

In the Stephens profile of an exemplary RESA the emphasis was on specialized services to local districts although some ministerial and administrative services were performed for state education agencies as well.[22] The high quality of the professional staff was another characteristic of the exemplary units.

One of the outstanding intermediate or regional service units is the Oakland schools headquartered in Pontiac, Michigan and serving 28 local school districts ranging in size from 2,300 to 24,000 pupils. It is an integral part of the state school system and has fiscal integrity and independence, with its board alone controlling fiscal and personnel resources. It also has taxing authority and bonding authority, and it qualifies for state education aids; it has authority to charge for some of its services and is accountable to its constituency in many ways.[23]

In addition to its hierarchy of well-prepared professional administrative staff it has a full complement of excellent specialists in a wide range of educational, psychological, guidance, evaluation, and technical areas. It provides services in electronic data processing, special education, compensatory education, student achievement monitoring, food service system, transportation, and leadership in professional development. Its film library, curriculum services and special projects for vocationally limited and others places it at the cutting edge of school leadership and services. Its total budget in 1972–1973 exceeded

[20]Ibid., pp. 187–189.

[21]Ibid., p. 16.
[22]E. R. Stephens, op. cit.
[23]W. J. Emerson, *This Is Oakland Schools,* Pontiac, Michigan: Oakland Schools, 1973.

$11 million. Oakland schools served over 260,000 pupils with a staff of 125 professional and 99 technical/clerical employees.

The Los Angeles County School District is perhaps the largest as well as one of the outstanding intermediate units in the nation. In 1973–1974 it employed 1024 certificated employees and had a total budget of over $51.4 million. The services of this unit were available to 95 local districts in the county, which had 1727 schools with a student and adult enrollment of more than 1.9 million. Its constituent districts cover an area of 4060 square miles. The sheer magnitude of numbers included in Los Angeles County should not obscure the high quality and comprehensiveness of this intermediate unit's leadership activities in curriculum development, programs for exceptional children, opportunities for outdoor education, expanded vocational education opportunities, instructional television, efficient handling of funds, computer based educational data processing, as well as audiovisual and library services. These programs were financed from the following sources: 6 percent from the federal government, 25 percent from state government, and 69 percent from local taxes (some of which can be levied by this intermediate unit), and through contracts with local school districts.

Structure of the RESA

The county and the supervisory union are too small in most states to administer the educational responsibilities of the revitalized intermediate unit efficiently. The great variance in size and population of counties points to the need for structuring the intermediate unit without regard to boundaries of existing political units, which were not created with the need of schools in

mind. There is evidence that an intermediate unit serving many local school districts should have no less than 5,000 to 6,000 pupils. If a revitalized intermediate unit is to perform its function with dispatch, it must have 25,000 or more pupils within its boundaries preferred.

The organizational structure for effective intermediate units would exhibit the following characteristics:

1. Provision should be made for an intermediate unit board of education and an executive officer. The board would serve as a policy-making body. Among its functions should be that of appointing a qualified superintendent.

2. Provision should be made for the administrative participation of representatives of the community schools in the area. The service nature of the intermediate unit requires that it be sensitive to the needs of the community schools. The intermediate unit board of education must determine policies with respect to the collective demands and interests of the community schools. Representation might be provided through an advisory council made up of the members of the community school boards of education.

3. Provision should be made for administrative coordination. An administrative advisory group, made up of all the community school administrators in the intermediate unit's area, could meet regularly with and advise the intermediate unit superintendent. Problems regarding the selection and functioning of intermediate unit staff, evaluation of specific services, schedules, and many other details of administrative duties must be planned cooperatively.

4. The intermediate unit should be large enough to provide efficiently a variety of services needed by the school districts in the intermediate area but which cannot be operated by

the district's acting alone. It should not, however, be so large that it precludes close personal relations among intermediate unit and community school staff members.

5. Provision should be made so that the structure can be adjusted to meet changing functions. The services the intermediate unit should provide will vary from place to place and from time to time. Services initiated by the intermediate unit may, in some instances, be transferred to the community schools, and vice versa.

6. Provision should be made for cooperation among intermediate units. The desirable service area for a few specialized services may be larger than a single intermediate unit. Considerable advantage may be gained through the sharing of such a service by two or more intermediate units.

7. Provision should be made for the adequate financing of a program of services.[24]

The financing of intermediate unit activities can come from one or more of the following sources: (1) federal support, (2) state grants, (3) county funds, (4) tax levies over the entire intermediate unit, and (5) contractual agreements with local districts. Authority to tax is important to the intermediate unit. The following can be used as a guide for financing a program of intermediate unit services:

1. Financial support should be adequate to provide those services that can most effectively and economically become a function of the intermediate unit.

2. The state should share in financing the intermediate unit's program of services.

3. The state should assume responsibility for a foundation program by underwriting the minimum program to

be provided by the intermediate units within the state.

4. The state's contribution should be based on the principle of equalization.

5. Intermediate units should be permitted and encouraged to exceed the foundation program. Necessary funds may be obtained by levying a tax equally upon the entire intermediate area as determined by the intermediate district's board of education. Funds may be collected by the general taxing authority of the district or by its constituent community districts.

6. The financial structure should provide for creative and experimental programs.

7. Indirect financing through contractual agreements between the intermediate administrative unit and local community districts should be used to support intermediate unit services of a special or temporary nature such as the development of pilot programs or the support of services not extended to all constituent community districts. When a service becomes a generally recognized function of the intermediate unit, however, contract financing should be replaced by direct financing to guarantee consistency of service and efficiency of administration.

8. A budget for all intermediate district activities should be prepared by the intermediate district superintendent and approved by the intermediate district board in accordance with state regulations and practice.

9. Compensation of employees of the intermediate district should be based upon a salary schedule that recognizes the experience, qualifications, and responsibilities demanded for efficient service on this level and should include all privileges accorded professional workers in other types of districts of the state.

10. The salary of the intermediate superintendent should be determined

---

[24]R. Isenberg, op. cit., pp. 197–198.

by a board of education that recognizes its responsibility for providing educational services and leadership that will make available to every community a comprehensive program of educational opportunities.

11. The financial structure of the intermediate unit should be reviewed at frequent intervals and kept sufficiently flexible that it can be changed in the light of experience and research.[25]

Emerson[26] pointed to the need for a reconfiguration of the various school administrative echelons in the state to cope with present demands upon school agencies. He recommended a rule of thumb for the allocation of educational functions in the multiechelon system: "Allocate the function to that echelon of the system closest to the student, where it may be carried out with completeness, equity, efficiency and responsibility. In testing for fit try the closest echelon first." In providing services, the revitalized intermediate units in Michigan, according to Emerson, have produced and are producing the following:

1. Intermediate-districtwide programs of special education—mature, complete, sophisticated, and serviceable.
2. Intermediate-districtwide programs of staff and curriculum development in the academic discipline served by Ph.D. specialists.
3. Intermediate-district-operated educational, diagnostic, and remediation centers for speech pathology, audiology and language development, reading, psychometrics, educational guidance, social work, and vocational rehabilitation.
4. Intermediate-districtwide educational research operations and systematic studies resources.
5. Intermediate-districtwide testing services, including a central lending library of tests, scoring and computing services, reporting and interpretation services.

6. Intermediate-districtwide cooperative purchasing and quality-control programs to acquire such items as foods, paper stock, standard machinery, fuel, and bus fleets.
7. Intermediate-districtwide staff-development programs for cooks, bus drivers, office staff, and maintenance personnel.
8. Intermediate-district-operated instructional materials centers.
9. Intermediate-districtwide data-processing systems employing second- and third-generation computers, random-access magnetic storage, and teleprocessing.
10. Intermediate-districtwide public-information service directed partly to news media and partly to the profession.
11. Intermediate-district-operated law enforcement functions performed on behalf of the state education department.
12. Intermediate-districtwide program of vocational education.[27]

To keep program development at peak efficiency, Emerson stressed the importance of periodically reevaluating and reallocating functions. He recognized the dynamic nature of educational enterprise and therefore the importance of reassessing the most effective ways of providing needed educational services from the various echelons.

Emerson stressed that successful intermediate district structure cannot be established casually by the state or members of the education profession. Certain kinds of cooperative arrangements are necessary to produce a truly effective three-echelon system. He indicated the seven significant conditions for the development of a revitalized intermediate administrative unit:

1. Product mix of the intermediate unit rests to a greater rather than a lesser extent on permissive legislation.
2. The degree of use of the product mix by the constituency is left largely to the choice of the local school adminis-

[25]Ibid., pp. 205–206.
[26]Emerson, op. cit.

[27]Ibid.

tration (law enforcement is one exception, but only a small one).

3. The intermediate district staff is selected and governed by a board popularly selected by the constituency.
4. There is some minimum taxing power exercised unilaterally by the intermediate district board.
5. There is some state aid for intermediate districts which issues with appropriate limitations from the state school office.
6. There are statutory arrangements for intermediate district housing to be acquired and held as intermediate district property.
7. There are statutory arrangements for the review of intermediate district programs by the constituents as well as the state school office.[28]

Significant developments are continuing in intermediate school districts or regional educational service units. It is a most encouraging trend. The complexity of education, with the many and varied demands placed upon local school units, points to a greater, not a lesser, need for an effective and revitalized middle echelon in the total school structural arrangement.

A number of model bills have been prepared for the establishment of revitalized intermediate units or RESAs in states seeking to move in this direction.[29] There is ample experience to prove the value of an effective RESA.

SUMMARY

Although the intermediate unit has been in existence for a long time, it is one of the least understood of ad-

ministrative units. It performs administrative and supervisory functions and provides supplementary educational services for two or more local school districts. It is also identified as the regional educational service agency (RESA). The intermediate unit began as an adjunct of the state educational agency.

The supervisory union is the intermediate unit serving districts in some New England states. Collections of several local districts, in all or parts of two or more counties, and the county superintendency perform similar functions for most of the remainder of the nation. There are states without intermediate units. In 13 states, located primarily in the south, the county is the basic, rather than the intermediate, unit of administration.

The intermediate or service unit superintendent is selected by a vote of the people or through appointment. Most of the county superintendents in most of the 13 county-unit states are appointed to office by a board of education. Election of the county superintendent is difficult to justify.

Much of the work of the county superintendent has been concerned with the weak and ineffective local school districts. Reorganization of local districts into more efficient units has necessitated a reorganization and revitalization of the intermediate unit. Newly reorganized and stronger local units structured along community boundary lines will require the services of intermediate districts.

The new role of the intermediate unit is to provide to two or more local districts those educational services that could not be provided by such local units in an efficient manner or at a reasonable cost per pupil. The range of services available to enrich educational opportunities in local districts is virtually unlimited.

---

[28]Ibid.

[29]E. Robert Stephens, *Recommended Statutory Provisions for the Establishment, Governance, Organization, and Operation of Regional Educational Service Agencies*, Washington, D.C.: Rural Education Association, National Education Association, 1970, p. 9.

QUESTIONS

1. Why is the intermediate unit sometimes called a "betweener"?
2. Will there be a need for intermediate school units after all local districts in the United States have been reorganized into effective school districts? Justify your stand.
3. What are the factors that have created a need for the reorganization of intermediate units?
4. What are the characteristics of effectively organized intermediate units?
5. List some of the educational services that the intermediate unit appears better adapted to sponsor or execute than is the local district. What educational functions should remain with local units rather than being delegated to intermediate districts?

SELECTED REFERENCES

Cooper, Shirley, and C. O. Fitzwater, *County School Administration,* New York: Harper & Row, 1954.

Emerson, W. J., "Intermediate School District," *Journal of State School Systems,* vol. 1, no. 1, Spring 1967, pp. 33–45.

Fitzwater, C. O., "Patterns and Trends in State School System Development," *Journal of State School Systems,* vol. 1, no. 1, Spring 1967, pp. 26–32.

Isenberg, Robert M., ed., *The Community School and the Intermediate Unit,* Yearbook, Washington, D.C.: Department of Rural Education, National Education Association, 1954, chaps. 1, 2, 6, and 7.

Rhodes, Alvin E., *Better Education Through Effective Intermediate Units,* Washington, D.C.: National Education Association, 1963.

Stephens, E. R., "A Profile of Exemplary Regional Educational Service Agencies," *Planning and Changing,* vol. 3, no. 3, Fall 1972, pp. 33–40.

11

THE STATE EDUCATION AGENCIES

Courts across the nation have reinforced, with some degree of finality, the concept of public education in the United States as a state function. How the state discharges this responsibility and the structural apparatus created for this purpose are the subjects of this chapter. The people of a state speak through laws enacted by their elected representatives in the legislature; through state constitutional mandates; and through rules, regulations, and policies enunciated by one or several executive agencies at the state level. Legislatures of every state except Hawaii have delegated considerable control over the operation of public education to the people and/or their representatives in local school districts. To enhance local efforts, various other agencies of the state have been fashioned—for example, the intermediate unit of school administration in most states and a state education department in all states. The influence of the state education agency on the operation of public education is growing, not lessening. A strong and effective state department of education is a necessity. The roles and structure of the state education agency are being reexamined and redesigned to meet new challenges; the quality and quantity of its professional staff have been enhanced and increased.

THE STATE LEGISLATURE

The legislature of each state determines basic policies in education such as: how local boards of education shall be selected, what specific subjects shall or shall not be taught in the public schools, how many years of education shall be available to all or various types of pupils, what standards shall be required for admission of pupils to schools, and even what textbooks shall be used. The state legislature approves laws applying to certification of teachers, the safety and quality of school facilities, and what financial resources shall be made available for the support of education in the state and in the local school districts.

No one today questions the authority of the state legislature to influence the organization and operation of public education within its boundaries so long as such actions do not violate principles and limits set by the state constitution or rights guaranteed to individuals by the United States Constitution. No state legislature may act in an arbitrary manner in discharging any of its responsibilities. A citizen may obtain relief through the state judicial system when the legislature exceeds its authority or acts in a capricious or unreasonable manner. Relief through federal courts may be sought when a citizen feels that the operation of an educational system as prescribed by the state legislature deprives him of rights guaranteed under the United States Constitution.

How the state legislature executes its educational responsibilities will have a decisive impact on local and state education agencies. Most authorities recommend that the legislature refrain from making detailed specifications of the curriculum for the schools, as well as delineating other dimensions of the educational operation. Detailed legislative prescription and excessive state-imposed restrictions could reduce the policy-making authority and status of school boards to mere implementation of decisions reached at the state level. Likewise, the assignment of state executive authority for educational or primarily school related policies to agencies other than the state department of education is a questionable practice. The state legislation should confine its activities to the determination of broad policy matters governing the organization, financing, and operation of public education, and then delegate establishment and enforcement of standards to a state education agency. The legislation should focus on establishing defensible minimums in education, with the proviso that local units may upon their own volition exceed such minimums. Above all, opportunities for leadership in improving education should be provided by both local and state education agencies.

The state education agency is a creature of the legislature and may be influenced by constitutional mandates. State concern for public education can be traced as far back as the Massachusetts laws of 1642 and 1647. These laws evidenced the willingness of the people of an area, later to be recognized as a state, to take governmental action to ensure establishment of schools—to resort to legal means to compel parents to respect their obligations for the education of the young. This point of view soon spread to all the original colonies, and by the time the nation was formed, widely varied legal provisions for public education existed in each of the 13 states. Very early in our history the United States Congress required that all new states make provisions for public education. The establishment of a state system of education became one of the conditions to be satisfied in the enabling acts drafted to transform a territory into a state.

THE STATE BOARD OF EDUCATION

Historical development

The first agency identified as a state board of education came into being in New York in 1784. It was created in response to the need for a statewide administrative agency for colleges and academies authorized during colonial days. In spite of its title, this board had no responsibility for the public elementary and secondary schools until 1904. Thus, credit for the establishment of a board in control of higher education belongs to New York, but it is questionable whether this deserves recognition as the first state board of education for public elementary and secondary schools.

The need to formulate state policy with reference to public education began to emerge with the federal land grants for education in the new states and the creation of state school funds in the original states. The first state board of education concerned with disbursing state school funds to local districts was formed in North Carolina in 1825; it was an ex-officio board to care for the newly created permanent school fund known as the "literary fund." Broader powers over education were granted to it in 1837. Vermont in 1827 established a rudimentary state board of education; it was abolished in 1835 only to be recreated subsequently.

The prototype of the modern state board of education was created in Massachusetts in 1837. It was the first board of education with an appointed secretary (Horace Mann), and it introduced a recommended pattern for state education administration and operation. By 1870 states then in existence established state boards of education. Typical practice in the states at that time was to create a number of special boards whose powers and duties were often limited to a unique purpose, such as operation of one type of educational institution, management of a state educational fund, or administration of a specific activity. The poorly defined terminology, which described state board functions, prior to 1900 makes impractical a detailed historical analysis of state boards of education.[1]

All states, the District of Columbia, and the outlying territories of American Samoa, Guam, Puerto Rico, the Trust Territory of the Pacific Islands, and the Virgin Islands now have some type of state board of education (see Table 11–1), for federal law requires a state board for vocational education if the state or territory is to be eligible to receive federal funds for these activities. Wisconsin is the only state or territory *without* a state board for public elementary and secondary school activities unrelated to vocational education.

In 1945 only 38 of the 48 states had

[1]R. F. Will, *State Education, Structure and Organization*, U.S. Office of Education, OE-23038, misc. no. 46, Washington, D.C.: GPO, 1964.

state boards of education with control over public elementary and secondary schools. Since 1945, boards have been established in Illinois, Iowa, Maine, Michigan, Nebraska, and North Dakota. The new states Alaska and Hawaii who entered the union since then make a total of 49 states with a state board of education concerned with public elementary and secondary education. Michigan in 1964 became the 48th state to establish such a board. A new state constitution was ratified by the voters of Illinois on December 15, 1970. Article J, Section 2, of the new constitution made Illinois the 49th state to create a more broadly based state board of education.

Duties of the state board

Early duties of the state board of education were usually general and included such responsibilities as "promoting education"; however, few funds were allotted for "promoting." Caring for school lands and funds, determining teaching qualifications, specifying courses of study and advising chief state school officers were other assigned functions. Their duties included broad discretionary powers considered essential to the administration of educational affairs.

The recommendations of the Council of Chief State School Officers with reference to responsibilities of the state board of education made over 20 years ago are still relevant today. These should be defined in the state statutes and include:

1. Formulate policies and adopt such rules and regulations as are necessary to carry out the responsibilities assigned to it by the constitution and the statutes of the state.
2. Appoint and fix the salaries of the professional staff of the state department of education on the recommendation of the chief state school officer.

TABLE 11–1

CHARACTERISTICS OF THE STATE BOARDS OF EDUCATION (SBE)

State	Designation	Elected by people or representatives of people	Appointed by governor	Ex-officio (by virtue of office or position held)	Total	Ex-officio	Term of membership (years)	SBE is board for vocational education	SBE is board for vocational rehabilitation
		Chief method of selecting members			Number of members				
Alabama	State Board of Education	—	X	—	10	2	4	Yes	Yes
Alaska	State Board of Education	—	X	—	7	0	5	Yes	Yes
Arizona	State Board of Education	—	X	—	9	1	4	Yes	Yes
Arkansas	State Board of Education	—	X	—	10	1	9	Yes	No
California	State Board of Education	—	X	—	10	0	4	Yes	Yes
Colorado	State Board of Education	X	—	—	5	0	6	No	No
Connecticut	State Board of Education	—	X	—	10	1	6	Yes	Yes
Delaware	State Board of Education	—	X	—	8	2	3	Yes	No
District of Columbia	State Board of Education	X	—	—	12	1	4	No	Yes
Florida	State Board of Education	—	—	X	7	7	4	Yes	No
Georgia	State Board of Education	—	X	—	10	0	7	Yes	Yes
Hawaii	State Board of Education	X	—	—	11	0	4	No	No
Idaho	State Board of Education	—	X	—	8	1	5	Yes	Yes
Illinois[a]	State Board of Education	—	—	—					
Indiana	State Board of Education	—	X	—	19	1	4	No	No
Iowa	State Board of Public Instruction	—	X	—	9	0	6	Yes	Yes
Kansas	State Board of Education	X	—	—	10	0	4	No	No
Kentucky	State Board of Education	—	X	—	8	1	4	Yes	Yes
Louisiana	State Board of Education	X	—	—	12	1	6,8[b]	Yes	Yes
Maine	State Board of Education	—	X	—	9	0	5	Yes	No
Maryland	State Board of Education	—	X	—	7	0	5	Yes	Yes
Massachusetts	Board of Education	X	X	—	14	3	5	Yes	No
Michigan	State Board of Education	X	—	—	10	2	8	Yes	Yes

State	Board								
Minnesota	State Board of Education	—	X	—	9	0	6	Yes	Yes
Mississippi	State Board of Education	—	—	X	3	3	4	Yes	Yes
Missouri	State Board of Education	—	X	—	8	0	8	Yes	Yes
Montana	State Board of Education	X	X	—	11	3	8	Yes	Yes
Nebraska	State Board of Education	X	—	—	8	0	4	Yes	No
Nevada	State Board of Education	—	—	—	9	0	4	Yes	Yes
New Hampshire	State Board of Education	—	X	—	7	2	5	Yes	No
New Jersey	State Board of Education	X	X	—	14	0	6	Yes	Yes
New Mexico	State Board of Education	X	—	—	10	0	6	Yes	Yes
New York	Board of Regents, University of the State of New York	X[c]	—	—	15	0	15	Yes	Yes
North Carolina	State Board of Education	—	X	—	13	2	8	Yes	No
North Dakota	State Board of Public School Education	X	X	—	7	1	6	Yes	Yes
Ohio	State Board of Education	X	—	—	23	0	6	Yes	Yes
Oklahoma	State Board of Education	—	X	—	7	1	6	No	No
Oregon	State Board of Education	—	X	—	7	0	7	Yes	No
Pennsylvania	State Board of Education	—	X	—	17	0	6	Yes	No
Rhode Island	Board of Regents	X	X	—	9	0	4	Yes	No
South Carolina	State Board of Education	X	—	—	16	0	4	Yes	No
South Dakota	State Board of Education	—	X	—	7	0	5	Yes	Yes
Tennessee	State Board of Education	X	X	—	15	3	9	Yes	Yes
Texas	State Board of Education	X	—	—	24	0	6	Yes	Yes
Utah	State Board of Education	X	X	—	11	0	4	Yes	Yes
Vermont	State Board of Education	—	—	—	7	0	6	Yes	Yes
Virginia	State Board of Education	—	X	—	9	0	4	Yes	No
Washington	State Board of Education	X[d]	—	—	15	1	6	No	No
West Virginia	State Board of Education	—	X	—	11	2	9	Yes	Yes
Wisconsin	No State Board of Education	—	—	—					
Wyoming	State Board of Education	—	—	—	10	1	6	Yes	No
American Samoa	Board of Regents	—	X	—	10	1	2,3	Yes	No
Guam	Territorial Board of Education	—	X	—	7	0	3	Yes	Yes
Puerto Rico	Commonwealth Board of Education	—	X	—	10	2	6	No	Yes

TABLE 11-1 (Continued)

State	Designation	Chief method of selecting members			Number of members		Term of member-ship (years)	SBE is board for vocational education	SBE is board for vocational rehabili-tation
		Elected by people or represen-tatives of people	Ap-pointed by governor	Ex-officio (by virtue of office or posi-tion held)	Total	Ex-officio			
Trust Terri-tory of the Pacific	Micronesia Board of Education	—	High Comm.	—	7	1	3	Yes	Yes
Virgin Islands	Virgin Islands Board of Education	X	—	—	10	1	2	No	No
Totals		16	36	2	562	48	—	46	32

Source: Sam P. Harris, *State Departments of Education, State Boards of Education, and Chief State School Officers*, DHEW Publication No. (OE) 73–07400, Washington, D.C.: GPO, 1973, pp. 60–61.

[a] To be determined by the state legislature.
[b] Three elected for overlapping 6-year terms; eight elected for overlapping 8-year terms.
[c] Elected by the legislature.
[d] Elected by members of boards of directors of local school districts.

3. Establish standards for issuance and revocation of teacher certificates.
4. Establish standards for classifying, approving, and accrediting schools, both public and nonpublic.
5. Prescribe a uniform system for the gathering and reporting of educational data, for the keeping of adequate educational and finance records, and for the better evaluation of educational progress.
6. Submit an annual report to the governor and legislature covering the areas of action of the state board of education and the operations of the state department of education and to support education throughout the state.
7. Consider the educational needs of the state and recommend to the governor and the legislature such additional legislation or changes in existing legislation as it may deem desirable.
8. Interpret its own rules and regulations and upon appeal hear all controversies and disputes arising therefrom.
9. Publish the laws relating to education with notes and comments for the guidance of those charged with the educational responsibility.
10. Provide through the state department of education supervisory and consultative service and issue materials which would be helpful in the development of educational programs.
11. Accept and distribute in accord with law any monies, commodities, goods, and services which may be made available from the state or federal government or from other sources.
12. Designate the extent to which the board is empowered to exercise supervision over public and nonpublic colleges, universities, state institutions and public and nonpublic elementary and secondary schools in accord with the law and sound public policy on education.[2]

In addition, the state board of education should stipulate the relation between the executive officer of the state board and the members of the department of public instruction.

Membership of the state board

An ex-officio committee of state officers was the earliest and most rudimentary state board of education. It included elected state officials such as the governor, secretary of state, and secretary of the treasury. Difficulties of travel and communication encouraged the creation of a board whose members were officials residing in the capital. The accomplishments were limited because the members' other duties as state officials supervened. In addition, such officials were not elected on the basis of their knowledge about state educational organization.

A second type of ex-officio board is illustrated by the state board of education in Indiana in 1852. This board was composed of the president of the university and the superintendents of certain cities on the theory that the schoolmen of the state were best qualified to handle the technical affairs of education. Conflicts of interest, however, were not unusual when individuals responsible for the administration of local school systems participated on a state board whose actions were bound to influence the operations of local districts.[3] Other states had both ex-officio and appointed members on boards.

In 1920, 35 state boards of education had ex-officio members. By 1974, of the 49 states with a state board of education, 22 had one or more ex-officio members, some of whom did not have authority to vote. The District of Columbia and four outlying territories have ex-officio members as well making a total of 27 boards with such posi-

[2]National Council of Chief State School Officers, *The State Department of Education,* Washington, D.C.: The Council, 1952, pp. 14–16.

[3]Ellwood P. Cubberley, *State School Administration,* Boston: Houghton Mifflin, 1927, p. 286.

tions. Only Florida and Mississippi have state boards wholly ex-officio in membership. Fifteen governors were ex-officio members on the state board of education in 1940 compared with only five governors serving in this capacity in 1973.

The question arises whether the chief state school officer should be a member of the state board of education. The superintendent is an ex-officio member in 22 of the 27 state boards with ex-officio members. In many of these boards he serves as chairman. The chief state school officer is more likely to be an ex-officio member of the board of education than any other state official. In 14 of these agencies he is the only ex-officio member. In the remaining agencies he serves only as executive officer. As a rule it is recommended that the chief state school officer not be a member of the state board. It is better to divide authority between those concerned with policy making and those concerned with policy execution. The chief school officer's primary contribution lies in the area of executing policy.

The use of ex-officio members appears to have increased since 1962 to reverse what seemed to be a trend. Thus, in 1940, 27 of the 56 state boards in the 50 states, District of Columbia, and outlying territories had ex-officio members. This number declined steadily in the following years to reach a low of 16 in 1962.[4] Boards with ex-officio members jumped to 27 in 1972 to equal the 1940 level.

The debate continues as to whether membership on a state board of education should be gained by appointment

[4]Sam P. Harris, *State Departments of Education, State Boards of Education, and Chief State School Officers*, DHEW Publication, No. (OE) 72-07400, Washington, D.C.: GPO, 1973, p. 68.

or through election. Arguments for the appointive board are based on the fact that the governor should have authority to appoint heads of all state departments. This system can be effective if the governor does not have the power to change the entire membership of the state board of education during one term of office. The elective type of state board has the support of experience, although there are problems related to election, particularly if it is looked upon merely as a stepping stone to other state offices. The cost of election might also prevent desirable individuals from running for such office.

In 32 states (36 if the outlying territories are included) board of education members are appointed to office by the governor. The popularity of this method may be because it is easy to administer. It works best in states with a strong tradition of nonpartisanship in selection and where governors are receptive and responsive to advice from citizens interested in education. The trend, however, seems to be away from the appointment of board members by the governor. In 1945, only two states, Nevada and Louisiana, provided for the popular election of state school-board members. Today, 14 states (16 if the District of Columbia and an outlying territory are included) provide for the election of the state board by the people, and in New York the election is by the state legislature.

As a general rule, the total membership on the state board should be large enough so that it cannot be dominated by a single personality and yet not so large that it becomes unwieldy and inefficient; from 7 to 11 members is recommended most often. At the present time the range varies from 3 members in Mississippi and 5 in Colorado to 23 in Ohio and 24 in Texas. Over half of all state boards of education have from 7 to 9 members, well within the recommended range.

Qualifications or legal requirements for membership on the state board of education are usually not prescribed by law. In spite of this, most state board members have attended college.

Term of office of board members

Four- and six-year terms of office seem to be the most popular; about 60 percent have terms of either four or six years duration. However, the length of term varies from two years to fifteen years in New York. As a general rule, it is recommended that members of the state board serve long, overlapping terms so that a comprehensive educational program can be developed and carried forward. A term of six to eight years seems most appropriate, for it would provide sufficient time to come to understand the problems and the methods of operation and still provide flexibility and adaptability in membership.

Recommendations for state boards

The following recommendations with reference to state boards were made by Cubberley in 1927 and are worth repeating. He recommended that the state board of education should be:

1. A lay board representing the people.
2. Neither too small nor too large, with 7 members as the optimum size.
3. Appointed or elected for relatively long and overlapping terms.
4. Appointed by a governor who does not have opportunity to change the entire character of the board during one term.
5. Appointed solely on the basis of ability to serve the people without reference to race, creed, occupation, party, and residence.
6. Elected by the people if this is preferred to appointment.
7. Removed only by action of the gover-

nor and then only for such causes as immorality, malfeasance, and gross incompetence.
8. Without ex-officio members, even the governor.
9. Organized so that the state superintendent is not a member of the board.
10. Paid an honorarium instead of a per-diem allotment.
11. Able to consider as its most important function the appointment of a state superintendent.
12. Organized in such a way that the subordinate officials for the state department are selected only on the recommendations of the state superintendent.
13. Empowered to make its own rules and regulations.
14. Organized so that there is a clear distinction between the legislative and the executive functions.[5]

THE CHIEF STATE SCHOOL OFFICER

The chief state school officer is most frequently referred to as the state superintendent, either of public instruction or education. The next most frequently used title is commissioner, which is gaining in popularity and some day may be the most popular designation. The position is established as a constitutional office in most states.

Historical development

New York is credited with establishing the first position of chief state school officer in 1812. He was called the superintendent of common schools and was appointed by a council. His salary was $300 a year, but there was a stipulation that he was not to come under pay until "he shall give notice of the first distribution of school money payable in the same way as is provided for other offices." His duties were to plan for improvement and management

[5]E. P. Cubberly, op. cit., pp. 290–294.

of the common school funds, to prepare and report estimates and expenditures of school money, to give information to the legislature respecting all matters referred to him by either branch, and generally to perform all services relative to the welfare of the schools. The position was abolished in 1821 and was not reestablished until 1854. The secretary of state served as the ex-officio state superintendent during the interim.

Maryland was the second state to establish the position, in 1826, followed by Michigan in 1829. Only three states in existence at that time had established the state superintendency. By 1850, however, the office had been created in 24 states and territories. At present all states have a chief state school officer. However, at one time or another the governor, the comptroller, the secretary of the treasury, the state auditor, and other state officials served as ex-officio state superintendent in about half the states.

Changes in this office during a relatively short period of time can be illustrated by what occurred in Iowa. The position was first created by the state territorial legislature in 1841, and the chief state school officer was appointed by the governor for a three-year term. In 1842 the position was considered a needless expenditure and legislated out of existence. The state superintendency in Iowa was reestablished in 1846, but as an elective office for a three-year term. In 1858 it was discontinued for a second time, but in 1864 was recreated and made elective for a two-year term. In 1913 the method of selection was changed from election to appointment by the governor for a four-year term. In 1917 the position was again made elective rather than appointive, also for a four-year term. The last and most significant change took place in 1953, when the position was made appointive, with appointment vested in a state board of public instruction. This appointment was subject to confirmation by the state senate every four years. The confirmation requirement is perhaps the most unfortunate aspect of the Iowa law, for it introduces some of the more undesirable elements of politics, which has manifested itself when needed but controversial actions such as reorganization of inefficient districts incurred the wrath of some rural legislators.

Duties and problems

The early duties of the chief state school officer were primarily clerical, with some advisory functions, for during the early years of our nation school systems were located in rural areas and were confined primarily to elementary education. As educational programs expanded, new functions were added to the state superintendency and its responsibilities were greatly increased after 1890.

One of the problems encountered in structuring this office was that its form was cast during the years when its functions were concerned mostly with clerical, statistical, and exhortatory activities. These early duties, rather than other possible ones, were crystallized into law and formed the traditions of the office. As a result, the potential of this office was not realized, and in many cases the salary was kept low. Changes were difficult, for in 35 states and 3 outlying territories the position is a constitutional office.

One of the most serious disadvantages of the position is that it remains political in nature, requiring that the chief state school officer campaign for office. In 1920, this officer was elected in 34 of the 48 states. From 1945 to

1974 the number of states electing the state superintendent declined from 33 to 19. The election is nonpartisan in only 6 states. It follows, of course, that where the superintendent is elected the choices are limited to those who are residents of the state.

Where the position is decided by balloting it is recommended that the election be held during the spring, when other state and/or national officers are not being selected, and that it be organized on a nonpartisan basis. The great weight of professional opinion is, however, that appointment is a better way to select the chief state school officer and is necessary to the continued professional development of the office. Selection by statewide election encourages opportunists to campaign for office and does little to stimulate the professionally well qualified to pursue the position. Of the three methods of selection of the chief state school officer (election, appointment by the state board, appointment by the governor) election is the least desirable.

In 37 of the 50 states, the District of Columbia, and the outlying territories the state superintendent is appointed to office (Table 11–2). In 28 of these situations appointment is made by the state board of education; in the remaining 9, it is made by the governor. The trend toward appointment by the state board is consistent with the adopted policy of the Council of Chief State School Officers. In the early part of the twentieth century the appointment power rested with the governor in most states (about 14). Rhode Island in 1845 was one of the first states that empowered the governor to appoint the chief school officer. By 1945 the appointment in 8 states was made by the state board; in 7 states it was made by the governor. In 1974 the appointment was made by the state

board of education in 28 states and other territories of the United States.

It is unfortunate that in many states there are no legal qualifications for chief state school officer. The salary for this position continues far lower than is justifiable, which fact can be traced to the political rather than the professional characteristics of the office. As late as 1957 the average chief state school officer received a salary of $12,900 (up from $7,180 in 1948) as compared with, at that time, an average salary of $20,610 for the local superintendent in cities of 20,000 or more. An upward trend continued for by 1964 the median salary was $17,000, by 1969 $23,000, and by 1972 $27,064. The spread in 1972 was from a low of $13,750 to a high of $51,275 (New York). Historically, the chief state school officers and their professional staffs received lower salaries than their peers in other local school or federal positions. This appears to be changing with state education personnel fairing better than before.

The Council of Chief State School Officers recommended that the state legislature enact laws defining the relation of the chief state school officer to the state board of education and to the state department of education.[6] These laws should indicate the functions of the chief state school officer in a general way, namely:

1. Keeping the board currently advised about the operation and status of the public schools.
2. Recommending to the board such policies and rules as he deems necessary for educational progress.
3. Serving as executive officer of the board and being responsible for promoting efficiency and improvement in the public-school system.
4. Delegating ministerial and executive

[6]National Council of Chief State School Officers, op. cit., p. 16.

TABLE 11–2

STATUS OF THE CHIEF STATE SCHOOL OFFICERS (CSSO)

State	Title	Method of selection				Relation to state board of education (SBE)	
		Elected by popular vote	Appointed by SBE	Appointed by governor	Term of office (years)	Ex-officio member	Official capacity
Alabama	Superintendent of Education	—	X	—	Indef.	Yes	Secretary and executive officer
Alaska	Commissioner of Education	—	X	—	5[a]	No	Principal executive officer
Arizona	Superintendent of Public Instruction	X	—	—	4	Yes	Executive officer
Arkansas	Director of Education	—	X	—	Indef.[b]	No	Ex-officio secretary
California	Superintendent of Public Instruction	X	—	—	4	No	Secretary and executive officer
Colorado	Commissioner of Education	—	X	—	Indef.[b]	No	Secretary
Connecticut	Secretary of the State Board of Education and Commissioner of Education	—	X	—	Indef.[b]	No	Secretary and executive officer
Delaware	Superintendent of Public Instruction	—	X	—	1	No	Executive secretary
District of Columbia	Superintendent of Schools	—	X	—	3	Yes	Seat on board, no vote
Florida	Commissioner of Education	X	—	—	4	Yes	Secretary and executive officer
Georgia	School Superintendent	X	—	—	4	No	Executive officer
Hawaii	Superintendent of Education	—	X	—	Indef.[b]	No	Executive officer and secretary
Idaho	Superintendent of Public Instruction	X	—	—	4	Yes	Administrative officer
Illinois	Superintendent of Public Instruction	—	X	—	4	Undetermined	Undetermined

							Chairman of each of three commissions into which SBE is divided
Indiana	Superintendent of Public Instruction	X	—	—	2	Yes	Chairman of each of three commissions into which SBE is divided
Iowa	Superintendent of Public Instruction	—	X	—	4	No	Executive officer
Kansas	Commissioner of Education	—	X	—	Indef.[b]	No	Executive officer
Kentucky	Superintendent of Public Instruction	X	—	—	4	Yes	Executive officer
Louisiana	Superintendent of Public Education	X	—	—	4	Yes	Executive officer and ex-officio secretary
Maine	Commissioner of Education and Cultural Services	—	—	X	Indef.	No	Secretary
Maryland	Superintendent of Schools	X	—	—	4	No	Chief executive, secretary, and treasurer
Massachusetts	Commissioner of Education	X	—	—	Indef.[b]	No	Chief executive and secretary
Michigan	Superintendent of Public Instruction	X	—	—	Indef.[b]	Yes	Chairman
Minnesota	Commissioner of Education	X	—	—	4	No	Executive officer and secretary
Mississippi	Superintendent of Education	X	—	—	4	Yes	Chairman
Missouri	Commissioner of Education	X	—	—	Indef.[b]	No	Chief administrative officer
Montana	Superintendent of Public Instruction	X	—	—	4	Yes	Secretary
Nebraska	Commissioner of Education	X	—	—	Indef.[b]	No	Executive officer and secretary
Nevada	Superintendent of Public Instruction	X	—	—	Indef.[b]	No	Secretary
New Hampshire	Commissioner of Education	X	—	—	Indef.[b]	No	Chief executive officer and secretary
New Jersey	Commissioner of Education	—	—	X	5	No	Official agent and secretary
New Mexico	Superintendent of Public Instruction	X	—	—	Indef.[b]	No	Chief administrative officer

TABLE 11–2 (Continued)

State	Title	Method of selection			Term of office (years)	Relation to state board of education (SBE)	
		Elected by popular vote	Appointed by SBE	Appointed by governor		Ex-officio member	Official capacity
New York	Commissioner of Education	—	X	—	Indef.[b]	No	Chief administrative officer
North Carolina	Superintendent of Public Instruction	X	—	—	4	Yes	Secretary and chief administrative officer
North Dakota	Superintendent of Public Instruction	X	—	—	4	Yes	Executive director and secretary
Ohio	Superintendent of Public Instruction	—	X	—	Indef.[b]	No	Secretary, executive and administrative officer
Oklahoma	Superintendent of Public Instruction	X	—	—	4	Yes	President and executive officer
Oregon	Superintendent of Public Instruction	X	—	—	4	No	Executive officer
Pennsylvania	Secretary of Education	—	—	X	Indef.[c]	No	Chief executive officer
Rhode Island	Commissioner of Education	—	X	—	Indef.[d]	No	Executive officer
South Carolina	Superintendent of Education	X	—	—	4	No	Secretary and administrative officer
South Dakota	Superintendent of Public Instruction	X	—	—	2	No	Secretary and administrative officer
Tennessee	Commissioner of Education	—	—	X	Indef.[c]	Yes	Chairman
Texas	Commissioner of Education	—	X	—	4	No	Executive officer
Utah	Superintendent of Public Instruction	—	X	—	Indef.[d]	No	Executive officer
Vermont	Commissioner of Education	—	X	—	Indef.[d]	No	Chief executive officer and secretary
Virginia	Superintendent of Public Instruction	—	—	X	4	No	Secretary

State	Title						
Washington	Superintendent of Public Instruction	X	—	—	4	Yes	President and executive officer
West Virginia	Superintendent of (Free) Schools	—	X	—	Indef.[a]	Yes	Chief executive officer
Wisconsin	Superintendent of Public Instruction	X	—	—	4	No SBE	No SBE
Wyoming	Superintendent of Public Instruction	X	—	—	4	Yes	
American Samoa	Director of Education	—	—	X	Indef.[a]	Yes	Executive officer
Guam	Director of Education	—	X	—	Indef.[a]	No	Executive secretary
Puerto Rico	Secretary of Education	—	—	X	Indef.[c]	Yes	No vote
Trust Territory of Pacific	Director of Education	—	—	High Comm.	2	Yes	Executive officer
Virgin Islands	Commissioner of Education	—	—	X	Coterm. with Governor	Yes	Secretary
Total		19	28	9			

Source: Sam P. Harris, *State Departments of Education, State Boards of Education, and Chief State School Officers*, DHEW Publication No. (OE) 73–07400, Washington, D.C.: GPO, 1973, pp. 76–77.

[a] Appointed for a 5-year term, but serves at the pleasure of the governor.
[b] Law is silent.
[c] Serves at the pleasure of governor.
[d] Serves at the pleasure of the state board of education.

261

functions to members of the state department of education.

5. Preparing a budget for the state education program under the jurisdiction of the state education agency, including the state department of education, and administering the same after approval.
6. Establishing and maintaining a system of personnel administration.

THE STATE DEPARTMENT OF EDUCATION

The state board of education determines policies, and the chief state school officer assumes responsibility for their execution. In present-day complex educational organizations, execution of policies calls for activities of many professionals rather than one. The state department of education has been created to perform those functions that the state board of education, acting through the chief state school officer, recognizes as important to the welfare of education in the state. The director or chief administrative officer of the state department of education is the state superintendent or commissioner of education. In a few states there is one state education agency for all levels, higher education as well as elementary and secondary. Some focus on an elementary and secondary education program other than vocational education; most combine these responsibilities.

Role of the state department

Fundamental changes in one part of the educational structure require alteration in others. When inefficiently organized local school administrative units existed and local school administrators were relatively unskilled, the state department of education had to perform a statistical and inspectoral service. The creation of more effective local school districts and the advent of professionally prepared local school administrators have permitted the state department to assume a leadership role.[7] The transition of the state department of education from one phase of development to another has necessitated emphasis on different functions and has called for substantially different personnel requirements.

Statistical stage. The first phase of development of the state department of education is referred to as the statistical stage. For most states this constituted a period from establishment to about 1900. During this time of evolution, the state department was concerned primarily with gathering, compiling, and publishing statistics; preparing forms; making biennial reports; publishing income studies; and similar duties. These activities need not be degraded, for they are important; criticism is warranted, however, when such activities remain the only or major function. Clerks were the only personnel needed. A few chief state school officers had no more than one or two clerks. During this period most of the state department personnel, including the chief state officer, could spend most, if not all, of their time in the central office. It is unfortunate that these were the activities of the office during the years when constitutional and legislative provisions established the state department of public education and specified the structure and conditions under which it would operate. All too frequently such statutory provisions were not altered in subsequent years.

Growth of state departments was slow during the statistical period. As late as 1900 there were only 177 em-

[7]F. F. Beach and A. H. Gibbs, *Personnel of State Departments of Education,* U.S. Office of Education, Washington, D.C.: GPO, 1952.

ployees of these departments in the nation: 47 were chief state school officers, and the remaining 130 averaged to a staff of less than 3 people per state.[8] In 1900, 5 state school officers had no staff assistant—not even a secretary or a clerk.

Inspectoral stage. The second, or inspectoral, stage lasted in most states from 1900 to 1930. (These dates are approximations; there is considerable overlap among the stages.) The inspector was not a clerical worker but a quasi-professional who provided service in the field. The inspector's functions were defined during the period when the legislature hoped to improve the quality of education through the establishment of regulatory controls over local school units. It was believed that local school improvement would be achieved if the state enacted standards and sent inspectors to determine if the standards were observed. It is one thing, however, for the legislature to prescribe a standard and another to understand its fiscal implications. Only in recent years have states come to comprehend the fiscal consequences of legislative requirements for education.

Inspectors were employed to determine whether state laws on compulsory school attendance, safe and healthful school facilities, efficient accounting systems, prescribed subject matter, and so on were observed. By 1950 most state departments had added inspectors to their staff. Sometimes the term "school visitor" or "supervisor" was used instead of inspector.

Inspectors were outnumbered by state department personnel concerned with clerical and statistical activities. During the 1900 to 1930 period the median state department staff grew from 3 to 28 employees, that is, there were almost ten times in 1930 the median number in 1900. Much of this growth could be ascribed to the passage of the Smith-Hughes Act and the beginning of the federal vocational rehabilitation program. In neither the statistical nor the inspectoral stage of development was the state department geared primarily to assist local education authorities in improving educational programs.[9]

Leadership stage. The leadership stage for the state department of education came into being when it became apparent that inspectoral activities were not achieving equalization of educational opportunity. The emphasis began to shift to leadership activities as a means of upgrading local educational programs.

This approach called for a new type of staff member—the professionally qualified state department consultant. Respect based on professional knowledge and leadership ability was emphasized in place of state authority vested in an inspector applying regulatory controls. The specialist or consultant was needed—a person competent in a particular professional area, but at the same time possessing a broad understanding of public education in general, familiar with important research and other information bearing on educational problems in the state, and able to work with professional and lay groups at the local level. The state department was no longer staffed by old superintendents waiting for retirement, but rather by dynamic and vigorous educators who carried on leadership, planning and research, consultation, coordinating, and professional-development activities.

[8]Ibid.

[9]Ibid.

Spectacular growth of state departments has occurred during the leadership period. The median department staff in the United States more than quadrupled as it grew from 28 in 1930 to 126 in 1950. In 1950 there were 9550 state department staff members, not counting the 48 chief state school officers, for an average of 200 per state.[10] By 1972 the size of the state department staff was almost double what it was in 1950. (See Table 11–3.)

As Harris observed in 1973, "in the past 25 years, growth in departmental staff size occurred largely in federally subsidized areas."[11] Some studies estimated that as late as 1949 at least two-thirds were either in vocational education or rehabilitation. This changed dramatically with other federal education activities in the 1950s and 1960s.

There remains wide variation in the number of full-time professionals in the state education agency. The smallest in 1972 had 47 and the largest 1421 or 972 if only the headquarters staff were included. The average for all of the 50 states for regional, special in-

---

[10]Ibid.

[11]S. P. Harris, op. cit., p. 38.

TABLE 11–3

PROFESSIONAL AND NONPROFESSIONAL STAFFS OF 50 STATE DEPARTMENTS OF EDUCATION, 1890–1972

Year	No. of staff members	Percent increase over preceding reporting year
1890	129	—
1895	155	20
1900	177	14
1905	219	24
1910	534	144
1915	610	14
1920	836	37
1925	1,416	69
1930	1,760	24
1935	2,256	28
1940	3,718	65
1945	5,403	45
1950	9,550	77
1955	15,375	61
1972	18,472	20

Source: L. M. Thurston and W. H. Roe, *State School Administration.* New York: Harper & Row, 1957, p. 117. Statistical information adapted from Fred F. Beach and Andrew H. Gibbs, *Personnel of State Departments of Education,* Washinton, D.C.: U.S. Office of Education, GPO, 1952. Sam P. Harris, *State Departments of Education, State Boards of Education, and Chief State School Officers,* DHEW Publication No. (OE) 73–07400, 1973, pp. 42–43.

stitutional, and headquarters staff in 1972 was almost 370.

Growth in size during the leadership period indicates only part of the changing role of the typical state education agency. More and more of the time and activities of the chief state school officer and professional staff members are now spent away from the central office. Utilization of a state department supervisor to visit many school systems once or twice a year for the sole purpose of evaluating them is destined to be abandoned. The regulatory functions of the state department must be discharged, but to make this the major or only duty of its personnel is to misuse the talent and potential of the department. While evaluative supervision from the state department was probably justified when school districts were fundamentally weak and their personnel limited in professional preparation, it is of questionable value for today's large and complex school systems. Violations of standards would have to be gross and ill-disguised indeed to be spotted during a short visit. Supervision has as its prime function the improvement of instruction. Supervision of teachers should be allocated to local districts, because these are in a better position to discharge this responsibility than is the state department. The staff of the state department must be used on a consulting basis by local districts interested in the improvement of the educational program.

To attract qualified personnel in a state department of education, a professional salary level must be maintained. One authority has recommended that a chief state officer should receive a salary equal to that of the highest-paid city superintendent or state university or college president. The division director of a state department should receive a salary similar to those of superintendents of large school systems

or deans of the university or state college. Consultants should command a salary similar to those of the highest-salaried specialists in city systems or full professors in the university or college with comparable preparation.[12] In most state departments, although there are a few exceptions, the salary scale is far below these standards. More effective support of state departments of education is needed if they are to fulfill their leadership role in the pattern of education in the state. Data presented earlier indicated considerable improvement in salary payments during the last decade.

Impact of federal legislation on state departments

A factor likely to have tremendous impact in the years ahead is the availability of federal funds to strengthen programs and personnel of state education agencies. State education departments received only meager support from the federal government in the years since 1784. The passage of the Elementary and Secondary Education Act of 1965 made federal funds available for strengthening the operations of state departments of education, as opposed to the traditional federal grants earmarked for specific aspects of educational programs in local school systems. The new grants made available through Title V of the act are of three types: basic grants, special-project grants, and assistance to allow interchange of state and federal educational personnel. Harris stated, "departments practically tripled the size of their professional staffs in the decade following passage of the National Defense Education Act," that is, during the 1960–1969 decade.[13]

[12]F. F. Beach and A. H. Gibbs, op. cit.
[13]S. P. Harris, op. cit., p. 39.

Title V funds were used to train state department staff members as well as to introduce data-processing techniques and study, planning, developing, and evaluating research.

Title V of the Elementary and Secondary Education Act allowed states to gain more balanced strength. Unfortunately, federal retrenchment in the 1970s resulted in reduced funds for state education agencies and produced widespread fears of substantial staff cuts to offset previously registered expansions.

**The future of the state
department of education**

The state education agency acting through the state board, the chief state school officer, and the state education department, has a most important role in public education. It is imperative that individual state governments, as well as the federal government, exert every effort to enhance the leadership capabilities and strength of state education agencies. Unfortunately, in most states the potential of the state department of education has gone largely unrealized, due in large measure to the inadequacy of resources allocated to the department. The state agency has been the most inadequately supported of the three echelons of education, even though no echelon has ever been granted all the funds desired. The lack of sufficient resources has made it impossible, in many cases, to employ a staff large enough and of sufficient quality to fulfill the leadership mandates of state education departments.

Fortunately there are exceptions to this generalization, and they demonstrate what can be done if adequate resources are forthcoming. For example, in New York a special study was made of the role of the state education agency in promoting change,

and in Florida and California electronic data processing for school systems has been developed.

It will be extremely difficult if not impossible to develop an excellent public school system without greatly improved state departments of education. Better organizational structure, with appointment rather than election of the state superintendent, and the creation of a nonpartisan state board of education are needed to translate sufficient resources and flexible personnel policies into imaginative programs. State education agencies have traditionally played a significant role in influencing legislative action on educational policies. This role needs to be strengthened to enhance the leadership image of state education agencies. In addition, state planning and evaluation systems must also be strengthened.

Harris identified the four major constraints that prevented state departments from providing quality leadership and services:

1. Lack of staff to maintain growing service expectations.
2. Low support levels from state legislatures.
3. Organizational and legal constraints placed upon the departments.
4. Lack of sensitivity or ability to cope with the political realities that determine the fate of state education agencies.[14]

SUMMARY

Public education in the United States is a matter of federal interest, a state function, and a local operation. No analysis of the structural framework for public education would be complete without reference to the state education agency.

[14]S. P. Harris, op. cit., pp. 41–51.

Our political system makes each state responsible for the organization and administration of education. The concern of the state for public education can be traced as far back as the Massachusetts laws of 1642 and 1647. The need for some formally designated state body for education gave rise to the formation of the state board of education, the position of chief state school officer, and eventually the state department of education.

Formulation of state policy in education began with the land grants for education in the new states. The prototype of the modern state board of education is the Massachusetts State Board established in 1837. By 1870 most of the states in existence at that time had some type of state board. In the late 1960s, 48 of the 50 states had state boards concerned with public elementary and secondary education. The trend has been away from a board composed of ex-officio members, and even the governor is no longer a board member in many states.

The position of chief state school officer was first established in 1812. The early duties were routine. One of the problems encountered in structuring this office was that its form was cast during the years when its functions were primarily clerical and statistical. The office remains political in nature because the state superinten-dent is elected to office in 19 states. The trend, however, is toward appointment by the state board of education.

The organization and operation of the state department of education are related to the whole educational system of the state. Changes in one part of the educational structure require some degree of alteration in other parts. The role of the state in education has changed in recent years and will continue to reflect the dynamic nature of public education. State departments have moved from the statistical stage (up to 1900), to the inspectoral stage (1900 to about 1930), to the leadership stage (1930 to the present). The leadership stage came into being when it became apparent that inspectoral activities failed to achieve equalization of educational opportunities. Most of the growth in personnel came during this period, particularly since 1950.

One of the most recent forces destined to have a profound impact on state departments of education is the allocation of federal funds to strengthen state agencies. These funds were made available under Title V of the Elementary and Secondary Education Act of 1965. The average state education agency in 1972 had almost 370 professionals although the variation in size from smallest to largest was very great.

QUESTIONS

1. What were the significant stages of development of the modern state department of education?
2. What arguments would tend to support the election of members of the state board of education? Appointment of members of the state board?
3. What factors appear to support the contention that there is a need for a reorganization within many of the present-day state departments of education?

4. Why should the state superintendent be appointed rather than elected to office?
5. What services can an effective state department provide local school districts?

SELECTED REFERENCES

Beach, F. F., and R. F. Will, *The State and Education*, U.S. Office of Education, misc. no. 23, Washington, D.C.: GPO, 1955.

Cubberley, Ellwood P., *State School Administration*, Boston: Houghton Mifflin, 1927.

Fuller, Edgar and J. B. Pearson, eds., *Education in the States: Nationwide Development Since 1900*, Washington, D.C.: Council of Chief State School Officers, 1969.

Harris, Sam P., *State Departments of Education, State Boards of Education, and Chief State School Officers*, DHEW Publication No. (OE) 73-07400, 1973.

Will, R. F., *State Education, Structure and Organization*, U.S. Office of Education, OE-23038, misc. no. 46, Washington, D.C.: GPO, 1964.

12

THE FEDERAL IMPACT ON EDUCATIONAL OPERATIONS

A fundamental characteristic of our form of federalism is that it precludes direct participation by the national government in the operation of public education. Nonetheless, the interest of the federal government in the priorities, direction, and operation of public education is an established fact; each can be traced to the activities of the Continental Congress several years before the adoption of the United States Constitution. The role of the national government in public education remains controversial. Federal contributions to development of public education in the United States, however, have been of great importance and are expected to become even more significant in the future. The interest of the federal government in public education has led to its increasing involvement in educational activities through the United States Office of Education, the National Institute of Education, and other agencies at this level. The evidence of past history and present involvement documents beyond any shadow of doubt that the federal government has had and will continue to have a decisive impact on educational operations. So complex is the federal involvement in recent years that a single total for federal educational funds is extremely difficult, if not impossible, to compile with a high degree of accuracy. The multiplicity of federal assistance means that there is no single total of federal funds that is meaningful or useful for all interpretations.

Growing federal involvement in education, and the increasing concern of people at the local and state levels about it, are characteristic of the years following the end of World War II in 1945. Never before in history have so much time and energy been devoted to comprehending federal legislation and direction in education. The excitement engendered by the Morrill Act in 1862 cannot match the intensity of present concern. Prior to the Morrill Act, only one major piece of federal legislation influenced education: the Northwest Ordinances of 1785 and 1787. A summary of selected major federal legislation on education in the years since 1867 is presented in Table 12–1. Over 70 laws—not all of which are included in Table 12–1—influencing some level of education were passed by Congress during this period of more than 100 years. Over two-thirds of such school-related legislation was approved after 1960!

Documentation, in part, of the ever increasing federal interest and involvement in public education is evident from the major legislation described in Table 12–1. This is only one indicator, for the federal government is a huge and complex system. A persistent

TABLE 12–1

SELECTED MAJOR FEDERAL LEGISLATION ON EDUCATION, 1867–1973

1867	*U.S. Department of Education created*	Now the U.S. Office of Education.
1890	*Second Morrill Act*	Provided federal funds for land-grant colleges and universities. (The first Morrill Act donated lands only to encourage establishment of land-grant institutions).
1917	*Smith-Hughes Act. P.L. 347*	64th Cong. Provided federal aid to states for vocational education in public schools below college level, and encouraged education for teachers of vocational education.
1936	*George-Deen Act*	Extended Smith-Hughes Act to include education in distributive occupations.
1941	*Lanham Act*	Provided federal assistance for school building aid for communities adversely affected by federal activities.
1944	*Servicemen's Readjustment (GI Bill). 58 Stat. P.L. 284*	78th Cong. Provided federal aid for readjustment to civilian life by returning World War II veterans, and provided educational training benefits for veterans.
1944	*Surplus Property Act*	Enacted a broad policy governing surplus property disposal for educational, health, and civil defense purposes.
1945	*Fulbright Act. P.L. 584*	79th Cong. Established Board of Foreign Scholarships.
1946	*Vocational Education Act (George-Barden). P.L. 586*	79th Cong. Provided further development of vocational education in several states and territories.
1946	*National School Lunch Act*	Provided for the distribution of funds and federally purchased foods to public and nonpublic schools. In 1954 provided for an accompanying School Milk Program.
1950	*P.L. 815*	81st Cong. Provided assistance for construction of schools in federally impacted areas.
1950	*P.L. 874*	81st Cong. Established operating expenses for schools in federally affected areas.
1953	*P.L. 13*	83rd Cong. Created Department of Health, Education, and Welfare with U.S. Office of Education a constituent unit.
1954	*Cooperative Research Act. P.L. 531*	83rd Cong. Authorized U.S. Office of Education to conduct cooperative research with colleges, universities, and state education agencies.

TABLE 12–1 (Continued)

1954	*Library Services.* P.L. 597	84th Cong. Established Library Services Program.
1958	*National Defense Education.* P.L. 85–865	Strengthened national defense and encouraged and assisted expansion and improvement of educational programs to meet critical national needs; set up college student loan funds.
1961	*Juvenile Delinquency and Youth Offenses Control Act.* P.L. 87–274	Authorized U.S. Office of Education to give technical education counsel.
1961	*P.L. 87–276*	Authorized grants to train teachers of the deaf (combined with P.L. 85–926 by P.L. 88–164).
1961	*Peace Corps Act*	Established a permanent Peace Corps to supply U.S. teachers and technicians to underdeveloped nations.
1962	*Manpower Development and Training Act,* Title II, Part B. P.L. 88–164	Authorized U.S. Office of Education to assist in retraining and occupational training programs.
1963	*Mental Retardation Facilities and Community Mental Health Centers Construc-tion Act.* P.L. 88–164	Expanded P.L. 85–926 and established a program of research and demonstration projects in the education of handicapped children.
1963	*Higher Education Facilities Act.* P.L. 88–204	Authorized financial assistance for con-struction and rehabilitation of facilities in higher education.
1963	*Vocational Education Act.* P.L. 88–210	Expanded and made more comprehensive vocational educational experiences and benefits.
1964	*Civil Rights Act.* (Title IV)	Allowed the U.S. Commissioner of Education to provide technical assistance, grants, and training institutes to help com-munities prepare for school desegre-gation.
1964	*Amendments to NDEA, Impact School Aid*	Extended and expanded both the National Defense Education Act (NDEA) and the impact school aid program. NDEA in-stitutes for the advanced training of teachers, previously limited to guidance counselors and teachers of modern languages, were broadened to include teachers of English, reading, history, and geography, teachers of disadvantaged youth, librarians and educational media specialists. The loan/ grant program for the acquisition of certain teaching materials was expanded to include his-

TABLE 12–1 (Continued)

		tory, civics, geography, English, and reading.
1965	Elementary and Secondary Education Act. P.L. 89–10 Bilingual Programs	Established new federal programs to strengthen education.
1965	National Vocational Student Loan Act. P.L. 89–287	Established a program of loans to students in vocational and technical schools.
1965	Higher Education Act of 1965. P.L. 89–329	Established seven new programs designed to strengthen institutions of higher education and provided student assistance.
1966	International Education Act. P.L. 89–698	Provided for strengthening American education resources for international studies and research.
1966	Child Nutrition Act	Amended the National School Lunch Act by authorizing a special milk program through 1970, a 2-year pilot school breakfast program, and a permanent nonfood assistance program for economically depressed areas.
1966	Demonstration Cities and Metropolitan Development Act	Authorized the Secretary of Housing and Urban Development to make grants and provide technical assistance to transform slum areas into "model" neighborhoods. Education services for the poor and disadvantaged must be a part of every project.
1967	Elementary and Secondary Amendments: Dropout and Bilingual Programs	Extended ESEA through fiscal 1970; transferred Title III and Title V to state control; established dropout prevention projects and bilingual programs.
1967	Education Professions Development Act	Extended Teacher Corps for three years; provided $1.1 billion for broadened training programs for education personnel.
1968	Vocational Education Amendments	Reorganized and expanded federal vocational education programs; making the basic state program authorization permanent and extending others for up to four years. With spending authorization of over $3 billion confirmed, the act redirects federal programs from training in specified occupational categories to preparation of all groups for adaptability to a rapidly changing job market. Provided an eventual quadrupling of federal funding and added new emphasis on dropouts.

TABLE 12–1 (Continued)

1970	*Drug Abuse Education Act*	Authorized $29 million over 3 years for drug abuse training, materials, seminars, and pilot projects, and $29 million for community-based programs.
1970	*U.S. Office of Education FY 1971 Appropriation Act: School Desegregation Aid*	Included $75 million to help school desegregation, and Whitten amendment prohibiting use of federal funds for forced busing.
1970	*Elementary and Secondary Amendments*	Extended ESEA through Fiscal 1973; consolidated Title III (supplementary service) with NDEA Title V-A (guidance and counseling); increased authorization for Title I; expanded impact aid to include children who live in public housing; however, no funds were appropriated for public-housing children; and extended the 1968 Vocational Education Amendents.
1971	*Office of Education and Related Agencies Appropriations Act, 1972. P.L. 92–48*	Section 309. "No part of the funds contained . . . may be used to force any school or school district which is desegregated . . . to take any action to force the busing of students"; to force on account of race, creed, or color the abolishment of any so desegregated; or to force the transfer or assignment of any student attending any elementary or secondary school so desegregated to or from a particular school over the protest of his or her parents or parent. Section 310. "No part of the funds contained . . . shall be used to force any school or school district which is desegregated . . . to take any action to force the busing of students; to require the abolishment of any school desegregated; or to force on account of race, creed, or color the transfer of students to or from a particular school so desegregated as a condition precedent to obtaining Federal funds otherwise available to any State, school district or school."
1972	*Education Amendments of 1972. P.L. 92–318*	Expanded and revised most higher education laws, creating new programs of institutional and student aid; established an Education Division within HEW, composed of the Office of Education and the National Institution of

TABLE 12–1 (Continued)

	Education, headed by an assistant secretary for education; increased federal support for career (vocational) education, Indian education, and consumer education; established ethnic cultural heritage studies; and provided financial aid for school desegregation.
1972 *State and Local Fiscal Assistance Act of 1972.* P.L. 92–512	Authorized a 5-year program for sharing $30.2 billion of federal revenues with state and local governments.
1972 *Supplemental Appropriations FY 1973.* P.L. 92–607	Included approximately $1.1 billion for programs under Education Amendments of 1972, P.L. 92–318.

question has been: Who speaks for the federal government on education? Is it the President (who recommends programs), Congress (which passes laws), or the Courts (which interpret legislation)? Is it the United States Commissioner of Education or some other agency official purportedly implementing congressional intent? Educational policy of the federal government is enunciated through laws, through court decisions, and through guidelines issued by executive departments.

The selected laws listed in Table 12–1 and discussed elsewhere in this chapter demonstrate that what started as a humble effort less than 200 years ago has mushroomed into total involvement in education by the complex federal governmental structure, with seemingly no end in sight. A number of government bureaus are involved, in varying degrees, in influencing the course of public education in the United States. Primary credit must be given to Congress, for it is the fountainhead of federal legislation dealing with education and the branch of the federal government duly authorized to make policy. On more than one occasion, however, the federal courts have undone congressional as well as

state legislative and state constitutional policy statements. Furthermore, a large federal bureaucracy whose employees enjoy tenure exceeding that of many congressmen occasionally interprets congressional intent to fit the interest and purposes of the executive agency.

Before examining the history of such legislative efforts it is appropriate to examine the impact on educational operation of the United States Supreme Court in its role as guardian of our Constitution and protector of our fundamental rights.

THE SUPREME COURT AND EDUCATION

The influence of the United States Supreme Court on the organization and administration of public education is derived primarily from its concern for the rights and privileges guaranteed to citizens by the United States Constitution rather than from its concern for education per se. The Court's many decisions regarding educational issues might suggest that this high tribunal has had a greater and more dramatic impact than the federal legislative and executive branches on education. But educational operations merely provided the Court with the settings in which to rule on fundamental constitutional issues such as the relation between church and state, impairment of contracts, freedom of speech, due process of law, and rights of citizens for equal protection under the law no matter where they reside in the nation or in a state. Spurlock's[1] review of 45 decisions of the United States Supreme Court dealing with education, and analyses of others since his review, indicate that one-third of the cases dealt with constitutional issues requiring interpretation of the First Amendment to the United States Constitution, another third with issues related to the meaning of the Fifth and Fourteenth amendments, and the remaining third with questions of state or federal powers or functions. In no case did the Supreme Court become involved because it was the final arbiter on educational matters in the United States. On the contrary, it remanded to lower courts or refused to review cases whose fundamental issue was operation of public educational institutions unrelated to constitutional interpretation. In short, the United States Supreme Court does not direct educational policy making. It has not upset or challenged the principle that education is a state function. It is involved in education only to ensure that educational decisions at the state level do not violate any aspect of the Constitution.

As social values and national outlook change, the Supreme Court's interpretation of the Constitution also changes and occasionally the Court reverses its prior position, as it did in the cases of *Plessy* vs. *Ferguson* and *Minersville* vs. *Gobitis*. The *Plessy* vs. *Ferguson* doctrine, affirmed by the Supreme Court in 1896, determined that so long as educational facilities provided Negroes were not unequal and inferior to those used by white children, separate facilities or separate school systems did not violate any rights guaranteed to citizens under the federal Constitution. In 1954, in the case of *Brown* vs. *Board of Education,* the Supreme Court ruled that maintenance of a separate school system was basically unequal and deprived black children attending separate schools of rights guaranteed under the Fourteenth Amendment. In the case of *Minersville* vs. *Gobitis,* the Supreme Court ruled that freedom of religious expression by members of the Jehovah's Witnesses was not abrogated by the requirement that children who were members of this religious group and who attended public schools must salute the flag of the United States as a condition of their attendance. Following this decision some children were expelled when they refused to salute the flag. The Jehovah's Witnesses argued that they believed a flag to be a graven image and that saluting was a form of bowing down before such an image. Approximately five years later, in the case of *West Virginia* vs. *Barnette,* the Court rescinded its earlier decision and declared that people have a right to avoid a practice accepted by others on the grounds that it is a violation of their fundamental religious precepts. Thus, public education authorities may not deprive any child of his or her fundamental religious beliefs on the grounds of patriotism or what is commonly accepted by others and may not expel a pupil who refuses to salute the flag of the United States on the grounds that it violates a fundamental religious belief.

[1]Clark Spurlock, *Education and the Supreme Court,* Urbana, Ill.: University of Illinois Press, 1955.

Whether the federal government can participate in the financing of public education, even though no mention of education is made in the Constitution and education is regarded as a state responsibility, presented another set of issues to the Supreme Court. President Buchanan vetoed the Morrill Bill in 1859 on grounds that, in his opinion, Congress had no power to appropriate money raised by taxes that were levied against all the people of the United States for the purpose of educating only some of the people in the respective states. Three years later President Lincoln signed the Morrill Act into law. He evidently disagreed with the legal interpretation of his predecessor in the presidency and recognized no constitutional barrier to the donation of public lands to the several states to help establish a particular type of public institution of higher learning. The constitutionality of federal participation in support of public education has been upheld by decisions of the United States Supreme Court.

The *Rodriguez* case (*San Antonio Independent School Districts et al., Appelants* vs. *Demetrio P. Rodriguez et al.*) decided by the United States Supreme Court on March 21, 1973 has been hailed as one of the most significant court statements since *Brown* vs. *Board of Education* in 1954. In a split 5–4 decision the Court rejected the position supported in several state supreme courts that school finance systems, although chaotic and unjust, violated the equal protection clause of the Fourteenth Amendment. The pending Supreme Court cases on federal court decisions to merge several districts into one to achieve a better racial balance between a large city district and its surrounding suburban systems may have a significant impact as well.

Social outlook and national values will continue to change, and new interpretations of the Constitution will be forthcoming. A number of matters pending before the Supreme Court may well affect public education as profoundly as did the *Brown* ruling in 1954. It appears that interpretations of the Fourteenth Amendment's application to educational operations and relationships with students may continue to be the focal point of litigation involving schools. The growing and controversial involvement of the federal government in education is bound to increase rather than decrease the number of cases brought to this tribunal from their educational setting. For example, in 1973 the United States Supreme Court by 6–3 decisions struck down efforts in New York and Pennsylvania to provide public aid to non-public schools by means of a tax credit to parents for tuition payments made to private schools or by means of reimbursing private schools for costs incurred in providing state required services. What the next efforts of the private schools seeking public aid will be remains to be seen. Thus far, the Supreme Court has decreed that there shall be a separation of church and state activities but that there must not be segregation of pupils no matter how equal the separate facilities may appear. The split decision on the state school finance systems' relationships to the Fourteenth Amendment may come back to the Court again.

FEDERAL INVOLVEMENT IN EDUCATION

Congress has done much to influence education in the United States without explicit and direct constitutional authorization for federal participation. One wonders what more could have been done with a constitutional mandate to promote the establishment and maintenance of a system of public education in the United States. Education appears so intimately connected with our national well-being that little question remains that when Congress appropriates federal funds for education it is expressing concern for the national welfare. Historical events as well as present activities make a mockery of the question that stirred much heated debate for over 100 years, namely, "Should there be federal aid to education?" This issue was settled well over a century ago, even though present arguments ignore the facts of history. The ever-increasing number of federal laws passed in the 1960s and 1970s influencing schools testifies that today federal involvement in education is total, complex, and becoming more massive when measured by the federal dollars appropriated. The federal role in public education, however, will continue to be more opportunistic than consistent. The concomitant confusion can be partly explained by lack of information on the history of federal activities in education; much of the controversy, however, is generated by emotion.

A review of the significant facts in the history of federal educational activities is in order. The interest of the national government in public education was evident as early as the Ordinance of 1785, passed by the Continental Congress several years before the Constitution of the United States became effective. This ordinance was concerned with the survey and disposal of colonial lands and declared that "there shall be reserved the lot number 16 in each township for the maintenance of public schools in said township, also one-third of all gold, lead, silver and copper mines to be sold or otherwise disposed of as Con-

gress shall hereinafter direct." The Ordinance of 1787, popularly known as the Northwest Ordinance, supported the land policy of 1785 with the statement that "religion, morality and knowledge being necessary to good government and happiness of mankind, schools and the means of education shall forever be encouraged." This federal land policy has been construed as a means of stimulating land sales to large land companies. Whatever the motives of the Continental Congress, the impact of the Ordinances of 1785 and 1787 on the formulation of state constitutions and the development of public education in the states carved from the Northwest Territory was most significant.[2]

Phase 1: land grants for elementary and secondary schools

Implementation of policies enunciated in 1785 and 1787 resulted in federal grants of land to the states for educational purposes and represented the first instance of federal aid to education. It was federal support of public education *without undesirable strings attached.* It established federal support of education as a policy or activity as old as the nation.

The original federal land grants were awarded to states that came into the Union after 1800. Although Tennessee was admitted to the Union in 1796, it did not receive its federal land grant until 1806. Ohio was the first to receive land grants for schools when it entered in 1802. The 13 original states plus Kentucky, Maine, Vermont, West Virginia, and Texas (all 5 contained no federally owned public lands) did not participate in the original federal land grants for schools. In

[2]L. M. Thurston and W. H. Roe, *State School Administration,* New York: Harper & Row, 1957, p. 56.

subsequent federal land grants, allocations were made to these and other states from salt lands, internal-improvement lands, and swamplands. Thirty-nine states (excluding Hawaii and Alaska) received over 154 million acres of land, estimated to be worth more than $1 billion,[3] for schools from the federal government. This includes more than 94 million acres received as original land grants for schools plus later federal grants of salt lands, internal-improvement lands, and swamplands.

Not all states received equal grants of land upon entering the Union. Starting in 1848 when the Oregon Territory was created, Sections 16 and 36 in every township were allocated to states entering the Union for the purpose of establishing public schools. Oklahoma received two sections in each township plus $5 million in gold for land held by Indians. Utah was granted four sections in every township in 1896, and Arizona and New Mexico were given similar allocations of Sections 2, 16, 32, and 36.

The concern of the federal government for public education was evident in enabling acts by which territories became states (admitted to the Union after 1800). In each case, enabling acts required that provision be made for a system of public schools in the territory that desired statehood, and "in this way the federal government may be regarded as the founder of the public school systems for many of the states."[4]

Additional land grants stimulated further development of public schools.

[3]Arvid J. Burke, Financing Public Schools in the United States, rev. ed., New York: Harper & Row, 1957, p. 241.

[4]A. R. Munse and E. D. Booher, Federal Funds for Education 1956–57 and 1957–58, U.S. Office of Education, Bulletin 1959, no. 2, Washington, D.C.: GPO, 1959, p. 3.

Unfortunately, most lands so acquired were administered poorly by states and their full potential to support education went unrealized. In only a few states do these early land grants remain an important source of public school revenue. By 1957–1958 the value of the "permanent endowments" created in states as a result of the federal land-grant policy for schools declined to total $69,788,282. Only 1.5 percent of the state grants to school districts in 1957–1958 were derived from the permanent school funds. Today the proportion is less than 1 percent, for school expenditures have increased far faster than the limited receipts from permanent school funds.

Phase 2: land grants for higher education

About three-quarters of a century were to pass before another major federal educational policy became a reality. The second major action influenced public institutions of higher learning not elementary and secondary schools. Federal land grants awarded under the Morrill Act of 1862 were in response to demands for improved and expanded agricultural, mechanical, and scientific educational programs in institutions of higher learning in the United States that previously focused primarily on classical literature. Federally owned lands totaling 30,000 acres to each state for each senator and representative then in Congress were granted with the proviso that the income from sale or rental of these lands be dedicated to organizing new agricultural and mechanical arts colleges. Such institutions were to include instruction in military science and tactics as well. States that established land-grant colleges but in which the federal government owned no lands were awarded rights of land ownership in another state where large acreages were available. This second major federal policy in public education, although focused on higher education, set the pattern for conditional grants. Some have suggested that this represents the beginning of some degree of federal control, because funds were awarded for specific educational programs.

The Morrill Act was not intended to exclude scientific and classical studies. It demonstrated that the federal government could and would take action in education (1) if it was important to common defense or general welfare and (2) if vital areas of education were neglected.[5] All states received land grants from the Morrill Act; 6 million acres of federal lands were donated to the states for the founding of agricultural and mechanical arts colleges.

The second Morrill Act of 1890, the Hatch Act of 1887, and others were enacted to further aid these agricultural and mechanical schools which were subsequently known as the land-grant colleges. These later acts initiated the federal outlay of money as well as the land which the federal government owned in such large quantities during the early history of our nation.

Phase 3: conditional, specific-purpose grants for secondary schools

Another 50 years with little federal activity in education was to go by before a new direction emerged. Actually because the Morrill Act dealt with higher education, it can be said that more than a century (about 130 years) was to pass before the federal government demonstrated new concerns for public elementary and secondary edu-

[5] E. L. Morphet, R. L. Johns, and T. L. Reller, Educational Administration, 2nd ed., Englewood Cliffs, N.J.: Prentice-Hall, 1967, p. 217.

cation. This is in sharp contrast to the 1960s and 1970s when almost every other year a new major federal thrust in some dimension of education appeared.

The third phase of federal activity in public education came with the conditional grants for highly specific purposes in public secondary schools. The Smith-Hughes Act of 1917 provided money grants for agricultural education and other activities. The original act required matching of federal appropriations for vocational education in agriculture, trades, and industry and in homemaking. Federal concern for vocational education in a relatively limited number of fields in public secondary schools was extended by various acts in 1929, in 1935, in 1937, and again in 1946. The Vocational Education Act of 1963 represented radical departure from past practices if for no other reason than the Act was far more comprehensive in scope, included post secondary institutions, and the dollars involved were much greater. The 1968 amendments expand the Vocational Education Act of 1963 even further.

The original 1917 federal vocational act represented the entry of the federal government into public secondary education and stimulation of specific educational programs with annual appropriations. At one time federal funds accounted for about one-half the expenditures for vocational education. This intervention came at the time when the public high school was concerned primarily with preparation of students for entry into institutions of higher learning. Federal stimulation of local financing of vocational education was successful for federal appropriations for vocational education in 1955–1956 represented less than 50 percent of the total expenditure of over $275 million for vocational education, $142 million coming from the state and local funds, and $133 million from federal funds.

By 1966 the authorization under the Smith-Hughes Act was a little above $7.2 million. By 1966, the authorization was almost $50 million for the various titles of the George-Barden Act compared with $235.5 million for the Vocational Education Act of 1963. In the early 1970s federal funds for various dimensions of vocational education, including post secondary and adult programs, exceeded $400 million annually. In contrast, state and local funds for these same broad ranges of vocational education in the early 1970s exceeded $2 billion annually.

**Phase 4: incidental aid
through relief programs**

A fourth phase of federal interest in public education came during the Depression of the 1930s. The declining economic wealth of the nation was reflected in the public school system, and the impact of the Depression on youth was of no less significance. It must be emphasized that federal interest in education during this phase was incidental to its concern for the welfare of youth.

In 1933 the federal government organized the Civilian Conservation Corps (CCC) for unemployed, unmarried males aged 17 to 23. These young men were to do useful work, much of which was concerned with conservation of our natural resources. It soon became apparent that there was a high incidence of insufficient schooling among those who joined the CCC. A very small percentage graduated from high school; nearly one-half had never finished grade school; and a substantial number were practically illiterate. These factors precipitated change in the 1937 CCC Act to include appropri-

ations for the education and vocational training of the young men. President Roosevelt indicated at that time that the major purposes of the CCC were to promote welfare and *further training*. Administration of the corps was then transferred from the War Department to the Federal Security Agency. About $5 million to $10 million was spent for education in CCC camps in 1938, when $308.5 million was expended for all CCC activities. The federal expenditures for education in CCC camps were more than triple those for all public elementary and secondary education at that point in time. More than 2.7 million of the approximately 3 million men enrolled in the CCC participated in some type of educational activity.[6] The CCC was abolished in 1943. Almost a generation passed before the CCC idea was brought back as one part of the Job Corps program of the mid-1960s.

The National Youth Administration (NYA) was established in 1935 as a welfare program for unemployed youths from 16 to 25. Educational programs at first were limited, but by 1938 the NYA was concerned not only with part-time work for youth but also with training programs. There developed a series of in-school and out-of-school projects. Most writers were impressed by the lack of cooperation between the NYA and local schools. The NYA did not work through state departments of education until 1940, so complete was the federal domination.[7] A less controversial activity of the NYA was the granting of money to needy students in attendance at secondary schools or institutions of higher learning. The recipients of such aid were to perform some useful function in the school. Although most such

[6]Ibid., p. 217.
[7]Ibid.

students first lived at home, others later were housed in NYA residences and dormitories.[8] The independent status of the NYA was changed in 1939 when the organization was transferred to the Federal Security Agency. The NYA was liquidated in 1944.[9]

Many educators during the 1930s expressed alarm over what could have been the development of a federal system of education. In some cases federally supported training programs were in direct competition with programs offered by local school systems with far less financial resources. There is little question that the CCC and NYA did much fine welfare work for youths. Nonetheless, the educational activities of the CCC and NYA programs could have been performed by school systems close to CCC camps if these had been awarded sufficient financial support. The same remark was made later with reference to the Job Corps of the 1960s.

Other federal welfare activities during the Great Depression had a more indirect impact on public education. The projects were for relief of the unemployed, and benefits to schools were incidental. Thus, many schoolhouses were repainted and renovated through funds and activities of the Civil Works Administration (CWA), organized to provide work for the unemployed. The Federal Emergency Relief Administration (FERA), established in 1933, allocated funds for adult education, vocational rehabilitation, and nursery schools, although its primary concern was for the unemployed. One of the first FERA releases was the expenditure of relief funds for the employment of unemployed rural teachers. Under the Works Progress Administration (WPA) which succeeded the FERA in 1935, substantial funds were

made available for school-plant construction and repair. The Public Works Administration (PWA), organized in 1933, had granted 30 percent (later 45 percent) of the cost of school construction and made loans for all or part of the remaining costs.[10]

The many communities that participated in the CWA, FERA, PWA, or WPA projects for school-plant construction were in a better position to meet the schoolroom shortage after World War II. The matching provisions of the federal grants, unfortunately, made wealthier districts with financial ability to raise money for matching the greatest beneficiaries. All federal relief agencies were terminated in 1940 because defense activities related to World War II solved the unemployment problem.

The only continuing federal "aid" for public schools that originated and grew out of relief measures of the 1930s was the school lunch program. The Federal Surplus Commodities Corporation was established by Congress in 1935 to purchase and distribute surplus commodities to nonprofit school lunch programs. Activities of this corporation were intended as a relief for agriculture and were administered by the Department of Agriculture. The School Lunch Program in the Department of Agriculture was initiated under Public Law 320, approved in 1935. The School Milk Program was initiated in 1940. The National School Lunch Act of 1946 established some degree of permanency for federal school lunch aid as a means of reducing surplus food purchased by the federal government to support agricultural prices. Federal funds totaling $666,121,279 were allotted under the National School Lunch Act from 1947–1948 to 1956–1957, inclusive. If the value of commodities

[8]Ibid.
[9]Ibid.

[10]Ibid., p. 220.

and milk were added to the actual money received, the total would be more than $11.5 billion for the ten years. In 1970 federal funds for school lunch and milk programs exceeded the amount granted in the first ten years of the National School Lunch Act. The annual grants thereafter exceeded $927 million and approached $1 billion.

The GI bills. During World War II the federal government engaged in many other educational activities. The Lanham Act of 1941 provided for grants to "federally impacted" areas where federal activities created special problems for schools or other community agencies. There also came a series of veterans' education laws in 1944 (Public Law 346) and 1952 (Public Law 550). About 10 million veterans received some training under these acts.

The Servicemen's Readjustment Act of 1944, known popularly as the GI Bill, was an educational "bonus" to returning World War II veterans. Funds allocated for veterans' education and training exceeded $2.7 billion in 1949, and then dropped to $1.94 billion in 1951 and $0.56 billion in 1958. Benefits were extended to Korean Conflict veterans and others in following years. This direct aid to the individual veteran benefited institutions of higher learning and special schools as well. Public Law 87–358, approved March 3, 1966, provided for a permanent program of educational assistance for veterans who served more than 180 days. The present act makes available from $100 to $150 a month to assist veterans who become full-time students.

Phase 5: the National Defense Education Act

After World War II, many forces combined to intensify federal concern for continued development of public education. The launching of the first Soviet Sputnik is generally credited for Congressional action leading to the National Defense Education Act (NDEA) of 1958. The importance of education to the national defense was declared in the first section of this act:

The Congress hereby finds and declares that the security of the nation requires the fullest development of the mental resources and technical skills of its young men and women. . . . The defense of this nation depends upon the mastery of modern techniques developed from complex scientific principles. It depends as well upon the discovery and development of new principles, new techniques, and new knowledge.

We must increase our efforts to identify in education more of the talent of our nation.

The Congress reaffirms the principle and declares that the states and local communities have and must retain control over and primary responsibility for public education. The national interest requires, however, that the federal government give assistance to education for programs which are important to our defense.

This rather broad act granted federal funds for:

1. College and university student loans.
2. Strengthening science, mathematics, and language instruction in schools.
3. Creating graduate-school fellowships.
4. Promoting guidance, counseling, and testing services in elementary and secondary schools.
5. Stimulating the teaching of certain languages that previously had been neglected.
6. Performing research and experimentation in various educational media.
7. Promoting the establishment of area vocational schools.
8. Improving statistical services of state educational agencies.

By June 30, 1960, nearly $400 million

had been spent in carrying out provisions of the NDEA—about $250 million from federal funds, and $143 million from state agencies, school districts, and institutions of higher education participating in the program.[11]

The NDEA was the first piece of legislation passed by Congress aimed specifically at improving instruction in academic or nonvocational school subjects. In Title III of the act, emphasis was placed on equipment and facilities improvement in the sciences, mathematics, and foreign languages. The NDEA was modified in 1961, 1963, and 1964. The last two changes broadened the act to include history, civics, geography, English, and reading as critical subjects.

Phase 6: the Elementary and Secondary Education Act

The Elementary and Secondary Education Act (ESEA) of 1965 represented a new high for federal support of public education. The amounts involved were measured not in terms of a few millions or even hundreds of millions of dollars, but rather in terms of one or more billions of dollars. The ESEA was an omnibus bill, with aid to education being a part of federal government's interest in an economic problem. When President Johnson signed the bill on April 11, 1965, he declared: "As President of the United States I believe deeply no law I have signed, or will ever sign, means more to the future of America."

The ESEA represented a new approach in that it provided means whereby federal tax funds could be made available to private and church-related schools as well as public schools: One of the conditions for ob-

[11]C. H. Moore, "The National Defense Education Act After 18 Months," *School Life*, vol. 42, no. 6, February 1960, pp. 29–35.

taining funds under Title II of the ESEA was that cooperative efforts be established with the parochial schools. In other respects, although the funds were far greater than any previously appropriated for public elementary and secondary education, the act did not provide federal funds for the general support of education. The funds were awarded primarily for specific purposes established by the federal government.

Title I of the ESEA was aimed at meeting the educational needs of children of poverty. The greatest concentration of funds went to rural areas of the South and the core areas of big cities. A little less than $1 billion was appropriated the first year and a little more than that the second year. Of the 22,000 projects approved almost two-thirds were for language-arts instruction and remedial reading. The major portion of the funds (51.6 percent the first year and 57.6 percent the second year) were for instructional services. Food services, particularly hot breakfasts and lunches at school, accounted for more than 2 percent of Title I funds. It is estimated that 8.3 billion educationally deprived children in 50 states were reached during the first year.

Title II of the ESEA granted support for three types of educational materials: school-library resources, textbooks, and other instructional materials. About $100 million was made available for these purposes during the first two years. Private schools received benefits from the appropriations as well.

Supplementary educational centers and services, sometimes called Projects to Advance Creativity in Education (PACE) were founded under Title III. Over 10 million public and nonpublic school pupils were touched by Title III programs, and 1085 proposals and $75.8 million for their support were approved, during the first year of operation.

The Cooperative Research Act of 1954 was amended and made Title IV of the ESEA. Grants or contracts were awarded under this title for research or related activities that could benefit education. From funds of only $1 million annually this program exceeded $100 million for research grants and contracts by the late 1960s. Federal educational research funds in all agencies, not simply the Cooperative Research Act, reached $320 million by 1972. It was estimated to exceed $450 million by the mid-1970s. As will be developed more fully later, the creation of the National Institute of Education (NIE) in the early 1970s increased emphasis on research even further. Planned ESEA expansions were curtailed in the late 1960s because of the Vietnam conflict.

Phase 7: multifaceted efforts

A number of specific federal efforts were instituted in the past ten years (since 1965) in an effort to cope with problems confronting the education of certain groups of learners. This includes such diverse activities as vocational education, the Job Corps and desegregation thrusts.

The Vocational Education Act of 1963 affected federally established vocational programs in existing public schools that had remained relatively unchanged since their founding in 1917. This act increased authorization for grants made to states to $60 million for 1964. By 1965 the expenditures from this act exceeded $100 million and by 1971 more than $317 million. The act led to the construction of area vocational schools for the use of pupils out of school hours and of adults. One-third of the states' annual allot-

ment was dedicated for the creation of such schools. The 50–50 matching provision was essentially unchanged from the 1917 Smith-Hughes Law. This 1963 Act continued to place federally supported vocational educational programs under the control of local school districts or specially created regional units within a state school system.

The Job Corps

The Job Corps was a vocational education effort that was radically different in the target population served. Of even greater significance is that its operation and control were outside state educational systems.

The movement toward the establishment of federally sponsored, supported, and controlled vocational institutions for school dropouts represents another type of federal involvement in public education. The Job Corps is similar in some respects to the CCC and NYA programs of the Depression, but goes beyond them. The creation of special educational institutions, known as Job Corps, was a federal response to defensible educational needs allegedly not cared for adequately through local initiative. High school dropouts had been the concern of professional educators for more than 50 years prior to federal interest in the problem. Federal concern for dropouts occurred at the very time significant improvements were evident in the holding power of public schools. Thus, for every 1000 children in fifth grade in 1957–1958, an estimated 710 graduated from high school in 1965 or about the time Job Corps came into being. Comparable figures show that there were 628 high school graduates in 1960, 505 in 1950, and 444 in 1940 for each 1000 pupils in fifth grade eight years earlier. The proportion of fifth graders in 1957–1958 who persisted (did not drop out) and graduated from high school eight years later, in 1965, was almost two-thirds greater than the proportion of fifth graders in 1932–1933 who persisted and graduated in 1940. This improvement occurred without federal funds. Limited resources, not lack of concern for dropouts, forced local school districts to concentrate on programs for pupils in Grades 1 through 12 who wanted to stay in school.

Administration and control of the Job Corps were vested in a specially created federal agency, the Office of Economic Opportunity, and not in the United States Office of Education. This fact demonstrates that the United States Congress will assign funds for educational purposes without regard to a centralized education department within the federal hierarchy. Of the more than $10 billion appropriated for education by the federal government in 1966, only about $4 billion was administered through the U.S. Office of Education. As a result of this dispersion, no agency now exists in the national government with adequate status or resources to assume effective leadership for the development of a consistent federal educational policy: One agency may even pursue a policy contradictory to that of another.

The Office of Economic Opportunity, which directed the Job Corps, was a special federal agency created to combat the problems associated with poverty. There were two main divisions of the Job Corps. One division directed the Urban Job Corps centers, which enrolled large number of youths and provided a comprehensive vocational program for them; the other directed Conservation Job Corps centers, which were more numerous than urban centers but enrolled fewer youths. The Urban Job Corps abandoned the coeducational concept for teenagers—an established part of public secondary school operations across the land—and set up the centers for men quite a distance away from those for women. Because all the funds were federal and most of the policy control remained within a federal agency, it can be said that the Job Corps was a federal system of education for youths 16 to 22. The federal government used the contract method to sublet actual center operations to private and a few public organizations.

The Job Corps was developed with little, if any, consultation with the professional people involved in teaching and administering public elementary and secondary education. It appeared with relatively little advance warning. It was by no means a federal response to a call from local school systems unable to cope with the dropout problem. As stated previously, federal involvement came at a time when the proportion of dropouts had been substantially declining over an extended period of time without federal help or concern.

The Job Corps can be defined as a residential, vocational, and compensatory education program with a massive welfare dimension for school dropouts in the 16- to 22-year-old group. It was not geared to serve all dropouts and only about a third qualified. Its main purpose was to overcome conditions of poverty, for one of the provisos for admission to a Job Corps camp was low economic status of the family of the applicant.

The Job Corps was a specialized effort and, therefore, did not provide a comprehensive program for all children and youths. Although Urban Job Corps centers were operated under contracts with private industry and a few public and semipublic educational agencies, the centers were financed completely with federal funds and were under close and continuing federal supervision. Over 300 of the Office of Economic Opportunity's Job Corps personnel were headquartered in Washington, D.C., and over 50 in the field. About three-fourths of the Urban Job Corps contractors in June 1966, were private corporations. These companies did not operate Job Corps centers on a nonprofit, good-will, or contribution-to-society basis; they sought to make money from Job Corps contracts. Comparatively little company capital was tied up in the process. In 1965 one private Urban Job Corps contractor made $80,000 annual profit from a center with a capacity of 300 women (about $266 per enrollee); another registered an annual profit of $364,000 for a center enrolling 1300 men (about $280 per enrollee). Some private industries used Job Corps centers to develop and try out educational systems that were to be sold as part of the company's product line at some future date. In this sense, part of the Job Corps grant can be considered profit beyond actual dollars earned or the image of being a "socially concerned" industry.

No public elementary- and/or secondary-school district ever has received a per-pupil federal grant to pursue a federally inspired program as massive as those awarded to agencies operating Urban Job Corps centers. No public elementary or secondary school has been allowed to make a profit on the federal funds allocated to it. On the contrary, federal grants to public schools have been conditional upon local and state matching funds or at least substantial contributions.

A double standard appears evident from the federal financing of educational ventures. If the grant was to a public school system, the local school system assumed part of the fiscal burden. Furthermore, additional facilities required to house the part of the educational program being stimulated were to be provided somehow by local educational authorities. Small sums per pupil were granted typically to local schools. On the other hand, if the federal grant for an educational program was awarded to a private firm, as in the case of Job Corps, not only was the private firm not required to make any substantial financial sacrifice, but a profit was expected and awarded. Furthermore, if facilities were rented, constructed, or refurbished, the federal government, rather than the private contractors, assumed full cost. Thus, during 1965, a special study by the author showed that the capital outlay costs for Urban Job Corps centers ranged between $3,500 to $7,500 per enrollee, with all funds being provided by the federal government. Whether this double standard will appear again now that Job Corps centers have been phased out remains to be seen.

Prior to its inception, various informal estimates of Job Corps cost placed the probable operating expenditures at around $5,000 per enrollee per year. This proved unrealistically low; published statements on the cost of keeping a single boy or girl in the Job Corps for one year range from $9,100 to $13,000 in one set of estimates and from $17,000 to $235,000 in another. As Oregon's Representative Green asked in 1966, could not public schools make breakthroughs if they were permitted to spend $13,000 each year on each student?

Certain factors must be kept in mind in analyzing Job Corps costs:

1. High starting costs along with unusual problems in some centers inflated many units' outlays.
2. The centers are residential—cloth-

ing is furnished and enrollees are fed three times a day seven days a week.

3. Extensive medical and dental services are available.

4. The corpsmen receive allowances of $30 per month plus a $50 terminal allowance.

A study by the writer, using financial data provided by the Office of Economic Opportunity, indicated that the annual cost was about $12,000 per enrollee for 1965. This is over 20 times the $501 per pupil in the average daily membership in the elementary and secondary schools of the United States in 1965–1966. By 1967 Job Corps expenditures had dropped to $7,500 per enrollee per year. Administrative costs of locating, screening, assigning, and paying corpsmen, as well as maintaining the Washington, D.C. headquarters operations, were in excess of $1,500 per enrollee per year, or about 12 percent of the expenditures for 1965. In contrast, only 3 to 5 percent of the budget of a public school system is allocated to administration.

There were early indications that the Job Corps could last for at least a decade assuming no new global warfare. Criticisms of this federal educational venture began to appear very early and it was evident that the Job Corps was not likely to be a permanent educational vehicle. By late 1967, there were over 123 Job Corps centers (93 conservation, 10 men's urban, 18 women's urban, and 2 special), enrolling almost 40,000 people. The extension of the Job Corps program beyond 1967 provided for 45,000 enrollees, 23 percent of whom must be women. The total allocated for fiscal 1966 was $303,400,861; about $211 million was allocated for fiscal 1967. By 1970 the Job Corps program was scheduled for

elimination having achieved but limited success in its mission and having become politically too controversial.

What kind of an impact could the Job Corps program have on the dropout problem? The most reliable estimates indicate that there were in 1963 about 3 million boys and girls aged 16 to 21 who dropped out of school. It is estimated by some that 750,000 yearly drop out of school before graduation from high school. As stated previously, the Job Corps did not attempt to serve all; only those who were (1) unemployable or unable to hold a job, (2) underprivileged from having lived in impoverished surroundings, or (3) in need of a change of environment to become productive. About 35 percent of the youngsters taken into Job Corps were illiterate. The average enrollee read at the fourth- to fifth-grade level. Since roughly a third of the total dropout population was eligible for the Job Corps, two-thirds of the school dropouts were not helped by this program. The idealists in the program had to learn that no single agency—no matter how dedicated—could serve *all* dropouts. After some difficult early experiences, the retarded, the emotionally disturbed, and the incorrigibles had to be dismissed or screened out of the Job Corps and sent to other social institutions if any existed.

If capacity in all Job Corps Centers remained at 40,000, the statistics would not be any more impressive. Less than 4 percent of the *total* dropout population eligible for the Job Corps (about one-third of the total, or 1,250,000) would have been served by all camps operating at full capacity. It would be safe to conclude that the federal approach administered by the Office of Economic Opportunity could not possibly make a substantial dent in the dropout problem in spite of massive federal funds and the alleged benefits of private industrial involvement.

The Job Corps itself had dropouts, as does any educational institution. The Job Corps was not the first federal venture for youths to experience this problem. About 26 percent of the average annual enrollment in the CCC from 1933 to 1941 terminated their education or training prematurely. The dropout rate in the Job Corps was in the neighborhood of 30 percent, depending upon how the term is defined; the Job Corps, after all, serves the dropout-prone. It was one of the most controversial of the antipoverty programs and one of the first to be phased out. The Job Corps was terminated, for all practical purposes, by 1970. OEO ceased to be a functionally operative agency by 1973 and most of its continuing programs (but not Job Corps) were transferred to other federal agencies.

Federal funds for dropout-prevention programs in the public schools have not even been mentioned, much less developed. Evidently it was better politics, for a time, to support the war against poverty and to treat the dropout rather than prevent his dropping out. The Job Corps failed to demonstrate that it was the ideal way to solve or even contribute substantially to the resolution of this problem. Nonetheless, the search for ways of minimizing the problem must be continued and new experiments must be attempted.

The Neighborhood Youth Corps (NYC) was the in-school counterpart of the nation's effort to combat poverty. Headstart deals with preschoolers, but the NYC dealt with the same age group as the Job Corps. NYC dealt with youths living in their own communities who were provided part-time paying jobs and with out-of-school, unemployed youths. Over one-half million youths were served by NYC during its first year. In 1966, $410 million was allocated for the program. It too was phased out by 1970.

Enforcement of desegregation

The growing concern for immediate assurance of civil rights and improvement of the economic condition of black Americans has been expressed, in large measure, in an educational setting. During the 1960s the federal government began to use its full force to promote the recommendations of the Supreme Court concerning the establishment of a desegregated public school system in all states. The Civil Rights Act of 1964 provided that programs receiving federal funds—including public education—must be nondiscriminatory and that financial assistance would be withheld or withdrawn from those school districts not giving clear evidence of their intent to establish a desegregated school system within a relatively short time. Federal guide lines, prepared by the Office of Education, were used to measure the extent to which organization and administration of public education in various states satisfied the spirit as well as intent of the law. The Civil Rights Act had an impact in the North, where de facto segregation in the operation of educational systems was alleged, as well as in the South. In 1967 primary responsibility for enforcement of the act was shifted from the Office of Education to the Department of Health, Education, and Welfare as a whole. The Department of Justice likewise assumed a more active role.

By 1973 the first northern school desegregation case reached the United States Supreme Court. The *Denver* and *Detroit* issues suggest that northern school systems may face desegregation problems similar to those encountered by southern school districts in the 1960s. Residential patterns, which are outside the control of schools, and movement of whites to the suburbs, again a factor beyond the control of schools, resulted in large concentrations of blacks and other minorities in certain school attendance areas. This situation is being attacked in the courts as illustrative of de facto segregation. The Department of Health, Education, and Welfare is being directed by the courts to cut off federal funds for school systems that fail to comply with desegregation requirements.

Other educational programs

In addition to supporting and encouraging general and specific educational programs, the federal government is engaged in operating such institutions as the Military Academy, the Marine Corps Institute, the Army Medical School, the Merchant Marine Institute, the Coast Guard Academy, the National War Colleges, the Naval Academy, the Air University, the Air Force Academy, and the Armed Forces Institute. It operates schools overseas for dependents of servicemen and specific government workers. The education of Indians has been in large measure financed by the federal government through the Department of the Interior.

Critique of federal educational efforts

Few things are less rewarding than the search for a piece of federal legislation that typifies the national government's approach to public education. There is no internally consistent federal policy on education. To illustrate, school lunch funds are provided through the Department of Agriculture, education of the Indians is the responsibility of the Department of the Interior, a large educational system for

dependents of the Armed Forces is operated by the Department of Defense, the NYC was the administrative concern of the Department of Labor, the Job Corps was under the direction of the Office of Economic Opportunity, the development of science curriculum materials is assigned to the National Science Foundation, and grant programs for schools are distributed through the Office of Education. On the basis of past action, it can be predicted that Congress will continue to assign funds for educational purposes without regard to a central education department within the federal hierarchy. The absence of a well-reasoned, commonly deliberated, and consistent statement of federal policy in education is not in the best interest of the nation.

One example of direct federal involvement in influencing educational curriculum is the program of the National Science Foundation (NSF). The NSF was created about 80 years after the Office of Education. Both are federal agencies. In spite of the time lag, it is said by some that in many areas the NSF has had a greater impact on education than the Office of Education. The NSF enjoys an independent status and a nonpartisan governing board. It makes no direct payments to school districts and state departments of education and is, therefore, less well known by local school systems than by colleges and nonprofit research groups that do receive direct grants from it. The NSF serves as an instrument of federal policy in education when it seeks to increase the supply of competent mathematics and science teachers, influences the writing of science and mathematics curricula, supports the design of instructional materials for science and math, and operates in-service education programs for mathematics and science teachers.

President Johnson in a message to Congress dated January 29, 1966, and dealing with the NSF's fifteenth Annual Report, stated that more than one-half of all high school science and mathematics teachers took part in NSF-sponsored refresher training programs. If one were to ask an Office of Education official whether the federal government is consciously attempting to shape curriculum and instruction in the local public schools, the answer would be an emphatic no. And it would be true that the Office of Education has not attempted to peddle new curriculum packages to replace the old. One activity does not establish an irreversible trend, but it is appropriate to speculate whether activities of the NSF, when placed in historical perspective, will represent the beginning of a federally sponsored curriculum-development program. The resources made available for mathematics and science curriculum development, as well as the ability of the NSF to attract scholars and others into curriculum-development activity, may well encourage the federal government to further exploit the role of prime developer of curriculum for public schools.

For fiscal 1965–1966, the NSF received a record appropriation of $420.4 million of which over $120 million was used for science education and over $60 million was allocated to institutional science programs. The remaining amount went to support basic research.

The federal government's schizophrenic policy of support of education has resulted in such a jungle of grants that books are now written on how to find your way around in the federal government's education program to be sure your district receives its share of the funds. Fragments of education are aided, often at the expense of balanced educational programs. Some federal programs are intended to compensate for deficiency in the school-tax base; others are intended to broaden the scope or improve the quality of public education; still others are for groups for whom the federal government accepts responsibility, such as Indians, children of war veterans, and Cuban refugees. Federal contributions to revenue receipts accruing to public elementary and secondary schools in 1965–1966 increased to 7.9 percent. In comparison, in 1964–1965 the federal contributions totaled only 3.8 percent. This was the most dramatic jump in the history of federal contributions to public school revenues. Since then federal contributions have hovered around 8 percent of all school revenues. Federal grants to elementary and secondary education remained below $1 billion through 1965. They jumped to almost $2.5 billion in 1966 and exceeded $4.3 billion in 1974. Total federal education grants and loans, including those for higher education, reached $6.21 in fiscal year 1974.

Categorical federal aids for education predominate and represent a well-established trend. Categorical aids allow maximum federal control and place a premium on grantmanship. Federal support programs in education shift with the political winds as the emergence of real or imagined crises determine which aspect of education shall be supported. During the twentieth century federal support started with the stimulation of vocational, agricultural, and home economics training; it later moved to include training in trades and industries, then science and mathematics, and now other instructional fields as well.

Categorical aids are more compatible with the regulatory functions of the federal government than with leadership. This approach to school finance implies that people and educators at the local level are neither imaginative nor concerned with educational improvement. Federal officials in contrast are assumed to be endowed with great imagination and complete dedication to quality education. To ensure that local educational systems make the best use of federal funds, centralized regulation of grants and guide lines for their use proliferate. Categorical aids are defensible when the support is limited in amount and confined to a few school programs. The greatly increased federal contributions to local schools as well as the ever-growing number of school program and curriculum areas being stimulated suggest that the time has come to abandon primary reliance on categorical aids and to move toward general support of education. General support would call for more emphasis on the federal government's leadership, as opposed to its regulatory, role as a means of directing local school efforts toward improvement.

THE UNITED STATES OFFICE OF EDUCATION

Although many federal agencies are concerned with education and administer federally appropriated funds for a variety of educational purposes, the United States Office of Education is the primary channel through which the federal government extends educational leadership and cooperation to the profession. It is the only federal agency whose sole concern is for all aspects of the country's educational system.[12]

The Office of Education has the specific role of promoting education by

aiding the people to achieve the objectives embodied in the *Handbook of the Office of Education*.[13] It seeks to encourage the citizen's understanding of, and responsibility for, education; to focus attention on the value of education to the individual and the nation; to promote agreement on common goals among educators and laymen; and through research and publication of research findings, to make accurate information available to all.

During the first week of March 1967, the Office of Education celebrated its one-hundredth birthday. In 1867 its first Commissioner, Henry Barnard, received a salary of $4,000 a year and had a staff of three clerks and a total budget of $18,592. Two years later, in 1869, a Congress that was not overly impressed with the need and importance of a Department of Education cut his salary and reduced his minimal staff. By 1974 the Office of Education had about 2800 employees and an estimated annual expenditures under its control of more than $6.12 billion. A dramatic increase in Office of Education expenditures took place between 1965 and 1966 when the total climbed from about $872 million to over $2 billion. The increase brought about by the Elementary and Secondary Act alone almost equalled the total expenditures for all purposes in 1965 and greatly exceeded that for all purposes in each year prior to 1965.

The National Defense Education Act (NDEA) that was passed in the late 1950s was the first large new program to be administered by the USOE in the post-World-War II period. Even more dramatic growth took place in the 1960s with the passage of several significant pieces of educational legislation by Congress. The year 1973 will

[12]U.S. Office of Education, *Progress of Public Education in the United States of America*, A Summary Report, OE-10005, Washington, D.C.: GPO, 1960, p. 4.

[13]U.S. Office of Education, *Handbook of Office of Education*, OE-11002, Washington, D.C.: GPO, 1972.

be remembered as a year of great change, when some of the functions and personnel previously assigned to the USOE were transferred to the newly created National Institute of Education (NIE). More will be said about the NIE later, but first a look at the historical development of the Office of Education.

Historical development

In 1838, Henry Barnard, then Commissioner of Education from Connecticut, came to Washington in search of reliable facts about the nation's school system. He found none, and for the next 30 years dedicated himself to the movement for the establishment of a federal education agency. Almost every national education meeting of any importance at that time gave its attention to the need for creating a federal office of education which would be the official agency for the exchange of educational information among the states, for diffusing knowledge of the science and art of education, and for organizing and administering education.[14] These early educational leaders contemplated an office that would not only collect and report educational information but also make comparative studies of schools and school systems in this country. They suggested that the head of the agency attend conventions, publish an educational journal, and make an annual report on the progress of education in the United States and foreign nations.

Activities and discussions among educational leaders culminated in 1866 in a request for the creation of a national bureau of education. James A. Garfield, then Representative from the state of Ohio, presented a bill to estab-

lish a "department of education." The bill was passed in the House in June 1866, but was not reported for the consideration of the Senate until February 1867. It was approved by the Senate shortly thereafter, and President Andrew Johnson signed it, creating the Department of Education on March 2, 1867.[15]

The historic purposes of what was then known as the Department of Education and now as the Office of Education were:

1. Collecting such statistics and facts as shall show the condition and progress of education in the several States and Territories.
2. Diffusing such information respecting the organization and management of schools and school systems, and methods of teaching, as shall aid the people of the United States in the establishment and maintenance of efficient school systems.
3. Otherwise [promoting] the cause of education throughout the country.

The Commissioner of Education was entrusted "with the management" of the Office of Education; he was to be appointed by the President, with the advice and consent of the Senate, and was to "present annually to Congress a report embodying the results of his investigations and labors" and prepare "a statement of the several grants of land made by Congress to promote education."[16]

Nine days after President Johnson signed the act creating the Department of Education, he appointed Henry Barnard as the first United States Commissioner of Education, a post that Barnard held until 1870. Even though it was known as a Department of Education, the Commissioner was not a member of the President's cabinet and was never intended to be one. The

---

[14]Lloyd E. Blauch, "To Promote the Cause of Education," *School Life,* vol. 35, May-June 1953, pp. 2–3.

[15]Ibid.

[16]Ibid., quotations taken from the original act.

title was unfortunate. The original draft of the bill presented by Garfield called for the establishment of a "bureau of education" in the Department of the Interior. In 1868 the new department was attached to the Department of the Interior and officially given the status of a bureau, although it was named "office" rather than "bureau" of education. An appropriations act for 1870 changed the title "office" to "bureau" without altering the status of the Commissioner, his salary, or his duties.[17] In 1929 the title Office of Education was adopted once again and has continued up to the present time.

The reorganization of government agencies in 1939 transferred the Office of Education, its functions and personnel, to the Federal Security Agency. On April 11, 1953, when the Department of Health, Education, and Welfare (DHEW) superseded the Federal Security Agency, the Office of Education became one of the units in this department. It remains in DHEW today.

Responsibilities of the office

The Office of Education focused primarily on the responsibilities and functions assigned it by the original act: collecting and disseminating statistics and facts and "promoting the cause of education," up until the late 1950s. Additional responsibilities were added to the historic functions by various acts of Congress or executive order. To illustrate, the conduct of educational and relief work among the natives of Alaska was administered under the Office of Education from 1887 until 1931, when it was transferred to the Office of Indian Affairs. During World War I the Office of Education received appropriations to carry on

[17]Ibid.

such war-related educational activities as school gardens, social studies, and the Americanization of immigrants. The educational program of the CCC, which involved several million enrollees, was placed under the general supervision of the Commissioner of Education. During World War II several extensive training programs enrolling more than 14 million people were instituted. The Federal Board for Vocational Education, established in 1917 to administer the Smith-Hughes Act, was transferred to the Department of the Interior in 1933 and later to the Office of Education. The large-scale programs for handling surplus property of the federal government were assigned to the office as well. The total acquisition value of surplus property transferred during the ten years from 1947 to 1956 was about $1.2 bilion. The acquisition cost of personal property of the federal government transferred to educational institutions during a more recent ten year period, 1962 to 1971, was in excess of $2.4 billion, or more than double that for the earlier ten year period. The estimated fair value of such property at the time of transfer was less than 10 percent of its acquisition cost.

The Office of Education carries on its work through

1. Publishing its research findings, studies, and survey reports.
2. Participating in conferences.
3. Lectures and writing.
4. Consultation and field work.
5. Contracting with colleges, universities, state departments of education, and others that conduct research.
6. Administering grant funds as stipulated by Congress.
7. Preparing guidelines covering conditions to qualify for federal funds.

Stated another way, the functions of the office are served by

1. Publishing educational information.
2. Establishing cooperative working relations with agencies and groups interested in education.
3. Engaging in educational research.
4. Providing leadership, consultative, and clearing-house services related to education.

It does not directly administer public education anywhere in the United States; other government agencies do. It was charged with enforcement of parts of the Civil Rights Act for a short period of time.

The office has become more of a grant-dispensing than a statistics-gathering and publications agency. Its influence has grown with the size of federal funds available. Its guidelines for disbursing grants have made it more controversial as well.

The five major programs in the 1960s and early 1970s, as measured by the magnitude of federal dollars invested, administered through USOE are: NDEA, assistance to school districts with enrollments affected by federal agencies or activities within such districts (federally affected areas), Elementary and Secondary Education Act (ESEA), Vocational Education Act of 1963 (with 1968 amendments), and Higher Education Act. Major programs vary from time to time as new ones are introduced through congressional action and others are phased out. Thus, the largest amount of money in the first half of the 1960s went for assistance to schools in federally affected areas, and the second largest was dispensed through NDEA. The second half of that decade saw funds for ESEA in the number one spot, assistance to schools in federally affected areas was second, grants for NDEA were third, money for the Higher Education Act fourth, and grants for Vocational Education fifth. In the early

1970s NDEA money reached a peak of $371 million in 1971 and then plummeted to about $98.7 million the next year. The five largest programs administered through USOE in the early 1970s showed the following order: ESEA, Higher Education Act, assistance to schools in federally affected areas, Vocational Education Acts, and finally NDEA. ESEA appropriations were below $1 billion annually only in the first year (1966). After that the ESEA grants climbed from $1.25 billion in 1967 to $2.12 billion in 1974.

Other programs of growing importance during the 1960s and early 1970s were federal funds for research and development, educational improvement for the handicapped, education professions development act, and higher education facilities support.

The Commissioner of Education

The Office of Education functions under the general direction of the Commissioner and Deputy Commissioner of Education. The list of men who have served as Commissioner of Education starts with Henry Barnard (1867 to 1870) and includes some of the most distinguished educators in the United States: John Eaton (1870 to 1886), N. H. R. Dawson (1886 to 1889), William T. Harris (1889 to 1906), Elmer E. Brown (1906 to 1911), Philander P. Claxton (1911 to 1921), John James Tigert (1921 to 1928), William John Cooper (1929 to 1933), George F. Zook (1933 to 1934), John W. Studebaker (1934 to 1948), Earl James McGrath (1949 to 1953), Lee M. Thurston (July 2 to September 1, 1953), Samuel Miller Brownell (1953 to 1956), Lawrence G. Derthick (1956 to 1961), Sterling M. McMurin (1961 to 1962), Francis Keppel (1962 to 1965), Harold Howe II (1965 to 1969), James E. Allen, Jr. (1969 to 1970), Sidney P. Marland, Jr. (1970 to 1972), John R. Ottina* (1973 to 74), and Terrell H. Bell (1974–). In more than 100 years 21 different men have served as Commissioner of Education. The shortest term was two months, caused by the death of the incumbent soon after assuming office, and the longest was 18 years (enjoyed by William T. Harris). The greatest turnover thus far was in the decade of the 1960s when five different men held office.

The Commissioner of Education is responsible for formulating policy and coordinating educational activities at the national level. The major functions of the position are:

1. To determine policy and program objectives.
2. To provide executive leadership for operations.
3. To render consultative services to educational agencies.
4. To coordinate office work with related programs within the Department of Health, Education, and Welfare.
5. To establish liaison with executive, legislative, and judicial branches of the government.
6. To advise national, state, and local officials and international bodies on educational problems.[18]

In addition, the commissioner is also an ex-officio member of the District of Columbia Commission on Licensure, an ex-officio representative of the Office of Education on the Board of Foreign Scholarships, and the governmental representative on the United States National Commission for UNESCO.

A deputy commissioner participates with the commissioner in the administration of the office and in the development of policies. Under the most recent office reorganization, there are in addition three associate commissioners: for international education, for federal-state relations, and for field services. An assistant and a special assistant are attached to the commissioner's office. Also included in the administrative staff are the offices of (1) construction service, (2) administration, (3) information, (4) legislation, (5) program planning and evaluation, (6) equal educational opportunity, and (7) programs for the disadvantaged. In addition there is the National Center for Educational Statistics, composed of the divisions of (1) data processing and analysis, (2) statistical analysis, (3) data sources and studies, and (4) operation analysis.

National Institute of Education (NIE)

In 1970 President Nixon proposed the creation of a new federal agency to be called the National Institute of Education (NIE). It took two years for the law establishing NIE to wend its way through Congress. What started as a simple 5-page bill ended up as a 200-page document, most of which is dedicated to higher education. Established in July, 1972, NIE was not an operational reality until almost a year later. Thomas Glennan was appointed as its first Director. NIE's first budget (fiscal year 1973) totaled a modest $142 million of which $110 million represented new appropriations and $32 million was transferred to NIE from other agencies.

NIE is an offshoot of the Office of Education. It inherited an assortment of ongoing research and development programs as well as personnel that were part of USOE. NIE is not a wholly independent agency such as the Environmental Protection Agency (EPA) or the National Aeronautics and Space Agency (NASA). The Institute Director, like the Commissioner of

---

*Acting Commissioner from October 1972; confirmed by the U.S. Senate as Commissioner in mid-1973.

[18]U.S. Office of Education, *Handbook of Office of Education*, p. 14.

USOE, is a presidential appointee. The NIE is coordinated through the office of an assistant secretary for education in DHEW and is parallel with the Office of Education.

The primary focus of NIE is research and development of research in education. Its mission is likened to its counterpart in health, the National Institute of Health, after which it was named. The Cooperative Research Act grew from humble beginnings in the 1950s to almost a $100 million effort, but it still is a relatively small program within USOE. Outlays for educational research under all federal acts reached $320 million in fiscal year 1972 and $452 million in fiscal year 1974. President Nixon's 1974 budget asked $162 million for all NIE functions, an increase of $52 million over 1973, but only a total of $75 million was approved. These figures should be compared with the more than $6.12 billion funneled through USOE in 1974. The early years have been very difficult ones for the newly established NIE. In 1973 the NIE's fiscal 1974 budget was slashed to $75 million by the Senate because it was reported to have been disappointed by NIE's lack of direction and action.

Transfers from USOE to NIE included Cooperative Research Act programs, Experimental Schools, Career Education, Dissemination (National Center for Educational Communication), the Research and Development Centers, and Regional Educational Laboratories. It also received the voucher demonstration project from the now defunct Office of Economic Opportunity (OEO) and some smaller projects from the National Center for Educational Technology.

There are several unique features to NIE. For the first time a small portion (about 15 percent) of the research monies can be kept in-house to con-duct educational research. This means that actual performers of research (rather than research grant administrators alone) will be employed by NIE. In addition there is a National Advisory Council on Educational Research and Development that is designed to be a policy-setting body for NIE.

The functions assigned to NIE could have continued, as it did earlier, under USOE. The creation of a new federal agency that focused primarily on education research was thought to enhance the image of such efforts as well as to give new vigor and promise to research. It is much too early to tell whether the promises will be fulfilled.

PATTERN OF FEDERAL SUPPORT FOR EDUCATION

As has been pointed out, the federal government has given financial support to public elementary and secondary education, and these contributions can be traced to the policies enunciated in 1787 and put into effect as enabling acts passed to organize territories into states. There have been over 180 years of federal aid to public education in the United States, and it exists at the present time. The major share of the total federal assistance for educational programs (over $18.2 billion in 1973) is distributed outside the Department of Health, Education, and Welfare (wherein the Office of Education is located) and for purposes other than elementary and secondary education (see Table 12–2). Less than 30 percent of all federal funds for education in 1971 and 1972 were administered through USOE, although this agency does disburse more than any other single federal agency. Over 10 percent of the total of federal assistance to education goes through the

TABLE 12–2

FEDERAL ASSISTANCE FOR EDUCATION PROGRAMS (IN THOUSANDS OF DOLLARS), 1950–1974

Federal agency	1950–1951	1956–1957	1966–1967	1972–1973	1973–1974
Department of Health, Education, and Welfare (Including Office of Education)	$ 111,370	$ 457,277	$4,125,500	$6,413,491	$ 7,013,480
Department of Agriculture	171,154	398,399	119,500[a]	1,517,254	1,604,987
Department of Commerce	5,292	2,884	18,100	10,309	9,893
Department of Defense[b]	27,807	73,216	1,534,200	1,078,204	1,133,640
Department of Housing and Urban Development	—	—	600	159,121	189,061
Department of Interior	45,834	90,794	199,600	287,392	317,679
Department of Justice	389	530	8,100	47,589	64,635
Department of Labor	3,927	5,940	403,000	1,594,000	1,657,000
Department of State	—	47,751	61,900	45,215	54,690
Department of Transportation	—	—	25,800	16,140	17,043
Department of Treasury	1,800	3,350	—	1,760	—
Veterans Administration	2,120,216	813,955	431,800	2,177,862	2,373,420
Appalachian Regional Development Commission	—	—	—	40,700	40,700
Atomic Energy Commission	18,908	30,717	14,400	9,695	10,140
National Science Foundation	—	34,952	199,800	58,600	57,200
Agency for International Development	—	—	204,600	140,529	140,943
Library of Congress	—	—	34,300	74,300	79,868
National Foundation for the Arts and Humanities	—	—	12,000	47,029	71,161
National Aeronautics and Space Administration	—	—	21,200	6,225	2,225
Office of Economic Opportunity	—	—	929,300	275,637	81,715
Research and Development (all federal agencies)	—	—	—	2,770,464	3,082,000
Smithsonian Institutions	—	—	19,200	60,000	62,306
U.S. Information Agency	—	—	7,600	2,227	2,232
Other (District of Columbia Schools, EPA. Government Printing Office, etc.)	5,132	8,481	96,500	119,113	146,149
Totals	$2,511,829	$1,968,246	$8,467,000	$16,952,856	$18,212,167

Source: Adapted from C. D. Hutchins, A. R. Munse, and E. D. Booher, *Federal Funds for Education 1958–1959 and 1959–1960*, U.S. Office of Education, Bull. 1961, no. 14, Washington, D.C.: GPO, 1961, pp. 14–17. 1966–1967 data based on data compiled by A. R. Munse for the U.S. Office of Education publication, *Digest of Educational Statistics*, 1971.
[a] Does not include $448 million for school lunch program.
[b] Includes Canal Zone assistance.

Veterans Administration and over 10 percent also goes through the Department of Labor. Expenditures for the Veterans Administration dropped from more than $3 billion during 1948–1949 to about $431.8 million during 1966–1967 and then climbed to $1.683 billion in 1972. Federal funds for education in all agencies declined during the late 1940s and into the early 1950s, hit a low of less than $1.5 billion in 1952–1953, and then began to increase again. Much of the decline could be traced to the phasing out of World War II veterans' education benefits. Growth in other federal educational ventures such as the Elementary and Secondary Education Act of 1965, Job Corps, and Neighborhood Youth Corps, raised federal assistance for educational programs of various types during the late 1960s and early 1970s.

The tremendous increase in federal educational assistance is evident from Table 12–2. The approximate expenditure of almost $8.5 billion in 1966–1967 does not include $2.3 billion dedicated to research and development in all federal agencies nor the $0.75 billion allocated to loan programs. In the space of 20 years following 1950 total federal assistance to education quintupled.

PURPOSES OF FEDERAL SUPPORT FOR EDUCATION

The Constitution charges Congress with promoting the general welfare. Some of the more prominent national purposes underlying the provision of federal funds for education are the following:

1. To encourage and support programs of education or services in the schools that are essential or beneficial to the national welfare and security.
2. To contribute to or provide for education where there is a federal responsibility or obligation.
3. To provide educational and training services essential to the national defense, but not separate responsibilities of any local community, state, or segment of the population.
4. To assist students, selected on the basis of tests and recommendations, to receive scholarships for advanced training that will serve the national welfare.
5. To assist the economically developing areas of the world and to improve international relations through the exchange of information and of students, teachers, professors, technicians, and leaders with other countries.
6. To maintain efficient governmental services and increase the effectiveness of the federal service through programs of education.
7. To promote the general welfare of the nation through research in the physical, biological, and social sciences that will develop new areas of learning and prepare more specialists with competencies in these fields.[19]

Thus far federal efforts in education appear to react more to emerging pressures than to predetermined purposes. It is more oportunistic than directional. New programs are launched with high hopes and funding only to fade away some five years later because more was promised than could be delivered. Categorical aids have not met expectations, perhaps the revenue-sharing efforts of the early 1970s will have more positive results. Only time will tell.

SUMMARY

The role of the federal government in education continues to expand and to become more significant. This has not lessened the confusion and controversy that surrounds it.

[19]Gordon Canfield Lee, *The Struggle for Federal Aid: First Phase,* New York: Teachers College, 1949, pp. 149–155.

The United States Supreme Court has had a profound impact on the course of education, an influence more noticeable since the famous Brown decision of 1954. This Court is more concerned with what happens to the rights guaranteed under the federal constitution in school situations than with education per se. Almost every decade since 1950 has experienced a major decision of the Supreme Court that has had profound impact on educational operations.

Federal concern for public education started with the federal land grants in the early 1800s, although its roots go back further in history. Federal involvement came in fits and spurts, and substantial time delays between major actions were common until after World War II.

The Morrill Act of 1862 signaled a shift in federal policy with conditional land grants. Monetary grants to public secondary education came with the Smith-Hughes Act for Vocational Education in 1917. The Depression years saw what started as welfare activities turn into educational activities. The CCC and NYA had a profound impact on education. The CWA, FERA, WPA, and PWA helped to build and remodel school plants. The only permanent federal aids for public schools that originated as relief measures during the 1930s were the school lunch acts. The GI bills, the NDEA, the Vocational Education Act of 1963, the ESEA, the Job Corps, and the Higher Education Act represent the quickening pace of federal legislation on education during the last 30 years.

Many federal agencies are concerned with education, but the most important is the United States Office of Education. It began as the Department of Education in 1867 and is now a part of the Department of Health, Education, and Welfare. The early functions of the Office were collecting statistics on education, diffusing such information, and otherwise promoting the cause of education. Other duties have been attached to it since then. The United States Commissioner of Education is appointed by the President, with the consent of the Senate. The Office of Education has been greatly expanded; its organizational chart is revised almost yearly. Other government agencies such as the National Science Foundation and the Office of Economic Opportunity do not share the same points of view on the control and stimulation of education.

The controversy over increased federal support for public education has continued since at least the end of the Civil War. The most recent federal activities in education have simply increased the controversy. Federal assistance for various educational programs is presently over $18 billion. The major share of federal funds is disseminated outside the Office of Education and for purposes other than public elementary and secondary education. The federal government continues to rely on categorical rather than general grants to public education.

The constitutionality of federal participation in school-support programs was tested in the early 1920s, and the Supreme Court upheld the constitutionality of federal aid at that time. Objection to federal support of public education on the grounds of constitutionality is indeed futile. The fact that over $18 billion is allocated annually by the federal government to education testifies to the magnitude of the impact of this branch on education.

The opening of a new federal agency called the National Institute of Education (NIE) in 1973 was a significant event in educational history. Many USOE programs related to research and development were transferred to

NIE as well as some personnel. NIE will focus primarily on educational research and will have in-house capability to perform research at its headquarters. A special advisory and policy making board was created for NIE. NIE is presently a smaller but parallel agency to USOE.

QUESTIONS

1. Enumerate the significant activities of the federal government in the field of public education.
2. What should be the functions or activities of the United States Office of Education?
3. Should there be an independent federal education agency with a special national advisory commission for education? Justify your stand.
4. Should the federal government operate educational programs for children and youth and thus compete with local school districts? Justify your stand.
5. Why has the federal government's involvement in education provoked so much controversy?

SELECTED REFERENCES

American Association of School Administrators, *The Federal Government and the Public Schools,* Washington, D.C.: The Association, 1965.

Educational Policies Commission, National Education Association, *Federal Financial Relationships to Educators,* Washington, D.C.: The Association, 1967.

Finn, Charles E., "What The NIE Can Be," Phi Delta Kappan, February 1972, pp. 347–351.

13

ALTERNATIVE SCHOOLS AND PROFESSIONAL AGENCIES THAT INFLUENCE PUBLIC EDUCATION

Nonpublic, or private, schools in the United States are the major operational alternatives to public education. They assume some of the responsibility for providing an educated citizenry in our nation. The magnitude and contributions of systems of private education in the United States are of a different order and influence than that noted in other nations of the world.

Professional societies serve teaching and administrative personnel of public schools and engage in activities and programs that influence public education almost as much as direct state and federal legislative efforts, local administrative policy decisions, and ruling case law. Only the large professional educational or administrator organizations—the National Education Association, the American Federation of Teachers, the American Association of School Administrators, the National Association of Secondary School Principals, the National Association of Elementary School Principals, and the quasi-professional group known as the National School Boards Association—will be examined herein. Last, but by no means least, special educational agencies of various sorts influence all or a part of public-school decision making and operations. Among these

are the regional accrediting societies. The National Congress of Parents and Teachers, one such informal agency with a strong and dynamic national base, will be discussed in Chapter 25. Civil-rights groups, special political groups concerned with what happens in the schools, local taxpayers' organizations, and agencies such as the Council for Basic Education are some of the agencies in the United States that must be considered a part of the total structural pattern through which society demonstrates its concern and influences public education.

PRIVATE SCHOOLS

Through most of history, and in most nations, educational control has been vested in private, or nonpublic, agencies which often had access to public funds. Where a state religion existed, the line between church and state has been blurred at best, and the state usually has delegated primary responsibility for the operation of educational institutions to the church.

Although public education dominates in the United States, private elementary and secondary schools enroll more than 5.2 million pupils. In the period just after World War II enrollments in private elementary and secondary schools grew at a proportionately faster rate than those in public schools. As a result, the private schools' share of elementary- and secondary-school enrollments in the nation as a whole increased from 10.9 percent in the fall of 1950 to 14.9 percent in the fall of 1959. After reaching the 1959 high point, the proportion of all pupils attending private schools declined to its present estimated 10.3 percent. Between the fall of 1965 and the fall of 1972 private elementary school enrollment lost over 1.4 million pupils to about 4 million. For the same period private secondary enrollment dropped 300,000 students to an estimated 1,155,000 in 1972.[1] There are indications that enrollments in private schools will stabilize at around 10 percent of those in public and private elementary-secondary schools.

Private schools are more likely to serve elementary-school (Grades K through 8) than secondary-school (Grades 9 through 12) pupils. There never were more than 11.2 percent of all secondary-school pupils attending private secondary schools and more often substantially less than that. Prior to 1956 secondary enrollment in private institutions was less than 10 percent of the combined public-private totals and since 1969 less than 8 percent. In contrast, since 1950 private elementary school pupils have constituted 11.4 percent or more of the total elementary school pupils. The low of 11.4 percent was established in 1972, which is substantially below the high of 16.1 percent in 1959.

A summary of the proportion of total public and private school pupils attending private school is presented in Table 13–1.

The responsibility of the state with reference to the operation, control, or regulation of nonpublic schools is not clear. In some states, laws dealing with maintaining buildings that are structurally safe, with a minimum of fire hazards, and with suitable sanitary facilities apply to nonpublic-school corporations. Some states enforce statutes requiring nonpublic schools to meet appropriate educational standards on attendance, and others do not.[2] In some instances, public schools and nearby nonpublic schools have entered into a type of cooperation referred to as dual enrollment.[3] In such cases a pupil enrolled in a private school may attend one or more special classes in a public school in the area. Private school pupils in Grades 7 and 8 or in Grades 11 and 12 are more likely to enroll in a public school class. Only a limited number of schools are involved in such cooperative ventures. Dual enrollment is also more likely to be found in specialized secondary-school courses such as homemaking, industrial arts, science, or mathematics.

Title II of the 1965 Elementary and Secondary Education Act (ESEA) created new opportunities for cooperative activities between public and nonpublic schools. For the first time, as a condition for receiving federal funds, local public schools are required to

[1]Research Division, National Education Association, *Estimates of School Statistics, 1972–73*, Washington, D.C.: The Association, 1973, p. 11.

[2]D. A. Erickson and L. L. Cunningham, *Non-public Schools in the United States*, Chicago: Midwest Administration Center, University of Chicago, 1970.

[3]J. E. Gibbs, Jr., J. J. Sokolowski, A. W. Steinhilber, and W. C. Strasser, Jr., *Dual Enrollment in Public and Non-public Schools*, U.S. Office of Education, circular no. 772, Washington, D.C.: GPO, 1965.

share with parochial schools some types of personnel and educational services under the control of public authorities. The materials shared belong to the public school and are loaned under Title II to libraries of parochial schools. This provision may yet be a source of litigation.

There is considerable variation from state to state in the percentage of children attending private as opposed to public schools. In large city systems as well as in comparatively small school districts, when a majority of students is enrolled in nonpublic rather than public schools community attitudes toward resources allocated to public education may be quite different than when relatively few attend private schools. In Wisconsin and Rhode Island about one-third of the elementary school pupils are enrolled in the nonpublic schools. At the other extreme, less than 2 percent of the elementary school pupils in North Carolina attend nonpublic schools. States with more than one-third of all

elementary school pupils enrolled in nonpublic schools are Massachusetts, New Hampshire, Rhode Island, New York, Wisconsin, and Minnesota. States with less than 10 percent of the total elementary-school students enrolled in nonpublic schools are Alabama, Alaska, Arkansas, Arizona, Georgia, Idaho, Mississippi, Nevada, North Carolina, Oklahoma, South Carolina, Tennessee, Texas, Utah, Virginia, West Virginia, and Wyoming. It is apparent that most of southern and southwestern states and some of the Rocky Mountain states have comparatively few pupils in nonpublic schools. In contrast, the mideast region (Delaware, District of Columbia, Maryland, New Jersey, New York, and Pennsylvania) have a substantial percentage, that is, above average national percentages, enrolled in nonpublic educational institutions.

More than 97 percent of the total enrollment in nonpublic elementary schools and almost 90 percent in nonpublic secondary schools are in church-

TABLE 13–1

PERCENT OF TOTAL PUBLIC AND PRIVATE SCHOOL PUPILS ATTENDING PRIVATE SCHOOLS, SELECTED YEARS FROM 1950–1972

Year	Grades K–8	Grades 9–12	Grades K–12
1950	11.8	8.1	10.9
1955	13.4	9.8	12.6
1959	16.1	10.9	14.9
1960	15.2	10.1	14.0
1965	14.5	11.2	14.2
1970[a]	12.1	7.9	10.9
1971[a]	11.6	7.4	10.4
1972[a]	11.4	7.6	10.3

Source: Committee on Educational Finance, National Education Association, *Financial Status of the Public Schools*, 1968, Washington, D.C.: The Association, 1968, p. 17.
[a] NEA Research Division estimates.

related institutions of learning. Over 90 percent of the elementary school and almost 90 percent of the secondary school enrollments in nonpublic institutions are in schools operated by the Roman Catholic Church. Schools operated by the Lutheran Church enroll about 3 percent of the students in nonpublic elementary schools. Lutheran schools were exceeded by Episcopal and Seventh Day Adventist schools in size of enrollment in nonpublic secondary schools.

There are indications that the Roman Catholic Church as well as the Protestant churches are reevaluating church-operated nonpublic schools. Rising costs as well as the increasingly complex educational demands being placed upon schools in American society today are stimulating such reexamination. Churches are having difficulty gaining additional resources to meet new demands. Church-related schools, as well as private nonchurch-related schools, have an option to continue or to abandon operation of certain grade levels. Public schools have no such option. As church-related schools cease to operate these grades, the burden on the public school becomes greater.

The educational structural pattern in the United States is significantly different from that in other nations, where sizable public tax resources are dedicated to nonpublic school operation. At present, public tax resources cannot be used directly for nonpublic institutions, although Title II of the 1965 ESEA provides some means whereby the nonpublic schools can share in federal funds for certain educational improvements.

A relatively new type of private school appeared in the 1960s. The so-called "white academies" appeared in several Southern states as an alternative to the public schools that were required by law to desegregate classrooms. Recent lower court decisions may force these special institutions to respect the mandates of the *Brown* decision of 1954. In the North and in the large cities the so-called "street academies" and "free schools" took root in abandoned stores and other spaces as alternative schools for those who drop out from or prefer something other than that which the public and more traditional private schools have to offer. The success of these alternatives appears to be considerably less now than when the alternatives first appeared. A 1973 directory of "free" or alternative schools listed 350 such institutions as entities separate from previously established public and private schools. How long the so-called "free" school movement will last in the face of difficult financing problems is a matter of conjecture.

PROFESSIONAL ORGANIZATIONS

There are about 2.7 million professional personnel—classroom teachers, principals, supervisors, and other administrators—employed in public and private schools. Over 2.43 million full-time-equivalent professional personnel worked in public schools, and about 260,000 worked in private schools. Although public school control, from a legal point of view, is vested in the state legislature and a large measure delegated to local school boards, this does not preclude professional organizations from exercising considerable influence in everyday as well as long-range operations of public schools. Professional workers face the dilemma confronting other individuals in an organized society. Few, if any, can muster the strength necessary to attain important objectives without cooperative effort and aid from others. Organization, which enables many to perform in unison, is a prerequisite for the attainment of power and significant achievement. The development of teacher militance and the application of the power of teachers' associations and unions to influence school operations will be explored in greater detail in Chapter 20. This section will review the history and development of organizations that include a large number of teachers and/or administrators: The National Education Association (NEA), the American Federation of Teachers (AFT), the American Association of School Administrators (AASA), the National Association of Secondary School Principals (NASSP), the National Association of Elementary School Principals (NAESP), and the National School Boards Association (NSBA). There are specialized organizations in selected subject matter teaching fields as well. Educators maintain a loyalty to their professional organization as well as to the school district or state that employs them. The propensity to form special societies, to support them, to become involved in their activities is a most important fact of life in public education.

The National Education Association

To begin with, there were state organizations of teachers; the creation of a national organization came later. The presidents of ten state education associations issued a call in 1857 to teachers of the country to form a national organization. Forty-three persons met in Philadelphia on August 26, 1857, to create the National Teachers Association. The original constitution of this national organization excluded women from membership—a restriction that was eliminated in 1866. In 1870 the National Association of

School Superintendents and the American Normal School Association merged with the National Teachers Association to create the National Education Association. The four chapter departments of the NEA were the Department of School Superintendence (now the American Association of School Administrators), the Department of Normal Schools (now the American Association of Colleges for Teacher Education), the Department of Higher Instruction (now the Association for Higher Education), and the Department of Elementary Schools (abolished in 1925). It is significant that in 1972, a little over 100 years after its founding, the NEA changed its appearance and thrust to become more like the original National Teachers Organization as several of the charter departments, particularly the administrators, broke their ties with the NEA.

In 1906 an act of Congress gave the NEA its charter, which was accepted in 1907 by its membership; its official title was expanded to the National Education Association of the United States. The charter determined to a considerable extent the organizational structure of the NEA. Change in this structure necessitates Congressional action, which has been obtained over the years. A significant shift in priorities and staffing took place in the 1960s.

The NEA is a complex organization. Its representative assembly meets annually and brings together about 9000 delegates to approve all resolutions, recommendations, and amendments to the associations's bylaws. The NEA board of directors has 94 members and the NEA executive committee 9 members. Its complicated governing apparatus includes a huge board of directors whose exact number varies with the membership number, a smaller executive committee of about 9, and a so-called review board. Many management surveys have recommended streamlining the NEA's organizational structure, but little has been implemented.

There is a headquarters staff consisting of an executive secretary, a deputy executive secretary, associate secretaries, assistant executive secretaries, and other personnel. The NEA executive secretary and his administrative assistants are responsible to the board of trustees, the executive committee, and the board of directors, as well as to the officers and representative assembly. Headquarters personnel direct the activities of headquarters divisions organized for educational services, federal relations, field operations and urban services, information services, and professional development and welfare, as well as of the number of commissions and committees in such areas as international relations, resolutions, teacher retirement, and professional ethics.

A number of specialized professional organizations are related to the NEA in some way. In some respects, the NEA acted as a holding company, wherein teachers and administrators of various specializations form groupings known as departments, national affiliates, or associated organizations to serve the needs of specialized personnel. In some cases membership in NEA is required to join a professional group related to NEA. The various administrator organizations for superintendents, high school principals, and elementary principals, as well as the Association for Supervision and Curriculum Development, were at one time related to NEA but now are completely separate and independent from NEA. The teachers of business education; health, physical education and recreation; music; mathematics; social studies; art; science; speech; industrial arts; and home economics have specialized departments within NEA. The largest department was at one time the now defunct Association (formerly Department) of Classroom Teachers. Most of the related professional groups have special membership fees. Significant changes between NEA and its related professional societies were approved in July 1968. In the 1970s several national professional societies in education severed their affiliations from NEA rather than accept new requirements. In 1973 there were 9532 NEA locals.

Some professional groups receive financial support from NEA for operation of activities, others are fiscally independent of the NEA. Most related organizations are housed rent-free in the NEA building at 1201 Sixteenth Street, N.W., Washington, D.C. This building and its land is listed as an asset of almost $14 million but would probably fetch a price several times that on the real estate market. The 1973 NEA budget exceeded $29.3 million.

From a total of 43 in 1857, membership in the NEA has grown to almost 1.4 million in 1973. In addition there were 1.76 million members in NEA state affiliates in 1973. Around the time of World War I, the membership of the American Federation of Teachers was greater than that of the NEA. NEA membership expanded immediately following World War I, and significant increases occurred after World War II. Not until 1930 did NEA membership exceed 200,000. Little change took place in the decade that followed. By 1945, however, the membership approximated one-third million, and after 1950 exceeded one-half million. The 1 million mark was not reached until March, 1967.

Until 1945 NEA dues were less than

$2. Presently the dues are $25 annually with every indication suggesting further increase in dues to support varied activities. Membership dues brought in almost $29 million in 1973.

NEA can also be considered as a cluster of state and local affiliated education associations. There are 50 state and about 9500 local affiliated associations. Separate state associations for white and Negro teachers have been eliminated. NEA's great strength is at the state and national level. Its weakest structural link is at the local level; the reverse is true for the AFT. Considerable effort is being expended, largely in response to the challenge of the AFT, to strengthen the local affiliated associations.

The NEA has had an impact on education in certain states through the use of sanctions to improve unsatisfactory educational conditions. Prior to 1967, very few NEA affiliates engaged in strikes. This changed dramatically after 1967, when the NEA indicated it would no longer frown on such activity. An NEA survey showed that the percent of public school teachers who favored strikes rose from 53.3 percent in 1965 to 68.2 percent in 1968. Over 80 percent of the strikes in the 1970s were triggered by professional associations rather than unions.

The NEA works through the state education association to influence the course of educational legislation in a given state, recognizing that education is a function of the state. At the federal level, the NEA has developed and recommended federal legislative activities.

At one time the NEA championed a united professional organization including teachers, supervisors, and administrators, but this led to the charge that it was "administrator-dominated." This charge embarrassed both the NEA, particularly in its dealings with local teachers' groups, and the administrators. Some pointed out that prior to 1918, the membership consisted largely of men in administrative positions, but this occurred when its membership was very small. Others pointed to the large number of administrators involved in NEA activities and elected to offices. In recent years the NEA president was more likely to be a classroom teacher. There was very little substance to support the accusation of administrator-domination,[4] but it remained. The separation of administrator associations from the NEA in the 1970s should put to rest once and for all 'the administrator-dominated" argument. This action likewise brought closer the possibility of an NEA-AFT merger.

The American Federation of Teachers

The AFT is a comparatively new organization. There were teachers' unions at the local district level prior to 1900. A national teachers' union was created on April 15, 1916, when four locals, in response to a call by the Chicago Teachers Federation, formed a new organization known as the American Federation of Teachers. The AFT became affiliated with the American Federation of Labor (AFL) in the same year.[5]

The Chicago Teachers Federation, formed in 1897, was the first significant independent organization of teachers. The San Antonio, Texas, Teachers Union, was the first to be affiliated with the AFL,[6] although the

[4]Myron Lieberman, *Education as a Profession,* Englewood Cliffs, N.J.: Prentice-Hall, 1956, pp. 280–296.

[5]Commission on Educational Reconstruction, American Federation of Teachers, *Organizing the Teaching Profession,* New York: Free Press, 1955, pp. 21–29.

[6]Lieberman, op. cit., p. 300.

Chicago Teachers Federation joined the AFL some two months later. By 1916, 20 teachers' groups in 10 states organized local affiliates with labor. The mortality rate was high. In some situations there was more than one teacher's federation in a city. Thus, during the early part of this century Chicago had the Chicago Teachers Federation, the Federation of Women High School Teachers, and the Federation of Men Teachers.

The teachers' union was a large-city phenomenon and was usually found where the labor movement in general was strong. Teachers' unions were founded in the following places (the dates indicate when the local affiliated with the AFL): Atlanta, 1919; New York City, 1915; Washington, D.C. (which had the first Negro local in the nation), 1917; St. Paul, Minn., 1918; Minneapolis, 1919; Chattanooga, 1932; Cleveland, 1932; West Suburban (Chicago), 1938; Toledo, 1933; Detroit, 1931; Gary, Ind., 1937; Wilmington, Delaware, 1943; Connecticut, 1944.[7]

The AFT, started just before the beginning of World War I, experienced considerable difficulty immediately following the conclusion of the war. It prospered for a while and at one time saw its membership exceed that of the NEA. Many locals were disbanded under heavy pressure from school boards.[8] The number of AFT locals increased from 24 (with a membership of less than 2,000) in 1918 to over 160 (with a membership of 11,000) in 1919. Less than one-fifth of the AFT locals previously chartered were still operating in 1927. By 1925, the membership had dropped to less than 3,500.[9] Between 1930 and 1940 membership in

the NEA dropped from about 216,000 to 203,000. In contrast, membership in the AFT during that period jumped from 6,872 to 29,907. The growth of the AFT after 1940 slowed, however, so that by 1955 there was only about a 50 percent increase over the 1940 level, to approximately 46,583. During the same period, NEA membership more than tripled to surpass 600,000 by 1955. At present, AFT membership is estimated to be around 368,000 or about 1 million less than that for NEA. In 1973 there were almost 1750 AFT locals compared with more than 9532 NEA locals. Some 15 AFT local affiliates constitute substantially more than one-half of the AFT membership. New York City accounts for over one-third of the total number in the AFT.

In the 1960s AFT moved its national headquarters from Chicago to Washington, D.C. The AFT lacks the strong financial base of the NEA. The Industrial Union Department (IUD) of the AFL-CIO has made substantial contributions to the AFT. Average dues of locals range from $3 to $5 per month or $36 to $60 annually; $1 per month goes to the national organization.

Historically, teacher unionism was an urban phenomenon in the United States. Today relatively few teachers' unions are found outside the very large metropolitan areas. The greatest impact of the AFT is upon education in the large urban centers. Thus, NEA membership in Chicago is less than 10 percent of the AFT membership in that city. In such cities as New York, Atlanta, Boston, Detroit, Cleveland, St. Paul, and Minneapolis, AFT membership exceeds that of NEA. The AFT has fewer state federations than the NEA. Again, the AFT is strongest at the local affiliate level and weakest at the state level of organization.

Dual membership is not unusual; the same person will join the NEA to re-

[7]Commission on Educational Reconstruction, American Federation of Teachers, op. cit., chap. 1.

[8]Lieberman, op. cit., p. 301.

[9]Ibid., pp. 301–303.

ceive its publications and alleged professional respectability and the AFT to take advantage of its concern for the individual teacher's welfare. In many school districts, the AFT has been elected bargaining representative for the teachers even though the NEA membership was significantly higher.

Whereas the NEA is accused of being dominated by administrators, the charge most frequently hurled against the AFT is that it is labor-dominated and therefore cannot serve the total community. The most potent weapons of the AFT have been its militancy in bargaining in behalf of teachers and its threat to employ the strike or some other form of work stoppage.

NEA-AFT impending merger

This writer was criticized by some in the mid-1960s when he predicted the inevitability of merger between the NEA and AFT. A decade ago this notion was anathema to many NEA members. The prediction made then was not an expression of what should be, but an analysis of the situation as it existed. One organization was much stronger, financially, than the other. Both were depleting resources in battling each other in jurisdictional disputes. One was strong at the state level and the other in local leadership. One dominated the large-city scene while the other was strong in smaller communities. It was apparent that if certain issues, such as strikes by teachers and affiliation of administrators, could be resolved the two teacher organizations would be seen as complementary rather than competitive and merger could be in the interests of both.

NEA resisted overtures from AFT during the 1960s to consider merger. The historic 1973 NEA convention put an end to resistance and signalled the beginning of a series of negotiations to bring the two together. At this writing all evidence points to a merger of the two organizations sometime during the 1970s. A new era in teacher and administrator organizations influencing the course of public education is now beginning.

The American Association of School Administrators

The AASA is now in its second century of service to school superintendents, assistant superintendents, associate superintendents, professors of school administration, college deans, and presidents. A handful of men gathered in Harrisburg, Pennsylvania, about four months after the assassination of Abraham Lincoln, to organize the National Association of School Superintendents. In 1870 five years after its creation, the National Association of School Superintendents merged with two other educational organizations to form the NEA. It developed into the NEA Department of Superintendence, as it was known until 1937, when it changed its name to the American Association of School Administrators. The first full-time executive secretary was S. D. Shankland. He was succeeded by Dr. Worth McClure and then Dr. Finis Engelman. Dr. Forrest E. Conner served as Executive Secretary of AASA until 1971. Dr. Paul Salmon is presently the executive secretary of that important and influential organization for superintendents and other administrators.

The influence of the AASA goes far beyond its membership of less than 20,000. Its national conference, with attendance in the 25,000 to 30,000 range and world-renowned educational exhibits, is one of the largest educational work conferences in the world. The AASA influences public education through its publications; its studies by special committees and commissions; its code of ethics for school administrators; and its series of conferences, seminars, and workshops. Its most recent innovation is the AASA National Academy for School Executives, which became operational late in 1968 as a continuing professional development vehicle for practicing school administrators.

At one time AASA demanded unusually high professional preparation standards for attainment of full membership. In January 1964 it became the first association to require two years of graduate study at an institution with an administrator-preparation program accredited by the National Council on the Accreditation of Teacher Education. This professional membership standard has had a profound impact on certification requirements for school administrators in various states. Unfortunately, the organization rescinded the professional preparation requirement in 1972 in an effort to attract more members.

The AASA Committee on Ethics has been in operation since 1964. In a relatively brief period approximately ten cases involving the ethical stature of a school administrator were referred to it. Disciplinary action was warranted and taken in one case.

The AASA Committee for the Advancement of School Administration (CASA) grew out of the Kellogg Foundation–sponsored programs for the improvement of school administration that started in the early 1950s. Various policies and programs recommended by CASA have had a profound impact on the course of school administration in the United States. This committee stimulated adoption of membership standards based on professional preparation, the code of ethics, and more

recently, the formation of the National Academy for School Executives.

The AASA is no longer an affiliate of the NEA. It has an independent governing board known as the AASA Executive Committee. The executive committee consists of the officers of the association, president, president-elect, and vice president, and other members elected specifically to the executive committee. Its headquarters staff consists of an executive secretary, a deputy and associate secretaries. The AASA was fiscally independent from the NEA even when it was headquartered in the NEA building in Washington, D.C. It was not until 1968 that AASA disaffiliation from NEA was discussed openly. The AASA continued to stress unity and did much to preserve the traditional relation with the NEA until 1972 when all formal ties were broken with NEA.

There were about 80 state associations of school administrators in the United States in 1967; these were not state affiliates of the AASA. Most state administrators' associations are departments in a state education association. In 1967 the Michigan Association of School Administrators called for its separation from the Michigan Education Association; this was the first such action, although some state associations were never affiliated with a state education association.

Associations of school principals

The National Association of Secondary School Principals (NASSP) and the National Association of Elementary School Principals (NAESP) are separate from the AASA. They likewise were at one time departments in the NEA. Both associations separated from NEA in the early 1970s. Each of the principals' associations operates its own national convention, elects its own officers, and has its own governing board.

NASSP was organized in 1916. It now has more than 30,000 members. It sponsors the National Association of Student Councils and the National Honor Society for secondary school students. Its annual national convention attracts approximately 10,000 people. NAESP was founded in 1921. Its present membership totals almost 24,000, and its annual convention attracts approximately 6,200. The state affiliates of each of the national principals' organizations are growing in strength and in memberships.

National School Boards Association

The NSBA had its beginnings as the National Council of State School Boards Association, organized in 1940 in St. Louis. It is significant that this event occurred at a meeting held in conjunction with the annual convention of the AASA. World War II interrupted activities that were revived in 1945.

To Pennsylvania goes the honor of organizing the first state association of schools boards in 1896. Progress was relatively slow, for by 1920 there were only seven state school board associations. By 1940 there were 27, and by 1957 there was a state association of school boards in every state.[10]

The National Council of State School Boards Association continued meeting in conjunction with the annual conventions of the AASA for many years after its organization. In 1948 its name was changed officially to the National School Boards Association. In 1949 Edward M. Tuttle was selected as the

[10]Edward M. Tuttle, *School Board Leadership in America*, rev. ed., Danville, Ill.: Interstate Printers and Publishers, 1963, p. 169.

first full-time Executive Secretary of the Association. He has since retired.

This national organization is essentially a federation of state school boards associations. It held its annual meetings just prior to the AASA meeting from 1950 to 1957. The first independent convention met in Miami in April 1958. From the approximately 100 who attended the NSBA conventions prior to 1950, the membership grew to more than 7000 in 1967. The NSBA is supported primarily from dues paid by school boards, rather than by individuals. Its impact on education stems primarily from its publications and convention resolutions. Its positions on certain sensitive issues such as federal aid to education and collective negotiation with teachers have involved it in a considerable amount of controversy.

ACCREDITING AGENCIES

Schools are accredited by the state department of education in most states, or by a state university or collection of universities in the state. There are, in addition, regional accrediting bodies that have no official relation with the state department of education. Primary emphasis here will be on the regional accrediting bodies.

The regional accrediting agencies include the North Central Association of Colleges and Secondary Schools, the Middle States Association of Colleges and Secondary Schools, the North West Association of Secondary and Higher Schools, the Southern Association of Colleges and Schools, the Western College Association, and the New England Association of Colleges and Secondary Schools. These associations are private and voluntary organizations. Membership of local schools is voluntary and dependent upon meeting membership criteria and paying dues. Recognition of these associations by a state department of education is voluntary as well. Nonetheless, these private agencies have a profound impact on public secondary school accreditation in many parts of the country. Recently the Southern Association has instituted programs for accreditation of elementary schools as well.

The responsibility for evaluating the quality of education of various schools has typically been a state function. The Office of Education in 1960 prepared a national survey of policies and procedures used in the accreditation of public schools.[11] According to this report, 29 states were involved in a general upgrading of requirements and status of their public schools at that time; 37 indicated procedures for a continuous review of the standards or criteria for the approval of accreditation of public schools. Thus, although regional accrediting agencies do not have the force of law behind their actions, they do have a significant impact in determining criteria for accreditation and which schools shall be admitted or continued on their list of accredited institutions.

OTHER INFORMAL AGENCIES

The National Congress of Parents and Teachers, as well as the various citizens' committees for the improvement of public education are reviewed in Chapter 25. Extremist groups of the right and the left have subjected schools to considerable criticism. Some

[11]W. B. Rich, "Approval and Accreditation of Public Schools," *Responsibilities and Services of State Departments of Education,* U.S. Office of Education, OE-20013, Washington, D.C.: GPO, 1960.

right-wing groups have attempted to infiltrate school-related organizations such as the local Parent-Teachers Association (PTA) or a citizens' group. Others have attempted to place their literature within the classroom and seek to influence the teaching of social studies by acting as censors of established textbooks. Many extremist groups seek to prohibit teaching about the United Nations in the local schools, and some attack the use of PPBS.

The civil-rights movement has often focused on education. Some within this movement have equated the neighborhood school concept with de facto segregation. Through the use of the demonstrations, and threatened or actual boycotts, the extremists have attempted to influence the decision-making authority of school boards as well as the structural arrangements of school operation.

The Council for Basic Education, which came into being in 1956, has attempted to influence public education through its publications and the speeches of some of its members. Taxpayers' groups in various communities wax and wane in influence. Some have been organized into state associations and have attempted to curtail the school board's right to levy particular taxes.

The number of informal agencies attempting to influence the organization and administration of public education has been growing in recent years. There is no indication that a reversal of this trend is likely.

SUMMARY

Nonpublic schools are primarily church-oriented institutions. They enroll a larger share of elementary and secondary-school students in some Eastern and Midwestern states than elsewhere; they attract fewer numbers in the South. Nationally, about 10 percent of the total enrollment in Grades K through 12 is in private schools. Nonpublic schools had a greater share of the total number of pupils attending school in the late 1950s than they do at present.

There are many general-purpose and special-purpose professional societies that influence in varying degree the behavior of teachers and administrators in education. The NEA, with almost 1.4 million members, is by far the largest and is one of the oldest. It is a complex organization of state and local affiliates, related specialized professional organizations, and a comprehensive collection of headquarters service agencies. Its cumbersome administration is in dire need of streamlining, but little progress has been made in that direction. The AFT as a teachers' union is challenging the NEA, but its membership is only a fraction that of the NEA. NEA and AFT competed through the early 1970s. Public announcements in 1973 now indicate an impending merger of NEA and AFT.

Most professional societies depend upon publications, resolutions, and conferences to influence education.

Their activities with state legislatures and the national Congress have an impact on laws dealing with education.

There are several professional societies for administrators. These organizations were NEA affiliates up until 1972. All have separated from NEA and act independently. The oldest (over 100 years old) and most powerful is the AASA. The NASSP and the NAESP have larger membership rolls and represent secondary and elementary principals, respectively. The NSBA is a recent development and is essentially a federation of state school boards associations.

Regional accrediting agencies are powerful informal forces working toward the improvement of education. They are voluntary associations and their membership criteria have an effect on secondary schools in particular. No state laws require accreditation by regional accrediting bodies, but the better schools seek such recognition.

The number of informal agencies seeking to influence the structure, organization, and operation of public education is increasing. This is testimony to the importance of education to the democratic way of life.

QUESTIONS

1. What influence do nonpublic schools have on public education in the United States?
2. Where in the United States are the nonpublic schools the most numerous?
3. Should the state attempt to regulate some or all aspects of nonpublic education? Justify your stand.
4. In what ways do professional societies have an impact on public education?
5. Should administrators' organizations at the state or national level be a part of an education association that includes teachers as well? Justify your stand.

SELECTED REFERENCES

Committee on Educational Finance, National Education Association, *Financial Status of the Public Schools 1968,* Washington, D.C.: The Association, 1968.

Gibbs, J. E., Jr., C. J. Sokolowski, A. W. Steinhilber, and W. C. Strasser, Jr., *Dual Enrollment in Public and Non-public Schools,* U.S. Office of Education, circular no. 772, Washington, D.C.: GPO, 1965.

Lieberman, Myron, *Education as a Profession,* Englewood Cliffs, N.J.: Prentice-Hall, 1956.

Rich, W. B., "Approval and Accreditation of Public Schools," *Responsibilities and Services of State Departments of Education,* U.S. Office of Education, OE-20013, Washington, D.C.: GPO, 1960.

Tuttle, Edward M., *School Board Leadership in America,* rev. ed., Danville, Ill.: Interstate Printers and Publishers, 1963.

III

THE ADMINISTRATIVE HIERARCHY AND TEAM: SPECIAL ROLES AND POSITIONS IN EDUCATIONAL ADMINISTRATION

School administrators function at various levels in the educational system. Some are concerned with problems and decisions that are system-wide in scope; others are responsible for a segment of the program as it operates throughout the system; still others are involved with educational problems in a given area or population sector of the district.

The local board of education serves as a general policy-making authority at the district level. The school superintendency functions as the executive arm of the board of education. Because the superintendency evolved from classroom positions, the chief school executive came to be viewed as the educational leader of the faculty as well. When the complexity of schools necessitated supervision and administration by more than one person, the central-office administrative and supervisory staff came into being. The principal is the chief executive officer at the attendance-unit level and rounds out the administrative team. There is considerably more emphasis now than ever before on the administrative team. One of the exciting developments in the period following World War II has been the growth of post-secondary institutions, notably the community junior college and the vocational-technical school.

In the following four chapters emphasis is placed on the complementary rather than the competing nature of the various major levels of school administration. The team concept of school administration calls for each level to perform those activities best suited to its place and role in the system and to the time and talents available.

14

SCHOOL BOARDS AND OTHER COMMUNITY AGENCIES FOR THE CONTROL OF EDUCATION

The local governing body concerned specifically with public education within a defined area of a state may be called the board of education, the school committee, the school board, the school directors, the school trustees, the school commissioners, or the school inspectors. The most popular terms in the literature are school board and board of education. Whatever the title, it is the local educational control agency whose authority, selection, term of office, and operating procedures are determined in large part by the state legislature. As such the members of the agency are representatives of the people residing within the district as a whole.

The number of local school boards is directly related to the number of school districts. A school district may not always operate a school, but there can be no school district without a school board. A decline in number of school districts means fewer local boards of education. In 1974 there were approximately 16,500 local school boards—significantly less than the more than 100,000 in existence 25 years previously. An estimate of the number of people serving as school-board members is more difficult. Assuming that the typical school board has seven members it can be com-

puted that in 1974 there were approximately 115,500 school-board members, far fewer than the estimate of one-half million 25 years ago.

Allocation of a considerable amount of legal authority and control over complex and technical operations of public education to local school boards is a distinctly American approach. The local school board is an American invention. How it should operate, what its missions are, and what its limitations should be have long stirred much debate and some misunderstanding among American educators and laymen. There is little to suggest that the local board of education is any less controversial today than it was 100 years ago.

As explained in Chapter 9, the local school district is a quasi-municipal corporation. It is also a civil subdivision of the state whose boundaries, and the procedures for altering such boundaries, are determined by state law. It is concerned specifically with the state's function of education. Members of the local board of education are thus corporate officers, specifically local officers of the governmental corporation known as the school district. As the governing body in each public school district, the board looks to the statutes of the state for a definition of its administrative powers. The state, through the legislature, enacts laws that influence public school operation. As numerous as state statutes and state department of public instruction regulations may be, even greater is the number of decisions on educational matters left to the discretion of the local board. Board members are public officers having a fiduciary relation to the school district.

The manner in which the local board of education exercises the legal authority granted it is the key to its role in the administration of public education. The board is confronted with the problem of determining which functions should be delegated to the professional chief executive and his assistant and which should be retained by the board. It attempts to balance the advice offered by lay citizens participating in specially organized citizens' committees or in the demonstration of the wishes of special-purpose groups with the fundamental responsibility for decisions that legally belong to it. Only the school board has the legal authority to determine salary and working conditions for teachers within the framework spelled out in state legislation. The desire of teachers to participate in the formulation of such policy decisions and the threat of some teachers' groups to engage in work stoppages if such a role is not granted has been duly recognized by the board as well.

Under the Hamiltonian concept of division of responsibilities between the legislative and executive branches, the school board is the legislative, or general policy-making, body. There is agreement at present that the execution of policy should be delegated to a full-time person with professional preparation and experience. Many of the difficulties in school administration can be traced to the inability to

ascertain the dimensions of the role of the board in the administration of education. Present trends indicate that the general policy-making authority of the board may be tempered to the extent that certain groups demand an opportunity to participate in those policies affecting their destiny. Likewise, the Supreme Court has been called a "national school board," so decisive has been its impact on the manner in which school boards act.

EVOLUTION OF THE SCHOOL BOARD

The New England town meeting was the classic expression of grass-roots democracy. People of the town gathered to discuss and decide such important matters as protection against Indian raids, building of roads, propagation of the religious faith, and education of the young. The school committee or board grew out of the New England town meeting and the committee of selectmen. Selectmen besieged with increasing local governmental responsibilities appointed, in turn, a temporary committee to report to them or to perform various approved functions such as recommending appointment of a schoolmaster or construction of a schoolhouse. This eventually led to a permanent committee on school visitation such as the one appointed in Boston in 1721.[1] It was later referred to as the school committee. The school committee was, at first, an agency of the selectmen of the town or of another governing body. Dispersal of population from the New England town and the rise of the district system led to a separation of the school committee from other municipal governing bodies.

[1] Charles E. Reeves, *Schoolboards: Their Status, Function, and Activities*, Englewood Cliffs, N.J.: Prentice-Hall, 1954, p. 17.

Legislation by the state was necessary to validate what existed in practice. Massachusetts legislation on education demonstrates the evolution of such laws. In 1693 a law was enacted that jointly charged towns and their selectmen with maintaining schools and that required selectmen to levy taxes for school support if so directed by vote of the people in the town meeting.[2] More than 100 years were to pass before the school committees of Massachusetts were recognized by a law approved in 1798 as a group devoted to school problems. Typically, selectmen or members of other town governing boards were included as members of school committees. The final step came with the law of 1826 which established school committees as separate from other governing authorities. These committees were delegated the general governance over all public schools in Massachusetts.[3] The school committee, as the governing body for public schools separate from other governing bodies of a city or town, was an early nineteenth-century product.

FUNCTIONS OF THE SCHOOL BOARD

Early in history, the local board of education was entrusted with considerable legal authority. It served as an executive as well as a legislative body. The extent of its control was limited only by state laws and the will of the people as expressed through selection of individuals as board members. It was the magnitude and complexity of the educational task, rather than laws or the will of the people, that precipitated a reexamination of the school board's role in the administration of

public education. The trials suffered in the process will be discussed later in this chapter. Of concern in this portion are the general and specific functions of the school board.

General responsibilities

Functions of the local school board are similar to those of boards of directors of other private and public agencies. In general, responsibilities of a board of directors of a corporation are to:

1. Establish general objectives, goals, or missions of the corporation.
2. Determine its major operating policies.
3. Determine the organizational structure.
4. Select major executives for the organization.
5. Appraise performance of executives to whom responsibilities have been delegated and evaluate how well the stated goals have been achieved.

Many of the responsibilities of the school board were assigned by the state government. The board must at all times stand ready to fulfill the constitutional demands of the state lawmakers. It is granted special powers for such purposes. These legally authorized powers and duties must be exercised by the board as a whole. More will be said about this later.

Powers delegated to a board by the legislature cannot be redelegated or allocated by the board to others. In other words, the school board cannot give committees or employees or other governmental officials authority to perform acts over which the board as a whole has discretionary powers.[4] This cannot be done even if the board desires it very much.

---

[2]Ibid.
[3]Ibid., p. 20.

[4]Robert R. Hamilton and E. Edmund Reuter, Jr., *Legal Aspects of School Board Operation,* New York: Teachers College, 1958, p. 6.

Although the board of education is one of several agencies concerned with the operation of public schools, it is the only one in a given community empowered by law to operate public elementary and secondary schools. Although its authority over public education is deeply rooted in law and accepted by the courts in all states, not all courts agree on the application of all points of law in specific cases. It is well established that the school board can exercise those powers that (1) are granted in express words, (2) can be fairly implied as necessary or incidental to powers expressly granted, and (3) are essential to realization of purposes of educational institutions. The board cannot employ discretionary powers to create authority not intended by law or to ignore demands of the state code or regulations which are properly the legal domain of the state department of public instruction. To illustrate, state laws or state department regulations on such matters as certification of teachers, length of the school term, preparation of special reports, and teaching of specific subjects must be accepted, and their violation is not a matter involving exercise of discretion by the local board of education. This points to the need for board members to know statutory and regulatory requirements or at least to have a ready source of reference or legal counsel on such matters.[5]

There has never been a time in this century when the school board could do whatever it wished. A variety of constraints have been placed on its actions. Some writers suggest that excessively detailed statutory prescriptions of educational operations have sapped the discretionary authority and reduced decision making by the board to a ritual rather than an exercise of

local initiative. In other words, the board's judgment on what can promote the cause of public education can be constrained severely by highly detailed state statutes, federal laws, or, for that matter, court decisions demanding specific educational programs, activities, or behaviors.

There are informal external and internal constraints upon a board's responsibility and authority, such as subtle political pressures or conflicts of interest. In addition, expectations of the community or of other school-board members, speaking at a state or national meeting of school-board members, may influence individual behavior. Expectations may be codified at a later time as a formal statement of ethics for school-board members. A code of ethics may be expanded to define appropriate relations with other board members, with the superintendent of schools, with members of the school staff, with parents, and with children. The effectiveness of such ethical constraints upon board members' behavior is determined largely by the machinery for investigation, disposition, and implementation of judgments by committees concerned with promoting high standards of behavior.

Responsibilities of the school board have changed in response to new demands upon public education. At one time school-board members were directly involved in details of operating a school system such as employing teachers, engaging in direct negotiations with a teachers' organization, purchasing school supplies, and supervising and evaluating instructional efforts. A school board that persists in performing such tasks today is considered a major obstacle in the effective operation of a school system. Preoccupation with "administrivia" during board meetings, such as the brand of floor wax to be purchased for the

[5]Ibid., p. 4.

school, is not in the best interest of the school system. Many writers— both professional school administrators and experienced school-board members—have stressed the importance of the school board recognizing where its particular talents are utilized best. Lay members whose occupational and other responsibilities limit the time they can spend on school problems find it necessary to order priorities carefully on the basis of a clear perception of school-board functions.

The significant responsibilities of the local school board can be summarized as follows:

1. To satisfy the spirit as well as the word of state laws dealing with education and of the regulations of the state education authority.
2. To ascertain goals or objectives of public education and to prepare general policies in tune with them.
3. To select a superintendent of schools, designate him as the chief executive officer, and work harmoniously with him.
4. To strive continuously to develop further and improve the scope and quality of educational opportunities for all children and youth in the district.
5. To create policies that will attract and retain professional and other personnel needed to realize educational objectives.
6. To provide educationally efficient and safe school-plant facilities.
7. To plan for and obtain financial resources necessary to achieve educational goals.
8. To keep the people of the district informed and aware of status, progress, and problems of their schools.
9. To appraise activities of the school district in the light of its objectives.
10. To discharge its responsibilities as a state agency by participating in state-wide efforts to promote and improve public education.[6]

[6]S. J. Knezevich and H. C. DeKock, *The Iowa School Board Member*, Des Moines, Iowa: Iowa Association of School Boards, 1960, pp. 17–18.

Policy making

Policy making is judged to be a most important function of a board of education. To better comprehend how this function is best realized it is important to know what is a policy, what kinds of policies should be generated, and what form the policies should take.

Definitions. A policy is a general statement of intent to act in a particular manner when confronted with a given situation or to achieve a given result at some future point in time. A policy statement represents a guideline to future courses of action to be pursued to ensure consistency and fairness. Policy making is the most important function assigned to a governing board. Policy statements are the means through which a board expresses and maintains control. Consistency of behavior and the ability to anticipate another's actions are important for any group of people who must work together in a complex institution. Policies written, published and disseminated to the public inform persons relating to the board as to the likely disposition of an issue covered by a policy statement.

A policy statement as a rational guide to future action is phrased usually in broad enough terms to include all issues likely to be involved, but at the same time is specific enough to apply to a particular situation. Policies are useful in arriving at decisions related to specific requests. A policy statement may be specific or broad, cover one or many dimensions of an issue, or simply define limits to be observed in reaching a decision on a given matter.

Rules and regulations grow out of and should be consistent with announced policies. A policy does not stipulate the strategy to be pursued to achieve objectives; it points the general direction. Specific directions on how, by whom, where, and when specific acts are to be accomplished may be written or merely implied by ongoing strategies.

A clear-cut distinction between a policy and a rule or regulation is not possible.[7] There is a large gray area between where one leaves off and the other begins. In general, however, it can be said that a policy is a general statement that serves as a guideline to future action. A rule or a regulation is concerned with rather detailed activities and establishes specific directions for implementation of a policy.

Value of policies. The development of a well-defined policy is no simple chore. It requires discipline, considerable debate and discussion, and much time. On occasion the value of policy formulation may be questioned in view of the time and effort required. Most authorities agree that written statements of policy are essential to effective school administration, particularly in complex institutions and in turbulent times. Without them boards may encounter considerable criticism. Policies are valuable because:

1. They help clarify responsibilities among board, administrative staff, teaching staff, and community.
2. They help promote more consistent and prudent decision making or, stated negatively, they minimize embarrassing inconsistencies in school-board action.
3. They provide continuity of action.
4. They can save the board time, money, and effort, for many specific questions deal with similar principles, that is, repeat themselves in a variety of forms, and therefore can be handled

in a manner suggested by a single policy.
5. They help improve public relations.
6. They help reduce pressure on the board from special-interest pleaders.
7. They help reduce criticism of board action when it becomes apparent to the community that board decisions are based on well-defined and consistent policies rather than on expediency.
8. They give the board a sense of direction.
9. They facilitate orderly review of board practices.
10. They ensure a better-informed board and staff.[8]

Policies are more likely to fulfill their potential if reduced to writing.[9] The development of written policy statements by boards of education is a relatively new phenomenon. References to written policies in the professional literature were practically nonexistent prior to World War II. One study concluded that as late as 1946 relatively few boards were concerned with written policies.[10] In contrast, since the end of World War II it is difficult to find a publication dealing with school-board activity that fails to emphasize the need for written policies. Boards have been slow in translating into practice the many exhortations to prepare written statements of policy to govern school operations.

Content of policy statements. A review of local school-board policy manuals revealed little consistency of content.[11] Nearly all manuals specified by-laws governing board operation and organization as well as school business management. A majority had provi-

---

[7]Alpheus L. White, *Characteristics of Local Schoolboard Manuals,* U.S. Office of Education, Bulletin 1959, no. 14, Washington, D.C.: GPO, 1959, p. 3.

[8]American Association of School Administrators and National School Boards Association, *Written Policies for Schoolboards,* Washington, D.C.: The Association, 1955, p. 6.
[9]Ibid.
[10]White, op. cit., p. 1.
[11]Ibid.

sions relating to school-community relations. Lists of personnel duties and responsibilities similar to those commonly set forth in job descriptions were prominent features in most manuals examined in an U.S. Office of Education study.[12]

What aspects of school operations should be covered by policy statements? This is best answered by an analysis of problems encountered in the local institution. In general, carefully written school-board policies should speak out on:

1. Legal status, functions, organization, and ethical conduct of the board of education.
2. Selection, retention, and duties of the chief executive officer or superintendent of schools.
3. Relations among personnel in the school system.
4. Scope and quality of the instructional program and school services within the system.
5. Function and operation of the school food services.
6. Procedures and other aspects of budgeting, accounting, auditing, and management of school property.
7. Operation of the pupil-transportation system.
8. Selection, retention, and other matters related to the professional personnel.
9. Selection, retention, and other matters related to the nonprofessional personnel.
10. Identification, admission, promotion, discipline, etc. of pupils.
11. Public relations.

Policy statements should encompass all aspects of school operations that command the attention of the school board.

[12]Ibid.

Methods of developing policy statements. There is no one best way of developing a set of written policy statements for all school districts. The steps recommended by the American Association of School Administrators and the National School Boards Association are as follows:

1. List problems that should be solved: This includes difficulties that seem to demand a large portion of the school board's time during regular meetings.
2. Review the minute book: Often records of previous decisions taken by the board shed light on items that should be included in statements of written policy.
3. Study what other boards have done: This does not imply that one school board can successfully adopt in toto the policy statements of another, but policy practices of other boards can be a valuable source of ideas.
4. Consult studies and writings concerned with policy development.
5. Check established practices: Some traditions of the school which were never reduced to writing previously can inspire policies.
6. Solicit suggestions from the school staff.[13]

Conditions that prompted development of some policies will change and trigger new concerns or demand a new priority schedule. Policies are dynamic and should be revised to keep abreast of the times. The process of formulating, reviewing, editing, revising, or deleting policies is continuous. Some boards set definite dates or times, such as once a year, to review policies and consider what revisions are necessary in the light of experience. If policies are to be a means by which the board can more effectively discharge its responsibilities, rather than a device that unduly restricts board deliberations, they must be flexible.

[13]American Association of School Administrators and National School Boards Association, op. cit.

There is a considerable body of opinion that supports the notion that one measure of a board's effectiveness is the existence of relevant policies to govern educational affairs. Working with and living by such policies is another measure of effectiveness. The existence of a written set of policies is documentation of the fact that the board is serious in the discharge of its policy-making role.

THE SCHOOL-BOARD MEETING

School-board members are state officers performing a state function. They are comparable to directors of corporations or other institutions. An individual board member away from a meeting of the total board cannot make decisions that bind the district, nor can his opinion be regarded, in a legal sense, as any different from that of an ordinary citizen. Some board members cannot resist the temptation to act individually and engage in an official visitation of a school or direct supervision of one or more teachers. This is particularly true of new board members, suggesting that one mark of a mature and experienced board member is the refusal to decide important issues outside of board meetings or to engage in individual acts of supervising school operations. The board is a deliberative body. Courts have ruled that public interest is served best when all board members gather to deliberate the course of action for the district. It is at the school-board meeting that members discharge their responsibilities for public education in the district.

The school-board meeting is, therefore, of great significance to the administration of public education. Skill developed at such meetings, when coupled with a clear understanding of the role of the school board in the administration of public education, determines in considerable degree the effectiveness of an individual school-board member.

Time and place of board meetings

The time and place of some board meetings, such as those dedicated to its formal organization, are specified in statutes. In general, however, the board has the authority to design a schedule to suit the convenience of its members. Most school-board meetings in small communities are held in the evening. It was reported that 82 percent of the school boards met in the evening, 10 percent in the afternoon, 6 percent in the morning, and 2 percent in the middle of the day.[14] The writer had the experience of meeting with the school board at 6:30 A.M. The members argued that they could deliberate best before the pressures of the day developed.

Most school boards meet about twice a month on the date agreed upon by the membership. In the large school systems enrolling 25,000 or more boards meet typically on a Tuesday but never on a Friday.[15] Some meet as often during the month as may be necessary to dispose of pressing issues. There can be too many meetings as well as too few. The board that must meet every week or more should inquire whether it is engaged in executing as well as formulating policy. Often what appears to be continuous labor on school problems covers up a basic weakness in school board-professional staff relations.

The meeting place is usually the board of education office or the office

[14]Reeves, op. cit., p. 195.
[15]Educational Research Service, "Local School Boards: Status and Structure," circular no. 5, August 1972.

of the superintendent. If a large group is expected, a meeting room large enough to accommodate the number anticipated must be located. Comfortable seating, ample work space, and easy access to needed data are some factors which should be taken into consideration.

Planning for the board meeting

During the legally convened meeting board action can commit, create, and interpret policies and consummate other school business. Above all, the meeting provides the occasion for board members to pool judgment on issues confronting them.

Many boards find the informal way a comfortable method of transacting the affairs of the institution, but informality should not be so extreme that the members do not know definitely what has been accomplished during the meeting. An informal tone can be maintained during discussion, but final disposition of the issue should follow parliamentary procedure.

The order of a typical business meeting of the school board might be as follows:

1. Call to order by the presiding officer.
2. Roll call and establishment of a quorum (a quorum is usually the majority of the total board).
3. Reading, approval, and signing of minutes of the previous meeting.
4. Reporting of communications to and from the board.
5. Hearing of any scheduled delegation.
6. Report of the superintendent.
7. Unfinished business from previous meeting.
8. New business.
9. Other activities.
10. Adjournment.

An effective school-board meeting (where the desired accomplishments are realized) follows an agenda—an itemization of matters to be considered during a scheduled meeting. The agenda may be a brief list of topics to be considered or a highly elaborate document that includes data related to decisions that must be made. A carefully documented agenda includes evidence such as charts, graphs, statistics, previous experience record, and/or precedents that bear on the matters to be reviewed.

Responsibility for preparation of the agenda for a board meeting is usually assigned to the superintendent. On occasion a full-time secretary may assume this function. Board members, school personnel, or lay people, of course, can submit topics that should be considered at the next meeting. The agenda can be confining or flexible. Some boards refuse to act on an item not included in the agenda on grounds of insufficient time for the consideration necessary for prudent decision making; others are more flexible.

The agenda is most useful when it is mailed with supporting evidence to board members about a week in advance of the meeting. Board members are justified in asking for careful documentation of matters included in the agenda plus an opportunity to study pertinent data on all issues prior to scheduled meetings. Study of the agenda mailed before the meeting, however, must not become an unofficial meeting, for if it does, the scheduled meeting merely formalizes action on decisions discussed elsewhere.

An agenda issued at the time of meeting is better than none. With an agenda before it, the board has some concept of the ground to be covered and the time it will take to discharge the business at hand.

Open versus executive sessions

Board meetings are concerned with public business, and the school board has a public mission to fulfill. These factors must be kept in mind in deciding whether the board meeting should be a private or a public session. The laws of some states, such as New Jersey, require that all business meetings of school boards be open to the public. One study showed that 68 percent of school boards permitted the public to attend all meetings, 6 percent held only closed or executive sessions, and 26 percent held both kind. Other studies completed over 25 years ago reached similar conclusions. An Educational Research Service review in 1966 showed that over 80 percent of the large city school boards held executive sessions to discuss personnel matters, land acquisition, and cases involving individual pupils.[16]

Occasionally a school board may find an executive session necessary to deliberate on matters that might prove embarrassing or harmful to an individual or costly to the school district. For example, if a teacher is accused of wrongdoing and the evidence requires careful scrutiny and interpretation, public discussion could prove embarrassing if the teacher were wrongfully accused. Similarly, discussion of disciplinary problems among pupils could prejudice the case of those involved. Anticipated purchase of a particular school site might justify deliberation in an executive meeting where the public is excluded. Executive meetings can be held at the request of the majority of members present after passage of a formal motion to that effect. Occasional execu-

tive sessions are understandable; their frequent use invites criticism and suspicion. All actions taken by the board of education should be at a public meeting. The purpose of executive session is discussion rather than decision. The public and the press have a stake in public school operations and have a right to be in attendance when discussions and decisions on public affairs take place.

In general, it can be said that unless specific statutes require otherwise, a board of education can exercise discretion in determining time and place of meeting and call special meetings. The board may move into executive sessions as per statutory demands. When there is evidence that an agreement or conspiracy took place during the executive session to determine how each board member would vote in the open meeting, courts have generally ruled that such an agreement is illegal and unenforceable.[17]

Delegations at board meetings are not unusual. The board is under no legal compulsion to act immediately on requests made by a delegation or for that matter even to hear out the delegation. A vocal minority may assume the guise of a majority. The board does owe any group in the district the courtesy of telling it when it may expect an answer from the board or the superintendent. Picketing the board session is a weapon used by some groups to force board decisions in harmony with their demands. Demonstrations that disrupt orderly procedures or that interfere with the right of any person or group to be heard are more common today than ever before. Board meetings tend to reflect the times. Disagreements and even vio-

---

[16]Educational Research Service, "Local School Boards: Status and Practices," circular no. 6, November 1967.

[17]R. L. Drury and K. C. Ray, *Essentials of School Law*, New York: Appleton-Century-Crofts, 1965, p. 11.

lence in a community or state will find its way into board sessions. Unfortunately threats and even casual assaults have been made upon board members in large urban school districts. Dissent can degenerate into arbitrary, undemocratic, and even violent behavior. Board members cannot avoid conflict; their challenge is to manage conflict to minimize dysfunction in the educational enterprise.

Role of the superintendent in the board meeting

School-board meetings are designed to encourage exchange of viewpoints and rendering of decisions by school-board members. Strictly speaking, the superintendent of schools is not a member of the board. In about 44 percent of the large school systems (25,000 or more) the superintendent also serves as board secretary. This office carries no vote. Presence of the superintendent at the school board meeting in all cases may be justified on the ground that he is the chief executive officer of the board. It would be difficult for a superintendent to perform his responsibilities effectively if he were not allowed to be present at the board's deliberations. There may be occasions when the board needs his counsel. The board, of course, reserves the right to make its own decisions which may or may not agree with the counsel of the superintendent.

The superintendent has no legal authority in meetings and cannot vote on any issues. It was pointed out previously that he is responsible for preparing the agenda of meetings. It is only when the superintendent's status and salary are under consideration that he should be excluded from participation in school-board meetings.

It is not unusual for designated members of the superintendent's staff to attend board meetings to help present educational matters. Such opportunities allow the staff members to contribute to the board's understanding of various problems and can strengthen morale and good working relations among the staff. Productive deliberative sessions often necessitate that a variety of human as well as material resources be available to the board of education during regularly scheduled meetings.

Minutes of board meetings

The minutes constitute the official record of board actions. Courts will not admit extrinsic evidence that adds or detracts from officially approved minutes or records of board action. Consequently, the careful preparation of minutes is essential.

School-board minutes are public records and are open to examination by taxpayers or by other persons who have good reason to examine them. It is no longer uncommon for board minutes to be duplicated and copies distributed to all board members, the administrative staff, newspapers, and other interested persons. The minutes become official records and official evidence when formally approved by the board and signed by the secretary and the president of the board.

Facts that typically are recorded in the minutes of the board are:

1. Type of meeting and its date, place, and time.
2. Name of presiding officer who called the meeting.
3. Names of members present and absent, as well as of other individuals in attendance in some official capacity.
4. Complete record of each motion, showing the vote of each board member.

5. Identification of all reports, documents, and contracts brought to the attention of the board.
6. Name and number of delegations appearing before the board and description of petitions or complaints submitted.
7. Time meeting was adjourned.
8. Signature of the secretary and president to acknowledge date of approval of minutes.
9. An addendum to show any corrections to the minutes.

Minutes are best kept as brief as possible within limits of comprehensiveness and coherence. A system of indexing board minutes simplifies identification of the time and nature of past board actions. These documents should be kept in a fireproof vault adjoining the board room.

ORGANIZATION OF THE SCHOOL BOARD

The local school board includes a chairman (commonly designated president), a vice president, a secretary, and a treasurer. Duties of each of these vary in different states.[18] Some boards are further constituted into standing or permanent committees. During the early educational history of the United States, the school board was an executive as well as a legislative body, and under such conditions there was some justification for large numbers of standing committees. It is of historical interest that there were standing committees of school boards before there were superintendents and other professional administrators. Standing committees were often necessary in cities where school boards were excessively large. Thus by 1849 Boston had 214 school-board

members, elected by wards, serving on its various committees.[19] Philadelphia as late as 1905 was reported to have 559 school-board members. The present size of school boards throughout the United States is much smaller, with most being composed of five to seven members.[20] Boards in large districts (25,000 or more) typically have seven members, only 25 percent have more than seven members.[21]

The growth and decline of school-board committees can be illustrated by events in Chicago. The Chicago board of 1861 constituted itself into 10 standing committees. This number grew to 19 "functional committees" by 1872, 70 by 1885, and 79 somewhat later. The trend was reversed in the twentieth century, so that by 1912 the board had reduced its standing committees by 13. There were only seven permanent committees by 1922, and the most recent study shows only one —a committee on finance.[22]

A 1962 nationwide study of school boards[23] indicated that nearly a third of the responding systems had one or more standing committees of the local school boards. Another 22.5 percent indicated operations through special committees but no standing committee. A recent study (1972) that was confined to large school systems, which are more likely to have standing committees than smaller districts, revealed

[18]Reeves, op. cit., chap. 8.

[19]Ibid., pp. 20 and 27.
[20]Morrill M. Hall, *Provisions Governing Membership on Local Boards of Education*, U.S. Office of Education, Bulletin 1957, no. 13, Washington, D.C.: GPO, 1957.
[21]Educational Research Service, "Local Boards of Education: Status and Structure," op. cit.
[22]Reeves, op. cit., p. 25; National Education Association, "Status and Practices of Boards of Education," *Research Bulletin*, vol. 25, no. 2, April 1946, p. 62.
[23]A. L. White, *Local School Boards: Organization and Practices*, Washington, D.C.: GPO, 1962, p. 41.

that 61 percent do not operate with standing committees.[24] Of those who do operate in this mode most have 4 or fewer standing committees although one goes to the extreme with 16. The most common type of standing committee is the finance committee. Others include permanent committees for legislation, buildings and grounds, complaints and appeals, public relations, publications, subdistricts, audit, salaries, school supplies, community use of school buildings, insurance, libraries, designated special subject areas, curriculum and instruction, textbooks, cafeterias, transportation, and school activities.[25]

Evidence compiled in many districts substantiates the claim that duties of standing committees are largely executive in nature. Most boards have assigned executive functions, often assumed by committees, to the superintendent. The professional staff of the superintendency is recognized as a better solution to the board's need for an executive agency.

The present prevailing practice is organization of the school board as a unit, with technical and professional assistance provided by the professionally prepared chief executive officer and his administrative staff. Operating as a unit rather than through standing committees in no way decreases the importance of the role of the board. It is a change in the manner of discharging responsibilities as the board is authorized by statutes to control educational affairs of the district. The key to effective control is who authorizes or adopts policies and practices rather than who is delegated responsibility to execute policies. As long as the board finally determines what educational policies

shall prevail it will control education.

Standing committees can lead to fragmentation of the school board. All too often reports of standing committees are uncritically accepted by the board as a whole. In effect the final action by the entire board is only a formality with the real decision determined by a convention of several "subschool boards." As Reeves stated:

It is no more logical to have committees of laymen dealing with technical education matters, such as promotion and grading, courses of study, curriculum, school supplies, and school buildings, than it would be for a hospital board to have committees of laymen dealing with technical matters such as skin and heart diseases, gynecology, pediatrics, and operations.[26]

Most authorities recommend that the board act as a committee of the whole, rather than permit itself to become fragmented into a variety of standing committees.

In all fairness it must be reported that this writer has observed a local school board with standing committees that was not fragmented. It created a unique communication system so that the discussions and actions of committees were shared with the board as a whole, and was able to complete board business expeditiously because of the deliberations of standing committees. This is the exception rather than the rule.

CHARACTERISTICS OF THE SCHOOL BOARD

The size of school boards, methods of selection, length of terms, qualifications for membership, and related factors have changed over the years. This is evident from the periodic surveys of board characteristics. The trend

[24]Educational Research Service, op. cit.
[25]Reeves, op. cit., p. 121.

[26]Ibid., p. 125.

seems to be away from either extreme —that is, those with fewer than five members to those with more than nine members. The reduction in numbers from over 125,000 school boards to fewer than 17,000 saw the elimination of many smaller school districts with three or fewer board members.

The size of local school boards ranges from 3 to 19 members. This is a much narrower range than previously reported. As late as 1905 the upper limit was over 500 members. Very few states (one in seven) have laws that mandate that all local boards be uniform in size. In contrast, laws in most states create boards of varying sizes—generally three, five, seven, or nine members. In three states the numerical size of boards is not precisely specified, but is related to such nonschool factors as the number of police jurors in a school district or the number of magisterial districts or wards. Pupil or total population is a common determinant of school-board size.

Despite the variation noted, school boards usually consist of from five to seven members. A study of large systems showed that almost three-quarters of the boards had either five or seven members, with seven being the most common.

Boards should be large enough to minimize domination by a single personality, but not so large as to become unwieldy. A school board of three members can be dominated by a single personality who needs only one other person to demonstrate majority control. The optimum size for a school board is seven members.

Local school-board members serve a specified term of office. The exception is Virginia, where a few boards serve at the pleasure of the appointing agency. In most states there are no statutory limitations on the number of

successive terms a person can serve. Systems with appointive boards are more likely to have limits on successive terms than those with elected boards. Only nine systems with such limitations were identified in 1972.[27] Only eight of the large districts (out of 186) were identified in 1972 where all board members serve concurrent terms, meaning that the entire board is elected or reelected at the same time. The overwhelming numbers provide for staggered terms where only part of the board membership is replaced, reelected, or reselected at a single election or occasion on a regular basis. Overlapping or staggered terms are recommended over the rare practice of designating concurrent terms. Most members serve a four-year term if elected and a five-year term if appointed. When a vacancy occurs in a majority of situations the remaining members on an elected board vote to determine who shall fill the unexpired term. On appointed boards, the appointive agency steps in to fill the unexpired term.

Local school-board members are popularly elected in most school systems. In 33 states, all school-board members are elected by popular vote; in the other 9 states most of the board members are chosen in this fashion. Appointive boards of education are in the minority. In three states—Indiana, Maryland, and Virginia—the appointive boards predominate.[28] The person or agency responsible for appointing school-board members may be the mayor, the governor, the county court, the city council, a grand juror, or a judge of the court of common pleas.

More than 95 percent of all local school boards in 1957 were elected to office by popular vote. Earlier studies

[27]Educational Research Service, op. cit.
[28]Ibid.

reported that 85 to 87 percent of all school-board members were popularly elected. A 1962 study of a sample of districts concluded that 85.9 percent of districts had elected school boards. Ninety percent of the elected boards were in the northeast, north central, and western parts of the nation. The larger the city the more likely that board members will be appointed to office, but even in the large systems about 80 percent of the board members were elected to office.

Any qualified voter is eligible for board membership in most school districts. Reference to educational qualifications of board members are found in statutes of 11 states. Thus, Kentucky requires a minimum of eighth-grade education or its equivalent. In other states such vague expressions as a "fair elementary education," "able to read and write," and "practical education" are employed. Maryland and North Carolina laws require "character and fitness" of those who aspire to board membership. All Arizona board members must be taxpayers or have a child in school. In New York board members of all except city districts must satisfy the following qualifications: (1) own, hire, or lease property within the district; (2) be a parent of a child who attended school for some time; (3) have a child attending school in a district residing with him. A 1946 report by the National Education Association[29] indicated that 61 percent of the school-board members had children attending school during their period of service, while 26 percent had children attending school at one time or another. Only 13 percent of the school-board members did not have any children attending school at any

time. Some would argue that having children attending school has little relation to the effectiveness of an individual as a board member. Education is important to everyone in society, not simply to parents of school-age children.

Most school boards (about 82 percent) are elected to office at non-partisan elections and from the district-at-large instead of by wards. Selecting board members from the district-at-large is used exclusively in 17 states and to some degree in 26 others. There is general agreement among authorities that boards should be elected at large and at nonpartisan elections. A reverse trend is evident in some states experiencing a considerable amount of reorganization which involves a partnership between rural and urban areas.

Compensation of board members is neither a rarity nor a common practice. There has been no discernable trend toward or away from payments of salary to board members. Where compensation is allowed and practiced the amounts paid have increased in recent years. In 1972 those that paid a salary to board members ranged from a high of $5500 in Florida to a low of $36 in Ohio. The majority of large systems paid no annual salary (57.5 percent) although mileage and expenses were permitted as incurred.[30]

It is difficult to determine what compensation school board members should receive. Participation in school-board activities is a public service and compensation is of secondary importance. Existing payments are nominal in all but a few cases and in no way approximate the worth or contributions of individuals, particularly those who are high-salaried executives in industry or business. There is some argument that board members should

---

[29]National Education Association, "Status and Practice of Boards of Education," *Research Bulletin*, vol. 24, no. 2, April 1946.

[30]Educational Research Service, op. cit.

not be paid, for otherwise they would tend to be executive.

A composite picture of the typical school board in large school systems in 1972 would show it to be:[31]

1. Representative of the entire district.
2. A seven-member board.
3. Elected.
4. With members serving four-year staggered terms.
5. Male-dominated.
6. Meeting twice a month.
7. Operating with standing committees.
8. Operating without salary compensation to members.
9. Served by a superintendent designated as secretary to the board.
10. Selecting replacement by board vote to fill the position vacated until the next election.

EFFECTIVENESS OF SCHOOL BOARD MEMBERS

The following six criteria have been suggested for evaluation of the effectiveness of school-board members:

1. Acceptance of the principle of board unity and subordination of self-interest. This calls for subordinating selfish or personal interests to achieve board purposes, adhering to the policy-making and legislative functions of the board, accepting and supporting majority decisions of the board, identifying with board policies and actions, and refusing to speak or act on school matters independent of board meetings.

2. Effective understanding of the executive function and willingness to support it when administering policies. This involves understanding the desirability of delegating executive responsibility to the chief executive officer, supporting the executive officer

[31]Ibid.

in his authorized functions, encouraging teamwork between the executive officer and the board, and recognizing problems and conditions that are of executive concern.

3. Demonstrating initiative and formal leadership. This includes suspending judgment until the facts are available, making use of pertinent experience, helping to identify problems, showing ability to determine satisfactory solutions to problems, devoting time outside board meetings as board business requires, and accepting ideas from others.

4. Effectiveness in personal relations. This involves willingness to work with board members in spite of personality differences, readiness to display both tact and firmness in relations with individuals, and forthrightness in treating patrons and teachers fairly and ethically.

5. Effectiveness in staff and group relations. This includes ability to speak effectively in public, believing firmly in democratic processes and in the right of all groups to be heard, working tactfully and sympathetically with teachers' groups, and understanding how a group thinks and acts in working effectively and having mature social poise.

6. Courageous action for the good of the school in spite of pressures and influences. This means being able to weather criticism, maintaining firm convictions, being willing to take sides in controversy, and sharing responsibility for board decisions.[32]

Effective working relations constitute the most important ingredients of team play. School-board members are people and they must work with other

[32]Richard E. Barnhart, "The Critical Requirements for School Board Membership Based on an Analysis of Critical Incidents," doctoral thesis, Indiana University, Bloomington, Ind., 1952.

people. Human relations are the basis of their effectiveness as board members.

THE SCHOOL BOARD AND THE SCHOOL SUPERINTENDENT

Board and superintendent face the same dilemmas and frequently are caught between the same cross pressures. It takes time for a new board member and a new superintendent to comprehend fully the significance of policies previously developed. Occasionally the new superintendent or board member will unwittingly violate or ignore an adopted policy. This could touch off a conflict whose ultimate resolution would be inimical to the district as a whole. An annual review of policies can reduce the probability of such errors.

In addition to the superintendent, the board must work with the parent-teachers association, other community groups, the professional staff, the state department of public instruction, and even militant demonstrators. It needs the support of all groups to make a major contribution to the administration of public education.

Hammering out desirable working relations between boards and superintendents was not without struggle. The late C. H. Judd, Dean of the School of Education at the University of Chicago, wrote in 1934 that school boards were an obstruction to good school administration and were survivals from an age when professionalization of schools was less advanced.[33]

[33]Charles H. Judd, "School Boards as an Obstruction to Good Administration," *The Nation's Schools*, vol. 13, no. 5, February 1934, pp. 13–15. Also note William McAndrew, "School Boards from Below" and "A Disease of School Boards," *The Nation's Schools*, vol. 3, no. 5, May 1929, pp. 21–23; vol. 3, no. 6, June 1929, p. 30.

He was not the first nor will he be the last to question the need for school boards. Mark Twain is reputed to have said: "First God made idiots. That was for practice. Then he made school boards." This unwarranted generalization from some inept rural boards in the last century persists despite its lack of substantiation.

Dr. Judd held that no private corporation could be successful if its board of directors behaved toward managers and operatives as boards of education commonly behaved toward superintendents and other members of the school staff. He concluded that there would come a day when school boards would be abolished. (There is no evidence some 40 years later to even hint at the probability of school boards being abolished in any state much less nationally.) His main argument was that ordinary citizens, even when honest, sincere, and intelligent, do not have the time, the patience, or the technical skill necessary to administer a modern school system properly. He represented an extreme form of professional impatience with school boards.

An almost immediate rebuttal came from another educator, Dr. Fred Engelhardt, Professor of School Administration at the University of Minnesota, who proclaimed that the general indictment of school boards contained in Judd's article was unfair, prejudiced, and not founded on fact.[34] He went on to say that if professional leaders in schools had been required to face the period from 1930 to 1934 without the assistance of lay school boards, the status of public education during the early depression years might have been much worse than it was. Many superintendents today would be

[34]Fred Engelhardt, "In Defense of School Boards," *The Nation's Schools*, vol. 13, no. 5, May 1934, p. 21.

the first to admit that public schools would have suffered more than they did from the vicious attacks upon public education immediately following World War II as well as the militant actions of the 1960s if there had been no school boards.

During recent times articles by laymen and by some professional educators have attacked the system of control of schools by a local board of education. Most publications about boards are concerned with the shortcomings of individuals selected for this position of high public trust. Hence, the primary emphasis today is on characteristics of effective board members, developing orientation programs for people newly elected to school boards, and preparing handbooks for school-board members. It is recognized that the American idea of keeping the schools close to the people by vesting control in representatives of the people elected to school boards is fundamentally sound.

Nevertheless, some of Judd's criticism is worthy of consideration. It is difficult to justify a board of education if its function is primarily to manage, directly administer, or execute the affairs of the schools. There is a danger of the board's overinvolvement in operating details at the expense of determining strategies, sensing new missions, and planning long-range activities. Board members are engaged in full-time occupations other than school-board work. The complexity of schools demands full-time, professionally prepared administrators and teachers. The importance of the board lies in nonmanagerial or nonexecutive functions. Direct administration must be delegated to professionally prepared school superintendents. This in no way decreases the importance of the board. Policy formulation, not policy execution, is the key to control.

A definition of desirable working relations between the professional school staff and the school board will be hammered out in most school districts. A board of education that almost ignores professional workers and tries to operate schools on opinions of the janitors or of alarmed and upset parents will continue to experience unnecessary problems. Everybody feels qualified to criticize the schools, but it is the board's *duty* to appraise the school. This appraisal must be based on facts and sound judgment.

The administrative team concept is rapidly gaining hold, whereby school-board members, superintendents, principals, and teachers are regarded as members of a team. Each has a specific function to perform, with one depending upon the other.

NEW DIRECTIONS FOR THE SCHOOL BOARD

Local boards of education are undergoing considerable stress and strain owing to unusual demands placed upon public education at the present time. Board members in some cities have suffered physical harm as well as emotional strain. Some forces that are redefining the role and influence of the school board in public education are:

1. The greater emphasis on quality, the increased demands placed upon schools, and the greater complexity of educational operations. These are manifest in many ways. To illustrate, national goals are receiving as much prominence as local needs or state demands.
2. The increasing militancy of teachers and the emergence of collective negotiation with teachers' groups. This is reinforced by threat of sanctions and strikes. Work stoppages

in the public schools are more numerous now than ever before and serve to compound greatly the problems of board members.

3. The increased involvement of the federal government as an enforcer of specific kinds of court decisions or laws, such as those dealing with civil rights, and as a stimulator of special programs in which the federal government has an interest.

4. The conception of the school as an institution capable of ameliorating social injustices.

5. The increased number of pressure groups, sometimes violent, and the greater use of protest and demonstrations in and out of school-board meetings to influence school policies.

6. The increased emphasis on innovations rather than on the continuation of operations as usual.

7. Changing expectations for public education at the local, state, and federal levels. Criticisms of public education wax and wane, but seldom disappear.

8. The involvement of many informal and formal agencies and professional and nonprofessional groups in the operation of public education.

9. The difficulty in obtaining additional resources for the operation of public education at the very time expectations are increasing and programs are becoming more complicated.

It is heartening to see efforts of state and national school-boards associations to improve the leadership quality of school-board members by operating clinics, workshops, and conferences. The ability to fulfill the responsibilities of the school-board member taxes the ability of the best. Special methods are needed to sensitize boards to emerging social demands as well as to the propensity of special power groups to mold schools to reflect selfish interests rather than to meet the needs of the district, state, or nation. It is much simpler for those concerned with specific programs to recommend a course of action than it is for those concerned with maintaining a balance in the public school system to fit the recommended program into the total system.

THE RESOLUTION OF CONFLICT

James[35] summarized a number of doctoral dissertations at Stanford University examining school-board conflict with the superintendent, the teachers, the community, the state, and the federal government. The studies were based on a sample of California districts. One concluded that rapid growth of the community was associated most prominently with a broken contract between the school board and its superintendent. Another reinforced a previous discovery that board members improve with experience, and members with long board service are better at managing conflict. A third study concluded that the recall election was not a satisfactory means for resolving board-community conflicts. Recall election campaigns intensify conflicts and polarize the community. The power of the board is misunderstood, and most citizens believe that the board has more authority and discretion than actually exists. A further study revealed that the traditional rule-making responsibility of the school board has degenerated into rule application and rule adjudication. James concluded that conflicts are inevitable,

[35]H. T. James, "School Board Conflict Is Inevitable," *American School Board Journal*, vol. 154, no. 3, March 1967, pp. 5–9.

and therefore, one mark of a vigorous and healthy school board is successful management of conflict.

Fowlkes presented a series of generalizations drawn from University of Wisconsin studies on citizens' perception of boards of education. These include:

1. Citizens have little knowledge of how school boards function.
2. Citizens' expectations vary on what a board should do.
3. Members of boards of education disagree on school functions.
4. Board membership is valued differently by people who are and are not on school boards.
5. Citizens have little knowledge of the functions of the superintendent and his importance to schools.
6. School-board meetings may fall short of potential value.
7. Citizens' knowledge and the specificity of their expectations of schools seem to be related closely to whether they have children attending school.
8. Teachers generally have little knowledge about school-board operations.[36]

Fowlkes concluded that improved communications are imperative to inform all citizens about board functions.

McCarty[37] reported that a board of education tended to exhibit the same kind of power structure as its community. He developed a model that depicted the school board as either dominated (looking to one member for a decision), factional (dependent on a majority for a decision), status congruent (dependent on discussion), or sanctioning (dependent on the recommendations of the superintendent).

[36]John G. Fowlkes, "What Does the Public Expect of the Board?" *American School Board Journal*, vol. 154, no. 3, March 1967, pp. 10–12.

[37]Donald J. McCarty, *Myths and Realities in School Board Research*, Washington, D.C.: American Educational Research Association, 1966.

SUMMARY

The local board of education is an American invention. It is the basic administrative agency for public education in the United States. The numbers of such boards have declined from over 125,000 to about 16,500. It represents the general policy-making level in school administration. The board evolved out of the town meeting and special committees of selectmen of the town. During colonial days and the early part of the nineteenth century, the board served as a legislative and an executive body. The growing complexity of educational institutions demanded a separation of these functions. The board of education is presently regarded as the legislative rather than the executive agency.

Consequently the most important contribution of a board of education to the administration of public education is the formulation of policies that can guide the institution toward its goals. A policy is the general statement of intent to act in a particular way when confronted with a given situation or to achieve a given result at some future point in time; rules and regulations are more specific statements derived from the general policy. Although there has been agreement among authorities on the desirability of written policies, most school boards have not as yet satisfied this requirement.

The board of education realizes its function at the school-board meeting. The meeting is a deliberative session of considerable consequence. Board members have the legal authority to commit the resources of the district at school-board meetings, but not individually or away from the meetings. Meetings of the board can be facilitated by adopting rules of order and by preparing an agenda. Because the board speaks through its minutes, these documents are of considerable consequence in school operations.

Standing committees of school boards were justifiable when boards were executive as well as legislative bodies. Standing committees are disappearing, and the superintendency is recognized as the executive branch of the school system.

Most school boards are elected on a nonpartisan ballot and from the district-at-large. Only in a few states are all boards of education appointed to office. Most school-board members serve without compensation, but where this practice prevails boards have received substantially increased payments in recent years. The typical school board has from five to seven members, although some have as few as three members and others as many as 19.

One of the fundamental responsibilities of the board today is the management of conflict. The traditional rulemaking responsibility of the board has degenerated into rule application and rule adjudication. A board tends to exhibit the same kind of power structure as its community.

QUESTIONS

1. Can an agency serve adequately as a legislative as well as an executive body? Justify your stand.
2. What conditions led to the development of the concept that a board of education should confine its activities primarily to the formulation of general policy?
3. What is a policy?
4. Why should a board prepare written policies?
5. What is the significance of the statement: "A board speaks through its minutes"?
6. Why are school-board meetings so important in the administration of public education?
7. What should be the role of the superintendent and other professional staff members at the school-board meeting?
8. How can school-board meetings be made more productive?
9. What is the best method of selecting school-board members?
10. What are the functions of the school board?

SELECTED REFERENCES

Educational Research Service, "Local Boards of Education: Status and Structure," circular no. 5, 1972.

Fowlkes, John G., "What Does the Public Expect of the Board?" *American School Board Journal,* vol. 154, no. 3, March 1967, pp. 10–12.

Hamilton, Robert R. and E. Edmund Reutter, Jr., *Legal Aspects of School Board Operation,* New York: Teachers College, 1958.

James, H. T., "School Board Conflict Is Inevitable," *American School Board Journal,* vol. 154, no. 3, March 1967, pp. 5–9.

McCarty, Donald J. and Ramsey, Charles E., "Community Power,

School Board Structure, and the Role of the Chief School Administrator," *Educational Administration Quarterly*, Spring 1968.

Reeves, Charles E., *Schoolboards: Their Status, Function, and Activities*, Englewood Cliffs, N.J.: Prentice-Hall, 1954.

Theisen, W. M., *The City Superintendent and the Board of Education, Contributions to Education, No. 84*, New York: Teachers College, 1917.

15

THE SUPERINTENDENCY: THE CHIEF SCHOOL EXECUTIVE AND HIS ADMINISTRATIVE TEAM

Carrying out the general school policy formulated by the board of education is an executive or administrative (as contrasted with a legislative) function. The general executive or administrative level of public school administration is empowered by the board of education to implement its policies and fulfill other responsibilities essential to an educational institution.

The professionally prepared individual serving as the general executive or administrator at the local level is referred to most frequently as the superintendent of schools or the general superintendent. In some states the executive may be called the school district administrator who has system-wide authority as opposed to those who function in a specific area or instructional center in the district.

The superintendent is the chief school executive and typically is the only professional employee in the chain of command reporting directly to the board of education. The superintendency is in reality a cluster of positions. The complexity of modern educational systems demands an administrative team at the general executive level to increase the effectiveness of present and future operations.

Section I: The superintendency

EVOLUTION OF THE SCHOOL SUPERINTENDENCY

The superintendency, which has served as the general professional executive branch of school administration, is almost 150 years old. It evolved after unsuccessful attempts to administer a complex system of public education via the part-time services of lay people. Delegation of executive responsibility to a full-time employee rather than a committee that met occasionally or the annual town meeting was not accomplished without debate and disagreement. A strong antiexecutive attitude was part of an emerging tradition among American colonists—an attitude evident in the state constitutions adopted from 1775 to 1800.[1] It is not surprising, therefore, that the appointment of a full-time administrator as an executive officer for the school system as a whole was delayed almost 200 years—two centuries after the start of the American system of public

[1]Leonard D. White, *Introduction to the Study of Public Administration*, rev. ed., New York: Macmillan, 1939, p. 20.

education. Recognition of the need for such a school executive had to await the development of complexities within the system that precipitated a crisis. The image of the executive as sort of a deposed royal governor lingered long after the royal governor had disappeared from the American scene.

School administration prior to the superintendency

There were no school superintendents in American cities at the time of the adoption of the federal Constitution. The first federal census in 1790 showed that about 5 percent of the people lived in urban communities. There were but five cities in the entire nation with a population of 8000 or more. The primitive school house and simple curriculum made management of the local community school fairly easy. Most administrative details were handled by lay people within the community. Policy making and policy execution were reviewed at the town meeting and the two were not separated during this early period.

The first half of the nineteenth century was characterized by rapid growth in urban population, development of manufacturing, and appearance of a multiplicity of important inventions. To illustrate, Detroit's population rose from 1,400 in 1820 to over 21,000 by 1850; New York's from 123,700 in 1820 to over 500,000 in 1850. Other cities registered similar gains. An executive system that worked well for schools in rural communities and small cities began to fall apart in the rapidly growing urban communities. It became apparent to many that the magnitude and complexity of school affairs made impossible the direct execution of policies by a public gathering acting in town meetings. The initial solution was to create a new format for lay admin-

istration of schools. The people in town meetings delegated to the school committee (the local board of education) both legislative and executive discretion. The school-committee members were thus the school administrators. But the work load grew far beyond the part-time attention that lay committee members could pay to it. The next response was the creation of a larger school board, as described earlier in Chapter 14. Unwieldy size complicated operations more than it helped. Standing committees were then established to supervise and inspect the schools at somewhat regular intervals. This fragmentation of the school board did not remedy the more fundamental problem, namely, that part-time lay citizens were attempting to execute important responsibilities that demanded full-time and professional expertise.

Standing committees were doomed to failure for they were not prepared for nor did they completely understand the intricacies of administration. Further, school affairs were demanding that board members devote an ever-increasing amount of time to education, and, therefore, less and less time was available for their private businesses. By 1850 many school boards in large cities were ready to admit that executive problems such as supervising instruction, grading schools, and keeping track of school property in rapidly growing systems were beyond the capabilities of a lay, part-time administration agency.[2] This started the search for alternatives. The creation of the American school superintendency was the alternative destined to survive in spite of resistance from those unacquainted with the complexities of

[2]Thomas M. Gilland, *The Origin and Development of the Power and Duties of the City-Superintendent*, Chicago: University of Chicago Press, 1935, chap. 9.

school operation. Some school committees urged the establishment of an executive position for 10 to 20 years before the post became a fact.

Establishment and development of the superintendency

Thirteen school systems established the city school superintendency between 1837 and 1850. Buffalo and Louisville are credited with the creation, in 1837, of the first superintendencies in public education. The number of teachers at the time of appointment of the first superintendent ranged from only 4 in St. Louis in 1839 to 2168 in Philadelphia in 1883. The dates of establishment (and in some cases reestablishment) of the superintendency in 39 cities are presented in Table 15–1. Only about a dozen cities created the school superintendency prior to 1850. Before the nineteenth century came to an end, the superintendency concept was to be recognized as the only promising solution to the administrative problems confronting public education.

Some of the early city school superintendents were elected to office by popular vote. This approach was short-lived and soon most were appointed to office by school boards. The county and state superintendents, in contrast, started as elected officials also but this method of selection persists today in many states. A hopeful sign is the established trend to appointive superintendents for intermediate and state education agencies. Election of the local school superintendent continued to be favored longer in the South as a reaction to the appointed carpetbag government officials that held office immediately following the Civil War. Today, even in the South, the trend is toward appointment of local school superintendents.

The school superintendency was well established in many jurisdictions by the time of the Civil War. Much more time was required to refine the position and to recognize the superintendent as the chief executive of the school board. It should be recalled that in the last half of the nineteenth century, the board was characterized by an increase in size as well as by the growth of standing committees. This pattern militated against the development of the effective superintendency. The involvement of both a professional executive and lay standing committees in executive details precipitated misunderstanding and conflict that continues at the present.

The brief tenure of office for the board of education often meant short tenure for the superintendent as well.[3] Board members were reluctant to appoint the superintendent for a term longer than their own. This short period of service deprived the early superintendent of the opportunity to concentrate on long-range policies and limited his ability to influence educational developments as well.

The early superintendent was considered an assistant to the board. There wasn't any question as to "whose man" the superintendent was. He came into being as an agent of the school board faced with perplexing educational problems. The typical board continued to exercise extensive executive power through executive committees during all of the nineteenth century.[4] The superintendent was assigned menial school chores or detail work, and was allowed little opportunity to exhibit professional skill and leadership ability. The concept of the superintendent as an agent whose prime function is to ascertain what the board hopes to accomplish and then to

[3]Ibid., p. 124.

[4]Arthur B. Moehlman, *School Administration*, Boston: Houghton Mifflin, 1940, p. 246.

TABLE 15–1

ESTABLISHMENT OF THE SCHOOL SUPERINTENDENCY IN 39 CITIES

City	Year of establish- ment	Year of reestablish- ment	Population as of nearest census	Population at time of reestablishment as of nearest census
Buffalo	1837		18,213	
Louisville	1837		21,210	
St. Louis	1839		16,469	
Providence	1839		32,171	
Springfield	1840	1865	10,985	15,199
Philadelphia	1840	1883	93,665	847,170
Cleveland	1841	1853	6,071	17,034
Rochester	1841		20,191	
New Orleans	1841		102,193	
Brooklyn	1848		96,838	
Memphis	1848		8,841	
Baltimore	1849	1866	169,054	267,354
Cincinnati	1850		115,435	
Jersey City	1851		6,856	
Boston	1851		136,881	
New York	1851		515,547	
San Francisco	1851		56,802	
Nashville	1852		10,165	
Newark	1853		38,894	
Los Angeles	1853		1,610	
Chicago	1854		29,963	
Indianapolis	1855		8,091	
Detroit	1855	1863	21,019	45,649
Worcester	1856		24,960	
Minneapolis	1858		2,564	
Milwaukee	1859		45,246	
New Haven	1860		45,267	
Savannah	1866		28,235	
Kansas City	1867		32,260	
Pittsburgh	1868		86,076	
Washington, D.C.	1869		109,199	
Richmond	1869		51,038	
Wilmington	1870		30,841	
Denver	1871		4,759	
Atlanta	1871		21,789	
Omaha	1872		16,083	
Portland	1873		8,293	
Seattle	1882		3,533	
Salt Lake City	1890		20,768	

Source: Theodore Lee Reller, *The Development of the City Superintendency of Schools in the United States,* Philadelphia: Published by the author, 1935, pp. 81–82. Selected cities over 100,000 in population in the 1930 census.

act accordingly persists in many communities today.

The early superintendent was literally the superintendent of instruction and little else. It was not until the beginning of the twentieth century that the superintendent was delegated responsibility for financial and school-housing functions.[5] These functions remained within the board's purview even longer in city school districts that were fiscally dependent or in which the city council controlled the finances. The image of the superintendent as the instructional leader concerned with grading schools, developing courses of studies, or organizing pupil promotional procedures was initially based on fact. The "scholarly executive" was thought to understand little of finance, buildings, services, and supplies and to have "little interest in many of the supplementary executive activities."[6]

A few boards were ready in the nineteenth century to think of the superintendent as their chief executive officer. In most communities, however, a wait of from 6 to 60 years was necessary for the superintendent to gain this status. Even today the position in many districts remains immersed in "administrivia" by choice of the superintendent or through the failure of the board to provide adequate clerical or professional assistance. The concept of the chief executive officer as one preoccupied with detail is not conducive to the realization of the leadership potential of the post; the concept of the superintendent as one preoccupied with maintaining the status quo is not conducive to the realization of his importance as a change agent.

Only in a few states is the superintendent of schools mentioned in statutes dealing with public education,

and more often than not, the mention is simply a statement that a superintendent can be employed in districts of particular size. The position of local school district superintendent is more likely to be defined clearly in those states where it is a constitutional office. Thus, in Florida, the position of county superintendent of schools (which is the local school district superintendent, since the county is a basic unit of school administration) is rather well defined in terms of authority, responsibility, and relations with the county board of public instruction. McCann reported that the school codes in only about half the states define the relation between the board and the superintendent.[7] The courts of 13 states have declared the superintendent to be an officer of the board, whereas 6 others have ruled that he is an employee. Often the language of the statute determines the status. It is more logical to consider the superintendent an employee of the school district and a special agent of the school board than to define him as an officer of the board or of the school system.

By and large, the school superintendency has evolved without much legislative direction. There are about 13,000 local superintendents of public schools and 1,700 intermediate school superintendents. There are more school districts than there are superintendents because many of the small ones do not employ nor do they have need for a full-time district administrator. Responsibilities and professional concerns have been defined on the basis of experience and recommendations of authorities in the field. The increasing complexity of public education, how-

[7]Lloyd E. McCann, "Legal Status of the Superintendent of Schools as a Public Officer," unpublished doctoral dissertation, Colorado State College of Education, Greely, Colorado, 1951.

[5]Moehlman, op. cit.
[6]Ibid.

ever, makes it more important than ever to provide an adequate legal basis for the superintendency in public education. The writer joins the many authorities who call for recodification of statutes dealing with public education and the determination therein of the status, authority, and responsibility of the superintendent of schools in public education. The present strife that besets many large urban systems serves to reinforce this recommendation.

THE SCHOOL SUPERINTENDENT AND THE SCHOOL BOARD

The superintendent's role

The superintendent of schools is a professional member of an administrative team which includes the board of education. Although there is general agreement that the board of education should be the legislative or policy-making body, and the superintendent should serve as the executive officer and the board's professional adviser this is easier said than done. The superintendent is obligated to execute policies approved by the board even though previously he has opposed their adoption. The superintendent cannot expect the board to shield him from all criticism, but he is entitled to its support when he conscientiously seeks to carry out the board's policies or directives.

A specific description of the superintendent's role involves the following:

1. The superintendent is the chief executive officer of the board.
2. He is responsible for carrying out all policies, rules, and regulations established by the board. In matters not specifically covered by board policy, he is to take appropriate action and report the same to the board not later than the next regular meeting.

3. All individuals employed by the board are responsible directly or indirectly to the superintendent of schools.
4. The superintendent has the authority to prepare regulations and to give such instruction to school employees as may be necessary to make the policies of the board effective. He may delegate responsibilities and assign duties. Such delegation and assignment do not relieve the superintendent of responsibility for actions of subordinates.
5. Except when matters pertaining to his reemployment are being considered, the superintendent is to be present at all meetings of the board and its special committees. He may be held responsible for preparing the agendas for board meetings.
6. He is responsible for preparing and submitting the budget to cover school operations.
7. The superintendent has the authority, within limits of major appropriations approved by the board, to authorize and direct all purchases and expenditures.
8. He recommends all candidates for employment. The board has the authority to reject specific candidates recommended, but personnel finally accepted should be employed only upon the recommendation of the superintendent.
9. The superintendent formulates and recommends personnel policies necessary to the functioning of the school.
10. The superintendent provides professional leadership for the educational program of the schools and is responsible for developing a system of regular reporting to the board on all aspects of that program.
11. The superintendent is responsible for keeping the school board informed on all vital matters pertaining to the school system.
12. He is responsible for the development of a program of maintenance and improvement or expansion of the buildings and the site. This includes recommendation for employment and supervision of all building custodians.
13. He is responsible for formulating and administering a program for supervision for all schools.

14. The superintendent is responsible for submitting an annual report on the operation of the school system.[8]

The American Association of School Administrators (AASA) has suggested that in his relations with the board of education the superintendent has a right to:

1. The support of his board members as long as he is superintendent.
2. Provision of the tools and clerical assistance necessary to carry on the work of his office effectively.
3. Protection from work days that are too long and from too close attention to his job (vacations should be provided for him as well as his staff).
4. Protection from an unreasonable termination of his contract.
5. Protection from people who would use his office for the personal gain of prestige.
6. Protection from factions.
7. Protection against excessive or unfair criticism.
8. Appreciation of the board when his work is satisfactory.[9]

A relatively new responsibility for the school superintendent is management of personnel negotiations. Problems will arise in the long run where the board of education fails to delegate responsibility for conducting professional negotiations to the superintendent, or to an individual on his staff designated by the superintendent. A third party, namely, the chief negotiator for the school board, could be placed between the board of education and the superintendent. Earlier in history, business operations were delegated to a school business manager who reported directly to the board of

[8]S. J. Knezevich and H. C. DeKock, *The Iowa School Board Member*, Des Moines, Iowa: Iowa Association of School Boards, 1960, pp. 57–58.
[9]American Association of School Administrators, *School Board-Superintendent Relationships*, Thirty-fourth Yearbook, Washington, D.C.: The Association, 1956, pp. 63–65.

education rather than to the superintendent of schools. A dual system of administration fraught with conflicts and problems was thus born, and over 50 years were needed to reestablish the unit system of administration with one executive officer responsible to the board. If the chief negotiator reports directly to the board, he will be coordinate with the superintendent, and once again a dual system of administrative organization will result. More will be said about this in Chapter 20.

Management of disagreements

There will be times when school-board members and the superintendent disagree. Disagreement can be healthy and conducive to the formation of new ideas. There should be full and free discussion of controversial ideas. When perspective is lost, trouble starts. It is the statesman on the school board who senses that the discussion may get out of hand and suggests a cooling-off period or moves on to points of agreement.

If the school board seriously questions the professional leadership of the superintendent, the situation should be discussed forthrightly between the board and the superintendent, not clandestinely at meetings involving school-board members only. In some states, the state school-board association in cooperation with the state administrator association attempts to help an individual board discuss differences with its superintendent. Disputes between the board and the superintendent are never pleasant, but reluctance to discuss openly the unpleasant situation should be overruled by the responsibility of both parties to act in the best interest of the children and youth of the district. Board members have an obligation to evaluate the effectiveness of their superintendent and to make their findings known to him. If, after exhausting all reasonable efforts toward corrective action, the board still finds the performance of the superintendent unsatisfactory, he should be informed of the decision and be asked to resign. The board has an obligation to present to the superintendent the specific reasons that have led to his dismissal.

A change in the superintendency is not a matter to be treated lightly or decided hurriedly, particularly if there has been emotional upset. A turnover in the superintendency can precipitate problems of morale among the professional staff and concern among school patrons. When a change is being considered there should be ample evidence that the present professional administrator is incapable of performing his duty or is otherwise unsuited for the position.

THE SCHOOL SUPERINTENDENT AND THE PROFESSIONAL STAFF

The superintendent's professional relations include contacts with teachers and central-office staff, as well as with the school board. The nature of his relations and authority in working with other school personnel is defined, to a large degree, by the board of education. Without authority, it would be extremely difficult for the superintendent to discharge his responsibilities. Delegation of authority by the board to other central-office staff is of particular significance to the superintendent. There is evidence that negotiations are radically redefining previously established school personnel relationships.

There is ample evidence to support the contention that the *unit system of* *school administration* is more effective than others. Under the unit plan, the board delegates responsibility for execution of all aspects of the educational program (for example, instruction, logistical support, and development) to a single executive officer. This single professional person, usually the superintendent, assumes concern for the total operation, and all operating personnel are subordinate to him. The superintendent, in turn, is the only professional employee who regularly reports to, and deals directly with, the board of education. All other employees, professional and otherwise, report to the superintendent and through him to the board.

Some boards assign executive functions within an educational system to more than one executive officer. This is the *multiple type of organization for school administration*. Under this pattern of operation, two or more persons report directly and independently to the school board. All executives are considered coordinate officers of the board. A few boards have gone so far as to divide responsibilities into such separate domains as instruction; auditing; logistical support and finance; and building planning, construction, and maintenance; and to employ an executive for each. Only one, the superintendent of instruction, may be professionally prepared. The superintendent of instruction, with whom most professional employees must deal, would have to be a strong personality to assume a position of importance in this type of organization.

The *dual system of school administration* is the most common type of multiple organization for execution of board policies. There is usually a director of business affairs (logistical support services) who reports directly and independently to the board. This individual is granted coordinate status with the superintendent of schools, who is responsible for instructional operations only.

The evidence showing the superiority of the unit type of administrative organization over any multiple type has prompted all but a few school systems to adopt the former. Few authorities, if any, recommend any other type of executive organization than the unit system of school administration. The unit pattern places a great responsibility upon the general superintendent of schools—a responsibility that must be discharged with humility.

Working relations between the teaching staff and the superintendent can be complicated if there are many layers of administration between the two. This is particularly true in large and complex school districts. If administration is looked upon as a means to an end, and due recognition is given the importance of the teachers' task at the class level, it is difficult indeed to justify teachers and administrators as opposing forces rather than as a unified body of professional educators assigned various functions to perform in a complex institution.

CHARACTERISTICS OF SCHOOL SUPERINTENDENTS

About every ten years since the early twenties the American Association of School Administrators (AASA) has reported on the characteristics of the American school superintendent. The first such reading was based on 1921–1922 data and published in 1923; others appeared in 1933, 1952, and 1960. (The study of the superintendency in 1940–1941 was not made because of World War II.) The latest study was published by AASA in 1971 and was based on 1969–1970 data. This was the last major project completed

by this writer as a member of the AASA staff. These data will prevail until the next survey which will be made at the end of this decade.

Mobility and tenure

The various studies by the AASA show that school superintendents as a whole are not a highly mobile group. The latest study based on 1969–1970 data concluded that "the vast majority of superintendents confine their experience as chief administrators to about two different school districts."[10] About 71 percent were superintendents in two or fewer districts; seven out of eight served in three or fewer systems. Movement from state to state is even more limited for better than nine out of ten complete their administrative career in a single state. Superintendents in large districts are more likely to move across state borders than those in small districts. Almost two-thirds of the administrators in districts of 100,000 or more pupils served in two or more states.

The length of time devoted to the superintendency in a given district is somewhere between 4.5 and 6.5 years depending upon whether the median or mean is taken as the indicator of tenure. The total years as superintendent in the sample studied in 1969–1970 ranged from 9.3 to 11.6 years depending upon whether the median or mean is used as the indicator.[11]

The length of the contract period varies throughout the United States. The smaller the school district enrollment the greater the likelihood that the superintendent's contract will be of

[10]Stephen J. Knezevich, ed., *The American School Superintendency, An AASA Research Study*, Arlington, Va.: American Association of School Administrators, 1971, pp. 39–41.
[11]Ibid., p. 33.

only one-year duration. In contrast, districts with 25,000 or more enrolled are more likely to have contracts of four or more years than those of shorter duration. Over half of the superintendents in the nation as a whole had contracts for two years or less. In 1931–1932, one- or two-year appointments were found in 50.1 percent of the urban superintendencies.

Data based on the 1965–1966 school year indicate that the turnover was such that 15 percent of those in positions as local school district superintendents during 1965–1966 were not in these positions at the start of 1966–1967 school year. These data were based on a study conducted by the writer for the AASA Committee for the Advancement of School Administration.

Death of a superintendent is an unusual occurrence in any given year. The majority of states reported no local school district superintendent had died; one state reported five superintendents had died. About 2.2 percent of the superintendents retired from their positions at the end of the 1965–1966 school year. The discharge rate for superintendents was less than 1 percent, about the same as those who die in office. The annual discharge rate would be less than 5 percent even if it were assumed that those who left the field entirely did so because of fear of discharge or actual pressure to leave the superintendency.

An expression of the demand for new superintendents can be seen in the number of persons who are new to the superintendency, that is, the number who have had no experience in the superintendency before assuming the present position. Based on a sample of approximately two-thirds of the states, roughly 6 percent of the persons in the superintendency in 1966–1967 were new to the position.

Entry into administration

Superintendents were about 23 years of age when they were appointed to their first full-time position in education. Almost 96 percent in 1969–1970 had classroom teaching experience, a far higher percent than the 74 percent of the superintendents in 1921–1922 who indicated classroom teaching experience. "The typical superintendent in 1969–1970 was more likely to have started service as a secondary school teacher."[12] No one discipline can be called a breeding ground for superintendents, although teaching courses in such fields as the natural sciences, social studies, or mathematics seem to be the most popular among the future administrators. Once again the myth that the typical superintendent was an ex-physical education teacher was exploded completely. The myth persists even though only one in eight taught courses in health or physical education. On the other hand over 70 percent of the superintendents reported being coaches of some kind of athletic teams as part of their extra-curricular responsibilities. About 29 percent were class advisors and about 10 percent directors of dramatics.

The typical administrator-to-be spent between six and seven and a half years in the classroom before entry into administration. A higher percent reported over 15 years of teaching than those who had no direct classroom experience. As yet there are no indications that a move directly from university preparation into practical administration has met with much success.

The superintendent-to-be was about 29 to 30 years old when appointed to his first administrative position. The entry position into administration was most likely to be the principalship (as-

[12]Ibid., pp. 24–25.

sistant principal or principal); almost 71 percent used this as the springboard position. Ages 25 to 34 seem to be pivotal, for over two-thirds became administrators or supervisors during these periods in life. Only one in eight started as an administrator before age 25. Less than 20 percent of the superintendents entered administration at age 35 or older. The probabilities of becoming a superintendent diminished rapidly if the person entered administration at age 40 or older. The greater demands for more extensive preparation prior to entry into administration may delay entry ages in future years.

The first superintendency, for the sample collected in 1969–1970, came about seven years after the first administrative or supervisory position, that is, about 13 years after being made a classroom teacher. The actual age at appointment to the superintendency was about 36 or 37 years. This is a little older than that reported in previous studies. Less than 5 percent were made superintendents at age 50 or older.

OTHER PERSONAL CHARACTERISTICS

The superintendency is a man's world; almost 99 percent of superintendents are men. They still come from rural and small city backgrounds; only about 14 percent come from the larger cities or their suburbs. The percent from the cities is larger than before, and half of the superintendents in districts with enrollments of 100,000 came from cities of 100,000 or more total population.

The median age of the superintendent in 1969–1970 was 48 years. This is younger than the median of 49 in 1950–1951 and the 51.8 in 1958–1959. The trend toward increases in age levels since the 43 years reported in

1921–1922 appears to have been broken. Even in the large school districts (roughly 25,000 or more enrolled) where the median age was 56 years, there are indications that younger persons are being selected. Thus as late as 1958–1959 there were no big city superintendents under the age of 40, whereas in 1969–1970 3.6 percent were under 40.

Almost 80 percent of the superintendencies in 1969–1970 were in districts with enrollments of less than 3,000. Only 1.2 percent of the districts enrolled 25,000 or more pupils, being a total of only 183 districts. There is evidence that districts enrolling less than 300 will disappear in the near future.

Professional preparation

In 1922 only about 35 percent of the urban school superintendents had earned a master's degree or a doctorate; in other words, about 65 percent had attained only a bachelor's degree or less. At that time about 13 percent had no degree. At the other extreme 2.9 percent had earned doctorates.

Dramatic changes in professional preparation were evident about 50 years later. The typical superintendent had at least a master's degree in 1969–1970. The following distribution of degrees prevailed in 1969–1970: Bachelor's degree, 2.1 percent; Master's degree, 55.1 percent; Specialist degree, 13.4 percent; and Doctor's degree, 29.2 percent.[13] There were ten times as many with a doctorate in 1969–1970 than there were in 1921–1922. For the first time additional work beyond the doctorate was recorded, with 6.1 percent in that category. The emphasis on the earned doctorate was particularly evident in the large school systems.

[13]Ibid., pp. 43–45.

Thus in 1969–1970 almost 65 percent of the superintendents in systems with 25,000 or more enrolled had earned doctorates. What's more, almost seven out of eight in districts with 100,000 or more pupils held a doctorate! The larger the system the more likely it is that the superintendent has an earned doctor's degree. The initial AASA study of the American School Superintendency published in 1923 made an observation that was prophetic in nature for it is borne out by subsequent studies:

While more than average training does not guarantee the superintendent's employment in the larger and hence in the more remunerative positions, still it is an important factor in the equipment of those who occupy the higher positions, one which contributes to their success and one which is largely taken into account in their employment. The superintendent, therefore, who is anxious to secure promotion will make sure that his training is at least equal to the median amount which is found in the city group to which he wishes appointment.[14]

[14]National Education Association, Department of Superintendence, *The Status of the*

FIGURE 15–1

Important steps in the professional development of superintendents.

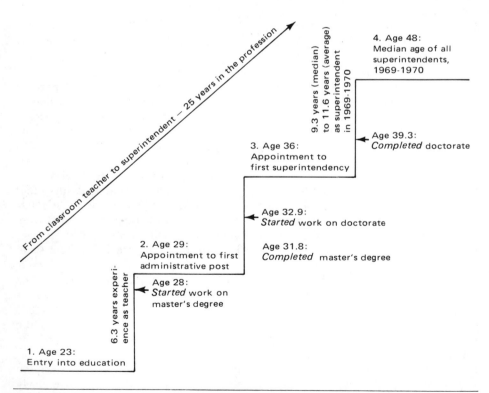

Source: S. J. Knezevich, ed., *The American School Superintendency, An AASA Research Study,* Arlington, Va.: The American Association of School Administrators, 1971, p. 47.

Announcements of superintendency vacancy increasingly declare: "doctorate preferred." The writer predicts that by the end of this decade an earned doctorate may be the minimum acceptable preparation for the school superintendency in most large school districts. In the 1980s the superintendency will become a field of post-doctoral specialization.

The movement of a typical superintendent from classroom teacher to his present job during the first 25 years of his career is depicted in Figure 15–1. Note that master's degree work wasn't started until age 28. Keep in mind that this was the generation whose careers were interrupted by first World War II and then the Korean War. Doctoral work was started by these superintendents while still in their early 30s. The typical investment in education by those completing a doctorate was about $10,000. Present prospective superintendents will have to invest even greater amounts.

The typical superintendent spends more than 55 hours per week on his position. This includes three or more evenings a week, two or more Saturdays a month, and at least one Sunday a month on the job.

Certification requirements

Certification requirements for superintendents are a post-World War II phenomenon, by and large. The standards for certificate holders vary from state to state but are based on increasingly higher professional preparation standards in each passing decade. As late as 1966 four states required the equivalent of a bachelor's degree. In 1970

only one state requiring a certificate for superintendents did not demand at least a master's degree or its equivalent. These data are summarized in Table 15–2.

Only Florida, Michigan, and the District of Columbia issue no certificates for superintendents. In contrast, some states have two or more certificate levels.

Professional preparation is only one requirement for certification as superintendent. Some states specify that the experience shall be in education. Others declare it must be in teaching. Still others allow it in teaching or in administration. A few demand experience in teaching plus additional years in administration. In some cases experience as a principal is necessary for a superintendency certificate. In 1953 and again in 1970, five years of experience was the most common requirement for certification as superintendent; three years was the next most common. Experience requirements have not changed as dramatically as those for professional preparation.

Typically the initial certificate as superintendent is valid for five years, three years, or life, in that order. Certificates after the initial one are valid for life in most states. The renewed certificate was valid for life, for five years, or for ten years, in that order.

There was considerable discussion of the competency-based approach to administrator certification in the 1970s. Thus far it is easier to talk about it than to translate it into actual operation. The competency-based certification issues may be resolved by the end of this decade.

Trends in certification requirements for superintendents clearly indicate that higher professional preparation standards are being incorporated into laws or board of education regulations

Superintendent, First Yearbook, Arlington, Va.: American Association of School Administrators, 1923, p. 20.

in most states. The superintendency is a demanding position, and an individual without adequate professional preparation and/or experience is not likely to enjoy a high degree of success. The answer to improving the quality of school administration in public education is to upgrade the quality of preparation programs and to increase the period of preparation. As the professional preparation re- quirement for the superintendency in- creases to six years or beyond, an internship program will be necessary to provide practical administrative experience. It is doubtful whether there is any advantage to employing persons ignorant of education or its administration, as has been suggested by those who argue for selecting school administrators from persons trained in other endeavors.

TABLE 15–2

PROFESSIONAL PREPARATION REQUIREMENTS FOR CERTIFICATION OF SUPERINTENDENTS, 1972

State or territory	Years of preparation	State or territory	Years of preparation
Alabama	5[a]	Montana	5
Alaska	5	Nebraska	5
Arizona	6[b]	Nevada	5 + 15 hrs.[d]
Arkansas	6	New Hampshire	6
California	7	New Jersey	5
Colorado	6	New Mexico	5
Connecticut	6	New York	6
Delaware	6	North Carolina	5
District of Columbia	5, NC[c]	North Dakota	5
Florida	NC	Ohio	6
Georgia	5	Oklahoma	5
Hawaii	5 + 20 hrs.[d]	Oregon	6
Idaho	5	Pennsylvania	7[e]
Illinois	6	Puerto Rico	5
Indiana	6	Rhode Island	5
Iowa	6	South Carolina	6
Kansas	6	South Dakota	5
Kentucky	6	Tennessee	5
Louisiana	5	Texas	6
Maine	5	Utah	6
Maryland	6	Vermont	5
Massachusetts	4 + 15 hrs.	Virginia	6
Michigan	NC	Washington	6
Minnesota	5 +	West Virginia	6
Mississippi	5	Wisconsin	5
Missouri	6	Wyoming	5 + 15 hrs.[d]

[a] 5 years is a master's degree or at least a bachelor's degree plus 30 hours.
[b] 6 years is a master's degree plus 30 hours or a specialist degree.
[c] NC = No certificates for superintendents issued. District of Columbia issues no administrator's certificate but requires a master's degree for all position holders.
[d] Designates a master's degree plus additional hours of study beyond that degree.
[e] Designates a doctorate or 70 semester hours of work including at least a master's degree.

CHALLENGES OF THE SUPERINTENDENCY TODAY

The superintendency is demanding, complex, and dynamic. Professional preparation is the initial step followed by participation in programs of continuing professional development, commonly referred to as in-service programs. Thus, the AASA recommended that "no school superintendent will serve his school district well who does not allocate a minimum of 6 hours a week to his professional improvement. . . . Professional growth is a part of his regular job. Time allocated for this purpose should be rigorously protected and used to the best possible advantage."[15]

Pressures that stem from the knowledge explosion, the technological revolution, and the social and economic ferment in contemporary society make imperative not only quality preservice education for the successful administrator but also the generation of a new vehicle dedicated to the continuing professional development of practicing school administrators.

During 1967 and 1968 an operational model for the AASA National Academy for School Executives was developed specifically to serve as a vehicle to respond promptly to pressing needs and to provide national leadership for continuing professional education of practicing school administrators.

A planning investment of over $100-000 culminated in the development of an operational model for an AASA National Academy for School Executives that already has had a significant impact on school administrators. It is the first time that a well-defined multidimensional and operationally feasible national in-service institution for school administrators has been translated into an action plan. Its problem-focus coupled with quick response capabilities helped to ensure the relevance of programs to meet the needs of career administrators. The multidimensional design concept permits the Academy to help school administrators develop new competencies through participation in short-term seminars now and longer term resident centers in the future. The affiliation of the Academy with AASA provides it with a national base denied to other agencies. This relationship offers stability, acceptability, and the established prestige of the Association.

The superintendency is a cluster of administrative responsibilities. It is no longer a one-person operation. It needs to be conceived more in terms of a function in the operation of educational institutions than in terms of a single person. This led to the development of an administrative team to help the superintendency meet the demands placed upon the educational institutions.

The superintendency is the same in principle in a small school district as in a large; its duties are the same in a metropolitan area as in a rural community.[16] In a system with a limited number of pupils and professional personnel, the superintendent of schools performs the functions of personnel officer, director of instruction, business manager, and public relations director, as well as of general administrator. In a large school district the need for specialized assistants stems from the complexity and size of tasks to be performed rather than from a difference in the principles of administration. When there is too much work

---

[15]American Association of School Administrators, *Inservice Programs for a School Administrator,* Washington, D.C.: The Association, 1966.

[16]American Association of School Administrators, *The American School Superintendency,* Thirtieth Yearbook, Washington, D.C.: The Association, 1952, p. 66.

for one full-time administrator to handle effectively, the responsibilities must be divided among members of the administrative team.

Although the superintendency is the same in principle in whatever size school district, the manner in which the superintendent executes his responsibilities in a large district is distinctly different from what happens in a small district. In a small school district, the superintendent comes to know in a face-to-face relation most members of his administrative and supervisory staff. From such contact he gains considerable information about how the system is operating and where incipient trouble spots may be. In a large and complex district it is physically impossible for him to have frequent personal contacts with the large professional staff. He must instead depend upon oral and written reports from members of the administrative team. Knowing what kind of information an executive officer needs to gauge progress and problems within a school district and who is best qualified to supply it is a significant challenge to the superintendent in the large urban district.

Section II:
The administrative team

EVOLUTION OF THE ADMINISTRATIVE TEAM

The first step toward improving the superintendent's effectiveness as chief executive officer of the board of education was to relieve him of such non-administrative activities as teaching and coaching. The second was to provide him with clerical and other non-professional assistants to handle the technical and mechanical chores of administration. The third and most re-

cent step was to permit him to develop a staff of professional assistants to constitute the administrative team. Like the superintendency itself, the concept of the administrative or superintendency team was long opposed.

Most boards sense when clerical and other nonprofessional employees must be added to perform the mountain of mechanical and technical chores of administration. But even when they approve addition of an administrative assistant, coordinator, or supervisor, they remain unsure as to whether they are contributing to a situation where there may be "too many chiefs and not enough Indians."

Team administration has emerged as the modern pattern, nonetheless, but in a grossly understaffed and overworked form. Whenever there is a financial crunch and the school budget must be slashed, these are among the first positions to be eliminated to further exacerbate the problem of creating a stable effective team. The number of school administration personnel is far below adequacy standards applied to effective management of business, industry, or government. As M. J. Rathbone, former board chairman of Standard Oil Corporation, put it: "Investment for modernizing plant and equipment is often wasted unless there is a corresponding investment in managerial and technical talent to run it." The typical school central-office administrative staff of today is barely adequate (in size) to keep the system operating efficiently and much less than adequate to cope with social issues, implement promising practices, and engage in professional negotiation. The size of the administrative teams in most school systems should be doubled or trebled. Some school boards demonstrate increasing concern for the problem, but most remain insensitive or lack the courage to allocate additional resources for expanding the superintendent's staff. Administrative leadership deserves recognition as one of the chief assets of the educational organization rather than as an overhead expense. The multiplier effect of administrative leadership at the superintendency level is impressive: One person at the first, second, or third echelon can influence 1,000 teachers and at least 20,000 students. If the systems approach to educational administration is to be implemented, the expansion of the central-office staff will have to be in terms of hiring new specialists rather than merely duplicating existing personnel.

THE TEAM CONCEPT

A team is a unit; it is more than a collection of individuals with offices at a single location. To function effectively it demands interplay and communication among members and usually with well defined roles and expectations for each. A team may be described in terms of its functions, structure, or individual personalities. The rationale behind the team concept emerged when it became apparent that one person was unable to do all things that are demanded in multipurpose and socially sensitive institutions; nor is it possible for a single individual to be in several places at the same time. Complexity and size of today's schools gave birth to and made the team approach to administration a necessity at the building and district-wide level.

There are relatively few studies or well developed analyses of the concept of the administrative team for educational institutions. From an organizational and structural point of view bureaucracy gives form to the team. Almost all modern administra-

tive organizations are bureaucratically organized. Weber viewed a bureaucratic organization as being necessary to maximize rational decision making and administrative efficiency. Bureaucracy, in the best sense of the term, is the most efficient form of administrative organization. It provides the structural and organizational dimensions for a team operation. The established relationships are usually translated into what is known as the organizational chart.

The structural pattern for the administrative team is not new; Weber's theory of bureaucracy provided the conceptual base some 50 years ago. It called for the very obvious division of labor in administration and the delegation of authority for the execution of certain functions. A chart was drawn to allegedly portray how members of the administrative team were related to each other. It failed to show how interrelationships were operationalized, the importance of communication, or the political and social forces that inevitably come into play where people are involved. The impersonality of the bureaucratic structure and the failure to recognize the human side of the enterprise generated a variety of problems in large industrial as well as educational operations. The team, therefore, must be viewed from the human relations as well as the structural point of view. This is a concern for the kinds of people as well as types of position created to insure that the organization will fulfill its reason for being, that is, its primary objectives. The unifying factor is the personal commitment of each team member to the objectives of the organization.

The administrative team can be perceived from the point of view of differentiated staffing as applied to administration rather than teaching. It is a differentiation that is based on a specialization of talents as well as authority as suggested in Weber's theory of bureaucracy. Differentiation may be made through an analysis of the roles to be performed. This in turn may reveal the diversity of talents or competencies required to achieve the many organizational goals. The team is held together by mutual respect and interdependency rather than authority of the captain or coach. In the MBO/R (management-by-objectives-and-results) approach a team or a task force may be created to meet job targets or objectives rather than for the execution of functions or activities that may or may not be focused on institutional outcomes. This approach leads to results-oriented administrative appraisal as well as a results-oriented position description system.

Differences in backgrounds, experiences, and preparation should be welcomed on the team rather than resisted. In the evolution of the superintendency as a cluster of leadership positions, the first addition was, by and large, in the form of a generalist with a background similar to that of the superintendent. The same thing can be said for the principalship. There was a desire to achieve interchangeability of individual team members, that is, everyone was prepared to handle anyone else's responsibilities. It was assumed in designing the administrative team that homogeneous administrative background was essential. In other words, it is the conception of the administratives team as a cluster of people trained in pretty much the same way, to do pretty much the same thing, and to complete assignments in pretty much the same fashion. You expanded a team by replication, that is, by adding more of the same kinds of units. This approach has serious limits and will not yield

effective team operations. A baseball team is not a cluster of players where everyone is able to pitch effectively but few can field well or hit consistently. Likewise no one would bet on a football team composed of eleven quarterbacks. It is the differentiation of roles that creates the effective team. Only through differentiation with excellence in diverse talent is the team able to achieve its goal of winning and the eventual championship.

Similar arguments could be used to visualize the administrative team as a picture of diverse specialists rather than similar generalists. It is not necessary for everyone to be able to teach, to prepare budgets with consummate skill, or to manage change. It is imperative for the leader of the administrative team to sense, to know, to articulate the special qualities needed by each member of his team to move toward a more productive educational organization. There is no reason why a data processing specialist must have ten years of classroom experience simply because extended classroom contact is important to those who are assigned the responsibilities for identifying, implementing, and managing new instructional strategies or innovative curricular experiences. The fundamental structure of the administrative team should be based on the clustering of specialists who are not interchangeable units and who do not reflect homogeneity in preparation, experience, or expertise.

HUMAN SIDE OF THE TEAM

Previous reference was made to the school as a social organization. It is a system where human behavior becomes socially organized—that is, there are observed regularities in the behavior of people that are influenced by the social conditions and constraints in which they find themselves. The administrative team is made up of people; it is a social unit. This is what is meant by the human side in contrast to the purely positional dimension.

The team is a living organism that is created, experiences growing pains, suffers maladjustments, and may even disappear through merger or replacement by another team. The organizational life thrives or dies with its communication system. Weber missed most of this. The more complex the team the more vital becomes the concern for the flow of information that influences prudent decision making among the variety of coordinated administrators. Practically all wrong decisions in history from Darius' attack on Marathon to the birth of the Edsel can be traced in large part to inefficient or inadequately processed knowledge among individuals. Boners in school administration happen for the same reason.

Each team has a personality. It may reflect the impact of a dominant chief executive, the uncertainties of a community in ferment, or simple individual hangups. To a large extent a chief executive is only as good as his subordinates. The caliber and personalities of professionals selected for key positions are as important as the total number of positions available. Administrative assistants can make the general superintendent look good or jeopardize his position. Often members of the leadership team are the unsung or unpublicized heroes. On the other hand, more than one ex-superintendent can tell the story of how his demise was hastened by some key assistants who failed to give 100 percent support and commensurate efforts.

Team skills don't come naturally. The team must be developed and re-

sources should be allocated for such functions. In some large corporations as much as 20 percent of a manager's time may be devoted to further training to sharpen team skills as well as to gain individual competencies.

RESEARCH ON THE ADMINISTRATIVE TEAM

What many are referring to as the "administrative revolution" refers in large measure to the emergence of professional managers and also to the use of team administration, that is, establishment of cooperative efforts among a variety of administrative specialists. The traditional design for an administrative team is based on a cluster of similarly trained generalists placed in positions that enable the superintendent to amplify his efforts. A 1971 AASA publication viewed the team as a "cluster of supportive administrative positions . . . created to enable the superintendent to amplify his efforts" and this leadership team was "composed of administrative specialists who hold the titles of deputy, associate, assistant and district, or area superintendent."[17] In relatively fewer instances, the team concept embraced personnel at lower levels such as supervisors, directors, and coordinators.

Often formal designation of membership on the administrative team was appointment to the superintendent's cabinet. The cabinet is an advisory body to the superintendent as well as a strategy planning group. It may be used as a decision making body as well. Principals were included as members of the administrative team, as witnessed by their

[17]American Association of School Executives, *Profiles of the Administrative Team*, Arlington, Va.: The Association, 1971, p. 11.

involvement as formal participants in the "superintendent's cabinet," in the smaller school systems only. There were a few large systems where principals were represented in the cabinet. The AASA study revealed that approximately 44 percent of the school systems included those holding the rank of assistant superintendent or above within the superintendent's cabinet.[18] The heads of the four educational functions typically included within "the administrative team," called the superintendent's cabinet, were the heads of instructional activities, business administration, pupil services, and staff personnel. Public relations and general administration were included less frequently than any of the above four. It is an interesting note that the research conducted by the Educational Research Service (ERS) for AASA demonstrated that only a limited number of systems considered the principal and the heads of such newer school district functions as research, federal projects, negotiations, intercultural education, and data processing to be members of the administrative cabinet. When this group was involved it was on a very limited basis. Data analysis revealed that the three functions of instruction, business administration, and general administration tended to hold higher rank positions on the leadership team than other functions such as staff personnel, public relations, and pupil services.

The larger the district the larger the size of the superintendent's cabinet. Membership of the cabinet ranges from 2 to 28, but the median size for districts of various enrollment groups is narrower from a low of 5 to a high of 12.

[18]Ibid., p. 19.

The AASA study likewise reported that in the last five years the factors that had the greatest impact upon the size of the central-office staff (which more often than not is conceptualized as the administrative team), have been the increases in the educational services for all pupils. People are demanding more. The second most influential factor in the expansion of the central office staff was the increase in compensatory programs. The third was larger school enrollments due to population growth, and the fourth was changes in organizational structure. Decreases in the size of central staffs during the last five years, according to the AASA study, have been rare among the school systems included within their research.

OPERATIONAL IMPACT OF THE ADMINISTRATIVE TEAM

Adding more people to the staff is only one dimension of strengthening the administrative team. The caliber of professionals selected for key central-office positions at the second or third echelon is at least as important as the number of positions. Administrative assistants can help the general superintendent or jeopardize his position. The general superintendent maximizes his leadership potential by selecting the right combination of administrative personnel; conversely, his best efforts cannot improve the administration if his assistants are without loyalty or the necessary qualifications.

The superintendency has been called an "impossible" position. It will remain so if practices inconsistent with realities are followed, such as operating with fewer administrative posts than are warranted or failing to staff key positions with qualified personnel. If the prime mission of the administrator is to cope with change, then the size of the central-office staff should be roughly proportional to the rate of innovation rather than to the number of pupils or teachers. A rapidly expanding and radically changing school district needs more administrators than a less lively one of similar size. If the general superintendent is to be held responsible for an effective and unified administration in a dynamic environment, he must be free to determine who shall occupy key administrative posts. This means he should not be restricted by poor administrative choices made prior to his coming to the district.

This leads to a most controversial point: When a superintendent of schools is dismissed, his key administrative assistants must be prepared to resign. A board that fires its superintendent implies dissatisfaction with the entire administrative team and not simply with the captain. One person cannot be held responsible for all the problems in a complex institution. "Fire me, fire my assistants" may sound brutal, but it is not unrealistic. Tenure laws that protect the assistant, associate, or deputy superintendent, but not the superintendent, are inconsistent with the realities of administration in complex educational institutions.

Tying the security of key administrative personnel to the fate of the superintendent yields benefits to the newly appointed executive. He gains freedom to fill key administrative posts and to develop a unified team. He can reappoint some of the incumbents if evaluation shows this would benefit the new team. He can accept or decline resignations and make appointments. Loyalty is due him and not a predecessor. Failure to support the superintendent by not keeping him fully informed, by slowing down the decision process, or by covertly planting doubt in the minds of his superiors as to his effectiveness becomes a threat to the administrative assistants as well as to the chief executive. If this is hard on administrative assistants, existing practices are hard on the superintendent.

The proposed method is similar to what is practiced at the national level in the executive branch of government. The cabinet resigns when the President goes out of office for any reason. The new President either accepts the resignation and appoints a new official or asks the incumbent to remain.

This controversial aspect of the superintendent's relation to his staff emphasizes the importance of the hierarchy in school administration. It suggests that prospective superintendents should study carefully the entire administrative organization of the system to ascertain the most appropriate team configuration. It forces careful analysis of the kinds of talents, experiences, or personal qualities that are most likely to produce effective administration. An administrative staff should help solve rather than contribute to the problems of the superintendent.

The composition of the administrative team is one of the most important decisions a new superintendent makes. When a board fires a superintendent, it implies dissatisfaction with his entire staff, including his key administrative assistants. When a board hires a new superintendent, it must allow him to select the kinds of people who are best suited by temperament and qualified by preparation and experience to work with him.

NEW DESIGNS FOR THE ADMINISTRATIVE TEAM

We are only beginning to recognize the ramifications of the concept called administrative team in the administration and operation of educational institutions. The administrative team should not be confined to the central-office staff only. This, for all practical purposes, effectively excludes principals as important building level personnel from regular and formal inputs at the superintendent's cabinet meetings. It is imperative that those who have close, continuing and daily contact with teachers and students be considered an integral part of the administrative team. This is true in negotiations, personnel selection and evaluation, and community relations. Administrators at the central office are important, but the traditional conceptualizations are much too limited to meet present day demands on schools.

Secondly, the emphasis in the creation of the administration team should be on results to be achieved. Instruction is the main thrust and an all-pervasive one. Everything that is done in schools seeks to promote learning as an activity viewed from the pupil's side, and instruction as an activity viewed from the teacher's side. A variety of specializations have been created to facilitate the improvement of learning and instruction. Instruction will always be a central focus in the formation of the administrative team. New concerns such as teacher militancy, student demands, conflict management, emerging technologies, urbanization, and organization to accept and manage change are parts of the superintendent's responsibilities. The administrative specialists in these areas—individuals who are responsible for achieving outcomes in these areas—must be given a voice on today's educational administration team.

There is an art to being number two in an administrative hierarchy: It is a challenge to ensure that the team doesn't end up with too many tigers and not enough lions. Naturalists have wondered what would happen if animals that are geographically separated and recognized as powerful in their own right would meet. Who would win if a powerful tiger were placed in the same cage as a lion of similar age, sex, strength, and ferocity? The answer is that there would be one dead lion. The tiger is much quicker, much more powerful than the lion. But what would happen if ten lions were put in the same cage with ten tigers of equal capability? There would be ten dead tigers. Tigers are individualists; they care nothing about a fellow tiger. In contrast, lions live with other lions (in a group called a pride). They work as a team to destroy tigers one by one.

There are many prima donnas, individuals of considerable intellectual power and ability who perform well by themselves but manage to foul up the operation of the team. It is a challenge for the team leader, the superintendent, to find the right combination of members whose special abilities will contribute to an effectively operating social and professional organization. If you look only for the best possible individual, you may end up with too many tigers and not enough lions and find yourself in a situation where proud personalities are going their separate ways without concern for others or the organization.

It can be argued that the racial and ethnic backgrounds of the community served or personnel employed should be recognized in the formation of the administrative team. This implies selection of team members in terms of their ability to communicate with a segment of the community or employed personnel. This is over and above the specialization of the team members.

Developing the team to make sure that administrative staff is on the cutting edge rather than the tattered, dragging end is a challenge as well. The needs of the organization will vary and therefore, a new team configuration must emerge. It is incumbent upon administrators to remain sensitive to forces within and outside the system that call for a fundamental change in the team's capabilities. Form follows function. The team, its size, and its form should be influenced by functions to be performed.

TITLES FOR TEAM MEMBERS

Members of the administrative team may include personnel carrying such titles as associate or assistant superintendent, director, supervisor, coordinator, and consultant, who are attached to the superintendent's office. Individuals in such posts are charged with responsibilities that are system-wide in scope but limited in range within the institution. Thus, the supervisor of music has functions that are system-wide in scope but confined to music; the assistant superintendent in charge of elementary education is responsible for elementary education only, but in all parts of the system. The central-office staff does not include itinerant teachers of art who are called erroneously "art supervisors" but actually teach in several buildings rather than supervise in any one.

When the work of the superintendent is divided among the central-office staff, the authority to accomplish tasks must be delegated. Authority should follow placement of responsibility. It was explained in Chapter 2

that delegation involves the assignment of duties by an executive to subordinates; the granting of permission or authority to make commitments, utilize resources, and determine other actions necessary to perform delegated duties; and the creation of an obligation on the part of each subordinate to the executive for satisfactory performance of duties. The larger the school system, the greater the series of redelegations to the point where the function can be performed without further assistance. Delegation does not relieve the chief executive of responsibility; it merely allows him to accomplish in a systematic way tasks for which he is responsible. In assigning responsibility and authority, the superintendent must decide how tasks of the organization are to be apportioned among his administrative co-workers. It is through delegation of authority and responsibilities that the central-office administrative and supervisory staff of a school system functions effectively.

There is a lack of research that specifies at what point in a school district's growth it becomes necessary and practical to establish or expand the administrative team. Practices vary considerably. The laws of some states call for the establishment of assistant administrative and supervisory positions when there are 30 or more teachers in a system, others when there are 50 or more, and others when there are 100 or more. Specialized positions vary with the characteristics of the system; these are discussed later in this chapter. It is useful here to review some of the basic concepts of organization developed in Chapter 2 and to apply them to central-office personnel.

The need for an assistant or a deputy superintendent is indicated by the number of individuals reporting *directly* to the superintendent of the school system. In other words, when the span of supervision of the superintendent becomes so large that he is unable to act in an effective manner, a subordinate position is needed. Effective span of supervision is related to such factors as:

1. Time available for supervision.
2. Mental capacity and personal adaptability of the executive responsible for supervision.
3. Complexity of the situation being supervised.
4. Other duties of the executive.
5. Stability of the operation.
6. Capability and experience of the individuals appointed to subordinate positions.

Whether the addition of new types of administrators will create a pyramidal or a flat organization is related to the number of executives reporting to another. A tall organization (where there are many administrative levels between principal's and superintendent's position) will result if each executive has relatively few others to supervise. A flat organization (where there are relatively few administrative levels between principal and superintendent) will result if each executive has a large number of others to supervise. The flat organizational structure is most likely to prove successful when there is a high degree of competence among subordinate executives as well as a relatively small turnover among individuals in the organization. A tall organizational structure, which is often inevitable in very large school systems, is subject to communication problems resulting from the distant relations between principals and the superintendent.

The line-and-staff concept has some value in determining types of central-office personnel needed in the system. A position subordinate to the superintendency and carrying authority to act in its own right (rather than in the name of the superintendent) in relation to positions subordinate to it, is a line position. For example, in a district with a large number of elementary schools, the superintendent might appoint an assistant superintendent in charge of elementary schools. The assistant superintendent would have authority over the principals of the elementary schools, and they would report to him rather than to the general superintendent.

A position subordinate to the superintendency but carrying authority to act only in a service capacity, is a staff position. For example, the director of personnel has no authority over assistant superintendents or principals, but he does perform the services of locating potential staff members and managing details of transfer, salary payment, and welfare benefits for the teaching staff. It is a service department for the system as a whole. Another example of a staff position is the administrative assistant to the superintendent, who performs a variety of chores, always in the name of the superintendent, and never under authority that he possesses because of his position in the operating hierarchy.

Functions of an advisory nature can be performed by personnel in staff or in line positions. Thus, an administrative cabinet composed of principals and/or central-office staff people might advise the superintendent on administrative policies. There is considerable question about the value of differentiating between staff and line on anything but a very broad basis. Considering a post in terms of its level in the administrative hierarchy is of greater significance.

The majority of professional central-office staff personnel are supervisors or consultants (an arrangement that appears to be gaining in popularity). These include elementary school supervisors and secondary school special-subject supervisors (for instance, in art, music, physical education). Individuals in these posts are actually supervising activities of personnel in attendance centers and should not be confused with itinerant teachers in certain special subjects. Special problems of supervision in public education will be reviewed in the last portion of this chapter.

It is traditional to think of administrative positions within the superintendency as concerned with a substantive problem, such as business management, curriculum, or personnel. New positions added to the administrative hierarchy should reflect the systems approach, the demand for innovation, and the problems of relating the school district to its internal and external environments. Such positions as systems analyst, educational program development specialist, federal relations director, and staff negotiation expert are examples. Individuals assuming responsibility for these areas can carry the title of director, coordinator, assistant superintendent, associate superintendent, or administrative assistant depending upon the size and the manner in which the system is organized and operates.

The appropriate size of a central-office staff cannot be determined only on the basis of number of pupils and teachers within a district because the nature of districts varies from one part of a state to another and from one section of the nation to another. As long as districts grow at varying rates; have pupils with significantly different social, cultural, or intellectual backgrounds; and are not likely to accept innovations in the same way or at the same speed they will need different numbers and types of central-office personnel to operate effectively.

The deputy and the area superintendent

The deputy superintendent is superordinate to the assistant superintendency. It is often mistakenly believed to be a central-office staff post. The deputy superintendent accepts any responsibility delegated to him as the immediate representative of the superintendent with operating authority. He is much more than an administrative assistant and executes responsibilities under the authority granted his office. He is often assigned to coordinating activities of various assistant superintendents for specialized areas, so that the general superintendent may be free to devote time and thought to long-range problems of the system. Unlike the assistant superintendent, the deputy superintendent is not responsible for a particular division of the school system, such as elementary or secondary education. Closely related to the deputy superintendency is the area superintendency in very large school systems organized to achieve some measure of decentralization. The term "district superintendent" may be synonymous with "area superintendent," if the district is thought to be a portion of a large city school system. The area superintendent is responsible for all aspects of administration of public education within a subdivision of a district in very large and populous school systems such as those in New York and Chicago. He is responsible directly to the general superintendent of schools, who in turn is responsible to the board of education. The area superintendent is a special type of deputy superintendent working in a given geographical area.

The deputy superintendency and the area superintendency should not be confused with the position of assistant to the superintendent, sometimes referred to as the administrative assistant. Deputy and area superintendents are delegated line, or operating, responsibilities. The administrative assistant is a staff official. As indicated in Chapter 2, the staff official is an extension of the superintendent's personality and assumes those functions that the superintendent would do himself if he had the time or the specialized knowledge. Often an administrative assistant is introduced into the school system of small size to relieve the superintendent of some of his many duties. Under such conditions the administrative assistant becomes in fact an operating official, even though not designated as such; it is not unusual to find that the title does not describe the responsibility assigned to a given position. Strictly speaking, however, the administrative assistant or assistant to the superintendent is a staff rather than a line position.

The assistant superintendent

The assistant superintendency is the most common administrative subdivision. It represents the top echelon of the central-office administrative and supervisory staff. The assistant superintendent's responsibility may be assigned on the basis of (1) large divisions of educational activity, such as elementary education, secondary education, business affairs (educational resources management), professonal personnel, pupil services, special services, curriculum, school plant, or combinations of these; (2) instructional areas, such as elementary education, secondary education, curriculum, or special services concerned with instruction; or (3) auxiliary or service

functions such as business and/or school-plant services. The assistant superintendent is directly responsible to the superintendent (or to the deputy or area superintendent, if such exists).

The assistant superintendency was created as early as 1854 in New York, 1868 in St. Louis, and 1870 in Chicago.[19] The position was established after the principalship and superintendency. The first assistant superintendents were concerned with supervision and coordination of instruction in various buildings of the large system, as well as with advising principals and teachers. Friction between assistant superintendents and principals resulted. Subsequent organization considered the principal as the administrative head of the building, but subordinate to the assistant superintendent in charge of the instructional area. Early assistant superintendents rarely had much authority and depended on persuasion or the soundness of advice.

The director or coordinator

The director, or coordinator, is subordinate to the assistant superintendent, the deputy superintendent, and the area superintendent, as well as the general superintendent. The two terms are synonymous. There is considerable confusion in the use of the title "director." In some quarters the term is unpopular because it is thought to connote autocratic direction instead of leadership. Other school systems, however, use the term "director" in place of "assistant superintendent" to avoid the appearance of being overstocked with superintendents.

Because there is a need for uni-

[19]Paul R. Pierce, *The Origin and Development of the Public School Principalship*, Chicago: University of Chicago Press, 1935, pp. 90–95.

formity in terminology in identifying various echelons in the administrative organization of school systems, it is suggested that the title "director" or "coordinator" be attached to administrative positions responsible to an assistant superintendent in charge of a particular division of the school system. Thus, a director of audiovisual education would be responsible to an assistant superintendent in charge of curriculum or instructional services; a director of secondary school supervisors would be responsible to an assistant superintendent in charge of secondary education or an assistant superintendent in charge of curriculum.

The term "manager" is popular in business and industry, but is infrequently used in educational administration. The assistant superintendent in charge of business services is sometimes called the "school business manager," but there appears to be a movement, to replace this title with "assistant superintendent in charge of business services," "director of business services," or better, "educational resources manager."

Supervisory positions

In business and industry the level immediately subordinate to middle management is referred to as supervisory management. It includes the general foreman and first-line supervisors or specialized foremen. The general-foreman level is analogous to the building principal and the specialized foreman to the special-subject or process supervisor in the public school. The supervisory positions in public education are staff rather than line positions. The special problems of supervision in public education are discussed later in this chapter.

GROWTH OF THE CENTRAL-OFFICE STAFF

For almost 100 years the very large school systems have maintained a central-office staff. Expansion of this level of administration in small systems has been inhibited by community opposition. However, all signs point to increasing use of central-office staffs in the small as well as the large school districts. Small systems may depend upon the intermediate unit for such staff functions. An important area of research and concern for those interested in the study of educational administration will be the organization and operation of the central office.

There have been many reports of the expansion of central-office staffs in American schools in the 1950s. A 1959 nationwide study of 468 urban, suburban, and rural school districts reported that almost one-fourth of the central-office (district-wide) administrative posts had been newly created during the past five years.[20] About 71 percent of these districts anticipated further change in administrative organization during the next 5 years. This expansionary mood was to be sharply curtailed if not reversed when the financial crunch hit in the early 1970s. Where the 1950s and 1960s were decades of considerable growth in the size of the administrative team, the 1970s appear to be a time of retrenchment and reduction in the size of the team.

In New York City there were 2544 full-time administrators with district-wide responsibilities working under the supervision of the general superintendent. No correlation exists be-

[20]Georgette N. Manla, "Administration in Transition," *American School and University, 1960–61, 32nd ed.,* New York: Buttenheim, 1960, pp. 144–154.

tween the number of central-office administrative positions and the size of a school district in terms of enrollments or number of buildings.[21] Other factors, such as scope and depth of educational services, rate of growth, and rate of innovation implementation, evidently influence the creation of these administrative positions. The pattern of increases is shown in Table 15-3.[22] These are average figures and do not show the great variation within categories. Thus, in the 66 districts with 4 central-office administrators enrollment ranges from 100 to 29,290 and buildings from 1 to 52.

The advent of federally sponsored programs has created a host of federal-project administrators.

SUPERVISION OF INSTRUCTION

"Supervision," as used in educational circles, has a very narrow meaning. It is interpreted narrowly as being related to teaching and learning activities and hence implies instructional supervision even though the more general and unqualified term supervision is used. Instructional supervision is only one responsibility of members of

[21]Ibid.
[22]Ibid.

the administrative team. Supervision is one dimension of the general practice of administration.

Supervision, as an administrative activity, is a controlling and coordinating device. It is not an end in itself. As such it may be viewed as a strategy to stimulate others toward greater effectiveness or productivity. It incorporates such functions as overseeing operations. It may even include the performance appraisal of personnel. The added expense in terms of organizational time and money can be justified only to the extent that the institution can function more efficiently with supervision or supervisory strategies than without it.

The functions of those engaged in supervision of the performance and outcomes of others may include in-service development; direction, control, and/or stimulation of effort toward goals; observation to determine when minor adjustments must be made in on-going plans and programs; and appraisal of progress and outcome. The more controversial supervisory activities, at least in the field of education, are those related to direction, control, observation, and appraisal. Supervision has an impact on people. As such it is a leadership function, for by definition, leadership involves people as well.

TABLE 15–3

SIZE OF CENTRAL-OFFICE ADMINISTRATIVE STAFF

No. of central-office administrators	No. of school districts	Average enrollment per district	Average no. of school buildings per district
1	80	1952	6.5
2	74	2442	7.0
3	61	2973	8.4
4	66	4191	10.5
5	37	4751	12.8

Newman called direction an essential step in administration, without which virtually nothing would happen.[23] What he referred to as "direction" has been called "influencing," "stimulating," or "leadership" by others. Direction starts action and is, therefore, concerned with the manner in which an executive issues instructions to and works with subordinates. There are many in education who are offended by the term "direction" and the suggestion that someone issues instructions to another. There is a decided preference in education for softer terms such as stimulating and leading. The outcome, if not the basic strategies, is the same, namely, starting, maintaining, and improving the performance capabilities of people in an organization. Subordinates crave specific information (instructions) on what is expected of them and suggestions as to preferred modes of operation.

Effective supervisory leadership, or "good direction," is based on effective communication of operational information (instructions) and includes the following considerations, according to Newman:

1. Compliance should be reasonable. An executive must understand the capabilities and experience of the staff. He should consider whether there are sufficient resources available to fulfill the assignment.
2. The instructions should be complete. They should leave no question in the minds of those assigned responsibilities as to what should be done.
3. The instructions should be clear. Clarity is measured at the person receiving the order. It is of particular importance with written instructions. Even Napoleon, supposedly the most autocratic of men, never gave an order without explaining its purpose. Mar-

shall Foch declared "Command never yet meant obscurity!"
4. Instructions should be followed up. Instructions should be executed or countermanded.
5. Standard operating procedures or practices should prevail where applicable. They can save time and greatly lessen the volume of directions issued.[24]

Control, likewise, has an undesirable connotation that to many implies manipulation or inflexible operation. In its broadest and best sense it is a means of assuring that the organization is not straying too far off course from previously agreed upon goals. Control of organizational direction and outcomes should not be confused with control of individual behavior.

Control in the organizational context merges with direction at one point and with appraisal at another. It requires an understanding of what is to be accomplished and the quality level desired. It is achieved by means of observation and reporting. Appraisal includes in-service development of personnel supervised, allocation of special resources to those being supervised, and similar activities. Direction, control, observation, and appraisal are aspects of the supervisory responsibility of administrators that cannot be shirked. It is the over emphasis of some aspects—such as control or evaluation, or misuse of authority—that creates problems in administration.

Supervision is a means of ascertaining how well assigned or assumed responsibilities are being discharged. It occurs when one person assumes responsibility for the performance of others. In terms of the organizational framework of public education board members are supervisors of the superintendent to whom they have delegated certain functions. The superin-

[23]William H. Newman, *Administrative Action*, Englewood Cliffs, N.J.: Prentice-Hall, 1950, p. 375.

[24]Ibid., pp. 376–378.

tendent supervises all deputy, area, and assistant superintendents, principals, and so on. The principal and special instructional supervisors supervise teachers, who in turn supervise pupils in their learning.

The purposes of supervision must be understood. All too often supervision is confused with inspection to insure compliance. Many of the negative images of this important function stem from the "snoopervision" interpretation.

ORGANIZATION OF INSTRUCTIONAL SUPERVISION

Eye, Netzer, and Krey defined supervision of instruction as "that phase of school administration which focuses primarily upon the achievement of the appropriate instructional expectations of educational systems."[25]

Supervision of instruction is a historic function of the professional administrator. As more people become involved in supervision there arises the problem of how they are to be related to each other. One approach is to place all concerned with supervision of elementary and secondary schools under the direction of an assistant superintendent in charge of curriculum. This type of organization permits better articulation among elementary- and secondary-school supervisors and simplifies the management of broad problems of curriculum, such as scope and sequence of subject matter and instructional materials, as well as methods of teaching.

Another approach is to place special-subject supervisors under the direction of an assistant superintendent for elementary education and an as-

[25]G. G. Eye, L. A. Netzer, and R. D. Krey, *Supervision of Instruction*, 2nd ed., New York: Harper & Row, 1971, pp. 30–31.

sistant superintendent for secondary education. Thus, the work of elementary school supervisors is coordinated by the administrator responsible for elementary education, and the work of secondary school supervisors by the administrator responsible for secondary education. This method has lessened the probability of conflict between the principal (who also has a role in instructional supervision) and special-subject supervisors, because both are serving under the assistant superintendent in charge of a particular division of education. It can be argued that curriculum is as much a concern of an assistant superintendent for elementary or secondary education as of an assistant superintendent in charge of curriculum.

While the most appropriate organization of supervision must be decided on the basis of local factors, there is ample evidence that the activities of many supervisors should be coordinated by an assistant superintendent or director, so that all supervisors will not have to report directly to the superintendent of schools.

In a small district, with too few special-subject teachers (for music, art, etc.) to warrant special-subject supervisors, the problem may be solved by the regional educational service agency (intermediate unit). Several such districts, federated as parts of a regional educational service agency, would have sufficient special-subject teachers to justify employment of a special-subject supervisor.

At the state level the trend is clearly toward the employment of consultants who provide specialized assistance to teachers in a single school system or a group of systems. Prevailing opinion recommends that state department personnel not be used as "supervisors" to evaluate performance on the basis of a brief visit. Supervision of instruction is a local function supplemented as needed by certain intermediate-unit supervisory services; it is not a state department of education function. The role of the state department of education is one of providing consultant services for highly specialized problems that cannot be managed by local or intermediate units.

EVOLUTION OF INSTRUCTIONAL SUPERVISION

There are at least four major periods in the evolution of instructional supervision in America. In the first phase, from the colonial era to about the time of the Civil War, instructional activities were supervised by laymen such as clergymen, school trustees, and selectmen. The primary purpose was inspection of operations. One strategy used to evaluate learning outcomes produced by the teacher was quizzing pupils directly. The supervisory techniques employed were crude, highly subjective, and of questionable validity. Citizens soon recognized the ineffectiveness of lay supervision, and other alternatives were sought.

In the second phase, from the Civil War to the early part of the twentieth century, supervisory responsibility was transferred from lay people to professional and full-time officials such as state, county, and local superintendents and principals. Supervision continued to be inspectoral in nature and served primarily to ensure compliance. This image of the supervisor as inspector or evaluator of teaching performance started at this point and remains deeply ingrained in the minds of teachers today.

The third phase ranging from the early twentieth century to about 1935 saw the emphasis turn to professional study of problems of instructional supervision. Writings on supervision were limited even as late as the end of the nineteenth century. Publications on supervision began to increase markedly during the early part of the twentieth century. They contributed to the development of the concept of supervision as a means of improving instruction using the strategy of direct classroom observation of performance levels. The focus was to help the teacher overcome weaknesses. Inspection and evaluation were not abandoned but lost out to the improvement of instruction. There came into being such techniques as classroom observation followed by conferences and/or demonstrations. Such methods called for professional talents of a high degree, and primary responsibility for supervision was placed upon principals and special supervisors. The role of the county superintendent and the state department supervisory officials began to diminish during this period. Effective supervision of instruction could be provided best at the local level.

In the fourth phase, from 1935 to the present, the concept of supervision as a means of improving instruction has been broadened to include out-of-classroom activities such as programs for continuous professional development and special curriculum studies as well as methods of classroom teaching. This is discussed further under "Modern Concepts of Supervision."

Eye, Netzer, and Krey recognized five major historical periods of change in the purposes and functions of supervision as follows:

1. The period of administrative inspection, 1642 to 1875, was the period when the supervisor was literally an inspector whose functions were more judicial than executive in character. There was established at that time a forbidding relation between the supervisor and the supervised.

2. The period of efficiency orientation, 1876 to 1936.
3. The period of cooperative group effort in the improvement of instructional learning, 1937 to 1959.
4. The period of research orientation, 1960 to the present time.
5. An emerging new period for the 1970s that may include systems analysis.[26]

Development of special-subject supervision

The introduction of special subjects beyond the traditional program eventually led to the use of special supervisory personnel to supplement the activities of principals, assistant superintendents, superintendents, and other general supervisory officials. There were a few special-subject teachers at the elementary school level prior to 1850, but the general trend was not evident until later. Thus, Cincinnati had a special teacher for handwriting in 1842 and two music teachers by 1845. Music was taught in the Chicago schools as early as 1850.[27] Drawing was taught widely in the Boston schools after 1856. Chicago attempted to utilize principals and other general supervisors to oversee teaching of special subjects, but the project was abandoned in favor of special-subject supervisors. There were supervisors in drawing, handwriting, physical education, and primary instruction in Cleveland by 1873. St. Louis employed supervisors of kindergarten by 1890.[28] The situation was somewhat confused because some regular classroom teachers taught special subjects and were supervised by special-subject teachers. Sizable staffs of special-subject supervisors even in large cities are a twentieth-century development.

Responsibility for instructional

supervision is often divided among principals, department heads, and superintendents, as well as special supervisors. The supervisory functions of principals will be discussed in Chapter 16. Although the subject matter content of secondary and elementary schools differs, the functions and techniques of supervision are the same at both levels. Supervision is concerned with people, and an effective supervisor must be able to work with and stimulate individuals or groups to higher performance levels. Recent emphasis on group processes in supervision is an attempt to develop important supervisory skills. What makes people productive and effective contributors to goals of the institution is the substance of supervision.

The day of the general supervisor as an agent capable of stimulating improvement of instruction is rapidly coming to an end. Each subject area within the school curriculum is facing a knowledge explosion. It is a challenge for a special-subject teacher to keep abreast of new knowledge, concepts, and skills in his field. A special-subject supervisor must know at least as much, and preferably a great deal more, of the current thinking, concepts, and skills in the field than the teacher. Clearly it is almost impossible for a supervisor to be sufficiently expert in more than one special subject.

The supervisor of a special field or one working with certain types of pupils (elementary school, secondary school, or exceptional) will take the place of the general supervisor of elementary or of secondary education. Each school system may need one general supervisor to coordinate efforts of specialized consultants or supervisors. In this sense the general supervisor becomes a director of professional development of special supervisors rather than the person who makes fre-

---

[26]Ibid., pp. 22–29.
[27]Pierce, op. cit., pp. 105–115.
[28]Ibid., p. 106.

quent and continuing classroom visits and works individually with teachers. As Wiles put it: "The number of people with the label of general supervisor who have responsibilities for all of these functions will probably decrease. School systems are being enlarged to make possible the provision of more services to the classroom teacher. It is being recognized that more specialized assistance is needed."[29]

EMERGING CONCEPTS OF SUPERVISION

Modern instructional supervision is characterized by programs of "cooperative study enterprises such as curriculum development, in-service training courses, etc., aiming toward improvement of instruction."[30] If supervision of instruction is to improve instruction, it must deal with all components of instruction.[31] Administrators, supervisors, teachers, pupils, parents, and other citizens all have a part to play in instruction. Instruction also involves curriculum in its broadest sense. Instructional supervision thus conceived is a body of knowledge and understanding rather than merely a body of techniques used in a classroom situation.

Instructional supervision is defined as:

1. A planned program for the improvement of instruction.
2. All efforts of a designated school official toward providing leadership to teachers and other educational workers in the improvement of instruction.
3. A program of in-service education and cooperative group development.
4. The efforts to stimulate, coordinate, and guide continued growth of teachers in school, both individually and collectively.
5. Assistance in the development of a better teaching-learning situation.
6. A means of maintaining existing programs of instruction as well as improving them.[32]

A staff of instructional supervisors increases the expense of operation and complicates organizational structure and relations among individuals. In periods of financial retrenchment poorly defined supervisory positions—those whose contributions to the educational system are obscure—are among the first to be eliminated. The additional costs are justified if improvement of instruction occurs or other objectives are satisfied. If the teacher continues to view the supervisor as an inspector or "snoopervisor," only a limited amount of improvement can be anticipated. The supervisor must not only identify and record poor teaching, but must also possess the professional competence to do something about it—and in a relatively short period of time. The teacher has the responsibility of developing a professional attitude toward supervisors. Ideally, the teacher should recognize when he is not working as effectively as he might and turn to the supervisor for advice. When this type of relation is realized, it will be appropriate to change the title of the central-office staff workers available on call to teachers from supervisor to consultant.

Supervisors have the task (however

[29]Kimball Wiles, *Supervision for Better Schools*, 3rd ed., Englewood Cliffs, N.J.: Prentice-Hall, 1967, p. 305.

[30]Harold Spears, *Improving the Supervision of Instruction*, Englewood Cliffs, N.J.: Prentice-Hall, 1953, p. 38.

[31]Robert C. Hammock and Ralph S. Owings, *Supervising Instruction in Secondary Schools*, New York: McGraw-Hill, 1955, p. ix.

[32]Kimball Wiles, "Supervision," in Chester W. Harris, ed., *Encyclopedia of Educational Research*, 3rd ed., New York: Macmillan, 1960, p. 1442.

distasteful) of ascertaining the effectiveness of personnel at the classroom level. A teacher who shows little promise of improvement must be reported to those responsible for the attainment of institutional objectives. Such a report could lead to the teacher's dismissal. Educational institutions exist to achieve certain goals, not to guarantee employment to any individual or group.

It is a responsibility of administration to facilitate the achievement of institutional goals. Supervisors can aid in the attainment of these goals by improving the quality of instruction. If the school system shows as little improvement with supervisors as it has without them, it is questionable whether the additional expense is warranted.

The supervisor of instruction must recognize a new role—that of a change agent—one of the many individuals responsible for introducing innovations within the school system. This suggests that the effective supervisor must be aware of promising developments, sense how a social invention can be adapted to his particular school system, and develop a series of appropriate strategies for disseminating promising and imaginative curricular and instructional practices within the school system. In dynamic educational school districts, the effectiveness of the specialized supervisory staff can be measured by the sensitivity of the instructional personnel to promising practices, the existence of a climate conducive to change rather than one that simply tolerates the necessity of some modifications, and the record of changes introduced and the proportion that persisted. The modern supervisor does more than maintain the status quo at an efficient level; he stays at the growing edge of his chosen area of specialization.

Yet another new role that may well radically alter the functions and contributions of the instructional supervisor began to emerge in the early 1970s. This is the concept of the supervisor as an educational auditor. The purpose of educational auditing is to verify teaching-learning outcomes. The emphasis on accountability has generated considerable interest in auditing of learning outcomes.[33]

SUMMARY

The American school superintendency has been in existence for almost 150 years. It became an executive position of importance to the administration of public education only after other attempts to administer public education effectively failed. The creation and growth of the position parallel the growth of urban communities. It is a position born of conflict and one that remains in a state of change. The traditional antiexecutive attitude, along with past images of the superintendent as an agent of the board of education, continue to inhibit the full development of this post.

The recognition of the superintendent of schools as the chief executive officer of the board of education is a fairly recent occurrence. The last half of the nineteenth century saw an increase in standing committees acting as executive bodies along with an increase in the number of school superintendents. This resulted in the peculiar arrangement of professional and lay executives sharing responsibilities. The failure of this approach led to the recognition of the superintendent as chief executive officer.

[33]G. G. Eye and L. A. Netzer, "Educational Auditing: From Issue to Principle," *New Directions for Education*, no. 1, Spring 1973, pp. 63–75.

Basic to effective school administration is a clear understanding of the difference between policy making and policy execution. There is a need for a specific enumeration of the superintendent's functions. The superintendent has a right to the support of his board as well as to the provision of the necessary tools and clerical assistants to accomplish his tasks. The management of disagreements between the board and the superintendent is essential for effective school operations.

The superintendent is also the professional leader of the staff. His relations to the staff are defined by the board of education. The unit type of administration is more effective than other types.

The typical superintendent in 1969–1970 was a man 48 years old who started as a classroom teacher at age 23. His first administrative position, typically a principalship post, was gained by age 29 and his first superintendency by age 36. The majority have at least a master's degree; the larger the district the more likely it is that the superintendent will have a doctorate. Certification standards for superintendents are being upgraded. More states demand six or more years of professional preparation prior to the award of a superintendent's certificate than ever before. Experience requirements for certification have not changed as much as those based on preparation. The emphasis on continuing professional development is increasing and new mechanisms such as the AASA National Academy for School Executives are in full operation.

Effective administration of public education depends upon the establishment not only of a professional superintendent of schools but also an administrative team. A team is a unit; a collection of individuals with diverse talents and differentiated roles. A team has a structure and a human side. The people in the social unit must be able to mesh their talents with diverse personalities.

The paucity of research makes it difficult to ascertain precisely at what point a need is created for the establishment of or increase in central-office staff and administrative positions. It is clear that this is related to size of faculty, complexity of educational goals, rate of growth, propensity to change, and quality desired.

Although very large school districts had assistant superintendents between 1850 and 1870, only in recent years have central-office administrative and supervisory personnel been common in most urban school districts. The growing complexity of education signaled the passing of the one-man office of school superintendent. The administrative team is now more important than ever before. It is imperative that the chief executive determine the configuration of the team and what persons are qualified to serve on it.

Division of responsibilities with other executives can result in the creation of such positions as deputy or area superintendent, to whom general administrative functions have been assigned. An assistant superintendent is often granted responsibilities of a division of the school system such as elementary education, secondary education, curriculum, or business. Immediately subordinate to the assistant superintendent are directors or coordinators of major bureaus or divisions within a given area of the school system.

Need for supervision arises whenever there is more than one administrative or nonadministrative worker in a system. Supervision entails overseeing of functions assigned as a measure of control, evaluation, and improvement. The term "supervision" in most education periodicals means instructional supervision. Supervisory tasks in the school system go beyond instructional supervision, as important as this may be.

Supervision of instruction has undergone four periods of development since colonial times. In the first period supervision was inspection for control and was performed by laymen. In the second period, from after the Civil War to around 1910, responsibility for supervision was transferred to professional workers such as principals, local superintendents, county superintendents, and state department personnel. Emphasis remained on inspection and control. In the third period, from 1910 to around 1935, supervision was conceived as a means of improving classroom work by classroom visits and observation. The fourth period, since 1935, has emphasized creative or democratic supervision of instruction, including many out-of-classroom activities such as continuous professional development programs and special curriculum studies, as well as methods of teaching in the classroom.

Although the introduction of supervisors increases the cost of operation, such additional expense is justified if improved instruction results. Classroom teachers will have reached a high degree of professional maturity when they conceive of supervisors as consultants who can help them work more effectively. Unfortunately, the continuance of the teacher's image of the supervisor as an inspector or "snoopervisor" is not conducive to such a relation.

New roles for supervisors include the change agent role and educational auditing. The verification of teaching-learning outcomes is made necessary by the increased emphasis on accountability.

QUESTIONS

1. Enumerate the conditions that stimulated the creation of the post of school superintendent. Enumerate those that inhibited its development.
2. Why are standing committees of the board in fundamental conflict with the functions of the superintendent?
3. What factors were responsible for an increase in the maturity and professional preparation of superintendents?
4. Should certification standards for the superintendent be based on no less than seven years of professional preparation? Justify your stand.
5. Why is it that the "one-man office of superintendency," is passing from the urban school scene?
6. Differentiate among the following posts on the basis of functions or responsibilities: (a) deputy superintendent, (b) director, (c) assistant superintendent, (d) supervisor.
7. Who should be on the administrative team?
8. When is it preferable to use the title director of elementary education instead of assistant superintendent in charge of elementary education?
9. Trace the evolution of the supervision of instruction.

10. Debate the following: Resolved, that supervisors of instruction shall never be permitted to evaluate teachers they supervise.

SELECTED REFERENCES

American Association of School Administrators, *School Board-Superintendent Relationships,* Thirty-fourth Yearbook, Washington, D.C.: The Association, 1956.

American Association of School Administrators, *Inservice Programs for a School Administrator,* Washington, D.C.: The Association, 1966.

Burbank, N. B., *The Superintendent of Schools,* Danville, Ill.: Interstate Printers and Publishers, 1968.

Eye, G. G. and L. A. Netzer, "Educational Auditing: From Issue to Principle," *New Directions for Education,* no. 1, Spring 1973, pp. 63–75.

Eye, G. G., L. A. Netzer, and R. D. Krey, *Supervision of Instruction,* 2nd ed., New York: Harper & Row, 1972.

Gilland, Thomas M., *The Origin and Development of the Power and Duties of the City-Superintendent,* Chicago: University of Chicago Press, 1935.

Knezevich, S. J., ed., *The American School Superintendent,* An AASA Research Study, Arlington, Va.: American Association of School Administrators, 1971.

Reller, Theodore L., *The Development of the City Superintendency of Schools in the United States,* Philadelphia: Published by the author, 1935.

Roesch, Winston L., *Statutory Basis for Administrative and Specialized Service Staffing in Local Districts,* U.S. Office of Education, Bulletin 1960, no. 1, OE 23000, Washington, D.C.: GPO, 1959.

Wiles, Kimball, "Supervision," in Chester W. Harris, ed., *Encyclopedia of Education Research,* 3rd ed., New York: Macmillan, 1960.

16

THE SCHOOL PRINCIPALSHIP: THE EXECUTIVE TEAM AT THE ATTENDANCE-CENTER LEVEL

The effectiveness of efforts expended at various levels of administration is determined finally at the attendance center. It is here where learning outcomes are in evidence. It is here that material resources are utilized and services of professional personnel are applied to promote learning. The administrative organization of any educational system must be designed to facilitate the teaching-learning process at the building level. The principal is the chief executive officer or administrator of the attendance center and influences to a considerable extent what occurs at this level. He likewise does not act alone; the administrative team concept applies here as well as at the system-wide level.

In the beginning there were single-room schools, where pupils of different maturity levels were taught by one teacher. The multiroom school attendance center and where a single grade level, or class, of pupils is instructed by the individual teacher came much later. Today very few one-room school attendance centers remain. The size and pattern of the attendance center have changed in response to such influences as the upward or downward extension of educational opportunities provided for elementary and secondary school pupils.

Data on the number of principals are imprecise and different sources provide different estimates. Thus, the United States Office of Education estimated that there were 85,507 principals and assistant principals in the public schools in 1967–1968. This is substantially above the 67,250 reported in 1961–1962. The National Association of Secondary Principals estimates that in the mid-1960s there were about 24,000 senior high principals and 7,000 junior high principals. The National Association of Elementary School Principals refused to give a specific number but estimated that around 1968 there were 45,000 to 50,000 persons in positions with functions similar to those called elementary principals. The estimates of the two principal associations would place the number of principals at somewhere between 76,000 and 81,000. Add to this an estimated 15,000 secondary assistant principals and 5,000 elementary assistant principals and the total would be far greater than that indicated by the Office of Education. The Research Division of the National Education Association reported that there were almost 101,000 principals and assistant principals in 1972–1973. Precisely how many principals and their professional assistants there are is a matter of conjecture. At this point in time this writer estimates there are 105,000 working in some capacity in the principalship at various levels.

In the fall of 1970–1971 there were 65,800 elementary school and 25,352 secondary school attendance centers, for a total of 91,152. It was in 1965–1966 that the number of public school attendance centers dropped below 100,000 for the first time. This decline promises to continue. In 1931–1932 there were 232,750 elementary school and 26,409 secondary school attendance units, for a total of 259,159. Not all attendance centers have principals. It is estimated that about 7,198 attendance centers are without either a part-time or full-time principal.

The total number of elementary school attendance centers in 1970–1971 was about 36 percent of those in 1931–1932. Most of the decline can be attributed to the decrease in number of one-teacher schools from 143,-391 in 1931–1932 to about 1,815 in 1970. Over 140,000 one-teacher schools were eliminated in about 40 years. In 1931–1932 one-teacher schools accounted for 61 percent of all elementary-school attendance units. By 1970 the number of one-teacher schools accounted for less than 2 percent of all elementary schools centers. By the end of this decade the one-teacher school may disappear from the American scene.

The total number of secondary schools reached a peak of 28,973 in 1943–1944, then declined to a low of 23,746 in 1951–1952. In the next 20 years there were fluctuations within a primary upward trend that hit a post-World War II peak of 27,011 in 1967–1968.[1] A primary downward

[1] K. A. Simon and W. V. Grant, *Digest of Educational Statistics*, 1971 ed., DHEW Publication, No. (OE) 72-45, Washington, D.C.: GPO, 1972, p. 45.

trend with some fluctuation is predicted for the 1970s.

There were an estimated 18,600 nonpublic school attendance centers in the United States in the fall of 1970. Of these 14,400 were elementary centers, and 4,200 were secondary school centers.

ORGANIZATION OF THE ELEMENTARY SCHOOL

The organization of the elementary school attendance center is influenced by the purposes of elementary education and by the type of pupil served. When the elementary school curriculum was limited and the educational aspirations of the pupils modest, the one-room or one-teacher school proved adequate. This pattern was characterized by a single room with a limited amount of equipment staffed by a teacher with a limited amount of professional preparation. All pupils were served the same educational menu, and individual differences were ignored to a large extent.

Evolution of the graded school

The first major improvements in the organization of the elementary school attendance center came with the grading of pupils. Graded elementary schools appeared first in urban districts, where population growth and the increased significance attached to education crowded the one-room ungraded schoolhouses beyond capacity levels.

Classification of pupils required professional expertise that was beyond the ability and time of lay administrative groups. The need for grading was one of the factors that stimulated the creation of the professional superintendency, and early superintendents devoted much time and study to this problem. Certain types of educational plans, such as the Lancasterian school and the Pestalozzian form of instruction, required grading for their most successful application.[2] The graded system permitted teachers to concentrate their talents and training on pupils of relatively similar chronological age, maturity and experience levels. Pedagogical reasons for grading, the chaotic condition of ungraded schools, and the increasing urbanization of the population that brought about sufficient concentration to assure enough pupils for each grade were mutually reinforcing factors leading to grading.

By the end of the Civil War graded elementary schools were established in most urban communities. Almost 70 more years were to pass before the graded school organization was the accepted practice in rural areas. The first graded elementary school was the Quincy School of Boston, erected in 1847 at a cost of about $60,000. It had 12 rooms, with a total capacity of 660 pupils; for the first time a separate seat was available for each child. Each classroom, with about 55 pupils, was assigned a single teacher. The Quincy school is still in use. J. D. Philbrick was its first principal; the organization he helped to create was influenced by the system then prevalent in the Prussian schools, which at that time were considered the best in the world.[3]

One of the major issues was how many grade levels there should be in an elementary school. Visits of American educators to Prussia, where an eight-grade common-school existed, led to the establishment of a similar pattern in the United States. Under the Prussian concept a child's education began when he was 6 years of age and ended at age 14, at which time he was considered old enough to start earning a living. The Prussian pattern was adopted in the United States, even though conditions that affected Prussian decisions did not prevail here.

Child development studies during the early part of the twentieth century suggested a more defensible base for elementary school organization. From the child-study movement came the concept of an elementary school terminating at the sixth-grade level, the time when most children enter the period of puberty. It eventually led to the idea of the elementary school as a school for children and the secondary school as a school for adolescents. A shift from this point of view is evident in the movement of Grade 6 from the elementary school to the middle school; no established trend in this direction is evident as yet.

Grading patterns

As late as 1960 an Office of Education study of urban elementary schools reported that about 24 percent of such systems terminate elementary school at Grade 8, 64.8 percent at Grade 6; and the remainder with other patterns. Another study completed ten years later showed over 85 percent terminating with Grade 6, less than 9 percent with Grade 8, and the remainder with other patterns. The trend is clearly toward the organization of an elementary school attendance center that terminates at Grade 6. Establishment of the middle school during the late 1960s and early 1970s has not altered this practice radically. Some middle schools had a Grade 6 and some a Grade 5. The traditional eight-grade pattern hangs on in too many

[2]John S. Brubacher, A History of the Problems of Education, New York: McGraw-Hill, 1947, p. 391.

[3]Fred Engelhardt, Public School Organization and Administration, Boston: Ginn, 1931, p. 226.

districts in spite of evidence favoring other types of organization. Government statistical reports on elementary school enrollments still persist in including pupils through Grade 8. This practice is difficult to justify and should be modified.

Downward extension of elementary education to include kindergarten and nursery school has likewise affected the organization of attendance centers. An Office of Education study showed that only 4.5 percent of urban communities maintain a public nursery school.[4] Well over 80 percent of existing nursery school programs are financed by *private* contributions only or by *combinations of public and private funds*. Nursery education is even more uncommon in rural areas. The nursery school is not yet an integral part of public programs of elementary education.[5] There were no observable trends toward establishing more public nursery schools until the federal legislation of 1965 stimulated Headstart programs in some urban areas for disadvantaged children. Kindergartens are far more likely to be included in the elementary-school organization in urban centers than are nursery schools. In 1958, 70.4 percent of the urban areas maintained public kindergartens. A great majority of kindergarten programs (80.8 percent) were supported entirely by public funds[6]; only 5.8 percent were supported solely by private contributions. Federal programs of the 1960s did not stimulate sizeable increases in the number of urban centers maintaining kindergarten programs. Kindergarten programs are more likely to be found in urban

than in rural areas; because kindergarten programs operate with half-day sessions, special transportation problems are involved in rural areas. A 1955–1956 study of rural counties in the United States, which compose 57 percent of the total of 3068 counties, showed that only 27.3 percent of the school systems in rural counties had kindergarten programs, compared with 57.6 percent of the systems in cities of less than 10,000 and 73.4 percent of the systems in cities of 25,000 or more.[7]

Flexible grading and departmentalization

Considerable interest was evident in the 1950s and 1960s in the development of what has been variously called a primary unit, an ungraded school, an ungraded primary school, a nongraded elementary school, a primary department, and a continuous growth plan. This type of ungraded organization is markedly different from the ungraded pattern of more than 100 years ago. In the modern context, "nongrading" is a relative term that actually means less rigid (more flexible) classification of pupil progress rather than no classification as to level of accomplishment. Its application is usually limited to a few grades at the elementary level. The term "flexible grading" describes the practice more accurately.

Public schools have been reporting an increase in adoption of this administrative and instructional practice. The volume of educational literature on the subject has grown during the 1960s. A 1958 nationwide report indicates there has been more talk about it than actual practice of it. Only 18

[4]Stuart E. Dean, *Elementary School Administration and Organization*, U.S. Office of Education, Bulletin 1960, no. 11, Washington, D.C.: GPO, 1960, p. 15.
[5]Ibid., p. 17.
[6]Ibid., p. 18.

[7]Mary Anne Harvey, *Statistics of Rural Schools*, 1955–1956, U.S. Office of Education, circular no. 565, Washington, D.C.: GPO, 1959.

percent of urban centers used a flexible-grading plan.[8] The most common pattern of flexible elementary organization includes Grades K through 3, or 1 through 3, depending upon whether the local system provides public kindergarten. Only 13 percent of the urban areas not now using this organization indicate its possible future adoption. The ungraded primary school is less likely to be found in rural than in urban areas.

Later studies revealed relatively slow progress in the 1960s toward more extensive use of nongrading. No standard meaning for nongrading had evolved by the late 1960s. One group of researchers was able to identify only 728 schools in 1967 that were reported to be nongraded.[9] Subsequent investigation revealed that more than 20 percent of these were no longer nongraded or had been so labeled erroneously to begin with. Personal observations and correspondence led Goodlad, one of the founders of the movement, to declare that "there are, indeed, precious few nongraded schools."[10]

An NEA Research Division survey of teachers in 1971 on the use of new techniques of instruction reported only 21.4 percent were in situations where nongraded classrooms were evident. This is consistent with data compiled in the 1960s and suggests that the nongraded concept has hit a plateau.

A survey of departmentalization was conducted by the Educational Research Service of the American Association of School Administrators

(AASA), using a sample of school districts of various sizes with enrollments of 12,000 or more in May 1965.[11] Less than one-half of the more than 400 school systems surveyed used departmentalization in elementary schools. Departmentalization was defined as present when students had more than one teacher for their academic subjects (English, social studies, mathematics, and science), and each teacher was solely responsible for a specific subject or groups of subjects. This should not be confused with the use of special-subject teachers, as in art or music, to supplement the teacher in an otherwise self-contained classroom. Less than one-fourth of the large school systems had plans that met these specifications and in less than 3 percent of the school districts studied were all the elementary schools departmentalized in 1964–1965. Departmentalization was more likely to be found at the seventh- and eighth-grade levels than at any other grade level. Grades 4, 5, and 6 (the intermediate grades) were more likely to be departmentalized than the primary grades.

Individualization of instruction began to be implemented in larger numbers in the nation's elementary schools in the late 1960s and early 1970s. This movement is contrary to departmentalization efforts. Some individualized instruction strategies such as what is called Individually Prescribed Instruction (IPI) may have a lesser impact on elementary school instructional organization than others, such as Individually Guided Education in the Multiunit School–Elementary (IGE/MUSE). There are many more IGE/MUSE organizational patterns than any others.

[8]Dean, op. cit., p. 24.

[9]G. F. Shearron and H. Wait, "Nongraded Elementary Schools," *The National Elementary School Principal*, vol. 47, no. 2, November 1967, pp. 39–42.

[10]J. I. Goodlad, "Editorial," *The National Elementary School Principal*, vol. 47, no. 2, November 1967, pp. 2–3.

[11]American Association of School Administrators and Research Division, National Education Association, "Departmentalization in Elementary Schools," Education Research Service, circular no. 7, October 1965.

The pioneer work of Klausmeier and others at the Wisconsin Research and Development Center on Cognitive Learning led to the design of the multiunit school that combines many of the instructional and organizational components into a unified package such as:

1. Organization of learners into units of 75 to 150 pupils for purposes in instruction.
2. Multi-age and cross-grade grouping of learners in units.
3. Nongrading.
4. Continuous promotion (progress) for students.
5. Team teaching.
6. Appointment of unit leaders for each learner unit.
7. Cooperative instructional planning by teaching teams.
8. Implementation of an instructional programming model to guide teaching efforts.
9. Emphasis on the use of behavioral objectives in all instructional activity.
10. Use of criterion referenced evaluation approaches.
11. The sharing of instructional leadership responsibilities in each school through the creation of an Instructional Improvement Committee.[12]

ADMINISTRATION OF THE ELEMENTARY SCHOOL

The first public schools organized in Massachusetts were the responsibility of the people of the town. The school was a primitive institution open for a limited period of time only, concerned primarily with a rudimentary curriculum, and staffed by a single teacher whose chief qualifications were some degree of competency in fundamentals,

his ability to maintain himself physically in the classroom, and his soundness of religious faith.[13] The school committee, or board of education, administered, supervised, maintained, and operated these primitive institutions, almost all of which were concerned with elementary education only. The teacher instructed pupils and cared for the building, but had little other administrative responsibility.

Evolution of the principalship

The growth of urban communities spurred development of the office of principal at the elementary school level. The principalship was created, as the superintendency was later, to cope with complexities that plagued urban school systems. One solution to these complexities was to increase the number of one-teacher schools. Another was to establish a "double-headed" school system, with authority divided between the grammar master, who taught reading, grammar, and geography, and the writing master, who taught other subjects and particularly writing. The third solution was to unite all school departments under a single head—the school principal. Although the Quincy School established in Boston in 1847 is usually cited as the first to have all departments united under a single principal, Pierce pointed out that Cincinnati placed all departments under a single head prior to 1838.[14]

The establishment and further development of the public elementary school principalship received encouragement from the following forces:

[12]H. J. Klausmeier et al., *Individually Guided Education and the Multiunit Elementary School: Guidelines for Implementation,* Madison, Wis.: The Wisconsin R and D Center for Cognitive Learning, 1971.

[13]Arthur B. Moehlman, *School Administration,* Boston: Houghton Mifflin, 1940, p. 233.
[14]Paul R. Pierce, *The Origin and Development of the Public School Principalship,* Chicago: University of Chicago Press, 1935, p. 9.

1. The rapid growth of the cities and the increase in numbers of pupils in each building.
2. The grading of schools.
3. The consolidation of the "writing" and "grammar" school departments.
4. The freeing of principals from teaching duties.
5. The recognition of the principal as a supervisory head of the building.
6. The establishment of specialized departments of the NEA concerned with elementary school administration.[15]

Factors that retarded development of the principalship include the influence of the Lancasterian, or monitorial, system; the inefficiency inherent in the double-headed school; and the small number of pupils (and hence also of elementary school teachers) in rural areas.

The elementary school principalship grew out of classroom responsibilities. First there were teachers; then teachers with some administrative responsibilities; still later the principal-teacher, who was more of an administrator than a teacher; and finally a principal. The idea of a principal serving as a teacher as well as an administrator continues today in many small urban communities and rural areas. It remains a deterrent to realization of the full potential of the elementary school principalship. It was not unusual to find one teacher in a multiroom building designated as the principal-teacher for purposes of controlling and managing school affairs. The early functions of the principal-teacher were:

1. To be recognized and function as head of the school attendance unit charged to his care.
2. To regulate classes and courses of instruction for all pupils in the building.
3. To discover any defects in the building and apply remedies.
4. To report defects to the trustees of the district if he is unable to remedy the conditions.
5. To give necessary instructions to other teachers in the building (such teachers being classified as his assistants).
6. To classify pupils.
7. To safeguard the schoolhouse and furniture.
8. To keep the school clean.
9. To instruct the other teachers referred to as his assistants.
10. To refrain from impairing the standing of other teachers especially in the eyes of pupils.
11. To require the cooperation of all the assistant teachers.[16]

Development of graded courses of study, classification of pupils by grade, and unification of separate departments led to relief of the principal from at least part of his teaching duties. The term "principal" became a noun rather than an adjective that modified "teacher." By the middle of the nineteenth century the duties of the typical principal in a large city were limited largely to discipline, routine administrative acts, and grading of pupils. It was some time later that the large city principals were relieved of teaching duties. As late as 1881 principals of Chicago schools were required to devote as much as one-half of their time each day to regular classroom instruction. In other large cities principals were relieved of responsibilities for classroom teaching prior to 1870.[17]

Released from teaching duties, the principal was able to visit other rooms and enhance his supervisory role; supervision became an important function of the elementary-school principal. Supervisory techniques, however, were rudimentary in character until well after the start of the twentieth century. Since 1920, supervisory techniques employed by elementary

---

[15]Ibid., p. 7.

[16]Ibid., p. 12.
[17]Ibid., p. 210.

school principals have showed considerable improvement.[18]

Early administrative responsibilities of the elementary school principal were largely clerical. A sampling of duties assigned to principals prior to 1845 showed that 58.8 percent were concerned with record keeping and reporting, 23.5 percent with organization and classification, 11.8 percent with care of the equipment and building, and 5.9 percent with discipline and care of the pupils.[19] Administrative responsibilities shifted in the last half of the century from records and reports to organization and general management.

During the twentieth century, functions of the principal were expanded to include participation in selection of teachers and assistants assigned to his building. More clerical help was provided urban elementary school principals during the early part of the twentieth century, but many principals in small school systems in urban and rural areas still have an inadequate number of clerical assistants and must, therefore, spend time performing clerical work that could be handled by personnel with far less professional preparation and who would command a lower salary.

Functions of the principal

By 1870 the typical elementary school was an attendance center with 8 to 16 teachers under the direction of a principal who frequently taught part time.[20] The curriculum included the three R's and, in large cities, music, physical education, and art. The kindergarten movement was received coldly by principals in the 1890s, but it was an innovation that was not to be denied.

[18]Ibid., p. 215.
[19]Ibid., pp. 210–211.
[20]Moehlman, op. cit., p. 526.

The growing complexity of the curriculum created special problems in the administration of urban elementary school attendance centers, although few curricular changes were noted in most rural areas. When urban districts began to experiment with various types of organization for elementary instruction, the debate began on the merits of departmentalization compared with the self-contained classroom type of organization. The same plan was called the Gary, Platoon, rotary, shift, or departmentalized plan. It, along with others, will be examined in greater detail in a subsequent chapter.

The principal was recognized as the building-level supervisor by 1900, and the introduction of special-subject teachers prompted upgrading of the qualifications for the principalship. The principal as special-subject supervisor, however, was soon replaced by central-office supervisory personnel. Employment of special-subject supervisors created problems of relation between the building principal and the central-office staff. There is considerable question whether an attendance center can be looked upon as an autonomous unit, headed by an administrator who is not concerned with systemwide policies and has no need of special resource personnel attached to the central office. The administrator of the attendance center is only one of several administrative levels in the public education system. Neither pride nor desire to be considered an autonomous unit is a good reason for depriving a teacher of the services of a special-subject consultant.

The supervisory role of the elementary principal has changed from that of being the only supervisor in the building to a position that relies more and more on specialized supervisory personnel attached to the central office. The knowledge explosion in traditional subjects such as reading or mathematics, as well as in such fields as art or music, calls for a considerable period of study for their mastery. The supervisory role of the present-day principal involves determining what specialized resources teachers need to perform more effectively. The principal cannot supply direct supervisory skills for all teachers himself.

The function of the principal is to administer all aspects of the attendance center. Administrative activity should not be confused with clerical chores. Leadership, which focuses on stimulating people to optimum performance, is the principal's most important single function. The principal, like all administrators, must make things happen through other people. He must know what resources are needed and available to realize the responsibilities at the building office.

An Office of Education study reported that elementary school principals in selected urban communities considered the following as the five most pressing problems facing the leader of an elementary school: supervising instruction, providing for the exceptional child, obtaining adequate physical facilities, providing programs of special education, and recruiting teachers.[21] It can be seen that the majority of the problems considered most important are related to instruction at the elementary school level. Less important problems, as judged by public elementary school principals, were reporting pupil progress and managing school-lunch programs.

Characteristics of elementary school principals

The National Association of Elementary School Principals (NAESP), for-

merly the Department of Elementary School Principals, has reported on the profile of the elementary school principal almost every ten years since the initial study released in 1928, with the sole exception of 1938. They differentiated between teaching principals and those who do no teaching and are identified as "supervising principals." The following major trends in selected characteristics were evident by 1968:[22]

1. Women supervising principals were in the majority in 1928 holding 55 percent of such positions, but were a relatively small minority in 1968 holding only 22.4 percent of the total positions.
2. There are more women in teaching principalships (35.8 percent) than in supervising principalships (22.4 percent).
3. Men dominate the elementary school principalships, but the larger the system the less the degree of disparity between the sexes. Thus, male, elementary principals represented 63.4 percent of the total in systems enrolling 300 to 2999.
4. Most elementary principals had experience teaching in elementary classrooms; only 14 percent did not have such experience.
5. Almost 90 percent of the supervising principals in 1968 had earned a master's or higher degree as compared to 16 percent in 1928.
6. About 88 percent of the elementary principals serve one school only.
7. The median age of the elementary principal is 46 years; the median age at time of entry into the principalship was 33.
8. Eight out of ten are married.
9. They put in a 50 hour work week.
10. Ninety percent would become a principal if they had to do it all over again, but only 56 percent saw it as a final career goal.

To summarize: In 1968 the typical elementary principal was a middle-

---

[21]Dean, op. cit., chap. 17.

[22]National Asociation of Elementary School Principals, *The Elementary School Principalship in 1968*, Arlington, Va.: The Association, 1968, 167 pp.

aged, married man with at least an earned master's degree who served only one attendance center with an enrollment of about 500 pupils. He taught elementary grades before becoming a principal, put in a 50-hour work week, and would choose to become a principal if he had to do it all over again.

A special study of elementary school assistant principalships was released in 1970.[23] In general this report concluded: The most popular title for this position was assistant principal; almost 62 percent were men, the median age was 42, over three-fourths are married, most had previously been elementary classroom teachers (72.5 percent), median classroom experience was ten years, and almost seven out of eight have at least an earned master's degree.

Relatively little is known about the number of elementary assistant principals or the functions assigned. Present practice shows that almost three out of every four are in schools enrolling 700 or more pupils and with 25 teachers or more. Most are of the opinion that an assistant principal is warranted when the elementary school enrollment reaches 400 or more. Typically the duties and functions of an assistant principal are defined by the principal.

ORGANIZATION OF THE SECONDARY SCHOOL

Evolution of secondary education

Circumstances different from those that led to the creation of the elementary school motivated the development of secondary education in the United States. Colonial secondary schools were copies of the English Latin grammar school. Young men were sent to grammar schools primarily to prepare themselves for college and then service in the church and state.[24] Some entered the colonial Latin school when they were as young as 7 or 8 years old. Secondary education during colonial times enrolled only a very small percentage of the population. Inability or unwillingness of the Latin grammar school to adjust to changing social conditions of the eighteenth century led to the formation of a new and competing form of secondary institution, the academy. It, too, was short-lived, even though its science program and other innovations represented an improvement over the limited curriculum of the Latin grammar school. The radically utilitarian studies suggested for the academy by Franklin eventually lost out in favor of the Andover program. The Andover curriculum included English grammar, practical geometry, logic, geography, and "such other liberal arts and sciences or languages" that may be permitted, as well as Greek and Latin grammar.[25] It became the model for the academy movement. The institution became oriented primarily toward college and, hence, could be called a "preparatory" institution.

Neither the academy nor the Latin grammar school popularized secondary education in the United States. The high school made its first appearance in American education when the academy was at the peak of its growth and popularity and, hence, did not come into being as a reaction to the academy (which was itself a protest against the shortcomings of the Latin grammar

---

[23]National Association of Elementary School Principals Association, *The Assistant Principalship in Public Elementary Schools– 1969, A Research Study*, Arlington, Va.: The Association, 1970, 96 pages.

[24]Brubacher, op. cit., p. 428.
[25]Ibid., pp. 430–431.

school). Originators of the high school in 1821 adopted the program of the academy, but added public support of the institution. It came to be considered a normal extension of a common-school education.

Although the first public high school was an immediate success, its influence spread slowly during the nineteenth century. The number of high schools was a little over 2,500 by 1890 with a total enrollment of about 200,000 pupils. There were well over 10,000 high schools by 1910, with a total enrollment of more than 900,000.[26] The growth and development of the comprehensive secondary school is primarily a twentieth-century event. The United States is one of the few nations in the world that supports a compulsory secondary education program. As an institution, the high school remains in a state of flux. Changes in its purposes and clientele have precipitated changes in its organization and administration.

Grading patterns

As discussed in the preceding section, the transfer point between elementary and secondary education is most likely to occur at the end of Grade 6. Secondary institutions are designed for adolescents; their terminal point has long been considered Grade 12. Recently, the last year of community (junior) college (Grade 14) has come to be recognized as the terminal point in some states. There is some question whether the word "terminal" is appropriate, because continuing education is generally considered desirable.

The traditional pattern for secondary education consisted of four grades beyond the traditional eight-year elementary school curriculum. It became

known as the 8–4 system (K–8–4 if kindergarten was part of the elementary school experience). The 8–4 pattern was popular during the early part of the present century; there were not many high schools prior to 1890. As late as 1920, 94 percent of the 14,300 public elementary and secondary schools were organized on an 8–4 or K–8–4 basis.[27] Furthermore, 83 percent of the 2 million pupils enrolled in secondary schools were in 8–4 or K–8–4 systems. By 1952, however, the 8–4 or K–8–4 pattern was reported in only 43 percent of the 23,700 secondary institutions, and only 25 percent of the 7.7 million pupils enrolled in secondary schools were in 8–4 or K–8–4 systems. In 1959 only 24 percent of the 24,000 secondary schools had an 8–4, or K–8–4 organization, and 18 percent of the 11 million pupils enrolled were in an 8–4 or K–8–4 system. The trend is clearly toward formation of junior and/or senior high school attendance centers.

In 1920 only about 5 percent of the systems were formed on a 6–6 basis. By 1952 systems organized on a 6–6 or K–6–6 pattern represented 36 percent of all schools and enrolled 35 percent of the 7.7 million students. More recent data show that the 6–6 plan is in disfavor, for less than 2 percent of the systems with 12,000 or more students utilized this organizational pattern in 1968. The 6–6 system consists of a six-grade elementary school, and a six-grade combined junior and senior high school. All pupils in the junior-senior high school are under the direction of one principal.

The reorganization of the secondary school into junior high school (for young adolescents) and senior high school (for older adolescents) is a

[26]Ibid., p. 435.

[27]Edmund A. Ford, "Organizational Pattern of the Nation's Public Secondary Schools," *School Life*, vol. 42, no. 9, May 1960, p. 10.

more distinct separation, with separate principals for junior and senior high schools. It is the 6–3–3 (or K–6–3–3) and the 6–2–4 (or K–6–2–4) form of organization. The secondary institution with various degrees of separation between junior and senior high accounted for only about 1 percent of the total secondary schools in 1920. By 1959, 34 percent of the schools and 50 percent of the enrollment were in 6–3–3 (K–6–3–3) or 6–2–4 (K–6–2–4) systems or systems with a separate junior high school. Most recent data show that at least two out of every three systems are organized on a 6–3–3 basis. Prevailing opinion appears to favor the 6–3–3 (K–6–3–3) organization.

A 1966 study of the junior high school principalship revealed that 67 percent of these principals were in a 6–3–3 system. Organizational patterns by states are shown in Table 16–1; the variations should be evident from the table data. The median practice in the United States is a state where 70 percent of the schools are organized on a 6–3–3 basis.

Attendance centers can no longer be dichotomized simply into elementary and high schools. The 8–4 (or K–8–4) type of organization is as much an anachronism as the one-room school. A better delineation is on the basis of elementary school, junior high school (two or three years), and senior high school (three or four years). Further investigation might suggest an even more elaborate division into primary grades (Grades K through 3); intermediate grades (Grades 4 through 6); junior high school grades; and senior high school grades. This would be represented symbolically as K–3–3–3–3. If junior college opportunities were also available, it would be a K–3–3–3–3–2 pattern.

Although the most common pattern

for secondary school organization is 6–3–3, there are other plans of organization. The 6–4–4 (or K–6–4–4) plan conceives of the junior high school as Grades 7 through 10 and the senior high school-community college as Grades 11 through 14. There has been a very small increase in the number of schools adopting this plan of organization. Another plan, the 4–4–4–4 (or K–4–4–4–4), is a block of four-grade units following kindergarten. It is not in operation in any public high school in the country at the present time.

The rapid development of junior colleges in the past 50 years cannot be ignored in the organization of secondary-school institutions. More will be said about these and other post-secondary institutions in Chapter 17.

The middle school

A relatively new plan, the "middle school," began quietly in the 1950s. The number of such schools increased from one to four annually in the 1950s, to five to nine new middle schools annually in the early 1960s. After 1966 25 or more were created each year. The middle school is an instructional center between the senior high school and the elementary school. It is found in the eastern states from Maine to Maryland and in Texas. Whether it is simply a new term for the junior high school or an entirely new school organizational concept is the subject of much debate. This debate will not be reviewed here. The focus will be on the prevailing practice.

Some argue that a new trend is being established. A 1968–1969 study by the Educational Research Service of the AASA[28] reported that their

[28]American Association of School Administrators, "Middle Schools in Action," Educational Research Service, circular no. 2, 1969.

efforts to identify existing middle schools in 1965 and again in 1968 showed that the number of middle schools in existence had grown. Thus, in 1964 only 63 middle schools clustered in 20 separate systems could be found; during the 1968–1969 school year there were 235 middle schools in 70 systems. Considering that there were about 95,000 school attendance centers at the time the percent that was called middle schools was very small as yet. There is no evidence as yet that there is an overwhelming ground swell in favor of the middle school title. The most middle schools and districts using this pattern were found in California and Texas.

There appears to be little consistency in grade grouping in the middle school in various systems. Some systems place Grades 6 through 8 in the middle school; some Grades 5 through 8; some Grades 5 through 9; and others Grades 6 and 7 only. Most seem to follow a 5–3–4 or 6–3–3 pattern.

Cuff reported data gathered at about the same time as those reported by the Educational Research Service indicating that 446 districts in 29 states

TABLE 16–1

PERCENTAGE OF SCHOOL ATTENDANCE UNITS OF VARIOUS PATTERNS IN EACH STATE, 1966

State	Pattern				No response	No.
	6–3–3	6–2–4	5–3–4	Other		
U.S. Median	70	15	2	10	—	—
Alabama	61	14	2	21	2	95
Alaska	38	25	25	13	0	8
Arizona	9	73	0	18	0	22
Arkansas	86	8	3	3	0	37
California	82	12	1	5	0	259
Colorado	70	22	3	5	0	96
Connecticut	70	14	8	8	0	64
Delaware	73	20	0	0	7	15
District of Columbia	100	0	0	0	0	16
Florida	87	5	0	8	0	161
Georgia	39	27	7	27	0	44
Hawaii	53	18	0	29	0	17
Idaho	59	24	8	10	0	51
Illinois	29	42	8	22	0	213
Indiana	59	29	5	7	0	97
Iowa	55	32	3	10	0	170
Kansas	74	14	1	10	0	77
Kentucky	69	14	6	11	0	35
Louisiana	70	11	5	11	2	61
Maine	46	33	12	10	0	52
Maryland	83	6	7	3	0	96
Massachusetts	56	29	8	8	0	167
Michigan	58	26	8	9	0	290
Minnesota	96	2	0	0	2	90
Mississippi	73	6	6	15	0	33
Missouri	62	26	2	10	0	86

were operating 499 middle schools during 1965–1966.[29] Yet another study claimed as many as 1000 middle schools in 1967. The apparent discrepancies are difficult to reconcile.

One reason for organizing these schools appears related to the desire for racial integration without busing or other costly maneuvers. Another is related to the desire to include in Grades 5 and 6 laboratory experiences,

[29]W. A. Cuff, "Middle Schools on the March," *Bulletin of the National Association of Secondary School Principals*, vol. 51, no. 316, February 1967, pp. 82–83.

particularly in home economics and industrial arts. In some situations, the desire for a four-year senior high remained strong and the middle school was an excuse to maintain it. In still other operations, the middle school appeared to be only a new name adopted to demonstrate the innovative qualities of the school district.

Sanders summarized various grading patterns as shown in Table 16–2. In his study of educational development Sanders concluded:

Grades six through eight do not constitute a more heterogeneous group than

TABLE 16–1 (Continued)

State	Pattern				No response	No.
	6–3–3	6–2–4	5–3–4	Other		
Montana	73	14	0	14	0	22
Nebraska	71	18	0	11	0	45
Nevada	80	20	0	0	0	10
New Hampshire	29	35	6	29	0	17
New Jersey	84	6	0	10	0	86
New Mexico	70	15	2	13	0	55
New York	88	3	1	8	0	180
North Carolina	74	15	0	10	1	82
North Dakota	71	10	0	19	0	21
Ohio	93	3	1	4	0	193
Oklahoma	88	8	0	2	2	103
Oregon	69	21	2	8	0	62
Pennsylvania	83	6	2	10	0	259
Rhode Island	78	17	0	4	0	23
South Carolina	49	37	2	12	0	49
South Dakota	70	15	0	15	0	20
Tennessee	75	3	3	19	0	63
Texas	48	21	18	12	0	330
Utah	79	4	6	6	4	48
Vermont	60	0	0	40	0	5
Virginia	75	18	2	5	0	44
Washington	83	6	1	10	0	164
West Virginia	71	13	3	14	0	95
Wisconsin	69	19	3	9	0	110
Wyoming	28	54	0	18	0	39
Foreign and U.S. Possessions	80	0	20	0	0	5
Canada	57	21	0	21	0	14

Source: D. A. Rock and J. K. Hemphill, *Report of the Junior High School Principalship*, Reston, Va.: National Association of Secondary-School Principals, 1966, p. 14.

seven through nine in the characteristics of mental and educational development measured by instruments, and the former could not be judged to be less satisfactory than the seventh, eighth, and ninth grade junior high school in this respect. Most differences which exist are too small to be educationally significant, and school districts choosing between the two grade combinations might just as well base their decisions upon other factors. What differences were found tended to favor grades six through eight as the more homogeneous. Variances between grades were much smaller than variances within grades. No combination of grades removes the need to provide for every substantial difference in intellectual development within each grade.[30]

ADMINISTRATION OF THE SECONDARY SCHOOL

Evolution of the principalship

The secondary school principalship is one of the oldest educational adminis-

[30]Stanley G. Sanders, "Differences in Mental and Educational Development from

trative positions, yet one that "has no history."[31] It can be traced as far back as 1515 to Johann Sturm, who was considered the greatest administrator of secondary education in his century. It is significant that Sturm did not teach much and hence must have had a considerable group of men under his direction to carry out the extensive, but largely classical, curriculum in the *Gymnasium,* a school for boys from ages 10 to 19 or 20. The great headmasters of the English Latin grammar schools are direct descendents of Sturm. Headmaster was the title assigned to a building-level administrator who was granted a considerable degree of responsibility for the control

Grades Six through Nine and Implications for Junior High School Organization," unpublished doctoral dissertation, University of Iowa, Iowa City, Iowa, 1960, p. 68.

[31]Forest C. Ensign, "Evolution of the High School Principalship," *The School Review,* vol. 31, March 1923, pp. 179–190.

TABLE 16–2

GRADING PATTERNS OTHER THAN 8–4 AND 6–3–3

Grading pattern	Year advocated	Advocates and occurrence
6–6	About 1900 by early reoroganization committees	Always common in small communities as a substitute for 6–3–3.
7–5	Existed in early 1900s	Prevalent in the South where 7-year elementary schools were common.
6–2–4	Late 1800s	Constantly common through the years.
6–4–4	1940s	Leading advocate: Koos; much recommended, seldom adopted.
4–4–4	1950s	Leading advocate: Woodring; receiving more attention in the 1960s.
5–3–4	1950s	Most common in Texas and some cities of the Northeast; now receiving support as more than an expedient.

Source: Stanley G. Sanders, "Differences in Mental and Educational Development from Grades Six Through Nine and Implications for Junior High School Organization," Unpublished Doctoral Dissertation, Iowa City, Iowa: The University of Iowa, 1960, p. 68.

of the Latin grammar school. He was required to be a great teacher and a great disciplinarian, not given to "wanton dalliances and unseemly behavior with women, [nor to be] a follower of vain, gaudy fashions of apparel, a papist, a wearer of long curled hair, a puffer of tobacco, or addicted to dicing, carding, or other unlawful games."[32] The basic ideas of administrative leadership that characterized the high school principalship during the early 1920s were evident in the English Latin grammar school.

The first secondary schools in the United States were also Latin grammar schools. They were, however, small institutions serving a limited number of people and, hence, had little need for administrators who did not teach. They were usually headed by a highly competent schoolmaster such as Ezekiel Cheever. A few academies with a half-dozen or more teachers were directed by a headmaster (also titled rector, preceptor, provost, and occasionally principal),[33] but even at the height of development of the academy (about 1850), the average number of teachers per school was two.[34] The need for teaching far overshadowed the need for administration in such small institutions.

Although there is a paucity of information on evolution of the public high-school principalship, there is evidence that this position existed prior to the establishment of the elementary school principalship and of the superintendency of schools. The high school principalship, as Ensign suggested in the 1920s, remains in the process of becoming.[35]

Moehlman pointed out that early superintendents were given no authority over secondary schools but concentrated on problems of grading and establishing unity among the many elementary-school principals.[36] As a result, secondary school principals achieved a high degree of independence from other administrators. It was unusual for the secondary school principal to confer directly with the board of education, even though in some cases he was regarded as co-ordinate with the superintendent. Relations between superintendent and high school principal were not always cordial. Not until well into the twentieth century were serious attempts made to bring the secondary school into a closer relation with elementary attendance centers.[37] Outdated concepts of the secondary institution as an independent empire in the school district remain to create problems of articulation between elementary and secondary grades and to stymie attempts at unification of administrative efforts.

The public secondary school principalship evolved from the headmaster's post. The headmaster was the best teacher in the building and the best informed in most, if not all, subjects in the curriculum. He had little need to develop a high degree of skill in the administrative process. Although the evolution of the high school into a comprehensive institution has long since rendered it obsolete, the headmaster concept of the secondary school administrator continues to dominate the profession. The introduction of special subjects and special teachers demands a more realistic appraisal of the role of the chief administrator of a public secondary school attendance center.

---

[32]Ibid., p. 184.
[33] Ibid.
[34]Ibid.
[35]Ibid.

[36]Ibid.
[37]Ibid.

Characteristics of secondary principals

The typical senior high school principal in the mid-1960s was a middle-aged married man with at least an earned master's degree.[38] About 89 percent were men and the median age was 44 years. The median number of years in the classroom before becoming a principal was eight. Over one-third of the principals served schools with fewer than 250 students; 90 percent had a master's degree; less than 4 percent of the senior high principals had a doctorate, a significantly smaller percent than that noted for superintendents.

Male domination was even more notable among junior high principals where 96 percent were men. The typical junior high school principal was a married man in his early 40s.[39] Ninety-three percent had an earned master's degree.

The assistant principal

The increasing complexity of the secondary school pupil population and curriculum in large institutions creates a need for other administrators at the building level subordinate to the principal. Such positions are no longer unusual or confined to large schools. Administrative personnel subordinate to the principal are given many different titles, among which are assistant principal, dean, vice principal, and administrative assistant: Assistant principal seems to be preferred. When there is only one assistant principal, he is usually considered second in command;

when there are more than one, the title may be specific, such as assistant principal in charge of attendance and scheduling or assistant principal in charge of student-body activities.

There is considerable variation in the number of pupils enrolled per high-school administrator. Median enrollments per administrator varied from 570 in four-year high schools, 550 in six-year junior-senior high schools, and 450 in three-year senior high schools.[40] There is some debate about the optimum size of the administrative staff for a high school. A rough index is one administrator for 400 pupils. The actual number will doubtless be influenced by the financial ability of the district, the complexity of student services, the number and turnover among staff, the total enrollment, the types of students served, and the nature of the area served. Justification for administrative staff increases must be based on an improvement in the quality of instruction or services.

What the assistant principals do appears to be determined by what the principal delegates. Wide variation in duties delegated to the assistant indicates that some aides have been used effectively, whereas others have been assigned primarily clerical chores. Functions assigned to most assistant principals include:

1. Assuming responsibility for the operation of the school in the absence of the principal.
2. Serving as a representative of the school in lieu of the principal.
3. Participating in parent conferences in matters of school discipline.

The assistant appears to be held par-

[38]J. K. Hemphill et al., *Report of the Senior High School Principalship*, Reston, Va.: National Association of Secondary School Principals, 1965.

[39]D. A. Rock and J. K. Hemphill, *Report of the Junior High School Principalship*, Reston, Va.: National Association of Secondary School Principals, 1966.

[40]Robert J. Keller, "Secondary Education: Organization and Administration," in C. W. Harris, ed., *The Encyclopedia of Educational Research*, 3rd ed., New York: Macmillan, 1960, p. 1243.

tially responsible for many things but seldom completely responsible for any one thing.

The position may be considered an internship for the principalship only if specifically designed for this function. An assistant limited to performing clerical chores cannot be said to be enjoying opportunities for professional growth and development. A principal should view an intern in a much different light from an assistant who is relieving him of a few chores. A principal who is participating in a program of executive development by working with an intern is assuming more responsibility than he is being relieved of.

The department head

The department head is at the classroom level of school administration. Because the post exists when there is more than one teacher in a given subject field, it is more likely to be found in the large high school centers. The department head was found in more than three-fourths of the large California high schools in 1950.

The position's usefulness is subject to debate. Communication difficulty owing to lack of coordination among departments is the most pressing problem. The formation of a principal's cabinet composed of department heads has been suggested to facilitate communication.

The duties of the department heads are usually those delegated by the principal and include:

1. Participation in budget planning at the building level by submitting needs of the department to the principal.
2. Detailed supervision of instruction primarily by working with central-office supervisors.
3. Organization and conduct of departmental meetings.
4. Recommendations of courses or educational experiences to be offered within the department.
5. Orientation of teachers within the department who are new to the system.
6. Investigation and recommendation of texts and other instructional materials.
7. Procurement, coordination, and distribution of departmental equipment and supplies.

It can be argued that department heads have a leadership function and should be held accountable for the relevance of the curriculum in their area of expertise, level of learning outcomes, and quality of teaching. To give department heads administrative responsibilities such as gathering appraisal data on the performance of teachers in their departments would call for the removal of department chairmen from the bargaining unit for teachers.

Department heads are justified when there are at least three and preferably five teachers for a given subject area. Departmental organization may introduce more complexity and inflexibility if it exists where it is not needed.

Functions of the principal

The principalship has evolved according to the following sequence: a classroom teacher, a teacher with a few administrative functions, the teacher-principal, and the supervising principal. Not all communities have moved from one phase to another. The principalship in some communities has been arrested at one of the earlier phases of development.

The principal can no longer fulfill the role of the headmaster or of an instructional supervisor competent to counsel all teachers. The instructional leadership role of the principal is one of marshaling resources—human and material—that classroom teachers require to perform effectively. It is suggested that the principal in future years be conceived as an administrator rather than an instructional supervisor for any and all fields. In other words, a principal fulfills his role as instructional leader by helping teachers obtain consultant services needed to do a more effective job, rather than by attempting to supervise teachers himself.

Nor is there justification any longer for the administrator of an attendance unit to teach one or several classes. A principal who must teach is deprived of opportunities to come to know more about the instructional program. Speaking from personal experience as well as from many empirical observations, the writer can well remember how the pressure of administrative activities made it impossible to prepare effectively for teaching during the day, and how many times he was prevented from supervising an instructional activity because it fell at the same time he was scheduled to teach a class. A full-time attendance center administrator is warranted when the enrollment exceeds 300 pupils.

The principal should not be overburdened with clerical work. Clerical tasks are a part of school operations and cannot be ignored, but they should be delegated to clerical personnel and not permitted to drain the time of the professional administrator. The administrator of the attendance center, like other administrators, makes things happen through other people. It is his ability to organize, to allocate resources, and to stimulate action among others that is needed most.

After an extensive study of competencies needed by superintendents, principals, and supervisors, Woodward concluded that 70 percent of the 203 competencies deemed essential were common to all three types of administrative positions.[41] The history of a principal moving into the superintendency of a small school moving into the principalship of a large school further suggests a unity among school administrators that is only confused by certification laws and preparation programs that tend to separate the areas.

The administrative process is the same at the attendance center as at the central-office and the superintendency level. A different degree of information concerning the substantive problems and the nature of the learner at various levels seems to be the only fundamental differentiation among types of administrators.

The principalship is changing due, in large part, to the pressures on society in general and on education in particular. The increasing pressure on the school to assume a more dynamic role in the amelioration of social injustices, the greater militancy and professionalization of teachers, the increased specialization of teachers, and the growing complexity of all educational institutions are modifying the nature of the principalship. The principal is still an instructional leader, but he must also be involved in matters such as professional negotiation. More and more the principal is recognized as an executive or administrator and the principalship as a constella-

[41]Pierce C. Woodward, "A Study of Competencies Needed by School Administrators and Supervisors in Virginia with Implications for Pre-Service Education," CPEA Project, doctoral dissertation, University of Virginia, Charlottesville, Va., 1953.

tion of positions. The importance of the position continues to grow even though its role is controversial.

Dean conceptualized the principal's office as a service center for the school.[42] The ten important services of this office were considered to be:

1. A communications center of the school.
2. A clearing house for the transaction of school business.
3. A counseling center for teachers and students.
4. A counseling center for school patrons.
5. A research division of the school, for the collection, analysis, and evaluation of information regarding activities and results.
6. A repository of school records.
7. The planning center for solving school problems and initiating school improvements.
8. A resource center for encouraging creative work.
9. A coordinating agency cultivating wholesome school and community relations.
10. The coordinating center of the school enterprise.

He also reported that there is a need to transfer more administrative activities (such as assignment of pupils to classes, improvement of instruction, selection of educational materials, reporting pupil progress to parents, evaluation of staff, management of lunch programs, curriculum improvement, community relations, pupil promotional policies, building maintenance, selection of staff, budget preparation, and pupil transportation) from the central office to the individual elementary school center. The least amount of change has taken place regarding business and staff personnel policies such as pupil transportation, budget preparation, and selection of staff. The greater the amount of change

in instructional procedures and the smaller the urban community, the more likely it is that the elementary school principal carries a high degree of responsibility for policy administration.

Briner visualized the three major dimensions of high school administration as technical, managerial, and conceptual.[43] Activities such as testing, measuring, interviewing, disciplining, coaching, scheduling, recording, accounting, spending, operating, and maintenance make up the technical dimension. Many members of the professional and nonprofessional building staff are involved in executing these responsibilities. Concern for the effectiveness of the staff, for the adequacy of plans, for conformity to rules, for economical use of space and funds, make up the managerial dimension. Principals spend a major portion of their time and energy on such duties. The conceptual dimension is directed to the entire school program, to the community setting, to learning, and to the pupil.

The principal in a public school, whether at the elementary or secondary school level, is a counselor of students, the school disciplinarian, the organizer of the schedule, the supervisor of the instructional program, the pupil-relations representative for the attendance area, the liaison between teachers and the superintendent, the director and evaluator of teaching efforts, the manager of the school facilities, the supervisor of custodial and food-service employees within the building, and a professional leader. Little wonder that this is a demanding position as well as one of considerable

---

[42]Dean, op. cit., p. 376.

[43]Conrad Briner, "Unhinging the High School Principalship," *The School Review*, vol. 48, Summer 1960, pp. 318–328.

significance in determining the direction of public education.

Selection of the principal

The American Association of School Administrators recognized that the responsibility for selection and assignment of principals should reside in the superintendency and not the school board.[44] Some of the major observations and recommendations of an AASA Committee on Selection of Principals were:

1. That the school board, as a matter of policy, elect only those persons recommended by the superintendent for a principalship.
2. That the superintendent execute his responsibility for principal selection with the consultation of professional administrators and/or instructional staff members.
3. That a better conceptualization of the principalship consistent with present demands maximizes the chances of selecting the right person.
4. That the uniqueness of each attendance center be recognized and defined with clarity; that expectations of the principalship vary with the times and referent group and help to define the demands in a given attendance center.
5. That no person be excluded from consideration as principal on the basis of sex alone.
6. That personal variables such as age, sex, marital status, intelligence, health, personality, and value patterns may be considered in the selection process, but that most systems ignore the existing research on the appropriate use of these factors.
7. That the issue of how much prior experience is necessary to become a principal remains unresolved, but unusually long periods are not recommended.
8. That each system may have its own group of "principal makers"—people who have the ear of the superintend-

[44]American Association of School Administrators, *The Right Principal for the Right School*, Washington, D.C.: The Association, 1967.

ent or contacts with the selection committees and those individuals whose recommendations carry weight.[45]

Not all selection information or devices used in principal selection have equal value. Biographical information blanks reveal the obvious characteristics; it has been remarked that the latest horoscope for the candidate may be as valid and reliable as letters of recommendation or credentials. Some of the factors used in principal selection and devices used in measurement are summarized in Table 16-3. No single device is perfect, nor can it provide all data necessary for prudent selection.

SUMMARY

Pupils learn and teachers instruct in the attendance units of the system. It is at this level that the efforts of the administrators at other levels are tested to determine their influence on the teaching-learning process and thus their value in the attainment of educational objectives. The administrator of the attendance center is commonly referred to as the principal. The importance of his role in the administration of public education is difficult to overestimate.

The trend in the organization of elementary and secondary school attendance centers is clearly away from the traditional 8–4 pattern. About two-thirds of the urban elementary schools now terminate at Grade 6; secondary education is now conceded to start at Grade 7. Elementary school experience has been extended downward to include kindergarten in about 70 percent of the urban school districts. Nursery schools are far less common, being found in less than 5 percent of the ur-

[45]Ibid.

ban districts and in far fewer rural communities. The ungraded, or flexible, primary school organization is found in only about 20 percent of the urban districts and appears to be growing slowly.

Most of the secondary schools have now been reorganized to include junior and senior high schools. By far the most common type of secondary school organization is the three-year junior high school and three-year senior high school each directed by a separate principal. No one knows the precise number of principals, but it is esti-

mated that there are about 105,000 in such positions.

The principalship evolved out of the classroom as one professional person was assigned varying degrees of administrative responsibility. The typical principalship is male dominated, although there are more women elementary school principals than women secondary school principals. The profile of elementary and secondary principals shows the typical person to be a married, middle-aged male with an earned master's degree.

The secondary-school administrator

TABLE 16–3

FACTORS USED IN PRINCIPAL SELECTION AND SOME RELATED MEASURING DEVICES

Factors used in selection	Devices used in measurement
1. Age, experience, family history	Biographical information blank, interview.
2. Breadth of general knowledge	Achievement tests, transcript, ratings by competent observers, interview, letters of recommendation.
3. Breadth of specialized knowledge of education	Achievement tests, transcript, ratings by competent observers, interview, letters of recommendation.
4. Command of the English language and ability to articulate thoughts	Tests, interview, ratings by competent observers.
5. Dependability, drive	Ratings by competent observers.
6. Emotional stability and other characteristics of personality	Tests, rating by competent observers, letters of recommendation, interview.
7. Human relations skills	Ratings by or conversation with competent observers, letters of recommendation, interview.
8. Interests	Interview.
9. Likely administrative behavior or creativity	Situational performance tests, interview, letters of recommendation.
10. Mental ability or intelligence	Intelligence tests.
11. Moral fitness	Ratings by or conversation with competent observers, letters of recommendation.
12. Scholarship	Transcript, letters of recommendation.
13. Value patterns	Tests of value, ratings by or conversation with competent observers, interview.
14. Physical fitness or health	Health examination.

Source: American Association of School Administrators, *The Right Principal for the Right School,* Washington, D.C.: The Association, 1967, p. 44.

is a direct descendent of the headmasters of the *Gymnasia* and Latin grammar schools. The role of the secondary-school administrator has changed as the institution's purposes and pupils have changed. Many schools are adding assistant principals (who are known by many other titles). The functions of the assistant principals vary widely.

The administrator of the attendance centers is part of the team of administrators operating at various levels whose major contribution is facilitating the attainment of educational objectives. Continuance of secondary schools as separate empires, unarticulated with elementary grades, is difficult to justify. The role of the administrator in the building center is clearly one of administration and should be based on abilities to work with people, rather than performing such tasks as teaching, clerical work, or even supervision of teachers in specialized areas.

QUESTIONS

1. What factors have influenced the organization of elementary school attendance centers? Of secondary school attendance centers?
2. What should be the professional relations between the building principal and the central-office supervisor?
3. How can a principal fulfill the role of instructional leadership?
4. When does it become necessary to add assistant principals at the building level?
5. Why should elementary-school attendance centers terminate at the end of Grade 6? What arguments would tend to support termination at Grade 8?
6. What is the profile of the typical elementary school principal? Secondary school principal?
7. Should the department chairmanship be eliminated? Justify your stand.

SELECTED REFERENCES

American Association of School Administrators, *The Right Principal for the Right School,* Washington, D.C.: The Association, 1967.

American Association of School Administrators, "Middle Schools in Action," Educational Research Service, circular no. 2, 1969.

Brubacher, John S., *A History of the Problems of Education,* New York: McGraw-Hill, 1947, chap. 18.

Dean, Stuart E., *Elementary School Administration and Organization,* U.S. Office of Education, Bull. 1960, no. 11, Washington, D.C.: GPO, 1960.

Ensign, Forest C., "Evolution of the High School Principalship," *School Review,* vol. 31, March 1923, pp. 179–190.

Ford, Edmund A., "Organizational Pattern of the Nation's Public Secondary Schools," *School Life,* vol. 42, no. 9, May 1960.

Jacobson, Paul B., James D. Logsdon, and Robert R. Wiegman, *The Principalship: New Perspectives,* Englewood Cliffs, N.J.: Prentice-Hall, 1973.

Mitchell, Donald P. and Anne Hawley, *Leadership in Public Education Study,* Washington, D.C.: Academy for Educational Development, 1972.

National Association of Elementary School Principals *The Elementary School Principalship in 1968,* Arlington, Va.: The Association, 1968.

17

POST-SECONDARY SCHOOLS: THEIR ORGANIZATION AND ADMINISTRATION

During much of the nineteenth century the typical public school in the United States offered a simple educational course that terminated at the end of what were then called the elementary grades, usually Grade 8. Secondary education, although it existed in the form of the academy and the Latin grammar school, did not begin to flourish until after 1890. During the first half of the twentieth century, secondary education was considered terminal education for most and preparation for college for the rest. Today, school districts are encouraged by patterns of state support and occasionally are compelled by legislative fiat to provide both elementary and secondary educational opportunities.

The educational history of the United States is one of rising expectations for public education. New educational institutions that extended educational opportunities beyond Grade 12 of the secondary level came into popularity. Since the end of World War II the public community junior college developed rapidly as an extension of public education. Like the high school, the junior college had existed for a half century before it began to gain acceptance, and within a relatively short time it has become the new terminal point in education for those not going on to college. In addi-

tion more specialized post-secondary institutions such as the regional vocational-technical schools expanded in numbers and programs in the 1960s and 1970s. The organization and administration of post-secondary schools will have an impact on elementary and secondary school systems.

THE COMMUNITY JUNIOR COLLEGE

The origins of this two-year post-high school institution in the United States are obscure. Some report the first community college to be Monticello College, established in 1835, and the second Susquehanna University, established in 1858.[1] These were private schools. Many nineteenth-century four-year universities had rudimentary programs and often the first two years were what is now considered to be of the secondary school level. This was often necessary in a nation that had few quality secondary schools during the nineteenth-century. It was not until late in the nineteenth century that the term junior college referred to the first two years in the undergraduate university program.

[1] C. E. Blocker, R. H. Plummer, and R. C. Richardson, Jr., *The Two Year College: A Social Synthesis*, Englewood Cliffs, N.J.: Prentice-Hall, 1965, p. 25.

Growth of the community college

Only a handful of junior colleges existed in the world in 1900; eight of these were in the United States.[2] Each had an enrollment of about 100 pupils. All were private schools. The first public junior college in the United States was established in 1901 at Joliet, Illinois. By 1921 there were 207 junior colleges, about one-third of which were public institutions, and by 1925 the number had reached 325, of which 42 percent were public. It is significant that although the number of private junior colleges exceeded the number of those publicly supported, enrollment in public junior colleges was greater than that in private ones in the years following 1925.

McDowell suggested the following as the four main stimulators of junior-college development early in the twentieth century.

1. Encouragement from universities to create a junior-college division.
2. Expansion of programs in normal schools to include studies in addition to education courses.
3. Extension of high-school programs.
4. Decision by many small colleges too weak to satisfy the accreditation standards of a full four-year institution to concentrate resources on the first two years of collegiate instruction.[3]

The number of junior colleges continued to increase during the Great Depression of the 1930s, reaching 610 institutions with an enrollment of slightly less than one-quarter of a million by 1940–1941. The enforced retrenchment during World War II created pressure for the dramatic growth in the postwar years.

Between the two world wars junior college functions were expanded to include occupational programs. The concept of the junior college as encompassing adult education and community service as well as occupational training and the courses found in the first two years of a four-year institution did not gain recognition until after 1945.[4] The dramatic growth paralleled acceptance of the comprehensive concept of the community junior college.

The growth in junior colleges following World War II was in numbers of publicly supported institutions. Even more significant is that the increase in enrollment in public community colleges far outstripped that in private schools, many of which chose to remain small and offer limited programs. During the first quarter of the twentieth century, enrollment in private junior colleges exceeded that in public ones. By 1931 enrollment in public junior colleges was more than twice that in private junior colleges, by 1941 more than three times, and by 1971 more than 15 times the enrollment in private junior colleges.

Enrollment in all types of junior colleges exceeded 1 million students for the first time in 1964. What appeared in the 1960s to be over-optimistic predictions of future junior college enrollments turned out to be conservative in the 1970s. In 1972–1973 enrollments in public two-year institutions hit 2,618,017 students, an increase of more than 5 percent over the previous year, and in private two-year colleges totalled 131,076. This amounts to almost 2.75 million students. Over 95 percent of those enrolled are in public two-year institutions. Enrollments in private two-year schools have been declining since 1968 in the face of overall increases. The 1972 enrollment in pri-

[2]J. W. Thornton, The Community Junior College, 2nd ed., New York: Wiley, 1966, p. 45.

[3]F. M. McDowell, The Junior College, U.S. Bureau of Education, Bulletin 1919, no. 35, Washington, D.C.: GPO, 1919.

[4]Thornton, op. cit., pp. 51–56.

THE ADMINISTRATIVE HIERARCHY AND TEAM: SPECIAL ROLES AND POSITIONS

vate schools was less than that recorded in 1966.

In 1964 there were no public two-year colleges in operation in Delaware, Hawaii, Louisiana, Maine, Nevada, South Carolina, South Dakota, and Tennessee. Various sources do not agree on the number of junior colleges in the United States at present. The best estimate is that in 1972–1973 there were 871 public and 247 private two-year colleges (a total of 1118).

Gleazer, in 1966, noted the tremendous development of junior colleges in California and Florida, as follows:

California's goal is for all of its high schools to be within a junior college district. This is now the case for 90 percent of the high schools. Florida aims for a junior college within commuting distance of 99 percent of its population. Publicly supported junior colleges are now within commuting distance of 80 percent of the population and will be within commuting distance of 95 percent when the junior colleges already authorized are established.[5]

In 1972 only the four states of Alaska, Kentucky, Maine, and South Dakota had no students enrolled in public two-year institutions. In contrast, in that same year two-year public institutions in California enrolled almost 500,000, in New York over 211,000, in Illinois over 107,000, and in Texas over 105,000. The Education Policies Commission, the President of the United States, and the President's Committee on National Goals have called for the establishment of a nationwide system of free public education through two years beyond high school. The nation is approaching achievement of this goal and at a quickening pace. By 1980, public education may no longer consist of Grades

K through 12 but may be extended upward to include Grade 14. We are close to becoming the first nation in history with a universal two-year postsecondary school.

Characteristics of the community college

The community college has at least three main purposes. The first (and the one that gave rise to the term "junior college") is the provision of courses found in the first two years of the typical four-year, baccalaureate-degree-granting college or university. Some states limit by law the caliber of college courses offered in community colleges to those given in the freshman and sophomore years of degree-granting four-year institutions.

The second function of the community college is adult education. Such programs are open to nonmatriculated students, and typically the only admission requirement is personal interest. The programs are geared to community needs. For example, some junior colleges in areas of Florida that are inhabited by large numbers of retired persons offer programs specifically directed to the needs of those living in the retirement community.

The third function of the community college is technical education to develop special occupational skills that require more than a high school education but less than four years of college. Included is training for such occupations as x-ray technician, dental hygienist, medical laboratory technician, practical nurse, data processor, accountant, and legal or other specially skilled secretary.

Thornton identified the generally accepted purposes of the community junior college as:

1. Occupational and technical education at the post-high school level.

American Association of Junior Colleges, "Emphasis," *Junior College Journal,* vol. 37, no. 3, November 1966, p. 5.

2. General education for all students.
3. College transfer or preprofessional education for the baccalaureate-degree-oriented student.
4. Continuing educational opportunities for part-time students.
5. Community services.
6. Counseling and guidance of students.[6]

Yet another function appears to be emerging, namely, remedial instruction. Most states require by law that public junior colleges admit all high school graduates and others of post-secondary school age who can profit from some type of instruction. This open-door admission policy, one of the more controversial issues in junior college education, necessitates one of the least publicized functions of the junior college—remedial instruction. It is to be expected that increasing numbers of the full-time student body will be low-ability students.[7] Results of remedial instruction have been somewhat less than encouraging in terms of students' subsequent educational accomplishments. These early conclusions do not suggest abandonment of remedial instruction, but rather the need for better conceptualization of its purposes and the best means to achieve them.

Fields suggested that the uniqueness of the community college could be traced to the following five characteristics:

1. It is democratic, having low tuition and nonselective admission policies, and is geographically accessible to large numbers of people.
2. It is comprehensive, serving a wide range of abilities, aptitudes, and interests.
3. It is community-centered, being locally

supported and controlled, and strives to serve community interests.
4. It is dedicated to life-long education and is concerned with learners of all post-secondary school ages.
5. It is adaptable, being concerned with differences in clientele and changing needs of society.[8]

The various functions do not necessarily dovetail. While some college-parallel courses may be useful for students of technical education, by and large, the various branches of the community college exist side by side, each having its own admission standards and staff requirements. It is possible for a public community college to become purely a preparatory school for a four-year degree-granting college. This happens when 90 percent or more of the students are enrolled in college-transfer courses to the neglect of adult and technical education. Because preparation for teaching adult and technical education courses is not universally accepted as adequate for teaching college-parallel courses, and vice versa, accreditation and preparation standards for the faculty are of prime concern in the community college.

The community college grants an associate in arts degree to designate the completion of the two-year college-parallel program. Usually the standards of admission to a college-parallel program in a community college are more flexible than those to a four-year, baccalaureate-degree-granting institution. It is possible for a student with a relatively inadequate scholarship record in senior high school to pursue freshman and sophomore college level studies through the community college program. Whether the community colleges will attempt to emulate baccalaureate-degree-granting

[6]Thornton, op. cit., pp. 58–70.
[7]J. E. Roueche, "The Junior College Remedial Program," *Junior College Research Review,* UCLA Clearinghouse for Junior College Information, vol. 2, no. 3, November 1967.

[8]R. R. Fields, *The Community College Movement,* New York: McGraw-Hill, 1962, pp. 63–95.

schools and raise entrance standards remains to be seen. Clearly such a move is contrary to the concept of the community college as a post-secondary school center.

An important characteristic of the community college is its accessibility to the people being served. A frequently mentioned goal is the location of a campus within driving distance of every pupil in the state. While this implies that the junior college is not a residential institution, those residing at the fringes of a community college area seek living quarters near the college, and in some cases pressures have developed for dormitory facilities for community colleges. Whether or not residential facilities should be provided for students is becoming an issue in community college administration. More seem to be amenable to building residential facilities.

Extracurricular activities such as the traditional football, basketball, baseball, and track teams are part of intercommunity college athletic programs. The junior college occasionally serves as a farm club for larger university football teams, with transfer taking place after the sophomore year. As yet sorority and fraternity programs have not been a problem in community colleges.

Administrative patterns of the community college

Whether the public community college should be considered an extension of education provided in local school districts, a state-wide two-year school system with its own state junior college board of control, an independent junior college district, or the two-year portion of the total system controlled by a state board for all higher educa-

tion is a controversial issue. There is no single organizational pattern.

Martorana and Morrison[9] reported on public junior college organizational patterns in the mid-1950s. The three predominant patterns were (1) a unified district with public elementary and secondary schools (41 percent), (2) a separate junior-college district (27.2 percent), and (3) a two-year extension center (18.3 percent). The state two-year college (5.8 percent) and the county normal-school pattern (6.3 percent) represent other approaches. Regional differences were noted: The separate junior college district was preferred in the South and West, the unified school and junior college district in the North Central region, and the off-campus university center in the Northeast and some North Central states.

The pattern in Florida up to 1968 exemplified the community college as part of the local school district (and each local district in Florida is coterminous with a county). The junior college represents an upward extension of the total educational opportunities provided in the basic unit of school administration. Although a special budget and separate state support were available, the community college was under control of the county board of public instruction, which was the local board of education in Florida until the late 1960s. The community college president was subordinate to the chief executive officer of the local school board (the superintendent of schools). The primary policy-making body was the local board of education, although a special community college advisory

[9]S. V. Martorana and D. G. Morrison, *Patterns of Organization and Support in Public Two-Year Colleges,* U.S. Office of Education, OE 52000, Washington, D.C.: GPO, 1957.

committee may make recommendations. Florida abandoned the concept of public junior colleges as an upward extension of a statewide system of elementary and secondary education. A junior college system separate from other schools came into being on July 1, 1968.

In California the public junior college may be organized as (1) a part of a high school district, (2) a part of a unified city school district, or (3) a separate junior-college district with an independent junior college board. Authorization to extend secondary school programs for an additional two years was passed in California as early as 1907. Educators who argue that the junior college is a collegiate rather than a post-secondary school institution subject to local jurisdictions appear to prefer a separate organization for junior colleges.

The Iowa organization for junior colleges was similar to the early Florida arrangement for a time. The Illinois pattern views the community college as a "special institution," standing between the termination of secondary education and the beginning of a senior undergraduate collegiate institution. A separate state-wide junior college board was created in Illinois to administer these institutions.

The perception of the junior college will ultimately determine its structure and organization within the system of public education of a state. If it is conceptualized primarily as an institution close to the student's home that offers collegiate-level courses similar to those given in the freshman and sophomore years of a four-year baccalaureate-degree-granting institution, there should probably be a closer alliance between the community college and institutions of higher learning. This could be achieved by establishing a separate state junior college board of control or by working with the existing state board for higher education for four-year and university-grade institutions.

On the other hand, if the community college is visualized as a multipurpose educational institution, of which college-parallel programs are a part, but not the dominant portion, its closest ties should be with local or intermediate-level administrative units. If the community college movement is perceived as the upward extension of secondary education, that is as a response to society's need for better educated, more highly skilled, more technically prepared citizens, then the argument for greater community involvement and control gathers weight.

It is the writer's contention that the more persuasive arguments are those that view the community junior college as a comprehensive post-secondary school institution supported by state funds but under the supervision and control of a local, rather than a state or separate, board of education. This is contrary to the opinion of those closest to the junior college movement. It is the opinion of this writer that just as the appearance of the high school near the end of the previous century caused some to argue in favor of a separate status for it, so the junior college specialists are fighting for a special status for two-year post-secondary schools. The trend seems to be in the direction of separate organization and control for two-year public institutions. Twenty years from now the nation will have another battle to integrate such units into a new and expanded local district.

The major sources of funds for support of a two-year college are tuition, state taxes, local taxes, and gifts. More and more states are assuming the major share for capital outlay and operation of community colleges.

Administrative staff of the community college

The chief executive officer of a community college is often referred to as a president and less frequently as a dean. When the community college is considered a special type of attendance unit, the broad policy-making authority resides in the local board of education. If the community college is a completely self-contained system similar to a small school district with one attendance unit, policy control resides in the junior college board.

The complexity of the community colleges necessitates a rather large administrative staff. Staff members usually carry the titles common in four-year institutions of higher learning rather than those in use in elementary and secondary schools. Thus, there is a vice president or a dean (but never a supervisor) for instruction, a dean or a director for technical education, a dean of students, and a vice president or dean (but not assistant superintendent) for administrative or for business affairs. Department heads are the rule rather than the exception in the junior college.

As yet professorial rank has not been awarded commonly to junior college instructors, but this may change.

It is evident from the titles of officers that the community colleges have emulated universities rather than elementary and secondary institutions. In most states, however, junior college teachers are certified by or through the state department of education as are elementary and secondary school teachers. No state requires the certification of four-year college and university teachers, whether they carry the title of teaching assistant, instructor, or professor. Instruction, not research, is the primary function of the junior college teacher.

THE AREA VOCATIONAL-TECHNICAL SCHOOL

The community college represents only one type of post-secondary school school center. The Vocational Education Act of 1963 stimulated formation of the area vocational-technical school that serves the needs of senior high school students, post-secondary school students, and adults. Federal funds provide resources for a variety of purposes related to these schools. One-third of the funds can be allocated for construction of new facilities. Because the vocational-technical school is a specialized institution, it usually serves a geographical territory larger than the local school district. Thus, in Wisconsin there are over 440 local school districts but only 15 or 16 area vocational-technical school districts that are controlled by a special board and operate with a separate set of administrators from local schools.

The area vocational-technical school was created to provide young people and adults with the skills necessary to gain and hold a remunerative job. Some of the schools provide complex vocational-technical training for senior high school students; others serve high school graduates and young adults seeking to learn specialized skills in such fields as automobile mechanics, culinary arts, refrigeration mechanics, data processing, and electronics. These functions overlap to some extent with technical education programs of the community college. There are many other post-secondary vocational education concerns that have not found their way into the typical community college program. In a few cases the area vocational-technical school and the community junior college are merged into one institution. In some instances the expansion of the educational program of an area vocational-technical school to include liberal arts courses as well as vocational and technical makes it operate as if it were a community college even though this name is not applied to it.

INTERRELATIONS OF THE POST-SECONDARY SCHOOL CENTERS

The community college may be evolving in many respects in a pattern similar to that of the secondary school. The Latin grammar school, the first secondary institution, was oriented toward academic pursuits and offered only college-preparatory programs. The academy and then the high school appeared, providing more diversified, but nonvocational, courses to meet the needs of many more students. The inclusion of vocational courses followed in spite of resistance from those who considered vocational instruction beneath the academic standards of the school. Federal funds stimulated comprehensive vocationally oriented programs in agriculture, home economics, and trades and industry within the local school districts. At present there are few who challenge the worth of the comprehensive secondary institution in the United States; there is general agreement that education for all youths can be achieved only through comprehensive secondary education programs that include vocational training.

Whether there shall be one or several post-secondary education institutions to satisfy the needs of the American society in the last quarter of the twentieth century has yet to be resolved. The multipurpose community college, providing college-parallel,

adult education, and technical education programs represents one approach. The area vocational-technical school represents another. The strictly collegiate, degree-oriented junior college is a third.

Out of present confusion will emerge a comprehensive community-oriented, as opposed to a baccalaureate-degree-oriented, post-secondary school institution. It will serve the three purposes of the community college, the functions of the area vocational-technical school, and the needs of late adolescents as well as adults. Although a college degree, whether at the undergraduate or the graduate level will be demanded by more and more students, there will still be many others who neither want nor need a college degree to become contributing, useful members of society. A strong nation needs to satisfy the educational requirements of both groups.

ADMINISTRATION OF THE POST-SECONDARY SCHOOL CENTER

The past few decades have witnessed a dramatic decrease in the number of basic administrative units in the public school system. Only about 10 percent of the local school districts existing in 1931 are operating at present. There is every indication that by the end of the next two decades there will be no more than 5000 basic administrative units. However, this trend might be reversed, not by an increase in local school districts but by the development of specialized educational administrative units for a variety of post-secondary school purposes, such as junior college districts and vocational-school districts. Early in this century the development of secondary education led to the organization of specialized high school districts separate from the elementary school districts, and consequently to a massive proliferation of local school administrative units. Today, the trend is toward a unified district providing elementary and secondary school opportunities.

Inefficient and overlapping school-district structures may reappear if post-secondary school institutions are managed by specialized administrative units rather than incorporated in a comprehensive local school district or intermediate unit. The enthusiasm for upward extension of educational opportunities beyond the secondary school level must be tempered with sound organizational procedures or the precious resources of the state, already strained to support expanding commitments in education, may be dissipated by duplication of administrative effort.

SUMMARY

What was once considered terminal education—completion of the elementary grades and graduation from high school—is being revised upward with the growth of the community junior college. The concept of terminal education should be abandoned in favor of continuous learning programs for all ages.

The handful of junior colleges in 1900 grew to about 900 by 1975. The private school dominated early in the century. After World War II, the publicly supported junior colleges were more numerous than private ones. Enrollment in two-year post-secondary institutions topped the 1 million mark for the first time in 1964, and 2.6 million in 1972 with the greatest gains registered in public institutions. Enrollments in private two-year institutions have been declining since 1968, in face of a general uptrend. In the 1950s and 1960s California and Florida

led the nation in developing extensive public community college centers. Four states have no public junior colleges. Others, such as California, have almost 500,000 enrolled in public two-year institutions. The nation is moving rapidly toward a system of free public education that extends two years beyond the high school level.

The community junior college is a multipurpose post-secondary school institution, offering college-parallel, occupational, and adult education programs. A remedial function is now being recognized as well. An important characteristic is the college's accessibility to the people being served.

Whether the public community junior college is an upward extension of the secondary school or a part of higher education is an unresolved issue. The many different functions have attributes of both. At one time most public community junior colleges were a part of the local school district. Separate junior college districts are becoming the most common organizational pattern.

The chief executive officer of a community college is referred to as president or dean. It is apparent from the titles of officers that community colleges have emulated universities rather than elementary and secondary schools.

The area vocational-technical school created by the Vocational Education Act of 1963 represents the newest of the post-secondary school institutions. To some extent its functions overlap with the community college's, but the latter institution seldom assumes comprehensive vocational instruction.

Whether there shall be one or several post-secondary school institutions has yet to be resolved. The organizational implications of new educational extensions may precipitate problems of proliferation of organizational units.

QUESTIONS

1. Are there other educational institutions better suited to assume adult education functions than the community junior college? Justify your response.
2. Why did the public community junior college grow so rapidly after 1945?
3. Should the open-door admission policy of public junior colleges be revised? Justify your stand.
4. How does the public community junior college differ from its private counterpart?
5. Debate the following issue: Resolved, that all community junior colleges in a state be under the control of a state junior college board, not the local board of education.

SELECTED REFERENCES

Blocker, C. E., R. H. Plummer, and R. C. Richardson, Jr., *The Two Year College: A Social Synthesis*, Englewood Cliffs, N.J.: Prentice-Hall, 1965.

Bushnell, David S., *Organizing for Change: New Priorities for Community Colleges*, New York: McGraw-Hill, 1973.

Fields, R. R., *The Community College Movement*, New York: McGraw-Hill, 1962.

Gleazer, Edmund J., *Project Focus: A Forecast Study for Community Colleges*, New York: McGraw-Hill, 1973.

Rarig, E. W., ed., *The Community Junior College: An Annotated Bibliography*, New York: Teachers College, 1966.

Roueche, J. E., "The Junior College Remedial Program," *Junior College Research Review*, UCLA Clearinghouse for Junior College Information, vol. 2, no. 3, November 1967.

Thornton, J. W., *The Community Junior College*, 2nd ed., New York: Wiley, 1966.

IV

THE PRACTICAL DIMENSIONS AND OPERATIONAL CHALLENGES IN EDUCATIONAL ADMINISTRATION

Traditional conceptualizations viewed educational administration as a cluster of operational challenges unique to schools. Skill in the practice of school administration has been related primarily to gaining professional competence in the subject matter of Chapters 18 to 25. These competencies remain a very important dimension of the practical art of administration.

Separate volumes have been written about each of the administrative areas dealt with in this part. The chapters that follow summarize the recent and important facts, trends, and issues in pupil personnel administration, professional personnel administration (with emphasis on negotiations), curriculum and instructional leadership, managing learning opportunity programs, economic dimensions of administration, management of school facilities, and political dimensions of administration. Particular emphasis is placed on the roles of various types of administrators and the competencies needed to fulfill the operational challenges.

The book concludes with a review of accountability and a summary of the trends and issues in the appraisal of administrators.

18

THE CLIENT SERVICE DIMENSION: PUPIL PERSONNEL ADMINISTRATION

Schools exist to provide educational services to learners. Pupils are the specific clients of educational institutions even though society as a whole may be the general beneficiary. Each school system must come to grips with the challenges of creating an organizational structure and administrative procedures to assure the delivery of the educational services desired by its clients. Another way of saying the same thing is to say that pupil personnel administration is one of the most important dimensions of an educational institution.

Pupil personnel administration comprises those administrative and supervisory functions and services, other than classroom instruction, that are concerned with (1) the identification, admission, registration, enrollment, and classification of school-age children and other learners; and (2) the comprehension and development of the abilities, interests, and needs of individuals at various levels of maturity within the school system. The first aspect of this definition, the quantitative dimensions of pupil administration, is the subject of part one of this chapter. The second part reviews qualitative dimensions.

Section 1: Quantitative dimensions

Early in this century pupil personnel administration was synonymous with keeping track of pupils, or "child accounting." As late as 1951, a well-known writer on school administration defined it as "the recording of all administrative, instruction, and appraisal information necessary to keep a pre-school, school, and post-school record of each student."[1] This emphasis on the quantitative dimension of pupil administration can be traced to the earliest writing in the field. Ayres in 1915[2] stressed record keeping—particularly locating, grouping, keeping track of, and reporting the progress of students. Some mention was made of special services and conditions favorable to the adjustment of pupils, but of overriding importance was keeping "accounts."

The qualitative dimension of student administration emerged when the

[1] A. B. Moehlman, School Administration, 2nd ed., Boston: Houghton Mifflin, 1951, chap. 14.
[2] Leonard P. Ayres, Child Accounting in the Public Schools, Philadelphia: William F. Fell, 1915.

records were analyzed and interpreted in the hope of improving pupil adjustment and learning in the school situation. The emphasis shifted from accounting for pupils to satisfying individual needs, and record keeping acquired a fresh purpose: to provide data on the growth and development of the learner. The qualitative approach to pupil administration stimulated an expansion of special services such as guidance and counseling, social work, and health services. The relation of guidance to administration of pupils was noted in textbooks on educational administration by no later than 1931,[3] but not until after World War II, and particularly during the 1950s, did the qualitative approach completely overshadow the quantitative. Today, pupil personnel administration is considered by many to signify guidance and counseling, clinical services, and other welfare activities to the exclusion of school census keeping, admission policies, attendance recording, and the like. Both aspects have a place in pupil personnel administration.

IDENTIFICATION OF PUPILS: THE SCHOOL CENSUS

The importance of an accurate census record for each child of school age has become obscured by innovations in public education in recent years. The purposes of the school census have changed over the years. Early in educational history it was the basis for the distribution of funds to the local school district; however, it left much to be desired and is seldom used for that purpose today. Some of

the present-day purposes of the school census are to:

1. Ascertain the nature and scope of educational services needed in the school district.
2. Provide data basic to planning school-plant programs.
3. Evaluate enforcement of compulsory-attendance laws.
4. Determine the number of children who will enter school for the first time and report any unusual characteristics of this group.
5. Locate children who move into, out of, or about the district.
6. Discover the employment of a child.
7. Check enrollment and absences in public as well as private and parochial schools.[4]

The school census is the first step in child-accounting. It is an official record of all persons of school age in a school district. Past enumerations were notoriously inaccurate. One nation-wide study revealed that 25 percent of school-age children were not reported in the school census. The reverse may result when census takers are paid in proportion to the number of persons counted. One study indicated overreporting of children by as much as 15 percent.[5] Many school enumerations were so inaccurate as to be useless in providing information important to planning new school-plant facilities. The census appears to be fairly accurate for children between the ages of 7 and 13. The count of the preschool (under age 5) population is the least accurate.

The census begins with a house-to-house canvass. Those who are to be counted are usually specified in state laws. By 1910, 33 states required an

---

[3]Fred Engelhardt, *Public School Organization and Administration*, Boston: Ginn, 1931, p. 361.

[4]William A. Yeager, *Administration and the Pupil*, New York: Harper & Row, 1949, p. 71.

[5]Jack Culbertson, "Attendance," in Chester W. Harris, ed., *Encyclopedia of Educational Research*, 3rd ed., New York: Macmillan, 1960, p. 95.

enumeration of school-age children, and by 1940 all states except Nevada did so. Culbertson reported a slight reversal in the trend, for by 1953 only 38 states required a census, 5 had permissive laws, and 5 had no laws. The most general practice is an annual enumeration. Census taking usually lasted about a month and was done sometime between April and September. In most states children between 6 and 21 were reported; this includes pupils under the jurisdiction of the compulsory-attendance laws.

Identifying children for the census roster immediately following birth is now recommended practice; the census age range would thus be 0 to 21. There is some argument for not reporting those over 19 if no community college experience is anticipated, but in view of the growth of post-secondary school institutions, people aged 19 through 21 should probably be counted.

Minimum information desired from the school census records would include name of child, date of birth, authority for birth information, address of child, names and occupations of parents, name and location of school attended, reasons for nonattendance, notation of physical or mental handicap, and movements within or out of the district. Whether a child is likely to attend a private school is useful in a district having a large percentage of the school population in private or parochial institutions. Census data may be organized to reveal the residential distribution of school-age children, for this is relevant to the location of new buildings or additions.

The continuous census

The continuous system starts with an initial house-to-house canvass, as does the periodic enumeration. Whereas the periodic enumeration (made annually or less frequently) produces data that become progressively more obsolete, the continuous census records changes in student population either weekly or monthly. By keeping track of pupil movements within, into, and out of the district, it increases the chances of discovering those missed in the initial house-to-house canvass.

The continuing census demands more personnel, more work, and careful organization: New data must be posted at the end of each week or month to update the original enumeration; additional clerical personnel and machines are required to gather and record such data. The additional expense is justified if the continuous census system makes possible more accurate counting of the preschool-age population and compensates for the incompetencies of the enumerators.[6]

The continuing census system has been recommended to all school administrators since at least the early 1920s. Its adoption has been slow. No district is too small to install it. The new data necessary to maintain a continuous census system accurately can be obtained from birth reports, death reports, and notices of moves into, out of, or within the district. Sources for the latter type of information include moving companies, utility companies, public and private school principals, school-bus drivers, and attendance officers. Data necessary to keep the census current can be obtained by subscribing to a local credit-bureau publication at a very modest cost. A continuous system requires validation by a periodic house-to-house canvass, but such canvassing can be spaced much farther apart than the usual one or two years.

[6]Ibid.

Processing of census data

Manual procedures were used in collecting and filing census data prior to the establishment of computer-based information systems. Manual processing is complex, inaccurate, time consuming, and expensive. Computer-based electronic data processing has greatly reduced the drudgery of census operations and improved the accuracy and accessibility of information.

With manual procedures, census data for each pupil are placed on an index card. The number of copies of each card is determined by the degree of cross-indexing desired. Thus, a card might be needed for indexing by pupil's age, another for alphabetical listing, and a third for indexing by type of school attended (elementary, secondary, or junior college). In addition a family card is needed, giving such information as parents' names, parents' occupations, and number of children of various ages. As census cards accumulate, the filing system becomes cumbersome. A live file and a dead file must be maintained. As soon as a child moves out of the district or reaches an age beyond that specified for the census, his card is moved to the dead file. Special markers are used to identify pupils with physical or mental handicaps. Thus a red tag on the census card might denote a seriously crippled child, a blue tag a child with a visual defect, an orange tag a child of subnormal intelligence.

It is difficult to retrieve data and to organize reports from manually processed census records. The use of electronic data-processing equipment can overcome most census record keeping defects and is feasible in large and small school systems. The information on pupil census can be classified readily into machine-usable form, stored in the computer's memory, and almost instantly be retrieved for the variety of reports necessary for the administration of the institution. There are a large number of programs available at the present time for use with a variety of electronic data-processing hardware to expeditiously handle the school census, attendance, registration, and similar reports.

A system large enough to justify its own computer operations should have little difficulty in converting census data into the information system. A small school system can obtain such services either through an intermediate unit or through cooperative arrangement with a university-based or privately owned data-processing service. The advent of electronic data processing greatly facilitates the installation and operation of a continuous school-census system and the effective utilization of the intelligence it provides.

ADMISSION OF PUPILS TO SCHOOL

Requirements for admission

Admission to a public school is not an absolute right. It is a right that can be exercised only upon meeting qualifications established by legal authorities. Thus, a child must usually attain a given age before being admitted to a public school. There is ample evidence that a child who enters kindergarten or Grade 1 before he is physically, socially, or intellectually ready experiences academic difficulties and is handicapped in adjusting to school. Although there are exceptions, research supports the contention that a child who enters first grade with a mental age of 6 years or older is more likely to experience academic success than a child with a younger mental age.[7] Boys mature about three or four months later than girls of the same chronological age. These factors should be taken into consideration in determining admission age. One study pointed out that four times as many under-age children had difficulty in school than did normal-age children. Both under-age and over-age children had more adjustment problems than those of normal age.[8]

Administrators are sympathetic to the idea of basing school entrance upon mental age plus physical, social, and emotional maturity. Although nationally there has been a steady decline in average entrance age since 1918, the trend today is toward raising the minimum admission age. There is wide variation among public school systems as to the minimum age attained for admission of pupils to kindergarten; the same is true for first grade. This is less true in states that mandate uniformity in minimum age requirements among all districts in the state.

There is need for selective admission of children who are as much as two months below the normal chronological entrance age requirement but have a mental age two or more months above the chronological age, who are in good physical health, and who are physically mature. Publicity about admission standards is often accompanied by parent education to reduce emotional reactions toward exceptions to rules which permit some children, particularly girls, to enter school sooner than others of the same chronological age.[9]

[7]Harold G. Shane and James E. Polychrones, "Elementary Education: Organization and Administration," in Chester W. Harris, ed., *Encyclopedia of Educational Research*, 3rd ed., New York: Macmillan, 1960, p. 425.

[8]Ibid.

[9]Ibid.

A second requirement for admission is residence within the district. A child's residence is normally where his father lives. The definition of residence for school purposes is much broader than that for domicile, which is the basis for determining the right to vote in a given area. A district has the right to reject pupils who do not reside within the district.

Certain health requirements must be met for entry into school. Thus, vaccination is legally required, according to some courts, for admission to a public school. The reduction in the incidence of smallpox in the United States may change this requirement if it is tested once again in court.

Effect of school integration

At one time in the history of public education the assignment of pupils to attendance centers was relatively simple and noncontroversial. Boundary lines designated the attendance area for a given building, and those living within the area were directed to register as students. Transfer problems arose occasionally, but seldom were they a source of unusual concern. Since the Supreme Court decision of 1954, which required all public schools to admit pupils from appropriate attendance areas regardless of race, admission and assignment of pupils to schools have become controversial issues.

In the years immediately following 1954, school integration was a problem primarily in the South, where the maintenance of separate schools for blacks and whites was supported by state laws. Little Rock and New Orleans were the battle grounds where the impact of the 1954 decision was tested. Progress toward desegregation in 17 southern states and the District of Columbia was relatively slow in the years that immediately followed that historic decision. During the 1960s the pace of desegregation in the southern and border states did not increase much. By 1966–1967 only 25.8 percent of the blacks were enrolled in integrated schools (up from 23.5 percent in 1960). Progress in the late 1960s is evident from the data which show that 29.4 percent of minority students attended schools where 100 percent of the enrollment was minority students in 1968 as compared with 10.5 percent in 1970. More dramatic gains were registered in the eleven southern states where in 1968 57.4 percent of the minority students were in schools with 100 percent minority students and in 1970 12.0 percent of the minority students were isolated in schools with 100 percent minority students.

The 1954 Supreme Court decision was followed by the enactment of a series of civil rights bills, each bolder than the last (in the years 1957, 1960, 1964, and 1965). A civil rights commission was organized and issued a detailed report on southern school desegregation that was scathing in its condemnation of the slow pace. It pointed out that the Civil Rights Act precipitated a boom in private white segregated schools that enjoyed both state and federal tax benefits. By 1973 there were almost 400 of these so-called "white academies."

Black leaders shifted from accommodation to protest, from subservience to challenge. Many organizations formed at least initially to further the civil rights of blacks focused on schools. Havighurst[10] depicted the many phases in the school's involvement in civil rights issues as follows:

[10]R. J. Havighurst, "Schools Face New Desegregation Phase," *Nation's Schools*, vol. 77, March 1966, pp. 80–82.

Phase I: Response to the court, 1954 to 1958;

Phase II: Rise of controversy, 1958 to 1963;

Phase III: Black revolution, 1963 to 1966;

Phase IV: Drive for integration, 1966 to 1970

A Phase V may be in progress with a drive for black control of schools where the majority of the student body is black. This includes more black school-board members and black administrators as well as more black teachers. The number of black school superintendents increases each year.

During the 1960s the Office of Education began to use its authority to withhold federal funds as a way to hasten desegregation of schools. In mid-1967, responsibility for civil rights enforcement was transferred from the Office of Education to a special office for civil rights in the Department of Health, Education, and Welfare.

By the middle of the 1960s large urban centers in the North came under attack for perpetuating (what is known as) de facto segregation. Although there was no intent to operate separate schools for blacks and for whites, the fact that blacks and whites often lived in separate areas caused many attendance centers to have a predominately black student body. Civil rights groups sought to establish a better balance. One proposed solution was to bus children from the predominantly black schools to predominantly white schools. Pupil busing to achieve a better racial balance in schools was an issue in the 1972 presidential campaign. It hit the northern schools as well as those in the South. The resolution of racial imbalance in assignment of pupils to attendance centers remained a controversial and unresolved issue some 20 years after the *Brown* decision.

Hauser and Taitel[11] reported demographical factors related to the movement of blacks into large urban centers. In 1910, 89 percent of the blacks of the nation were in the South. By 1950 the migration of Negroes from the South to other regions left only about two-thirds in the South. By 1960 less than 60 percent of all blacks remained in the South. This trend continued and by 1970 there were as many Negroes in other regions as in the South.

The southern black was primarily a rural resident. In 1910, prior to the migration of blacks to the North, only 27 percent lived in urban places, defined by the census as places of 2500 inhabitants or more. By 1960, 58 percent of the blacks in the South, and 95 percent of those in the North and West, lived in urban communities. Blacks settled in the central core of the metropolitan areas rather than in suburbs. Hauser and Taitel described the central core of the city as the blacks' port of entry into northern regions and into urban America. Recently a movement toward the suburbs has been in evidence.[12] In many cities the great majority of residents are blacks. In many urban school systems black students constitute the largest proportion of those enrolled in the public schools.

The Coleman report published results of a study of racial segregation in public schools and the effect that school characteristics have on student learning.[13] Done at the behest of the United States Congress, the report was based on 1965 data. It concluded that the great majority of American children were segregated, the blacks being the most segregated of the minority groups. For the black segregation was nearly complete in the South, but was extensive elsewhere as well. It also concluded that the social class of the school's student body was the most important factor in determining student achievement. The report boldly declared, and in great opposition to a mass of other educational research, that the amount of money spent per pupil for books, buildings, and other resources had little direct effect on achievement. The report stated: "The achievement of minority pupils depends more on the schools they attend than does the achievement of majority pupils" and "improving the school of a minority pupil will increase his achievement more than will improving the school of a white child."[14] Many attacked these conclusions as unwarranted and not clearly related to the data. Some critics contended that the Coleman report was based on relations among factors that were not isolated and that the methods used to measure the background of Negro students were inadequate. In short, the Coleman report's methodology as well as its conclusions became controversial.

The school system is asked to cope with problems, many facets of which are beyond its control. As long as residential areas are determined by the availability of housing to particular ethnic groups, it will be difficult to obtain the degree of school integration

[11]P. M. Hauser and M. Taitel, "Population Trends: Prologue to Educational Programs," *Perspective Changes in Society by 1980: Designing Education for the Future,* Denver, Colo.: The Eight-State Project, July 1966, pp. 23–55.

[12]Ibid.

[13]U.S. Department of Health, Education, and Welfare, *Equality of Educational Opportunity,* Office of Education Summary Report, OE 38000, Washington, D.C.: GPO, 1966.

[14]Ibid., p. 21.

sought by many groups. In addition, the school has no authority to prevent persons from selling their homes and moving to the suburbs, and the migration of whites from the city to the suburbs is largely responsible for the increased proportion of blacks in the total enrollment of large urban schools. It is apparent that other agencies in addition to public schools must be involved in promoting the established goal of better racial balance in school attendance centers.

ENROLLMENT AND ATTENDANCE OF PUPILS

The large increase in enrollment in public schools over the years can be deduced from Table 18–1. These data, based on United States Office of Education statistics, are quoted in preference to others, which differ slightly. Enrollment in public nursery, elementary, and secondary schools totaled only 6,872,000 pupils in 1869–1870. Most were elementary school pupils, for only 1.2 percent of the total enrollment was in high schools. Fifty years later, in 1920, public school enrollment had tripled to 21,578,000. Enrollment increased again during the next decade.

A decline was evident, particularly at the elementary school level, during the Depression decade of 1930 to 1940. Although elementary school enrollment increased during the 1940s, secondary school enrollment declined, so that once again total enrollment dipped. Total enrollment in public schools in 1939–1940 and 1949–1950 was lower than in 1929–1930. Enrollment during the 1950s and 1960s set new records each year. There was an increase of over 9.5 million pupils in the 1960s, that is, from 1959–1960 to 1969–1970. The peak enrollment was hit in the fall of 1971 with an estimated 46,081,000 pupils. Declines have been recorded, but in the early 1970s pupil enrollments did not fall below that indicated for any year prior to 1969–1970. The nation's schools are moving from a robust expansionary mood that was characteristic of the first 25 years after World War II to one of cautious retrenchment based on slowly declining pupil population in the 1970s. It should be assumed that the drop in pupil enrollment in the mid- and late-1970s will not be precipitous. It is more likely to equal or exceed that found in the late 1960s, which at one time was considered to be a record high, and will exceed that noted in the early 1960s.

Acceptance of the public secondary schools as an important part of the American school system is a twentieth-century achievement. During the nineteenth century less than 2 percent of the total enrollment in public schools was found in high schools. By the end of the first decade of the twentieth century only about 5 percent of the total enrollment was in high schools. Since the end of World War II enrollment in public high schools has constituted approximately 22 percent of the total in public elementary and secondary schools. About 88.5 percent of the school age population is enrolled in the public elementary and secondary schools.

Enforcement of attendance

Part of the dramatic gains in public school enrollment can be traced to compulsory-education laws. The first modern public school compulsory-attendance law, enacted in Massachusetts in 1852, required three months' attendance in public school during the year; in 1873 this was extended to five months.[15] By 1890, 27 states and the District of Columbia had enacted similar compulsory-education laws, and by 1914, all but 6 Southern states had such laws. Mississippi, in 1918, was the last state to enact a compulsory-education law. Compulsory education was delayed until after 1850 because (1) providing education only for those who wanted to go to school was in itself a tremendous task, and (2) children were valuable as workers. It was not until the early part of the twentieth century that most states enacted child-labor laws compatible with compulsory-education laws. As a result of the Supreme Court decision on school integration, South Carolina and Mississippi repealed compulsory-attendance laws in 1955 and 1956,[16] and Virginia did the same in the late 1950s.

Establishment and enforcement of compulsory-education laws were accompanied by debate and difficulty. Such laws were considered undemocratic and unenforceable, but events proved them otherwise. Early compulsory-education laws placed school-leaving age at 13 or 14 years. By 1954 school-leaving age was 16 years in 39 states, 17 years in 4 states, and 18 years in 5 states.[17]

Most state departments of education have some responsibility to enforce compulsory-attendance laws. The most common age at which a pupil must begin regular attendance is 7 years, and the most common school-leaving age is 16 years; 31 of the 50 states specify 7 through 16 as the compulsory-education age range.

There are limitations to the compulsory-education laws. The case of *Pierce* vs. *Society of Sisters of the Holy Name of Jesus and Mary* (268 U.S. 510) established that a pupil can discharge education requirements by attending a parochial or a private rather than a public school. An individual completing the highest grade offered within a district is likewise exempt from further conditions of the compulsory-attendance laws in some states. Exemptions have been recognized for illness, physical or mental handicap, and special religious reasons. On the other hand, the courts have repeatedly held that a married pupil cannot be excluded from school on the grounds of marriage alone. Although a married pupil is excused from conditions of the compulsory-education law, she has a right to attend school if she chooses. Board action cannot override the law.

When school attendance first became compulsory, truant officers employed by the school district or the city police department invoked police power to enforce attendance. The present-day attendance officer relies less on police power (although it is still employed where necessary), than on understanding why the child is not attending and applying corrective measures in place of force.

The individuals charged with the enforcement of school attendance during the 1920s had such occupations as police officer, real estate agent, meat cutter, glass blower, painter, and electrician; only about 14 percent could be classified as professionally trained; the majority were 51 years of age or older.[18] The White House Conference on Child Health and Protection in 1932 suggested an attendance officer for every 1500 to 2000 children enrolled in public, private, and parochial schools. It also suggested that the office should be oriented toward social work rather than policing, and that the attendance officer should have

[15]Culbertson, op. cit., p. 93.
[16]Ibid.
[17]Ibid.

[18]Yeager, op. cit., p. 77.

TABLE 18–1

HISTORICAL SUMMARY OF PUBLIC ELEMENTARY AND SECONDARY SCHOOL ENROLLMENT AND ATTENDANCE, 1869–1870 TO 1972–1973

	1869–1870	1899–1900	1919–1920	1929–1930	1939–1940	1949–1950
K-8 enrollment	6,792,000	14,984,000	19,378,000	21,279,000	18,833,000	19,387,000
9-12 enrollment	80,000	519,000	2,200,000	4,399,000	6,601,000	5,725,000
Total K-12 enrollment	6,872,000	15,503,000	21,578,000	25,678,000	25,434,000	25,112,000
Percent of total population enrolled	17.3	20.4	20.6	21.1	19.4	16.9
Percent of school-age population (5-17) enrolled	57.0	71.9	78.3	81.7	84.4	83.2
Percent of total enrollment in high school	1.2	3.3	10.2	17.1	26.0	22.7
Percent of enrolled pupils attending daily	59.3	68.6	74.8	82.8	86.7	88.7
Average length of school term in days	132.2	144.3	161.9	172.7	175.0	177.9
Average number of days attended by each pupil enrolled	78.4	99.0	121.2	143.0	151.7	157.9

	1959–1960	1967–1968	1969–1970[a]	1970–1971[a]	1971–1972[a]	Fall 1972–1973[a]
K-8 enrollment	27,602,000	31,642,000	33,249,000	33,229,000	32,910,000	31,800,000
9-12 enrollment	8,485,000	12,250,000	13,282,000	13,599,000	14,092,000	14,100,000
Total K-12 enrollment	36,087,000	43,891,000	46,531,000	46,828,000	47,002,000	45,900,000
Percent of total population enrolled	20.1	22.2	DNA	DNA	DNA	DNA
Percent of school-age population (5-17) enrolled	82.2	85.1	DNA	DNA	DNA	DNA
Percent of total enrollment in high school	23.5	27.9	28.3	29.0	30.0	DNA
Percent of enrolled pupils attending daily	90.0	91.3	90.4	DNA	DNA	DNA
Average length of school term in days	178.0	178.8	178.9	DNA	DNA	DNA
Average number of days attended by each pupil enrolled	160.2	163.2	161.7	DNA	DNA	DNA

Source: K. A. Simon and W. V. Grant, Digest of Educational Statistics, 1971 ed., DHEW Publication No. (OE) 72–45, Washington, D.C.: GPO, 1972, pp. 28–29.
[a] Data for 1969–1970, 1970–1971, 1971–1972, 1972–1973 are estimates compiled by the author from various sources of Office of Education data.
DNA = Data not available at this writing.

some professional preparation for his job.

The visiting-teacher movement during the early part of the twentieth century (1906 to 1921) was a type of school-attendance service. The visiting teachers were to provide services that would help the child adjust better to school and to attack such problems as nonattendance, juvenile delinquency, and tardiness.[19]

Administration of pupil attendance involves building-level administrators and certain central-office administrative and supervisory staff. In a large school system an assistant principal may be in charge of attendance services at the building level and may work with attendance officers in the central office.

Evidence points to the need for replacement of the truant officer with a social worker, supplemented by a psychologist, psychiatrist, school nurse, and school counselor. The attendance worker retains his police powers, being able in most states to pick up truants, enter and inspect places of employment, prepare cases, and, in some circumstances, prosecute cases.

The six major functions of attendance personnel in a school system are:

1. Determining causes of absence through interviews at home and school.
2. Providing liaison between home and school.
3. Providing liaison between school and a law-enforcement agency.
4. Offering intensive casework on social and emotional problems.
5. Providing liaison with other social agencies in the community.
6. Interpreting the program to the community.

Such individuals function at the central administrative and supervisory level, but rely upon attendance officers at the building level for basic information.[20]

Length of school term and daily attendance

The average length of the school term has ranged from 132.2 days in 1869–1870 to about 179 days at present. The average number of days attended by each pupil enrolled has ranged from 78.4 in 1869–1870 to about 163 at present. The average length of the school term and the number of days attended by each pupil enrolled increased by significant amounts until about 1939–1940; since that time very small gains have been registered. Only 59.3 percent of enrolled pupils attended daily in 1869–1870; at the end of the nineteenth century the figure was only about 64.1 percent. Average daily attendance, as a percent of average daily membership, is presently around a very high 94 percent. Variation among states both in daily attendance and in length of school term has been reduced considerably in the past ten years.

By far the major cause of absenteeism is illness. Investigations have shown that 50 to 80 percent of absenteeism is due to illness. These data also indicate that primary-grade pupils are absent for illness more often than older children, and girls more than boys. Most absences are for two days or less. Truancy, or willful absence, accounts for only about 2 percent of absenteeism. Attendance at school varies with the month of the year and the age and sex of the child. Girls appear to have a slightly better attendance record than boys.

The public schools have steadily increased their holding power over the nation's youth. Of 1000 pupils who

---

[19]Ibid.

[20]Culbertson, op. cit., p. 94.

enrolled in fifth grade in 1924, 612 entered ninth grade in 1928. During the high-school years the dropout rate increased sharply so that only 302 graduated from high school in the spring of 1932. In other words, about 70 percent of the 1000 fifth graders in 1924 failed to graduate from high school; only 118 of the 302 who graduated from high school entered college in the fall of 1932.

Dropouts, those who terminate their education prematurely, declined in number in the years since 1932. Of 1000 fifth graders who enrolled in public school in the fall of 1962, 963 entered high school (9th grade) in the fall of 1966, 752 graduated in the spring of 1970, and 465 entered college in the fall of 1970. The dropout rate in 1932 was 70 percent; in 1970 it was less than 25 percent. These are national figures and there is considerable variation in this rate between states and within a given state.

Without question, the comprehensiveness of the program, the availability of remedial instruction, and the improvement of instruction methods and guidance services have contributed to the improvement of the holding power of the secondary school. More remains to be done, however.

CLASSIFICATION OF PUPILS

After admission and enrollment, pupils must be classified for instructional purposes. Perhaps the most significant change in the classification of pupils came with the grading of the elementary schools in Boston in 1847. Such grading today represents merely a rough attempt at grouping pupils for the purposes of instruction. Further classification is necessary when there are more than enough pupils to fill one grade room or one high school class section, and considerable attention has

been devoted to developing methods of grouping that will facilitate the learning or the teaching process.

Heterogeneous grouping can be defined as class sectioning on the basis of chance factors or arbitrary standards unrelated to learning ability or past performance. Homogeneous grouping implies placement of pupils into class sections on the basis of some measure of ability. Because it is impossible to organize a section or grade in which all students have the same kind and quantity of ability or social background, "homogeneous" implies *approximately* the same kind and quality of ability as measured by some instrument. Stated another way, the range of some type of student ability is less in a homogeneous than in a heterogeneous section.

A number of bases can be used for sectioning classes for purposes of instruction. Among these is grouping by special ability. Implicit is the assumption that a considerable amount of some type of ability or aptitude is related to facility in mastering a skill or gaining special knowledge. Thus, those who possess certain aptitudes in music and art can be expected to gain considerable skill in learning experiences concerned with music or art. Homogeneous grouping through what might be called "natural selection" occurs at the secondary level in advanced courses in specialized fields of learning. Only the highly interested who possess special aptitude in a given field will undertake advanced and elective courses in the field.

Another basis for grouping is general learning ability. This is commonly used in sectioning elementary school classes and the required classes at the secondary level. General learning ability is usually measured by one of the standard intelligence tests and is reported in terms of mental maturity as indicated by mental age or intelligence quotient. It can also be deduced from the pupil's past achievements as determined by his score on a standardized test, by his grade-point average, or by informal evaluation by teachers. A pupil's general aptitude for learning also includes such factors as social maturity and emotional stability. A combination of factors, such as mental age, reading skills, grade-point average, and emotional stability, provide a better indication of general ability to learn than does intelligence alone. The most frequently reported bases for grouping pupils are intelligence quotient from a group mental test, scholarship marks in all subjects, an average of several teachers' ratings of the pupil's academic ability or intelligence, scores on group intelligence tests, mental age, and average scholarship marks in certain and related subjects.[21] The validity of each or a combination of bases remains to be established.

A number of experiments have attempted to measure the effect of ability grouping on instruction. Most compared learning in an experimental group of pupils selected on the basis of one type of ability and in a control group of randomly selected pupils. The data failed to establish any clear superiority for homogeneous grouping, and researchers have been exceedingly cautious in reporting findings. The data tend to support the contention that grouping is most advantageous for those at the extreme ends of a curve of normal distribution of ability or intelligence. Thus, the very dull and the very bright appeared to succeed better under homogeneous rather than heterogeneous grouping, although the evidence was less positive for the bright than for the dull children. Differentiation of those pupils in the broad normal range was more difficult to relate to learning ability.

Grouping does not solve educational problems. It is an administrative device that can facilitate learning only if teaching techniques are adapted to the group's potential or if special resources are available. The inconclusiveness of experiments with homogeneous grouping may be traced to failure on the part of the instructor to teach differently when confronted with a narrower range of talents or interests. Of significance for this volume is the usefulness of classifying pupils into more homogeneous groups as a means of stimulating learning.

Following a survey of research on the effects of ability grouping, Goldberg et al. made the following comment: "Many of the issues concerning grouping remain unresolved and most questions are still unanswered despite 70 or 80 years of practice and at least 40 years of study. Insufficient and conflicting data are being used to support partisan views concerning the consequences of grouping rather than to resolve the persistent issues."[22] The writer concurs that an effective class organizational pattern for instruction is far more complex and elusive than the champions of specific approaches would have us believe.

The most recent data suggest the typical elementary school pupil is not likely to be carefully grouped in all school situations. As one source put it,

[21]S. J. Knezevich and Stanley G. Sanders, "Research on Ability Grouping with Special Emphasis on Its Effect on the Education of the Intellectually Gifted," Iowa Center for Research in School Administration, Iowa City: State University of Iowa, 1959, mimeographed.

[22]M. L. Goldberg, A. H. Passow, and J. Justman, The Effects of Ability Grouping, New York: Teachers College, 1966, pp. 21–22.

grouping has yet to prove itself as an administrative device to meet individual needs.[23]

Section II: Qualitative dimensions

Education for all is an ideal whose realization demands adequate resources and services to meet the varied needs of a heterogeneous student body —some bright, others dull; some mature, others immature; some emotionally well balanced, others disturbed; some sound of body, others physically handicapped; some highly motivated to learn, others apathetic or even antagonistic to school and learning; some from privileged socioeconomic backgrounds, others from deprived areas; some white, others black. The qualitative aspects of pupil administration concern the educational institution's responsibility to serve students of almost infinite variety by providing the special instructional, counseling, health, welfare, and other services (in addition to classroom teaching) required to describe, understand, and if possible to direct and treat students and help them to become more effective social beings and better learners. Pupils are not seen as statistics in a school report, but as individuals who may require special services.

Despite the growing tendency to view pupil administration solely in terms of its qualitative dimensions, the quantitative aspects should not be dismissed. Both approaches are important, and the school administrator must maintain a balanced view of school operations.

It has been estimated that there are 60,000 full-time-equivalent public school personnel with professional background (in addition to teachers) providing special services to pupils.[24] These specialists are guidance counselors, school social workers, attendance workers, school psychologists, speech and hearing clinicians, school nurses, and other health personnel. The growth and development of each of these areas have been tremendous.

GUIDANCE SERVICES

Vocational guidance started as a humble service in 1908 with the creation of the Vocation Bureau in Boston. Limited in the beginning to helping the student obtain initial employment, it has expanded to a point where today it is considered indispensable at all levels of education. Comprehensive educational-guidance services trace their origin to vocational guidance.[25] The development of objective and scientific methods of individual testing added impetus to the movement. Increased concern for mental health and the evolution of a body of knowledge and skills related to the counseling process further extended the potential of the field.

Guidance focuses on the individual. It is concerned with the ways each person can better comprehend and interpret his potentials and limitations so as to plan realistic life goals. It is defined more formally by the American Personnel and Guidance Association in cooperation with the National Education Association as "services

[23]Research Division, National Education Association, *Ability Grouping*, Research Summary 1968–1969, Washington, D.C.: The Association, 1968, 52 pp.

[24]L. O. Eckerson and H. M. Smith, eds., *Scope of Pupil Personnel Services*, U.S. Office of Education, Washington, D.C.: GPO, 1966, p. 9.
[25]Ibid., p. 25.

available to each student to facilitate his academic success in school; to help him better understand his strengths and limitations; to identify his interests; to aid him in planning for and attaining realistic goals. The emphasis is always on the individual even when students meet in groups for guidance purposes."[26]

Guidance, therefore, is a service that can have profound impact if rendered at crucial points in the growth and development of children, youths, and adults. It is not confined to one age group with one set of problems; it is a continuous process to cope with a broad range of problems.

Guidance—a cluster of particular kinds of services to individuals—should not be confused with one of its most common techniques—counseling. Guidance is the responsibility of many different kinds of professional persons: teachers, counseling specialists, psychologists, psychiatric specialists, social caseworkers, and administrators.

Counseling in a guidance program

Counseling is the central service of guidance. It is usually a relation between a counselor and a single counselee who seeks to understand himself, to formulate plans, to make decisions, or to demonstrate feelings and attitudes. The counselor employs his special understanding of human behavior, his skill in interpreting data, and his knowledge of interview techniques to understand and perhaps subsequently to direct efforts of the counselee. Small-group counseling has been hailed by some as an exciting current trend. So important is counseling to the en-

tire guidance program that often the two are held to be synonymous.

As Bishop put it: "Whoever counsels touches the delicate web of an individual decision-making personal adjustment and self-image. Those who counsel may beckon, consult, or direct."[27] The teacher is not just a subject matter specialist or a purveyor of information. The teacher is also a person who knows the learner well enough to understand the learner's needs and problems through use and interpretation of a variety of instruments. The teacher's concern for the development of the individual learner is as much a part of guidance and counseling as the work of those who identify themselves as specialists in the field. Counseling is not solely the prerogative of the guidance counselor. This is not to depreciate the role of the professional full-time counselor as a strategic person in the total educational enterprise; rather, it suggests the concern of the entire educational organization for guidance and counseling. Nor should recognition of the teacher's role in the process suggest that no special preparation is necessary to achieve skill in the use of the counseling procedures; on the contrary, it suggests the importance of the teacher's gaining skill in guidance techniques.

The guidance program includes appraisal of students, placement of school graduates, and related services, as well as counseling. Guidance and counseling can help pupils in elementary as well as in secondary institutions.

Guidance and counseling services have expanded rapidly since 1958 owing to the provision of federal funds under the National Defense Education

[26]American Personnel and Guidance Association and National Education Association, *Answers to Questions About Guidance*, Washington, D.C.: The Association, 1963, p. 3.

[27]L. J. Bishop, "Who Is the Counselor?" *Educational Leadership*, January 1967, p. 301.

Act (NDEA) for support of programs of testing, counseling, and guidance in secondary schools. In 1962–1963 there were 27,180 full-time equivalent counselors.[28] Of these, 17,928 were full-time counselors. This number represents an increase of 143 percent over the 1958 (or pre-NDEA) figures. By 1967–1968 the number of public school guidance personnel jumped to 41,716.

Usually the consultant was a former teacher with preparation in guidance, a psychologist, or a social worker. State departments of education also have added counseling and guidance personnel to their staffs. The number of such specialists in state departments of education increased significantly in the 1960s.

The counselor-student ratio in the secondary schools has declined from 1:960 in 1958–1959 to 1:500 at present. The recommended counselor-student ratio at the secondary-school level is 1:250 or 1:400. This implies that more counselors will be needed. The desired counselor-student ratio at the elementary school level has been variously estimated as 1:300 or 1:600, depending upon the characteristics of the student body and availability of other services. On the basis of a 1:600 ratio, it is estimated that 54,000 guidance counselors should be employed in elementary schools.

Studies have shown that pupils benefit from guidance services. Those with access to such services tend to learn more, learn better how to solve their own problems, make more realistic vocational choices, persist longer in attendance at institutions of higher learning, enjoy greater success in the vocational world, and are better adjusted from the standpoint of expressed behavior. Guidance needs increase

with school size, for with the availability of greater opportunities comes the difficulty of making the most prudent choices.

Guidance and counseling specialists should not be called guidance directors, because this implies administrative responsibilities. If several specialists in guidance and counseling services are employed in one building, they may be attached to the principal's office, with an assistant principal assuming responsibility for supervising such services. In large school operations, a person of central-office rank may be concerned with supervising the work of guidance and counseling experts at the building level and developing programs for their continued professional growth.

School counselors and guidance specialists have their own professional society, the American Personnel and Guidance Association, with a membership of 20,000. In addition, there is a counseling psychology division of the American Psychological Association.

Certification of school counselors is provided in 47 states, although the requirements vary from a few hours of graduate credit to a master's degree or more.

It is well to recognize the limitations as well as the contributions of counseling. The counselor may apply his techniques to understanding problems confronting the counselee and, if necessary, recommend therapy by professionals in the treatment of human behavior problems. He should not himself attempt psychotherapy.

SOCIAL WORK SERVICES

Like guidance and counseling, school social work began at the turn of the present century. Visiting teachers were the first specialized school personnel

[28]L. O. Eckerson and H. M. Smith, op. cit., pp. 10 and 11.

with a social work orientation. They were part of the program for enforcing attendance at school and worked primarily with children who were unable to adjust to school and refused to attend. Concerned with the fundamental causes of absenteeism, they endeavored to correlate the student's background and his relation to the community with individualized casework and counseling. In the course of enforcing compulsory-attendance laws, they became involved in juvenile court activities to determine the scope and nature of the child's problem and his right to an education. Their interest extended to unmarried mothers of school age who sought special services.

The early school social workers dealt primarily with disadvantaged youngsters from socially and economically deprived areas of the district. The school's interest in helping the disadvantaged predates present popular concern and attendant publicity. Today, school social workers are concerned also with able students from high socioeconomic backgrounds who suffer from the stress of high social and academic expectations and develop internally directed rather than overt patterns of maladjustment.

School social work and guidance services overlap; the former arose from concern with attendance and absenteeism in the school, and the latter from concern with adequate vocational choices after leaving. The close relation between the two services is illustrated by the following enumeration of the social worker's responsibilities. The social worker is described as:

1. A caseworker who counsels with students and their parents.
2. A collaborator concerned with working with teachers and other members of the school staff.
3. A coordinator who serves as a liaison agent between school and home and school and community in order to bring each in a better working relation.
4. A consultant available to other school staff members to add his perceptions to problems that students may have and that may not directly involve the social worker.[29]

About ten years ago there were 5432 full- and part-time attendance workers in the public schools, of whom 2254 were full-time social workers or visiting teachers. About 53 percent of public elementary schools with over 100 pupils had services of social workers available to them. In one-fourth of these, the services were evaluated as adequate.[30]

By 1950 nearly all states that certified attendance workers required a minimum of a bachelor's degree. Such workers are called by a number of titles. One study reported 29 different titles. The two most frequently used were school social worker and visiting teacher. Other terms are school counseling consultant, adjustment teacher, welfare worker, caseworker, and attendance officer.

Case loads vary greatly and there is little uniformity in reporting the number of pupils served. It is not unusual for such specialized personnel to work longer days and weeks than the typical teacher.

PSYCHOLOGICAL SERVICES

School psychological services were inaugurated just before the turn of the century but were confined primarily to large cities and a few wealthy suburban districts until after World War II. They became more common during the 1950s. One study reported that

[29]Ibid., p. 38.
[30]Ibid., p. 12.

there were only 520 school psychologists in the nation in 1950. The number jumped to 2724 in 1960, an increase of more than 500 percent. This is corroborated by the fact that in 1950 there were no school psychologists in 22 states, whereas in 1960 only in 4 states was this true.[31]

The school psychologist employs the clinical approach and devotes most of his time to individual pupils referred to him because of learning problems. His background and special preparation in interpretation of data and observations on the child enable him to determine the child's problem and potential growth and development. He is skilled in the use of psychological instruments to detect special aptitudes, interests, and personality characteristics. He is sensitive to the child's cultural background, his home situation, and his physical condition, particularly whether there are sensory or perceptual handicaps.

Placement of a pupil in a special class for exceptional children is commonly based upon the judgment of the school psychologist. In some unusual cases, he may recommend that a child be excused from school attendance because mental immaturity or a complex of factors makes it impossible for the school to serve the child.

Like other pupil-service workers, the school psychologist works with teachers and parents as well as with pupils. In working with pupils he is not confined to counseling alone but may engage in psychotherapy. Typically, however, the school setting is not conducive to extended psychotherapy even by those certified to engage in this practice.

At least 23 states and the District of Columbia have some form of certification requirement for school psycholo-

gists.[32] The American Psychological Association recommends that full certification of a school psychologist be contingent upon attainment of a doctor's degree in psychology and that the minimum certification requirement be two years of graduate work. For certification as psychological assistant, one and a half years of graduate work are required; such personnel may work only under the supervision of a certified school psychologist.[33]

The employment of school psychologists is not yet widespread. Only a fraction of the schools have adequate services, and usually the psychologist's time must be carefully budgeted. Typically his commitments are far greater than time and talent will allow her to fulfill.

PSYCHIATRIC SERVICES

As limited as psychological services are in most schools, psychiatric services are even more limited. This is true even though approximately 7 to 14 percent of the children attending school each year have an emotional, behavioral, or psychosomatic disturbance or a learning problem of psychological origin that is clearly beyond the capabilities of teachers to cope with. It is most unfortunate that today in only a small proportion of schools (37 percent of public elementary schools surveyed) do pupils receive the services of a psychiatrist at no cost. Usually psychiatric services

[31]Ibid., p. 51.

[32]W. L. Hodges, "State Certification of School Psychologists," *American Psychologist*, vol. 15, 1960, pp. 346–349.

[33]James I. Barden and The Division 16 Committee on Training Standards and Certification, "Report of Division 16 Committee on Training Standards and Certification," *American Psychologist*, vol. 18, 1963, pp. 711–714.

are limited to examination and consultation. The greater concern for the mental health of the child may some day increase the number of child psychiatrists and other mental health workers in schools, but in the beginning these services will be only diagnostic and consultative. Direct therapy for disturbed children under school auspices is still a long way off.

The larger the system, the more important the psychiatrist becomes in the school's physical and mental health program. One authority stated that a school system of 5000 or more children may encounter almost daily behavioral, emotional, and psychosomatic disturbances in its students and staff.[34]

The school psychiatrist can also serve as a consultant to teachers, parents, and school administrators. The development of special psychological clinics, school social-casework divisions, and guidance services may help maintain mental health of those served by or serving in the school.

SPEECH AND HEARING SERVICES

By far the most common services available in schools are those related to remediation of disorders of communication. These services are concerned with impairment of speech, hearing, or language, or some combination of these. One survey reported that 76 percent of elementary schools provided services in speech and hearing.[35] Next to attendance services, concern for communication disorders was most frequently offered in the public elementary schools.

It is estimated that more than 3 million children have speech or hearing so seriously impaired that it interferes

[34]Eckerson and Smith, op. cit., p. 66.
[35]Ibid., p. 13.

with their educational, social, or emotional adjustment. About 5 percent of school-age children are said to have speech defects. The estimated number of children per 10,000 school population with each type of speech disorder is presented in Table 18–2. These are conservative estimates. About 0.7 percent of school-age children have a hearing loss that is significantly handicapping; another 1 million children have a nonhandicapping reduction in hearing acuity.

The typical case load for a specialist in this area varies. It is estimated that a child with a significant communication handicap should be seen at least twice a week for 20 to 25 minutes. A total of 12 such children would require the full-time services of a speech clinician. By grouping, the efficient clinician could work with as many as 100 children per week. Thus, depending upon the work performed, the case load will be more than 12 but less than 100.

Screening can be done under the supervision of a specialist with semi-

TABLE 18–2

ESTIMATED NUMBER OF SCHOOL-AGE CHILDREN PER 10,000 SCHOOL POPULATION WITH VARIOUS SPEECH DISORDERS

Disorder	No. of children
Articulation difficulty	300
Stuttering	100
Voice disorder	10
Speech defects due to cleft palate	10
Speech defects due to cerebral palsy	10
Retarded speech development	20
Speech defects due to impaired hearing	50
Total	500

Source: L. O. Eckerson and H. M. Smith, eds., *Scope of Pupil Personnel Services*, U.S. Office of Education, Washington, D.C.: GPO, 1966, p. 71.

professional help from students majoring in speech pathology and audiology in neighboring universities or colleges. Ten students can assist in the screening of as many as 1800 children in a single day. It is imperative that the equipment be in excellent order. Some studies report that the audiometers are not maintained in the good condition necessary for accurate reading with instruments.

The speech and hearing specialist requires extensive training to deal with speech problems from such diverse causes as mental retardation, bilingualism, cleft palate, and impaired hearing.

NURSING SERVICES

School nursing began around the turn of the century. In 1952 there were over 6,300 school nurses; today there are more than 12,000. A defensible nurse-pupil ratio has yet to be defined. Such a ratio depends on many factors, such as the availability of nonprofessional assistants to handle clerical and housekeeping duties.

MEDICAL SERVICES

The physician's participation in school health services is limited to periodic visits for diagnosis and referral and for immunization. The need for physicians in the public schools is far greater than for psychiatrists but far less than that for nurses. Typically the school medical adviser acts as physician to the athletic teams, examines pupils not examined by their personal physicians, and consults with the school administrator on a variety of health problems in the school. He is paid on a fee-for-service basis.

SERVICES FOR EXCEPTIONAL PUPILS

The administrator of a public school system may not refuse schooling to any pupil who satisfies the general requirements for admission. It is consistent with democratic traditions that everybody be given an opportunity to develop to his or her fullest capabilities. This creates problems of a magnitude never before envisioned, because a wide variety of human talents and deficiencies clamor for attention in the public schools. For example, if the gifted child is to be offered special opportunities, the meaning of "intellectually gifted" must first be defined; then it must be decided whether to devote a special attendance center to such children, or to set aside special rooms in an attendance center, or to require the regular classroom teacher to provide the special opportunities. At the opposite extreme are the mentally retarded. These are usually divided into educable and trainable children. In a small school system such pupils can be organized in rooms operated by the intermediate unit. In a large system it must be decided whether to set aside a special building for such pupils or to assign them rooms in regular school buildings. Similar problems arise in providing educational services for the physically handicapped, the visually handicapped, and those with hearing defects.

The number of exceptional children enrolled in special-education programs in local public school systems more than doubled between 1948 and 1958, but the total was still less than 1 million. This rate of growth is three times the rate of enrollment increase in public elementary and secondary schools for the same period. Almost 2 million were enrolled in such public school classes for exceptional children in 1966. By 1970 the total of excep-

TABLE 18–3

TOTAL ENROLLMENT AND NUMBER OF HANDICAPPED PUPILS IN LOCAL PUBLIC SCHOOLS, BY SCHOOL LEVEL AND BY TYPE OF HANDICAP: 50 STATES AND THE DISTRICT OF COLUMBIA, SPRING 1970

Type of handicap	All schools		Elementary schools		Secondary schools		Combined schools[a]	
	Number	Percent	Number	Percent	Number	Percent	Number	Percent
All pupils	44,389,000	100	24,321,000	55	17,802,000	40	2,265,000	5
Total handicapped pupils[b]	4,752,000	100[b]	3,438,000	72[b]	1,045,000	22[b]	269,000	6
Speech impaired	1,793,000	100	1,520,000	85	198,000	11	76,000	4
Learning disabled	1,160,000	100	779,000	67	314,000	27	67,000	6
Mentally retarded	936,000	100	606,000	65	257,000	28	73,000	8
Emotionally disturbed	556,000	100	371,000	67	160,000	29	25,000	5
Hard of hearing	131,000	100	71,000	54	50,000	38	10,000	8
Deaf	23,000	100	18,000	79	3,000	13	2,000	8
Crippled	82,000	100	40,000	49	36,000	44	5,000	6
Partially sighted	64,000	100	30,000	47	24,000	37	10,000	16
Blind	6,000	100	3,000	51	3,000	45	*	4

Source: "Number of Pupils and Handicaps in Local Public Schools," Spring 1970, National Center for Educational Statistics.
[a] Schools with both elementary and secondary grades.
[b] The actual total numbers and percent of handicapped pupils may be somewhat less than the figures presented because in some cases the same handicapped pupils may have been reported in more than one category.
*Number greater than zero but less than 500.
NOTE: Detail may not equal totals due to rounding.

tional pupils being served was over 4¾ million (see Table 18–3).

By 1966 eight out of every ten systems with 300 or more pupils made some provision for mentally retarded children, and seven out of ten provided for children with severe speech impairments; 46 percent of the systems provided for visually impaired children and 42 percent for emotionally disturbed and socially maladjusted children.[36] The larger the enrollment, the more likely that the system will provide for the exceptional child. Most of the progress has been in programs for the blind, those with impaired speech, the intellectually gifted, and the mentally retarded. The least progress since 1948 has been in programs for crippled children.

Further expansion in this area can be expected. Such programs are expensive because the pupil-teacher ratio is smaller than usual and often special space or equipment is necessary for effective learning. Federal grants have helped to expand such services.

Children normal in mental ability and physical health may experience other problems ranging from simple nervousness and confusion to serious emotional disturbance. Guidance and counseling services have greatly facilitated the management of such children. Psychiatric or psychological services may be provided to identify the nature of the emotional disturbance, and the child may be referred to an appropriate agency for treatment.

ADMINISTRATIVE IMPLICATIONS OF SERVICES FOR PUPILS

The number and variety of specialists in guidance, social casework, speech

and hearing, health, and psychological services are growing. These specialists serve pupils with learning, adjustment, and self-image problems, and their mission is to improve the pupils' learning and adjustment. They have a fundamental commitment to work with teachers, parents, and school administrators, as well as pupils.

The coordination of the ever-increasing number of specialists, who are not in the classroom on a daily basis, and the determination of their contributions to the improvement of the educational process constitute a significant challenge to the school administrator. The systems approach offers a solution to the problems of administering large numbers of highly specialized personnel whose knowledge and skills the administrator just barely understands.

One of the dangers of specialization is loss of perspective: The specialist tends to view his work as an end in itself rather than as a means to an objective, specifically of helping the teacher teach and the student learn. It is the responsibility of the administrator to prevent such loss of perspective. The effectiveness of special services can be evaluated only in terms of their impact upon the individual pupil and individual teacher at the classroom level.

The addition of supportive-service personnel increases the school costs but does not reduce class size; it improves the quality of education but does not modify the pupil-teacher ratio. It is likely that as schools become more concerned with improving the quality of education and reaching all types of pupils, the increase in special-service personnel will be greater than the increase in number of pupils reached. Further, with the expansion of supportive services, the pupil-teacher ratio will become less meaningful; indeed its validity has

[36]National Education Association, "Programs for Handicapped Children," *Research Bulletin*, vol. 45, no. 4, December 1967, pp. 115–117.

already been questioned. The pupil-teacher ratio was significant when pupils were instructed by only one teacher; today, when pupils are instructed by many teachers, who in turn are advised by consultants or supervisors, the pupil-professional staff ratio (number of pupils per professional staff member or number of professional staff members per 1000 pupils enrolled or in average daily attendance) is a more meaningful index. Professional staff members include full-time-equivalent nurses, doctors, psychiatrists, psychologists, guidance counselors, and special consultants, as well as teachers.

Almost 30 years ago the Institute of Administrative Research at Teachers College, Columbia University, developed a comprehensive measure called numerical staffing adequacy or professional staff per 1000 pupil units.[37] Mort and his students completed many studies of the relation of numerical staffing adequacy to other quality-related criteria.

There are more pupils in school than ever before, the schools are serving a greater variety of pupils, and many constraints are placed upon admission and assignments of pupils to school by groups concerned with protecting the civil rights of pupils. Improvement of the quality of instruction depends not only upon the time and talents of individual teachers but also on the availability to pupils and teachers of a host of special services.

STUDENT DISCIPLINE, CONTROL, AND ACTIVISM

By the mid-1960s the civil disturbances that swept the nation were being felt on university campuses. College stu-

[37]B. H. McKenna, *Staffing the Schools,* New York: Teachers College, 1965, p. 4.

dent protests accompanied by disruptive and destructive behavior on the part of large groups precipitated confrontations with administrators and clashes with the police and, in some cases, the National Guard. The large university that experienced no student-originated campus conflict during the last half of the 1960s was the exception. These campus civil disturbances were triggered by a variety of causes but the Vietnam War, the draft, civil rights of minority students, student interpretations of the relevance of course programs, and student behavior and dress codes were the major factors. The appearance of drug subcultures on campuses enhanced the atmosphere of protests and violent demonstrations.

It was inevitable that junior and senior high school students, particularly those near university campuses, would begin to emulate their older counterparts, albeit in a milder form. By the end of the 1960s one survey of over 1000 secondary school principals reported that a majority experienced some kind of protest. This marked the beginning of an unusual challenge for school administrators. Discipline, or school pupil control measures, focused primarily on individual rather than group or crowd behavior. There were occasions when an intense athletic rivalry led to a large-scale disorder following a bitterly fought game. These were embarrassing to school administrators but were usually brought under control and the incident didn't remain smoldering for long. The appearance of student "underground newspapers" and student walkouts to protest undesirable school food services, dress and discipline codes, and actual or purported denial of civil rights to minority students are of a different order of student discipline concern. Administrators were hard-pressed to cope with the tactics of secondary school activists during a decade of dissent. It led to greater involvement of students in the secondary school government, in the formulation of school building policies, and on local boards of education. Parents were recruited to help curb the excesses of some of the activists.

At this writing in the mid-1970s, the disruptive behavior of students seems to have run its course. It could be that the basic causes have been removed such as the termination of an unpopular war, the ending of the draft, and the modification of restrictive and arbitrary dress and behavior codes. Perhaps more meaningful school programs have been developed. The feeling of greater student involvement and contributions to the operation of the educational enterprise could have helped to minimize such student behavior. On the other hand, given a similar set of conditions antisocial behavior by large groups could strike the schools again. At any rate, administrators should be in a better position to "rap" with students, modify archaic practices, and generate strategies that will contain and reduce the destructiveness of civil disruptions by students should they occur at some future point in time.

SUMMARY

The administration of pupils has moved from the quantitative aspects of accounting and reporting the whereabouts of pupils to the qualitative aspects of interpreting all data available on pupils and providing special services to help them adjust in the school situation. So great has been the emphasis on the qualitative aspects that the term "pupil personnel administration" appears synonymous with guidance and counseling.

However, school census taking remains necessary. Properly collected, classified, and kept up to date by a system of continuous census reporting, it can provide the data necessary for planning school-plant alterations, determining the number of professional personnel needed, and estimating the school budget. All enumeration starts with the house-to-house canvass, but need not stop there. Periodic census taking is notoriously inaccurate and the data become progressively more obsolete. The continuous system of reporting is recommended as a means of overcoming the inadequacies of periodic canvassing. The advent of computer-based electronic data processing greatly facilitates the operation of a continuous census system.

Admission to school is not an absolute right. Admission is contingent upon satisfying certain conditions of age, residence, and mental and physical health. It is generally agreed that pupils who start school too soon may experience difficulties throughout the school career. Assignment of pupils to attendance centers has become controversial since 1954. Integration started primarily as a southern problem, but now involves all parts of the nation. Progress toward school integration has been painfully slow, with greatest achievement evident in the border states. The Coleman report concluded that only massive school integration will allow educational progress for blacks; this conclusion has been questioned by others.

Enrollment increased almost yearly in public elementary and secondary schools until 1971–1972. Since then, slight declines appear annually. The attendance of pupils is improving, as evidenced by the fact that approximately 94 percent of those enrolled now attend school daily. The length of the school term has been extended as well. The school dropout rate has improved dramatically from 70 percent in the early 1930s to less than 25 percent in the early 1970s.

The most common cause of absenteeism is illness. Truancy, or willful intent to be absent, accounts for about 2 percent of the absenteeism in public schools. The emphasis in administration of attendance has shifted from the truant officer's compulsion to the social worker's identification of causes and their correction.

Attempts to classify pupils into more or less homogeneous groups based on ability is a refinement of grading pupils, which was the first attempt to reduce the range of abilities that confront the teacher. Research in this area has been inconclusive. The purpose of designing homogeneous groups is to provide an administrative means for improving learning. Unless teachers take advantage of the reduced range of abilities and interests by developing new techniques and employing appropriate materials, the advantages of homogeneous grouping will be lost.

The qualitative dimensions of pupil administration include special instructional, counseling, health, welfare, and other services required to describe, understand, direct, and possibly treat individuals to help them become more effective social beings and better learners. A school administrator must maintain a balanced view of pupil administration.

There are more than 60,000 full-time-equivalent public school personnel working as guidance counselors, school social workers, school psychologists, speech and hearing clinicians, school nurses, and other health personnel. Each of these areas has grown and developed during the last two decades.

Comprehensive educational guidance services grew out of vocational guidance narrowly conceived as helping individuals gain initial employment. Today guidance is concerned with understanding the potentials and limitations of each individual in order to help him attain realistic goals. Guidance is a cluster of functions and many different types of personnel may have a role in it. Counseling is its central service. The counselor employs his special knowledge of human behavior and interview techniques to understand the counselee better. Small-group counseling is a comparatively recent development.

The federal government, particularly through the NDEA of 1958, has done much to increase guidance services in the schools. These services continued to improve in the 1960s. The recommended counselor-student ratio has been reduced over the years; it is presently 1:250 or 1:300. There is evidence that shows pupils benefit from guidance services.

Like guidance and counseling, school social work began around the turn of the present century. The movement grew out of efforts at enforcement of compulsory-attendance laws. Counseling is an important technique for school social workers, as is casework. School social work focuses on the fundamental causes of a pupil's difficulty in adjusting to school, which often manifests itself as absenteeism or premature termination of education. Nearly all states require certification of these specialists.

The number of school psychologists has increased dramatically since 1950. Often decisions about placing a child in a special school or excusing him from school are made by the school psychologist. The demand for such services is far in excess of the number of specialists available. Psychiatric services are even more limited. The school setting does not always permit therapy for emotionally disturbed children.

By far the most common special services available to schools are those of speech and hearing clinicians. The school nurse was one of the early service experts. Relatively few physicians, however, participate in school health services beyond diagnosis and immunization programs.

Special-education programs for exceptional children have increased greatly to the present level of almost 5 million pupils served by public schools. The most common are special classes for the speech impaired, the mentally retarded, and the intellectually gifted.

The coordination of the ever-increasing number of specialists and the determination of their contribution to the improvement of the educational process are significant challenges facing school administrators. The systems approach to administration offers a solution.

The great increase in supportive services to the classroom teacher has made the pupil-teacher ratio less meaningful than when only teachers were employed in schools. Other indexes such as numerical staff adequacy or pupil-professional staff ratio are being developed as better measures of the qualitative aspects of school staffing.

QUESTIONS

1. Differentiate between the qualitative and quantitative aspects of pupil administration.
2. What are the advantages of the continuous census system over the traditional periodic census systems?
3. How does the present-day attendance officer differ from the truant officer of the past?
4. What are the advantages of homogeneous grouping? Disadvantages?
5. What were the major conclusions of the Coleman report?
6. Should counseling be restricted to guidance specialists? Justify your stand.
7. What were the significant historical developments in the school social work movement?
8. What services can be provided by a school psychologist?
9. Why has the advent of more supportive services complicated the administration of public education?
10. What factors have been responsible for the lessening of the significance of the teacher-pupil ratio?
11. Is it better to dedicate special buildings or special classrooms within a building for handicapped pupils, or to enrich regular classroom work for the following types of pupils: (a) the mentally gifted, (b) the mentally retarded, (c) the physically handicapped, (d) the emotionally disturbed?

SELECTED REFERENCES

Bishop, L. J., "Who Is the Counselor?" *Educational Leadership,* January 1967, p. 301.

Culbertson, Jack, "Attendance," in Chester W. Harris, ed., *Encyclopedia of Educational Research,* 3rd ed., New York: Macmillan, 1960.

Eckerson, L. O., and H. M. Smith, eds., *Scope of Pupil Personnel Services,* U.S. Office of Education, Washington, D.C.: GPO, 1966.

Goldberg, M. L., A. H. Passow, and J. Justman, *The Effects of Ability Grouping,* New York: Teachers College, 1966.

Mackie, R. P., and P. P. Robbings, "Exceptional Children in Local Public Schools," *School Life,* vol. 43, November 1960.

U.S. Department of Health, Education, and Welfare, *Equality of Educational Opportunity,* Office of Education Summary Report, OE 38000, Washington, D.C.: GPO, 1966.

Walden, John C. and Allen D. Cleveland, "The South's New Segregation Academies," *Phi Delta Kappan,* December 1971, pp. 234–239.

Yeager, William A., *Administration and the Pupil,* New York: Harper & Row, 1949.

19

THE STAFFING DIMENSION: SELECTION, ASSIGNMENT, AND EVALUATION OF PROFESSIONAL PERSONNEL

Traditionally, the administration of professional personnel has consisted of recruiting, selecting, assigning, orienting, paying, and stimulating the professional growth of a school staff at the attendance-center, central-office, or general administrative level. These concerns remain important, but the 1960s brought a dramatic new dimension to personnel administration, and school systems will never be the same for it. It is professional negotiation (also termed collective negotiation or collective bargaining), that is, the involvement of the professional staff in decision making. It has profoundly altered the life styles and strategies of educational administrators. Professional negotiation is the subject of Chapter 20. The traditional dimensions of the administration of professional personnel will be reviewed in this chapter.

MAGNITUDE OF THE PERSONNEL CONCERNS

The numbers, types, and deployment of professional and nonprofessional personnel in schools are influenced by many factors, the most important of which are pupil enrollment and the nature and scope of the learning experiences provided. Thus, an increase in public school enrollment between 1956–1960 and 1969–1970 that totaled about 9.5 million students saw a concomitant increase in the number of teachers during the same period of over 610,000. Likewise, stable and slightly declining enrollments in the early 1970s has produced a decline in the number of elementary classroom teachers since 1970–1971. A drop at the secondary level in later years of this decade can be predicted.

There are presently about 2.1 million classroom teachers in public schools and about 263,000 in private schools. The number of public elementary school teachers will continue to fall in the 1970s below the peak level of about 1.3 million reached in the very early 1970s. Some estimate that the number of secondary teachers may exceed elementary teachers by the mid-1970s. All indicators point to either stable or slightly declining numbers of teachers employed during the 1970s. In contrast, during the mid- and late 1960s, 70,000 to 80,000 additional persons were added to the teaching facilities each year. The primary concern of school personnel administrators during that time was to find new teachers. Presently the concern has reversed, as administrators ponder how to process hundreds of applications for few vacancies. The situation is reminiscent of the conditions that prevailed during the 1930s. The teacher shortage that prevailed for almost 25 years since the end of World War II has now become a shortage of teaching jobs.

During the 1940s the numbers of elementary teachers grew slightly while the numbers of secondary teachers actually declined. Both types of classroom personnel increased substantially during the 1950s, with growth at the elementary level outstripping the secondary level. But during the 1960s the gain in secondary teachers was far greater than that for elementary teachers. The growth rate of secondary teachers in the early 1970s tapered off but an actual decline was noted for elementary teachers.

Classroom teachers constitute the largest group of professional personnel employed in the public schools by far; they account for about 89 percent of the total instructional personnel. In 1972–1973 there were 2,110,368 teachers, about 141,000 other instructional personnel, almost 101,000 principals and assistant principals, and 67,715 other administrators. This was a grand total of 2,420,144 full-time professional staff members. This is an increase of about 700,000 over a ten-year-period, with teachers accounting for almost 587,650, or 84 percent, of that increase. During most of the 1960s the annual rate of instructional staff increase fluctuated between 4 and 5 percent. In 1972 the annual rate of increase over the previous year was less than 1 percent.

Secretarial and clerical workers, custodians, maintenance employees, transportation workers, food-service workers, and others accounted for an additional 1 million public school staff members. Approximately one noninstructional person of some type is employed for every 2.4 professional personnel. This does not include the approximately 115,500 school-board members or the more than 75,000 part-time noninstructional personnel. It is estimated that about 3.6 million lay, professional, and noncertified people are engaged in teaching, administration, supportive services, and operation of public education.

Proliferation of federally sponsored educational programs during the 1960s greatly strained the ability of local school districts to expand their staffs rapidly enough to man new programs. This factor has stabilized during the 1970s.

Teachers are not distributed equally among the approximately 16,500 school districts. Thus, the 187 systems with 25,000 or more enrolled make up only 1.1 percent of the public school districts but employ 27.1 percent of all full-time teachers.[1] At the other extreme, the 4,731 of the operating districts with fewer than 300 pupils employ only 1.8 percent of all teachers. About two-thirds of all classroom teachers are women.

CERTIFICATION

Investments of time, money, and effort in the recruitment of teachers was a serious concern for more than two decades. School districts are less likely now to send teams of administrators scouring the nation in search of teachers. The emphasis is now on higher selection standards and counseling

[1]National Education Association, *Twenty-sixth Biennial Salary and Staff Survey of Public School Professional Personnel, 1972–73*, Research Report 1973-R5, Washington, D.C.: The Association, 1973, p. 6.

only the best students to pursue teaching as a career. All those recruited or selected are required to possess a certificate to teach. A teaching certificate is a license to practice a profession and carries no guarantee of employment. There is considerable variation among states about conditions for certification. Certification requirements for teachers at the elementary and secondary school levels are based on increasing levels of preparation in most states. From 1900 to 1920, no state required a bachelor's degree for elementary school teachers. At present, practically all states have declared the bachelor's degree to be the minimum standard for certification of new elementary school teachers.

In 1930 less than half the states required a bachelor's degree for high school teachers. By 1964 no state certified secondary school teachers without a bachelor's degree. The nondegree elementary or secondary teacher is a relic of past ages and has almost disappeared. At present less than 3 percent do not have at least an earned bachelor's degree.

Some significant trends in certification of teachers are discussed below.

1. Certification is becoming centralized. In past years teaching certificates were issued by the local school board and the county superintendent of schools. In most states certification is now the responsibility of the state department of education.

2. Certification is based on professional preparation. In past years the certifying authority usually required that all candidates for a teaching certificate submit to a written or oral examination. At present certificates are granted after completion of a specified program at an institution approved beforehand by the state department of education.

3. Certificates are valid for specified

periods of time only. At one time a "life" or "unlimited" certificate to teach was issued after completion of a specified number of years of successful teaching (usually two or more). A teacher with little professional preparation who had been granted a life certificate could not be stimulated to additional study even if standards for new teachers were raised. The present trend is to limit validity of the certificate to two to five years.

4. Certificates are limited to special areas or subjects. In previous years one teaching certificate enabled an individual to teach at the elementary or secondary level and in any subject, whether special preparation was evident or not. This is no longer true.

5. Increased professional preparation is required. This may be the most significant trend in teacher certification. Requirements have moved from completion of high school to completion of two years of normal school to completion of four years of college. In a few states, five years of preparation after high school are required; this may be the new standard in the years ahead.

6. Dual or certificate-conversion programs are common. Such programs permit high school graduates with teaching credentials to pursue a further, but limited, amount of college work to become certified for elementary school teaching. These programs were developed to remedy the shortage of teachers, and their value remains to be determined.

7. Members of the profession determine standards for certification. For many years, most teachers had little to say about the requirements for entry into the profession. There is a definite trend toward involving local teacher organizations as well as national groups in formulating standards for certification. The authority to issue

certificates remains lodged in a centralized state agency, but the formulation of policies regarding certification involves members of the profession.

8. Fewer types of certificates are issued. In the past some states have had as many as 25 different types of certificates for teachers. Classes of certificates are being reduced in numbers, which greatly simplifies satisfaction of requirements. The number of separate certificates has declined in the last five years from about 1000 to 550. Further reduction is needed.

9. Reciprocity—the recognition of a teaching certificate from one state to another—is increasing. It is developing slowly and is hampered by the variations in standards among states. The mobility of our population indicates the necessity of such programs. Accreditation by the National Council for the Accreditation of Teacher Education facilitates the reciprocity movement.

10. Cooperation regarding teacher certification is evident between subject-matter specialists in liberal arts colleges and colleges of education.

11. The National Commission on Teacher Education and Professional Standards and the National Council for the Accreditation of Teacher Education have been established and are contributing to the improvement of teacher education and certification.

12. There was evidence in the 1970s of a growing interest in relating preparation more closely with performance, giving rise to what is known as competency-based teacher preparation and competency-based teacher certification.

ROLE OF THE SCHOOL BOARD AND THE SUPERINTENDENT

The local board of education, as the policy-making agency, is responsible for determining the type, quantity, and caliber of teachers to be employed in the school system. Legally, the board is the only agency authorized to employ school personnel. All teachers are employees of the board of education, no matter what other individuals are involved in the selection process. The board cannot employ teachers who do not meet state certification standards, but it can require more professional preparation or experience than is demanded by state certification agencies. In addition, the board of education determines the financial resources available for teachers. The adopted or negotiated salary schedule is a statement of financial policy of the board of education with reference to teachers.

There is little question of the school board's authority in personnel matters. It is the manner in which the board exercises its authority that is at issue. It is physically impossible for board members in a large school district to interview and employ all teachers personally. The superintendent, who has the professional preparation, as well as the time, to assess applicants is delegated the responsibility for nominating personnel, but the power of appointment rests with the board of education. The board exercises the legal authority to appoint only upon the recommendation of its chief executive officer. Only in a few small districts does the board insist upon interviewing all teacher candidates and determining who shall be appointed.

As early as 1950, 84 percent of city school systems delegated responsibility for nominating school personnel to the superintendent of schools or his recognized representatives. At this point in time it is the unusual school system that fails to delegate the responsibility of teacher selection to the superintendent or his professional assistant.

There is general agreement that the location and nomination of candidates for school positions are best executed by the superintendent, who may turn to other administrative personnel for assistance. Professional understanding is necessary to interpret the qualifications of candidates by reviewing placement-office credentials or by interviewing.

CRITERIA FOR EMPLOYMENT OF TEACHERS

Professional qualifications

Education. Local district professional standards, beyond those required for certification, for the employment of teachers are increasing. In 1923 a two-year normal school certificate was the minimum requirement for elementary school teachers in 79 percent of cities; 20 percent had still lower requirements. That elementary school teachers might need four years of preparation was not even admitted in the 1923 inquiry. By 1951 only 18 percent of the cities studied accepted a minimum of two years of preparation, and 74 percent required at least four years. State certification laws are now based on four years of preparation for elementary teachers in practically all states. With a surplus of applicants, most school systems may demand more rather than less than four years of training.

In 1923 four years of professional preparation were required for junior high school teachers in only 26 percent of cities; by 1951 the proportion had risen to 95 percent. By 1951, 99 percent of cities required four or more years of preparation for senior high school teachers. Since 1964 every state

has required four years of preparation for a secondary school teaching certificate.

Although the back of the teacher shortage has been broken there are other factors that may restrain districts from demanding more than four years of professional preparation. The salary factor is one. Teachers with master's degrees or higher command a higher salary at all experience levels than those without advanced degrees. The present job market differs markedly from the 1930s when greater experience and preparation helped a person to find a teaching position. With the extended financial crunch facing education, districts are seeking the less experienced to balance out the total staff so that not all are at the high end of the salary scale.

Experience. Previous teaching experience is often considered a requisite for employment. The National Education Association expressed forceful opposition to experience as a condition for employment as long as 40 years ago. This practice has the approval of tradition. At one time large cities relied on small school districts to give experience to new teachers. The lack of adequate supervisory services in some small districts, however, allowed the development of undesirable teaching styles, which caused more problems than benefits for the large districts that insisted on employing experienced teachers only. The teacher shortage of the 1950s and 1960s forced the large systems to employ inexperienced teachers and to develop adequate orientation, in-service, and supervisory programs to stimulate professional growth. This along with the current financial difficulties brought about a change in the traditional practice. Large as well as small districts, for reasons indicated earlier, now actively seek to include a number of inexperienced new teachers.

Personal characteristics

Age. As the period of required preparation for teachers increases, age limits for new teachers become less important. In 1951 less than 12 percent of cities reported age limits for new teachers, and only 7 percent reported a minimum age. Now about 34 states still enforce a minimum-age requirement for certification: 18 is the minimum age in most. The requirement of a college degree eliminates the need for a minimum-age stipulation.

Marital status. Policies discriminating against the married woman teacher have all but disappeared for various reasons. The teacher shortage of previous decades and the emphasis on equal employment opportunities of the present decade brought an end to such discriminatory practices. Striking progress in removing discrimination against married women teachers occurred between 1931 and 1951. In 1931, 77 percent of city school systems refused even to consider employing qualified married women. By 1941 the proportion had dropped to 58 percent, and by 1951, to only 8 percent. Any system refusing to consider employing a qualified married woman would, in all likelihood, face court action.

The debate over the employment of married women as teachers was a carryover of the attitude common during the depression that there should not be two breadwinners in one family, whether husband and wife taught in the same or different systems. The limited evidence available—and there were some studies during the 1920s and 1930s concerned with the efficiency of single versus married women teachers—yielded inconclusive results, but suggested that the married woman teacher is slightly more efficient than the single women teacher.[2] If quality of teaching is given priority over such noneducational factors as social welfare and economics, then married women deserve the same consideration.

Most recent data show that the unmarried school teacher was a thing of the past by 1961; only 14 percent of teachers are presently single women. About 72 percent of all teachers are married; four out of five men teachers and two out of three women teachers are married. The discriminatory policies of the 1930s against married women have been completely repudiated by the practices of the 1960s and 1970s.

Sex. Women dominate the teaching profession. There was a time when school masters outnumbered "school marms," but teaching began to be primarily a career for women around the middle of the nineteenth century. In 1880, 43 percent of all teachers were men and 57 percent women. By 1920 only 14 percent of all teachers were men and 86 percent women. An upsurge was noted after that. At present about 36 percent of the teachers are men and 64 percent are women.[3] Most of the women teachers are in the elementary grades (two out of three women are elementary teachers). There are now more women than ever before in senior high schools, but men outnumber women at this level.

[2]Committee on Equal Opportunity, National Education Association, *Status of the Married Woman Teacher,* Washington, D.C.: The Association, 1938.

[3]National Education Association, "New Profile of the American Public School Teacher," *Today's Education,* May 1972, pp. 15–17.

Women dominate the teaching of secondary school English, but men are more likely to teach science and social science.

The typical teacher

The description of the typical teacher has changed and continues to do so. The National Education Association (NEA) studied teachers' characteristics in 1960–1961,[4] in 1965–1966,[5] and in 1970–1971.[6] In each case, a questionnaire on personal and professional status and attitudes was sent to a probability sample of American public school teachers. The typical teacher in 1971 was younger, less experienced, better educated, and better paid than her counterpart of years past. The median age dropped from 41 years in 1961 to 35 years in 1971. Teaching experience dropped from a median of 11 years in 1961 to 8 years in 1971. The typical teacher in 1971 was a college graduate. The nondegree teacher all but disappeared. Teachers with a master's degree (27.1 percent) far outnumbered those without a bachelor's degree (2.9 percent) in 1971. Eight percent of all teachers in 1971 were black. Ethnic background is changing. NEA in 1974 showed 9.5 percent of the teachers were black, 1.2 percent Spanish speaking, 0.2 percent American Indian, and 0.4 percent Asian American. The remainder were identified as "nonminority" teachers. This same source reported that 15.2 percent of the public school enrollment was black, 5.4 percent Spanish speaking, 0.5 percent American Indian, and 0.5 percent Asian American. Efforts are being mounted to hire more teachers from the minority populations.

The typical teacher in 1971 was a married women in her late thirties with a bachelor's degree. She was likely to be teaching elementary pupils, reporting to a male principal, and working in a school with a teaching staff of 25. She put in about a 47-hour work week and taught about 181 days during the school year.

ASSIGNMENT AND TEACHING LOAD

The contract signed by the board of education and the individual teacher consummates the formal employment act. Practically all states require a written contract between the board and the individual teacher. It refers to functions to be performed by the teacher in a very general way. Seldom is the name of the building to which the teacher is assigned included within the contract. The contract must be supplemented by executive action to assign the teacher to a building and to specify the class or grade level to be taught. Prior to employment, a teacher has a right to information about the grade level and teaching load for which he is being considered. There may be some reasons to change later, due to emergency situations. The assignment of a teacher to an attendance center is a function of the superintendent, but the central-office staff and the principal should be consulted. It is no longer unusual to develop many of the work conditions by mutual agreement between teachers and board members via the negotiating process that yields the general contract for all teachers.

[4]National Education Association, "The Status of the American Public School Teacher," *Research Bulletin*, February 1962.

[5]National Education Association, *The American Public School Teacher, 1965–66*, Research Report 1967-R47, Washington, D.C.: The Association, 1967.

[6]National Education Association, *The American Public School Teacher, 1970–71*, Research Report 1972-R3, Washington, D.C.: The Association, 1972.

A teacher should be assigned to those classes which she is qualified to teach and in which she has a particular interest. Where a compromise must be made, the teacher should be fully informed of why it was necessary and should be granted an opportunity to transfer at the earliest practical moment. These procedures are now being formalized by collective negotiation in many schools.

The focus of personnel administration shifts to the attendance center and, therefore, involves principals to a greater extent than before, following employment and assignment. Teaching load is predicated on general and central-office administrative decisions that are not at variance with any negotiated agreement. Execution of policies on numbers of pupils and/or subjects assigned to a teacher is the domain of the principal.

Various devices have been developed to equalize the work load of teachers in a school system, or at least within the same building. Most of the current practices specify a maximum of from five to seven periods per day of teaching plus supervision of study hall and other activities. This is a heavy standard, and a more desirable level is at least one period less than the maximum. About 19 percent of the secondary teachers in 1971 had no unassigned period. The typical elementary teacher in 1971 had a class of 27 pupils, but secondary teachers had 130 pupil contacts per day. High school instructors average 26 periods a week with 53 minutes for each period.[7]

Many factors influence the measurement of load. Among these are student-teacher ratio, classes per day, total enrollment in classes taught, number of different subjects taught

or preparations required, total clock hours, nature of students in classes (particularly if the mental ability is unusually low or high or if the pupils have handicaps), nonclassroom responsibilities such as corridor or playground supervision, extracurricular activity commitments, and administrative responsibilities.

In elementary school, number of pupils in the classroom, ability range in the room, nonclassroom supervisory chores, number of special subjects taught by the regular teacher, and number of grade levels within a room are considered in measuring teaching load. The average work week of an elementary-school teacher is 47 hours per week, of which about 30 hours were spent in classroom, 6 hours in out-of-class instructional duties, and 10 hours in miscellaneous functions such as monitorial activities, meetings, and community service.

Computation of work load for secondary school teachers is more complex. A formula developed by Douglass in 1932 and revised in 1950 took into consideration number of classes per week; length of class period; amount of time spent in class sections of the same subject and grade level; time per week spent in study-hall supervision, classroom teaching, preparation, and other activities. The Douglass formula attempted to compensate for difficulties in preparing and teaching certain subjects by developing a "subject matter difficulty" coefficient.

Various surveys show that the average secondary school teaching load has diminished from six to five sections per day. The average work week for secondary school teachers was 48 hours, of which 29 hours were spent in classroom instruction, 8 hours in out-of-class instructional duties (correcting papers and preparation), and 11 hours in miscellaneous functions

[7]Ibid.

such as supervising study halls, sponsoring clubs, monitorial duties, and community service.

In an effort to relieve teachers of some of the stresses of the school day, as well as to lighten the teaching load, some states have enacted legislation that prescribes a duty-free lunch period for classroom teachers. In 1971 over 30 percent of the teachers ate lunch with their pupils. The percentage of elementary teachers without a duty-free lunch period is twice as high as that for secondary teachers (40.5 percent versus 19.6 percent). The duty-free lunch is more common in the larger districts. Some districts achieve this by insisting that all pupils go home for lunch; others have only the principal supervise the lunchroom.

CONTINUING PROFESSIONAL DEVELOPMENT

Completion of a preparation program that terminates with a bachelor's or a master's degree is the beginning of a lifetime of learning. Teachers are part of a dynamic profession and must keep abreast of improvements in instructional methods at the classroom level. In-service education, more appropriately titled "continuing professional development," is not unique to teaching; other professions, too, utilize refresher courses, special readings, observations, and visiting.

Stimulation of professional improvement calls for a variety of devices that must be unified into a total program. It can be started simply through the creation of a professional library. Filling a room with books is not difficult; stimulating the staff to utilize it effectively is. Providing special consultative services to teachers can be used to influence continuing professional development of classroom teachers. Granting teachers time off to observe promising practices in other schools is another method, though not always a satisfactory one, since not all highly publicized projects live up to expectations. Demonstrations of new procedures may be designed with local or special resources. Sabbatical leaves for elementary and secondary teachers are relatively rare. Continuing professional development is not an institutional responsibility only; each educator has a personal and professional obligation to keep informed of new developments.

Workshops organized and sponsored by school systems or universities are the most common type of professional growth activities. Faculty meetings can contribute to professional development if organized to do so. If teachers' meetings are what the name implies, rather than the principal's meetings, teachers should participate in their planning. A major problem encountered in organizing staff meetings aimed at contributing to professional growth is tremendous variation in teachers' talents and interests. In a small school all faculty members, regardless of grade or subject level, can occasionally gather and participate in profitable discussions. However, because the concerns of elementary and secondary school instructors are usually different, faculty sessions are often arranged on a grade or subject basis. The approach is not without problems, for teachers from all over the system must gather at some central place, and fighting city traffic jams does not develop a mood conducive to professional growth.

The best time for faculty meetings whose prime purpose is professional growth seems to be immediately following or before the school year. Such meetings may last a few days or all summer; the usual period is one or two weeks. Seven out of eight teachers attend faculty meetings regularly. The average length is about one hour. They are most likely to be called monthly.

Involving faculty members in curriculum revision is still another way to stimulate staff growth. Some systems relieve certain teachers from instructional responsibilities to participate in curriculum projects which may last several months. Substitute teachers are employed and paid by the board.

The procedures suggested above are but means of releasing the creative energies of the teaching staff; their effectiveness depends on the leadership ability of the administrator.

SALARY SCHEDULES

The authorization of a contract for personal services is the initial step in the management of salary payments. The amount of payment can be an arbitrary figure or part of an overall salary policy.

One of the significant developments in personnel administration has been the growth and use of salary schedules. Prior to 1920, less than one-half the cities had salary schedules. By 1922–1923, however, approximately 65 percent of city school systems had inaugurated a schedule for salary payments to instructors. At the present time, it is difficult to find a city school district that does not use a salary schedule for teachers.[8] Collective negotiation may well spell a significant modification in traditional salary scheduling.

The development of salary schedules requires a number of board of education policy statements as well as

[8]Stephen J. Knezevich and John Guy Fowlkes, *Business Management of Local School Systems*, New York: Harper & Row, 1960, chap. 6.

administrative decisions. Among these are statements regarding minimum or starting salaries. The minimum or initial salary for teachers with a bachelor's degree has risen from less than $1,000 annually during the Great Depression of the 1930s to more than $7,300 in the early 1970s. The 1973 NEA convention called for a starting salary of $12,500 for qualified beginning teachers. The average annual salary for classroom teachers for 1972–1973 was about $10,250, not quite double what it was ten years earlier (about $5,750 in 1962–1963). These figures should be interpreted in the light of inflation during this period and its impact on purchasing power. Thus, in 1967–1968 dollars the 1972–1973 salary is reduced to only about $8,220. The larger the system the higher the salary. Thus, the mean salary of $11,215 was noted in large systems in 1972–1973; this is over 9 percent above the national average.

Salary schedules require decisions about how long it should take an employee to move from initial to maximum salary level. It is generally felt that the number and size of annual increments should permit a teacher to move from minimum to maximum salary in 12 to 15 years. In past years, $50 to $100 was considered a reasonable annual pay raise. Most school systems presently award annual increments of five times these amounts. The average size of the increment may be determined by dividing the difference between the minimum and maximum salaries by the number of steps in the schedule. It should not be assumed that all annual increments must be the same size. There is some argument for allowing smaller increments during the earlier period of employment and much larger increments subsequently to career teachers.

There is a distinct trend toward using a single salary schedule, that is, a schedule in which salary is based on professional preparation and experience, without regard to position in the system. Prior to 1920, no city system had a single salary schedule. By 1956–1957 the proportion of city systems that did not have a single salary schedule was negligible. The position type of schedule, which bases salary payments on the position held in the school system, is rapidly disappearing.

An examination of trends in salary scheduling discloses that salary differentials between men and women teachers have been decreasing; cost-of-living bonuses have all but disappeared; minimum salaries have risen more rapidly than maximums; the number of annual increments has re-

mained constant; and the average salaries paid to teachers have increased sharply. It is evident from the data in Table 19–1 that in spite of improvements, average annual salaries for instructional personnel over the years remained below that for federal government civilian employees and others.

There remain a number of controversial issues with reference to salary payments. Among these are development of a differentiated salary scale for differentiated school staffs, extra pay for extra work, and merit salary increases. Merit payments should not be confused with the entire problem of wage and salary payments. They are only a single factor in the determination of salary. Merit rating calls for

TABLE 19–1

AVERAGE ANNUAL EARNINGS OF PUBLIC SCHOOL INSTRUCTIONAL STAFF AND CERTAIN OTHER GROUPS, 1929 THROUGH 1971 CALENDAR-YEAR BASIS

| | Average annual earning | | | | Index: Teachers = 100.0 | | | |
Calendar year	Public school teachers	Wage and salary workers, all industries	Employees in manufacturing	Civilian employees of federal government	Instructional staff	Wage and salary workers, all industries	Employees in manufacturing	Civilian employees of federal government
1929	$ 1,400[a]	$1,405	$1,543	$ 1,933	100.0	100.4	110.2	138.1
1935	1,255[a]	1,137	1,216	1,759	100.0	90.6	96.9	140.2
1940	1,450[a]	1,300	1,432	1,894	100.0	89.7	98.8	130.6
1945	1,900[a]	2,189	2,517	2,646	100.0	115.2	132.5	139.3
1950	2,823	3,008	3,300	3,503	100.0	106.6	116.9	124.1
1955	3,907	3,847	4,351	4,595	100.0	98.5	111.4	117.6
1960	5,088	4,707	5,342	5,946	100.0	92.5	105.0	116.9
1965	6,292	5,710	6,389	7,613	100.0	90.8	101.5	121.0
1970	8,846	7,571	8,155	10,519	100.0	85.6	92.2	118.9
1971	9,414	8,061	8,638	11,503	100.0	85.6	91.8	122.2
1972[b]	10,254							

Source: For 1929 through 1945 data National Education Association, *Economic Status of Teachers*, 1967–1968, Washington, D.C.: The Association, 1968, p. 27. For 1950–1971 data National Education Association, *Economic Status of The Teaching Profession*, 1972–1973, Washington, D.C.: The Association, 1973, p. 49.

[a] Based on all instructional staff that includes public school teachers.

[b] Based on data from the National Education Association, *26th Biennial Salary and Staff Survey of Public School Professional Personnel, 1972–1973*, Washington, D.C.: The Association, 1973, p. 13.

evaluation of teachers, and an objective and accurate measurement of a teacher's efficiency has not yet been developed. For this reason, most groups of teachers have expressed opposition to merit raises. However, such instruments may be developed and merit increases may then be practical.

Merit increases in scheduled salaries have been referred to as quality-of-service provisions. A study of practices in urban school districts revealed the following:

1. One in six urban districts provided a reward or a penalty to recognize quality of service in the salary schedule.
2. The percentage of large urban school districts providing superior-service maximums, after decreasing for 14 years, was increasing slightly.
3. Over one-fourth of the urban districts having superior-service maximums in 1957–1958 dropped them in 1958–1959.
4. One in ten urban school boards authorized the granting of superior-service maximums, but only 6 percent actually used such provisions in 1958–1959.
5. About 13 percent of urban systems had salary provisions for penalizing teachers for unsatisfactory service, but only 3 percent imposed a penalty in 1958–1959.
6. About 46 percent of the reporting superintendents of districts having quality-of-service provisions stated that they thought such a provision had a good effect on the level of performance of nearly all teachers.[9]

In 1938–1939 about 20 percent of all urban schedules examined had superior-service maximums. By 1958–1959 the proportion was reduced significantly to a low of 6.2 percent. The provisions for additional compensation for superior-service varied from year to year with about 10 percent of the school systems including such a provision. As of 1971–1972 only 7.9 percent of the school districts included some type of merit salary provision. It can be concluded that very few include merit pay even though the pressure to do so continues unabated.

A 1970 Gallup poll revealed that 58 percent of the general public polled were of the opinion that teachers should be paid on the basis of the quality of work (merit) rather than on a standard scale. In contrast the polling of teachers' opinions demonstrated that 67 percent of the teachers favored payment on the basis of a standard scale and only 28 percent supported the quality of work (merit) criterion as the basis for determining remuneration. The disparity between public desires and professional opinions on whether merit salary plans should be implemented in the schools is substantial.

Other issues regarding salary schedules have emerged as a result of professional negotiation. The salary schedule was developed as an alternative to individual bargaining by teachers with superintendents and school boards. The practice of teachers as a group bargaining for salary and working conditions may bring an end to the salary schedule as presently conceived. Some argue that a salary schedule assumes a given increase and that such a declaration weakens the bargaining power of the board and the administrator in the salary-agreement-reaching process. It may well be that salary schedules will be developed every two years on the basis of collective negotiation rather than constructed by administrative personnel and representatives of the teachers.

[9]National Educational Association, "Salary Provisions for Quality of Service," *Research Bulletin,* vol. 37, no. 4, December 1959, pp. 106–110.

TEACHER TURNOVER

One purpose of the salary schedule is the retention of qualified teachers.

Teacher turnover is a far more complex phenomenon than would appear at first glance.

The typical loss rate in the 1950s was about 11 percent. This does not include teachers moving to a teaching position in another public school district; it includes only those who ceased to practice classroom teaching in public schools. These transfers constituted about 6 percent of all teachers. The total separation rate in the 1950s, which includes loss to the profession as well as transfer between school districts, was 17 percent of all teachers. To summarize, out of 100 teachers who started in one year, 83 returned the following year, 6 moved to another teaching job, and 11 left the profession.

The highest separation rates occur among women teachers in secondary schools (19.5 percent) and the lowest among men at the same level (11.5 percent). The lowest separation rate was in districts with enrollments of over 25,000 (about 15 percent) and the highest in districts with an enrollment under 500 (29 percent). In other words, the smallest districts experienced the greatest turnover.

Studies during the 1960s showed that the teacher turnover rate fluctuated between 11 percent to 13.6 percent annually, or below the total for the 1950s. The larger the school system the lower the annual teacher separation rate.

Whether the separation rate of from 11 to 13.6 percent is high, low, or average is determined by comparison with turnover in other professions that have a high percentage of women. The turnover among caseworkers in 53 state child-welfare agencies is 28 percent, or considerably higher than the turnover among teachers. The turnover among nurses in general hospitals is even higher (66.9 percent). Thus, the turnover rate in education is not high by these standards.

The dramatic turnaround in teacher supply and declining, rather than rapidly increasing, enrollments during the 1970s suggest an annual turnover rate of much less than the 11 to 13.6 percent noted in the 1950s and 1960s. The present turnover rate is probably about one-half of that noted in the 1960s. This is an estimate that may prove to be too high rather than too low.

Once again the 1970s will provide a situation much different from that recorded in the 1950s and 1960s. The number of graduates prepared to teach grew from about 129,700 in 1961 to about 266,260 in 1969. This number continued to establish new high records until it reached 337,619 by June, 1972. Projections for the rest of the 1970s assume that graduates prepared to teach may grow, if unchecked, to 412,000 by 1979. This fantastic but possible growth in teacher supply comes at a time when the number of teaching positions will first stabilize and then decline (unless unforeseen developments occur). The imbalance between supply and demand for teachers will create an even tighter job opportunity market in the late 1970s than was experienced in the early 1970s. The NEA predicted that a surplus of almost 104,000 beginning teachers (excess of supply over demand) in 1971 would grow to an excess of almost 196,000 by 1979. In addition the numbers of unemployed *experienced* teachers "will increase by 172,800 between 1975 and 1980."[10] They pointed out, however, that needed massive improvements in school quality could substantially reduce the critical surplus and delay its onset until 1975. Another, but evidently less palat-

[10]National Education Association, "Teacher Job Shortage Ahead," Research Bulletin, vol. 49, no. 3, October 1971, pp. 69–74.

able, remedy is to reduce the numbers allowed in teacher preparation programs. There is evidence now that enrollments in teacher preparation programs are declining.

RETIREMENT, TENURE, AND LEAVES OF ABSENCE

Retirement provisions for teachers are a twentieth-century development. Some states did not have such provisions until after World War II. Amounts dedicated to retirement have had to be increased owing to the continued pressure of inflation. The programs are retirement rather than pension plans because both teacher and the state contribute; an employee makes no contribution toward a pension. In some states the employer's contribution to the retirement program is paid by the local district rather than by the state; this procedure is of questionable merit. Federal participation in teachers' retirement programs started in 1952.

Tenure laws must be considered in the administration of professional personnel. There is a difference between tenure laws and continuing-contract laws. A tenure law guarantees employment indefinitely after completion of a probationary period; it implies that a teacher can be discharged only for definite causes specified in the tenure law, and only if certain procedures are followed. A continuing-contract law merely specifies that a teacher must be notified by some definite date in the spring of the year whether she is or is not to be offered another annual contract. If no notification is given by the specified date in the spring, the teacher's contract is automatically continued. Continuing-contract laws specify that the notification shall be given not only by a certain date but in a certain manner; special hearings are granted in some states.

Considerable progress has been made in the development of sick leave plans. The NEA reported that in 1927–1928 only 57.7 percent of urban school systems had sick-leave provisions. Sick-leave plans with full salary and cumulative sick-leave provisions are now established throughout the nation, often by state law covering all types of school districts. Leaves may also be granted for professional preparation, maternity, or other appropriate reasons. Granting leaves generates the need for substitute teachers. The recruitment of a core of well-qualified and skilled substitute teachers has lagged. Substitute-teaching plans must be developed to minimize lost days of instruction for pupils. Most substitute teachers work because they want to, not because they have to.

EVALUATION AND IMPROVEMENT OF MORALE

Teachers are evaluated for many reasons, the most important of which is to improve their effectiveness in promoting learning. Teachers have a stake in evaluation, for as one writer put it: "Teachers must realize that evaluation is as vital to their self-interest as the salary schedule, the retirement benefit, the insurance program, or other conditions of employment."[11]

Identifying the effective teacher is not simple. Mitzel reported: "More than a half century of research effort has not yielded meaningful measurable criteria around which the majority of the nation's educators can rally. No standards exist which are commonly

[11]R. P. Klahn, ed., *Evaluation of Teacher Competency*, Milwaukee: Franklin, 1965, p. 3.

agreed upon as the criteria of teacher effectiveness."[12] Redfern concurred: "The appraisal of teaching performance has baffled both teachers and school administrators for half a century."[13] The 1950 edition of the *Encyclopedia of Educational Research* concluded that, although research has added materially to an understanding of abilities, traits, and qualities desirable in the teacher, the identification and definition of competency are as yet unsatisfactory. There is no "adequate definition of teacher efficiency and consequently no satisfactory means of measuring this variable."[14] These were typical statements prior to 1965.

More recently Redfern claimed to see some "light at the end of the tunnel" with reference to performance evaluation of teachers. There is a definite move toward modifying traditional unilateral rating schemes in favor of results-oriented and competency based evaluation.[15] More state legislatures are mandating teacher evaluation. Five states have enacted laws, three states used the initiatives of the state departments of education, and four other states were in 1973 in the process of demanding local school systems to design and implement more systematic evaluation approaches.[16]

It can be argued that evaluation of teacher performance can be a positive force for teacher and organizational improvement. The systems approach to staff evaluation is described in greater detail elsewhere.[17] Its outlines include developing an overall evaluation systems model with specification of evaluation objectives; identification of teacher effectiveness models; designing evaluative data-gathering instruments, personnel, and procedures; storing and retrieving evaluative data; designing decision-making subsystems to act on evaluative data gathered; and personnel actions based on evaluative data. Evaluation must produce more than simply a label for a teacher. It should provide information vital to the design of professional development programs. Great strides in the improvement of teacher evaluation systems were noted during the early 1970s.

Morale is difficult to define and even more difficult to measure. It is a state of being more easily felt intuitively than described and verified. Morale is not necessarily an end in itself. It is a means of promoting a smoothly functioning and productive institution. It is possible to have high morale and little accomplishment. The administrator must try to promote this general feeling of well-being so that all people in the institution will work together consistently in pursuit of the common purpose.

The development of good morale starts the day the individual is employed. Teachers new to the school system experience a variety of problems: adjusting to assignments; getting acquainted with the community, the system, and the school; coming to

---

[12]Harold E. Mitzel, "Teacher Effectiveness," in Chester W. Harris, ed., *Encyclopedia of Educational Research,* 3rd ed., New York: Macmillan, 1960, p. 1481.

[13]G. B. Redfern, *How to Evaluate Teaching,* Worthington, Ohio.: School Management Institute, 1972, p. 6.

[14]A. S. Barr, "Teaching Competencies," in Walter S. Monroe, ed., *Encyclopedia of Educational Research,* rev. ed., New York: Macmillan, 1950, pp. 1453–1454.

[15]G. B. Redfern, "Competency-Based Evaluation: The State of the Art," *New Directions for Education,* vol. 1, no. 1, Spring 1973, pp. 51–61.

[16]Ibid.

[17]See S. J. Knezevich, ed., "Creating Appraisal and Accountability Systems," *New Directions for Education,* vol. 1, no. 1, Spring 1973, pp. 21–61.

know colleagues within the building and the system as a whole. A number of monographs and books have focused on problems of the teacher new to the school system.[18] The administrator alert to these difficulties will institute such practices as preschool workshops, carefully prepared handbooks for new teachers, special letters and programs of welcome, and assigning existing staff members or special supervisors to help new teachers.[19]

Conditions of employment, such as the work load, sick-leave policy, provision for substitute teachers, and planning periods, as well as salary and retirement benefits, affect morale. Analysis of the typical teaching load shows that a 40-hour week in teaching would be sheer luxury. Reasonable class size would ease the teacher's load. Above all, teachers desire a brief respite during the day from the pressure of activities. A planning period at the secondary school level, and special time off at the elementary school level, would be most welcome. Pleasant and comfortable surroundings help a great deal. Special lounges for teachers contribute to feelings of well-being and acceptance in a school system.

Morale is improved by the general atmosphere in the school system. Although salaries are important, an increase in pay will not reduce emotional pressures. Democratic school administration which attempts to release the abilities of teachers, develop a democratic spirit in supervision, and open lines of communication may be even more conducive to development of good morale.

[18]See Glen G. Eye and Willard R. Lane, *The New Teacher Comes to School,* New York: Harper & Row, 1956; also National Education Association, "First Year Teachers, 1954–55," *Research Bulletin,* vol. 1, no. 1, February 1956.

[19]Eye and Lane, op. cit., chap. 10.

NEW PERSONNEL ISSUES

Faculty integration

Faculty integration became a significant personnel issue in the 1960s owing to the civil rights movement and the desegregation process that resulted in the closing of previously all-black schools. Some states developed special programs to relocate displaced black teachers. The criterion of teacher competency was compromised in some cases as administrators were pressured to employ teachers to achieve racial balance for the total staff of a school. Statistics on the extent of faculty desegregation were not available until 1966. Pressures for faculty integration in Northern as well as Southern schools will continue during the 1970s. To adequately reflect the proportion of minority students in its school population, NEA estimated in 1974 the need for 13,706 Spanish speaking and 15,375 black teachers to be employed in the New York City schools alone. Nationwide, the achievement of a better balance would necessitate the entry into teaching of 116,000 black, 84,500 Spanish speaking, 7,400 American Indian, and 3,000 Asian American teachers for the public schools.

Team teaching

Team teaching (also called cooperative instruction or cooperative teaching) gained popularity in the 1950s and 1960s. Teachers were selected not purely for ability to teach a given grade or subject but for ability to work with other teachers to fill team needs. That team teaching poses problems of matching teachers' personalities has gone unrecognized thus far in the enthusiasm to implement the practice.

It is not unusual for teachers to share insights about pupils each has come to know or to share teaching skills, but the deployment of teachers into a team has acquired a special meaning. The Franklin School in Lexington, Massachusetts, is credited with the introduction of team teaching in 1957, and its program became the prototype for several other projects.[20] The concept has spread to all parts of the nation although it appears to have peaked out in the early 1970s. The team leader is a pivotal position in the Franklin School team-teaching experiment. The team leader coordinates the work of several others responsible for instruction and guidance for as few as 50 or as many as 200 pupils. She does some teaching, but most of her time is allocated to curriculum planning, staff leadership, and pupil evaluation. The team leader is more highly paid than other members of the cooperative arrangement. (This is a controversial point resisted by some districts and teacher organizations. There are those who argue for a $400 differential between a team leader and other qualified teachers of equal preparation and experience; others want differentials of several thousand dollars or more.) The other two team members are the master teacher—a fully certified and experienced instructor—and the auxiliary teacher—typically a trainee, a student teacher, or a teachers' aide.

Team teaching represents a departure from the self-contained classroom arrangement in which one teacher has complete responsibility for planning lessons, developing appropriate methods and materials, and evaluating pupil learning. No single pattern for team teaching has emerged. The

Franklin School plan is one pattern. Another employs three teachers plus a clerical assistant for 75 or more students of similar age and grade level.

Team teaching may be conceived as part of a continuing effort toward what some call differentiated staffing. In differentiated staffing a hierarchy of teaching positions with various salaries is created. The team leader is at the top of this teaching hierarchy with a cluster of pupils. It is an approach that can be incorporated in a number of individualized and other instructional organization patterns such as IPI and IGE/MUS-E.

The team leader holds a line position under the direct supervision of the principal, and in some respects is similar to a department chairman of a secondary school. Like a department chairman, the team leader prepares schedules, recommends procedures for grouping students, selects materials, plans techniques, and helps evaluate the program. Because such tasks are concerned with organization and stimulation, the position is more an administrative than an instructional one. The team leader must be an experienced teacher of unusual talent, however, and she should have a considerable amount of professional preparation beyond the master's degree.

Team teaching will not reduce the number of teachers in a school; more often than not, it will necessitate more personnel, although the increase may be in auxiliary teachers or teachers' aides. Team teaching is an arrangement to facilitate professional cooperation, in the belief that such cooperative effort will lead to more effective instruction by utilizing the special knowledge and talents of individual teachers. It has been used in both elementary and secondary schools.

Hilson pointed out that the full value of team teaching remains to be

[20]National Education Association, *Planning and Organizing for Teaching,* Project on the Instructional Program of the Public Schools, Washington, D.C.: The Association, 1963, p. 85.

measured.[21] He identified the following advantages of the method:

1. Superior teachers can exercise greater influence in the school and still remain in classroom teaching.
2. It facilitates grouping.
3. During large-group teaching periods, other teachers are free for small-group work, lesson planning, and parent-teacher conferences.
4. Pupils spend more of their school time receiving instruction than they do in the self-contained arrangement.
5. More extensive use is made of visual aids.
6. There appears to be more efficient use of space, materials, and equipment.
7. Teachers find it helpful to exchange information and viewpoints.
8. Evaluation of pupils is a combined judgment of several teachers.
9. It allegedly furnishes impetus to improve curriculum.
10. It may be effective for training student teachers.
11. The beginning teacher is not isolated; she has the benefit of the supervision from experienced teachers.
12. Part-time teachers with special competencies can be employed.
13. Illness of one member of the team does not necessitate a substitute teacher, who often does little more than baby sit.
14. Teachers work hard on improving the instructional ability of the team.

He listed the following disadvantages:

1. Complex problems of human relations may result from the frequency and intensity of contact of team members.
2. The problem of status is created when teachers are pyramided under a team chairman.
3. To attain the flexibility of team teaching, much time and effort must be spent on scheduling and planning all group and individual activities.
4. Mechanical aspects of evaluation may be more difficult.
5. Questions children have during large-group sessions or demonstrations must wait until completion of the lecture.
6. Opportunities for pupil leadership may be lost because of the large size of the group.
7. Noise may be a problem in large-group operation.
8. Instruction may tend to be formal and hence reduce pupil activity.
9. Interaction between the superior teacher and the learner may be minimal, since such teachers are involved chiefly in the administrative aspects of the program.
10. It is difficult to locate teachers with the special competencies and high qualifications necessary to be team leaders and senior teachers.
11. It will probably cost more, since team leaders and senior teachers will be paid more and secretarial help must be provided.

There appears to be more talk than practice of team teaching. An NEA survey in 1971 showed only about one in eight teachers involved in a team teaching situation, although almost 37 percent noted the practice in their school building; not all participated in it.

Teachers' aides

Teachers' aides, sometimes called paraprofessionals, may be defined as "all nonprofessionals who relieve regular teachers of some nonteaching duties, whether they are paid or volunteer their time."[22] The use of teachers' aides to provide clerical assistance on an individual or a group basis is not a new idea. For many years lay readers and library and lunchroom aides have been employed, and on occasion the assistance of parents, high school students, and college students has been enlisted. The availability of fed-

---

[21]M. Hilson, *Change and Innovation in Elementary School Organization*, New York: Holt, Rinehart & Winston, 1965, pp. 163–167.

[22]American Association of School Administrators, *Teacher Aides in Large School Systems*, Educational Research Service, circular no. 2, Washington, D.C.: The Association, 1967.

eral funds for employment of non-professionals in education, through such agencies as the Office of Economic Opportunity and Title I of the Elementary and Secondary Education Act of 1965, stimulated use of auxiliary school personnel. Such personnel may be clerical aides who enter marks on report cards, compute averages, and type and mimeograph class material; library aides who assist in processing books; housekeeping aides who take care of ventilation and lights, clean up after art classes, put up and take down displays, and help young children with their clothing; non-instructional supervisors who oversee lunchrooms, study halls, and playgrounds; or instructional assistants who help teachers in classrooms, read to youngsters, keep attendance registers, work in laboratories, and prepare instructional materials. This listing is by no means complete.[23]

The use of teachers' aides creates such personnel questions as what qualifications should be demanded of paraprofessionals, how should they be screened and selected, should they be certified, and who is to determine the extent of their responsibilities.

There is no accurate count of the number of aides. An estimated 10,000 aides were working in poverty projects across the nation in the 1960s. By now this number may exceed several hundred thousand. The various types of auxiliary personnel may some day outnumber teachers. In 1971 only about 30 percent of the teachers had an aide of their own or shared one with others.

Most volunteer aides work less than 6 hours a week, and most paid ones

work over 20 hours a week. Most are paid hourly wage rates rather than a salary. The development of a teachers'-aides association or a union of paraprofessionals cannot be discounted, as these workers, too, may clamor for collective negotiation to determine wages and working conditions. The National Education Association has created a special membership classification for paraprofessionals.

Recruiting paid paraprofessionals has not posed a problem as yet. Paid teachers' aides are retired teachers, former substitute teachers, and young married women. Mothers receiving aid to dependent children are given priority in some large urban centers. Educational requirements vary, with high-school education being the most common. A few states have established certification requirements for teachers' aides. The teacher surplus in the 1970s has created a most unusual situation with some unemployed teachers who qualify for a full teaching credential accepting employment on an hourly basis as an aide. This could create controversy in the future years should the practice of employing qualified teachers as aides become more widespread.

SUMMARY

Over 3.6 million people are involved in teaching, operation, and administration of public education. In 1973 there were over 2.1 million classroom teachers, with comparatively small annual increases in staff in the early 1970s and the distinct possibility of stability first and decline next in the remaining years of the present decade.

Personnel policies developed by the board of education and executed by the superintendent of schools or his assistants represent the first step in

[23]National Commission on Teacher Education and Professional Standards, National Education Association, *Auxiliary School Personnel*, Washington, D.C.: The Association, 1967.

the development of effective personnel administration. The role of the board is to formulate such policies rather than to execute details of locating and interviewing teacher candidates. The trend is clearly in the direction of assigning responsibility for identifying and nominating teacher candidates to the superintendent or his staff. The typical teacher today is a married woman in the late 30s who is better prepared professionally than ever before. She is likely to be teaching in an elementary school with 25 teachers and puts in a 47 hour work week. Certification requirements are continually being upgraded, so that the overall professional preparation levels of teachers are continuing to improve.

The principal has considerable responsibility for assigning the teaching load. This load is affected by class size, number of class preparations, time spent in study hall supervision, ability range of pupils, and similar factors. Some attempts have been made to develop more objective procedures for measuring teacher load. Salaries paid to teachers continue to rise. By 1972 the salary paid to beginning teachers with a bachelor's degree exceeded $7,300. The average annual salary in 1972 for teachers was only about $10,250, not quite double the $5,750 registered ten years earlier.

Although the turnover rate among teachers in the past two decades was about 17 percent, turnover in education is less than in certain other fields. The turnover rate in the 1970s is likely to be more than one-third of the previous rate as a result of a growing surplus of persons prepared to teach. The oversupply of beginning teachers by 1979 may reach 196,000.

Salary schedules are a statement of board policy with reference to salary payment. Most school systems now employ salary schedules based on professional requirements only. Merit-increase provisions remain a point of controversy. Collective negotiation may modify the traditional concept of salary schedules and their development.

Tenure provisions are found in most states. Tenure laws should not be confused with continuing-contract laws, which merely guarantee notification of termination or renewal of contract.

An adequate definition of teacher efficiency has not been developed to date. Recent developments in the systems approach to staff performance appraisal show promise of considerable improvements in a persistent problem area. A number of state legislatures and departments of education are stimulating the development of more effective evaluation systems for teachers.

Morale is difficult to define and even more difficult to measure. It is possible to have high morale and limited effectiveness. Conditions of employment and the general tenor of administration and supervision influence morale.

Developing integrated faculties, team teaching, and teachers' aides are creating new challenges in the professional personnel field.

QUESTIONS

1. Enumerate the major trends in the certification of teachers.
2. What should be the role of the school board in personnel administration? Of the superintendent? Of the principal?
3. What factors influence the measurement of teaching load?

4. How can teachers' morale be improved?
5. Why is it so difficult to develop valid and reliable measures of teachers' effectiveness?
6. Why are salary schedules used to the extent they are today?

SELECTED REFERENCES

Bolton, Dale L., *Selection and Evaluation of Teachers,* Berkeley, Calif.: McCutchan, 1973.

Eye, Glen G., and Willard R. Lane, *The New Teacher Comes to School,* New York: Harper & Row, 1956.

Klahn, R. P., ed., *Evaluation of Teacher Competency,* Milwaukee: Franklin, 1965.

Knezevich, Stephen J., ed. "Creating Appraisal and Accountability Systems," *New Directions for Education,* vol. no. 1, Spring 1973.

National Education Association, *The American Public School Teacher, 1970–71,* Research Report 1972–R3, Washington, D.C.: 1972.

20

PROFESSIONAL PERSONNEL LEADERSHIP: PROFESSIONAL RELATIONSHIPS AND NEGOTIATIONS

Since 1960 a new pattern of relations has developed between teachers and administrators and between teachers and school-board members. Professional negotiation (also called collective negotiation and collective bargaining) is destined to be a most important factor in fashioning the professional relationships between administrators and teachers. It is the most dramatic development in professional personnel leadership in this century. The American Association of School Administrators declared in the late 1960s that "were school administrators to name their most pressing current problems, negotiation would undoubtedly be near the top of the list."[1]

Demands for professional negotiation are forcing school administrators and school boards to reexamine previously established personnel relationships and general policy-making procedures, and to determine what new roles and new skills must be developed to operate successfully in this mode. Professional negotiation is not the first challenge to school personnel administration; upgrading preparation

standards, determining certification requirements, developing salary schedules, and delegating responsibility for the selection of teachers were once revolutionary concepts. Each required decades for diffusion among public-school systems, but none depended for realization upon angry marches or threatening postures. The suddenness and intensity of real or threatened strikes, sanctions, and work slowdowns among the teaching personnel caught the nation as well as school administrators off guard. The furious and persistent saber rattling of militant teachers' organizations is now heard round the nation. The number of times since 1960 groups of teachers have seen fit to picket and demonstrate to dramatize their cause is measured in the hundreds. This ferment is forming a new configuration for the teacher's relations with the community, the school board, and the school administrators.

The complexity and confusion surrounding school personnel relations in the 1960s can be examined from many angles. The emphasis in this chapter is on its effect upon professional administrators, particularly with regard to new patterns of relations with teachers' groups, the need for understanding new

[1] American Association of School Administrators, *The School Administrator and Negotiation*, Washington, D.C.: The Association, 1968, p. 5.

concepts, and the urgency for developing new administrative competencies.

DEFINITION OF TERMS

Professional negotiation was a new term in the vocabulary of employer-employee relations in education during the 1960s. In 1960 the Pasadena, California, Board of Education became the first to adopt a professional negotiation agreement as a result of a resolution by the National Education Association (NEA). Collective bargaining is an older term, used by labor and industry (but less frequently in education) for a century in the United States and even longer in Britain. The Wagner Act of the 1930s stimulated the use of the negotiating process in labor disputes but did not invent the term. Collective negotiation, a combination of the other two terms, is likewise a recent addition to the nomenclature. In the 1970s the modifying word "professional" was dropped and the process was referred to simply as negotiation.

Stinnet et al. defined "professional negotiation" as a "set of procedures written and officially adopted by the local staff organization and the school board which provides an orderly method for the school board and staff organization to negotiate on matters of mutual concern, to reach agreement on these matters, and to establish educational channels for mediation and appeal in event of an impasse."[2] The significant factors in professional negotiation are:

1. A written and officially adopted set of personnel procedures.
2. An orderly method through which

to negotiate matters of mutual concern.

3. An established pattern for resolving an impasse.

"Collective bargaining" is defined simply as group action concerned with reaching common points of agreement. It is a way of arriving at decisions that influence terms and conditions of employment, that is, "governance of the shop." It is basically a negotiating and agreement-making process involving give and take by both sides. It begins with flexible positions from which both sides can retreat with honor. It presumes a similar degree of bargaining power for representatives on each side of the table. It focuses on substantive matters of mutual concern. It is group action involving debate and discussion that may be peppered with varying degrees of histrionics to impress the public, that is, to win public opinion to a given side of the bargaining table. The psychology of human relations in group situations is part of the total picture of collective bargaining. It is an art and not a science. It is conflict management at its most basic level, for the parties involved proceed from contrary, often antagonistic, viewpoints and concepts of self-interest to collective agreement.

Lieberman and Moskow[3] defined "collective negotiation" as "a process whereby employees as a group and their employers make offers and counteroffers in good faith on the conditions of their employment relationships for the purpose of reaching mutually acceptable agreement." As an agreement-making process between a group of employees and employers, it should not be confused simply with the right of teachers to be consulted

---

[2]T. M. Stinnet, J. H. Kleinman, and M. L. Ware, *Professional Negotiation in Public Education*, New York: Macmillan, 1966, p. 2.

[3]M. Lieberman and M. H. Moskow, *Collective Negotiations for Teachers*, Chicago: Rand McNally, 1966, p. 1.

or to be heard. As defined it applies to all fields, not simply education.

Wynn adds another dimension by using the term "informal negotiation" to mean "informal customs of faculty-board collaboration in attempting to reach agreement on matters of mutual concern."[4] The employer negotiates with teachers as a faculty, not as a teachers' association. In informal negotiation there are no officially adopted contracts or agreements, no mediation or arbitration procedures developed, no formally designated representatives of either side, and no threats of force or power by either party in event of failure to reach agreement. A pattern of informal problem-solving discussion among peers replaces the complex machinery of collective bargaining. It suggests a process of discussion "around the table" rather than in an atmosphere of conflict. This pattern has gained few adherents and in the early 1970s appears to have lost out completely to formal negotiations or bargaining.

The NEA prefers the term "professional negotiation," whereas the American Federation of Teachers (AFT) tends to use "collective bargaining" or "collective negotiation." AASA refers to it simply as "negotiation." At present there is considerable debate about the full meaning of these terms as well as about which should be employed in education. The differences in meaning are slight. The terms have more in common than the advocates of any one term would care to admit. Preference for one over another is based more on connotative than on substantive differences. For the purposes of this volume, the terms are synonymous.

[4]D. R. Wynn, *Policies of Educational Negotiation Problems and Issues,* Research Monograph, Pittsburgh: University of Pittsburgh, Tri-State Area School Study Council, October 1967, p. 1.

GROWTH OF NEGOTIATION

Negotiation is a means whereby teachers formalize their access to the school power structure. The causes behind its growth and development are multiple and complex. They include the doubling of the percent of men in the teaching profession (only 17 percent of teachers in 1945 were men, compared with almost 34 percent in 1972); the better preparation of teachers; and the highly impersonal style of teacher administration that resulted from attempts to meet the staffing requirements of congested urban school districts in the face of a shortage of teachers and a high turnover rate in the 1950s and 1960s.

The desires for greater economic security and advancement may not have been primary motives in the beginning but appear to receive more emphasis at present. There had been a significant increase in the average salary paid to teachers before the outbreak of teacher militancy. Salaries more than doubled from 1949 (about $2900) to 1965 ($6485). The average annual salaries of teachers increased at a faster rate than the average annual earnings of workers, other than civilian federal government employees, in the decade 1955 to 1965. Furthermore, nearly 97 percent of AFT members are from the 25 wealthiest states. In short, professional negotiation emerged in spite of economic improvements. Many felt that the salaries paid to teachers were still unjustly low and represented the failure of society to recognize the full contribution of professional personnel in education. It appears logical, therefore, that the posture of aggressiveness among teachers was precipitated by a strong desire to be a significant part of a creative enterprise and to achieve self-respect and self-determination, rather than by the desire for greater economic security alone. If the latter were the prime motivating factor, teachers in rural rather than urban areas and in the South rather than the North would have been the first to engage in strikes or work stoppages.

Both the NEA and the AFT advocated collective action by teachers. Such action began, for practical purposes, in 1960, when the United Federation of Teachers (UFT) started a drive to establish a collective-bargaining relation with the New York City Board of Education. This drive culminated in an election in December 1961, that recognized the UFT as the system-wide bargaining agent. Collective negotiation began shortly thereafter, but broke down in April 1962, when the UFT called another strike.[5]

Collective bargaining, however, is not new to American labor. The Norris-LaGuardia Act of 1932 guaranteed labor the right to engage in strikes, boycotts, picketing, and other activities in labor disputes and limited the role of federal courts in labor affairs. The National Labor Relations Act (Wagner Act) of 1935 recognized the rights of employees to form, join, or assist labor organizations to bargain collectively through representatives of their own choosing and to engage in concerted activities for purposes of collective bargaining.

Most of these gains for labor were made during the presidency of Franklin D. Roosevelt. It is interesting that President Roosevelt in 1937 did not consider collective bargaining appropriate for public employeess. He stated:

The process of collective bargaining, as usually understood, cannot be translated into the public service. It has its distinct and insurmountable limitations when applied to public personnel management. . . . Particularly I want to emphasize my conviction that militant tactics have no place in the functions of any organization of government employees.[6]

President John F. Kennedy, in Executive Order 10988, took the opposite point of view and authorized collective bargaining as a way of reaching agreements between organizations of federal employees and federal administrators.

State laws are basic in employer-employee relations in public education. The drive by the NEA and the AFT to have negotiation laws covering teachers enacted in every state is now in progress. Wisconsin was the only state that had a comprehensive law regulating negotiation in public education prior to 1965. Between 1965 and 1967 14 states—Alaska, California, Connecticut, Florida, Massachusetts, Michigan, Minnesota, Nebraska, New Hampshire, New York, Oregon, Rhode Island, Texas, and Washington—enacted legislation guaranteeing the right of teachers to join or not to join various types of employee organizations as well to participate in professional negotiation. By 1972, 29 states enacted legislation defining in some manner teacher-school board negotiations. Maguire reported that "many state statutes have taken major portions of their collective negotiations act verbatim from the Taft-Hartley Act (1947)" and "used precedents established by the National Labor Relations Board in deciding disputed cases in teacher negotiations before state appeals boards."[7]

[5]Lieberman and Moskow, op. cit., pp. 35–40.

[6]Letter from Franklin D. Roosevelt to L. C. Stuart, President of the National Federation of Federal Employees, August 16, 1937. Reprinted in Charles S. Rhyne, *Labor Unions and Municipal Employee Law*, Washington, D.C.: National Institute of Municipal Law Officers, 1946, pp. 436–437.

[7]John W. Maguire, "Professional Negotia-

The content of such state laws varies greatly in scope and substance. In general, the basic elements of a comprehensive state negotiation law would include: key definitions and purposes of the law, rights of teachers to join a professional organization, prohibitions against coercive actions by school districts, methods of ascertaining the composition of negotiation groups, what constitutes "good faith" negotiation, conditions conducive to negotiation, resolution of impasses, stipulation of fact finding procedures, what constitutes unfair labor practices, prohibition against strikes and work stoppages, development of agreements and contracts, and periods of duration of negotiated agreements.[8]

In 1965 the Minnesota legislature passed one bill for collective bargaining for all public employees except teachers, and a second bill that dealt with teachers exclusively. The governor signed into law the bill that covered all public employees except the teachers, but vetoed the bill for teachers. The Minnesota Federation of Teachers contested the law that was signed, and a county judge ruled that the section of the public-employee law that excluded teachers was unconstitutional. On appeal by the Minneapolis Education Association, an NEA affiliate, the state supreme court reversed the county judge's opinion and held that exclusion of teachers from a law was not unreasonable and arbitrary, because for purposes of classification teachers had been treated by the legislature as a separate group. The court cited tenure laws, certification acts, and other statutes that dealt primarily with teachers. It further

ruled that in the absence of statutory authorization for collective bargaining with teachers, the school board had no authority to conduct an election to designate an exclusive representative of the teachers. Furthermore, without express statutory authority and where no prohibitory state statute exists, there is nothing to prevent collective bargaining entered into voluntarily.

The growth of interest in negotiation led the NEA to establish a Negotiation Research Unit. Its initial report came out in April 1967, in a publication known as *Negotiation Research Digest*. The initial survey in 1966 of written negotiation procedures between local school boards and organizations of the teaching profession revealed that 1,097 school systems had agreements for recognizing an organization representing the instructional staff.[9] Considerable progress has been evident since then, and presently it is the unusual system that has no negotiated agreement in most states.

There is little question, from a legal point of view, that certified school employees have the right to organize whether affiliated with a union or not. Several states have passed specific statutes stipulating that public employees have the right to join unions or other types of organizations. On the other hand, compulsory membership in such organizations is not likely to be upheld by a court, particularly if there are no statutes specifically permitting compulsory membership. Furthermore, the traditional judicial view is that teachers do not have a legal right to strike. In a great majority of states teacher strikes are prohibited by

tions: State or Federal Legislation?", *School and Society*, vol. 98, no. 2324, March 1970, pp. 176–177.

[8]American Association of School Administrators, op. cit., pp. 27–28.

[9]Research Division, National Education Association, "Preliminary Data from 1966–67 Survey of Written Negotiation Procedures Between Local School Boards and Organizations of the Teaching Profession," *Negotiation Research Digest*, no. 1, April 1967, p. B1.

law. In some no specific provisions are made with reference to strikes. Only in Hawaii are strikes legal under certain conditions. The lack of legal authorization to strike has not prevented teacher organizations or unions from engaging in strikes. In several states a "no strike" pledge is required for recognition of the bargaining organization or union. In others the penalties may be as severe as termination of employment whereas still others include no specified penalties for striking. In North Carolina and Virginia negotiating with public-employee organizations is specifically prohibited.[10] It was prohibited in Texas until 1967.

NATURE AND ART OF NEGOTIATION

If agreements covering relations between employees and employer and various conditions for employment are to be determined by negotiation, the following conditions and procedures must be determined:

1. Who is to represent the teachers and who is to represent the board of education.
2. What is the scope of the subject matter of the negotiations.
3. How the negotiating sessions are to be structured, conducted, and scheduled.
4. How agreements are to be reached and reported (in oral or written form).
5. Whether, if an impasse is reached, mediation or arbitration shall prevail, and under what conditions.

After an agreement has been concluded, the conditions that govern the execution of the negotiated contract, the person responsible for its execution, and the rights and responsibilities

of parties during the term of the negotiated contract must be determined.

Choosing representatives

Determining who is to represent the professional staff involves defining who is to be considered a classroom teacher, specifically whether the principals are part of the teachers' group, as in Canada, or part of administration, as is likely in the United States.

Also to be decided is whether, if two or more teachers' organizations are involved, representation should be joint, proportional, or exclusive. In joint representation, each group represents its own members but not members of the other groups. Most authorities reject this as highly impractical.[11] In the proportional method, each group is represented in proportion to its membership number. In exclusive representation, the one organization which will represent all groups is selected by vote. The advantages of empowering one organization to speak for the professional staff in the negotiating sessions are:

1. It is simple, clear-cut, and direct.
2. It provides a single clear-cut organizational authority for the negotiating committee.
3. It provides for negotiation by unified groups selected by, and working on behalf of, a majority of those being represented.
4. It provides for testimony rights for individuals in minority groups who may not wish to be represented by the majority organization.
5. It is in keeping with the majority-rule principle of democracy, whereby the representative chosen by the majority speaks for all until replaced.
6. It makes possible the responsible use of organization resources.
7. It is in harmony with the concept of free choice among alternatives, which

---

[10]Stinnet et al., op. cit., chap. 2.

[11]Lieberman and Moskow, op. cit., pp. 105–106.

lies at the heart of the democratic process.[12]

The disadvantages are that exclusive recognition may exploit nonmembers and that in the absence of state laws, boards are legally prohibited from recognizing an exclusive representative.

Typically, the teachers' representative is chosen in an election called by and supervised by the board of education, by a special state labor agency, or by an independent group experienced in holding negotiation elections.

In the past considerable sums of money have been expended by rival organizations battling to gain exclusive representation rights for teachers. In large cities the competing organizations may spend as much as $100,000 each on the election alone. This is one of several reasons why merger of the NEA and AFT appears to be attractive to both organizations. Each side questions the wisdom of one group of teachers battling another instead of joining forces against those who would thwart the ambitions of teachers.

Also to be decided is how long certification of the winning organization as exclusive representative shall prevail before another election must be held. In the absence of specific legislation, school boards have adopted a wide range of practices, usually granting exclusive representation for from one to three years.

The question of selecting the negotiation representative for the board of education will be examined later in this chapter, under Role of the Administrator in Professional Negotiation.

Defining subject matter for negotiation

Determining the scope of what is and what is not negotiable is crucial and

[12]Stinnet et al., op. cit., pp. 167–168.

controversial. Some negotiators say flatly that everything affecting the teacher is negotiable. Others argue that certain matters are part of "management rights" and not subject to negotiation. State legislation may define dimensions of the subject matter for negotiation in a general manner (as in Wisconsin, where questions of wages, hours, and conditions of employment are negotiable) or specifically (as in Oregon, where only salaries and related economic policies are negotiable). Washington state allows discussions to include "school policies related to but not limited to curriculum, textbook, selection, inservice training, student teaching programs, personnel hiring and assignment practices, leaves of absence, salaries and salary schedules and noninstructional duties." As many as 45 different items could be subject to negotiation.

The NEA believes that decisions affecting what the teacher does in the classroom and working with pupils, as well as economic interests, are subject to negotiation. The AFT similarly refuses to limit the scope of bargaining.

To specify that anything is subject to negotiation is not the same thing as declaring that everything is negotiable. Board selection of a superintendent is not negotiable with a teachers' organization, nor are other administrative decisions that are clearly prerogatives of the board and administrators and with which teachers are not concerned.

What is negotiable must be agreed on by both parties prior to entering into discussions. In private industry and commerce, there seldom are legislative guides to the scope of negotiations. The substance of bargaining is not prescribed in the Wagner Act or other labor legislation, but is left to the parties involved. Obviously, what specific textbooks will be adopted is not subject to negotiation, but it can be argued that procedures for selecting textbooks are.

Setting up the negotiating sessions

The negotiation process itself, even after the issues of representation and scope of subject matter have been resolved, is long and complex. Time is necessary for preparation, although the line between preparation and actual negotiation is fuzzy. Negotiation appears to be headed for continuous, year-round activity; it may well be that preparation will also be a continuous activity. Each side searches for data to support its point of view. On occasion facts may be interpreted from a different perspective, or data presented by one side may be suspect, but in general negotiations are conducted in good faith. Redfern referred to organizing data into a "negotiation book" that included: board policies in general; board policies for making salary adjustments; salary, fringe benefit, and working condition improvements of the past five years; data on practices in other systems; dollar value of fringe benefits; number of certificated employees and average salary of each type of employee; approximate amount of money available for salary adjustments; items to be presented by the board in negotiation; items not granted in previous negotiation and why, and a prognosis.[13]

Collective negotiation involves human-relations skills, discussion of issues and facts, and the understanding that a silent third party—the pupil, for whom the institution exists—is also participating. Time and place are significant. The tactics of each group will be determined by constraints and

pressures on each. A crisis atmosphere may be generated with the approach of the expiration date for the existing contract, the beginning of school, or the time for recording fiscal decisions affecting the school budget. Sometimes the crisis tends to hasten the agreement-making process, and sometimes an impasse results and the search for a way out begins in earnest.

Meetings may be scheduled on a regular basis at some point in the school year or they may be called on the basis of requests filed with one or both parties. When the negotiating process begins in earnest, there are no rules. Psychology as well as sudden shifts in community and national sentiment influence the process. The points raised in early discussions are seldom the concluding points. Just when concessions begin, that is, when modifications of initial offers start to appear, is difficult to ascertain. Application of pressure and other tactics may create shifts. When firmness sets in is likewise a crucial point but is difficult to pinpoint.

Reporting and administering the agreement

The goal is to reach an agreement between the parties involved that can be formalized in a written contract. The weight of legal opinion has shifted toward the acceptance of collective agreements, and laws are being written to allow schools as public agencies to negotiate and sign such agreements. The traditional point of view is that the board cannot delegate its discretionary authority without specific statutory permission. This had been interpreted to mean that negotiated agreements cannot be substituted for the board's discretionary authority. New laws have changed this traditional conception.

[13]American Association of School Administrators, op. cit., p. 55.

Once the agreement is reached, a zipper clause may be included to ensure that negotiation will not be re-opened for a specified period of time. In other words, the conditions agreed upon cannot be interrupted in a period shorter than the one designated.

Emphasis upon written agreements appears to be relatively recent. Lieberman and Moskow state that until the first agreement was signed between the UFT and the New York City Board of Education, the AFT was little concerned with written agreements. As late as 1962, only 12 local affiliates of the AFT had written agreements with school boards. Since 1962, and particularly since the 1965 edition of the NEA *Guidelines on Professional Negotiations,* considerable emphasis has been placed on developing written contracts that set out the term and other conditions of agreement.

The execution of policy is an administrative concern, and, therefore, the administration of the negotiated contract between employer and employee is the responsibility of school administrators, the principal, and the superintendent. Grievance procedures must be developed to handle conflicting interpretations of an agreement or a direct violation of it. Arbitrators are called in unusually to decide when discussions cannot produce agreement about interpretation. Binding arbitration is the terminal point in approximately 95 percent of all grievance procedures in private industry. It is still relatively uncommon in education although more and more states are moving toward binding arbitration by mutual voluntary agreement.

Resolving an impasse

Agreement is not always the end result of negotiation. When each side has yielded maximum concessions (from its own point of view) and con-flicting viewpoints have polarized some distance apart, an impasse has been reached. Impasses can occur even though both parties are bargaining in good faith and are represented by skillful negotiators.

When an impasse is reached, usually a third party is called in to assist the negotiators in arriving at some common ground. Mediation is the term used when a third party is called in voluntarily and in a strictly advisory capacity. Mediation differs from consultation in that the mediator recommends settlement terms, whereas the consultant only assists parties to arrive at some point of agreement. The question of who should be the mediator is controversial. It is important that both sides of the bargaining table have confidence in the integrity and competence of the mediator.

Fact finding is another procedure for resolving an impasse. Independent fact finders may investigate and search out true conditions. In 1965 Massachusetts, Michigan, and Wisconsin were the only states providing for fact-finding in employment disputes involving public school teachers. Many more have joined that list since then. The fact finders conduct a study of the facts and file a report of their findings. Public approval of the fact finders' objective and independent recommendations provides a strong incentive for the disputants to agree to the terms recommended. The process is voluntary, and either party is free to reject all or part of the fact-finding report.

Binding arbitration may be used to resolve an impasse. It may be compulsory or voluntary. In either case, the recommendations are binding on each group involved in the negotiation. There is opposition to compulsory binding arbitration on the grounds that if it becomes common practice, it will diminish the usefulness of collective bargaining. Procedures for handling an impasse should be decided prior to the start of negotiations.

Bernstein challenged the point of view that collective bargaining in industry is breaking down because of its lack of "social vision," the change in the nature of the work force, and the impact of automation in a stagnant economy.[14] He claimed a misreading of collective bargaining was responsible for the accusation that it was too limited for the solution of current problems. To Bernstein collective bargaining cannot be equated with an academic collective search for truth. Not all problems can be solved by its local approach to conflict. Others argue that government must step in because the public interest is often ignored by selfish groups. It is interesting that education has become involved in an agreement-reaching process at the very time many experts are questioning the appropriateness and effectiveness of that process.

STRIKES, SANCTIONS, AND WORK STOPPAGES

The exercise of raw power may result from lack of an agreement or from the belief on the part of a teachers' group that the board of education is not negotiating in good faith. Power implies access to or possession of a resource—physical, personal, or psychological—that is desired by others. The exercise of power exacts a cost. If the cost of exercising the power appears less than the cost of doing nothing, the chances of a power showdown are great.

The use of power by a teachers' association or a union to influence the activities of a school system is nonlegitimate. This is a statement of fact and not a moral judgment. The laws of all states place legal control over educational systems in the hands of school boards or other lay groups, but never with teachers. Legitimacy is a matter of the law. Efforts of teachers, or others without legal authority, to control an organization must be directed through other channels. The success of such group efforts lies in their ability to bring an organization's work to a halt by refusing to work and by inhibiting others from working. This is the power of the strike or slowdown. The show of such force is effective during times of teacher shortage, in locations where democratic traditions flourish, and when community opinion, existing laws, and other associations or unions at the state and national level support the strike. When the protesters lack access to the conference table, or when the conference fails to bring capitulation of holders of legitimate power, then wielders of nonlegitimate power take to the streets to demonstrate in behalf of the social change desired. There are limits to nonlegitimate show of force as a means of influencing an organization's policies: It must stop short of a complete takeover of the administration of the organization.

The strike is the ultimate and also the most controversial weapon of teachers. The NEA at one time opposed striking; it no longer opposes it, but recognizes that there may be conditions that warrant such action. For a while euphemisms such as "withdrawal of services" were preferred, but there is no longer any hesitancy to label a strike as a strike. The American Association of School Administrators does not condone teacher strikes under any condition.[15]

14Irving Bernstein, "The Cockeyed World of Paul Jacobs," *AFL-CIO American Federationist,* May 1964, pp. 20–22.

15American Association of School Administrators, *School Administrators View Professional Negotiation,* Washington, D.C.: The Association, 1966.

In 1964 the AFT convention recognized the right of locals to strike under certain circumstances and called upon the AFL-CIO and affiliated international units to support such strikes when they occur. Even prior to this national policy, the local affiliates of both NEA and AFT had gone on strike. The number of work stoppages was relatively small prior to 1945, less than a dozen. In the early 1960s there were, on the average, only about two or three teacher strikes a year. The strike became a relatively popular weapon in the last three years of the 1960s, hitting a peak of 181 in 1969–1970 and averaging 142 per year during the three-year period. The early 1970s witnessed a decline in strikes, to 130 in 1970–1971 to 89 in 1971–1972, but then back up to 143—the second largest number ever—in 1972–1973. These numbers average ten or more times the numbers registered in the early 1960s. Prior to 1966 the majority of strikes were sponsored by a teachers union. Today, most teacher strikes are conducted by NEA affiliates. Historically, NEA affiliate-sponsored strikes are the most numerous and involve the majority of personnel. Teacher union sponsored strikes are much longer, as evidenced by the work days lost (see Table 20–1).

Strikes receive considerable publicity. This obscures the obvious fact that in 99 percent of the school districts in any one year, up to this point in history, there were no teachers on strike. Only in 1969–1970 did the number of school systems experiencing a teachers' strike come close to one percent of the total operating school districts in the nation.

By the end of September 1973 there were more than 100 teacher strikes in 14 states during the opening of the 1973–1974 school year as compared with 82 during the same period a year earlier. Once again NEA affiliates were responsible for the majority, 86 percent, and AFT affiliates for the minority, 14 percent. Michigan had more strikes in 1973–1974 than any other state, keeping its historic number one position intact.

September seems to be the most popular strike time, with 281 of the

TABLE 20–1

SUMMARY OF TEACHER STRIKES, JANUARY 1940 THROUGH JUNE 1973

Type of organization	Strikes or work stoppages		Estimated no. of personnel involved		Estimated man-days involved	
	No.	Percent	No.	Percent	No.	Percent
Professional association	656	67.7	397,607	51.5	1,999,024	25.0
Teacher union	241	24.9	352,126	45.6	5,647,494	70.7
Independent organization	17	1.8	3,103	0.4	9,158	0.1
No organization	46	4.7	2,479	0.3	21,400	0.3
Joint union association	9	0.9	16,731	2.2	310,741	3.9
Total	969	100.0	772,046	100.0	7,987,817	100.0

Source: National Education Association, "Teacher Strikes, Work Stoppages, and Interruptions of Service, 1972–1973," *NEA Research Memo*, RM 73-9, December 1973, Washington, D.C.: The Association, p. 7.

863 (32.6 percent) occuring during that month. May is the next most popular strike month; December is the least popular time.

There have been strikes in 37 of the 50 states and the District of Columbia. There were more strikes in Michigan (178) in the 1960–1973 period than in any other state. Pennsylvania, with 145, is the only other state with a record of more than 100 strikes in the period. In contrast New York with only 56 teacher strikes during 1960–1973 accounted for almost 43 percent of the man-days lost.

The majority of strikes are of relatively short duration, lasting one to five days. Over 80 percent last ten days or less. Only about 10 percent of the strikes involve 1000 or more school personnel.

Selden, of the AFT, declared in the mid-1960s: "What American schools need most is more teacher strikes."[16] He argued that school strikes were not so terrible, and pointed out that as a result of a one-day shut-down of New York City schools in April 1962, $13 million was "added" to the school budget. With questionable logic, he described school vacations as a kind of "work stoppage" that no one believed was harming children. He concluded with a call for the release of teachers "from their conformist bondage."

The president of the New York local spent 15 days in jail after a 1967 strike, and the union was fined $150,000 (approximately $3 per member). A second person, a national organizer for the AFT, was sentenced in 1967 to a jail term for his role in a teachers' strike in Woodbridge, New Jersey, in January 1966. In 1970 the AFT president went to jail for his participation in a Newark, New Jersey, strike by teachers. In 1973 some teachers in New York who were not officers of the association on strike went to jail for the first time.

An alternative to the strike is the imposition of sanctions against a school district or an entire state. This is a weapon supporting professional negotiation.[17] A strike illegally violates or terminates an existing contract by withholding services. The imposition of sanctions involves the withholding of services by refusing to sign a new contract until the conditions are met. The profession is informed by the NEA, the local association, or the state association proposing sanctions that working conditions are undesirable and teachers should not sign contracts to serve in such districts. In the past, sanctions have been imposed by the NEA and its state affiliates in Oklahoma, Utah, and Florida. The California Teachers' Association placed the Little Lake, California, school district under sanctions at one time. The strength of sanction lies in the impact of public opinion and the total profession on undesirable working conditions.[18] About two-thirds of the teachers sampled by NEA in 1968 favored strikes, a remarkable shift in sentiment from years past.

ROLE OF THE ADMINISTRATOR IN NEGOTIATION

Negotiation places the administrator in a new role in his relations with teachers and his professional colleagues. In many respects, negotiation is based on the concept of a democratic school administration. The basic precept of democratic school administration is that those affected by a policy should have a voice in its determination. The

[16]David Selden, "Needed: More Teacher Strikes," *Saturday Review of Literature,* May 15, 1965, p. 75.

[17]Stinnet et al., op. cit., chap. 6.
[18]Ibid.

difference is that democratic school administration provides a permissive atmosphere for teachers' participation and involvement in vital educational affairs. Negotiation agreements formally guarantee the teacher's right, whether or not the superintendent and the board practice democratic school administration, to exert formal and deliberate influence upon school-board policy. Administrators not in sympathy with democratic school administration view negotiation as an encroachment on the administrative authority and resist its development. Such resistance is not likely to meet with success. More and more teachers' groups are pressing for state laws granting teachers the right to participate in the determination of policies under which they work and of economic reward they receive.

The superintendent

The role of the superintendent of schools in formal collective negotiation continues to evolve. Nor can it be said that the nation's school administrators agree on their role in professional negotiation. During most of the 1960s there were some who pictured the superintendent as a resource person for both the board of education and the teachers' group; in other words, he supplied information to both sides and acted as a referee, but was a formal representative of neither.

Another group viewed the superintendent as the chief executive officer of the school board, a role in which he cannot remain uncommitted in the face of sensitive educational issues raised during professional negotiation. This side argued further that the superintendent is associated with the implementation of school-board policy and cannot avoid being the board's agent in accomplishing many tasks within the school system. He need not, so the argument goes, sell his professional soul when he acts in behalf of the school board in negotiation or in other administrative responsibilities, so long as he is not called upon to violate his code of ethics. Further, his status as a leader could be jeopardized if he stands apart while the board and the teachers arrive at an agreement which, like it or not, he must implement. To the argument that alignment of the superintendent with the board and against the teachers would destroy the unity of the educational profession, its proponents answer that an adversary role with teachers in one situation does not preclude united professional action with them in other situations and that collective negotiation has produced a defacto fragmentation of the educational profession in spite of the talk about unity.

In the mid-1960s the conflicting attitudes and policies of the various educational organizations did little to clarify the superintendent's role in collective negotiation. Much of the argument was set in the historical context that all educators—teachers and administrators alike—were members of a single professional association. There were top echelon leaders in NEA and AASA who sought to preserve this image in spite of pressures from the field from both sides that historic relations were being modified by new and powerful forces. The NEA's initial position assigned the superintendent a central role in the negotiating process, but as an information-supplier and stimulator of both negotiating groups, not as an active representative of either side.[19] A 1966–1967 survey by the NEA Research revealed that most superintendents at that time considered themselves as advisors

[19]National Education Association, *Guidelines for Professional Negotiation,* Washington, D.C.: The Association, 1963, p. 14.

rather than negotiators; most of the time as advisor to *both* the board and to teachers. At that time only in California and Michigan did the superintendent view himself as a negotiator with full authority. The AASA, in a 1966 publication, declared that the superintendent "should be an independent third party in the negotiation process,"[20] but at the end of the same paragraph stated: "In no instance should the responsibility for negotiations be delegated outside the profession." The AASA appeared to recommend a role for the superintendent midway between nonparticipation and acting as chief negotiator representing only the board. Shils and Whittier after some analysis declared: "The AASA and NEA positions on the role of the superintendent are much alike."[21] The AFT declared that the superintendent is not an acceptable spokesman for both teachers and board at negotiation sessions; it put the superintendent on the board's negotiating team. There never was any question in the mind of any AFT leader that all administrators, superintendents, and principals belonged on the board's side of the bargaining table and not the teachers' side. They insisted that teachers could speak for themselves through the union and were not dependent upon administrators as oracles to describe what is or as spokesmen to plead a case for teachers.

Redfern developed five "across the table" negotiation models for education.[22] In all models, members of the teacher association ratified the agree-

ment approved by its negotiation team and the board ratified the agreement accepted by its negotiators. The difference in the models was in who represented the school board as negotiator, namely, the superintendent, the professional negotiator, the administrative team of which the superintendent was chairman, the administrative team of which an assistant superintendent was chairman and which reports to the superintendent, and an administrative team that does not include the superintendent and which reports directly to the school board. Thus, the AASA in the late 1960s was beginning to change its perception of the superintendent's role in negotiation.

In previous editions the author took what some in the 1960s viewed as a radical position on the role of the superintendent in negotiation. The author believed that the alternatives to the superintendent's involvement in direct negotiation with teachers would be more injurious to the image of the superintendent as an educational leader and the development of effective administration than whatever loss would occur by his temporary assumption of an adversary role. Now that all administrator organizations have separated from the NEA and the merger between NEA and AFT appears imminent this writer is no longer viewed as radical. The air has cleared considerably and there is considerable agreement that, like it or no, administrators cannot be on the same side of the bargaining table as teachers.

Board members, as lay individuals without special preparation in negotiation or in administration, and usually with full-time occupations outside education, have neither the skills nor the time to participate directly in negotiations or, for that matter, in any other administrative or executive activities. Typically, in all educational activities

[20]American Association of School Administrators, op. cit., p. 54.

[21]E. B. Shils and C. T. Whittier, "The Superintendent, the School Board, and Collective Negotiations," *The Record—Teachers College*, vol. 69, no. 1, October 1967, p. 49.

[22]American Association of School Administrators, op. cit., pp. 33–36.

they turn to the superintendent for special advice and counsel. He provides it through his personal knowledge, through the knowledge of his staff, or through arrangements with consultants. Negotiation is one of the few activities which some educators feel would be better left to others. This writer rejects this position and argues that the superintendent must assume a dynamic and leadership role in the negotiation process or lose much of the status and leadership inherent in the position.

If the board were to employ a negotiator other than the superintendent to meet with teachers' representatives, what would be the relation between the professional negotiator for the board and the superintendent of schools, who is the professional executive for the educational activities? Are these coordinate positions, each reporting independently to the board? Is the negotiator subordinate to and responsible to the superintendent and then to the board? Some writers imply that the negotiator for the board is coordinate with the superintendent and is involved in an activity with teachers' groups on an equal basis with the superintendent. This is a dual system of school administration in which more than one person reports directly to the board of education. The dual-headed monster has been condemned in other situations and is equally bad in this situation.

Of no less consequence is the superintendent's relations with teachers when the specialist in negotiation, not the superintendent, makes important decisions concerning welfare during bargaining sessions. By avoiding a controversial stance, the superintendent is eliminated from crucial decisions. The avoidance of controversy in the name of something called unity of the educational profession results in a loss for

superintendents tantamount to evisceration of the chief school executive's position in educational organizations. This statement appears less controversial than it was when it first was written in the late 1960s.

The superintendent, therefore, must accept the challenge of representing the board in the hard-nosed and often frustrating activity of hammering out significant personnel decisions in negotiating sessions with teachers' groups. If the superintendent abdicates his role in negotiation, a new educational leader who assumes that role will eventually replace the superintendent.

To argue that the superintendent cannot shirk executive responsibility for negotiation is not to imply that the superintendent must participate in person in all bargaining sessions, but rather that negotiation is part of the chief executive's responsibility in public education as it is in private industry. No board of directors is concerned actively and directly in bargaining with labor unions; nor is the chief negotiator independent of the industry's management.

In large school systems where collective bargaining consumes an inordinate amount of time, additional people must be added to the superintendent's staff. As a matter of policy it must be declared that persons engaged in negotiation on behalf of the school board are subordinate to the superintendent of schools, so that the unit system of administration can be maintained. The superintendent is responsible for the action of negotiators, and they can commit the district only to the extent board policy concurs. When an impasse is reached and concessions or modifications must be made, caucus among the negotiator, the superintendent, and the board must determine what the next policy position should be. The school board must endow the superintendent and his staff with decision-making authority in negotiation and specify what limits shall prevail.

In all bargaining, the end product must be ratified by all parties involved. The representatives reach agreement, but their total memberships must ratify the agreement. Thus, representatives for teacher groups must submit the agreement to the vote of the entire membership; the superintendent and his staff must receive approval of the agreement from the school board.

The personnel director

The personnel director in the large school system is concerned more with preparing for and developing a negotiated agreement than with other activities. Complexity of the school personnel director's office has greatly increased as a result of staff negotiation.

The principal

The principal's role in negotiation is less controversial now than it was in the 1960s. He is a member of the total administrative professional negotiation strategy team. He advises the superintendent on matters of concern at the attendance-unit level. He stands ready to counsel with the superintendent and the school board about the implications of particular concessions for the operation of a school system. The principal is an administrator and does not belong with teachers' groups. The AFT places the principal in the same perspective but for different reasons. He is an executive at the building level, and the position is an extension of the superintendency. Whether or not he has a dynamic role in negotiations depends on whether the superintendent has a dynamic role. In 1967 and 1968 the principals in Detroit and Philadel-

phia began to talk seriously about forming a union to gain collective bargaining authority. Principals in some districts have formed their own negotiating unit in dealing with the school boards, but this has not put them in the teachers' negotiating group.

The NEA Research Division reported that whereas in 1968 teachers were evenly divided as to whether teachers and administrators should have the same or separate negotiating units, in 1971 a significant shift occurred with a higher percent favoring separate units.[23] Some states demand that the two groups be represented by different bargaining agencies.

The advent of negotiation is disturbing the established relation within the education family. It is effecting a fundamental realignment of power for decision making in education. It may prove to be the most important single factor that determines how administrators and teachers will work and live together. The competition between the NEA and AFT for the membership and loyalties of teachers confuses the issues, but the impending merger will resolve these.

Strategy sessions in which negotiating skills are discussed are imperative for all administrators, principals, and superintendents. The focal point for developing such skills will be the personnel director or associate superintendent for personnel services office.

SUMMARY

Negotiation may prove the most important factor in determining future relations within the educational profession as well as between teachers and school

[23]National Education Association, "Teachers and Administrators: Same or Separate Negotiation Units?", *Research Bulletin*, vol. 49, no. 3, October 1971, pp. 77–79.

boards. The old term is collective bargaining, but new ones—collective negotiation and professional negotiation —are very similar. Professional negotiation, coined by the NEA, appeared as part of the educational vocabulary around 1960. The purpose is to gain agreement among parties with conflicting demands and interests on matters of mutual concern.

The reasons for the growth and development of negotiation are many and complex. The desire for greater economic security is only one reason, for concern with negotiation developed at a time when teachers' salaries were improving dramatically. Teacher militancy seems to be related to the desire of teachers to have a more significant role in the operation of educational institutions.

More and more states are enacting statutes governing negotiations with teachers. Certified employees have a right to join employee organizations, whether affiliated with labor unions or not. The traditional judicial view is that teachers do not have the legal right to strike, even though they sometimes do strike.

Most authorities agree that a single representative, rather than a proportional representative council, should be selected to act in behalf of teachers. The selection should be made in an election run by the school board or an independent agency. State legislators may define what is or is not subject to negotiation. Some argue that every decision affecting what a teacher does in the classroom or affecting his economic interests is negotiable. What is negotiable is a matter of agreement among the parties concerned.

Collective negotiation involves human-relations skills, discussion of issues and facts, and recognition of

pupils as a silent third party. There are no hard-and-fast rules to govern the process. It is an art, not a science.

The goal is to reach agreement, and a zipper clause should be inserted in the agreement to ensure that negotiations will not be reopened for a specified period of time. Written contracts summarize the agreements. Execution of the written agreement is an executive matter and involves the superintendent.

There is no guarantee of reaching agreements in all bargaining sessions. Impasses may be resolved by mediation or arbitration. Strikes or sanctions, rather than agreement, may result from negotiating efforts. Strikes by teachers grew rapidly in the late 1960s to reach a peak of 181 in 1969–1970. The strike is a common resort of teachers' unions and is no longer denied to NEA-affiliated groups. There have been more strikes by NEA affiliates than by AFT affiliates. The strike is the ultimate weapon. Sanctions are an alternative to strikes.

Whether the superintendent is to play no role, to be the chief negotiator for the board, or to act as middleman in collective negotiation is subject to less debate in the 1970s than in the 1960s. The pending NEA and AFT merger and the departure of administrator groups from NEA has helped to place all administrators on the school board's side of the bargaining table. The role of the personnel director, the principal, and other middle-management persons in the educational hierarchy depends on whether the superintendent has a dynamic or passive role in the process.

Negotiation is here to stay. It is disturbing previously established relations. It demands that administrators acquire new insights and skills.

QUESTIONS

1. What are the forces that led to teacher militancy in the 1960s?
2. Should teachers be allowed to strike? Justify your stand.
3. Are sanctions more effective than teachers' strikes? Justify your position.
4. What is collective negotiation?
5. What should be the role of the superintendent in the negotiating process? The role of the principal? The role of the supervisor?
6. Why is single representation for teachers' groups recommended over a proportional representative council?
7. What is mediation?
8. Should compulsory arbitration be a part of all state laws governing negotiation with teacher groups? Justify your stand.

SELECTED REFERENCES

American Association of School Administrators, *The School Administrator and Negotiation,* Washington, D.C.: The Association, 1968.

Education Commission of the States, "Survey of Teacher/School Board Collective Negotiation Legislation," *Compact,* vol. 6, no. 2, June 1972, pp. 24–33.

Epstein, Benjamin, *What Is Negotiable?,* Professional Negotiations Pamphlet Number One, Reston, Va.: The National Association of Secondary School Principals, 1969.

Knezevich, Stephen J., "Professional Subculture Impacts on Innovation," in *Educational Administration and Change,* New York: Harper & Row, 1970, pp. 56–75.

Lieberman, M. and M. H. Moskow, *Collective Negotiations for Teachers,* Chicago: Rand McNally, 1966.

Maguire, John W., "Professional Negotiations: State or Federal Legislation?", *School and Society,* vol. 98, no. 2324, March 1970.

Shils, E. B. and C. T. Whittier, "The Superintendent, the School Board, and Collective Negotiations," *The Record—Teachers College,* vol. 69, no. 1, October 1967.

Stinnet, T. M., J. H. Kleinman, and M. L. Ware, *Professional Negotiation in Public Education,* New York, Macmillan, 1966.

21

CURRICULUM AND INSTRUCTIONAL LEADERSHIP

Curriculum can be defined as all of the experiences that are provided the learner under the direction of an institution for education. It is an instrument by and through which the schools seek to translate educational hopes and aspirations into reality. Broadly conceived, it is the "means of instruction used by the school to provide opportunities for student learning experiences leading to desired learning outcomes."[1] Means of instruction include classroom studies, guidance and counseling programs, school and community service projects, school-related work experience, school health services, school camps, and school library, as well as those activities called "extracurricular" or "cocurricular." Curriculum planning includes identifying and stating educational objectives, developing the all-school program, teaching and learning, providing curriculum guides, and providing instructional aids and materials.[2]

In this volume, curriculum is considered to include the scope and sequence of learning experiences that are provided in the school as well as the teaching-learning process (commonly referred to as methods of instruction) and instructional aids and materials. To facilitate discussion, that which is to be learned is sometimes separated from the methods that are used to promote learning. Curriculum is what the school is all about. Every school administrator at every level must keep in touch with what is being taught, and how much is being learned.

Taba observed that "one is struck by a seeming lack of rigorous, systematic thinking about curriculum planning."[3] She commented that the literature about curriculum development is eclectic in quality and lacks a conceptual framework to determine crucial elements and their relation to each other. The dynamic nature of the curriculum necessitates the design of a strategy for implementing curriculum change in schools. This is one of the many challenges confronting those in leadership positions in educational institutions.

The prime focus of curriculum and instructional leadership is the pupil-learning outcomes. Administrative and supervisory personnel have a professional obligation to develop a conceptual framework for the study of curriculum and the instructional strategies that show promise of yielding the desired results. It necessitates, at the very least, comprehending and evaluating the learning experiences provided in the system, the methods used in the teaching-learning process, and

[1] Edward A. Krug, *Curriculum Planning,* rev. ed., New York: Harper & Row, 1957, pp. 3–4.

[2] Ibid.

[3] Hilda Taba, *Curriculum Development,* New York: Harcourt Brace Jovanovich, 1962, p. 3.

the nature and availability of instructional resources and materials.

It is beyond the scope of this volume to review in detail the various elementary and secondary school learning experiences (curriculum). There are a number of curriculum books that may be reviewed and that should be on every administrator's reference list if not shelf.

THE ADMINISTRATOR'S ROLE IN INSTRUCTIONAL LEADERSHIP

It is of historical interest that the employment of a full-time, professionally experienced school administrator in public education was motivated by the desire to improve the quality of educational programs in schools. Early principals and superintendents were concerned primarily with instructional problems such as grading of pupils, determination of courses of study, and supervision of instruction.[4] Responsibility for buildings and finance was not delegated to the school superintendent until many decades later.

Instructional leadership is a much talked about and dynamic role for school administrators at all levels. How well this responsibility is discharged is vital to the success of the school's mission. The complexity of programs, the increasing specialization among teachers, and the increasing diversity of the student body have precipitated shifts in priorities and generated new demands for instructional leadership. As a result there is considerable confusion about how an administrator should fulfill his obligations as a leader in curricular and instructional affairs. Perhaps the least

[4]Thomas M. Gilland, *The Origin and Development of the Power and Duties of the City School Superintendent,* Chicago: University of Chicago Press, 1935, chap. 9.

desirable way to fulfill the instructional-leadership role is the simplistic solution which demands that all administrators continue to teach a class or two during every semester. This was a common practice in the early years of the superintendency and the principalship and has not disappeared completely in small districts. Teaching is a specialized function and is best performed by those who are interested, qualified, and have the time to concentrate on it. In a varied and complex educational institution the administrator must work with and through large numbers of people to fulfill all educational missions. The purpose of administrative leadership in curriculum and instruction is to make great teaching possible, that is, to stimulate greater effectiveness among all teachers. Instructional improvement does not result from the performance of a single administrator as a classroom teacher. The far more difficult challenge is to motivate improved performance from other personnel. The strategies for achieving this vary. It may come by freeing classroom teachers from the time-consuming and often frustrating tasks of organizing, obtaining, allocating, and coordinating resources necessary for effective teaching. It may be the result of sensing when new technologies, research findings, or promising practices are ready to be introduced at the classroom level and helping teachers to utilize these new developments. It could be realized by designing a new instructional organization pattern.

When the superintendent is criticized for spending too much time on "buildings, bonds, and budgets," the critic is implying that his time might be better spent on curriculum and that the three B's have nothing to do with curriculum. Such an attitude fails to comprehend the nature of the administrative process, the leadership role of the administrator in curricular affairs, and specifically the relationship between buildings, bonds, and budgets and the teaching-learning process.

It is impossible to plan and design a functional school building without knowledge of the educational experiences and methods of instruction to be provided therein. As will be discussed in Chapter 24, a building is the physical expression of the school curriculum. The size, shape, and arrangement of space and the type of equipment provided are dictated by the educational program. The purpose of the school plant is to facilitate learning. Often improvement in the scope of educational experiences and in the quality of teaching have had to await the construction of better facilities. When a superintendent dedicates time to the planning and design of functional school buildings, he is setting the stage for better instruction and fulfilling one instructional-leadership role. The physical remoteness of the administrator from the teaching process at the classroom level does not mean that he is professionally remote from what goes on there.[5]

Searching for additional funds to employ better teachers and to retain outstanding ones or to purchase needed instructional materials is one component of instructional leadership. Likewise, the careful accounting and safeguarding of school funds to minimize waste and misappropriation contributes to the improvement of educational experiences. In the last analysis, the school budget is the fiscal interpretation of the educational program. Everything done in public education must sooner or later be translated into dol-

lars and cents. Time spent on planning and organizing the school system helps to make great teaching possible. The seeming remoteness of some administrative tasks from where learning occurs should not be interpreted to mean that such tasks have no impact on the quality of learning. They are more often than not important instruction support roles necessary to insure quality teaching in complex organizations.

There is always the danger that an administrator will confuse means with ends. He may become so preoccupied with the technical aspects of administrative activities that he forgets about the relation of these to the teaching-learning process. Criticism is justified when facilities are constructed and budgets planned without regard to what goes on at the classroom level. School buildings, bonds, and budgets are significant resources in a comprehensive educational program, without which classroom teachers could not function effectively.

In a more positive sense a leader is a person who knows where he is going and has the means to get there. One of the basic issues in curriculum and instructional leadership is the choice of goals. What is the mission of education in our society at this point and in the near future? An instructional leader is one who has deliberated on this issue and formulated at least a tentative answer. There is no way an administrator can serve as a leader in curriculum and instruction without perceiving and working with the relevant objectives for education.

The setting of objectives is the first step in instructional leadership. Knowing what kinds of learning experiences (curriculum) at what levels of human development can be attained by pupils to satisfy objectives is also a part of the total picture. Of no less significance is the ability to translate the ob-

[5]American Association of School Administrators, *The Superintendent as Instructional Leader*, Thirty-fifth Yearbook, Washington, D.C.: The Association, 1957, pp. 18–19.

jectives and the related curricular experiences into an effectively operating organizational pattern. The administrator must demonstrate a knowledge of objectives and curriculum, and also the competency to design and operate a system that will deliver these promises.

RESPONSIBILITY FOR CURRICULUM

The public school curriculum is far too important and complex to be the sole responsibility of only one agency. Involved in determining what should be taught and how it can be taught most effectively are the state department of education, classroom teachers, local school administrators working at various levels, and local boards of education.

Role of the state education agency

Responsibilities of the state education agency for curriculum planning, development, and change are:

1. Ensuring that a minimum educational program is available in all public schools of the state. This is a regulatory function.
2. Sponsoring leadership and coordinating activities to bring together large numbers of persons with first-hand experience to plan state educational programs. Developing curriculum guides is preferred to specifying required courses of study prepared by a few people or a single specialist.
3. Employing supervisors or consultants in special subjects to improve general educational programs for schools in the state.
4. Organizing programs for continuous statewide evaluation of curriculum.
5. Planning changes and possible improvements in curriculum through development of workshops, conferences, meetings, and committees.
6. Sponsoring research and experimentation on curriculum as a means of pro-

moting new ideas that could be of value to local school programs.
7. Selecting textbooks in those states in which the same textbooks are used throughout the state. In too many school systems a textbook is considered equivalent to the course of study, and, hence selection of textbooks has considerable influence on the educational experiences provided in local districts.[6]

Role of local school administrators

The local board of education is responsible for determining policies governing scope, sequence, continuity, and integration of the curriculum organization and for procuring the resources necessary to realize goals. The superintendent, at the general administrative level, is concerned with executing these policies and organizing, coordinating, stimulating, and allocating human and material resources necessary to achieve curriculum and instructional goals. The central-office staff is responsible for coordinating curriculum study among teachers, organizing demonstrations on new methods of teaching, and supervising execution of teaching responsibilities. Principals have functions similar to those of central-office staff members, but confined to the building level. Principals and central-office staff often unify efforts on curriculum projects. Administrators at these two levels are much closer to the teaching-learning process than the superintendent and the board. It would be difficult, however, for central-office staff and attendance-center administrators to realize their aspirations for curricular improvement without guidance and direction from superordinate

[6]Howard H. Cummings and Helen K. Makintosh, *Curriculum Responsibility of State Departments of Education,* U.S. Office of Education, misc. no. 30, Washington, D.C.: GPO, 1958.

officials who control allocation of necessary resources.

It behooves an administrator either to become personally acquainted with the dominant issues or to have a staff of sufficient size and competence to interpret curriculum issues, organizational problems, and change efforts. Superintendents and principals are generalists who look to curriculum specialists for data and counsel on, for example, the strategies to be used in the introduction of new learning experiences; the elimination of nonrelevant content; and the value of such new developments as team teaching, nongrading of schools, or computer-assisted instruction. The complexity of today's educational institutions makes it impossible to be an expert in all fields and areas.

Activities of administrators in curriculum programs include:

1. Stimulating staff members and others to study cooperatively new approaches to instructional improvement.
2. Helping staff members to become more skillful in research or problem solving in curriculum.
3. Providing staff members and others engaged in study and research with the resources they need.
4. Obtaining from such study groups the kinds of information required for prudent decision making on changes in the curriculum, for allocation of various resources within the system, or for introduction of new approaches.

Curriculum planning and development is a continuous process, with activities becoming more intense as new data or situations warrant. Within the school organization, there should be a means of alerting the system to intensified efforts in curricular affairs as the need arises. In large systems, this

may be the duty of the assistant superintendent in charge of curriculum or instruction; in others, of the director of elementary or secondary education; in still others, of a cabinet of principals or an individual principal or even an organization of classroom teachers. Educational program development, not merely maintaining present programs at effective levels, is of prime importance to the administrator.

Eye and Netzer placed the instructional leadership roles of principals and superintendents in a dynamic perspective and related it to the pressure of the times.[7] In the most definitive statement yet, these writers called for development of valid indicators of instructional improvements that went beyond the usually laudatory self-appraisal of projects and the accumulation of new but seldom used curriculum reports. They argued that administrators must sharpen competencies to render prudent judgment about the instructional program if schools are to fulfill newly defined missions as well as the traditional ones.

CLASSIFICATION SCHEMES FOR EDUCATIONAL EXPERIENCES

What the task of the schools should be has been debated for hundreds of years and there is little likelihood that the arguments will ever cease. There is no shortage of writers and ideas about what should be taught. The impact of technology and science, the knowledge explosion, and the social revolution have complicated the issues and intensified the debate. Even if there were agreement on "what knowledge is of most worth" or what function deserves the highest priority, only

[7]G. G. Eye and L. A. Netzer, *School Administration and Instruction,* Boston: Allyn and Bacon, 1969.

part of the many difficulties would be solved. Purposes are important, but all too often are stated in general terms that obscure the practical ways of achieving them. If the systems approach is to be utilized, educational objectives will have to be expressed in behavioral and operational terms capable of more precise evaluation. Identifying specific learning experiences to be provided in the school program on the basis of statement of general objectives is no small task, and when a pattern of courses has been decided on, the specific problems related to each instructional field must still be solved.[8]

Educational programs or fields of study must be systematically organized and then scheduled to be completed by the learner over a given period of time. Taba[9] declared that scope, sequence, continuity, and integration are central problems of curriculum organization. School studies are derived from general objectives and can be classified in various ways. The most widely used curriculum-classification schemes are based on (1) subjects, (2) broad fields, (3) problems or areas of living, and (4) experiences.[10] Other patterns, such as the programmatic curriculum format, may yet emerge.

The subject curriculum

The traditional and the prevailing pattern defines educational experiences in terms of subjects, or categories of knowledge or skills, arranged in a particular sequence and with a defined scope for the purpose of teaching. Much of the prevailing and traditional emphasis in curriculum can be stated succinctly as "teach the disciplines." It is pursuit of knowledge, to transmit

the great cultural heritage, that is most relevant. Taba indicated that "part of the philosophy of subject organization is that there is a hierarchy of priority among the subjects according to their value as mental disciplines."[11] Thus, there are "hard" or "soft" courses. Some are called "solid" subjects with an inference that others may be more gelatinous. The pattern has been criticized as an arbitrary basis used to fragment human knowledge and skills. The existing division of knowledge into subjects has been criticized as arbitrary and artificial, and hence, a deterrent to effective teaching and learning. Despite its shortcomings, the subject pattern continues to be the most popular because of certain practical advantages: It is backed by long tradition, it makes the counting of educational progress clearer, and it is related to teacher training. Much of the current curriculum reform, particularly that sponsored by the National Science Foundation, buttresses the traditional format. The primary thrust of such efforts is to revitalize the content of the subject matter to produce the "new" mathematics, science, social studies, and the like.

The broad-fields curriculum

A reaction to the compartmentalization of knowledge and skills into discrete and artificial subjects led to the broad-fields classification for educational experiences. This pattern emphasizes correlation among subjects to permit greater integration of substantive knowledge. Correlation is more easily accomplished if the identity of the subjects related to each other is maintained; thus, American history as a subject can be correlated with American literature.

[8]Krug, op. cit., p. 132.
[9]Taba, op. cit., p. 382.
[10]Krug, op. cit.

[11]Taba, op. cit., p. 386.

This approach is feasible in the self-contained, or undepartmentalized, elementary school classroom, where one teacher teaches both subjects. In the departmentalized secondary school, where two or more instructors teach these subjects, correlation is more difficult to operationalize. The broad-fields classification disregards the division of knowledge established for the convenience of specialists but not necessarily learners. It is, in effect, a modification of the subject organization. The difference between the two is not one of basic principle but one of comprehensiveness of the division of knowledge and skills for purposes of teaching geography, history, sociology, and economics.[12] High school biology is a fusion of botany, zoology, anatomy, physiology, and other life-science subjects. The fusion process has contributed to formation of new subjects without engendering much conflict. Only when the field becomes so broad that the subject content is not readily identifiable, or when too many subjects are being fused is debate stimulated. Such terms as "social living" or "senior science" create "curriculum conglomerates" that may precipitate a violent reaction.

The areas-of-living curriculum

Organization of school studies on the basis of problems or areas of living is a radical departure from the traditional subdivisions of the curriculum. Learning experiences are grouped on the basis of human needs, such as selecting and preparing for an occupation, selecting a mate and getting ready for marriage, developing skills for more effective human relations, and becoming an effective citizen. Proponents argue that the areas-of-living curriculum is intimately related to the pupil's day-to-day life pattern. It is also closely related to Herbert Spencer's categories of common features of life in any culture.

Its use necessitates defining the important problems in living, assigning each to a grade or maturity level, and arranging them for teaching purposes. Subject matter can be used, but the emphasis is on how to deal with situations confronting the learner in his lifetime. The pattern represents a shift from a classification designed for the convenience of scholars and teachers to a classification directed to the learner. The pattern is difficult to implement, due primarily to the traditional teacher-oriented outlook and secondarily to the difficulty of deciding whether the problems to be discussed should be selected by the adults or the learners.

The experience curriculum

The experience curriculum is a long distance away from the traditional curriculum-classification schemes. The emphasis is upon improvement of human growth through group contacts. The curriculum is conceived as a series of experiences, but the experiences are not fixed; hence, the experience curriculum is said to be "in a continuous process of development in which the learner participates."[13] For these reasons, this classification is called the "emerging" curriculum. The vagueness and elusiveness of the terms "experience," "interaction," and "improvement of human growth" make definition and illustrations of the emerging curriculum difficult. There are no schools using it at present, and the few that did were experimental schools.

[12]Krug, op. cit., p. 105.

[13]Ibid., p. 106.

Programmatic curriculum

Curriculum-classification schemes are differentiated on the basis of the same central thing or focus. Learning experiences may be organized around the achievement of certain outcomes. This is the focus of the so-called programmatic curriculum. It is essential to the implementation of other dimensions of educational operations such as PPBS and MBO, described in Chapter 8. A program was defined therein as a set of activities clustered around an objective, that is, functions executed to reach an objective. A programmatic curriculum format is one where the achievement of an objective, rather than subject matter divorced from an objective, is the primary focus in clustering a set of learning experiences for learners.

The core curriculum

During the 1930s the term "core curriculum" or "core classes" came into popular usage. Unfortunately, it acquired several unrelated definitions, such as (1) the required subjects in a program of studies, (2) any high school class combining two or more subjects, and (3) "common learnings organized not around subjects, but around common problems and needs of children and youth regardless of subject lines."[14] The last definition is accepted in this volume. The nature of the core curriculum can be understood from the following list:

1. It seeks to establish relations among areas of living by the study of problems that challenge the pupil to explore and utilize the knowledge and skills of more than one subject.
2. It aims at larger objectives than would characterize any single subject area.
3. It involves the joint planning of those objectives, and of means of achieving them, by both teachers and pupils. It is directly geared to the goal of increased skill in the processes of cooperative planning.
4. It requires a block of time longer than the traditional period.
5. It involves either a single teacher for two or more periods or a team of teachers who work together.
6. It is dedicated to improved guidance of individuals and groups of pupils.
7. Its basic emphasis in instructional planning is the present psychobiological and social needs of the pupils themselves.[15]

The core curriculum has had a brief but stormy history. It was launched with ambitious aims. To many who have not worked with it, it is too vague. Interest in it waxes and wanes. Its death knell has tolled several times, but it has always been revitalized. The success of the core approach in some places cannot be denied. One writer claimed that the "most damaging one-two punch to the existence of core programs is the combination of the Conant reports and the current emphasis on college-preparatory secondary school programs."[16] There is some evidence that the core curriculum may be revived in the 1970s as one part of an effort to individualize instruction at the secondary school level in particular.

THE HUMANISTIC CURRICULUM

The 1970s saw a new or renewed emphasis on the humanistic school based on a humanistic curriculum. The learning activities are designed to focus on person-centered values; self-growth and self-learning are major missions.

[14]Ibid., p. 108.

[15]Roland C. Faunce and Nelson L. Bossing, *Developing the Core Curriculum,* Englewood Cliffs, N.J.: Prentice-Hall, 1951, pp. 8–9.

[16]Earl W. Harmer, "Le Mort de Core?" *Phi Delta Kappan,* vol. 42, no. 2, November 1960, p. 67.

The individualization of the school program is seen as one way to achieve a humanistic school that looks to people and not inanimate subject matter that need development. This was a theme sounded by Dewey and his followers early in this century, but appears to be revived in a new form in the 1970s.

FACTORS STIMULATING CURRICULUM CHANGE

The scope and sequence of experience within the public school curriculum have changed in the past, are changing today, and will continue to do so in the future. Hardly a decade passes without some course being added, dropped, or substantially modified in the elementary and secondary schools. This reflects the dynamic nature of society. Knowledge is being expanded at a tremendous rate and in many fields. The first doubling of knowledge occurred in 1850, the second in 1900, the third in 1950, and the fourth in 1960. New instructional materials and systems are appearing at an increasingly rapid pace as well. The programmed approach to instruction, whether based upon computer-assisted instructional systems, a teaching machine, or a programmed text, is destined to have a profound effect on the role of the teacher. Educational TV may not be living up to expectations, but it is a significant part of the instructional system.

Shifts in the grade levels at which a subject is taught occur often. Biology, once thought to be a tenth-grade subject, is now placed at the ninth grade. The improvement of science instruction at the elementary school level may have made this possible. Algebra was taught at tenth- and ninth-grade levels for many years, but of late at least some pupils study it in the eighth grade. Reading-readiness programs are part of kindergarten experience in some schools and of first-grade learning elsewhere. Calculus, at one time considered a university-level course, was offered in 40.6 percent of the more than 2000 high schools studied by Conant in 1966.[17]

Developments in nuclear physics and space exploration have influenced the teaching of science and mathematics in the schools. The curriculum-reform movement in mathematics, started in 1951 by the University of Illinois Committee on School Mathematics, has expanded to encompass such groups as the School Mathematics Study Group (SMSG) and the Greater Cleveland Mathematics Program. This movement has influenced instruction in mathematics at all grade levels. Appraisals in the late 1960s and early 1970s questioned the effectiveness of SMSG math and doubtless a new revision of math content may be in the offing. Efforts to restructure the elementary school science curriculum have cost in excess of $2 million to date. The high school science curriculum was first modified to include the physical science study committee (PSSC) physics course for high school students; that was followed shortly by the biological science curriculum study (BSCS biology) and the chemical bond approach (CBA) and chemical education material study (CHEMS) chemistry courses for high school. The teaching of the social studies and English has been altered as well. Foreign languages are now introduced in elementary school, and their teaching has been the subject of study and modification at all grade levels. In

[17]J. B. Conant, *The Comprehensive High School: Second Report to Interested Citizens,* New York: McGraw-Hill, 1967, p. 56.

short, practically every course offered in the schools has been or is presently undergoing some degree of study and modification.

Influence is exerted on the school curriculum through federal agencies such as the National Science Foundation and through private foundations. As Goodlad pointed out:

Curriculum planning is a political process, just as it is an ideological process of determining ends and means for education. Proposals either find their way to the political structure in educational institutions or slip into obscurity. The unique and sensitive relationship among local, state, and federal governments in the support and conduct of school affairs has materially affected the way in which the various curriculum projects have entered the bloodstream of American education.[18]

At present the enthusiasm for curricular change remains high. The mere fact of newness often has been sufficient reason to introduce a different course organization or instructional approach. Evaluation of the results of such changes has been slow. Evidence is accumulating that the superiority claimed for many publicized curricular reforms was not warranted. In some cases, undesirable side effects were evident, and modifications subsequently were introduced. Goodlad reported at least three different weaknesses following his survey of the current curriculum-reform efforts:

1. Program development in social sciences, humanities, especially the arts, health and physical education is as yet only embryonic at both elementary and secondary levels.
2. Many subjects that could be included in the curriculum are not included as part of the reform efforts.

[18]J. I. Goodlad, *School Curriculum Reform in the United States*, New York: Fund for the Advancement of Education, 1964, pp. 10–11.

3. There is an absence of experimental effort to fit together the various subjects or combinations of subjects into a reasonably unified curriculum.[19]

He submitted a series of recommendations to overcome such deficiencies.

Present curriculum-reform efforts are far more conservative than those noted during early parts of this century. The traditional subject-matter mold is assumed, and no radical curriculum reorganizations are being recommended.

Changes in the curriculum influence the size and design of school buildings, the number and type of personnel to be employed, the size of the budget, and the means of financing schools. Unless the administrator gives primacy to matters of curriculum, he may be guilty of designing classrooms that fail to function because they are based on an outmoded concept of teaching, of employing teachers who lack the ability to teach pupils to meet the problems of today's world, or of planning budgets for educational experiences of another era.

NEW METHODS FOR PROGRAM DEVELOPMENT

Instructional leadership demands the capability to generate new educational programs. It is no longer enough to keep existing programs operating at efficient levels. A variety of new agencies at the local, state, and federal level, along with private groups such as foundations, are required to produce the creative curricular and instructional innovations capable of promoting more effective learning as well as learning in tune with the challenges of the time.

[19]Ibid., section 3.

Regional education laboratories

The federally sponsored and supported regional education laboratories were created under Title 4 of the 1965 Elementary and Secondary Education Act (ESEA). Twenty regional laboratories were established by 1965; by 1973 less than half that number survived the many federal evaluations and budget cuts. The founding legislation specifies that the laboratories are to identify specific problems confronting public education today, conduct and coordinate research and research-related activities in problem areas, and disseminate findings for implementation in the schools. The grouping of states in the cooperative effort is not specified in the law but is left to the states themselves.

It is still too early to determine the effectiveness of regional educational centers and programs that may influence public education. Their purposes have not been defined with sufficient clarity. There is little uniformity of effort among the various regional centers. Financial shortages have been experienced as a result of the curtailment of federal expenditures in the late 1960s and early 1970s.

Pilot programs

Federal efforts must dovetail with local and state determination to identify research that shows promise for the improvement of education. Readiness on the part of local school districts to select promising research ideas to be tested at pilot centers is one function of curricular and instructional leadership of administrators and supervisors. The classrooms in the pilot centers with particular student ability, social and economic backgrounds, and grade levels, and with teachers and administrators of speci-fied competency, must be described and recorded. Experimental controls must be identified beforehand to ensure the validity of subsequent evaluations. It should be understood that not everything attempted will prove successful. The limitations as well as the advantages of a pilot program should be recognized.

Implementation of innovations begins with willingness to try out, on a limited scale, those of greatest promise. The next step is to move from a pilot operation to dissemination in the school system, and for this there must be created a readiness for change. Usually this will occur if the educational personnel come to recognize difficulties that have been experienced with existing approaches or organizational patterns. In other words, there must be a felt need before there can be readiness for change. When this readiness exists, the consequences of the shift, particularly the nature, quantity, and availability of resources required to accommodate a new approach, must be determined by administrators. Additional resources must be budgeted. In effect, the change must be programmed either throughout the system as a whole during a relatively short period of time, or in various parts of the system over a more extended period of time.

Alternative schools

Free schools, street academies, and even "deschooling of society" were publicized with increasing frequency in the late 1960s and early 1970s. The public school has been called a monopoly and there is the desire among those disenchanted with established patterns to create alternative school patterns. Most of the time such alternatives are in competition with established schools. There are some school districts with alternative schools within the system, that is, they are off-shoots of the established system.

All instructional leaders must come to know the alternative patterns and assess the possible contributions of each because educational reform will remain a part of the 1970s. Leaders who become defensive and who are anxious to preserve the status quo in the face of whatever odds are adopting a self-defeating strategy: One mark of a leader is that he knows his options and seldom allows himself to run out of them.

ORGANIZATION OF THE ELEMENTARY SCHOOL DAY

The length of the elementary school day is usually an administrative decision. It has an impact on the number of learning opportunities and their duration in a given school situation. The minimum length of the day is often specified in state laws, state department of education regulations, and general local school-board policies. The number of hours in the elementary school day varies with grade level. Thus, kindergarten pupils attend only a half day, or from 2 to $2\frac{1}{2}$ hours. Pupils in Grades 1 through 3 attend for shorter periods than do pupils in Grades 4 through 6; those in Grades 7 and 8 attend for longer periods than those in Grades 4 through 6. A study of urban school districts indicated that, nationally, 85 percent of elementary schools have a school day of between 5 and 6 hours.[20] No primary school pupils and few intermediate-grade pupils are in school longer than 6 hours. In general, it can be said that

[20]Stuart E. Dean, *Elementary School Administration and Organization,* Bulletin 1960, no. 11, U.S. Office of Education, Washington, D.C.: GPO, 1960, chap. 5.

the length of the school day for pupils in Grades 1 through 6 is $5\frac{1}{2}$ hours; for those in Grades 7 and 8 it is 6 hours. A change in the length of the school day is not likely, although about 42.7 percent of the urban school systems studied thought there might be an increase in length of the school year.

Double sessions were common in the 1950s and 1960s, but the anticipated decline in enrollments portends their disappearance in the 1970s in all but very unusual school situations.

ORGANIZATION OF THE ELEMENTARY SCHOOL CURRICULUM

The curriculum of the elementary school comprises seven broad subject fields: language arts, arithmetic, science, social studies, art, music, and health and physical education. The problem facing administrators of elementary attendance centers, as well as many central-office staff members, is how best to maintain a proper perspective among these curricular obligations—how much time to allocate to each field. The most common administrative policy is to suggest the number of minutes per week per subject for the first six grades and to prescribe it for the seventh and eighth grades.[21] Another important administrative decision is how to organize pupils for purposes of instruction. This raises the issues of pupil grouping, departmentalization, and nongrading among others.

A study of the use of grouping as a basic policy in public elementary schools shows that about 17 percent of urban schools use homogeneous grouping and 72 percent use heterogeneous grouping for Grades 1 through 6. Homogeneous grouping in Grades 1 through 3 was less likely than in the

[21]Ibid.

upper grades. For Grades 7 and 8, 34 percent of urban schools use homogeneous groupings. Nationwide, pupils in the elementary grades appear to be organized without consideration for homogeneous grouping. About 46 percent of urban elementary school systems predicted an increase in homogeneous grouping; these were primarily the largest cities. It is significant that almost three-fourths of the elementary school administrators did not consider grouping a major administrative problem.[22]

As indicated previously, grading was the first major change in the organization of instruction at the elementary-school level. There is concern today over further change in organization to facilitate learning. Two conflicting points of view emerge, one advocating self-containment and the other advocating departmentalization. Proponents of the former view argue that the scientific data on human growth and development point to the importance to the child of elementary school age of having close contact with a single teacher who can understand her and provide for her individual differences in ability, maturation, and potential.[23] Those who favor departmentalization believe that the increasing accumulation and importance of knowledge make it no longer possible for the traditionally prepared elementary school teacher to be qualified as an effective instructor in all subjects to all children.

There are various degrees of self-containment. In a completely self-contained classroom situation, the teacher teaches all seven broad subject fields that constitute the elementary curriculum; no specialists intrude into such rooms. In the modified (or enriched) self-contained classroom, specialists may teach art and music, but the general classroom teacher instructs in most subject areas, particularly the language arts, arithmetic, and social studies.

In a departmentalized program, the students move from one classroom to another (rather than having special teachers do so) and obtain instruction from a variety of teachers (each being assigned a given specialty). Partial departmentalization, where children move to some rooms rather than the teachers moving, bears a strong resemblance to the modified self-contained organization, where special teachers move from room to room but the children do not. In the partially departmentalized program, the pupils remain with one teacher all morning, studying language arts, arithmetic, and social studies. In the afternoon they move to various classrooms to be instructed by special teachers of science, art, music, or physical education. The teacher of the fundamental subjects has a second class of pupils to teach in the same areas all afternoon. The partially departmentalized plan increases the number of pupil contacts for a homeroom teacher or teacher of the fundamental subjects. Complete departmentalization requires students to move to different teachers at the end of each instructional period and for each subject offered in the curriculum. In a sense, each teacher is a specialist in the completely departmentalized school. There are many variations possible within the range of departmentalization.

A study of the urban elementary schools indicates that the self-contained instructional organization prevails in over three-fourths of the buildings housing Grades 1 through 6. Only about 2 percent were multigraded, 77 percent were self-contained, and 11

[22]Ibid.
[23]Ibid.

percent were partially and completely departmentalized. Departmentalization was the usual plan for the seventh and eighth grades.

As indicated elsewhere individualized organizational patterns such as IPI and IGE/MUS-E began to emerge in the 1960s and spread in the 1970s. As yet such patterns are found in only about 1000 to 2000 schools.

Curriculum changes influence instructional organization. Greater demands made upon the general elementary school teacher as a result of an enriched program of studies spurs use of special teachers and makes possible an instructional organization of a different type. Use of school-plant facilities at the elementary school level is affected by instructional patterns. Thus, departmentalization results in more efficient utilization of the school plant. At the primary school level, however, the maturity level of the pupils may necessitate special teachers coming to the classroom, rather than the elementary pupils moving to the special teachers. In other words, building utilization notwithstanding, a self-contained organization is more likely to create a desirable learning situation. Administrators at the building level as well as at the general or central-office level have a responsibility to gather data and determine what procedure seems most acceptable for the system.

INSTRUCTIONAL MATERIALS

Administrative leadership carries the responsibility for obtaining and allocating instructional materials necessary to promote educational program development and student learning. The proliferation of instructional devices and aids has greatly complicated the job. Today there are FM radios, tele-

vision, sound and color motion-picture projectors, slide projectors, teaching machines, and computers, as well as the traditional textbooks, maps, globes, charts, and models. The availability of federal funds has greatly increased the purchase and use of teaching materials.

Audiovisual aids

The use of audiovisual devices has increased. Educational institutions own one-third of the 600,000 16-mm. sound motion-picture projectors. The Federal Communications Commission reserved a total of 259 TV channels for non-profit educational institutions. By March 1, 1960, 46 educational TV stations were operating in 31 states. Within five years the number of ETVs more than doubled and were operating in practically all states. Later the name preferred became public television stations, rather than educational TV, suggesting the broader use of these vehicles. The number of licensed public TV stations grew to 193 by 1971 and then jumped to 270 by 1972. Local public school systems operated almost 12 percent, institutions of higher education about 30 percent, community organizations almost 27 percent, and various other state and municipal agencies over 31 percent of the public TV stations. TV programing prepared specifically for classroom use in local schools accounted for only 12.4 percent and in institutions of higher learning for only 21.8 percent of the total public broadcast hours. The typical ETV station is on the air an average of almost 71 hours per week.

Laboratory facilities

The laboratory approach to teaching has extended beyond the science courses. There is a growing demand for foreign language, as well as chemistry, biology, and physics, laboratories. The laboratory approach might well be employed in social studies, English, and mathematics as well. The library is already recognized by some English and social-studies teachers as a laboratory.

Library facilities

About 70 percent of the schools (nearly all the secondary, but less than half the elementary, schools) have centralized libraries serving about 75 percent of the pupils. Elementary school pupils use the public library and the mobile library more often than junior or senior high school pupils do. There are about 200 million volumes in public school libraries The major users of the library materials are English and social studies teachers, followed closely by science teachers. Instructors in business education, mathematics, physical education, health, industrial arts, music, foreign language, and art make limited use of the library. Large systems are likely to have a paid librarian. Title II of ESEA provided funds for the improvement of school libraries in the years following 1966.

The library has expanded its functions and is no longer considered to be merely a depository for certain types of books. It has been reconceptualized as the Instructional Materials Center (IMC) and has become an integral part of the educational process at all levels. The facilities have been attractively designed and made more functional.

Some of the other trends in school libraries and book buying are:

1. An increase in free textbooks provided by states, many of which never provided free books before, particularly in the South.

2. Greater cooperation between public and private schools because of the provision that books purchased under Title II must be available for lending to private schools.

3. More frequent additions to state textbook lists and more revisions of textbook-adoption lists.

Textbooks

The textbook continues to be an important part of the instructional program despite the proliferation of other instructional aids. The selection of textbooks is determined in different ways by various states and territories. According to the most recently available data, local school authorities in 27 states selected textbooks without recommendation or control from any state authority. In the remaining 23 states, the local school authority was required to select books from an approved list of texts adopted by a state committee. State textbook lists are prepared by the state board of education, a state textbook-purchasing board, or a state textbook-selection committee. Ten states do not specify the number of texts in any given field that may be placed on the state approved list. One state has as many as 10 texts in each field on the approved list and the local agencies may select one or all. Most states place 5 texts in one field on the approved list for local adoption. The multiple listing of texts is a recent development that has displaced the more traditional single-textbook list. A summary of textbook-selection practices by states is presented in Table 21–1.

The shift from local and county adoption of textbooks to state adoption occurred between 1897 and 1927. In 1897, 21 states permitted local school districts to adopt textbooks, but by 1927 the number had dropped to 17. The number of states using the same textbooks statewide increased from 18 to 25 by 1927. The changes since 1927 have been negligible, although the new states of Hawaii and Alaska have state textbook-adoption systems. Most of the states using the same books statewide have adhered to the plan for well over 30 years, and most are located in the South and Far West; likewise, no states in which local districts select books were planning any changes in the near future.

Some of the arguments for statewide uniformity of textbook adoption are:

1. It ensures a uniform course of study.
2. Textbooks may be purchased at lower prices because of large orders.
3. The mobility of the population makes statewide uniformity of texbooks helpful for children who change school often.[24]

The arguments against statewide uniformity of textbook adoption are:

1. No state is a homogeneous unit, so neither uniform text nor uniform courses of study will satisfactorily apply to all districts.

[24]L. W. Burnett, "Schools Are Gaining in the Battle Against State Control of Textbooks," *The Nation's Schools,* vol. 45, no. 5, May 1950, pp. 49–50.

TABLE 21–1

TEXTBOOK-SELECTION PRACTICES

State	Local adoption	State adoption for subjects multiple texts	Term of adoption (years)
Alabama		x	3–6
Alaska		x	NS[a]
Arizona		x	5
Arkansas		x	4–6
California		x	4–8
Colorado	x		NS[a]
Connecticut	x		NS[a]
Delaware	x		4
Florida		x	5
Georgia		x	5
Hawaii	x		NS[a]
Idaho	x		NS[a]
Illinois	x		NS[a]
Indiana		x	5
Iowa	x		5
Kansas		x	NS[a]
Kentucky		x	4
Louisiana		x	NS[a]
Maine	x		NS[a]
Maryland	x		NS[a]
Massachusetts	x		NS[a]
Michigan	x		5
Minnesota	x		NS[a]
Mississippi		x	4–5
Missouri	x		NS[a]
Montana	x		3
Nebraska	x		NS[a]
Nevada		x	NS[a]

2. The state text-adoption plan will stifle local initiative and irritate teachers.
3. State adoption involves long periods of time during which new and better books cannot be adopted.

Free textbooks are being made available in more and more states. In 1966 about 85 percent of all systems with enrollments of 12,000 or more provided free textbooks to all students. A very small percent require student purchase of texts. A higher percent of elementary pupils have free texts (about 90 percent) as compared with secondary pupils (about 73 percent). Title II of the Elementary and Sec-

ondary Education Act accentuated this trend to free use of texts. Where the rental plan is used, the students pay a nominal fee. Philadelphia in 1818 was the first district to provide free textbooks to pupils. Massachusetts in 1848 was the first to have a state-wide free-textbook law for all public schools. All states except one have legislation which provides that a textbook must or may be furnished to students. Free textbooks are mandatory for some or all grades in 30 states and permissive in 18 others.

California was the last state to require a single basic textbook for each

TABLE 21–1 (Continued)

State	Local adoption	State adoption for subjects multiple texts	Terms of adoption (years)
New Hampshire	x		NS[a]
New Jersey	x		NS[a]
New Mexico		x	6
New York	x		5
North Carolina		x	5
North Dakota	x		NS[a]
Ohio	x		4
Oklahoma		x	4–6
Oregon		x	6
Pennsylvania	x		NS[a]
Rhode Island	x		NS[a]
South Carolina		x	4
South Dakota	x		NS[a]
Tennessee		x	3–5
Texas		x	5
Utah		x	4
Vermont	x		NS[a]
Virginia		x	6
Washington	x		NS[a]
West Virginia		x	4
Wisconsin	x		NS[a]
Wyoming	x		NS[a]
Total	27	23	4.5 (median)

Source: Institute for Educational Development, *Selection of Educational Materials in the United States Public Schools,* (New York: Institute for Educational Development, 1969), pp. 27, 55, 91.

Howard H. Cummings and Helen K. Makintosh, *Curriculum Responsibility of State Departments of Education,* U.S. Office of Education, misc. no. 30, Washington, D.C.: GPO, 1958.

[a] NS = None specified.

elementary school subject and the last to print all elementary textbooks. It went to multiple adoption in 1970. After 1972 California continued to use the state printer to produce some elementary texts but only when it was economically advantageous to do so. Until 1957 Kansas printed textbooks for schools, renting the plates from the publisher, but gave up the undertaking. Georgia, Florida, Indiana, and Louisiana also printed textbooks at one time.[25]

SUMMARY

A traditional and honored role for the school administrator is that of instructional leader. To fulfill this role, he must be sensitive to, and able to comprehend, the educational problems at the elementary and secondary school level as well as to design the administrative strategies needed to resolve these issues. The role of the administrator is to make great teaching possible. Insisting that the administrator teach a class or two is the simplistic solution to instructional leadership. Far more significant is the administrator's capability to stimulate desirable changes in the professional behavior of other teachers. Administrative leadership in the curriculum involves organizing and evaluating to improve instruction as well as making

resources available to groups studying means of improving the curriculum and instruction. The administrator is primarily a change agent rather than one involved in teaching or curriculum projects. His involvement in building, planning, and budgeting can contribute to the improvement of instruction. A leader knows where he is going and how to get there. He must make choices as to which curriculum and instruction goals to pursue. The next step is to translate objectives into operational programs.

Curriculum refers to all the educational experiences provided under the auspices of a school, including the scope and sequence of educational experiences as well as methods of teaching and instructional materials. Educational programs can be classified by subjects, by broad fields, by areas of living, and by experiences. Recent developments have given birth to the programmatic and to the humanistic curriculum.

The development of instructional materials is part of the instructional leadership responsibilities of the administrator. This includes providing adequate textbooks, supplies, and equipment as well as special devices such as audiovisual materials and teaching machines. Special facilities, such as libraries and laboratories, are larger aids for instruction. Very little change has occurred in state textbook-adoption patterns. The trend among the 23 states that now use the same textbooks statewide is toward the preparation of multiple listings of textbooks.

[25]B. R. Buckingham, "Textbooks," in Chester W. Harris, ed., *Encyclopedia of Educational Research*, 3rd ed., New York: Macmillan, 1960, p. 1522.

QUESTIONS

1. Why is the curriculum of such importance to the administration of public education?
2. What is the role of the school board in curriculum planning and improvement?

3. How does a superintendent realize the role of instructional leader? The building principal?
4. What are the characteristics of a core program?
5. What factors have compounded the problems of providing instructional aids and materials for schools?
6. What are the advantages and disadvantages of the use of the same textbooks statewide?
7. What are the advantages and disadvantages of the following curriculum-classification schemes: (a) by subject, (b) by broad fields, (c) by areas of living, and (d) by experiences?

SELECTED REFERENCES

American Association of School Administrators, *The Superintendent as Instructional Leader,* Thirty-fifth Yearbook, Washington, D.C.: The Association, 1957.

Cummings, Howard H. and Helen K. Makintosh, *Curriculum Responsibility of State Departments of Education,* U.S. Office of Education, misc. no. 30, Washington, D.C.: GPO, 1958.

Eye, G. G. and Netzer, L. A., *School Administration and Instruction,* Boston: Allyn and Bacon, 1969.

Krug, Edward A., *Curriculum Planning,* rev. ed., New York: Harper & Row, 1957.

Lutz, Frank W., ed., *Toward Improved Urban Education,* Worthington, Ohio: C. A. Jones Publishing, 1970.

Purpel, David E. and Belanger, Mark, eds., *Curriculum and the Cultural Revolution,* Berkeley, Cal.: McCutchan, 1972.

Saxe, Richard W., ed., *Opening the Schools,* Berkeley, Cal.: McCutchan, 1972.

Taba, Hilda, *Curriculum Development,* New York: Harcourt Brace, Jovanovich, 1962.

22

MANAGING LEARNING OPPORTUNITIES: INSTRUCTIONAL ORGANIZATION, PUPIL ASSESSMENT, AND PROMOTION POLICIES

Determining instructional objectives, designing related learning experiences, and developing instructional strategies were the important components of curriculum and instructional leadership reviewed in the previous chapter. These functions demand an organizational framework to become operational. Likewise, there are other challenges that confront an administrator who must manage the learning opportunities that are available in the particular educational institution.

Organization is only one variable affecting learning. There is at present no evidence supported by well-designed and carefully executed research concerning the degree to which the single variable of organization for instruction can influence the amount learned by a pupil or the performance level of a teacher. Even less clear is whether the instructional organization has more, equal, or less impact on a pupil's learning than other variables in the learning process such as the pupil's ability, interest, socioeconomic background, and motivation; the teacher's preparation, attitudes toward particular groups of pupils, knowledge of

subject matter, and skills in using particular instructional devices; the availability of instructional materials and equipment; the values attached to education by parents from a given cultural or socioeconomic background; and the skill being learned. The list of variables that influence the complex process of learning by a pupil or group of pupils is sizable indeed.

It bears repeating that instructional organization is a means and represents potential; it is not an end or a guarantee of given outcomes. It is what people do, particularly what teachers and pupils do within a given organizational pattern that is most likely to determine the outcomes. There is no guarantee that a teacher will or will not make use of advantages that are inherent in an instructional organization. More information is required on the teacher's instructional behavior and attitudes toward pupils in one type of instructional pattern as opposed to another. The crucial question is: What is it that teachers, in attempting to stimulate learning among pupils, can do or cannot do to promote educational objectives in one type of instructional organization as opposed to another? The instructional leader is challenged to probe for an adequate response to this question.

The present period is by no means the first time in history that new ways have been suggested of organizing pupils to facilitate learning. The *Encyclopedia of Education Research* records a long list of organizational plans proposed in the nineteenth and the early part of the twentieth centuries to overcome the rigidity of existing instructional approaches and to make learning more meaningful and more efficient. There is complete agreement that improvement of instruction is a worthy goal. The argument is whether the means suggested will accomplish the goal. Much the same can be said about the many phrases that are part of our educational heritage, such as "individualizing instruction," "enriching learning," "special provisions for the slow learner," "better adaptation to individual differences," "allowing each child to progress at his own pace," "continuous growth," "learning to think," "emphasizing problem solving rather than mere accumulation of bits and facts," "effective social personal development," "education of the whole child," "providing better educational programs for children," "meeting the needs of the individual and society," and developing the "humane school." No one questions the importance and desirability of designing school structures to reach these goals. These phrases, which carry a favorable or desirable connotation, have been part of our educational heritage for at least 50 years. Not everyone using them can design better approaches to realizing educational goals. No one can claim that his post-World War II pattern for instructional organization was the originator of concern for "individualizing instruction," "allowing each

child to progress at his own speed," "learning to think," and "providing better educational programs." The problem is to gather objective evidence that the goal is being realized better through a novel instructional approach. The administrator attempting to fulfill his role as change agent may find it difficult to separate research evidence from unsupported claims from a variety of publicized instructional organizations. History records when a given mode of organization is adopted by a substantial number; it does a less adequate job of reporting discontinuance. Unless claims meet the test of reality within a relatively short time, say one generation, the innovation is discarded. Sometimes it is promoted again later on and acclaimed as progress, though such repetition constitutes little more than senseless dissipation of resources.

A variety of constraints are placed on those who would create a realistic and significant pattern of instructional organization. Because there are over 45 million elementary and secondary school pupils to be educated, it is futile to preach a tutorial approach to instruction, namely, one teacher for one pupil. The large numbers of learners and the limited resources of the schools necessitate grouping pupils for learning. Grouping must be based on some kind of classification. Basic to every pattern of instructional organization is the manner in which pupils of similar or different chronological age levels are assigned to one teacher or to teams of teachers within school attendance centers. Additionally, the pupil's growth in learning must be measured so that he can be transferred to other teachers with different specializations. This process goes on from the time the learner is admitted initially to school until he has completed the formal, full-time learning opportunities available in the school district

--usually at the end of secondary school. Of no less concern is what types of pupils shall be placed in what types of instructional centers and how these instructional centers shall be related to produce a unified and interrelated educational system.

Instructional organizational problems result from complexity. Organization is not difficult when there are only enough pupils to justify one school plant. The one-room, one-teacher school is satisfactory when the curriculum is simple and educational objectives are limited.

ORGANIZATION OF THE SCHOOL YEAR

Time is an important element in the teaching-learning process. It takes time to participate in experiences and to learn from them. Time must be organized by the instructional leader at the attendance center or system-wide level to promote learning in the most effective manner. Length of the school year should be related to present-day educational demands. The professional school administrator has an obligation to continue to review the need for a change in the length of the school year, whether to make schooling more efficient, to extend pupil services, or to provide special opportunities for the continuous professional development of the staff.

The length of the school year has increased steadily during the nineteenth century and the first seven decades of the twentieth century. The average length of the school term in 1869–1870 was 132.2 days; in 1909–1910, 157.5 days; in 1929–1930, 172.7 days; and presently almost 180 days.

It is frequently said that the long summer vacation is the vestige of an agriculturally oriented society which found children of considerable value on the farm and around the home during the planting, growing, and harvesting season. But this can be questioned, for school terms during the 1700s and much of the 1800s were 3 or 4 months out of the year at most. Pupil attendance was even worse in the early years of all educational history; less than 90 days was common up until 1890. In short, there was far more vacation than school up to the twentieth century.

In addition, demands for organized educational experiences during summer months were practically nonexistent through the beginning of the twentieth century. The traditional school calendar was molded when there was no shortage of teachers, when school facilities were not crowded, and when the pressures for quality education were not as intensive as they are today.[1] The 9-month school year was a maximum that could be supported until recently, but to meet present-day demands, a 12-month school year has been suggested. The idea is not new. Even before 1840 schools in some cities were conducted almost all year round: Buffalo operated schools for 12 months, Baltimore and Cincinnati for 11 months, New York for 49 weeks, and Chicago for 48 weeks. The school year was divided into four terms of 12 weeks each, with 1 week of vacation at the end of each term. Gradually the pattern was altered to 1 week of vacation at Christmas, 1 week at Easter, and 2 weeks in the summer. In the 75 years following 1840, cities gradually adjusted programs, shortened the school year, and increased the vacation period. At the same time rural areas, which held school primarily during the winter

[1] American Association of School Administrators, *Year-Round School*, Washington, D.C.: The Association, 1960.

months (except for the very young), slowly lengthened the school year to approximate the shortened year in the cities. By 1915 most of the nation had a 9-month school year.[2] Between 1924 and 1931, again between 1947 and 1953, and again in the 1960s and 1970s interest in year-round school was renewed.

The following reasons have been advanced for extending the school year to 12 months:

1. It would allow fuller utilization of school-plant facilities and possibly forestall the need for new school construction.
2. It would reduce certain unit costs of operation, such as fixed charges and administration.
3. It would utilize the staff more fully.
4. It would keep urban youngsters engaged in constructive programs during the summer.
5. It would permit moving some non-academic experiences, such as driver education and typing, to the summer, leaving more time for academic subjects during the rest of the year.
6. It would permit use of school facilities for the professional growth and development of teachers.

Saville outlined the major year-round operating schemes as follows:

1. The Four Quarter Plan
   1.1 Standard four quarter
   1.2 Quadrimester
   1.3 Staggered quarters
2. The Trimester
   2.1 Standard trimester
   2.2 Split trimester
3. Summer School Program
   3.1 Extension of regular year (standard) (voluntary)
   3.2 Modified summer program
4. The Multiple Trails Program
5. The 45–15 Plan
6. Other Combinations
   6.1 Continuous Progress Plan
   6.2 Split Semester Plan[3]

[2]National Education Association, "All-Year School," Research Memo, 1958–9, Washington, D.C.: The Association, 1958.
[3]A. Saville, Instructional Programming, Columbus, Ohio: Chas. E. Merrill, 1973, p. 178.

The four-quarter plan

The most frequently suggested year-round plan is the four-quarter system with rotating attendance. This is sometimes called the staggered quarter plan because pupil vacations are staggered with a different group enjoying time-off during each quarter. Schools are operated all year, but each pupil spends only 9 months attending classes. Teachers are employed for three or four quarters, depending upon arrangements—some teachers may work for less than three quarters. This system could lead to a contract period of 3 rather than the usual 9 months.

The first four-quarter plan with rotating attendance was put into operation in Bluffton, Indiana, in 1904 and was discontinued in 1915. Some systems employing this plan by 1925 were Gary, Indiana; Mason City, Iowa; Eveleth, Minnesota; Omaha, Nebraska; Albuquerque, New Mexico; Ardmore and Tulsa, Oklahoma; Ambridge and Aliquippa, Pennsylvania; Nashville, Tennessee; Amarillo and El Paso, Texas.

Under the standard quarter plan the school year is 48 weeks, as opposed to the more traditional 36 weeks. Each quarter may be called a quadrimester. Full attendance for all four quarters may not be mandatory. If all four quarters are attended a student could theoretically complete five traditional school years in three years. Most extended year programs were designed primarily for secondary schools.

The advantages claimed for the four-quarter plan with rotating attendance are:

1. Each child continues to receive as much instruction time as under the traditional school year, but theoretically 25 percent more pupils are cared for by approximately the same staff and with the same number of classrooms, laboratories, libraries, and playgrounds.

2. Pupils continue to graduate on schedule and attend 6 years of elementary school, 3 years of junior high school, and 3 years of senior high school.
3. A double shift or a shortened day is unnecessary.
4. Demands for new school buildings and equipment are drastically reduced.
5. Expenditures for personnel, new construction, and new equipment are reduced.
6. Teachers have an opportunity for full-year employment and, therefore, better annual salaries, which should reduce teacher turnover. Men teachers, in particular, would not be forced to seek summer employment or eventually to turn to occupations offering greater remuneration.
7. Fewer books are needed at any one time.
8. Pupils have a better opportunity to make up lost work because of extended absence or failure since they can attend school an additional quarter.
9. The work of the pupil is evaluated more often and his progress is reported more frequently to his parents.[4]

The disadvantages inherent in the four-quarter plan with rotating attendance are:

1. Because the total pupil enrollment should be the same for each quarter, a school system with a relatively small enrollment would have trouble registering equal numbers. If the alleged economy is to be realized, optimal conditions must prevail. In other words, unless enrollment is large and the distribution in all four quarters is about the same, inefficiency will prevail.

2. Existing patterns of family living and working militate against acceptance of the four-quarter plan with rotating attendance. Families with two or more children in school would want all of them to be in school during the same quarters; relatively few families would want children out of school

during the winter or in school during the summer. An elective system would result in a very uneven distribution of pupils in the four quarters.

3. Because schools in some sections of the country would have to install air conditioning and raise teachers' salaries, the economies are not as great as claimed.

4. The large numbers of youngsters who are not in school during each quarter have to be profitably engaged to keep them out of trouble. Programs similar to the summer work opportunities, special recreation programs, camps, and family vacation plans will have to be developed for the other three quarters. Part of the savings in school costs (and probably more) would be needed to finance these additional welfare and community recreation programs.

5. Certain kinds of activities are difficult to administer under the staggered term approach. Thus, if coaches have their way, all football players will be enrolled during the fall term, basketball players in winter and spring terms, and track- and tennis-team aspirants during spring and fall terms. The band master, dramatic coach, orchestra leader, and debate coach, too, will want certain pupils to attend during certain terms.

6. The burden of administration and supervision is increased by the need for complete rescheduling four times a year and for keeping special records on vacation periods for each student.

The four-quarter plan with rotating attendance appears, on the surface, a simple way to improve the utilization of facilities and of personnel. It may be justified as a temporary approach in preference to the double session. Careful examination of facts indicates, however, that it may precipitate more problems than it solves. For this reason, many communities that have examined the plan carefully, or have ac-

[4]Ibid., and American Association of School Administrators, op. cit.

tually tried it, have eventually abandoned it.

The trimester

A trimester is, theoretically, one-third of a school year. Each such period is longer than a quadrimester but shorter than a semester, usually about 14 weeks. More universities have operated under the trimester plan than have local school systems, but most that have used it have abandoned it.

One problem at the university level has been the summer sessions. The summer trimester may be split into two seven-week sessions.

Summer school for pupils

A voluntary summer-school program to extend the school year is not a new idea, but the present concept differs in philosophy from the traditional summer school. Summer school used to be for the slow learners, the retarded, and those who failed for whatever reason. In effect, it was punishment for not doing well during the school year. It carried a stigma, so that a pupil did not boast about attending summer school and resisted going to school at that time.

The new summer school is viewed as an opportunity for enrichment of all—the bright and the average, as well as the inefficient learners. Remedial programs and make-up work are but a small part of present-day summer-session programs. Enrichment, through advanced courses in chemistry, physics, mathematics, creative writing, and painting, and through the study of typing, shorthand, nature, woodworking, music, crafts, or driving constitutes the real substance of the program. It adds a new dimension to the quality of the instructional program during the regular year. It gives each pupil an opportunity to learn more during the time he spends in elementary or secondary school. Summer-school programs also provide supervised recreation, but even here new skills are developed or old ones sharpened to make leisure time more enjoyable.

Summer-school attendance has increased as the programs have been expanded to meet remedial, avocational, recreational, and strictly academic interests of children and youth. Additional costs for teachers, equipment, and care of facilities are a part of such summer schools. In other words, this pattern of year-round school use will require more funds rather than less. In times of financial retrenchment summer school is one of the first programs to be curtailed or special tuition charges may be assessed for those who attend.

Summer program for professional personnel

A special summer program for professional personnel provides teachers with an opportunity to be employed on a 12-month basis. Children go to school during the traditional 36- to 40-week period. During summer sessions, when children are not in school, teachers, administrators, and supervisors engage in instructional and curricular planning. Usually teachers are not required to participate in a 12- or 8-week summer program of professional improvement. Experience in Glencoe, Illinois, Lexington, Kentucky, and Rochester, Minnesota, which have organized such programs, shows that a fairly high percentage of the teachers do participate. Such a program increases the current expense budget by about 10 to 20 percent. It places a tremendous burden (or challenge) on the leadership responsibilities of administrative and supervisory staff.

The 45-15 plan

The most highly publicized year-round school plan in recent years by far is the 45-15 plan. It is a variation of the staggered-quarter plan; about a fourth of the students at any one time are on vacation. The duration of the vacation period at any one time is for 15 school days (3 weeks) rather than the full quarter of 60 school days (12 weeks). In short, the pupil attends for 45 school days (9 weeks) and has a 15 school day vacation (3 weeks); this pattern is repeated four times during the total school year with 180 days of pupil school attendance.

As yet this plan has been implemented in relatively few districts. It appears to be an acceptable alternate to double sessions rather than to the traditional school year in systems with adequate facilities.

The economies of year-round school operation

Greater "efficiency," somewhat loosely defined, is the purported objective of year-round school operation. It is argued that school facilities (the site, building, and equipment) represent sizable physical capital investments that are under-utilized during summer months. It is implied that greater efficiency is the direct result of using physical facilities during every month of the calendar year and that the cost of operating schools for 12 months would be little more than for 9 months since the facilities are there. The following illustration, developed by the writer, indicates that this simplistic type of reasoning won't hold up under critical examination.

A $5 million classroom building represents a sizable expenditure. This gross sum may be three or four times the annual salaries paid to instructors using the instructional unit. If no further analysis is made, the comparison between annual salaries paid to instructors using a structure and building costs help "prove" the efficiency of year-round operation. The initial difficulty lies in the failure to distinguish between current expenses and capital outlay. Salaries for professional personnel are annual expenditures and are included in current expenses. The $5 million for the building is capital outlay; the gross amount of $5 million is amortized over a 20- or 30-year period. The annual cost of the building depends upon the interest rate and length of term of the debt; in other words, it is no greater than the annual debt-service payments (interest plus a portion of the principal retired). But because the building continues to be used for 50 to 75 years, or for more than twice the debt-amortization period, the annual cost of the structure is less than the debt-retirement cost. Let it be assumed that there will be a 20- or 30-year amortization period and a relatively high rate of 5 percent annual interest will be charged for tax exempt bonds in the 1970s. The average annual debt-retirement cost (principal plus interest) would be about $381,250 for 20 years or about $295,850 for 30 years. This annual cost places the $5 million gross cost of building, equipment, and site in another perspective.

The average annual economic cost, defined as the total cost of construction and site plus financing charges for the period of debt divided by the life span of the structure, is yet another measure. If a conservative 50-year life span is assumed, the average annual economic cost of the building would be $152,500 if the debt were paid off in 20 years, and $177,525 if paid off in 30 years at the relatively high rate of 5 percent interest.

Further refinement suggests that by far the biggest cost in an educational institution is salary and not physical capital investment. It can be estimated that a $5 million instructional structure will provide 125 teacher stations. This is based on the fairly liberal assumption that construction and equipment will cost around $40,000 per classroom. All supporting services of halls, toilets, utilities, faculty offices, etc., are included in this unit cost figure per classroom. If it is further assumed (and this is a very conservative estimate) that only one teacher will use a given classroom, this $5 million capital structure can be said to have a "capacity" of 125 teachers.

In this light a $5 million building that has an average annual economic cost of $177,525 (using the higher of the two figures quoted above) can accommodate 125 teachers. Dividing $177,525 by 125 teachers yields a cost of about $1500 per year per teacher over the life span of the building or $125 per month (for 12 months) per teacher. In contrast to the investment in physical capital per teacher (or "production worker in education") the investment in average annual salary for the teacher in 1972–1973 was $10,240. On a monthly basis this is a salary cost of about $853.

Salary and physical capital costs have been presented in comparable annual cost units. The monthly salary payments to teachers are more than six times the monthly investments in physical plant. This is a very conservative ratio. Actual data may show that monthly salary is ten times the monthly rate investments in plant and equipment. Education is a human capital intensive system rather than a physical capital intensive system.

It is not uncommon to hear that business and industry could not operate at a profit if the same low degree of utilization of physical capital investments were permitted as is presently characteristic of most educational institutions. Although plant shutdowns for 2 to 4 weeks are not uncommon in some industries, 2- or 3-month shutdowns are unusual. Such statements assume, without adequate basis, that conditions of physical capital utilization appropriate for one industry are appropriate for all. The increase in efficiency from year-round operation of an industry characterized by a large physical capital investment per production worker (physical capital intensive) may be greater than that for an industry characterized by a limited physical capital investment per production worker. For example, assume that an industry purchases a $120,000 machine whose useful life is 10 years and that only one worker is needed to use it for production purposes. The average annual cost of the machine over the 10-year period is $12,000; with three shifts using it, the capital investment per production worker, not including building costs, is $4,000. It can be seen that the physical capital investment per production worker is sufficiently high to warrant 24-hour use (by three shifts) as well as year-round operation. The $12,000 per year per worker for physical plant and equipment investments is eight times that in education.

Although the absolute amount of physical capital investment per teacher probably increases with the educational level of the pupil, the importance of human capital (teachers) probably increases even more.

There is a need for more realistic appraisals of the economics of year-round school operation to answer such questions as:

1. Because physical capital costs are mainly fixed in the short run while

salaries are variable, how large would savings in cost per unit of output or per production worker be if year-round schooling were universal?

2. How would such savings vary between different levels of schooling? For example, would they be important at lower levels and less significant at upper levels?

3. What percent of the students at each educational level would have to be willing to attend summer sessions in order to lower the unit cost of education at each level?

More hard data are required to determine whether industries of various types, within educational as well as noneducational sectors, differ in amounts of physical capital investment per production worker. Likewise, the relation between physical capital inputs, nonphysical capital inputs, periods of operation, and efficiency needs to be analyzed.

The writer, in conjunction with economists at Florida State University, Dr. George Macesich and Dr. Marshall Colberg, submits the following statements that deserve further testing:

1. Industries with relatively low amounts of physical capital investment per production worker will gain less in efficiency from continuous operation than will industries characterized by relatively higher amounts of physical capital investment per production worker.

2. The cost of labor inputs is at least as significant in promoting efficiency in industries employing relatively high wage and specialized manpower resources as is full-time utilization of physical capital investments in the form of land, buildings, and equipment.

3. Educational institutions can be classed with industries having relatively low levels of physical capital investment per production worker.

4. Educational institutions can be classed with industries having a unit of labor cost that is significantly higher than the unit of physical capital investment; therefore, any increases in efficiency (at a given level of quality) must concentrate on the productivity of human capital inputs rather than greater utilization of physical capital inputs.

The key to year-round school operation resulting in saving money lies in pupil acceleration, that is, a pupil completing the traditional 12 grades in 9 or 10 years rather than in 12. If the year-round school plan includes a summer program that enriches without accelerating, the plan will simply cost more. The most recent review of the research on the extended school year and its financial impact was reported by Johns,[5] who in 1969 claimed that sufficient evidence was available to indicate the following about extended year plans.

1. When initially installed such plans will increase school costs a maximum of 10 to 11 percent.

2. After a transition period there may be no increase or even a small reduction in costs while providing better quantity and quality of services.

3. Enrichment with no pupil acceleration may increase operating costs more than can be saved through more intensive building utilization.

4. If designed primarily to save classroom space, such plans will have a short life, for operating cost increases will exceed building cost decreases.

5. There will be no substantial increase in the number of districts operating in the extended year mode in the next ten years.

[5]R. L. Johns et al., *Dimensions of Educational Need,* Gainesville, Fla.: National Educational Finance Project, 1969, pp. 203–204.

One local school system study by a relatively small city school system in Wisconsin revealed that more would have to be spent to introduce a year-round school operation than could be served through more intensive physical plant utilization or not constructing a new facility. Other data demonstrate that year-round school operations have failed to reduce school costs measurably. The lack of nationwide implementation of such schemes may be traced to the failure of year-round schemes to demonstrate any measurable cost advantages. The various schemes have gained publicity at least three different times since 1945 but have never caught on for long.

The major point in this extended analysis of the economics of year-round school operations is that the major gains in the improvement in efficiency of school operations will come from improvements in the productivity of its professional work force, namely, teachers and administrators. Eighty-five percent of the school budget goes for personnel and it is there that the largest efficiency gains are to be made. It is predicted that because new school plant construction in the 1970s will be far below that of the 1950s and 1960s plus the initial stabilization and then decline in pupil enrollments in the 1970s, the popularity of various year-round school operations will decline as well.

Energy and the school calendar

The school calendar may be viewed as an instrument for conserving energy as well as a respite from the rigors of learning. The traditional factors influencing the design of the school calendar were program, staff, space, and past practices. Concern for the conservation of energy immediately following the Arab oil embargo of October, 1973, added a new dimension to calendar design.

There are many types of school calendars. There is the daily schedule with fixed starting and stopping times plus a number of class periods of so many minutes or hours per day. There is the weekly calendar, which assumes a five-day week starting on Monday and concluding on Friday. Saturday has not been part of the school's weekly calendar nor has a period of less than five days received serious consideration. Lastly, the annual calendar has been fixed to include nine or ten months with appropriate vacation periods.

A variety of alternative calendar arrangements may be designed to satisfy schools in various locations in the nation. In designing such alternatives, the year-round calendar, which has more to offer where increased building utilization and teacher deployment concerns predominate, may be more of a problem than a help when energy conservation is paramount. Obviously the utilization of facilities during every month to meet learner and program demands precludes the shutdown of facilities for weeks or months to reduce heavy heating or cooling demands when fuel and electrical demands for schools are at a peak. Much the same can be said where double sessions prevail. To employ the calendar in the development of strategies to save heat and electricity demands periods of non-building use.

A number of winter energy-saving schedules are possible. No hard data are available to suggest which are most likely to produce lower energy consumption in a particular portion of the country. The traditional school calendar of starting some time around Labor Day and concluding some time around Memorial Day is not designed to do much about nonhuman energy conservation. A winter energy-saving schedule for schools in climates experiencing severe winters may well necessitate an annual school schedule that would eliminate a spring recess, or an Easter recess, or limit release from instruction during a religious holiday to one or two days at most. These Easter, or spring, vacations occur during a time of year when consumption of heating energy in the form of gas, oil, or coal and/or electricity for cooling is likely to be nominal. In contrast, the times of severest cold may necessitate extended winter school vacations. Thus, a four to six week winter vacation could be scheduled any time from December 15 to February 1, instead of the usual two weeks. To avoid the very hot months of the summer there would be the compensation of eliminating one week of spring vacation and starting school one or two weeks earlier and concluding school one or two weeks later. Obviously in warmer climates where the convening of school earlier than Labor Day and concluding significantly later than Memorial Day would call for more cooling, that is, use of greater amounts of electrical energy for air conditioning with relatively little gain in energy saving, the winter vacation could be shorter.

Another contingency plan would be a school calendar based on a four-day week and extending each day from the typical 6 to 6½ hours to 8½ hours. The important point is the total number of minutes of instruction per week and the total number of weeks per academic year rather than the distribution in any fixed pattern. Schools could start as early as 8:30 A.M. and conclude as late as 5:00 P.M. when four-day weeks are employed. It may not be necessary to operate four-day weeks during the full nine or ten months of the total school term or

academic year. Thus, an energy saving schedule calling for a four-day week could operate between November 1 and March 1, a period of approximately four months, with its duration varying with the severity of the climate in various regions during these particular time periods. The impact of such shifts on the working mother should not be overlooked.

The point is that there are possible ways of adjusting the weekly and academic calendars to cope with severe energy shortages. The least that can be said is that an emergency plan calling for four-day weeks or long winter vacations could be developed to deal with the crisis if an energy crunch more severe than now being experienced should hit the nation. Data are lacking to identify the savings potential from the possible patterns.

Reducing the number of buildings in use may or may not be a viable alternative depending on whether the majority of students walk to buildings or are transported to them. Likewise, whether or not the buildings are operating at capacity will determine whether this is a viable option.

Busing for school transportation may demand such adjustments as the use of shoestring routes, which call for student drivers who live at the end of the route, or the shoestring, being selected as drivers. Fewer and larger-capacity buses may also be needed. An administrative arrangement may be needed that requires pupils who live as much as two miles away to walk to school.

In short, October, 1973, signaled the need for energy crisis plans, generation of energy budgets, and more careful control of energy utilization within the schools. The great variation in climatic conditions and the maturity of learners precludes setting up one plan for the entire nation. Emotional reactions are likely to be generated, as evidence by what happened when the switch to daylight savings time during the winter months meant that pupils had to leave for school in the dark. Nonetheless, the schools can and should demonstrate the kind of foresight and creativity necessary to cope with the situation, whether it lasts for one year or ten years. By the same token the willingness to make these adjustments should in no way be interpreted as vindicating the designation of schools as low-priority energy users. Their function is much too crucial to the continued greatness of this nation.

ELEMENTARY SCHOOL INSTRUCTIONAL ORGANIZATION

It is important for an instructional leader to know the various alternatives to organizing a school to facilitate pupil learning and teaching. References are made to elementary school grading patterns in Chapter 16. A more detailed review of the arguments pro and con grading from the standpoint of instructional development rather than structural analysis follows.

Graded versus nongraded patterns

Grading and grouping of pupils within grades were reviewed in part and from different perspectives in Chapters 16 and 21. These concepts impinge on the administration of education in many different ways. When the graded school organization was introduced in this nation over 130 years ago it was heralded as one of the most significant instructional innovations of all time. During the latter part of the nineteenth and the early part of the twentieth centuries, the innovative schools were those that adopted the graded organization; the traditional, noninnovative schools were the nongraded ones. A reverse opinion was promulgated during the 1950s and 1960s.

Grading, as an instructional organization system, was sometimes implemented in a rigid fashion and differences in individual learning rates were all but ignored. All pupils at a given grade level were required to learn a specific quantity of subject matter before being permitted to move up to the next grade. Such inflexible implementation of grading produced a significant amount of nonpromotion or pupil failure, and, more often than not, repeating a grade became a social punishment rather than an extension and improvement of learning experiences. This misinterpretation of the grade concept produced the undesirable lock-step approach that is presently and rightfully severely criticized. Curriculum and instruction began to search for alternatives to such rigidity.

Not long after grading came into being various proposals aimed at correcting the inflexible operation of the graded pattern began to emerge. Most plans were identified with the particular school system wherein they were developed. Some of the most famous were the St. Louis, Pueblo, Cambridge, Portland, Batavia, North Denver, Santa Barbara, and Winnetka organizational plans. These patterns aimed at a modification of grade standards but *did not seek to eliminate grading*. The St. Louis plan, introduced in 1868, sought to lessen grade rigidity by classifying students at six-week intervals. The Pueblo approach, in operation from 1888 to 1894, required all children to study all grade units, but allowed each to progress through the units at his own rate. The Gary plan was a continuation of the original platoon school and represented refinement of the principles first tried out in Bluffton, Indiana, in 1900. The Winnetka plan of 1919 provided enrichment opportunities in addition to commonly accepted elementary school studies; each pupil was allowed to progress at her own rate through the standardized grades. The Burke approach of 1913 represented one of the earliest efforts to permit individual rates of progress in promotion. The Dalton contract system of 1919 permitted the student to move to another contract upon completion of requirements according to his own rate of learning. The modern and more sophisticated development of the contract plan is known as Individually Prescribed Instruction (IPI) at the elementary level and "unipacks" at the secondary level. The Cooperative Group plan of 1930, a forerunner of the team-teaching approach, provided for a group of teachers to work together, each offering one part of the curriculum but all trying to coordinate efforts. In summary, there were attempts to recognize individual differences, to express concern for continuous progress, to individualize instruction, and to enrich learning experiences over 50 years prior to present efforts. Current reform movements are an extension of earlier ones even though some proponents of the new lack a sense of history and fail to recognize the continuing desire to improve learning and organizational patterns to achieve improvements. After World War II, the term "nongraded" became used to designate an organizational pattern first used in schools in Western Springs, Illinois in 1936, and in the Maryland Avenue Elementary School in Milwaukee in 1942.[6] Goodlad and Anderson did much to stimulate the development of the nongraded instructional pattern for elementary schools.[7]

It is extremely difficult to find a standard definition of the nongraded school. What grades are involved and even the name of the organizational scheme are not the same in all schools. The common denominator of nongraded schools is reaction to the rigidity characteristic of the graded pattern. Beyond this, definitions of nongradedness are vague, and the lack of organizational uniformity makes it difficult to ascertain when a school is or is not nongraded. Anderson in 1967 commented: "For all the publicity it has received, nongradedness apparently remains a somewhat nebulous, even confusing, concept."[8] Advocates of the nongraded school do agree on one thing: that the graded school pattern is bad and should be replaced with a nongraded pattern. Anderson concluded: "Nongradedness is a clumsy and unsuitable term, since it refers primarily to what is not rather than to what it is."[9] He pointed out that it is not a new staffing pattern such as team teaching, not a technological innovation, not a part of a curriculum reform movement, and should not be confused with departmentalization and self-containment. A full-fledged nongraded program, according to Anderson, would have:

1. Suitable provision in all aspects of the curriculum for each child (flexible grouping and subgrouping; adaptable, flexible curriculum; and a great range of material and instructional approaches).

[6]R. I. Miller, ed., The Nongraded School, New York: Harper & Row, 1967, pp. 3–5.

[7]J. I. Goodlad and R. H. Anderson, The Nongraded Elementary School, New York: Harcourt Brace Jovanovich, 1963.

[8]R. H. Anderson, "The Nongraded School: An Overview," The National Elementary Principal, vol. 47, no. 2, November 1967, pp. 4–10.

[9]Ibid.

2. Learning experiences pertinent and appropriate to the needs at the moment for each child.
3. Just the right amount of pressure for each child.
4. Success for all kinds of learners, even some degree of failure and frustration occasionally.
5. No grade levels and related promotion machinery.
6. A revised reporting system with no numerical or letter grades.
7. More sophisticated curriculum planning, evaluation, and record keeping.[10]

It may be appropriate to seek an objective definition of the word "grade" without regard to the connotations applied by promoters of the nongraded system. A grade is a class of people who are at the same stage or have the same relative position, level, rank, or degree. It can mean as well "a stage in the process." The verb "to grade" means to classify according to some appropriate standard. In education it means to classify pupils for some particular purpose and on some basis.

Every institution composed of large numbers of people must develop some systematic way for grouping or classifying them so they can benefit from the services of the institution. Even in the nongraded school it is necessary to have some kind of systematic organization, that is, some means for determining which pupils shall be assigned to which teachers. Likewise, there must be some way of determining when a pupil is to start to learn to read or write or cipher and whether he has made any progress. No proponent of the nongraded school has recommended distributing pupils to a teacher on the basis of pure chance, for this could place in one class pupils ranging in maturity from kindergarten to senior high school levels. The classification standard frequently proposed by the proponents of nongrading is the

pupil's reading level. Reading level, therefore, rather than age or years in attendance, serves as the basis upon which the pupil is "graded," or placed at a particular level in the school. In this sense, the term nongraded is a contradiction. There is a scheme for classifying a pupil to determine what learning exercises are appropriate for her and to what teacher she shall be assigned, and classification is another name for grading. But the classifying, according to the proponents of nongrading, is done on a basis purportedly more closely related to learning or to a significant achievement such as reading, rather than on the basis of some arbitrary standard such as age. (Classification of pupils is the first step in organizing into groups of various sizes for purposes of instruction.) It can be argued that proponents of the nongraded school instructional organization are reacting negatively to classifying pupils on the basis of age rather than to the classification process per se.

Learning materials, such as textbooks on reading, spelling, or arithmetic classify concepts and skills in terms of difficulty and, supposedly, the ability of the average pupil at a given age to master the concepts or skills. If the term nongraded were interpreted literally, not only would the grade designation disappear from the classroom, but no books with graded designations, obvious or disguised, could be employed. If no standards are allowed in any educational activity, we can never know where a pupil is, much less how far he has progressed; there are no bench marks against which to measure progress.

Objective analysis reveals that to grade pupils means simply to develop a system for determining where pupils can best start or continue their learning activities with teachers in instruc-

[10]Ibid.

tional centers. Pupils are placed in one situation as opposed to another to maximize learning. In Individually Guided Education and the Multiunit School the composition of groups of learners varies from skill to skill and such groups are of short duration, continuing until a performance objective is realized. It is implied that the teacher can work best with a group of pupils whose range of ability is minimal and whose backgrounds are fairly similar. What differences exist should not be permitted to interfere with learning; rather, pupil achievement potentials and other variables related to success are clustered to facilitate the teaching-learning process. Such an environment carries a greater potential for (but not a guarantee of) more effective instruction.

Research on advantages of the nongraded compared with the graded instructional organization is neither voluminous nor conclusive. Some favor the nongraded approach whereas others give advantages to the graded structural pattern.[11]

In the last analysis, it is what the teacher in the classroom does or fails to do within a given pattern of instructional organization that has the greatest impact on pupil learning, not the organizational pattern per se. Search for improvements in the educational structure must demonstrate concern for teacher arrangement, pupil classification, technology, and materials that help or hinder attainment of the most learning for a given cluster of learners. If the word "grading" is unacceptable, perhaps a better word can be found for arranging a large number of students with varied backgrounds in a systematic way to maximize services

[11]See R. F. Carbone, "A Comparison of Graded and Nongraded Elementary Schools," *The Elementary School Journal*, vol. 62, no. 2, November 1961, pp. 82–88.

and to minimize the confusion that limits learning.

To some educators, nongrading is another name for a continuous-promotion, or no-failure, policy. Because promotion implies that a child must learn a given amount within a specified period of time (a semester or a school year) and failure suggests that she has not learned the standard amount for the given period of time, there can be neither promotion nor failure if no time limit is placed upon learning a certain amount or acquiring specific skills. A major idea behind what is called "criterion-referenced" evaluation is that evaluation of learning is not based on some predetermined norm but on whether a criterion level of performance has been satisfied. How long it takes to satisfy the criterion is not supposed to be relevant, for pupils are allowed to learn at their own rate. At some point, however, those who require five years to learn to read and cipher and those who acquire the same level of reading and ciphering in two or three years must be separated in different learning situations lest one impede the progress of the other.

There is a subtle difference between continuous promotion under flexible interpretation of grade norms in a graded school, and continuous promotion in the nongraded school. In the nongraded school, there is no failure because a child works at her own pace or within the confines of her ability to learn. If it takes her four years to do something that others achieve in three, this cannot be called failure because the pupil does achieve. This works fairly well in the primary grades, but engenders difficulties in the secondary grades. The underlying premise is that any pupil can learn any skill, concept, set of facts, or appreciation of social relations if she is given enough time. The validity of the premise is questionable. Very few people have the physiological make-up to run one mile in less than four minutes no matter how long or how hard they practice; likewise, there may well be certain types of reasonings and specific intellectual skills that cannot be learned by individuals without the intellectual make-up to do so, no matter how long or how hard they work or attend school. This assumes present methods of instruction and insights into learning will prevail. Obviously if new pharmacological, electrophysical, or electronic devices are generated to carry us beyond present knowledge, then new and higher standards will have to be used. Further research is needed to determine what human limitations are; there may be far fewer than presently is suspected.

The no-failure policy in the graded school pattern is based on promotion whether or not the student has learned the required skill or the facts within the allotted time. The justification is that social development would be inhibited if the pupil were not allowed to accompany his peers into the next grade level. The problem is that at the next grade level it is assumed that pupils promoted for social reasons have achieved as much as have pupils promoted for academic achievement, and instruction at the new grade level proceeds on that basis for all pupils. Thus, it is imperative that remedial programs be provided either during the summer or continuously during the year in the next grade.

Goodlad and Rehage recognized that confusion could result if the nomenclature concerned with school organization were not clarified.[12] They

suggested vertical and horizontal dimensions to organization. Procedures for initially classifying students and for describing their progress upward through various learning levels to the point of departure from the school constitute the vertical dimension. The division of students with similar achievements into class groups or levels constitutes the horizontal dimension. Grading and nongrading are alternatives in vertical organization for instruction. Goodlad and Rehage concluded that benefits with respect to the pupils' well-being and achievement in the nongraded as opposed to the graded school have not been proved. Part of the problem is inadequacy of research, particularly the failure to identify essential organizational characteristics to differentiate a nongraded from a graded school. Although the graded school can be defined with some degree of precision, the most that can be said about the nongraded arrangement is that grade levels have been removed from some or all classes. The horizontal organization generates a variety of alternatives such as homogeneous versus heterogeneous grouping and team teaching versus single-teacher instruction.

The extent to which the nongrading is employed in public education is difficult to ascertain with precision. Usually a district is said to employ nongrading in elementary school organization if it has a nongraded primary arrangement in only one school. Data on the extent of nongraded operations in the early 1970s were presented in Chapter 16. "There are few models of nongrading—conceptual, simulated, or real."[13] It can be concluded that more continues to be written about nongraded organizational patterns than is being practiced.

[12]J. I. Goodlad and K. Rehage, "Unscrambling the Vocabulary of School Organization," *National Education Association Journal,* vol. 51, November 1962, pp. 34–36.

[13]Ibid.

Is nongraded instructional organization an innovation? It is clear that during much of the history of education, schools were nongraded. Grading, on this basis, is the more recent concept in school organization. On the other hand, modification of pupil classification to allow individual rates of progress within the school on the basis of factors other than age is of more recent origin. It can be argued, however, that if nongradedness is equated with a continuous-promotion or no-failure policy, it cannot be called new, for such policies have existed for at least 30 years. Comments by two writers confirm that the nongraded pattern is a new grouping of established concepts rather than a completely novel approach. Goodlad stressed that "nongrading has given a fresh thrust to some respectable ideas of relatively long standing."[14] Anderson pointed out that "nongradedness is by no means a new idea in American education."[15] He went on to identify four arrangements in the elementary school in 1967: "(1) uncompromising gradedness; (2) nominal but eroding gradedness (possibly the prevailing arrangement); (3) nominal nongradedness (but with disappointing evidence of gradedness still in the atmosphere); and (4) nongradedness."[16]

Class size

Size of the elementary school classroom enrollment has a bearing on instruction. The median size of the elementary school class in large urban districts was 30 pupils. Less than 5 percent of the elementary school classes contained more than 40 pupils. Class size has remained at or below

[14]Ibid.
[15]Ibid.
[16]Ibid.

this level for the last decade. It must be pointed out, however, that to millions of elementary school children enrolled in classes with 35 or more, national average has limited meaning.

The continuing educational challenge for administrators working with teachers and others to improve instructional practices is to determine classroom patterns that preserve and enhance the significant differences among students. At the same time there is a need to preserve unity in content and effective utilization of teaching resources. All these factors must be understood, along with funds available, traditions, administrative expediencies, and the like.[17]

The administrator is responsible for all aspects of the educational institution. Reducing class size has fiscal and school-plant implications. The Chicago school district reduced the average class size in Grades 1 through 8 from 36 in February, 1959, to 34 in September, 1960. To do this required 1001 additional teachers at an annual salary cost of $7,007,000.[18] This is a sizeable sum even in a district that spent $213,796,703 in 1960 for current expenses (exclusive of capital outlay and debt service). It was estimated that to reduce average elementary school class size further by only one pupil in 1961 would require approximately 375 additional teachers at an additional annual cost of $2,625,000, plus 375 additional classrooms at a cost of $11,250,000. In a much smaller school district in Madison, Wisconsin with about 31,500 pupils, the reduc-

[17]John I. Goodlad, "Classroom Organization," in Chester W. Harris, ed., Encyclopedia of Educational Research, 3rd ed., New York: Macmillan, 1960, pp. 221–225.
[18]Benjamin C. Willis, Quality Through New Directions, Annual Report of the General Superintendent of Chicago Public Schools, 1960, pp. 27–28.

tion of the pupil-teacher ratio by one during the 1974 school budget year was estimated to necessitate the employment of 67 new teachers at a cost of about $771,000, elevating a previously estimated budget of $47.6 million by about 1.6 percent. Keep in mind that "pupil-teacher ratio" is not precisely the same as "class size." Quality in public education carries a price tag as well as a program.

SECONDARY SCHOOL INSTRUCTIONAL ORGANIZATION

Secondary schools are schools for adolescents. The junior high school was organized as an institution for early adolescents, and the senior high school as a school for late adolescents. The history of the secondary school curriculum reveals four major patterns:

1. The single fixed curriculum, in which all subjects are prescribed for all students.
2. The multiple curriculum, with two or more "tracks," each of which offers a sequence of subjects designed to help the student toward common as well as specific objectives.
3. The constants-with-variables curriculum, in which certain subjects are required of all students but other subjects may be selected.
4. Combination plans that include features of both the constants-with-variables and the multiple programs.[19]

New curriculum plans attempt to compensate for the growing compartmentalization of knowledge and have led to such developments as the correlation of subjects and the core curriculum.

Between 1860 and 1900 there was a gradual increase in subjects offered. Curriculum patterns were concen-

[19]William G. Brink, "Secondary Education Programs," in Harris, ed., op. cit., p. 1262.

trated largely in traditional areas of English, mathematics, social studies, science, and foreign languages. By 1930 high schools included commercial arts, industrial arts, household arts, fine arts, and noncollege-preparatory subjects. Continued expansion of the curriculum led to establishment of the comprehensive secondary school. Extraclass activities began to develop in the 1920s and have broadened learning activities in secondary schools.

New developments, as well as dissatisfaction with existing secondary school programs, led to further experimentation and the development of the "Random Falls Plan" and the Commission on Experimental Study and Utilization of the Staff in Secondary Schools. As high schools grew in size and complexity, guidance and counseling services were added to compensate for the increasingly impersonal character of the institution. Cafeterias, health services, and transportation services were added for other reasons. The variety of services, magnitude of enrollments, and comprehensiveness of objectives have made administration of secondary institutions a complex undertaking.

Instructional programming (scheduling)

Instructional programming is the process of relating the learning opportunities available to the pupil needs and the instructional resources such as time, space, and personnel. The more popular term is scheduling; both will be used in this chapter.

The school schedule is a timetable for accomplishing previously agreed upon and stated instructional goals. It indicates what educational opportunities are available at what hour, on what days, and who is to teach them. Instructional programming is the process whereby specific teaching resources and given instructional facilities are arranged at specific times to facilitate the educational development of pupils attending an institution of learning.

Implementation of a comprehensive curriculum resulted in a departmentalized organization based on a six-period day in most secondary schools. A perennial problem for the secondary school principal is the scheduling of classwork for the semester. The schedule can be a boon or a barrier to realization of curriculum objectives. The schedule is a means of translating the educational program for the semester into units of study or learning during the school day. Length of the secondary school day varies from 4½ to 7½ hours, with the median being 7 hours, including intermissions and lunch period.

The traditional organization was an eight-period day, with each period lasting 40 to 45 minutes. The inconvenience of such a short period, particularly for classes in physical education, industrial arts, and laboratory work, in which time is needed for dressing or obtaining materials of instruction at the beginning of the period, as well as for showering, redressing, and cleaning up at the end, prompted consideration of a longer period. The supervised-study movement also contributed to a longer class period.

The usual secondary school schedule today consists of six or seven periods per day, of which one is an activity period. The length of each period varies, although the 50-minute period plus passing time is becoming standard. The median length of period is about 53 minutes in junior and 56 minutes in senior high school.

As such the schedule is a means to an end. Its value is derived from its capability to maximize the educational opportunities available to pupils and/or the ability of teachers to instruct such pupils. There is no inherent virtue in a 55- or a 40-minute period, a rotating schedule or a floating schedule over a fixed daily class period, or in a modular schedule over a nonmodular one. One schedule is superior to another only in terms of how it improves instructional opportunities and how it facilitates instructional methodology or learning psychology.

Modular schedules

New technology, particularly the computer, was tapped during the 1960s to enable the development of school schedules with instructional periods of variable length during the day, week, month, or longer period. It produced what is referred to as the modular, flexible, or flexible modular schedule. The time module, or the basic time period, in the schedule varies from school to school and ranges from 10 to 30 minutes, with most preferring a 15 or 20 minute time module. The number of such time modules in any given day devoted to a subject can also be flexible; thus there is no requirement that all classes each day be convened for the exact number of minutes demanded in most traditional schedules. For purposes of illustration assume that the basic time module is 15 minutes. If school starts at 8 A.M. and dismisses at 3 P.M., the total school time would be 7 clock hours of 60 minutes each which translates into a 28 module day. If desired, a single subject could be scheduled for three modules (45 minutes) one day and five modules (75 minutes) the next day. The flexible schedule is often linked with the team-teaching approach and the rotating schedule discussed below. The issue is not whether it can be done; there exists technology in the form of hardware and several computer programs to create an extremely flexible schedule for instructional activities. The issue is whether it should be done and whether it is necessary to vary the length of the instructional period from one day to the next or one month to the next. There are some case histories that purport much "success" and superiority for the flexible modular type of scheduling. There are others who tried and then abandoned the approach. There is no well-designed research which suggests that the flexible modular schedule produces greater learning than other types of school scheduling. There is conflicting evidence from the case studies that exist.

Other types of schedules. The rotating schedule is a variation of the six- or seven-period conventional schedule with the innovation of alternating times when classes meet. Thus, period one meets during the first time slot during one week, the second time slot during the next week, the third time slot during the third week, and so on. Other periods are rotated so that the time slots each occupies are changed each week. The rotation of period meeting times may be done daily as well as weekly. Thus, if there are seven periods per day, the same period would be in the same time slot only on every seventh school day.

The floating schedule is a more radical departure from the conventional schedule where each class meets every day of the week. Under this approach one period of the schedule "floats," or is not convened each day. Thus, what starts out as a six-period schedule actually has only five class periods meeting each day. It per-mits five periods from 60 to 75 minutes to occupy a time schedule where six or more could convene. Variations of this schedule are shown in Tables 22–1 and 22–2.

Preparation of schedules. The preparation of a schedule requires a variety of information, such as number of pupils likely to enroll. The basic procedures in constructing a secondary school schedule (instructional programming) include the gathering of the following kinds of data and activities:

1. Identify policies that may influence the schedule making.
2. Register students.
3. Determine courses or other educational experiences to be offered.
4. Determine student choices of subjects offered by grade, that is, enrollments in courses.
5. Compute number of sections needed in all courses with sizeable enrollments.
6. Determine number of faculty needed and areas of expertise.
7. Assign faculty to courses and class sections.
8. Determine school day starting and ending time.
9. Determine instructional period or module length in time and number per school day.
10. Identify rooms available for various classes.
11. Assign courses and teachers to available rooms.
12. Identify potential scheduling conflicts, that is, when two or more courses with one or a few sections desired by students may be offered during the same period.
13. Resolve or minimize schedule conflicts or have students seek alternative choices when confronted by irreconcilable conflicts.

TABLE 22–1

HORIZONTAL VERSION OF THE FLOATING SCHEDULE: A WEEKLY CLASS SCHEDULE FOR A COLLEGE PREPARATORY SOPHOMORE

Time	Period	Monday	Tuesday	Wednesday	Thursday	Friday
65 min.	1	English 10 Rm. 108	English 10 Rm. 108	English 10 Rm. 108	English 10 Rm. 108	X-Pd.[a] Typing 10 Rm. 5
65 min.	2	German 10 Rm. 11	German 10 Rm. 11	German 10 Rm. 11	X-Pd.[a] Typing 10 Rm. 5	German 10 Rm. 11
65 min.	3	Plane Geom. 10 Rm. 203	Plane Geom. 10 Rm. 203	Z-Pd.[b]	Plane Geom. 10 Rm. 203	Plane Geom. 10 Rm. 203
65 min.	4	Biology 10 Rm. 115	X-Pd.[b] Typing 10 Rm. 5	Biology 10 Rm. 115	Biology 10 Rm. 115	Biology 10 Rm. 115
65 min.	5	X-Pd.[a] Typing 10 Rm. 5	World History 10 Rm. 103	World History 10 Rm. 103	World History 10 Rm. 103	World History 10 Rm. 103

[a] X-periods can be scheduled for the first or fifth period each day, if desired, to avoid interrupting extended periods.
[b] Z-period: First and third Wednesdays, science club; second Wednesday, assembly; and fourth Wednesday, class meeting or guidance.

TABLE 22–2

VERTICAL VERSION OF THE FLOATING SCHEDULE[a]: A WEEKLY CLASS SCHEDULE FOR A NONCOLLEGE PREPARATORY STUDENT

Time	Period	Monday	Tuesday	Wednesday	Thursday	Friday
65 min.	1	Work Expr.	Work Expr.	Prob. of Democ. 12 Rm. 105	Short-hand 11 Rm. 3	X-Pd.[b] Phys. Ed. 12
65 min.	2	Work Expr.	Work Expr.	Prob. of Democ. 12 Rm. 105	X-Pd.[b] Chorus	English 12 Rm. 109
65 min.	3	Work Expr.	Work Expr.	Z-Pd.[c]	Short-hand 11 Rm. 3	English 12 Rm. 109
65 min.	4	Work Expr.	X-Pd.[b] Spanish 10 Rm. 13	Prob. of Democ. 12 Rm. 105	Short-hand 11 Rm. 3	English 12 Rm. 109
65 min.	5	X-Pd.[b] Spanish 10 Rm. 13	Work Expr.	Prob. of Democ. 12 Rm. 105	Short-hand 11 Rm. 3	English 12 Rm. 109

[a] The square pattern of the schedule facilitates a shift from horizontal position to vertical position. Pupils scheduled for work experience may be scheduled to work all day without interruption in the vertical plan. In such a schedule, the X-periods involved are either eliminated or rescheduled.
[b] X-periods: This pupil has chosen Spanish for 2 periods (120 minutes) per week, chorus for 1 period, and physical education for 1 period.
[c] Z-period: First and third Wednesdays, commercial club; second Wednesday, assembly; and fourth Wednesday, class meeting.

14. Construct preliminary schedule.
15. Try out schedule with shortened time period sessions.
16. Revise final schedule for the ensuing year.

These procedures may be executed manually, that is, without a computer. The advent of electronic data-processing equipment has greatly facilitated the development of schedules in large secondary institutions, particularly those using flexible modular schedules.

Trends in scheduling. Trends in scheduling reveal that:

1. The schedule is no longer developed by an administrator only; the judgment and experience of all members of the staff are sought and used.
2. The traditional practice of scheduling each class to meet five times per week no longer confines the schedule maker. The floating period, the two-week cycle, and the "5 by 5" plan illustrate this trend. The last allows one class to meet in an all-day session, permitting long consecutive study of one project or participation in a lengthy field trip. Modular schedules represent yet another variation.
3. Two or more periods are often allotted for a given teaching situation. This is common practice in junior high school and apparently its use is increasing in senior high school.
4. An increase in total length of the period, allowing more laboratory time or more study time with a given teacher is generally accepted as desirable. This tends to reduce the number of student contacts for each teacher each day, but also reduces elective choices for each student because of the fewer number of periods in the day.
5. The assignment of teachers to otherwise unscheduled classrooms is recommended as a temporary expediency for increasing building utilization.
6. The difficulty of feeding many students in a short time has stimulated much lunch-hour experimentation. Successive groups of classes are scheduled to the service area as facilities become vacant. Instead of several distinct lunch periods, there is a constant flow of students and teachers to keep facilities in constant use. Total length of time devoted to the lunch period is reduced for such purposes.
7. In large high schools a departmental program schedule is made through the leadership of the department chairman and then related to the total school program in order to avoid conflicts.
8. The large amount of clerical work involved in preparing a schedule, whether decentralized or not, is being simplified through use of punch cards or electronic equipment.[20]

Size of instructional centers

Most research on high school size has concentrated on minimums required to achieve a comprehensive program at a reasonable cost per pupil. Wright[21] summarized 18 research studies on high school size. Variables involved in determining optimum size were curricular offerings, extraclass activities, staff qualifications, relations, and pupil achievement. The variety of curriculum offerings increased with an increase of enrollment, up to approximately 2000 students. Beyond that point, there was duplication rather than more program variety. An enrollment of at least 1000 in a four-year high school was considered essential for a minimum variety in educational course offerings. Qualifications of teachers generally increased with size of enrollment. Schools enrolling fewer than 400 pupils usually did not attract the best-

[20]American Association of School Administrators, *The High School in a Changing World,* Thirty-sixth Yearbook, Washington, D.C.: The Association, 1958, pp. 202–203.

[21]Grace S. Wright, *Enrollment Size and Educational Effectiveness of the High School,* U.S. Office of Education, circular no. 732, Washington, D.C.: GPO, 1964.

qualified teachers. Most studies reported that in larger schools there were more experienced, better prepared teachers; larger percentages were in their major fields; less teacher turnover was evident. Some studies found little or no significant relation between pupil achievement and school size. Three reported that student achievement in school with a minimum enrollment of 500 was superior to that in schools with a smaller enrollment. There was general agreement that small schools provided greater pupil participation in extraclass activities; the most active participants in extraclass activities were pupils in schools of fewer than 300. Studies that considered school community, staff, and teacher-pupil relations recommended enrollments of 1200 to 1600.

The optimum size of the high school for all-around educational effectiveness appears to be less than 2000 pupils, but how much less is not clear. Organization of secondary schools for more than 2000 pupils does not further improve educational opportunities. In the mid-1960s Pittsburgh planned to build the five "great high schools," with enrollments of 6000 in one center, suggesting a departure from the trend of reducing attendance-unit size. This did not come to pass. In the past three or four decades there has been evidence of a movement away from the very large high school. The three largest high schools in 1934 enrolled more than 10,000 pupils each; three others had from 9000 to 10,000 pupils each. No high school in 1946 had as many as 9000 pupils and not one in 1952 enrolled as many as 7000. There is no evidence to substantiate the educational superiority of enrollments of 6000 or more in a given center. As indicated previously, a high

school with more than 2000 pupils tends to lose its economic advantage, for duplication rather than extension of opportunities results. The "great high school," like the educational-park concept, appears to be more closely related to attempts to deal with social conditions within large urban areas than to improvement of educational opportunities alone.

Grade grouping within instructional centers

The evolution of educational opportunity determines to some extent the grade groupings within instructional centers. Thus, when the common school was limited to elementary education only, and it was assumed that at age 14 a boy or girl was ready to enter the world of work, this age was the terminal point of formal education. The school terminated at Grade 8. The secondary school started as a separate institution composed of Grades 9 through 12. The community junior college also started as a separate instructional institution with its own facilities for similar reasons.

Early in this century it was argued that separation of pupils in instructional centers should be based on natural factors such as human growth and development rather than on arbitrary concepts. It was reasoned that the coming of adolescence, typically at age 12 or 13, is a significant time that corresponds for most children with the period between Grades 6 and 7. If a child enters first grade at 6 or kindergarten at 5, he will with continuous promotions be approximately 12 years old at the end of Grade 6. Elementary school was thus conceived as terminating at Grade 6, because it was a school for preadolescent children.

Because the next 6 years, corresponding to Grades 7 through 12, constitute two stages of adolescence, it seemed desirable to separate early adolescents from late adolescents. The junior high school, Grades 7 through 9, was designed for the early adolescent; the senior high school, Grades 10 through 12, for the late adolescent. These concepts provided a defensible approach to school organization.

There were, however, problems. One was articulation between Grades 6 and 7, for the elementary school was usually self-contained and the junior high school departmentalized. Articulation problems were attacked and difficulties minimized, for the junior high school maintained some features of the elementary and some of the high school. It took at least a generation to move from traditional 8–4 organization to the 6–3–3 pattern. All data available today indicate that the 6–3–3 pattern predominates.

In the 1960s a new pattern, the middle school, came under discussion. It was conceived as an instructional center between the senior high and the elementary school. As indicated elsewhere there appears to be little consistency in defining which grades constitute the middle school. Some place Grades 6 through 8 in the middle school, some Grades 5 through 8, some Grades 5 through 9, and others Grades 6 and 7 only. Because so few instructional centers operate under this plan, no general statements can be made about the middle school today.

The very large high schools are introducing the school-within-a-school concept. Thus, one large high school of 4500 pupils on the same site organized three 1500 pupil units with each being given a special identity. It was one way to cope with the problem of school bigness where an individual pupil could be lost easily.

EVALUATION OF LEARNING AND PUPIL PROGRESS

National education assessment

During the 1960s the national assessment of educational performance was one of the most significant and actively debated issues in American education. It seemed less of an issue in the 1970s. According to the Exploratory Committee on Assessing the Progress of Education, very little information is available on a national basis regarding educational progress and purposes: how much students really know, what subjects they do best in or poorest in, and the relation between income levels and learning. The Exploratory Committee was financed initially by the Carnegie Corporation; its work was led by Dr. R. W. Tyler. The major purpose of the national assessment project was to provide the lay public with census-like data on educational levels for various sections of the population.

Those promoting national assessment argued that a new approach to educational evaluation was needed to help people understand educational problems and needs, and to guide their efforts in developing sound public policy on education. The national assessment would evaluate the educational progress of large populations; it would not be focused on individual students, classrooms, schools, or school systems; it would not evaluate the effectiveness of a given teaching method or type of school or classroom organization. New tests were developed for large-scale assessment of a large population sample from various sections of the nation.

Those opposed to national assessment were concerned that it really meant "national testing." Even though it was to be based on a sample in a given region, it would indict all schools and pupils, good or bad, within the area. It was the opinion of this group that such national testing would tend to create a national curriculum. There would be a great likelihood that teachers would teach to help youngsters do well on the national tests of achievement. The opposition registered no objection to creating new instruments of evaluation to improve understanding of pupil achievements at the extremes of the ability spectrum. They stressed testing as a diagnostic instrument that would lead to the design of learning exercises to correct shortcomings. However, they pointed out that volumes of census-like data on education are already available to the public. They argued that the strained analogies between gross national product, consumer price, and mortality indexes and the national assessment were a coverup for the real purpose of the program, namely, to produce a national curriculum.

Marking systems

Marking systems represent attempts at reporting the progress of learning. They are results of whatever instruments teachers employ to evaluate learning.

The variability and unreliability of school marks have long been of concern to teachers, administrators, and parents alike. Marking systems generally were based on percentage up to approximately 1920. After 1920 the percentage system began to be replaced by letters or other symbols representing a range of percentages.

The ABCDF symbols, or their equivalent, remain based on the quantitative approach to marking. Percentage or letter marking is quite different from the descriptive system of marking which attempts to measure how much progress the individual has made in relation to his ability. Descriptive systems are less well understood than the quantitative systems.

Marks and reports on pupil progress have been developed to inform parents, to enable school and home to work together, to motivate and stimulate learning, to form an administrative shorthand to measure learning, and to serve as a means of comparison among schools. To inform parents, marks and the report card upon which they are inscribed must be easily understood. Too much emphasis on marks as a means of stimulating or measuring learning can lead to student short cuts to good marks through such devices as cheating.

Studies of marking and report cards show considerable concern over the validity of marks and their lack of objective meaning. Many desirable learning outcomes resist precise mathematical measurement. The reliability and validity of teachers' marks are questionable. For example, the same English test, graded by 142 different teachers, received marks of from 50 to 98 percent; the same history paper, examined by 70 teachers, was marked from 43 to 90 percent; a model-answer paper made by a teacher was marked from 40 to 90 percent by other teachers; and even the same geometry paper was scored from 28 to 90 percent. Poorly designed tests further confuse the issue.

Most school systems issue four or five progress reports on pupils to parents during the school year. More than three-fourths of the districts report pupils' progress by means of conferences with parents and report cards. This combination method is used less frequently in junior and senior high school than in elementary school. The trend, however, at all levels is toward a combination of reporting by card plus conferences with parents.

The so-called passing mark ranges from 60 to 75 percent for no apparent reason. "Marking on the curve" is not as uniform as it may appear. For example, in some systems, 3 percent of pupils receive A's, in others 7 percent, and in still others 10 percent. In some systems, 50 percent of pupils receive C's, in another 38 percent, and in still others 40 percent. The curve of normal distribution is derived from an adequate and representative sampling of a characteristic that is amenable to objective and precise measurement.

Marks can reflect achievement only or incorporate such ideas as effort, attitude, or neatness. Most schools consider only achievement in awarding grades. Over two-thirds of the schools use letter grades in preference to numerical marks. Some use a dual mark that includes two symbols such as a large letter with a small numerical subscript. The letter indicates achievement only, and the numerical subscript, such attitudes as effort.

Ability grouping compounds the problem of marking. Some students in high-ability groups receive low marks when in competition with all mentally-gifted pupils. These same students could have received much higher marks had they been in a heterogeneous group. Such students in gifted sections complain that lower marks hurt their chances for college scholarships. To circumvent this problem, some school systems use the same letter but award a higher honor point-count for a B in sections of the gifted than for a B in regular sections. Thus, the honor point-count in regular sections is A = 4 points, B = 3 points, C = 2 points, and D = 1 point; in gifted sections it is A = 5 points, B = 4 points, C = 3 points, and D = 2 points.

Promotion and failure

Current thought on pupil failure and nonpromotion in the elementary grades is as follows:

1. Since 1900 there has been a decrease in the rate of pupil failure leading to nonpromotion and repetition of a course of study.
2. Threats of failure do not necessarily motivate children to work harder.
3. Nonpromotion and subsequent repetition of the subject do not always increase mastery of subject matter.
4. The fact that boys fail more often than girls, despite insignificant differences in scores on intelligence and achievement tests, raises the question whether promotion is based on factors other than academic achievement, such as deportment and neatness of written work.
5. Failure of an individual pupil is usually caused by a number of factors sometimes beyond his control.[22]

Nonpromotion occurs only about one-third as often today in the elementary school as it did 50 years ago. Nonpromotion in elementary schools dropped from approximately 16 percent in 1909 to about 5 percent in 1949. In the past, the graded school organization demanded a certain level of academic achievement before promotion. In the elementary grades, a student delinquent in a single subject was retained in that grade even though he did well in other subjects. The grade-standards approach resulted in failures of 10 to 20 percent of all pupils, and this was considered defensible and proper. Studies indicated that the most fail-

[22]National Education Association, "Pupil Failure and Non-Promotion," *Research Bulletin,* vol. 37, no. 1, February 1959, pp. 16–17.

ures in elementary school occurred in the first grade, and the next most in the second grade. The fewest failures were in the eighth grade. A 1933 study showed that 20 percent of all pupils in the first grade failed each year. This created a serious administrative problem in the primary division. The situation was alleviated somewhat when underage children were prevented from entering, because these pupils experienced the greatest amount of difficulty in learning. Although at present almost all systems report that 90 percent of the pupils in each of the first two grades are promoted at the end of each year, in many districts the rate of promotion is somewhat lower in Grade 1 than in other grades. Causes of failure and reasons for nonpromotion are being given more consideration and study. A prominent reason for demanding repetition of a grade is irregular attendance.

Early studies of the rate of failure at the secondary-school level showed the range among schools to be from 2 to 80 percent. More recent studies indicate a range of from 0.02 to 10.6 percent. Great efforts are being exerted at this level to determine the reasons of failure.

Annual promotion is presently the dominant pattern. Promotions at the end of a quarter or a semester were developed as a means of making failure less serious. Prior to 1940, semiannual promotion was the typical pattern in the large cities. Experience proved seminannual and quarterly promotion plans too cumbersome. By 1948, 93 percent of the public-school systems had annual promotion policies.

Continuous-promotion policies

Far more controversial than when promotion shall occur is whether there shall be a continuous-promotion policy or no-failure plan. The continuous-promotion policy is based on the concept that success is a better regulator of conduct than is failure. Failure as a mode of learning is deemed inadequate because lasting failure ends in frustration rather than stimulation. There is evidence that elementary school children and others who have not been promoted one or more times are rated by both teachers and pupils as having more undesirable personality and behavior traits than do regularly promoted children. Beneficial effects of nonpromotion are limited.

A continuous-promotion policy is not without problems. These difficulties can be compounded if serious consideration is not given to the following factors:

1. Some teachers can motivate pupils to study only through fear of failure. Continuous promotion removes the only prop supporting this teaching method. An attempt must be made to rehabilitate such teachers before a continuous-promotion policy can be effective.

2. The curriculum must be adapted to the interest and needs of the pupils.

3. A remedial program is necessary to help those promoted with the age group who lack the necessary skills to succeed at the higher grade levels.

4. Smaller classes are necessary so that the teachers can know each pupil as an individual and work with her from her present level of accomplishment.

5. There is a need to promote public understanding because past experiences indicate a resistance within the community to accept new ideas that conflict with the traditional approach.

6. A continuous-promotion system re-

quires understanding what practices contain motivational features desirable for efficient instruction and learning.

Requirements for graduation

An analysis of high school graduation requirements shows that almost 80 percent of the schools have only one required course of study. During the last five years, most high schools have been increasing their requirements in mathematics, science, English, and social studies for graduation from high school. A study by the Research Division of the National Education Association indicated that 90 percent of high schools offer only one type of diploma. Some offer a certificate of attendance for those members of the graduating class who are unable to meet the requirements for this diploma.[23]

The Bureau of the Census reported that high school completion more than doubled during the 1960s for persons 25 years or older. Thus, 52.3 percent of those over 25 had high school diplomas in 1970 as compared to 24.1 percent in 1960.

Performance contracting

During the 1960s experiments were designed to determine if the instructional responsibilities, traditionally the most important challenge confronting a school, could be better discharged by agencies in the private sector by employing special contractors who would be paid according to how much the pupils actually learned. Teachers are typically employed under a contract calling for performance of specified services over a given period of

[23]National Education Association, "High School Diplomas," *Research Bulletin*, vol. 37, no. 4, December 1959, pp. 114–117, 121–127.

time without regard to actual learning outcomes. The so-called performance contract for instructional services is actually a variable payment contract with the payment scale increased or decreased according to how much pupils actually learned.

Results reported and audited in the early 1970s demonstrated that the highly publicized claims of private contractors were not substantiated. More was promised than could be delivered. Much less is heard now about performance contracting as a viable alternative for instructional leaders. Nonetheless, under special conditions the concept may prove to be worthy of further consideration. The performance contracting experiment did serve to focus on learning outcomes rather than simply on inputs such as teacher salaries or books. Vendors of school instructional materials may be asked to indicate the impact of such materials on learning outcomes.

SUMMARY

The objective of any scheme of instructional organization is to differentiate and coordinate time, personnel, and resources available to schools to maximize learning opportunities for all students. Organization is a means to an end. There is little evidence whether the variable of instructional organization has more, equal, or less impact on pupil learning than other variables influencing the learning process. The present period is not the only time in which new ways of organizing pupils have been developed. There is agreement on the desirability of fostering lofty objectives, such as individualizing instruction, allowing each child to progress at his own pace, and improving learning. There is less consensus on which instructional organization patterns realize such goals most efficiently.

Instructional organization is necessitated by complexity. It was of limited concern when there was only one school plant in the district or only enough pupils to need one teacher.

Time is an important aspect of the teaching-learning process. How the school day should be divided into time periods and how much of the year a pupil should attend school are controversial issues that affect the instructional program. The school year has been influenced by traditional practices of an agricultural society. It has been changing slowly. In the past century the school year has been lengthened from three to nine months. The year-round school idea is debated anew, but it is not a new concept. Some variations are the four-quarter year with rotating attendance, the 48-week school year, 45–15 plan and summer school. Perhaps the most practical approach is compulsory attendance for nine or ten months, plus voluntary attendance in summer sessions. Summer sessions have been broadened to include remedial work, developing avocational interests, enriching educational experiences, and providing special opportunities for study on the part of professional staff members.

The length of the typical elementary-school day is between 5½ and 6 hours. The typical school day for secondary school is approximately 7 hours. Most elementary grades (1 through 6) are nondepartmentalized, whereas most junior and senior high schools follow departmentalized programs. Schedule making in the secondary school is undergoing considerable reevaluation in spite of recent developments.

The graded school at one time was heralded as a significant instructional innovation. Today many proponents of the nongraded movement consider it an abomination. There were a number of previous proposals aimed at correcting rigidity in the operation of graded school patterns. There is no standard definition of the nongraded school. It appears to be a new clustering of some highly respected concepts in education. More has been written about the nongraded school than has been translated into practice. Relatively few districts employ the system. It is most likely to be found in large districts and in the primary grades. There is little research to support adoption of nongraded school organization.

The secondary school schedule is a timetable for accomplishing instructional goals. In the process, specific teaching resources and instructional facilities are arranged in time slots. New technology, particularly the computer, has enabled this development and rapid change of schedule modules. Modular flexible scheduling appears to be a new effort to improve a traditional concern.

There appears to be some evidence that optimum high-school enrollment is around 2000. Schools larger than this suffer duplication rather than extension of educational opportunities.

National assessment was one of the most hotly debated issues of the 1960s. Interest in it waned considerably in the 1970s.

Marks and marking systems in public schools aimed at evaluating learning have long been the subjects of investigation and concern. The movement has been away from percentage systems to those based on letter grades. Attempts have also been made to move from a strictly quantitative evaluation to a description of individual growth and development. The number of adults 25 and over with a high school diploma more than doubled in the 1960s.

Performance contracting for instruction outcomes gained considerable attention in the 1960s. The results reported in the early 1970s showed that private contractors promised more than they could deliver.

QUESTIONS

1. Why should there be any type of instructional organization?
2. What are the essential elements of the nongraded school?
3. Trace the history of significant efforts aimed at overcoming rigidity in the implementation of the graded school pattern.
4. What are the advantages and disadvantages of year-round school operation?
5. What is flexible scheduling?
6. What is the difference between the no-failure policy in nongraded and graded schools?
7. What is meant by national assessment of education?

SELECTED REFERENCES

Anderson, R. H., "The Nongraded School: An Overview," *The National Elementary Principal,* vol. 47, no. 2, November 1967, pp. 4–10.

Carbone, R. F., "A Comparison of Graded and Nongraded Elementary Schools," *The Elementary School Journal,* vol. 62, no. 2, November 1961, pp. 82–88.

Carpenter, Polly and George R. Hall, *Case Studies in Educational Performance Contracting, Conclusions and Implications,* R-90011 HEW, Santa Monica, Cal.: RAND Corp., 1971, p. 51.

Education U.S.A., *Individually Prescribed Instruction,* Special Report, 1201 Sixteenth Street, N.W., Washington, D.C.: Education U.S.A., 1968.

National Education Association, "Grade Organization and Nongrading Patterns," *Research Bulletin,* vol. 4, no. 4, December 1967, pp. 118–120.

National Education Association, *Planning and Organizing for Teaching,* Project on Instructional Program of the Public Schools, Washington, D.C.: The Association, 1963, p. 7.

Saville, Anthony, *Instructional Programming,* Columbus, Ohio: Chas. E. Merrill, 1973.

23

ECONOMIC DIMENSIONS OF ADMINISTRATION: SCHOOL FINANCE AND LOGISTICAL SUPPORT SERVICES

Schools consume resources in the pursuit of desirable educational objectives. Administrators are charged with identifying, procuring, and managing the variety of resources that are required to operate an educational institution. While the administrator should not become so engrossed in financial details that he neglects to keep abreast of educational developments, neither can he ignore the financial implication of instructional programs without endangering the welfare of the school system. Finance and the curriculum are interrelated in a school system. (The teacher may ignore the former to concentrate on the latter, but the administrator cannot pursue such limited strategies.) What is done in one area will influence the other, and the superintendent of schools must exercise administrative leadership in both areas.

In this chapter the economic dimension of administration will be examined in terms of the procurement and management of financial resources for education. School support, once primarily a local matter, has become increasingly the concern of the state and more recently of the federal government. A whole new series of fiscal relations for public education is evolving. After resources have been secured, school business management becomes important. The terms "logistical support services" or management of educational resources will be used more frequently here than "school business management" because they more accurately describe the contributions of such services to the educational system.

SUPPORT FOR PUBLIC EDUCATION

Approaches to school support have always mirrored the times, particularly the economy and value systems of the given period, and have been modified continually to cope with emerging challenges. Early in our history a large part of school support came from nonmonetary sources. Patrons provided services to schools (supplying fuel or wood, boarding teachers, taking care of the fire, or making repairs to the school building) in lieu of money. Later there was an attempt to support public education from income derived from land endowments and rents, lotteries, and gifts and bequests. (Lotteries appear to be making a comeback in recent years.) During the early part of the nineteenth century, it was hoped that income from lands received from the state and federal governments would provide all the money needed to operate schools. The futility of this hope became evident as the nation grew and demands upon public schools exceeded all expectations. Clearly, limiting school support to non-tax resources was creating a financial crisis, and a new method was tried—financing education almost entirely by means of a local property tax. It made sense during a period of our history when local units of government, such as school districts, were the predominant tax-collecting and tax-spending bodies. Prior to 1930 the tax collected by state and federal governments combined was less than that collected by local governments.

By the last quarter of the nineteenth century, the local property tax had become the backbone of public school support. Local initiative could be expressed if funds from property tax were available in the quantity necessary. If financial resources were lacking, local initiative degenerated into inertia. State regulations were developed to minimize the differences in quality of educational programs within the state. The use of property tax during the last half of the nineteenth century enabled schools to meet the challenges of the times. Today, this nineteenth-century support system dominates twentieth-century educational institutions which are facing problems of a magnitude and complexity never envisioned in the nineteenth century and barely comprehended at present. Public school enrollments remain at high levels. Widespread inflation has taken its toll of the school dollar. Teachers call for higher salary levels. In addition schools are asked to do more, to keep pupils longer, and to teach those who either resist learning or lack the ability for

success under normal conditions. The resources allotted to public education have in fact been increasing somewhat faster than enrollment, though clearly less than is necessary to meet the widespread desire for excellence. School boards and administrators charged with procuring adequate resources for quality school programs during the early 1970s encountered increasing resistance from taxpayers at all levels.

Magnitude of school expenditures

Expenditures for public elementary and secondary schools, exclusive of the cost of new buildings and other items not considered current expenditures, showed relatively small increases during the 1930s. Since then the total spent doubled or almost tripled in every decade. Thus, total annual current expenditure for schools in 1939–1940 was $1.94 billion, but by 1949–1950 hit almost $4.69 billion. Expenditures almost tripled in the 1950s, hitting about $12.33 billion by 1959–1960. By 1969–1970 the current expenditures exceeded $34.22 billion or almost tripled again. What was recorded for the annual current expenditures for education over a thirty year period, from 1939–1940 to 1969–1970, jumped from less than $2 billion to more than $34.2 billion, an increase of over 1700 percent! Local school districts in New York City, Los Angeles, and Chicago now have budgets that exceed $1 billion per year. It is nothing short of remarkable that taxpayer resistance to further increases is not more vehement than it is presently or that it didn't appear sooner. Estimates for 1973–1974 place the annual school expenditures at about $49.2 billion. If gains registered in previous decades continue in the 1970s the $100 billion annual expenditures could be reached by the end of the present decade. If the rate of increase abates somewhat the $100 billion figure will not be reached until the 1980s. A major concern for educators and lay persons alike is whether existing school finance systems are capable of generating revenues on the magnitude of $100 billion annually. There is every indication that a dramatic new system of educational finance will have to be produced very soon in the 1970s or else a severe financial crisis will be faced in the late 1970s or the 1980s at the latest.

An analysis of the increase of $14.9 billion in school expenditures between 1957–1958 and 1967–1968, revealed that 40 percent could be attributed to additions for quality of education (about $6.0 billion), 25 percent to growth in school enrollment (about $3.7 billion), and 35 percent to inflation (about $5.2 billion).[1] Inflation promises to be a continuing factor in rising school costs during the 1970s.

Larger enrollments usually imply larger expenditures. A unit cost figure such as current expenditures per pupil in average daily attendance (ADA) may be used to show how much more is being spent to educate each pupil in present versus previous years. Current expenditures per pupil in ADA were about $88 in 1939–1940; $208.83 in 1949–1950; $375.40 in 1959–1960; and $816 in 1969–1970. In 1972–1973 it reached $1,026 per pupil in ADA. It is apparent that the expenditures per pupil increased substantially between 1939–1940 and 1969–1970, but at a significantly lower rate than that for gross current expenditures for the same period.

[1]Committee on Educational Finance, National Education Association, *What Everyone Should Know About Financing Our Schools,* Washington, D.C.: The Association, 1968, pp. 11–12.

There is considerable variation among the states in expenditures per pupil. Thus, the current expenditures per pupil in ADA in 1972–1973 in Alabama was $590, the lowest, and in New York was $1,584, the highest. States in the mideast showed expenditures per pupil in 1972–1973 of $1,376, the highest in the nation, compared with the southeast of $789, the lowest.

About one-fourth of the increase in expenditures during the 1960s could be attributed to enrollment increases. In contrast, about two-thirds could be traced to increased spending for teachers and other instructional personnel.

Capital outlay expenditures for new facilities for school systems increased as well. Thus, capital outlay rose from almost $258 million in 1939–1940 to $1.01 billion in 1949–1950; $2.66 billion in 1959–1960; and $4.66 billion in 1969–1970. The 1972–1973 capital outlays were $5.0 billion.

Annual interest payment on the school debt demonstrated a more dramatic rise than did capital outlay. Interest payment grew from approximately $130.9 million in 1939–1940 to $489.5 million in 1959–1960. Owing to the tremendous amount of school-plant construction in the years after World War II, financed in large part by bonded debt, annual interest payments totaled more than $1.66 billion in 1973–1974 and will stay at a very high figure during the rest of the 1970s.

Total school expenditures (current expenditure, interest payment, and capital outlay) grew from $2.344 billion in 1939–1940 to almost $40.683 billion in 1969–1970. In 1972–1973 the $51.9 billion annual total expenditures for public elementary and secondary schools only exceeded the $50 billion level for the first time; then in 1973–1974 it climbed to about $55.86 billion. *Total* educational expenditures may exceed $100 billion annually before the end of the present decade.

The total expenditures in 1967–1968 for the nation's private and public education at all levels (from kindergarten through graduate programs in higher education) were $57.2 billion. They reached a total of $90.2 billion in 1972–1973. Expenditures for all educational programs in the United States exceeded $100 billion by 1974–1975.

Expenditures for education during the 1960s increased at a rate greater than increases in the nation's wealth as measured by the GNP (Gross National Product). The percent of the GNP devoted to expenditures for private and public schools at all levels from kindergarten through universities remained between approximately 3 and 4 percent in the 1930s; dropped below 3 percent during most of the 1940s; increased from 3.4 percent in 1951 to 5.1 percent in 1959; and climbed even further from 5.6 percent in 1961 to 7.6 percent in 1969. By 1971 the ratio between educational expenditures and the GNP reached the record level of 8.0 percent. The nation, indeed, has invested an increasing percent of its resources in education (public and private) at all levels.

Sources of school revenues

The challenge confronting education administrators is where the school revenues (money) to support the increasing magnitude of school expenditures will come from. A brief review of sources of revenue follows, but first some basic concepts must be defined.

All school revenues are receipts but not all receipts are revenues. Revenue receipts produce additions to assets without increasing school indebtedness and without reducing the value of or degrading school property; they include money from taxes and tuitions.

Nonrevenue receipts accrue to the district as the result of incurring an obligation that must be satisfied at a future date or of reducing the value of school property through the exchange of a property asset into a cash asset.[2] Revenue receipts are derived from local, federal, and state sources.

As indicated earlier, taxes levied by various governmental units are the primary sources of revenues for public education. A relatively recent development, this practice is only about 100 years old. The percentage of taxes coming from various units of government to support education has varied over the years. In the beginning the local school district property taxes provided the dominant source of funds. Thus in 1920–1921 about 83.0 percent of school revenues came from local resources, only 16.5 percent from state sources, and 0.3 percent from the federal government. In contrast, by 1972–1973 an estimated 52.1 percent of school revenues were derived from local sources, 40.0 percent from state sources, and 7.8 percent from federal sources. The trend since then has been first to have a larger proportion coming from the state level, and second to increase the assistance from the federal level. The percentage of contributions of local govermental units to the support of public elementary and secondary schools will continue to decline. Federal support of education increased slowly until 1963–1964, but jumped dramatically in 1967–1969, as shown in Table 23-1. Since then federal contributions have been around 8 percent, state contributions 41 percent, and the local school district an all time low of about 52 percent.

During the twentieth century the

[2]S. J. Knezevich and John Guy Fowlkes, *Business Management of Local School Systems,* New York: Harper & Row, 1960, p. 47.

state has moved from a relatively insignificant role in the financing of public education to one of considerable importance. Only in recent years have taxes collected by state governments approached the combined total taxes collected by local units. Using their broader range of taxing power, the states will be in a position to reduce extreme variations in financial ability of local units to support education. Of particular significance will be distribution of state-collected taxes to promote quality education within local districts.

Federal involvement in the support of educational programs has a long and stormy history. The issue is clouded by emotional considerations of the role of the federal government in our way of life. In 1966, the federal government raised 68 percent of all tax revenues; the states and localities, 16 percent each. The federal government is a superior tax-collecting agency simply because it has access to the greater wealth of the na-

tion. For this reason, it has been necessary to turn to federal support for highways, housing, agriculture, hospitals, welfare, and other public enterprises.[3]

At present, the contribution of each level of government to the support of public education is in inverse ratio to the amount of taxes collected. Thus, although the federal government collects 68 percent of all the taxes, it provides about 8 percent of the school revenues; the state collects 16 percent of the taxes and supports about 21 percent of school costs, whereas the local units gather 16 percent of all taxes and contribute approximately 51 percent of the total school revenues.

The property tax. The property tax has been the backbone of local district tax resources. In 1957 school districts collected $4.4 billion from property taxes, which constituted 98.6 percent

[3]Committee on Educational Finance, op. cit., pp. 53–56.

TABLE 23–1

PERCENT OF REVENUE RECEIVED FROM FEDERAL, STATE, AND LOCAL SOURCES FOR PUBLIC ELEMENTARY AND SECONDARY SCHOOLS

School year	Federal sources	State sources	Local sources
1955–1956	4.6	39.5	55.9
1959–1960	4.4	39.1	56.5
1961–1962	4.3	38.7	56.9
1963–1964	4.4	39.3	56.3
1965–1966	7.9	39.1	53.0
1967–1968	8.8	38.5	52.7
1969–1970	8.0	39.9	52.1
1972–1973	7.8	41.0	52.1

Source: R. N. Simon and W. Vance Grant, *Digest of Educational Statistics, 1971 Edition,* DHEW Publication No. (OE) 72–45, Washington, D.C.: GPO, 1972, p. 54 and NEA Research Estimates for 1972–1973.

of all taxes collected by local school districts. This high level continued through the 1960s and into the 1970s. For all its shortcomings, the property tax is peculiarly well adapted to administration by small units. Property taxes provided over 50 percent of the nonfederal school revenue in the nation throughout the 1960s. Recent federal court decisions threaten the continued use of the local property tax in states with local districts with great disparities in property wealth. The famous *Rodriguez* decision will be reviewed more completely later in this chapter.

Early studies suggested that the local property tax is slow to respond to general economic growth, comprises a declining portion of total tax capacity, and often correlates poorly with ability to pay. The estimated proportion of local and state school revenues derived from property taxes in the United States varied from zero in Massachusetts to over 80 percent in Connecticut and New Hampshire. More recent data have shown the property tax to be more elastic and more responsive to economic growth than was previously thought possible. It is one of the most productive and stable revenue producers for local units and will probably continue to be so in the years ahead.

The local property tax is notorious for inequality in assessment of individual properties. Studies of average practice show that assessment of residential property for purposes of taxation varied from less than 10 percent of its sale value in one state to 66 percent in another; assessment of acreage and farms varied from 5 to 45 percent of sale value; assessment of vacant lots varied from 5 to 50 percent of sale value; and assessment of industrial property varied from less than 20 to almost 80 percent of sale value.

Reform of property-tax assessment procedures is long overdue. The computer is being used to cope with the problems of tax assessment equalization on a more frequent basis.

The value of taxable property is reduced not only by unrealistically low assessments but also by exemptions for homestead property, veteran's status, or class of property. Some states exempt all types of personal property and some completely exempt intangible personal property; partial exemption from the general tax base is less common. The total value of partially exempt property (usually homestead property) in the states is in the billions. Few authorities on taxation concur with the political expedient of partial exemption of some property from taxation.

The psychological limit on the tax rate for real property was approached in many states in the early 1970s if the taxpayer's revolt is indicative of such a limit. Further increases in school revenues may have to be sought in other forms of taxation.

Nonproperty taxes. Nonproperty taxes have been employed to support schools for many years, but the yield of such revenues did not add materially to school finance until recently. Nonproperty taxes have been collected by state governments during most of the twentieth century and have contributed to the growth of states as important tax-collecting agencies. Within the category of nonproperty taxes are those levied on such items as food, luxuries, restaurant meals, tobacco, admissions, gasoline, deed transfers, use of polls, mercantile licenses, income, and retail sales.

Income and retail-sales taxes are the most productive of all nonproperty taxes levied by the various local governmental units. Local nonproperty taxes are difficult to administer by small units and must be looked upon as purely a supplementary device. Such taxes respond quickly to business trends, and yields rise and fall in prosperity and recession. It is questionable whether an increase in number or rates of local nonproperty taxes will solve all problems of finance for a typical school district. Nonproperty taxes produce a far greater yield when the administrative unit is large in area, such as the state or federal government, and thus are far more important to state and federal governmental agencies than to local units.

Greater state support for public education is predicated on the financial capability of the state to raise the necessary revenues. Sources of state tax revenue vary considerably. All but eight states tax individual income. Most but not all states tax general sales. More states tax corporation income than individual income. All but one state tax cigarettes. All states levied taxes on gasoline and on alcoholic beverages. Rates of such taxes varied as well.

State sales and gross receipts taxes are by far the biggest producers of state nonproperty tax revenues. The next largest source of state revenues is the state income tax. State property taxes yield less than 3 percent of total state revenues.

Personal- and corporate-income taxes are the largest sources of revenues for the federal government. At one time customs duties accounted for the largest share of federal tax collections, but this pattern changed with the advent of the income tax early in the twentieth century. Other taxes, such as special sales and gross-receipts taxes and those on alcoholic beverages, represent a poor third and fourth in the total revenue sources for the federal government. Personal- and corporate-income taxes accounted for 81 percent of all tax collections by the federal government.

Availability of wealth to support education

The question usually arises whether the people of the United States have the financial capability to support expanded programs of public education. In 1971 current expenditures for public elementary and secondary schools totaled $48.8 billion. In the same year, the purchase and operation of automobiles totaled $84.3 billion, various types of recreation cost $42.5 billion, and money spent for alcoholic beverages and tobacco totaled $30.8 billion. Expenditures for user-operated transportation far surpass those for public education. Expenditures for alcoholic beverages and tobacco in 1966 fell below those for public education for the first time. Expenditures for public elementary and secondary schools do not take a lion's share of the consumer's dollar. Nor does most of the nation's tax dollar go to schools; of the $369 billion spent for all government services and facilities in 1971, $48.8 billion were expended on local schools. In other words about 13 cents out of each government dollar is spent for public schools.

Perhaps even more significant than the existing consumer expenditure patterns and tax allocations is whether the United States economy can stand an increased investment in education. The gross national product (GNP) represents the total value of all goods and services in the United States. The GNP has been increasing steadily, for we continue to produce more and more per year. In 1939 the GNP was about $90.5 billion; in 1949, $265.5 billion; in 1959, $483.7 billion; and in

1969, $930.3 billion. The GNP in the 1970s exceeded one trillion dollars, hitting $1,155 billion in 1972; $1,287 billion in 1973; and an estimated $1,390 billion in 1974. Most of the growth was the result of inflation. Thus, in 1958, or constant, dollars, the GNP was $791 billion in 1973, $837 billion in 1973, and $851 billion in 1974. Nonetheless, ours is and will continue to be an affluent economy. An 8 percent growth in 1974 was estimated for the GNP, which includes personal consumption expenditures, gross private and domestic investments, export of goods and services, and government purchases. This translates into a one percent real growth, that is, in constant dollars. The Committee for Economic Development predicted that about 3.12 to 3.2 percent of the future GNP will be needed to meet the total public school elementary and secondary expenditures, assuming that there will be no changes in the resources utilized per student.[4]

The evidence is overwhelming: The nation has the wealth to support quality schools. We must be willing to allocate a higher percent of the future GNP to support public education. The ultimate decision is based on the value that is assigned to an educated populace as a great national resource. Administrators together with lay leaders have the challenge to convince the public of the value of investing in public education.

Cost-quality relations

The determination of cost-quality relations in education is far more complex than appears at first glance. Among the requirements for such a determination are an acceptable defi-

nition of quality education, a measure of quality, comparable cost data, and information on community differences in percentage of each school dollar that can be applied directly to instruction. It is little wonder, therefore, that although available evidence on the cost-quality relation may be significant, it is neither final nor complete.

Some of the interesting conclusions and observations on cost-quality relations in education are stated below:

1. A higher quality of education is generally provided in school systems that spend larger amounts per pupil; a lower quality of education is generally provided in school systems that spend smaller amounts per pupil.

2. Spending more money does not automatically produce better schools. Inefficient district organization, divisive community factions, and other negative factors may be more powerful in reducing educational quality than high expenditure is in increasing it.

3. Specifically, when communities spend more money on their schools, they generally are able to and do employ more and better teachers. They are able to and do provide better materials and other aids to good teaching. They get better teaching. The amount of schooling provided is greater because longer school terms are maintained. There is better attendance and youths remain in school longer. Higher scores on achievement tests are made both in the three R's in elementary school and on academic tests in high school. The quality of the educational program as a whole and of teaching procedures is generally rated higher by trained observers in the school systems that spend more money.[5]

---

[4]Committee for Economic Development, *Paying For Better Schools,* New York: The Committee, 1959, p. 14.

[5]Committee on Tax Education and School Finance, National Education Association, *Does Better Education Cost More?* Washington, D.C.: The Association, 1959.

Exceptions to these general conclusions began to appear in the much publicized Coleman report of the late 1960s and the Jencks report of the early 1970s. These two reports, based on the same Coleman data, conclude that more money is not necessarily the answer to better schools and that schools don't make all that much difference in helping those from disadvantaged backgrounds to succeed. On the other hand there are researchers with data in hand who contend that the level of schooling does influence earning power.[6]

Trends and issues

A National Educational Finance Project was launched in 1968 to cope with the fact that state school finance programs were increasingly proving inadequate to meet the growing expectations for education.[7] The design of new school finance models for the years ahead was a major objective of this study.

The federal government, as indicated in previous chapters, has increased its involvement in education in general and in financing schools in particular. In 1972 the federal government began the historic revenue-sharing effort whereby taxes collected by the national government were shared in part with state and local governments. A $30.2 billion five-year general revenue sharing started in 1972 with the initial installments being disbursed to 38,000 states and communities. How much of these new funds will be dedicated to the improvement of education remains to be

seen. Tax relief seemed to be the initial concern in the early 1970s rather than more money for schools.

A constitutional challenge in about five states threatened the way most states finance local public schools. The argument raised was that inequality in the distribution of property-tax wealth among the school districts resulted in discrimination against the poor or the disadvantaged in violation of the Equal Protection Clause of the Fourteenth Amendment of the United States Constitution. The *Rodriguez* case was the first to reach the United States Supreme Court which ruled in 1973 in a split 5–4 decision that the Texas State School finance system was not unconstitutional. If the Supreme Court had ruled otherwise, many states would have been forced to levy state rather than local property taxes to support schools. Nonetheless, needed reform in school taxation is being talked about, if not acted upon, with increasing frequency in the early 1970s.

The plight of public education in large cities began to be dramatized in the years following World War II. The wealth of the big cities and the quality of their educational programs were the envy of rural and suburban schools during the last half of the nineteenth and the first half of the twentieth centuries. Then certain shifts occurred. The more affluent of the population moved to the suburbs, and in their place, the deprived and disadvantaged came to live in the core cities. Municipal services were added and expanded to help the migrants to the city adjust to urban values and work their way out of conditions that approached poverty. The schools were faced with students of significantly different character from those who previously had been served well. The many individualized and special services required increased greatly the

---

[6]J. W. Guthrie et al., "The More Schooling, The Higher the Individual's Income," *Compact*, vol. 6, no. 6, December 1972-January 1973, pp. 6–8.

[7]R. L. Johns et al., *Dimensions of Educational Need*, Gainesville, Fla.: National Educational Finance Project, 1969.

costs of operation. Expenditures began to rise faster than enrollment increased. Development of superhighways and urban-renewal projects removed more property from the tax rolls to intensify problems of school finance. The term "municipal overburden" appeared to explain why a city school district with wealth equal to that of a noncity district could not dedicate the same amount to education that a noncity district could. Competition for tax dollars is keener in large urban areas.

New patterns of financing education in large urban communities will have to be developed. State support, once distributed to compensate for sparsity of population, must now be apportioned to compensate for the concentration of large numbers of low-income families in the big cities.

The voucher system of educational finance was the subject of experimentation during the late 1960s and early 1970s. Supported by the now defunct federal Office of Economic Opportunity the experiment called for payments to parents with children of school age rather than directly to a public school system. It was argued that the parent could then choose where to send the child to acquire an education giving the voucher to the institution selected as payment for costs for the year. This is the competitive conceptualization of accountability. It assumes that parents can assess competing public and private systems or competing attendance centers within a system. This assessment challenge is difficult for professionals, and parents could substitute advertising claims for hard facts. The idea purports to use the market as a determiner of which schools deserve support. Education is primarily a social good rather than purely an individual benefit. Social goods are not well regulated by the market mechanism. The voucher system has had little impact on educational finance as yet and does little to resolve the fundamental issues confronting education.

Distribution of state support

The role of the state is to equalize educational opportunity. The trend is clearly toward establishment of a foundation program of education which guarantees to all pupils of the state a certain minimum education. State laws requiring better-qualified teachers, safer school facilities, and compulsory attendance at school have contributed to the increased cost of education, and as many state legislatures have recognized, it is unrealistic to demand quality in local school units without helping to pay for it.

Distribution of state-collected taxes to promote quality education within local districts will be primarily foundation-program oriented. More effective school districts can contribute to quality programs, and more equitable assessments will make foundation programs simpler to administer. More sophisticated bases for the distribution of state funds are being developed to ensure that state support comes closer to achieving avowed purposes. Flat grants based on average daily attendance, long the standard by which states allocated their share of the cost, are no longer adequate. A foundation program conceived in terms of current operating costs fulfills only a part of the educational goal. It will become increasingly difficult to justify a state support program that ignores capital outlay. Research since the 1920s has identified components of the foundation program; these findings must be put to practice.

Because the state and federal governments, to a greater degree than ever before, are providing the resources necessary to promote quality education, local school-board members and local school superintendents must become involved in state and federal projects concerned with the improvement of educational finance. Members of the board of education are state officers performing a state function; their concern for purely local educational problems must be replaced with concern for public education throughout the state.

CONTRIBUTION OF EDUCATION TO ECONOMIC DEVELOPMENT

More and more economists are awarding to the nation's system of public education some of the credit for the fact that the standard of living in the United States is about twice that of the advanced countries of Europe. This stands in contrast to the Coleman and the Jencks reports of recent years. The United States has only 6 percent of the earth's population and 7 percent of the world's land area, but it produces more than 30 percent of the world's goods and services. The median family income more than tripled as it increased from $3,031 in 1947 to $10,285 in 1971 (based on actual dollars and not corrected for the effects of price inflation).[8]

Although the classical economists Adam Smith and Alfred Marshall believed "the most valuable of all capital ·is that invested in human beings,"[9] most economists thereafter failed to see the relation between economic

growth and education. Most of the nation's economic growth was credited to physical capital investments (instruments of production) and very little to improvements in human capital until about the middle of the 1950s. Output of workers improves with more and better tools and machines, that is, with quantitative and qualitative changes in physical capital. Machines are products of the creative mind, and the poorly trained lack the capability to operate them efficiently. Today economists recognize readily that economic productivity is affected not only by the quantity of physical capital but also by the quality of human capital a society possesses.

Schools improve human capital through education. In this sense, expenditures for public education are investments in human capital development, just as expenditures for physical tools and machines used in the production of goods and services are investments in development of physical capital. Local, state, and federal taxes allocated to educational purposes can be viewed as funds to promote economic growth of the nation as well as to promote other benefits an educated populace contributes to society. As Harbison and Myers put it, "Progress is basically the result of human effort. It takes human agents to mobilize capital to exploit natural resources, to create markets and to carry on trade."[10] No country can move forward politically, socially, or economically without developing its human resources.

This broader view of factors related to economic development grew out of the realization that only about 20 percent of the economic growth of the United States could be traced to increases in size of work force and

[8]National Education Association, Research Division, *Economic Status of the Teaching Profession*, Research Report 1973-R3, Washington, D.C.: The Association, 1973, p. 86.

[9]See F. Harbison and C. A. Myers, *Education, Manpower, and Economic Growth*, New York: McGraw-Hill, 1964, p. 3.

[10]Ibid., p. 13.

amount of tools and machinery used in production.[11] The other 80 percent of economic growth was first credited to improvement in quality, as distinct from an increase in quantity, of physical capital goods. But qualitative changes in physical capital goods failed to explain all unaccounted for gains in economic output, and the positive relation between educational level of population, income, and productivity began to emerge. Education began to be perceived as a process of building human capital, and investments in education were granted a more prominent place in economic analysis.

An early and influential study, completed by Theodore W. Schultz, produced a measure of the value of education in America. Schultz examined the relation between educational expenditures and income or capital formation for the period 1900 to 1956. He computed that the total "stock" of educational capital rose in the United States labor force from $63 billion in 1900 to $535 billion in 1957. He considered that investment in education included not only actual outlay for operation of educational institutions, but also "opportunity costs." The opportunity cost of education was the possible earned income given up by the person who chose to go to school during years he could have been working and earning.

Schultz then computed the return, that is, the ratio between lifetime earnings to the cost of differing amounts of education. He estimated that 21 percent of the $152 billion increase in real income between 1929 and 1957 could be attributed to additional education.[12]

This and other studies led the American Association of School Administrators to conclude:

In quantitative terms it is not unreasonable to say that about 20 percent of our economic growth stems from technological progress, the kind of progress that, for example, sustains our health and reduces the physical burden of work. If all of technological progress could be attributed to education, then our school system would be responsible for about 40 percent of economic growth (20 to 23 percent through improvement in labor skill and 20 percent through technological progress). No other field of human endeavor can claim so large a share.[13]

Harbison and Myers further suggested that the underdeveloped nations of the world must develop a strategy of human-resource development if they hope to move forward in political, social, and economic modernization. They designed a blueprint for action useful to economic, educational, and manpower planners. They analyzed qualitatively the problems of education and training faced by various types of undeveloped, partially developed, semiadvanced, and advanced countries and outlined a human-resource-development pattern related to economic growth.

Education benefits the individual as well as society as a whole. The evidence continues to mount that the level of education of a person is related to his ability to earn. Miller[14] summarized the lifetime earnings as related to education as ranging from $143,000 for a person with less than eight years of schooling to $454,000 for a person with five or more years of college. The disparities in earning power in various years for persons completing various levels of schooling are shown in Tables 23–2 and 23–3. The high school graduate of 1968 will

[11]American Association of School Administrators, op. cit., p. 13.

[12]Ibid., p. 34.

[13]Ibid., p. 36.

[14]H. B. Miller, *Rich Man Poor Man*, New York: Cole, 1964, p. 145.

earn $60,000 more during his lifetime than the student who drops out prior to graduation. This is true even though the high school graduate starts work a year or two after the dropout. The college graduate of 1968 will accumulate $180,000 more than the high school graduate, even though his life's work started 4 years later. It is estimated that today's college graduate will receive 9.5 times more in extra income than his college education cost him or his parents.[15] These differences

[15]Ibid., p. 2.

in earning power related to the completion of education levels appear to be increasing over time. Such hard data over an extended period of time is strong evidence to counter the arguments of some recent sociological studies that claim that schools and the educational level achieved don't contribute much to the breaking of the cycle of poverty.

There is evidence that workers in the same field with more education earn more than those with less education. Thus, in 1960 a carpenter who completed high school earned $5,700

TABLE 23–2

LIFETIME INCOME FOR MALES, BY YEARS OF SCHOOL COMPLETED[a]

Years of school completed	1949	1961	1968
Income from Age 18 to Death			
Elementary:			
Less than 8 years	$ 98,222	$151,881	$213,505
8 years	132,683	205,237	276,755
High school:			
1 to 3 years	152,068	235,865	308,305
4 years	185,279	273,614	371,094
College:			
1 to 3 years	209,282	335,100	424,280
4 years	296,377[b]	432,617	584,062
5 years or more	—	475,116	636,119
Income from Age 25 to 64			
Elementary			
Less than 8 years	$ 79,654	$125,044	$174,240
8 years	106,889	168,967	226,708
High school:			
1 to 3 years	121,943	193,265	258,455
4 years	148,649	224,626	306,786
College:			
1 to 3 years	173,166	273,309	356,297
4 years	241,427[b]	350,699	386,643
5 years or more	—	379,908	525,997

Source: K. A. Simon and W. V. Grant, *Digest of Educational Statistics 1971,* (OE) 72–45, U.S. Office of Education, Washington, D.C.: GPO, 1972, p. 17.

[a] These figures are estimates derived from a sample survey of households and, therefore, are subject to sampling variability as well as errors of response and nonreporting.

[b] Data not available in 1949 on earnings with 5 years of college or more. The figure shown is based on 4 years or more and not on 4 years alone.

on the average; a carpenter with an elementary-school education earned $4,800. An electrician who finished elementary school but dropped out of high school had an average income of $6,100; an electrician who graduated from high school received $6,600. Among toolmakers, those with a high-school education earned $600 more than those without, and firemen who graduated from high school earned $800 more a year than those who did not.[16] Table 23–3 presents further evidence confirming the relations between money income and educational level. These data are based on selected years up to 1971.

In general, the benfits that accrue to a person through education include extra income, a broader range of job opportunity, greater job security, and a happier family life. The rate of unemployment is lower among those with more education.

Education benefits business as well. It generates sales receipts for business firms through enlarged markets; it reduces production costs. Furthermore, schools produce a talent pool from which private industry recruits personnel.

Almost a century ago the English economist Alfred Marshall remarked that the cost of educating a generation of children in a whole city would be repaid amply by one important scientific discovery by one graduate of the city schools. The benefits of scientific discoveries by those with educated and creative minds are enjoyed by the nation as a whole. The payoff in agricultural research and development in this nation is a case in point. For all types of research expenditures, the annual rate of return is between 100 and 200 percent.[17]

Abundant natural resources represent potential, but educational development of people is necessary to translate potential into per capita income. A frequently quoted illustration shows

[16]American Association of School Administrators, op. cit., p. 2.

[17]Ibid., p. 10.

TABLE 23–3

ANNUAL MEAN INCOME (OR EARNINGS) FOR MALES 25 YEARS OF AGE AND OVER, BY YEARS OF SCHOOL COMPLETED

Year of school completed	1939	1949	1961	1968	1972[a]
Elementary:					
Less than 8 years	—	$2,062	$2,998	$ 3,981	$ 5,235
8 years	$1,036	2,892	4,206	5,467	6,756
High school:					
1 to 3 years	1,379	3,226	5,161	6,769	8,449
4 years	1,661	3,784	5,946	8,145	10,433
College:					
1 to 3 years	1,931	4,423	7,348	9,397	11,867
4 years	2,607	6,179	9,342	12,418	15,256
5 years or more	—	—	9,987	13,555	17,346

Source: K. A. Simon and W. V. Grant, *Digest of Educational Statistics 1971*, No. (OE) 72–45, U.S. Office of Education, Washington, D.C.: GPO,,1972, p. 17.
[a] U.S. Department of Commerce, *Money Income in 1972 of Familes and Persons in the United States*, Series P60, No. 90, December 1973, p. 121.

Brazil and Colombia rich in natural resources but low in educational development, and Switzerland low in natural resources but high in educational development. Analysis of wealth in these countries reveals that the per capita GNP in Switzerland was over eight times that in Brazil and Colombia.

Quality schools contribute to economic development and their absence can adversely affect the economy and other aspects of a nation. Individuals most prone to unemployment, mental irresponsibility, and delinquency are those with an inferior education. Limiting the resources necessary for education merely transfers expenditures from education to welfare programs. To deny the educational system the resources to reach ever-growing numbers of students and/or to improve its quality is to starve the goose that lays the golden egg.

RESOURCE SHARING WITH NONPUBLIC SCHOOLS

The Research Division of the National Education Association[18] completed a study in 1966 of public-school systems which gave assistance to nonpublic schools. The study was limited to systems enrolling 12,000 or more students. About half these districts cooperated in some way with nonpublic schools. The most common way was lending or giving materials to nonpublic schools; the next most common was allowing nonpublic school pupils to use public school facilities. Many of these practices were stimulated by the 1965 Elementary and Secondary Education Act. The various types of re-

source sharing by nonpublic and public schools are summarized in Table 23–4.

LOGISTICAL SUPPORT SERVICES

Decisions on resources that are made available to schools are consummated in the halls of state and/or federal legislatures. The typical administrator seeking to improve finance systems works in a political milieu. After the resources have been received by the school system, the administrator plays a very important role in managing them to insure attainment of educational goals.

What has been traditionally referred to as school business management—the planning, expenditure, and management of the school's financial resources—is a significant part of educational administration. The term "business management" is misleading because, as used in fields other than education, it refers to the administration of all aspects of an organization known popularly as a business and operated usually for a profit. The term thus connotes concern with money rather than with quality of education, a concept alien to the fundamental purpose of the public-school system.[19] This in turn may give rise to a flury of old wives' tales such as: "Business management is the greatest force undermining intellectual standards," "When business practices come into the school system the quality of education goes out the window," "Efficiency is a cult that destroys a funda-

---

[18]National Education Association, "Sharing of Resources by Public Schools with Nonpublic Schools," *Research Bulletin*, vol. 45, no. 3, October 1967, pp. 90–92.

[19]See S. J. Knezevich, "Fiscal and Material Resource Management as an Aspect of Educational Logistics," in W. E. Gauerke and J. R. Childress, eds., *The Theory and Practice of School Finance*, Chicago: Rand McNally, 1967, chap. 7, where these ideas were developed originally.

mental purpose of school," or "The dollar bill dictates educational decisions." The fact that these statements, half-truths at best, have reappeared in recent publications illustrates that well-encrusted clichés are passed on from one generation to the next.

The terms "logistical support services" and "fiscal and material resource management" more precisely describe the nature of the activities involved and minimize the chance of misconception of the importance and contributions of these activities. "Logistics," as used herein, refers to the process of supplying, maintaining, transporting, storing, accounting, and renewing the human, fiscal, and material resources necessary to initiate,

sustain, or modify activities of organized institutions in pursuit of predetermined goals. In the case of educational institutions resources are managed to pursue instructional objectives. The term has a military connotation, but military organizations are not alone in requiring coherent logistical systems to transport, feed, fuel, and munition organized efforts intent on fulfilling missions.

At one time teachers had to forage for themselves to accomplish educational purposes. The one-room, one-teacher school remains a classic illustration of a "self-contained logistical pattern." Thus, the teacher in the one-room school gathered wood, started fires, swept floors, created rudi-

TABLE 23–4

TYPES OF RESOURCE SHARING BETWEEN PUBLIC AND NONPUBLIC SCHOOLS, 1966

Shared resource	Systems enrolling 12,000 or more (%)	Enrollment group of school systems			
		100,000 or more (%)	50,000–99,999 (%)	25,000–49,999 (%)	12,000–24,999 (%)
No cooperation	49.5	25.0	44.7	54.4	51.2
Public schools give or lend materials to nonpublic schools	21.0	37.5	19.1	24.1	18.8
Nonpublic school pupils use some public-school facilities other than classrooms	17.5	29.2	17.0	19.0	16.0
Nonpublic school pupils take some classes in public schools under public school teachers	15.0	16.7	14.9	15.2	14.8
Public schools send some educational specialists to nonpublic schools	13.2	20.8	14.9	10.1	13.2
Public schools send teachers to nonpublic schools to teach some classes	2.7	—	8.5	2.5	2.0
Public school pupils take some classes other than religious instruction at nonpublic schools	1.5	—	2.1	—	2.0
Nonpublic school pupils take some classes in public schools but under nonpublic school teachers	0.7	—	2.1	—	0.8
Other cooperative arrangement	10.5	16.7	12.8	2.5	12.0
Number of systems reporting	400	24	47	79	250

Source: Research Division, National Education Association, "Sharing of Resources by Public Schools with Nonpublic Schools," Research Bulletin, vol. 45, no. 3, October 1967, p. 91.

mentary instructional devices, and copied materials out of textbooks. Children walked to school and teachers were often paid in services and board rather than in cash. Financial records were limited.

Keeping the massive front-line forces in complex educational organizations supplied with consumable and non-consumable materials; housed in clean, safe, esthetically attractive, functional facilities; and satisfied with prompt and accurate monthly salary payment requires a much more sophisticated logistical system. Today's money-based economy (as opposed to the pioneer barter-based or payment-in-kind economy) has created logistical problems of prodigious proportions.

Fiscal and material resource management is one part of educational logistics and one of many responsibilities of an educational administrator. Fiscal and material resource administration is a means, not an end. It includes such activities as budget making, procuring and handling funds, purchasing or expending funds, controlling inventory, accounting, auditing, financial reporting, analyzing cost, maintaining property records, insuring against unexpected financial losses, operating school food services, and operating transportation systems. In short, it is the phase of educational logistics or administration that is concerned primarily with procuring, expending, accounting for, protecting, organizing, and maintaining fiscal and material resources in an efficient manner so that they may aid human resources and efforts in the achievement of educational goals.

Administrative organization

The school board usually delegates responsibility for execution of the entire educational program, both instruc-

tional and business affairs, to a single executive officer—the general superintendent of schools. This is what has been previously referred to as the unit type of school organization. There is ample research to indicate the superiority of the unit type of administrative organization over any form of multiple organization. The delegation of responsibility for the execution of various facets of the logistical support program to a person who is independent of or coordinate with the superintendent of schools is difficult to justify. It is emphasized that fiscal and material resource administration should be subordinate to the purposes of the educational institution and to general school administration. If the business official is coordinate with the superintendent of schools, there is a real danger that the quality of public education may be sacrificed to perfectionism in business details.[20]

Within the framework of the unit type of administration, particularly in a large organization, it becomes physically impossible for one executive to manage all aspects of the educational institution, and the subordinate executive positions of the central-office administrative and supervisory staff are needed. Some superintendents have been criticized for spending too much time on financial matters and too little on instructional activities. Such difficulty may be traced to the lack of sufficient central-office staff to perform the detail work of fiscal and material resource administration. General executive responsibility for all business affairs remains with the superintendent of schools; all other individuals, such as an assistant superintendent in charge of logistical support services, are subordinate to him and report to

[20]Knezevich and Fowlkes, op. cit., pp. 12–13.

the board of education only through him.

Budget making

The budget is the heart of fiscal management. Through the budget the board can approve and determine the expenditures of the school system. The budget is the fiscal interpretation of the educational program. This implies that reducing the proposed expenditures or refusing to approve the procurement of receipts stipulated in the budget has more than merely monetary significance. Such acts affect the quality and quantity of educational services available in the district. In one sense, the budget can be regarded as an expression of the educational hopes and aspirations of the people. It is by nature future oriented.

Budgeting is stimulated by the need for economy and efficiency in financial operations. In this sense the budget becomes a disciplined way to handle school expenditures. It is traditionally conceived as a control device. It appeared in United States governmental affairs early in the twentieth century, although it was used in private business and industry prior to that time. Local school districts were among the last of the governmental units to develop and use the budget. Prior to 1920 budgetary practices in local school systems were relatively undeveloped and nonstandardized. Even at the present time, the recommendations cited in the voluminous literature on this subject have been practiced in only a very limited way. One of the significant contributions of the professionally prepared school superintendents in the 1920s and 1930s was to design and introduce the budget as an important instrument in school operations and to utilize budgeting as a meaningful planning and control process.

The budgetary process. The phases in the budgetary process are preparation, presentation, adoption and authorization, administration, execution, and appraisal.[21]

Responsibility for budget preparation rests with the superintendent, or in a large school, with the assistant superintendent in charge of business services. The three major phases of budget preparation are (1) determination of the educational program for the period in question, (2) estimate of expenditures necessary to realize the program, and (3) estimate of revenues or receipts anticipated from local, state, or federal sources. These phases are often referred to, respectively, as the educational plan, the expenditure plan, and the revenue plan. Although there is considerable agreement that the educational plan is the most important part of budget preparation, few executives include the statement of the educational program to be realized in the budget document. It is difficult to defend a budget request professionally without justification based on educational goals envisioned. The educational plan must be translated into reasonably accurate expenditure estimates. This does not mean that no consideration is given to the revenue plan until expenditures are known. The three phases of budget preparation are considered at the same time.

It can be called "long-term budgeting." It is one aspect of the planning-programming-budgeting system, which is explored in greater detail in a previous chapter.

The budget document is the general financial and educational plan for a stated period of time. It evolves from continuous fiscal and educational planning. The budget document contains a balanced statement of estimated revenues and estimated expen-

[21]Ibid., chap. 2.

ditures. The justification of anticipated expenditures is based on the desired educational program. The budget document also includes exhibits that report in some detail the current financial condition of various funds at the start of the fiscal year.

The prepared budget document is submitted to the board of education, which adopts, rejects, or modifies it. Presentation of the budget document is an executive activity. Adoption of the budget is a board of education function; authorization of the budget, after review and evaluation, is a legislative function.

Administration of the budget follows approval and authorization. This, again, is an executive activity. The authority to expend the amounts stated in the budget document should be delegated to the chief executive officer of the board of education. So long as he expends funds within budgetary allotments, there should be no need for board approval prior to a purchase. A different set of circumstances prevails when extrabudgetary purchases are envisioned.

Appraisal of the budget document is a function of the board and the superintendent. Primary responsibility, however, rests with the policy-making agency.

The term "balanced budget" is a relative one that means usually an excess of revenues over expenditures. The budget serves as a means of controlling future fiscal operations after the estimated expenditures and receipts have been approved.

The planning-programming-budgeting system (PPBS). PPBS is more than a new approach to budgeting. It is a part of what is known as the systems approach to school administration. It thus might be more accurately labeled a "resource allocation decision system" (RADS). PPBS focuses primarily

on the educational plan and expenditures plan in budgeting. It ignores the important financing plan (the receipts side) of the budget document. The concept of PPBS as a decision system is reviewed more fully in Chapter 8 on management science.

PPBS is more than a new fiscal instrument, although it does give rise to a different looking budget document. Its primary concern is with expenditures. Though dynamic relations exist among its many dimensions— planning, programming, budgeting, analyzing, and evaluating—it focuses on the total configuration of activities. PPBS allows the systematic analysis of alternatives; it provides a way of improving how limited resources are to be allocated among various programs.

The school fiscal officer and many other second-echelon administrative personnel are involved in several phases of the total PPBS system. It is the general school executive at the top level who directs PPBS rather than the school business official. As an outcomes-oriented management system, the PPBS budget is a planning tool as well as an instrument to control expenditure patterns. It demands interrelations of key executives—the team or task force approach—which is basic to systems approach to administration.

Program budgeting. Program budgeting has become a popular term during the last decade. Some use the term as a synonym for PPBS even though the originators of the PPBS seldom mentioned program budgeting; others insist that the two phrases are not synonymous.

Whether program budgeting is a more meaningful fiscal analysis and control device or a comprehensive systems approach is a matter of definition. For the purpose of this writing, program budgeting is a subset of the PPBS. It is concerned primarily with developing programmatic classifications for educational budget categories. Its purpose is to facilitate operations analysis. It focuses on output-oriented (or mission-oriented or program-oriented) categorization of budgets. It involves restructuring budget presentations to reveal outputs as well as inputs and to relate each to objectives.

Accounting

The system of accounting grows out of the production of records of financial transactions. From the basic documents and their subsequent classification, a picture of the educational program develops as contained in the budget. Accounts reveal changes in financial status of the district. The central aspects of accounting are the maintenance of essential records in which are summarized financial transactions of the institution and the reporting and interpretation of them.[22] Accounting involves recording, classifying, summarizing, and reporting in terms of money, the activities and events affecting the financial character of the administrative unit and its programs. The exact records to be kept and the manner in which fiscal information is to be classified and summarized depends upon: (1) the purposes of the institution, (2) the financial information required for prudent administration, and (3) the principles and practices of accounting. There is no one set of records or one type of bookkeeping procedure that must be employed in all types of in-

stitutions. Although some principles and standards apply both to public school and commercial accounting, there are fundamental differences between the two.

Computer-based electronic devices promise to facilitate school-accounting procedures in small and large districts alike. The advent of machines makes it difficult to justify the keeping of only minimum or inadequate financial records on the grounds that too many workers are needed to discharge financial responsibilities adequately.

Purposes of accounting. Purposes of public school accounting are:

1. To safeguard school-district funds from loss, theft, waste, or misuse.
2. To promote budgetary control.
3. To provide information to management that is necessary in policy formulation.
4. To provide information necessary to the public and the school board to appraise the management of the local school system.
5. To provide data required for state reports.
6. To show that legal mandates have been complied with.[23]

If financial information among communities in various states is to be comparable, there is a need for uniformity in terminology in accounting. The United States Office of Education financial accounting manual, which has been revised several times, provides a basis for such uniformity among school districts in the United States.[24]

If operations analysis and cost-effectiveness studies are to be possible in education, present accounting sys-

---

[22]Knezevich and Fowlkes, op. cit., chap. 3; see also B. K. Adams et al., *Principles of Public School Accounting*, U.S. Office of Education, OE 22025, Washington, D.C.: GPO, 1967, p. 260.

[23]Knezevich and Fowlkes, op. cit.

[24]C. T. Roberts and A. R. Lichtenberger, *Financial Accounting Classifications and Standard Terminology for Local and State School Systems*, Handbook II, rev. ed., DHEW Publication no. (OE) 73-11800, Washington, D.C.: GPO, 1973.

tems must be redesigned, in terms of outputs rather than inputs, to permit establishment of the PPBS.

Fund accounting

As indicated previously, a fund does not refer to money per se, but an independent accounting for specific activities that may be related to the attainment of objectives. The USOE Handbook II, Revised, called for the following types of funds to be established, as needed, in local schools: General Fund, Special Revenue Fund, Debt Service Fund; Capital Projects Fund; Food Service Fund; Pupil Activity Fund; and the Trust and Agency Funds.[25]

Receipt accounts. Various funds and receipt accounts specified in the Office of Education pattern will be identified in this section. A fund is a sum of money or other financial resources segregated for specified activities within limits set by laws or regulations. Thus, each fund must be an independent fiscal and accounting entity. Any fund can be divided into a number of accounts for the purpose of systematizing financial transactions. Those financial transactions related to receiving money are classified as receipt accounts; those related to spending money are classified as expenditure accounts.

The receipt accounts for public schools can be classified as revenue-receipt accounts, nonrevenue-receipt accounts, and incoming-transfer accounts.

Revenue-receipt accounts record money that increases assets without increasing school indebtedness by reducing the value of, or by depleting, school property. Included is revenue

[25]Ibid., p. 4.

from local sources, from intermediate governmental units, from state sources, and from federal sources. Most of the tax funds and grants received are classified in revenue-receipt accounts.

Nonrevenue-receipt accounts record money produced as a result of incurring an obligation to the district which must be amortized at some future date or money produced from the sale of school property. In such accounts are recorded sale of school bonds, loans, and similar financial transactions. The term "nonrevenue" appears contradictory if revenue is equated with money, and "nonrevenue" receipts is translated as "nonmoney" receipts. A better term is needed, but for the present nonrevenue applies to a type of receipt.

Incoming-transfer accounts record money received from other school districts for services rendered. Included are tuition receipts, which could distort the picture of total school receipts in a state or nation if they were not identified by the special terminology. Incoming-transfer accounts avoid duplication of data on school receipts and, therefore, ensure more reliable and more comparable state and national figures on receipts.

Clearing accounts. Clearing accounts or "revolving funds" record gross amounts of money received for various school activities and allowed to accumulate for a specified period of time before being disbursed or distributed to appropriate agencies or other accounts. In the conduct of school business affairs certain financial transactions involve a double handling of money. To illustrate, money may be received from the operation of a given activity and then spent again for the same activity in a cycle of operations. Recording these activities in regular receipt and expenditure accounts would greatly distort financial operations.

Clearing accounts are used when the single-entry system of bookkeeping is employed. They are not required in the double-entry system; in the double-entry system a profit-loss statement is prepared and either profit or loss is transferred to another fund at the end of a given accounting period.

Expenditure accounts. Schools incur liabilities through the purchase of materials and supplies and through contracts for personal services. It is necessary in all school systems to purchase and manage school supplies and equipment with the greatest amount of efficiency, so that loss or misuse will be minimized. Procurement of school materials begins with a requisition, a request by the teacher for approval of the purchase of supplies and equipment. It in turn leads to the purchase order, a document authorizing the seller to deliver described merchandise or materials at a specified price. When accepted by the seller, the purchase order becomes a contract. After materials specified have been shipped to the school system, the seller submits an invoice, a document calling for payment for merchandise delivered. The invoice activates expenditure of funds from the school treasury.

A major revision in school accounting classifications recommended in the USOE appeared in 1973. Expenditure accounts for schools classified according to function in the most recent USOE recommendations in Handbook II, Revised, are:[26]

Code 1000: *Instruction.* Includes expenditures for activities concerned directly with or aiding in the teaching of students or improving the quality of teaching, such as salaries for teachers aides, and assistants.

[26]Ibid., pp. 36–49.

A further breakdown of the major *Instruction* classification includes Regular Programs (Elementary, Middle High or High, Senior High etc.); Special Programs (Gifted and Talented, Mentally Retarded, etc.); and Adult and Continuing Education Programs (Adult Basic, Occupational, Life Enrichment, etc.)

Code 2000: *Supporting services.* All of the instructional support services such as administration, guidance, media, etc. are collected under this broad umbrella of accounts. It is not meaningful until broken down into major subfunctions and then into other account levels. In this sense the *Supporting Services* is a sizeable collection of significant function accounts. The major subfunctions within Code 2000 are:

2100: Support services—pupils. This must be subdivided further into: Attendance and Social Work Services; Guidance Services, Health Services; Psychological Services; Speech and Pathology Services.

2200: Support services—instructional staff. This may be subdivided into Improvement of Instruction Services and Educational Media Services.

2300: Support services—general administration. This may be subdivided into Board of Education Services and Executive Administration Services.

2400: Support services—school administration. This is primarily for the principal's office expenditures.

2500: Support services—business. This is a very large category that must be subdivided into the following services: Direction of Business Support; Fiscal; Facilities Acquisition and Construction; Operation and Maintenance of Plant; Pupil Transportation; Food; and Internal.

2600: Support services—central. This may be broken down into the following types of services: Direction of Central Support; Planning, Research, Development and Evaluation; Information; Staff; Statistical; and Data Processing.

Code 3000: *Community services.* This major account classification includes expenditures for services not directly related to instruction such as community recreation and other services, public library, child care or custody programs, and nonpublic school services.

Code 4000: *Nonprogrammed charges.* This classification is designed primarily to cope with payments or transfers to other governmental units in or outside the state.

Code 5000: *Debt services.* As the title implies the payment of the principal and interest on bonded indebtedness is included herein.

A number of new account classifications are evident in the 1973 USOE recommendations. It is noted that the principal is no longer included in the *Instruction* category. It is recognized as being a part of administration. Likewise the peculiar *Fixed Charges* category of years gone by is no longer a part of the accounting system. As new educational services or operations are included, the complexity of the accounting increases.

Encumbrance accounts. Encumbrance accounting is rapidly becoming an important part of school fiscal management. There is a difference between an encumbrance and an expenditure. An encumbrance is a commitment of resources prior to actual disbursement of funds to liquidate a liability. It ensures that the money cannot be used for anything else until the expenditure has been realized. Encumbrance accounting enables a school district to know how much money has been spent or has been committed to be spent at any given time. Without encumbrance accounting, the exact financial situation at any period of time can only be estimated.

Auditing

The audit is a systematic investigation, verification, and critical review of financial operations within the school

district. Its primary purpose is to verify the financial status of the school system.[27]

Audits may be classified as general or special audits, or complete or limited audits. A general audit is concerned with all fiscal transactions and records for every school fund; it is a comprehensive review. A special audit is limited to a particular aspect of school fiscal transactions. A complete audit is a thorough analysis of operations, necessitating a careful study of the system of internal control and of all books and accounts, including subsidiary records and supporting documents. A limited audit reviews only selective items; it is based on sampling rather than a complete review of every financial transaction. There are complete general audits, limited general audits, complete special audits, and limited special audits. A complete general audit checks all funds and is based on an intensive examination and verification of all items during a given account period. A complete special audit is concerned only with specific parts of the school's financial operations.

Preaudits, continuous audits, and postaudits are classifications based on time. A preaudit is an investigation and critical review prior to consummation of a transaction. It is a means of avoiding expenditures of borderline validity and preventing money appropriated for one purpose from being used for another. Preauditing takes place in the normal careful accounting routine when this involves the checking of an expenditure to ascertain that it is authorized in a budget and that unencumbered funds are available. A postaudit takes place after the transaction has been completed. It is the most common type of audit and is frequently referred to as the "annual

[27]Knezevich and Fowlkes, op. cit., chap. 8.

school audit." The most common type of audit required by state law is the annual independent audit, which is a postaudit.

An auditor functions most effectively as an expert in accounting or auditing and least effectively as an expert in educational philosophy and curriculum. Educational policy should never be exercised through school audits.

There is evidence to indicate the need for improvement in school-district audit laws. Relatively few laws stipulate the time and scope of the audit, or the qualifications of the school auditor. The school district, rather than the state department of education, is the most suitable agency for directing the school audit.

Cost accounting and unit-cost analysis

The purposes of unit-cost analysis are to ascertain the costs of operating a given school facility, to judge the efficiency and practicality of certain school activities, to help in the budgeting of activities that can be reduced to measurable units, to estimate costs of proposed projects, and to compare educational costs among communities. Perhaps the most dangerous of these steps is comparison. The temptation to analyze the cost of educational programs is very great despite the many chances of misinterpretation.

One difficulty in unit-cost analysis is ascertaining appropriate units of measurement. Unless units are comparable for the area under investigation, unit-cost analysis is of questionable value. Cost accounting for schools endeavors to ascertain and evaluate the cost of operating various phases of the educational experience. It is limited by the financial information available and the design of procedures in accounting. A well-designed and well-kept accounting system will facilitate the gathering of cost data but cannot guarantee correct interpretation of such information.

Unit-cost figures for different school systems should be qualified if they are not based on the same educational program. It is erroneous to assume that the same educational program is being purchased with the same or differing amounts of money in all school systems. The selection of appropriate units for cost analysis compounds the problem.

Cost accounting may be confused with cost effectiveness or cost-utility analyses. The last two terms are related to the systems approach to administration and involve far more than unit cost analysis. The cost-accounting procedures may provide basic data in the cost-effectiveness analysis.

Financial reporting

Financial reports are a means of informing the school board, professional administrators, and public and state officials of the fiscal state of the school. Reports are prepared on a monthly, quarterly, or annual basis. Some reflect the status of receipts and expenditures; others are concerned with the general financial condition of the school system. It is usually the function of the school superintendent to prepare the financial reports. The form and content of a report vary with its purpose. The systems approach requires reporting by outputs as well as inputs.

School records accumulate fast, and there is a need for legislation and policy to determine which records should be kept and which destroyed. Microfilming is useful to reduce storage requirements of permanent records, but the high cost and possible legal problems cannot be overlooked. As long as there are no specific statutory requirements to the contrary, many school records and reports can be disposed of after ten years without adversely affecting school administration.

Management of student-body activity funds

The practice of storing student-organization monies in fruit jars, filing cabinets, personal checking accounts, or even the left-hand pocket of the activity sponsor can no longer be justified. A system for managing student-body activity funds is urgently needed in every local school system. A number of suggestions have been made. The Association of School Business Officials and the United States Office of Education have each developed a financial accounting handbook for student-body activities funds. It has been proposed that these funds be placed under school-board jurisdiction in clearing accounts. While students can formulate policies related to management of student-body activities funds, actual business operations, such as purchasing, disbursing, accounting, and reporting, should be performed by professionally prepared adult members of the school staff.

Management of the school debt

The school debt is part of the public state and local government debt. The present public state and local government debt is about ten times the 1945 debt of $16.6 billion. The increase in private debt since the end of World War II has exceeded the increase in the public debt for the same period. School indebtedness is growing primarily because of the tremendous spurt in school-plant construction. New school facilities were required to meet expanding enrollment and to re-

place obsolete units. The indebtedness program is closely related to the plant and equipment needs of the instructional program. These needs will level off and decline in the 1970s.

Although some states practice capital-outlay financing, most school-plant construction must be financed through the sale of bonds. Some districts finance construction through pay-as-you-go procedures, but by and large plant needs are growing too fast to be satisfied by this means.

A bond is a written financial instrument issued by a corporate body to borrow money; time and rate of interest to be charged, method of principal payment, and term of debt are clearly expressed.[28] A school bond is not a mortgage on the real or personal property of the district. If a school district defaults on the bonds, its property cannot be assumed by bondholders. To compensate for this, courts earmark a part of the taxable income accruing to defaulting districts until the debt settlement is reached. Most states permit the levying of an irrevocable tax for purposes of retiring a debt as part of the district's bonding authority.

Often restrictions placed upon bonding appear too onerous. A review of municipal and school-district borrowing reveals, however, that legal restrictions may not be bad in themselves. For example, requirements that promote better management, such as those that demand the issuance of serial bonds only, are commendable; statutory regulations of school debts can make bonds easier to market and command a more favorable rate of interest. On the other hand, legal limitations of school debts to an unrealistically low percentage of assessed valuation of property impair the ability of the school district to provide quality education.

[28]Ibid., chap. 12.

School bonds must have the approval of the electorate before they can be issued. During the early part of the 1960s about 72 percent or more of the bond issues were approved in various elections across the country. In the late 1960s, the success rate dropped so that in 1969–1970 only 53.2 percent of the bond elections were accepted. Approval of bond elections in the early 1970s fell below 50 percent. Thus, only 46.7 percent of school bond elections were approved in 1970–1971 and 47.0 percent in 1971–1972. Maguire observed that success in bond and millage elections "was associated with absence of controversy and low voter turnout."[29] He noted as well that the voters were more likely to be parents, professional people, and those satisfied with their own education.

Limitations on indebtedness, or restrictions on the total school bond that can be issued, vary among states. Debt limits, as percentages of the assessed value of taxable property, range from 2 percent in Indiana and Kentucky to 50 percent for certain school districts in Minnesota. Because property value for tax purposes is not assessed at the same rate in all states, the debt-limit percentages are difficult to interpret.

School bonds are usually unsecured, for the physical assets of the district do not guarantee principal and interest payments. In this sense, all school bonds are debenture bonds (a type not secured by collateral or the tangible assets of the district). Bonds are most frequently classified according to the maturity of principal and the method of making principal payments. Straight-term bonds were used widely

[29]John W. Maguire, "Political Techniques in School Bond and Millage Elections," *School and Society*, December 1971, pp. 514–515.

to finance the construction of school buildings a generation ago. Principal payments for this type of bond are not made until the complete issue reaches maturity at the end of 10 years, 20 years, or whatever period. In other words, the total principal of a bond of $100,000 or $1,000,000 falls due at one time. Failure to set aside a certain amount of money voluntarily each year for principal payment, or the mismanagement of sums accumulated for principal payment, often necessitated issuing new bonds to pay the principal on the old bonds. This often led to a vicious fiscal circle.

To correct the difficulty inherent in deferring principal payment until maturity date, the voluntary annual allocation of a certain sum for principal payments was changed to mandatory accumulation. This was not successful because the amount that accumulated to pay principal could be mismanaged or diverted to other purposes.

The serial bond proved the best solution. A serial bond issue is a collection of many term bonds so organized that a certain number of term bonds reach maturity each year. In other words, the total issue is broken down into several bonds of $1000 or larger denominations, which are numbered serially and which mature periodically in serial order. Principal payments are made on certain numbers of the series each year, along with the interest.

Bonds can also be classified as callable and noncallable. Callable bonds include a special provision which gives the district the privilege of paying the entire debt earlier than the maturity date stipulated at the time of sale of the issue. Noncallable bonds can be paid only at the stipulated date of maturity.

The advantages of issuing serial bonds can be negated if careful scheduling of debt amortization is neglected.

Prudent debt management is based on the knowledge of existing and future debt requirements, as well as the size of issues to be amortized. Improperly developed serial bond retirement schedules can prove most embarrassing in financing future capital outlays for rapidly growing school districts.

The total amount paid annually as interest on the school debt now exceeds $1.66 billion. Interest rates on school bonds increased all through the 1960s and into the early 1970s. The lowest average interest rate on school bonds was 1.29 percent in February 1946. The highest average annual rate, 5.69 percent, was experienced during the Great Depression. This high average annual interest rate may be exceeded during a time of great prosperity in the 1970s.

Accounting for school property

The total value of school property exceeds $20 billion. This is a tremendous investment that must be safeguarded and carefully identified with a system of property accounting.

The status of school property accounting is at least 30 years behind that of accounting for other school financial transactions. Inadequate property records characterize most school districts. This is in stark contrast with the capital-accounting procedures in a business or industry. Property accounting for schools is necessary, but for different reasons than those which prompt it in the business and the commercial world.

The development of the Office of Education property accounting handbook[30] eliminates whatever reason there may have been for delaying the

establishment of property accounting in most schools. A property account can be defined as a descriptive heading under which is posted specific information about land improvements and buildings and equipment owned and/or controlled by the school district. The term "account" is used in the sense of a formal record rather than a descriptive classification of a financial transaction.

The various types of property accounts can be classified under the following headings:

1. Type of plant (elementary, secondary, or other used for instructional or noninstructional purposes).
2. Land facilities.
3. Improvements to school sites.
4. Building facilities (type, kind, cost, and size of building).
5. Equipment (instructional as well as noninstructional).

Protection of school personnel and property

At one time attacks on teachers and vandalism of school property were a rarity or not a significant concern. This changed dramatically during the 1960s. The school administrator is now confronted with the challenge of making the school a secure place.

One measure of concern is the statistics on crime in elementary and secondary schools, which are shown in Table 23–5.[31]

School insurance. Insurance affords protection against financial loss from loss of life, crime, destruction of personal property, destruction of another person's property, or other causes. In

[30]U.S. Office of Education, *Property Accounting Handbook,* Handbook no. 3, Washington, D.C.: GPO, 1958.

[31]W. N. McGowan, "Crime Control in Public Schools: Space Age Solutions," *NASSP Bulletin,* vol. 57, no. 372, April 1973, pp. 43–48.

return for a relatively small payment —a premium—that is collected from many individuals, a company assumes risk of the possibility of a substantial, even though unknown, financial loss to each party who pays a premium. Insurance companies are professional risk bearers. Insurance is a means of gaining some measure of financial security even though catastrophe may strike.

The major classifications for insurance are property, liability, crime, and personal welfare.[32] Property insurance commonly gives security against financial loss from property damage or destruction arising from fire, windstorm, and explosion. Liability insurance provides some measure of security to the insured if his unintentional acts injure or damage another person's body or property. Crime insurance protects against financial loss through the commission by others of intentional and illegal acts such as robbery, theft, and embezzlement. The various types of health, accident, and life policies constitute personal-welfare insurance.

[32]Knezevich and Fowlkes, op. cit., chap. 15.

Insurance firms make use of the mathematical theory of probability and the law of large numbers. The method is based on an understanding of which kinds of perils and losses are experienced with certain types of structures. Statistics cannot predict the loss of a certain school building, but past experience points to the likelihood that one school building of a given type somewhere in the United States will suffer the peril or loss under question during a given time. The insurance premium is computed, at least in part, on statistical experience with losses inflicted on properties of any given classification in a given location. In commercial insurance companies the premium charged must pay the expenses of the business and return a profit, as well as cover all anticipated losses.

If the number of properties at risk is not sufficient to permit the free play of the law of large numbers, prediction of losses is more certain. Under such conditions, insurance companies reinsure a major portion of all the school buildings in one large city to

TABLE 23-5

CRIME IN ELEMENTARY AND SECONDARY SCHOOLS, 1964 AND 1968

Crime category	1964	1968	Percent increase
Homicides	15	26	73
Forcible rapes	51	81	61
Robberies	396	1,508	306
Aggravated assaults	475	680	43
Burglaries, larcenies	7,604	14,102	86
Weapons offense	419	1,089	136
Narcotics	73	854	1,069
Drunkenness	370	1,035	179
Crimes by nonstudents	142	3,894	2,600
Vandalism incidents	186,184	250,549	35
Assaults on teachers	25	1,801	7,100
Assaults on students	1,601	4,267	167
Other	4,796	8,824	84

lessen the hazards of great loss in any one place.

There are stock types and mutual types of insurance companies. A stock company has behind it a reserved capital stock provided by individual investors. Capital stock guarantees that the company will pay losses even though premiums collected during any period are insufficient to cover them. Mutual companies do not issue capital stock; they depend primarily upon insurance premiums for the payment of losses. They select risks more carefully and refuse the more dangerous. The policyholders of a mutual company are the stockholders. The cushion necessary to meet unexpectedly large losses is made possible through the promise that mutual company policyholders are liable to additional assessment if the losses exceed the premiums paid. Some mutual companies sell nonassessable policies after they have accumulated a substantial reserve.

A large number of careful studies show that insurance payments for fire loss suffered by school districts are a small fraction of premiums paid by the school district. This has changed somewhat in the 1960s as the result of riots in urban centers and the greater incidence of vandalism against school property. School property should be classed as a preferred risk; subsequently, insurance rates should be adjusted downward. A higher-than-justifiable rate for school insurance has led some states to establish state-operated insurance programs. The loss experiences with fidelity bonds, crime insurance, and transportation insurance likewise indicate that school districts are preferred risks.

Self-insurance. Some districts attempt self-insurance programs. Self-insurance is practical in the very large district with ample financial resources and with a large number of school buildings scattered throughout the district. The various systems of self-insurance can be classified as no-insurance, insurance reserve, or partial insurance. Under the first system, the school has no insurance payment to make and does not attempt to accumulate reserves to pay for losses; this is practical if losses are so infrequent that they can be met by tax payments or bond issues. Under the second system, the school district creates a reserve fund to defray future financial losses suffered through destruction of property; the school system becomes its own insurance company and losses are covered from the reserve. Under the partial insurance plan, the district insures only the most hazardous risks and carries no insurance on the select risks.

Coinsurance. The insurance rate that is actually charged a school district is influenced by factors within the community and the nature of the risk. Insurance can also be paid at a special coinsurance rate. The coinsurance concept was developed when investigation showed that the sum of partial losses paid exceeded the aggregate sum of total property losses. In other words, in the great proportion of fires, the property damage and loss incurred are a small percentage of the total value of the property.

The principle behind coinsurance is simple. The insurance company agrees to lower the rate per unit of insured value if the insured promises to carry a given amount of insurance stated at a certain percentage of the full insurable value of the risk. The coinsurance clause is an inducement to keep insurance in force equal to at least a certain percentage of the insurable value of the building. If partial loss occurs and commitments of the coinsurance clause have been satisfied by the district, the latter will receive full payment for the partial loss. If the district failed to keep the correct amount of insurance in force, only a percentage of the partial loss will be paid by the company. This does not apply if total loss occurs, for then only the amount indicated on the face of the policy will be paid. Most authorities recommend that districts take advantage of 80 to 90 percent coinsurance rate reductions.

Management of transportation and food services

Pupil transportation and school food services are among the more rapidly growing school operations. About 45 percent of the total enrollment—close to 20 million pupils—are transported to school and are fed daily in school food-service operations. Total expenditures of public funds for pupil transportation jumped from $54.8 million in 1929 to $1.22 billion in 1969–1970. The overall cost per pupil increased only from $28.81 in 1929 to almost $67 in 1969–1970. Prudent business management of these services, which are significant and related to instruction, is most important. More and better-organized data are needed in both these fields if more efficient management of these growing services is to be achieved.

All indications are that school transportation will become more important, particularly if it is used in an attempt to obtain better racial balance in school systems.

SUMMARY

Schools consume resources in the pursuit of objectives. All goals in the instructional program carry a price tag. This necessitates the procurement of financial resources, as well as the careful management and control following procurement. These are the economic dimensions of school administration.

School finance patterns have changed through the years to meet new conditions. At one time, nontax sources dominated; by the last portion of the nineteenth century, schools were supported primarily by local tax funds. The property tax provides the lion's share of school revenues.

Increasing enrollment, growing complexity of educational objectives, and the insistent demand for quality have created conditions which necessitate a new approach to school finance. School expenditures, for current expenses, have increased from less than $2 billion in 1939–1940 to $34.2 billion in 1969–1970. In 1973–1974 annual expenditures reached $49.2 billion. A major concern is whether existing finance systems are capable of generating revenues in the magniture estimated for the rest of the 1970s and 1980s. Unit cost figures show that the cost per pupil in ADA in 1972–1973 reached $1,034. The most recent figures indicate that approximately 52 percent of school funds come from local sources, 40 percent from the state, and 8 percent from the federal government. This occurs even though 68 percent of the taxes are collected at the federal level, 16 percent at the state level, and 16 percent at the local level. All estimates for the future indicate that school costs will continue to climb. To meet these increases, the state and federal governments will have to allocate a larger percentage of their resources to public education. The question is not whether the United States has the wealth to support public education, but whether it is willing to do so. It is true that increases in school expenditures have outstripped the rate of increase in the nation's wealth as measured by the GNP.

Education is now recognized by more persons than ever before as an investment in the development of human resources. The quality of education influences the economic development of a nation, enhances the earning capacity of individuals, and lessens social and welfare problems. Progress is basically the result of human effort. Economic productivity of a nation is affected not only by the quantity of its physical capital but by the quality of its human capital.

Some recent studies have questioned the value of education in breaking the cycle of poverty. The preponderance of research documents the fact that the higher the level of educational accomplishment the higher an individual's earnings.

We are undergoing a revolution in educational finance. Court tests, such as the *Rodriguez* case, have unsucessfully challenged the use of the local property tax in school districts as being discriminatory and in violation of the Fourteenth Amendment of the United States Constitution. Others are suggesting the use of the voucher system of educational finance where payments are made directly to parents who in turn present vouchers to the schools that they select to educate their children. New patterns of urban school financing are demanded as well.

Political decisions influence the design of school finance systems. Administrative expertise becomes more important in the management of resources received for education. Fiscal and material resource management becomes important after funds have been procured. Funds obtained must be cared for and mismanagement or loss prevented. The school board is the legal agent of control over school affairs. Its task is to formulate policies that constitute the framework for business management, not to execute these policies. School business managers should be subordinate to the superintendent.

Effective fiscal administration is based on budget making, accounting, auditing, and financial reporting. A major revision in school accounting procedures was recommended by USOE in 1973. The budget is the heart of financial management and is the fiscal translation of the educational program; the accounts reveal financial status, and the audit verifies its accuracy. All cost accounting depends on the accuracy of financial records. A well-designed and well-kept accounting system will facilitate the gathering of cost data, but cannot guarantee the correct interpretation of such information.

The planning-programming-budgeting system (PPBS) is the school's part of the systems approach to administration. A fundamental reorganization of fiscal accounting and budgeting systems and the restatement of objectives for schools will be needed to facilitate the introduction and use of PPBS in education.

The growing school debt has necessitated more prudent debt management. The debt is related to the need for more school facilities. These facilities are financed largely by the issuance of bonds. Most schools issue serial bonds, for this provides a more systematic means of making principal payments. School property represents a tremendous investment and should be protected by a system of property accounting. Crimes against persons and vandalism of school property increased dramatically in the 1960s. School security has become a major concern for administrators. Property accounting for schools lags far behind the recording of other financial transactions.

Insurance is protection against the likelihood of financial loss from various sources. Stock and mutual insurance companies are the most common types. There are a variety of school self-insurance plans, such as no-insurance, insurance reserve, and partial insurance. School districts are preferred risks, and insurance rates should be adjusted to this fact.

QUESTIONS

1. What factors stimulated the changing patterns of finance for schools during the nineteenth and twentieth centuries?
2. What evidence is there to support the contention that the United States has the financial capability to finance expanded educational programs?
3. Which taxes yield best for local governments? State governments? The federal government?
4. Does better education cost more? Justify your position.
5. What should be the fundamental purposes of school fiscal and material resource management?
6. What are the instruments necessary for efficient financial administration?
7. What is PPBS?
8. What changes in school accounting are necessary to develop a school program-budgeting system?
9. What is the relation between education and economic development of a nation?

SELECTED REFERENCES

American Association of School Administrators, *Education Is Good Business*, Washington, D.C.: The Association, 1966.

Berke, J. S. et al., *Financing Equal Educational Opportunity Alternatives for State Finance*, Berkeley, Cal.: McCutchan, 1972.

Committee on Educational Finance, National Education Association, *What Everyone Should Know About Financing Our Schools*, Washington, D.C.: The Association, 1966.

Education Commission of the States, "Education's Financial Dilemma," *Compact*, vol. 6, no. 2, April 1972.

Harbison, F. and C. A. Myers, *Education, Manpower, and Economic Growth*, New York: McGraw-Hill, 1964.

Johns, R. L. et al., *Dimensions of Educational Need*, Gainesville, Fla.: The National Educational Finance Project, 1969.

Knezevich, S. J., "Fiscal and Material Resource Management as an Aspect of Educational Logistics," in W. E. Gauerke and J. R. Childress, ed., *The Theory and Practice of School Finance*, Chicago: Rand McNally, 1967.

Knezevich, S. J. and John Guy Fowlkes, *Business Management of Local School Systems*, New York: Harper & Row, 1960.

Maguire, John W., "Political Techniques in School Bond and Millage Elections," *School and Society*, December 1971, pp. 514–515.

Reischauer, R. D. et al., *Reforming School Finance*, Washington, D.C.: The Brookings Institution, 1973.

Roberts, C. T. and A. R. Lichtenberger, ed., *Financial Accounting Classifications and Standard Terminology For Local and State School Systems*, Handbook II, rev. ed., DHEW Publication no. (OE) 73-11800, Washington, D.C.: GPO, 1973.

24

MANAGEMENT OF SCHOOL FACILITIES

The decade from 1950 to 1959 was one of great vigor in school-plant construction. The average annual expenditure during the 1950s for new educational buildings, public and private, was $2.7 billion. During the 1960s the average annual expenditures for capital outlay in public schools only was about $3.7 bilion. In 1973–1974 capital outlay expenditures hit a new high of $4.95 billion.

A record 75,400 public elementary and secondary instruction rooms were completed during 1967–1968. There was an average construction of over 70,000 classrooms per year during the 1960s. Most of the new schools in the 1950s were elementary school centers. In the 1960s nearly twice as many new secondary school plants were built as new elementary school plants. The United States Office of Education estimated that there were 1,918,000 publicly owned instruction rooms in the fall of 1971. The number of classrooms abandoned each year ranged from a low of 16,400 to a high of 24,000. Recent changes in enrollments plus the feverish construction of the 1950s and 1960s suggests a cooling off of the classroom construction rate during the 1970s.

Providing facilities for instructional purposes demands the attention of the school board, the superintendent, specialists in school-plant planning and design, as well as formally organized lay advisory committees. The professionally prepared school administrator, the architect with special training and experience in school-house design and construction, and the school-planning consultant are resource persons who stand ready to help the school board more effectively discharge its responsibilities in this area.

NATURE OF THE SCHOOL-PLANT

The school-plant is the space interpretation of the school curriculum. The curriculum finds its physical expression in construction and arrangements of the school-plant. The size, proportions, and relations of learning spaces influence the type and quality of instruction. The school site and the school building are part of the broad concept known as the school plant.

This functional concept of the school-plant emphasizes the effect of plant facilities on the educational experiences provided and the educational methods employed within it, rather than on the materials used in its construction. The school-plant is viewed as a controlled environment that facilitates the teaching-learning process while it protects the physical well-being of the occupants. Caudill suggested that school planning starts and ends with the pupil and that the building should be designed to satisfy the pupil's physical and emotional needs.[1] His physical needs are met by ensuring a safe structure, adequate sanitary facilities, a balanced visual environment, an appropriate thermal environment, a satisfactory acoustical environment, and sufficient shelter space for his work and play. His emotional needs are met by creating pleasant surroundings, a friendly atmosphere, and an inspiring environment. This humanistic, pupil-oriented approach to school planning and construction views design and equipment as means of enhancing the pupil's learning and comfort.

Not a single line should be sketched upon a drawing board until the curriculum to be housed has been defined. Determination of the educational program precedes designation of the physical pattern and materials of construction.[2] The kinds of spaces to be included in the educational plant depend upon the school curriculum. If vocational agriculture, home economics, industrial arts, and music are part of the educational experience, then spaces for learning in these areas must be designed. The amount of each kind of space needed for learning depends upon the size of the school enrollment. If school size does not justify separate instructional areas for each field of learning, multiple-purpose rooms become necessary. In addition, the total area, shape, and special design of a classroom are determined by the curriculum. Thus, the lecture method of teaching requires an en-

tirely different type of classroom than does the activity or laboratory method of instruction.[3]

To recapitulate, educational specifications are prepared as a prelude to architectural design. Of crucial importance is the translation of educational needs into space requirements. The curriculum and the method of teaching become meaningful for school design when the spatial implications of the program are clarified.[4]

The challenge is complicated by the fact that the "form and substance of the educational program for tomorrow's school is just emerging."[5] Technology is coming into the classroom, special services are being added, content of instructional program is being shifted to more appropriate grade levels, and new learning experiences are designed—all these factors influence planning, construction, and utilization of school facilities. A building design that is functional can no more remain static than the educational program it was created to serve.

Fredrickson identified the essential information to be described in an educational specifications document as: statement of philosophy; grade levels to be accommodated; enrollment capacity expectations; curricular programs and activities; specific utilization plans; instructional procedures; teaching space requirements; specialized instructional facilities; auxiliary areas;

[1]W. W. Caudill, *Toward Better School Design*, New York: McGraw-Hill, 1954, chap. 1.

[2]Council of Educational Facilities Planners, *Guide for Planning School Plants*, Columbus, Ohio: The Council, 1964.

[3]S. J. Knezevich, "The Curriculum and the School Plant," *Educational Leadership*, May 1953, p. 495.

[4]S. J. Knezevich, "Your New School: Procrustean Bed or a Functional School Plant?" *The American School Board Journal*, March 1960, pp. 35–37, 48.

[5]American Association of School Administrators. *Schools for America*, Report of the AASA School Building Commission, Washington, D.C.: The Association, 1967, p. 7.

miscellaneous concerns; and summary statement.[6]

SCHOOL-PLANT NEEDS

Despite the greatest rate of new school-plant construction in history that took place in the 1950s and 1960s there were in the fall of 1972 over 422,000 pupils on curtailed sessions because of inadequate housing. The continuing shortage of physical facilities for educational institutions can be traced to:

1. The Great Depression of the 1930s, during which school boards were barely able to keep schools operating, much less carry out extensive construction programs.
2. The global war of the 1940s, during which school construction was almost completely halted.
3. The increased number and rate of births during and immediately following World War II, which resulted in the enrollment boom of the 1950s and 1960s.
4. The expansion and extension of the educational program that required more generous space allotments.
5. Inflated site and construction costs.
6. Population mobility, which has led to a concentration of school-building needs in the peripheral areas of large towns and cities and in certain counties and states.
7. School-district reorganization, which has created a demand for larger, better equipped, centrally located buildings to replace the abandoned school plants.
8. The long history of inadequate plants for public schools.

The last item requires further explanation. Throughout our history as a nation, the public school system has been plagued with overcrowded and inadequate school plants.[7] As early as 1848, Barnard wrote that almost all school plants were badly located; exposed to the noise, dust, and danger of highways; and built at the least possible expense of labor and material. He criticized them for being too small, badly lighted, poorly ventilated, imperfectly warmed, and not furnished with seats and desks suitable for pupils.[8] Apathy of the public toward inadequacy of school-plants is related to a lack of understanding of the importance of the plant to the educational process. All too often the schoolhouse is considered merely a shelter. Belatedly, the vociferous expressions of dissatisfaction with the antiquated school-plants in the core city are stimulating interest in school-plant improvement. The measure of adequacy has become more than structural soundness. The cost of replacing these functionally obsolete but structurally defensible plants will be tremendous and will require state and federal, as well as local, financial contributions.

SCHOOL-PLANT PLANNING

The educational administrator is by the nature of his position responsible for stimulating effective school plant planning. He must know the major steps in building a new school plant. These include:

1. Analyzing the educational needs of the community and determining the fu-

[6]J. H. Fredrickson, "The Principal and School Plant Planning," *The Bulletin of the Wisconsin Secondary School Administrators Association,* vol. 1, no. 3, Spring 1973, pp. 13, 16.

[7]S. J. Knezevich, "Inadequate School Plant Facilities," *The American School Board Journal,* May 1954, p. 44.

[8]Henry Barnard, *Principles of School Architecture,* Hartford, Conn.: Case, Tiffany, 1858, pp. 11–12.

ture school program desired as a basis for evaluating existing facilities as well as planning new or remodeled ones.

2. Surveying the facilities of the school district and establishing a master facilities plan giving due consideration to the possibility of district reorganization.
3. Selecting and acquiring the sites needed to implement the approved master plan.
4. Preparing educational specifications for each separate project or facility recommended in the approved master plan.
5. Employing architectural and other services required to design each separate project in accordance with the approved educational specifications.
6. Securing bids, letting contracts, and erecting the building in accordance with the approved working drawing.
7. Equipping the completed building and putting it into use.[9]

The respective responsibilities of owner and architect in school-plant construction are summarized in Table 24–1.

Educational Facilities Laboratories has counseled those contemplating school-plant construction to anticipate, because schools are usually planned too hurriedly; to think of what the school is to do before making decisions about it; not to plan in isolation, because there may be others close by with similar problems; and not to buy permanence at the expense of performance.[10]

SCHOOL-PLANT COSTS

While the cost of school-plants has definitely increased since the end of

World War II, there is evidence that the cost of constructing other facilities has increased at a far greater rate. Thus, during the 20 years before 1957, the cost of school buildings rose about 150 percent, whereas the cost of all buildings jumped 210 percent. The cost of general construction has risen 270 percent; of brick residences, 225 percent; of frame residences, 225 percent; of highway construction, 200 percent; and of automobiles, more than 200 percent.[11] The increased cost of construction and manufacturing is not surprising, for during the past 20 years the price of structural steel has risen 215 percent; the price of face brick, 200 percent; the cost of common labor, 330 percent; the cost of skilled labor, 220 percent; and the price of materials and components of construction, 200 percent.[12] The continuing inflation rate, rising labor costs, and increasing materials cost combined to elevate school-plant construction expenditures during each year since the end of World War II. The 1970s is not likely to show any decline in costs per square foot despite new building systems and greater cost consciousness.

A building whose initial cost is low is not necessarily an economical building. Indeed, there appears to exist an inverse relation between the initial cost of a building and its subsequent maintenance cost. In other words, the lower the initial cost of a building, the greater the likelihood of early and continued high maintenance expenses during the lifetime of the structure. A study of Zimmerman indicated a correlation between initial price and subsequent maintenance cost that is

[9]Council of Educational Facilities Planners, op. cit.

[10]Educational Facilities Laboratories, *The Cost of a Schoolhouse,* New York: The Laboratories, 1960, p. 138.

[11]American Association of School Administrators, *Stretching the School Building Dollar,* Washington, D.C.: The Association, 1958.

[12]Ibid.

TABLE 24–1

RESPONSIBILITIES OF OWNER AND ARCHITECT IN SCHOOL-PLANT CONSTRUCTION

Owner	Architect	Owner and architect
1. Seeks architectural service		
		2. Preliminary conferences
		3. Owner/architect agreement
		4. Establish building program
		5. Set production time limits
	6. Program analysis	
	7. Schematic designs	
8. Approves schematic documents		
	9. Preliminary drawings	
	10. Preliminary specifications	
	11. Preliminary estimates	
		12. Conference on preliminaries
	13. Revisions to preliminaries	
14. Approves preliminary documents		
15. Authorizes final documents		
16. Approves special consultants, if any		
		Special:
		17. 25 percent of fee now payable
	18. Final working drawings	
		19. Conference on specifics
	20. Final specifications	
	21. Final estimates	
		22. Set construction time limit
		23. Conference and review
	24. Revisions, if required	
		Special:
		25. Review by city, state, and federal groups
		26. Conference and acceptance
27. Approves final documents		
		Special:
		28. 50 percent of fee now payable
		29. Selects contractors for bidding
	30. Issues documents for bidding	
31. Receives bids		
		32. Bid tabulation and review
	33. Advises on contract award	
34. Awards contract		
	35. Assists in execution of contract	

TABLE 24–1 (Continued)

Owner	Architect	Owner and architect
36. Executes contract		
	37. Approves bonds and insurance	
38. Arranges for waiver of liens		
	39. Issues proceed letter to contractor	
		40. Field construction begins
	41. Supervises construction	
	42. Prepares field inspection reports	
	43. Reviews and approves shop drawings	
	44. Inspects and approves samples	
	45. Prepares monthly certificates	
46. Pays construction costs monthly		
		47. Reviews construction reports Special: Emergencies Special: Construction delays
	48. Prepares and signs change orders	
49. Countersigns change orders		
		Special: 50. 25 percent of fee prorated
	51. Receives special guarantees from contractor	
	52. Makes final inspection	
53. Receives release of liens		
54. Makes final payment		
55. Accepts building		
56. Assumes maintenance		
		57. Celebration

Source: *The Cost of a Schoolhouse,* New York: Educational Facilities Laboratories, 1960, p. 70. This building sequence chart was prepared by Nolen and Swinburne, Architects/Planners, Philadelphia, Pa.

greater than can be accounted for by chance.[13]

Nevertheless, a number of authorities have recommended ways of economizing in school construction. Caudill suggested the following economies in structure and construction methods:

1. Using repetitive structural units.
2. Using fewer and larger products.
3. Using speedy erection techniques to save labor costs.
4. Using modular coordination to take

[13]William J. Zimmerman, *"The Relationship of Initial Cost and Maintenance Cost in Elementary School Buildings,"* Doctoral Thesis, Stanford, Calif.: Stanford University, 1959.

advantage of standard shapes and sizes of building materials and to eliminate waste costs by cutting and fitting these materials on the construction job.[14]

The Council of Educational Facility Planners outlines 13 principles of economy in school-plant planning and construction:

1. Carefully selecting consultants, architects, and school sites.
2. Careful educational planning.
3. Tailoring the school plant to facilitate functioning of the educational program.
4. Planning the building so that internally it is easily adaptable to changing educational conditions.
5. Planning the building so that it can be enlarged or extended at a reasonable cost.
6. Preparing complete, exact, and accurate drawings and specifications.
7. Using a simple design.
8. Making the building as compact as practicable.
9. Planning certain areas or rooms in the building for multiple use.
10. Designing the building according to a system of modular dimensioning.
11. Using recurring structural units and repetitive installation procedures.
12. Using materials that minimize future maintenance and replacement costs.
13. Having standardized parts of the building prefabricated at the factory.[15]

Educational Facilities Laboratories recommended the following economies based on careful planning:

1. Selecting the best architect and professional advice before buying a site.
2. Eliminating waste space, especially in corridors, boiler rooms, and other noninstructional areas.
3. Using out-of-doors areas where possible.

4. Using a short, simple perimeter to reduce expense on exterior walls.
5. Simplifying detail and using repetitive modular building elements where possible.
6. Carefully selecting building materials.
7. Using movable partitions to reduce future remodeling costs when alterations are needed to keep the building from becoming obsolete.
8. Using space flexibly.
9. Including foundations designed for imposed loads.
10. Using walls that can be moved to subdivide space.
11. Considering acoustical problems.
12. Considering quality and quantity of light.
13. Avoiding overdesign (more capacity than needed) in the heating system.
14. Consulting with an insurance agent during design.
15. Using building alternates with moderation.
16. Avoiding confusion of cheapness with economy.
17. Keeping in mind the purpose of everything that goes into the schoolhouse.[16]

The American Association of School Administrators warned, however, that in the long run it is sometimes wiser to spend a little more money on school-plant construction.[17] The emphasis should be not on producing cheaper schools but on making best use of the school construction dollar.

TRENDS IN SCHOOL BUILDING DESIGN

Buildings are a tribute not only to the creativeness of architects who employ a variety of materials and construction techniques but also to the many school superintendents and consultants who have devoted a great amount of time

---

[14]Caudill, op. cit., p. 105.

[15]Council of Educational Facilities Planners, *Thirteen Principles of Economy in School Plant Planning and Construction,* Columbus, Ohio: The Council, 1955.

[16]Educational Facilities Laboratories, op. cit., pp. 112–113.

[17]American Association of School Administrators, *Schools for America,* Report of the AASA School Building Commission, Arlington, Va.: The Association, 1967, chap. 16.

to school-plan planning and design. Not all new construction is good, but many forward-looking approaches are evident in the school plants constructed since the end of World War II. The significant trends in school-plant planning and construction will be discussed below.

1. Planning the school building from the inside out. The present-day concept of the school building as the physical expression of the curriculum calls for the preparation of educational specifications prior to the creation of working drawings and physical specifications of the building.

2. The team approach to planning. No longer is planning the domain solely of the school board and the architect, with the superintendent acting as an informed bystander. Teachers who use the building and laymen who help pay for it are involved in advisory committees. The number of citizen's committees for school-plant planning rose from 1,000 in 1950 to almost 20,000 in 1959.[18]

3. Greater use of specially trained resource persons in the planning process. The architect, who has the necessary architectural design and engineering services available in his office, is only one of many specialists involved. Services of the school-plant consultant as well as specialists in other areas, such as the planning and design of home economics facilities, art rooms, and lunch rooms, are used to a greater extent than ever. Complexity has made it necessary for school boards to turn to individuals with specialized talents as resource persons in the school-plant planning process.

4. Increased size and more specialized design of instructional spaces.

Classrooms now are larger and are designed around the functions performed within them. The typical elementary-school classroom of the 1920s and 1930s measured 600 to 750 square feet; today, the size is 800 to 900 square feet. The use of laboratory and activity methods of instruction has resulted in larger general-purpose and special-purpose classrooms at the junior and senior high school level as well.

5. Flexibility in design. Buildings are long-lasting structures, and the educational program may change several times during the physical lifetime of a building. Planning for change calls for consideration of such things as classroom areas that are square, end walls or partitions that can be moved readily, and building design that facilitates expansion of the structure in many different directions. Flexibility can be built into a structure without greatly increasing initial costs. It is primarily a matter of careful design at the time working drawings are being created.

6. Concern for shape and form of the building. The relative merits of one-story and multiple-story structures are still debated. The concensus seems to be that in most cases a one-story building costs from 3 to 5 percent less than a multiple-story structure.[19] However, some schools, particularly secondary schools, are so large as to be unmanageable on one floor. Also, the amount of land available and needed for recreational and instructional purposes may dictate whether a single- or multiple-story structure is used. The desire to keep a school in scale with homes around it may dictate a single story. Climate must be considered, too; a one-story building may permit the use of outside corridors.

[18]"Educational Building in 1959," *American School and University,* 32nd ed., 1960–1961, New York: American School Publishing Corp., 1960, pp. 117–124.

[19]Educational Facilities Laboratories, op. cit., p. 74.

Single-story structures are more flexible in layout, can be designed for lighter structural loads (this is important in areas of poor subsoil conditions), permit nonfireproof construction of a type prohibited in multiple-story design, and generally reduce costs of window areas and exterior walls by eliminating need for scaffolding. On the other hand, multiple-story buildings require less square footage of ground and less lineal footage for foundations. Although this may not reduce the cost because the foundation must be stronger to carry live loads at multiple-story levels, it permits greater use of a site that is rolling or otherwise difficult. Multiple-story structures have a smaller roof area that reduces heat loss and maintenance cost. Plumbing costs are also lower because toilet layouts can be stacked and pipes, ducts, and conduits can be shorter.[20]

Nevertheless the trend appears clearly in favor of the single-story structure for both elementary and secondary schools.

7. Use of larger sites. The minimums recommended by the Council of Educational Facilities Planners are being accepted. No longer is an elementary school built on a half-block or block area, and no longer is a secondary school constructed on a crowded downtown site. The elementary school with 5 to 10 acres and the secondary school with 30 to 40 is no longer unusual.

8. Concept of the building as more than a collection of classrooms. Classrooms are no longer all exactly the same size, but vary in area and design in accordance with the instruction carried on in them. Highly specialized spaces such as auditoriums, gymnasiums, swimming pools, shops, and laboratories are considered an integral part of secondary schools. A new elementary school without a multiple-purpose room and a suite of offices for the principal and the nurse is a rarity.

9. Concern with quality as well as quantity of lighting. The importance of a "balanced visual environment" is now almost universally recognized, although implementation lags far behind. Contributions of the Council of Educational Facilities Planners cannot be overlooked in this field.[21]

10. Concern with thermal environment (temperature, humidity, and air flow) and research to determine conditions most conducive to human comfort for learning. This includes adequate heating and ventilating in winter and air-conditioning in summer. Air-conditioned schools are now commonplace in all regions of the country not simply the south. The writer recalls being a member of a jury reviewing school plants worthy of exhibition and citation in the early 1960s. Several buildings earned high praise plus a special citation simply because they were air-conditioned; five years later, a high percentage of school plants submitted for review by another jury were air-conditioned and this factor was no longer crucial in determining whether the building was worthy of exhibition or citation.

11. Use of a variety of materials and techniques of construction. Brick and wood are no longer the basic or only construction materials. Glass (in various forms, such as glass block, plain plate glass, tinted glass) is used extensively. Steel and other metal panels for curtain walls are replacing solid masonry exteriors. New materials are being coupled with new techniques of construction.

[20]Ibid.

[21]Council of Educational Facilities Planners, *Guide for Planning School Plants,* Columbus, Ohio: The Council, 1964.

12. Concern for esthetics. In recent years it has been recognized that beauty does not necessarily mean useless ornamental fabrication but can be a part of functional buildings. Treatment of masses within the structure as well as blending building design and site has enhanced the appearance of many school structures. The beauty of a school is a tribute to the artistry of the architect who is able to blend educational demands, structural requirements, and building materials into an esthetically pleasing structure.

13. Use of carpeting. Carpeting in libraries, classrooms, cafeterias, and administrative suites became common during the 1960s and widely accepted in the 1970s. Studies have appeared on the economics of carpeting.[22]

14. Improved design of components. The establishment of the School Construction Systems Development (SCSD) in the early 1960s by Educational Facilities Laboratories led to improved design for various components used in school construction. This promises to have a significant impact on speed and economy of construction. SCSD has compiled a list of performance specifications for four construction components: long-span structures, movable partitions, thermal environment systems and control, and effective low-brightness lighting for desirable visual environments. The purpose is to achieve maximum flexibility without loss of quality or variety. It is an alternative to the stock building approach.

SCHOOL CONSTRUCTION IN LARGE CITIES

A large number of school-plants were constructed in the large cities during the 1920s and 1930s. Owing to the high quality of initial construction and to maintenance and operation programs, the plants remain physically sound although many are functionally obsolete. The educational program has changed so much that it no longer fits into a building designed during the 1920s or 1930s.

Construction of new facilities in the core city, where land values are usually high, calls for novel approaches. The proposed solution in Pittsburgh was the "great high school." Other solutions have been the high-rise school building, the incorporation of instructional centers in commercial high-rise apartment structures,[23] and the incorporation of instructional centers in large downtown office buildings. New York City proposed converting the luxury liner Queen Mary into a school to be anchored off the old Brooklyn Navy Yard. A committee of architects estimated that the conversion would cost about $3 million, some $7 million less than the cost of building a land school. New York City was outbid on both the Queen Mary and the Queen Elizabeth, and this imaginative approach to urban school construction has yet to be tested.

The educational park concept, a revival of the idea of combining facilities for kindergarten through Grade 12 on a single site, gained popularity during the 1960s—not because any unusual advantages accrue in terms of building construction but because of a desire to hasten the end of de facto segregation. Unless the site is large enough (about 100 acres) and access roads are adequate to handle sizable traffic volume, however, the educational park concept can precipitate

---

[22]G. M. Parks, The Economics of Carpeting and Resilient Flooring, Philadelphia: Wharton School, University of Pennsylvania, 1966.

[23]American Association of School Administrators, Schools for America, Report of the AASA School Building Commission, Arlington, Va.: The Association, 1967, chap. 7.

many problems in a congested urban area.

OPERATION AND MAINTENANCE OF FACILITIES

The time it takes for a building to become physically obsolete depends on the quality of the original construction and materials as well as the quality of housekeeping and maintenance. Some buildings have a useful physical life of less than 50 years, whereas others have functioned effectively for more than 75.[24]

Operation includes cleaning, disinfecting, heating, caring for grounds, and similar housekeeping duties, which are repeated somewhat regularly. Maintenance is concerned with keeping grounds, buildings, and equipment in their original condition of completeness or efficiency. Repair and replacement are an essential part of maintenance. Operation and maintenance have the common objective of keeping school property in the best possible condition for effective education at all times. Because housekeeping activities can be looked upon as preventive maintenance, separation of operation and maintenance is rather artificial; new terminology is needed.

The men given primary responsibility for the care of school buildings and grounds are called janitors, custodians, porters, and cleaners; the women are called maids, janitresses, matrons, cleaners, scrubwomen, and charwomen. The term custodian will be used here. These individuals play an important role in the management of the school plant or property.

There is considerable agreement that

[24]S. J. Knezevich and John Guy Fowlkes, *Business Management of Local School Systems*, New York: Harper & Row, 1960, chap. 13.

custodians should be selected carefully on the basis of skill, knowledge, and personal character rather than for low wages or as political and sentimental favors. Employment of custodians by the school board without consideration of recommendations by the administrators responsible for their performance is poor personnel procedure. In some states, employment of all nonteaching personnel is subject to civil-service rules, and permanent employees are selected only from a list established as a result of examinations. This is an encouraging development, for it removes a post vital to preservation of school property from political favoritism or sentimentality.

The custodian's social contacts with pupils, teachers, principal, central-office staff members, superintendent, board, and the public are many and varied. At the building level the custodian looks to the principal for directions. The principal, therefore, is the immediate superior of the building custodian. The director of plant operations and maintenance for the district and his staff are a source of professional aid to the custodian in solving technical problems related to the cleaning and care of the building. They also direct the in-service programs for custodial personnel.

The relation between the custodian and teachers must be defined as well. It is not the function of the teachers to command activities of building custodians. Failure to define lines of authority can result in conflicts among teachers, principals, school-plant supervisors, and building custodians. The teachers and pupils can complicate housekeeping by failure to exercise disciplinary control. There is little justification for any youngster to throw paper on the floor. Undesirable habits or sloppiness in students do not contribute to the care and upkeep of the buildings. Perhaps the antilittering campaigns and the general emphasis on maintaining a clean environment will have its impact on school operations and maintenance.

The building custodian must accomplish a large number of varied tasks to keep the building in operating condition. Custodial work schedules can be used to facilitate their efficient execution. Such schedules can save work, simplify tasks, and improve performance. The custodial requirements of a school building vary with the type and age of the structure. Not all rooms are of the same area and not all are cleaned with the same ease. Studies have shown that the custodial manpower needs of a building can be determined on the basis of (1) the nature and number of school tasks of the custodian, (2) the setup time and total time required for each and all tasks, (3) the accepted standards for the number of minutes in a man-unit, and (4) the computation of man-units by dividing (2) by (3).[25]

There is a close relation between the quality of custodial services and the need for building maintenance. Systematic inspection of each school building at least annually is an important first step toward an effective maintenance program. Regular inspections can detect small difficulties. Record keeping is necessary to obtain the full benefit of periodic inspection.

The question sometimes arises whether maintenance work should be done by custodians, special maintenance crews, or through contracts with outside agencies. The general rule is that the more out of the ordinary the maintenance work is the more likely it will be done on a contract basis by outside staff. Compli-

cated maintenance work that necessitates a highly specialized staff is likely to be done by a contract force. This is true, for instance, of major electrical repairs, which may take a considerable period of time and require special skills.

Age and use deteriorate buildings and equipment. It is a responsibility of the superintendent and the principal to formulate the kind of building operation and maintenance program that will extend the useful physical life of building and equipment. Davis indicated that the principal has primary responsibility for the utilization and care of the building. He outlined procedures for analyzing a variety of facility concerns including procedures for analyzing custodial problems.[26] Vandalism of school property has grown at an alarming rate and has exacted a cost measured in millions of dollars annually in large city systems. Security systems consisting of special alarms and a force of security guards have been installed in some large districts. Vandalism of sizeable proportions was rare prior to World War II and now has emerged as a problem of concern to administrators.

SUMMARY

The school-plant is a means to an end. It exists to facilitate the instructional program. There is a close relation between the school curriculum and the school-pant. The school-plant can be defined as the physical expression or space interpretation of the curriculum. The 1950s and 1960s were periods of great school-plant construction as well

---

[25]Ibid., p. 236.

[26]J. Clark Davis, The Principal's Guide to Educational Facilities, Columbus, Ohio: Chas. Merrill, 1973, chap. 4.

as of advances in design and architecture.

The continuous shortage in building space, even in the face of unprecedented construction over an extended period, can be traced to such factors as the Depression of the 1930s, curtailments in World War II, increased mobility of the population, school-district reorganization, and the long history of inadequate school pants.

At one time school buildings were simple structures. Today they are complex structures and a wide variety of talents are required to plan, design, and construct them. The school board has the fundamental responsibility for providing such facilities. It must depend upon its chief executive officer to coordinate the various specialists involved and to provide special advice when needed. The services of an architect or an educational consultant are important, but the board must evaluate the advice in the light of community needs and traditions.

Major steps in school-plant construction include analysis of educational needs, development of a master building plan, procurement of the necessary site, preparation of educational specifications for each project, design of the building, securing bids and letting contracts to erect the building, and equipping and using the building.

School costs have increased, but not as much as the cost of other types of construction. Low initial cost of a building is not necessarily an indication of an economical structure. There are many ways to economize in schoo! construction, nonetheless.

The significant trends in school construction in the years following World War II are planning from the inside out, the team approach to planning, greater use of specialized resource persons, increase in size and specialization of instructional spaces, flexibility of design, concern for the shape and form of the building, use of larger school sites, expansion in complexity of a building, concern for lighting and for thermal environment, use of a variety of techniques and materials of construction, and concern for esthetics in building design.

Age and use deteriorate school buildings. This creates a need for the special staff of custodians and maintenance men to keep the building functional. The quality of custodial services is reflected in the condition of the building and its years of usefulness. The building custodian is responsible to the building principal.

QUESTIONS

1. What is a school building?
2. What have been the significant trends in school-plant construction?
3. What is the role of the school board in school-plant planning? Of the superintendent? Of specialists?
4. How can school building costs be minimized?
5. How can the physical usefulness of a building be extended?
6. How can the educational usefulness of a school-plant be extended?

SELECTED REFERENCES

American Association of School Administrators, *Schools for America*, Report of the AASA School Building Commission, Arlington, Va.: The Association, 1967.

Caudill, W. W., *Toward Better School Design*, New York: McGraw-Hill, 1954.

Council of Educational Facilities Planners, *Guide for Plannning School Plants*, Columbus, Ohio: The Council, 1964.

Davis, J. Clark, *The Principal's Guide to Educational Facilities*, Columbus, Ohio: Chas. Merrill, 1973.

Educational Facilities Laboratories, *The Cost of a Schoolhouse*, New York: Educational Facilities Laboratories, 1960.

Frederickson, J. H., "The Principal and School Plant Planning," *The Bulletin of the Wisconsin Secondary School Administrators Association*, Spring 1973., vol. no. 3, pp. 13, 16.

Knezevich, S. J., "The Curriculum and the School Plant," *Educational Leadership*, May 1953.

Knezevich, S. J., "Your New School: Procrustean Bed or a Functional School Plant?" *The American School Board Journal*, March 1960.

25

POLITICAL DIMENSIONS OF ADMINISTRATION: THE POLITICS OF EDUCATION AND PUBLIC RELATIONS

Throughout history school administrators have been admonished to remain out of politics. To be called a politician or to be accused of playing politics was a rebuke. More recently what seems to be an opposite recommendation has gained prominence with the declaration that schools operate in a political environment and that education is one dimension of public policy making. Traditionally politics has suggested its worst side: partisanship, the spoils system, the employment of office for personal advantage or for favored friends. In the more recent views of politics the schools are seen as part of the political system or branch of government and are influenced by formal and informal power coalitions in the community, state, and nation. This is politics in the best sense of the term and it is this latter point of view that prevails herein. There are political dimensions to the art of school administration. As Gregg put it "politics . . . is public, not private, in the sense that its aim is the influencing of decisions relating to public issues within a political system."[1] In this sense the school is a

political system itself within which power and influence swirls and is, as well, part of a broader political system for the state and nation. Education is the public's business and it is necessary too for administrators to comprehend how public policy is shaped, that is, the nature of the political decision-making process of local school boards, state legislatures, and the federal congress. The power structure at various levels is dynamic and the administrator must sense when a new power elite emerges. To illustrate, the impact of the young vote on school politics is not yet known. Maguire declared that school boards and administrators should be aware that the changing voter profile could have serious consequences in school elections.[2]

Public education has always been close to the hearts of the people of the United States. The idea of a system of public education was born and nourished at the grass-roots level. The people, through the town meeting, watched over the schools they organized to satisfy certain ideals. The public's perceptions of educational functions influenced its approaches to decision making, its choice of leaders,

[1]Russell T. Gregg, "Political Dimensions of Educational Administration," *Teachers College Record,* LXVII, November 1965, pp. 118–128.

[2]John W. Maguire, "Changing Voter Profiles and School Elections," *Intellect,* vol. 101, no. 2344, November 1972, p. 110.

576

and its ranking of values. A description of the way power and influence are exercised in one community is not necessarily valid for others.

The complexity of the educational system influenced the manner in which public decisions on education were made. Schools multiplied as the community grew in size and became more heterogeneous and as the one-teacher school grew to many and large attendance centers, the distance between teachers and the people widened. The involvement of the citizenry through the town meeting was no longer feasible. The people and their leaders found access to information difficult and consequently lost understanding of what schools were doing. Information-disbursing procedures effective in the small district failed in the complex ones. The problem was intensified when professional administrators assumed executive responsibility for complex institutions, for then even school-board members, representatives of the people, had to depend upon another agent for information. The times demanded an executive organization, but the widening gap between school and community was an unwanted corollary. Nevertheless, public apathy could be tolerated as long as educational needs remained relatively unchanged, most needs were satisfied, and resource demands did not grow at unprecedented rates.

After World War II, however, the demands on public education did indeed increase at an unprecedented rate. More teachers and more buildings were urgently required, and the money to buy them had to come from the public. It began to dawn on school officials that what the public *didn't know* about school problems *could hurt the system's development.* The basic notion that public education needs public sympathy and support

for its continuance and expansion was rediscovered in the late 1940s. The criticism of public education following World War II further spotlighted the importance of effective relations between school, home, and community. Those responsible for the administration of public education started to redevelop the art of keeping people informed and interested in public education and of identifying and understanding the community power structure. Closer ties between the people and their schools, were encouraged anew despite the ever-growing size and complexity of districts. Administrators became more sensitive to the need for a better understanding of the politics of school administration.

CRITICISM OF PUBLIC EDUCATION

Progress in public education has come as the result of actions varying from pitched battles to dogged delaying tactics. The criticism of public education immediately following World War II reached a peak shortly before 1950 and then died down, only to be triggered anew by the first Soviet success in orbiting a space satellite. In the 1970s it is less a criticism of some dimension such as the teaching of reading or science and more a general reaction to the escalating costs and lack of accountability. No battle in public education is final; even what many consider the basic traditions of public education are not immune to challenge. For example, that resources would be expended to educate all children and youth, rather than reserved for an intellectual elite group, was decided (finally, it was thought) by the beginning of the twentieth century; nevertheless heightened interest in moving rapidly toward spectacular space accomplishments, and the concomitant need for gifted scientists, refocused debate on this issue.

One might postulate a "law of attack on social institutions" as a variation of what sociologists refer to as the crisis theory of social change. This law would proclaim that whenever a nation or a culture is experiencing social or physical duress of any kind— a depression, a shooting war, a "cold" war, loss of face from not being first in almost everything, or a propaganda disadvantage—its social institutions will come under attack from within, and its own people rather than foreigners will lead the attack. It is not unusual for the attack to continue long after charges that prompted it have been proved wrong or of doubtful validity. Emotion overcomes logical consideration. Revolution, usually preceded by a civil war of words and ideas, may be the end result. Thus, no one began to praise schools when the United States began to score one dramatic space success after another until it was acknowledge that American capability in space technology was at least equal to the Soviets'.

Throughout history, the social institutions responsible for education of children and youth have been prime targets of criticism during periods of social upheaval. This has predictive value: Schools will be criticized when difficult times are being experienced. The waxing and waning of criticism of public education follows the cycle of social unrest and stability. Even when the education scene is relatively peaceful, there is no guarantee that schools will never again face criticism. How well the public schools weather these periods is related to their proximity to the community.

The school administrator works in a socially sensitive institution. If there is to be progress, schools must be attuned to the times. Change in educa-

tion is inevitable, and the stress of change can be faced best when the people of the community remain close to the schools. Public apathy is of far greater concern to the administrator that public criticism. Criticism betrays an interest, even though it may be negative. The important thing is to keep people fully informed on what is happening in educational institutions and what is needed to improve them.

A fundamental thesis in this book is that conflict in education is inevitable. For a long time it was believed that conflict betrayed a lack of ability —that difficulties resulted from ineptitude. This is true in some cases, but even the best led school district will experience conflict. Conflict is characteristic of the times, and no one can avoid it perpetually. The measure of the administrator is how well she manages conflict. Her behavior under stress and criticism will determine success. Conflict is the name of the game, and the public school administrator is right in the thick of it.

GROUPS ASSUMING PUBLIC LEADERSHIP ROLES IN EDUCATION

There are many groups outside of the educational system that have been organized to allow individuals to pursue their special interests in education. They form part of the political setting for schools and often interface with administrators.

The PTA

One of the earliest formally organized groups of citizens interested in promoting the cause of education was the National Congress of Mothers founded in 1897 for education in motherhood, child health, child feeding, and morality through the development of a strong body and healthy mind. In 1908 this organization changed its name to National Congress of Mothers and Parent-Teacher Association, which was shortened in 1924 to the National Congress of Parents and Teachers.[3] Today this group is usually referred to as the PTA.

The national organization is made up of a series of state and local PTAs. Membership has been growing. The number of organized PTA units rose from about 26,000 in 1946 to more than 46,000 in 1967. Total membership increased from about 3,900,000 in 1946 to more than 11,500,000 in 1966, and then stabilized in the mid-1960s. Membership is made up largely of teachers and parents of children who are attending schools, although it is not confined to such individuals.

The PTA is concerned with developing closer relations between home and school, parents and teachers. Some of its other objectives are:

1. To promote the welfare of children and youth in the home, church, and community.
2. To raise standards of home life.
3. To secure adequate laws for care and protection of children and youth.
4. To bring closer relations between home and school so that parents and teachers may cooperate intelligently in training the child.
5. To develop between educators and the general public such united efforts as will secure for every child the highest advantages in physical, mental, social, and spiritual education.

The PTA is a general type of citizen's organization, concerned with

[3]Arthur B. Moehlman and James A. Van Zwoll, *School Public Relations*, New York: Appleton-Century-Crofts, 1957, chap. 18.

the total educational program rather than a specific part only. Special-interest groups, such as "parents of athletes" and "band mothers," focus on one aspect of the school program to the exclusion of others. The more general PTA is a way for lay people to team up with professionals to further the cause of education. The purpose of the PTA is not to raise money to buy special equipment for a given building. Units that devote all or most of their time to raising funds to buy motion picture projectors, curtains for the auditorium, or other special school equipment fail to fulfill their potential. Instead they develop the stereotype of the PTA as a bunch of cookie pushers, money-thumpers, and do-gooders concerned with issues peripheral to the child's education and neglectful of the crucial ones.

The PTA as a public-leadership agency experienced some intraorganizational battles during the 1960s when extremist groups attempted to take over local school organizations. Some were successful and used the PTA as a platform to attack educational policies and to peddle extremist propaganda. Special interest groups unable to take over the local school PTA organized the PTO (Parent-Teacher Organization) and capitalized on being confused with the PTA, which has state and national dimensions. The organization seems to be strongest at the elementary school level and weakest at the high school level. It appears to exert less impact on core city areas where large numbers of disadvantaged pupils may be located. The more militant groups from low socioeconomic backgrounds tend to be critical of the PTA as being dominated by middle class values. The administrators of attendance centers tend to interact more with the PTA than do those at the central office level.

The National Citizen's Commission

A considerable amount of citizen activity in behalf of public education was stimulated during the brief history of the National Citizen's Commission for the Public Schools (NCCPS). This organization rekindled an idea and served as a mechanism for citizens banding together to act in a common cause which was positive in nature and dedicated to the improvement of the schools.

The NCCPS was organized in 1949 at a time when the public schools were in the midst of many difficulties and faced a growing volume of criticism. Many outstanding men in business, labor, law, and publishing joined this lay public action convinced that America's prime need was for a wise and informed citizenry and that the quality of the public schools were critically important to the nation. The first chairman of the new commission was Roy E. Larson, then president of Time, Incorporated. He declared: "Problems of public education concern all of us and it is time for all of us to do something about it."[4] Dr. James B. Conant, then president of Harvard University, suggested the importance of stimulating people to work toward improving public education. The NCCPS was an important development for it influenced public policy and decision making to promote the advancement of public education. This is political action at its best: NCCPS was an organized way to encourage greater people participation in political activity in support of improved schools. Its goals were to help Americans realize how important public schools are to an expanding democracy and to arouse in each community the intelligence and will to improve the public schools. Its credo was set forth as follows:

The problem of its children's schools lies at the heart of a free society. None of man's public institutions has a greater effect upon his conduct as a citizen, whether of the community, of the nation, or of the world. The goal of our public schools shall be to make the best in education available to every American child on completely equal terms. Public-school education should be constantly reappraised and kept responsive both to our educational traditions and to the changing times.[5]

The NCCPS contained a built-in provision for its termination after six years. It became the National Citizen's Commission for Better Schools in January 1956. This second organization terminated all formal activities on December 31, 1959. The total life span was a little over ten years, but it was a most significant decade.

Initial goals of arousing citizen interest and helping communities organize for school improvement have been substantially achieved through the work of the NCCPS and of the Advertising Council, a nonprofit organization representing advertisers, their agencies, radio, television, newspapers, magazines, and outdoor advertising. Through a giant campaign conducted by the NCCPS and the Council, citizens everywhere heard of the importance of improving schools through recruiting teachers and building new facilities. The NCCPS published a monthly bulletin, *The Citizens and Their Schools,* and later a newspaper, *Better Schools.* In the first months the NCCPS could find only 17 local citizen's committees in the entire United States.[6] A year later there were 175 committees, the following year 1000, and by mid-1955

[4]David B. Dreiman, *How to Get Better Schools,* New York: Harper & Row, 1956, chap. 7.

[5]Ibid., p. 71.
[6]Ibid., p. 77.

there were 2500 local and state committees in regular communication with the NCCPS. It was estimated that 7500 more were in operation in 1956 but most were on their own. Another source estimated 20,000 citizen's committees in action in 1960.

It was a coincidence—but a most fortuitous one—that the NCCPS came into being at the very time when education was under the most vicious attack in decades.[7] Professional administrators lacked a broad public power base to contain or reduce such attacks. It is the opinion of the writer that the NCCPS did much to counteract the unwarranted criticism of public education and laid the foundation for a positive program of improvement of public education through the involvement of lay advisory committees.

Roundtable of public schools

Another informal public organization that promoted interest in public schools was the Roundtable of Public Schools, which came into being in March 1953. It was based on the idea that the most effective way to reach the people (influence public opinion) was through existing organizations of all kinds—service clubs, business and industrial groups, farm and labor organizations, etc.—rather than create new mechanisms. Top-level representatives of more than 30 national organizations met twice a year to discuss the school situation and ideas for its improvement. The Roundtable was not an action body; it did not commit its component organizations to anything, but its work improved the character and effectiveness of the organizational efforts on behalf of the school. One illustration of successful organizational activity was the program of teacher recruitment sponsored by Kiwanis International at a time of a severe shortage.[8]

Lay advisory committees

The involvement of lay advisory committees as a political force in education reached a high point during the 1950s. Presently lay committees constitute a latent force whose efforts are sporadic rather than continual. The purpose of such committees is to provide two-way communication between the schools and the community. They communicate information about schools to the people and funnel facts about the community to educators. It was hoped that through this process misinformation, misunderstanding, and mistrust could be minimized. The previously mentioned NCCPS was instrumental in stimulating formation of many lay advisory committees and served as a national clearing house for describing their activities.

Lay advisory committees are usually selected to include:

1. People who have a vital interest in public education.
2. People who are willing and able to give time and study to problems of education.
3. Enough people to provide cross-representation of social groups within the school committee.

It is difficult to get agreement upon who should be excluded from appointment to a lay advisory committee. Even the general principle of excluding individuals who do not believe in public education deserves some qualification, for it need not be assumed that parents who send their children

[7]Ibid., p. 81.

[8]Edward M. Tuttle, "Neither Alone nor Aloft," *NEA Journal,* November 1956, pp. 512–513.

to private schools do not believe in the principle of public education. The selection of people with a vital interest in the school need not exclude the "antischool" forces, because interest can be negative as well as positive.

Sumpton and Engstrom, is a systematic approach to school-community relations,[9] reviewed community participation in education through formal and informal approaches and identified three levels of citizen's participation: (1) collecting and assembling information, (2) classifying and interpreting data, and (3) making judgments and developing recommendations. These authors declared that lay advisory committees have demonstrated their value to school communities across the land.

Responsibility for appointing or organizing a lay advisory committee should rest with an agency which has the confidence of the public. Many individuals shy away from participation unless some sort of public recognition or status is granted to the lay advisory group. Furthermore, a self-appointed group that serves without public recognition is often a pressure group fighting for special favors or power rather than trying to solve a community problem. In communities where the board of education enjoys the respect of the citizenry, it usually takes the initiative and responsibility for appointment. If the local board is not held in good repute, some other public agency must assume this responsibility.

Activities of lay committees. A lay advisory committee should not be organized unless there exists a felt need for such an organization. In some

[9]M. R. Sumpton and Y. Engstrom, *School-Community Relations,* New York: McGraw-Hill, 1966.

communities, an awareness of this need may be felt, but in other cases educational leaders may have to make the community aware of the existing need. Tenure of the committee is related to the number and intensity of problems that require attention. If there is a need for a special group, then concern about how to keep the committee busy is without foundation. The advisory committee should think of itself as a work group that gathers facts and information about the school and community. It should not be looked upon as a means of airing opinions that are usually without foundation. However, it should not arbitrarily disallow the ventilation of feelings in such mechanisms.

The process of working out the answer to an educational problem is as significant as the conclusions reached. Although professional educators can sometimes perform research on community educational problems in a shorter time, a lay group may be in a better position to communicate the special problems and answers to the community. In some instances, the lay group may be in a better position to obtain the information needed. Lay participation in solving educational problems can result in lay awareness of them. The community comes to appreciate those things which it helps to create.

Relations with the school board. The relation between the lay advisory committee for education and the board of education often needs clear definition. Schools belong to the people, and members of the board of education are representatives of the people. The local board is the legally constituted authority on all educational matters affecting the district and is legally responsible for all official actions. A lay advisory group is not organized to take the place of the board. It may act as a sounding board for the legal school board. It often derives its status from the board. The lay advisory committee movement is an attempt to bring schools closer to the people, for it is through such committees on education that the people hope to recapture some of the feeling they had earlier for the one-room school.

The board of education cannot be forced to accept recommendations of a lay advisory group. It follows, however, that if the recommendations of such a group are repeatedly ignored or rejected, the morale and effectiveness of the group will be gravely impaired. The board of education has an obligation to inform the group when it disagrees with the advice offered.

The superintendent of schools is usually not a member of the lay advisory committee. He stands ready to serve in an advisory capacity if and when his professional services are requested. The need for professional assistance from the superintendent or other members of his staff will become apparent as the committee pursues its attack on educational problems.

Relations with the PTA. The question sometimes arises whether a lay advisory group duplicates the work done by the local PTA. If the PTA has become a mother's club, if its membership is limited to parents and teachers, and if it is made up only of people who have a positive interest in the schools, there may be a need for a lay advisory group. If the PTA is effective, there is little need for another lay group. The NCCPS recognized the PTA as a lay group on education if the organization was actually functioning as such within the community. The citizen's committee movement ac-

tually stimulated membership in the PTA rather than decreased it.

POLITICS OF ADMINISTRATION: COMMUNITY DECISION MAKING

There was a growing interest in the politics of educational administration during the 1960s—in sociological analysis of the nature of the community, its power structure or public leadership, and the process of public policy and decision making. This is the politics of education, that is, the interaction between the school and the political system in which it is located.

Probing the social class and power structure in American communities started in the late 1920s and early 1930s with the work of the Lynds.[10] These were efforts outside the field of education. The Lynds reported that the power, or influence in decision making, in Middletown (Muncie, Indiana) was concentrated in the hands of established families, called the "old elite." The Lynds were among the first to describe the power elite of a community and the manner in which economic power was utilized in daily decision making in small American cities. Warner's group studied another locale identified as "Yankee City" in the 1930s.[11] They depicted the impact of shifting ownership and managership functions within the highly industrialized city from local people to others outside the community. Warner developed the well-known classifica-

[10]R. S. Lynd and H. M. Lynd, *Middletown*, New York: Harcourt Brace Jovanovich, 1929; and *Middletown in Transition*, New York: Harcourt Brace Jovanovich, 1937.

[11]There are many volumes published by the Warner group, one of which is W. L. Warner and T. S. Lunt, *The Social Life of a Modern Community*, New Haven, Conn.: Yale, 1941.

tion system for the various social class, economic status, and other major components of Yankee City. These studies supported the conclusion that people of high socioeconomic status are more likely to hold office in formal associations than people of lower socioeconomic status. Other writers prepared case studies of social, political, economic, and cultural factors in communities in the South and West as opposed to the midwestern and eastern cities examined by the Lynds and Warner's group. They reported the nature of economic and political controls and described who was and was not a part of the power elite in such cities. Hunter's studies of the community power structure in "Regional City" (Atlanta, Georgia)[12] suggested that a small homogeneous group of men formed a power elite and directed the affairs of this southern city. Sociologists ventured out into an analysis of the political world of the community. It was a surprise to no one when such efforts received the criticisms of political scientists, who considered themselves to be the real experts on politics.

Hunter's work opened a new dimension in community analysis and understanding of public decision making. Political scientists continued their interest in community decision making but preferred to call it "public leadership." Bell et al. classified various methods of studying community power structure or pubic leadership as one or a combination of the following five:[13]

1. Positional, or formal leadership, method. A public leader, or a member of the power elite, is identified by the organizational position he holds, which in the researcher's judgment is important, influential, or indicative of his status. A person is thus identified as a public leader if he is one or more of the following in the community: (a) an elected political leader, (b) a high civil servant or political appointee, (c) a major business executive, (d) a military officer of high rank, or (e) an officer holder in a voluntary or civic-minded association. Influence or power is related to the position held in private or public agencies. It is implied that a person with influence in some aspect of the political, social, or economic life of the community will have a platform from which to influence community affairs. The essential arbitrariness of the positional approach is apparent when the researcher is forced to select types of positions judged important in community decision making or public leadership. Disagreement among experts about the power positions in a community is common.

2. Reputational, or nominal leadership, method. This method relies on identifying public leaders or community power elite through opinions of other members of society whom the researcher thinks are qualified to identify members of the power structure. Emphasis is on the reputation a person enjoys, not the position she holds. The method's validity depends upon the informant's knowledge of community affairs and sensitivity to power relations. There is always the danger that the informant relied on by the researcher is biased, brainwashed, or uninformed. To overcome these potential shortcomings, some researchers consult a sample and cross-section of a population of informants; others identify a limited number of key informants or a panel of experts who

[12]Floyd Hunter, *Community Power Structure*, Chapel Hill, N.C.: University of North Carolina Press, 1953.

[13]S. Bell, R. J. Hill and C. R. Wright, *Public Leadership*, San Francisco: Chandler, 1961, chap. 2.

are judged by others to really know the community; still others combine the two by starting with a small number of key people or judges and then broadening the sample. Hunter utilized both positional and reputational methods. He started with lists of recognized leaders as persons in prominent positions in business, government, civic associations, and society. From these, a panel of experts was developed. Panel members were then queried to identify top leaders in Regional City. Researchers who compared persons identified as leaders by means of the reputational and the positional methods concluded that some individuals appear on one list but not on the other. In other words composition of the community's power elite differs significantly depending on method of selection employed. This doubtless led some researchers to combine the positional and reputational methods. The reputational approach may also be referred to as the informal leadership pattern. Many significant decision makers at the local level are not in leadership positions in government, business, military, or civic associations. Those in the state and national power elite are more likely to occupy such posts.

3. Social participation method. Another assumption is that an individual's participation in a variety of activities is an index of his social participation and, therefore, of his access to the community's network of power and communications. Social participation can be used as an operational definition of public leadership. Researchers do not use this method as frequently as the first two.

4. Influence, or opinion leadership, method. Opinion leaders or personal influentials in a community are not necessarily holders of formal positions of leadership. This implies that one person looks to another as a well-informed individual whose opinions carry weight. Whatever its validity, the method is based on asking individuals to whom do they turn for advice and counsel on given matters. This approach rejects the concept of a generalized leadership type and suggests instead that each special area of decision making develops its own opinion leaders. One person may be asked about a network of roads, another about welfare problems, and still another about education.

5. Decision-making, or event-analysis, method. This is an historical approach based on tracing the history of a particular decision or event and determining who was influential in making this come about. It works backward, but again depends upon opinions of others to determine who in effect is part of the power structure.

Another approach to community power-structure analysis involves identifying the number of times the person's name is mentioned in a local newspaper. This is of doubtful valadity if top decision makers avoid publicity and contact with the mass media.

Bell et al. summarized a tremendous volume of research (over 570 items are listed in their bibliography) and reported the major finding as:

1. Public leadership in the nation is a man's role.
2. The public leaders are most likely in the middle years of life; some elder members of society are powerful, but rarely are young adults described as leaders.
3. Leadership is not often in the hands of members of ethnic or religious minority groups. Where the concerns of the entire community or nation are involved, the vast majority of dominants are native-born white protestants, although exceptions are noted in some large urban areas.

4. Formal reputation and social participation types of leadership are displayed more often by people in the middle and upper social classes as well as by those with above-average formal education.[14]

Concern for identifying the power structure of the community and its impact on school decisions started in the late 1950s and continues to attract considerable interest. Vidich and Bensman analyzed school politics in a small rural community called Springdale.[15] Goldhammer observed the effect of the formal and informal behavior of board members on community affairs in a small Oregon school district in the early 1950s.[16] Kimbrough reported on power structure in two Florida school districts.[17] Other studies were of school communities in Tennessee. A whole host of school community case studies have followed since then. It is difficult to arrive at generalizations about public decision making on education from the case study approach.

That there are individuals and groups within communities who exercise considerable influence on vital issues has been sensed intuitively by the more skillful practicing school administrators. Research on community power structure analysis has provided a theoretical framework for studying the interaction between the school and the political leadership in the community, state, and nation. For better or for worse the educational system cannot be divorced from the quality of the political system in which it is located. It is difficult to develop a quality city or county school system located in a corrupt or inadequate city or county political system.

The following limitations should be considered in interpreting the significance of various research efforts on community power structure or public leadership. First, just about all are case studies confined to description, analysis, and interpretation of individual cities or rural communities. Generalizations from individual cases studies are fraught with danger. A description of a power elite in one community is not necessarily valid for another.

Second, the methodology employed in determining the power elite influences the outcome of the study, as does the care the researcher uses in analyzing his data. Personal prejudices or predispositions can affect interpretation of the facts.

Third, and perhaps most important, communities are dynamic. It is erroneous to assume that even a well-entrenched power elite in a stable community will remain dominant forever. Public leadership is not static. Shifts occur through time as well as because of new issues. Every administrator must be sensitive to the emergence of new groups which previously had no access to the community power elite. Subtle shifts can catapult new groups into positions of dominance. This is particularly true at present when the use of demonstrations amplified through the mass media, TV in particular, and coalitions can wrest control from what appear to be well-entrenched community power groups. Civil riots and other forms of unrest, as well as changing political climates, can significantly alter membership in the circle of community decision mak-

[14]Ibid., chap. 9.

[15]A. J. Vidich and Joseph Bensman, *Small Town and Mass Society*, Garden City, N.Y.: Doubleday, 1958.

[16]Keith Goldhammer, "Community Power Structure and School Board Membership," *American School Board Journal*, vol. 130, March 1950, pp. 23–25

[17]R. B. Kimbrough, *Community Power Structure and Analysis*, Englewod Cliffs, N.J.: Prentice-Hall, 1964.

ers. A school administrator insensitive to changes in community power structure risks failing to sense the emergence of a powerful new ally or foe. Killian pointed out the sudden shift of the black community from accommodation to protest from subservience to reaction.[18] He reported on the function of the black elite and the emergence of black leaders skilled in the techniques of bargaining.

When approval is needed for increasing taxes for school operations or financing a bond issue for new school facilities, the support of community decision makers is essential. Identifying the community power elite is not an easy task and it cannot be done with an inadequate staff. Every administrator needs sufficient staff to delegate the responsibility to study of the social, political, and economic factors within the community; to determine the power elite on the variety of economic, social, and political issues within the community; and to recognize the emergence of new groups which may some day be a dominant force.

PUBLIC RELATIONS

The public-relations movement in education, as an effort to keep the public better informed about schools, started soon after the turn of the century and came into its own shortly after World War I.[19] It has at times been almost indistinguishable from other vigorous movements, such as the community school, the citizen's advisory committee, politics of education, or the accountability movements. Much of the literature consists of rule-of-thumb techniques and common-sense observations, sometimes assembled by means of a canvass of experiences only.[20]

Public relations is so firmly established as a "good thing" that any attempt to analyze the movement in the hope of developing a more precise understanding of its dimensions, or at least of formulating an operational definition, is viewed as unwarranted criticism. Administrators of the school system have a responsibility, nonetheless, to be community leaders as well as educational leaders. Realization of one role may be dependent on the other. Bernays defined public relations as:

1. Information given to the public.
2. Persuasion directed at the public to modify attiudes and action.
3. Efforts to integrate attitudes and actions of an institution with its publics and of the publics with that institution.[21]

Others have vaguely defined it as a two-way interpretive process between society and an institution. The definitions imply that public relations is concerned with personal and corporate behavior which has social and public significance. An individual responsible for the public relations of an institution is involved in directing, advising, and supervising those activities of the institution which affect or interest the public. Such an individual interprets the institution (or client) to the public and the public to the institution.[22] The purpose of all such activities is to promote harmony and

[18]L. M. Killian, "Community Structure and Role of Negro Leader Agent," *Sociological Inquiry*, vol. 35, Winter 1965, pp. 69–79.

[19]W. W. Charters, Jr., "Public Relations," in Chester W. Harris, ed., *Encyclopedia of Educational Research*, 3rd ed., New York: Macmillan, 1960, pp. 1075–1081.

[20]Ibid.

[21]Edward L. Bernays, *Public Relations,* Norman, Okla.: University of Oklahoma Press, 1952, p. 3.

[22]Ibid., p. 94.

understanding between the group and the public it serves and upon whose good will it depends.[23] One may rightfully question the broadness of activities defined as public relations, because they appear to encompass almost the entire range of public-school activities.

The word "public" is sometimes misinterpreted as implying a homogeneous mass of people. To counteract this misconception, the plural of the word—"publics"—is suggested. The word "public" is synonymous with "groups," and because groups differ in size, organization, interests, methods of communication, and systems of control or guidance, it is just as appropriate to speak of several groups that have contacts with the school as it is to speak of the many publics involved in public relations.

The phrase "public relations" is used in many ways. For example, as applied to school personnel, "good public relations" may mean:

1. A good public opinion (which unfortunately is not described in any further detail).
2. The absence of political crisis in the community with respect to the school or a minimum of potentially disruptive criticism of the school.
3. The involvement of the citizens in formulating school policies (it is not always clear whether this is regarded as a means or an end in itself).
4. The attainment of a favorable vote on a bond or a tax referendum.[24]

Considering public relations as information, persuasion, and integration between the institution and the public helps to avoid some of the confusion. It is a way of influencing public policy or decision making and, hence, may

[23]American Association of School Administrators, *Public Relations for America's Schools,* Twenty-eighth Yearbook, Arlington, Va.: The Association, 1950, p. 12.

[24]Charters, op. cit., p. 1076.

be seen as a part of the politics of education.

Out of public relations has grown a new profession, "adjustment." The complexity of society, technical improvement of the mass media of communication, increased education and literacy, accelerated transportation and communication which have widened the market for ideas and things, development and acceptance of the social sciences, substitution of persuasion and suggestion for threat and intimidation and force, and extension of the right to vote have created a need for public-relations specialists.[25]

In its broad sense, school public relations involves all the contacts through which an impression or image about the public schools is established in the minds of various groups of people. The image of the school held by an individual or a group results from the intentional or unintentional creation of such an image. The development of the most desirable image of the public school system depends, some feel, upon following a prescribed pattern of activities. There is little empirical evidence, however, to determine the effectiveness of various devices for evaluating public-relations programs and activities. Most of the "research" in public relations is little more than a collection of judgments of panels of educators regarding the suitability, effectiveness, and success of practices employed. This leaves unresolved the question of the criteria utilized by panel members "judging" the "public-relations practices."

PURPOSES OF SCHOOL PUBLIC RELATIONS

It is not the purpose of school public relations to create a more desirable

[25]Bernays, op. cit., p. 3.

image of the educational institution. Rather, the purposes are:

1. To inform the public about the schools.
2. To establish confidence in the schools.
3. To rally support for proper maintenance of the educational program.
4. To develop an awareness of the importance of education in a democracy.
5. To improve the partnership concept by uniting parents and teachers in meeting the educational needs of children.
6. To integrate the home, school, and community in improving educational opportunities for all children.
7. To evaluate the offerings of the schools and the needs of the children of the community.
8. To correct misunderstanding about the aims and objectives of the school.[26]

HUMAN RELATIONS AND PUBLIC RELATIONS

School public relations is concerned with informing people, persuading the public to some kind of action, and integrating the attitudes of some people with those of other people. The public is people. What is known as public relations might better be called human relations, for the latter term more accurately describes its essential nature, provides a more appropriate setting, minimizes concern for rule-of-thumb techniques and procedures in favor of a study of human behavior in society, and shifts the emphasis from gimmicks and journalistic talent to an understanding of social psychology of groups and individual human behavior under various conditions of stress.

Human relations is the way in which people learn to relate to their social surroundings. It is a way of acting—or not acting—toward other human beings in terms of the ideals and values of the society. Human-relations skill

is the capacity of people to communicate their feelings and ideas to others, to receive such communications from others, and to respond to their feelings and ideas in such a fashion as to promote congenial participation in a common task.[27]

The basis for effective human relations is the desire of the individuals responsible for the direction of the institution to keep all those affected informed and involved in the operation or outcomes of the institution. The shallow approach of keeping people in ignorance by releasing only information thought to be complimentary is ultimately a contradiction of human-relations procedures. Communications should convey feelings and ideas. The right words are those that succeed in conveying feelings and ideas. What influences other groups is a problem of social psychology, not a question of knowing how to formulate and time press releases. As Berelson pointed out, communications influence public opinion, but by and large, many of the statements on the effectiveness of communication are misleading. The more defensible conclusions about it are that "some kinds of communications on some kinds of issues, brought to the attention of some kinds of people under some kinds of conditions, have some kinds of effects." The complexity of the "effect" problem has defied the superficial analysis of the proponents of the school public-relations movement.[28] Where an effort is made to influence public opinion in a particular way, what is called public relations merges with what others are wont to identify as the politics of education. The primary concern of what has been called public relations

[26]American Association of School Administrators, op. cit., p. 14.

[27]F. J. Roethlisberger, *Training for Human Relations,* Boston: Division of Research, Harvard, 1954, p. 172.

[28]Charters, op. cit., p. 1078.

is human relations, and the answer to effective motivation of human behavior within a community is more likely to be discovered through an understanding of the social psychology of human behavior in organization than through the typical approach (of stories and reports released by a particular officer of the school) of public relations. The communications challenge increases in significance when the primary role of the administrator becomes that of mediator among groups contesting for power or where he is attempting to influence public decision making.

THE SCHOOL PUBLIC-RELATIONS PLAN

The usual admonition that the school administrator has a responsibility to communicate the school story to the people does not answer the question "what story"? There are many that could be told, and to tell the wrong one would be unfortunate. While it is encouraging that all media—newspapers, radio, and television—exhibit a growing interest in the school story, their avidity puts even greater pressure on school officials to relate the educational program to the community effectively and to help the people interpret its significance. It is not possible to "manage" school news, but the impact of each story should be known beforehand.

The first step in carrying out this important responsibility is the generation of a model public-relations program in terms of the missions of the school to be projected. Model creation is a responsibility of the total staff, not simply the public-relations department. It is a top-echelon function that requires creativity, understanding of the totality of educational operations,

and knowledge of the technical aspects of public-relations operations. The model provides the framework for action. It is useful in deciding the priority of various school stories and what aspect of each story deserves prominence. It provides the criteria for determining what voids exist in the school's public-relations program and how to fill them. The model is based on the identification and ranking of significant factors that help the various publics comprehend the missions of the school and judge its contributions and activities. It is a representation of the reality that confronts the educational institution, but it includes only those elements essential to describing the missions, sensing who is to be reached, knowing what kinds of information in what format reaches the various publics, and developing an organization to execute the operation of a public relations subsystem.

The public-relations model is a generalized plan of action. It defines what is to be achieved before it specifies how it is to be achieved. It is concerned with all aspects of school operation, school growth and development, the resources available to the school system, the media available for telling the school story, and the variety of publics to be reached. Day-by-day school activities, future educational plans, and communication with external and internal environments are some of the subsystems in the model. What stories should be written (and how released, how slanted, and how timed) about any of the school subsystems can be answered through a public-relations model.

For the purposes of this writing, image (or posture) is defined as the total impression people, usually outside the school environment, have of the educational system—its staff, its clientele, and its activities. Again, to suggest that the public-relations plan starts with a definition of the missions (or image or posture) of the educational institution that are to be crystallized in the minds of people is not to infer management of school news. On the contrary, the release of distorted or unsupported information on school activities will surely backfire and place the school and its administration in an embarrassing position. An attempt to cover up is a bad strategy as well as questionable professional ethics. Rather, it is insisted that school personnel comprehend the impact of every release on the audience.

To present a balanced view of educational affairs, it is imperative to prepare positive information on many programs. Thus, various releases should project the special skills, preparation, and insights of the teaching staff; how well various types of pupils are learning; and how efficiently school funds are expended and protected. Communication is an art, which, when done well, presents not a sales pitch, but accurate and objective information on school operations. Determination of what kinds of communications will help or hinder the projection of a given school posture is a difficult task, but one that deserves high priority in education.

Knowing what to say is the beginning. The public-relations model must also recognize the various avenues of dissemination and the audience each will reach. This assumes comprehension of the various publics in the community and the fundamental characteristics of each. Publics can be classified by religious inclination, socioeconomic status, race, national background, economic orientation (industrial or agricultural, union or management), political belief (conservative or liberal), age grouping (senior citi-

zens, young adults, or mature citizens), and civic affiliation. Publics can also be classified by school orientation —PTA members, childless couples, singles, parents of children attending private schools, and parents of children attending public schools. One individual can play a role in many different publics. An effective program of communication has the capability to reach all segments of a community. What appeals to one dimension of a community may miss another. The public-relations plan must use many avenues to reach the different publics.

Once these policies have been outlined, an organization to execute them can be fashioned. The continuing involvement of many people is desirable, but a specially skilled public-relations team should be in charge. Sufficient human and fiscal resources must be allocated to keep the program functioning. Lastly, there must be continuous evaluation to determine how well the public-relations model corresponds with reality and whether the desired image of the school has been in fact projected.

The development and execution of a public-relations plan can be summarized as follows:

1. Define the missions (or image or posture) of the educational system to be projected.
2. Determine whether the specific purpose is for straight information giving or for influencing public decision making in a given way.
3. Determine what kinds of communications will help or hinder the de-development of the posture desired, recognizing that distortion of the truth or news management must be avoided.
4. Identify the optimum avenues for projecting the missions of the school (based on an understanding

of the appropriate media, frequency of communication, and the tone of the message).

5. Know the variety of publics to be reached (classified by religion, socioeconomic status, nationality grouping, political belief, age level, educational orientation).
6. Develop an organization unit or division to operate the plan that involves many people but recognizes that a team of specialists is needed.
7. Allocate the resources to accomplish the public-relations program.
8. Execute the program.
9. Evaluate its effectiveness on a continuing basis.

Public relations is more than telling and selling; it is a sensitivity to community interests and desires. What the people want to know about schools is not always the same. The extent of misinformation to be corrected varies from one aspect of the school to another. Just pumping out data may not get the job done. Certain insights and attitudes can be gained best by participation in citizen committees. Involving people in school activities and designing ways to help them participate in arriving at significant educational decisions are as much a part of public relations as writing a story for release to the press. No less significant is allowing interested citizens the opportunity to express their concern about public education, for example, at board meetings. Community involvement in education is a characteristic of a dynamic and effective school public-relations program.

TECHNIQUES OF SCHOOL PUBLIC RELATIONS

There is no dearth of suggestions about who should be involved and what approaches are most effective in establishing the desirable image of the school. A high quality of classroom education is rightfully considered basic to satisfactory school and community relations. No amount of press, radio, or TV releases will overcome dissatisfaction by the child and parent about what is being accomplished in the classroom. Thus, the classroom teacher plays the paramount role in fostering desirable school-community relations. This does not suggest that the teacher employs special techniques in dealing with the public or the pupil, but rather that the teacher's deep concern in meeting the educational and other needs of the child and in working in close and harmonious relation with parents and other interested adults is a keystone in effective school-community relations.

However, school public relations does not stop at the classroom level. Schools are complex institutions in a complex society, and this, according to some, has created a need for the professional public-relations person. This profession took hold in the 1920s and came of age at approximately the end of 1941.[29] It served to fill the gap caused by the lack of organization and information within the school system about how to gather data and release stories about educational activities to the various mass media of communication or to individuals and groups.

The responsibilities of the school public-relations division include organizing and releasing school publicity to news outlets, maintaining a calendar of school publicity, searching out news and information in the system, and maintaining a file of stories released. The variety of media available for communication necessitates decisions

[29]Bernays, op. cit., chaps. 9 and 10.

on use of the correct tools to gain the attention of the public for a particular purpose. Determining what makes a good news story; developing steps in preparing a news story; using newspapers, radio, and television effectively; preparing graphic and pictorial materials; creating a letter or other ways of sending messages to parents; utilizing school-oriented or school-operated publications; and creating special reports to the public are some of the more technical aspects of school public-relations procedures.[30]

SCHOOL REPORTING

An ever-widening range of school topics is of interest to the people of the community. This interest in school news is a recent phenomenon and it has brought an improvement in newspaper coverage of school events. Gone is the time when the journalist assigned to education ranked somewhere below the real-estate editor and above the chief copyboy.[31] Educational reporting, long neglected by the nation's daily press, is now more exciting than ever. Many people learn most of what they know about schools from the newspapers. Major newspapers may have a number of full-time education reporters plus students as paid education "stringers" working under an education editor. It is not unusual to find education stories on the first page of a metropolitan paper, along with many others on the inside pages devoted to education. There is ample evidence that people are interested in school news and that the school can benefit from the release of such news.

Dapper observed that good public relations begins with a good product and continues with skillful use of every device available to inform people about it.[32] This has to be done openly and with faith in the public. Writing from the point of view of the reporter, she said that a school public-relations officer "can be a blessing or a curse." To some education reporters, his job appears to be providing a way for the superintendent to dodge the press. Dapper recounted the mistrust and misinterpretation that can arise on both sides. Education reporters complain about the school's fear of the press, failure to recognize deadlines, and inability to understand that the editor, not the reporter, determines headlines and the position in the paper of the school news item, and that the reporter is rarely consulted about what appears on the editorial page. Schoolmen complain about inaccurate reporting or outright distortion. Dapper pointed out that a school system has public relations whether it tries or not.

The superintendent, the board, and the newspaper editor have a common interest. Administrators, therefore, have a responsibility to keep the newspaper informed, to work with reporters, and to supply effective photographs and stories. Most administrators lack journalistic talents, and hence those who have such gifts as well as the ability to get along with representatives of the mass media must become an important part of the administrative team.

ADMINISTRATION OF PUBLIC-RELATIONS PROGRAMS

A study of public-relations administration in all school systems with en-

---

[30]American Association of School Administrators, op. cit., chap. 12.

[31]"Boom on the School Beat," *Time*, February 29, 1960, pp. 69–71.

[32]Gloria Dapper, *Public Relations for Educators*, New York: Macmillan, 1964, p. 5.

rollments of 25,000 or more and in a sampling of systems with smaller enrollment was conducted by the Educational Research Service.[33] It can be seen from Table 25-1 that school systems with large enrollments were more likely to have a full-time public-relations director, but that about 60 percent of all systems studied had a full-time director. The position of public-relations director exists when the system has unified its communications program under the direction of an individual. The titles for the position vary, but the term "information" is frequently a part of the title. "Public relations" is less commonly included in the title, the incumbent is likely to have the position status of director, administrative assistant, or coordinator, in that order. The position is so new that in 1967 the majority of systems had not set up definite job requirements.

[33]Educational Research Service, American Association of School Administrators, *The Administration of Public Relations Programs in Local School Systems, 1966–67*, Washington, D.C.: The Association, 1967.

The number of staff persons working with the public-relations director ranged from 33 full-time personnel in seven different positions in New York City to no staff in five systems. The six major responsibilities of the PR director were press, radio, and TV contacts; press releases; staff newsletters or publications; community newsletters or publications; election and bond referenda campaigns; and superintendent's annual report. The director's functions are summarized in Table 25-2.

SUMMARY

The term politics of education has changed from implying partisanship to connote the understanding of power structures and the influencing of public decision or policy making. Schools serve the educational needs of the community and, in turn, draw support and strength from the community. Public schools are the product of the people and as they become more complex, the distance between the people and the schools increases.

TABLE 25–1

SUMMARY OF ADMINISTRATION OF PUBLIC RELATIONS PROGRAMS IN 1968 SCHOOL SYSTEMS

Administrative arrangements	Percent of school systems responding				
	Stratum 1	Stratum 2	Stratum 3	Smaller	Total
Full-time public relations director	87.5	74.0	40.6	60.0	60.1
Part-time public relations director	4.2	6.0	20.3	30.9	17.7
Other arrangements	8.3	20.0	39.1	9.1	22.2
Total	100.0	100.0	100.0	100.0	100.0

Enrollment strata:
   Stratum 1: 100,000 or more
   Stratum 2: 50,000 to 99,999
   Stratum 3: 25,000 to 49,000
   Smaller: Less than 25,000
Source: Educational Research Service of the American Association of School Administrators and the National Education Association, 1967.

Attempts to reduce the distance between the people and their schools appear to come in cycles: Whenever a society experiences duress, its social institutions, and particularly the schools, come under attack. When such conditions occur, the public can be the foremost ally of educational institutions.

Many groups have formed that affect the politics of education. Citizen interest in public education has a long history. Attempts to bring the schools closer to the people resulted in the organization of the National Congress of Parents and Teachers and the short-lived, but most influential, National Citizen's Commission for the Public Schools. These organizations have done so much to stimulate citizen interest in the improvement of public education. The PTO (parent-teacher organization) came on the scene in the 1960s as a challenge to the PTA.

The lay advisory committee in education reached a maximum during the

TABLE 25–2

RESPONSIBILITIES OF FULL-TIME PUBLIC RELATIONS DIRECTORS IN 119 SCHOOL SYSTEMS

Public relations function	Percent of school systems reporting degree of responsibility for each function		
	Major responsi-bility	Minor responsi-bility	Not a responsi-bility
Press, radio, and TV contacts	90	8	2
Writing press releases	84	16	0
Staff newsletters or publications	82	14	4
Community newsletters or publications	76	16	8
Election and bond referenda campaigns	55	26	19
Superintendent's annual report	53	23	24
Work with community, civic, or service groups	46	50	4
Special projects (e.g., American Education Week, teacher-orientation programs, B-I-E Day[a])	38	51	11
Development of teacher recruitment	35	46	19
Photographic services	32	43	25
Assessment of public attitudes	31	46	23
Speakers' bureau	29	52	19
Publicity on federal projects	29	63	8
Editorial services for central-office staff	18	63	19
Writing speeches, reports, or papers for central-office staff and/or board	17	60	23
In-service public-relations training or school staff	15	50	35
Supervision of duplicating plant	14	14	72
Planning and/or programming for educational TV	12	18	70

Source: Educational Research Service of The American Association of School Administrators and the National Education Association, 1967.
[a] Business-Industry-Education Day.

1950s. Such committees are advisory in function and do not replace the board of education. They serve a purpose when a need exists for such groups. They are primarily study and advisory groups and need special resources to accomplish their purposes effectively. The school board has the right to accept or reject the recommendation of advisory groups.

A growing interest was evident among school administrators in the 1960s in analysis and understanding of community power structure as one dimension of the politics of education. There are many approaches to identifying people who occupy positions of public leadership. The formal leadership method identifies the power elite on the basis of formal positions of authority. The reputational approach relies more on the reputation a person enjoys than on the position he holds. Another method relies on activity in civic or voluntary community organizations.

One of the dangers in analysis of community power structure is generalizing from a few case studies. Another is assuming that communities are static and that social changes do not alter the power structure. Subtle shifts can catapult new groups into positions of dominance. Every school administrator needs sufficient staff to study the nature of and modifications in the social, political, and economic factors within the community.

The school public-relations movement came into its own after World War I. School public relations is concerned with giving information to the public and modifying and integrating attitudes and actions of the institution with its publics and of the publics with the institution through persuasive efforts. It focuses on developing a desirable image of the institution.

Unfortunately, rule-of-thumb techniques are often emphasized without an adequate research base for justifying faith in them. Human relations can change the emphasis from techniques and procedures to understanding the social psychology of human behavior in groups and a means of influencing it. To the extent it attempts to influence public decision making, it merges with the politics of education.

The development of a public-relations model helps determine what story to use, how to slant it, what kind of communication will help or hinder the development of a given posture, what avenues of dissemination are best, what specific publics are to be reached, and what the requirements are for a public relations organization; it also serves as the basis for subsequent evaluation.

A heartening feature of recent years is the great attention being devoted to schools in the nation's newspapers. Educational reporting has improved. The interest of the people in the schools is evidenced by the frequency with which school news appears on the front page. Misunderstanding occurs between education reporter and school when either side is insensitive to problems and limitations of each. A school system has public relations whether it organizes to do so or not.

One study showed that the larger the city school district the more likely it was to have a public-relations director. About 60 percent of all districts had a full-time public-relations director. The number of staff persons working with the public-relations director varied from 33 to none. The functions of the public-relations director were mass-media contacts, writing press releases, and handling school or community publications.

QUESTIONS

1. Why have the political dimensions of educational administratio gained more prominence in recent years?
2. Is public apathy toward schools a greater danger than public criticism? Justify your stand.
3. How do lay or citizen advisory committees differ from the PTA?
4. Should a school administrator actively promote the installation and/or support of the PTA? Justify your stand.
5. How can an administrator stimulate greater interest in the school?
6. What are the major methods of identifying members of the community power structure?
7. What are the purposes of school public relations?
8. What is the difference between human relations and public relations?
9. What functions are assigned typically to a public-relations director?
10. What are the essential elements of a public-relations model or plan?

SELECTED REFERENCES

Bell, W., R. J. Hill, and C. R. Wright, *Public Leadership*, San Francisco: Chandler, 1961.

Dapper, Gloria, *Public Relations for Educators*, New York: Macmillan, 1964.

Gregg, Russell T., "Political Dimensions of Educational Administration," *Teachers College Record*, LXVII, November 1965, pp. 118–128.

Kimbrough, R. B., *Community Power Structure and Analysis*, Englewood Cliffs, N.J.: Prentice-Hall, 1964.

Kirst, Michael W., *Politics of Education*, Berkeley, Cal.: McCutchan, 1970.

Maguire, John W., "Changing Voter Profiles and School Elections," *Intellect*, vol. 101, no. 2344, November 1972, p. 113.

Sumption, M. R., and Y. Engstrom, *School-Community Relations*, New York: McGraw-Hill, 1966.

Wayne, Edward, *The Politics of School Accountability*, Berkeley, Cal.: McCutchan, 1972.

26

ACCOUNTABILITY AND THE APPRAISAL OF EDUCATIONAL ADMINISTRATORS

The opening chapter declared that administration is a critical function in complex institutions, is dynamic with new competencies being demanded for achievement of effectiveness at various times, and is a means rather than an end in itself. In the early 1970s there was heard the call that administrators should be held accountable for what happens in schools. Accountability has replaced relevance as the most popular word in the vocabulary of writers and speakers on education. It is a catchy concept that has fired the popular imagination, but it is also subject to conflicting interpretations that compound the problems of those who seek to implement accountability systems. This chapter examines accountability as a concept and its system of operation as well as its implications for educational administrators.

There were so few school districts prior to 1960 with administrator appraisal systems that one could almost assume that school executives were immune from evaluation. This is not the case today; the pressures behind administrator appraisal are now intense for a variety of reasons. Since the 1960s more and more school districts have dedicated themselves to the design and implementation of ways and means of assessing administrator behavior and decisions. Accountability and appraisal go together and, therefore, are placed in a single chapter.

ACCOUNTABILITY

The tremendous number of books, articles, and speeches on accountability in education generated since 1970 provide the documentation for growing national interest in it and also reveal the confusion that surrounds what accountability means for educational administration. About 31 states passed some kind of accountability legislation or joint resolution by the fall of 1973. The substance of the idea can be traced to the Biblical idea of an impending Judgment Day when all will be accountable to the Creator. The concept was not strange to secular literature nor did administrators of secular institutions overlook the fact of an eventual day of reckoning for decisions and actions. Over 50 years ago educational administrators confronted with financial accountability pressures designed systems of financial accounting, budgeting, fiscal auditing and reporting to satisfy the then existing demands for better accountability in education. This was the traditional notion of accountability that implied that you could spend public money only on the purposes for which it was legally raised, and you had to demonstrate that educational resources met all legal constraints and were cared for in an honest and careful manner.

Lessinger, one of the early and extensive writers and scholars in educational accountability, emphasizes that it is not the traditional perceptions that make accountability so popular or that will make it endure.[1] He recognized "three distinct, but interactive types," namely, performance accountability, professional accountability, and system accountability. He cited the "exponential cost increases," public dissatisfaction with educational outcomes, and public interests in adapting "modern management procedures" to educational institutions as reasons for the "rediscovery of and widespread demands for accountable education."[2]

Accountability today is a more comprehensive concept that embraces all of education and not simply the safeguarding inputs to assigned uses. The current interpretations of accountability stress the relevance of educational goals, effectiveness of instructional and administrative strategies at all levels, and the assessment of educational outcomes achieved through its programs and activities. In short, accountability applies to the educational system as a whole and demands clarification of the relationship between inputs and outputs.

To avoid vagueness and to serve as a guide to executive planning and action, it is imperative that accountability be defined. Accountability is a system of operation for delivering desired educational outputs that specifies the desirable and measurable outcomes to be achieved, the assignment of responsibilities to members of the organization to achieve these objectives, and the assessment of achievements to ascertain relationships between inputs and outputs. In short, it requires setting goals, assigning responsibilities, and verifying how well resources are utilized.

In an operational accountability system *every person (or group) in the organization is answerable (or responsible), to some degree, to another person (or position) for something (or objectives) expressed in terms of performance levels (or results or achievements) to be realized within certain constraints* (such as a specific time period or within stated financial limits.)[3] The implementation of such a system demands the definition of who is answerable to whom and for what—accountability is a goal-referenced term. Accountability means identification of responsibility for satisfying the entire range of goals and objectives for an organization as well as for how resources are allocated and utilized for such ends. Unfortunately, some misconstrue the true meaning of accountability by assuming that the obvious root word "account" reveals its basic business orientation. A modifier is introduced to place focus on the total and comprehensive concept as *educational* accountability.

Accountability in politics is often the model in the minds of many. Precinct captains and ward bosses are held responsible for delivering votes in their domains to candidates favored

[1] Leon M. Lessinger, "Accountabiltiy: Present Forces and Future Concerns," New Directions For Education, vol. 1, no. 1, Spring 1973, pp. 1–9.

[2] Ibid.

[3] The ideas that follow were published originally in S. J. Knezevich, "Implementing Accountability Systems," New Directions for Education, vol. 1, no. 1, Spring 1973, pp. 11–20.

by the political organization. Following each election, the political party analyzes voting outcomes on a precinct-by-precinct basis. Those responsible for getting out and for influencing the vote for a favored candidate must answer to the political party chief.

This precise type of accountability is possible when single or limited objectives are pursued and when results can be measured with a high degree of precision, as in the case of actual voting behavior. Measuring accountability with the same degree of precision, and objectivity, is far more difficult in multipurpose institutions. This is particularly true in education because the end products are difficult to define and even more perplexing to measure with certainty.

As conceptualized here the fundamental purposes of accountability are to focus on objectives, to fix responsibility, and to optimize relationships between resources—human, physical, and/or fiscal—and results. Through accountability a clearer definition of where the institution is going, more prudent resource allocations, improved resource utilization patterns, and better information on the performance qualities of personnel and teachers as they relate to organizational objectives become possible. An accountability system gives administrators and other policy makers an important new capability by providing them with data necessary to make more definitive judgments on how well (or poorly) the organization's resources have been used to achieve stated purposes. For that reason policy makers and administrators alike should welcome rather than resist the design and implementation of an educational accountability system at local and state levels.

Every accountability system demands clarification of whether personnel will be responsible for the execution of a process or for the development or achievement of a product related to some goals. At present schools are designed to hold teachers accountable for the execution of an instructional process or activity with so many pupils in so many classes per day over so many months in a school year. This is the process called teaching. Procedures have been developed to insure that teachers are present by a given time and leave no earlier than a stated time. This is accountability for performance of a service. The traditional teaching contract is a "performance" contract, but teachers are held accountable for rendering a service only. This is similar to "contracts" with a physician, lawyer, architect, or TV repairman, who make no guarantees about outcomes but simply agree to perform stated functions in a given time.

Teachers may be held accountable for results as well, that is, for pupils learning up to a previously specified level. This is what parents along with others, called taxpayers, are clamoring for and mean by accountability. They yearn for accountability for a product or outcome and are no longer satisfied if someone performs a process faithfully over a stated period of time. The so-called performance contract in education is in reality a variable payment contract for the fulfillment of instructional outcomes. Payments are not fixed but related to the outcome levels satisfied. Clearly then, the so-called performance contract is not an effort to bring accountability into education for the first time so much as it is an effort to switch the focus from accountability for instructional inputs and processes to accountability for instructional outcomes.

The conceptualization of accountability being argued herein bears a close relationship to what others have called the "management-by-objectives" (MBO) approach, which was described more fully in Chapter 8. This approach stresses results and not processes and is based on the assumption that the clearer an idea one has of what he is trying to accomplish, the greater are his chances of accomplishing it. Progress, it is believed, can best be measured in terms of what one is trying to make progress toward. An accountability system may be viewed as a way to manage more effectively by stressing outcomes. Clearly, operation in a MBO mode could contribute much to the realization of an overall accountability strategy. Obviously, the success of the system depends in part on the sharing common goals by all personnel. It won't work if the administrator has one set of objectives and teachers another.

CONFLICTING CONCEPTUALIZATIONS OF ACCOUNTABILITY

Accountability, simply because it is a popular term, has been appropriated by those with special interests to pursue. Writers feel free to pour their special meanings into accountability. In some instances it may even be used as a ploy or subterfuge or to cover for other aspirations. All this confuses the fundamental issues. It may suggest why teacher's organizations express concern over accountability—particularly when it appears to be a subterfuge for establishing a merit pay system, which has been resisted by teacher's associations as well as unions.

Still others have used accountability as the mechanism to justify tax support of private as well as public educational institutions. To produce a set of competing schools a voucher system of educational finance is recommended as a viable mechanism for bringing about what they call greater accountability in education. The assumption is that there can be no truly operative accountability system without direct payments to parents who will determine which school shall be supported to provide educational opportunities for children and youth. This is the competitive conceptualization of accountability and is quite different from the approach suggested earlier to bring about optimum resource utilization or "management-by-objectives" within existing, publicly supported educational institutions.

A voucher system of educational finance is not crucial to an optimum resource utilization conceptualization of accountability. But voucher proponents claim that alternatives to the public schools are imperative and essential to this uniquely, but vaguely, defined notion of accountability. Implicit is the assumption that the individual consumer has the ability to make complex evaluations of comprehensive educational institutions, even though this challenge presently perplexes experienced professionals and educational evaluation experts. The consumer has difficulty choosing between comparatively simple products, such as competing refrigerators and automobiles. Independent and careful evaluation of alternative school systems is necessary if the voucher system is to have any hope of delivering on its promises as being a mechanism for better education. The very premise on which it is based is suspect. Subjective, incomplete, and emotionally charged rather than rational and precise evaluations may be the end result of the efforts of nonprofessionals with a limited understanding of the art and science of evaluation as well as the learning process. Nonetheless, voucher advocates hold that accountability, improvement of education, and the basic financial support system for educational institutions, public and private, rest on the individual consumer's determination of where to place his resources for the best education of his offspring.

It is recognized that the consumer-choice model is not without its problems in setting prices and survival of private goods in the market place. This is burden enough, and inept choices abound even when relatively simple products are involved. Consumer protection legislation is now being demanded because of difficulties encountered. An almost impossible demand is placed on the consumer, who is expected to separate the glib charlatan and his advertising gimmicks from the competent professional when both offer difficult-to-measure instructional services in a complex social institution.

Of no less importance is the fact that education is properly perceived as a class of social goods that benefits all society and not a strictly individual consumption of goods that benefit only individual students and/or their parents. The point is that the market mechanism may not be the best means of generating improvement in a product or for determining what constitutes adequate support for activities related to social goals. One reason for public support of certain social institutions is that wise choices do not always come from individual consumers who are ill-equipped to make complex decisions alone.

Voucher advocates have made claims for competitive accountability that are unsupported by objective data. The methods of evaluation necessary to determine the outcomes of voucher experiments are much too general and too far beyond the capabilities of many involved to allow for the objective exercise of control. Accountability in these so-called experiments loses much of its precision. Better schools are more likely to result from research on the nature of learning and the learner than from subjective and incomplete evaluation of schools. Improved health and medical practices do not result from cutthroat competition among medical practicioners or hospitals.

ACCOUNTABILITY STRATEGIES

Designing a system of educational accountability that is meaningful, flexible, economical, and simple to operate —and then implementing it—is easier to talk about than to execute.[4] Simplistic pronouncements obscure the fact that it is a complex undertaking demanding the formulation of an accountability "game plan."

The school executive's accountability strategy would include establishment of accountability centers through the system—at the classroom, building, and/or district level. As in the case of ward-by-ward review of voting behavior, the chief executive may have an attendance center-by-attendance center review of learning or other outcomes. In the internally directed comprehensive educational accountability plan, at least the following practices or techniques should be in operation:

1. *Identification and clarification of significant objectives* to understand their operational implications and to determine whether attainment of any or all is realistic in view of the constraints under which the institution functions. The emphasis on objectives

[4]The ideas presented herein, to repeat, were published originally in S. J. Knezevich, op. cit.

is not unique to accountability and is similar to the initial steps in MBO and PPBS. There is little hope for the installation of an operational accountability system unless the administrator demonstrates skill in preparing quality performance objectives. In addition, the success of the system depends in part on acceptance of common goals by all personnel.

2. *Creation of an accountability team Within the school system.* No single person can satisfy the complex requirements of the total educational accountability strategy. It is not a burden carried by the superintendent alone. His first responsibility is to create a team with each member accepting a definite assignment or set of responsibilities that is part of the total plan. Hopefully, the performance level demanded of a player will be in line with his professional capabilities. Accountability is off to a promising start when all personnel know and accept the missions they are expected to fulfill and the degree of responsibility each has (as a person or as a member of the team). Fairness dictates that the persons held accountable be informed of whom he is answerable to and how the execution of his responsibilities will be monitored.

For example, the superintendent's accountability strategy could start with a conference with a principal to discover why pupil performance in a given attendance center is significantly lower than that in another district center of the same size which serves pupils with similar socioeconomic backgrounds and fairly similar intellectual levels. If additional resources were allocated to that principal to overcome the discrepancy, he could be held accountable at a later time for how well the additional inputs were converted into improved pupil performance levels. By the same token,

the principal could hold the professional staff accountable to some degree for what happens at the classroom level.

3. *Development of an accountability chart* indicating who is to be responsible for what. Such a chart is drawn from data obtained after fulfillment of points 1 and 2 mentioned in the previous paragraphs. Obviously, not everyone is responsible for everything. In general, the higher the position in the administrative hierarchy, the greater the number of assigned responsibilities. Keep in mind that it is possible to hold someone accountable for the wrong thing. By summarizing the specified responsibilities for all personnel, the chart of accountability provides data on who is answerable to whom, for what, when, and to what degree.

A related question is whether the individual alone, the group with which he works within a building, or those employed within the total system should be held responsible for realization of particular goals. This is part of the debate on individual versus joint accountability. Joint accountability is the more rational basis when learning specialists have collective responsibility for a certain impact on the lives of the learners. This avoids the difficult operational problem of disentangling the contributions of many who influence learner's progress.

4. *Continuation of the search for alternative approaches to educational objectives.*

5. *Development and implementation of output-oriented management systems, such as the Planning-Programming-Budgeting System (PPBS) and Management-by-Objectives (MBO).* PPBS is a decision system related to the allocation of resources among the competing ends within an institution. It along with other systems techniques

can contribute to realizing accountability through analysis of resources used and determination of the productivity of each resource.

6. *Development and utilization of computer-based information systems* capable of providing the data needed to fulfill the demands of educational accountability. Accountability calls for a variety of and frequent reports and analyses of data. No administrator can hope to install an operational accountability system without a solid information base.

7. *Creation of a system for education auditing* to verify the quality of reports and activities. This is one of the key concepts in the operation of an educational accountability system. To avoid the "unverified information trap," the prudent administrator must include within his accountability network an educational audit dimension to verify the authenticity of perceptions submitted. An audit substantiates progress (or lack of it) toward achieving goals and verifies other data available; it is one of the culminating steps in the control and feedback process. Through the independent audit—carried out by both internal and external agencies or personnel, independent of the person completing the task—the accuracy, integrity, and authenticity of previous reports and documents can be ascertained. Independent external audits occur less frequently than in-house audits by someone on the superintendent's staff.

8. *Design and operation of a total staff appraisal system* that would include specification of effectiveness models, performance indicators, ways of measuring performance (instruments used), and decision points for the interpretation of evaluative data. The total appraisal system calls for personnel, program, and resource use evaluation. Every system of account-

ability has a day of reckoning—a time for appraising how well objectives were satisfied, stewardship over resources was discharged, and/or delegated tasks were fulfilled. There is no avoiding this Judgment Day, even though it makes "the judged" uneasy. By the same token, those evaluated have a right to know how their performances will be monitored, what standards will be applied, when periodic evaluations will occur, what rewards or penalities are in store, and what feedback they can expect on their performance appraisals. More will be said about this in the section on administrator appraisal.

9. *Dedication of ample resources to make the accountability system work.* "From nothing, comes nothing" applies to all things. An educational accountability system will consume resources, and the public must expect to invest resources for an operational system. The amount will vary with the comprehensiveness and complexity of demands placed on the institution. Investment increases in magnitude of from 1 to 1½ percent should be considered reasonable. Spending less may simply mean less meaningful accountability.

10. *Recognition of educational accountability as being as much an attitude as a set of techniques.* It is a point of view that must prevail in the entire school system, with the superintendent informing principals, supervisors, and others that they will be held responsible and answerable to him for the achievement of specified goals.

People who seek to establish greater accountability among schools do not all subscribe to the same beliefs. They range from those who see accountability as a way to stem the tide of increasing education expenditures, to the critics of education who see accountability as a way to pin the blame on someone for shortcomings, to proponents of public finance of private institutions. Whatever the reasons, the forces triggering the cry for greater educational accountability are not to be denied—they are more likely to increase than decrease in intensity. There is limited agreement among the 31 states that by 1973 had passed some form of accountability legislation. In 11 states accountability was equated with PPBS, in 2 a management information system, and in 5 a uniform accounting system. Twenty-two such states view it as a state testing or assessment program. In ten states accountability demanded evaluation of professional employees.

Accountability puts the stress on performance in the achievement of objectives rather than on promises or inputs alone. It recognizes that while money helps, it isn't everything. Accountability is defined as a system that clarifies who is answerable to whom, for what, when, and within what constraints.

ADMINISTRATOR APPRAISAL

The status studies of the Educational Research Service of the AASA completed in 1964, 1968, and 1971 document the growing trend toward appraisal of administrators. The data are based on large school systems, those most likely to have extensive evaluation systems. In the early 1960s the minority that appraised school executives had rather informal approaches. In 1968 only about 40 percent of the large system respondents did so, and about a quarter of these evaluated administrators in practice for a period that covered 10 or more years. By 1971 a majority (about 55 percent) assessed administrators. Before this decade is out practically all school systems will have formal administrator appraisal systems.

All who implemented such procedures evaluate principals, and more than half appraise other types of administrators. Tradition has the immediate superior evaluating the subordinate official. Some use the client-centered approach, where evaluatees (teachers) participate in the evaluation of the evaluators (administrators). By 1971 two school systems included evaluation of principals by teachers as part of the negotiated contract.

The pressures for extending evaluation of administrators to all levels and in all systems are many and varied. They include:

1. The social ferment of our times that brings all things into question.
2. The escalating costs of schools and of salaries paid to administrators.
3. The accountability thrusts that have been described previously.
4. The pressures for teacher appraisal that lead teachers to ask for administrator evaluation.
5. The growing concerns for managerial obsolescence that focus on ways to detect such problems early.
6. The efforts to identify the right principal for the right school that assume the effectiveness of the principal has been assessed.
7. The school boards that feel that administrator appraisal is one of their job responsibilities.

More than a rating scale is involved. The development of a total evaluation system includes agreement on the theory undergirding evaluation, specification of objectives for the evaluation; development of an administrator effectiveness model; creation of a monitoring subsystem to design data gathering instruments, prepare evaluative data gathers, and outline evaluative procedures; collection of relevant evaluative data; determination of who shall interpret evaluative data; and finally specification of alternative courses of action based on appraisal information.[5]

Appraisal should be a positive force with emphasis on analysis of administrator performance leading to additional learning experiences to produce greater individual effectiveness. In other words, there is more to it than labelling a person good, bad, or indifferent. Orderly dismissal of incompetents is a very narrow rationale for evaluation, for less than 1 percent of the personnel would face such action if quality selection procedures were operative.

The purposes of administrator appraisal are not always explicit and some may be in conflict. Appraisal may aim at identifying those who should be promoted from probationary to tenure status, determining regular and merit compensation, providing documentation for orderly dismissal of incompetents, satisfying state legislature or local school board demands for appraisal, and/or collecting data important to the design of professional development programs. The appraisal system created should be capable of providing data needed to satisfy one or more objectives.

Appraisal assumes that a model of an effective administrator is known. The data collected about a given individual is compared with the effectiveness model and a judgment is made as to how closely the real person matches the ideal of effectiveness. The many alternative models are summarized in Table 26–1. In most cases where eval-

uation systems exist, the effectiveness model has to be assumed from the kinds of data being collected, that is, there is no explicit statement of what constitutes effectiveness. Research and the existing literature have little to offer and most conclude that we know next to nothing about managerial effectiveness.

The data-gathering instrument helps to focus the attention of the data gatherer on important elements. The instrument designed should help provide data on how well the administrator is:

1. Fulfilling the legal responsibilities of the position.
2. Fulfiling the position description or responsibiities demanded.
3. Satisfying the change agent demands the position.
4. Satisfying the leadership roles and team demands.
5. Fulfilling the service functions of the office.
6. Bearing under the pressures or conflicts inherent in the position.
7. Meeting the necessary personal growth and productivity demands.

These are some of the major dimensions to be considered in the construction of a data-gathering instrument.

There are a number of issues to be met in the actual implementation of an administrator evaluation system. These include:

1. Where do you go to obtain evaluative information on administrators?
2. Who should evaluate the administrator?
   a. Should teachers, superiors, board members, community leaders, students, and custodians be involved?
   b. Should cooperative appraisal be encouraged (where the evalu-

[5]See S. J. Knezevich, "Designing Performance Appraisal Systems," *New Directions For Education*, vol. 1, no. 1, Spring 1973, pp. 37–49.

atee and evaluator get down to agree on job targets and procedures)?

c. His peers? (Should a team of administrators occupying similar positions be involved in providing evaluative data?)

3. How often should an administrator be appraised? Annually or more often?

4. What kind of instrument should be used?

5. Should the emphasis be on MBO or the results-oriented appraisal approach?

6. How much time and what magnitude of resources should be allocated for such purposes?

7. What are the legal ramifications of such procedures?

TABLE 26–1

ALTERNATIVE MODELS OF ADMINISTRATOR EFFECTIVENESS

Type A: Input models

Effectiveness is:

1. A constellation of administrator traits or personality (such as honesty, dependability, and industriousness). Some call this charisma determination. It is the most common model assumed in the historic and traditional approaches to evaluation.

Type B: Process or behavior models

Effectiveness is:

2. A series of administrator behaviors or role-performances (such as diagnosing problems, managing operations, and introducing change).
3. A series of teacher and/or pupil activities within the system (This is the "reflection theory," that is, effectiveness is reflected in what others are doing who are influenced by the administrator).
4. A set of interactions between the administrators and others (teachers, pupils, lay persons, supervisors, etc.).
5. A set of skills in utilizing technology or media (such as knowing how to use a computer in administration).
6. Competency in management of the technical dimensions of administration.

Type C: Outcome models

Effectiveness is:

7. A set of teacher and/or pupil performance levels.
8. A given standard of building appearance, safety, and security.
9. A specified level of pupil, teacher, and/or community control or influence.
10. A concensus of teacher, pupil, parental, or community reactions to the principal.
11. A set of decisions rendered by the administrator—the ultimate impact of these on the organization.
12. A cluster of problems resolved by the administrator.
13. What the evaluator says is effectiveness.
14. Attainment of any set of predetermined objectives or growth levels (management-by-objectives).

Type D: Eclectic models

Effectiveness is:

15. Any combination of two or more models of types A, B, and C.

8. How should compensation approaches be tied to administrator evaluation?

At this writing there is considerable discussion but comparatively little agreement on these issues. They will have to be resolved by the next decade. It is the opinion of this writer that the results-oriented emphasis identified with MBO/R will have more to offer in the design of administrator evaluation than any other approach.

A competency may be defined as the skill or capability to achieve an objective or demand of a position within a predetermined level of quality. Competency-based evaluation (CBE) is a relatively new development that is consistent with the spirit of the systems approach to performance appraisal and is an extension of the results-oriented appraisals approach in MBO/R. It can be outlined as:[6]

Step 1: Specification of objectives or results to be achieved by a person in a given position. Effective performance of responsibilities is equated with outputs. The first step specified determination of "competency for what"?

Step 2: Identification of professional competencies needed to satisfy pre-

determined objectives. In short, the skills or abilities related to objectives become the requisite competencies. Sometimes competencies may be classified around roles to be played.

Step 3: Conversion of competencies into performance or observed behaviors that can be measured. Indicators and measures must be specified for each competency.

Step 4: Design of an assessment system to measure competencies from at least two vantage points, namely, were objectives achieved and did the person have the skills necessary to meet the situation? Effectiveness is a matter of degree and not an all-or-none proposition.

Step 5: Determination of which competencies are lacking in order to improve performance by coaching.

Step 6: Operation of inservice or "coaching" clinics to improve effectiveness of personnal.

The flow of ideas may be summarized as: objectives → competencies → performance objectives → appraisal → coaching → effectiveness. tiveness.

The emphases of conventional appraisal and CBE may be contrasted as shown below:

[6]Ibid.

Conventional	CBE
Do things right →	Do right things
Emphasize inputs →	Specify outputs
Identify traits →	Measure competencies
Discharge duties →	Obtain results
Solve problems →	Produce creative alternatives
Safeguard resources →	Optimize resources
Performing functions →	Satisfying objectives

SUMMARY

Accountability has replaced relevance as the most popular educational term of the 1970s. It is an old concept that has been expanded to apply to all dimensions of the educational institution. It no longer applies only to the financial dimension. As a more comprehensive concept it includes performance, professional, and system accountability. It demands a review of the relevance of goals, effectiveness of strategies, and assessment of educational outcomes actually achieved.

Accountability as a system of operation is based on specification of desirable and measurable outcomes, the assignment of responsibilities for the achievement of objectives, and subsequent assessment. Within an operational system every person is answerable to another for something expressed in performance terms and realized under certain constraints. It is a goal-referenced term whose meaning is clarified when "accountability for what" is known.

Accountability in education is less precise and more difficult to achieve in education than in other endeavors. Educational institutions have multiple objectives and their end products are more difficult to measure. It is a means to an end whose fundamental purpose is to optimize relationships between resources and results. It should be welcomed rather than resisted for the new capabilities given to administrators.

There can be accountability for services as well as for achievement of a product related to a goal. The traditional teaching contract is a "performance" contract with emphasis on services performed rather than outcomes achieved. This is similar to the kinds of contracts under which physicians and lawyers may work. The so-called accountability movement seeks to switch the focus from accountability for inputs to instructional outcomes. It is closely related to the MBO concept.

There are other and conflicting interpretations of accountability. Teacher organizations express concern about accountability. Some individuals use the concept to justify tax support of private schools. These are the competitive conceptualizations of accountability that are different from the optimum resource utilization to achieve desired goals.

The design of an educational accountability strategy would include definition of objectives, creation of an accountability team, development of an accountability chart, searching for alternatives, implementation of output oriented management systems, utilization of computer based information systems, creation of educational auditing approaches, design of staff appraisal systems, allocating resources for accountability, and viewing accountability as a frame of mind as well as a set of techniques.

The pressures and the facts all attest to a growing trend toward establishing administrator appraisal systems. Appraisal and accountability are complementary concepts. The development of a total evaluation system calls for more than a new rating scale. Its rationale should be based on more than the orderly discharge of incompetents. The emphasis belongs on analysis of administrator performance leading to inservice activities contributing to the attainment of greater effectiveness.

Appraisal, by implication or explicit statements, rests on a model of administrator effectiveness. The evaluative data collected is then compared to such a model. There are a number of input, process, output, and eclectic models. The trait or personality model is the most common one and undergirds the historic and traditional approaches to appraisal. Research has little to offer and most writings conclude we know next to nothing about managerial effectiveness. It is the writer's opinion that the results-oriented, MBO/R, or competency-based administrator appraisal systems, will predominate in the years ahead. There are many perplexing and unresolved issues in instrument construction as well as in other general dimensions of administrator appraisal.

QUESTIONS

1. In what ways are accountability and appraisal similar? Dissimilar?
2. Why is the pressure for greater accountability likely to intensify rather than decrease during the 1970s?
3. Who should be on the accountability team?
4. Why is accountability more difficult to implement in educational institutions?
5. What are the essential elements of an educational accountability strategy?
6. Which of the many models of administrator effectiveness do you feel hold the most promise? Justify your stand.
7. What are the major issues in administrator appraisal?
8. Who should assume primary responsibility for the design of an administrator appraisal system?
9. Why is administrator appraisal more than a matter of designing a new rating scale or other type of evaluative instrument?
10. How does the competency-based evaluation approach differ from the traditional?

SELECTED REFERENCES

Browder, L. H. Jr., ed., *Emerging Patterns of Administrative Accountability*, Berkeley, Cal.: McCutchan, 1971.

Browder, L. H. Jr., and W. A. Atkins, Jr., and Kaya Esin, *Developing an Educationally Accountable Program*, Berkeley, Cal.: McCutchan, 1973.

House, Ernest R., *School Evaluation, The Politics and Process*, Berkeley, Cal.: McCutchan, 1973.

Knezevich, Stephen J., ed., "Creating Appraisal and Accountability Systems," *New Directions for Education*, vol. 1, no. 1, Spring 1973.

Lessinger, L. M., *Every Kid a Winner: Accountability in Education*, Palo Alto, Cal.: Science Research Associates, 1970.

NAME INDEX

SUBJECT INDEX

SUBJECT INDEX